Growth and Productivity in East Asia

NBER–East Asia Seminar on Economics
Volume 13

National Bureau of Economic Research
Productivity Commission, Australia
Korea Development Institute
Chung-Hua Institution for Economic Research
Tokyo Center for Economic Research
Hong Kong University of Science and Technology

Growth and Productivity in East Asia

Edited by Takatoshi Ito and Andrew K. Rose

The University of Chicago Press

Chicago and London

Takatoshi Ito is a professor at the Research Center for Advanced Science and Technology, University of Tokyo, and a research associate of the National Bureau of Economic Research. Andrew K. Rose is the Bernard T. Rocca Jr. Professor of International Trade at the Haas School of Business, University of California–Berkeley, director of its Clausen Center for International Business and Policy, and a research associate of the National Bureau of Economic Research.

The University of Chicago Press, Chicago 60637
The University of Chicago Press, Ltd., London

Printed in the United States of America
13 12 11 10 09 08 07 06 05 04 1 2 3 4 5
ISBN: 0-226-38680-5 (cloth)

Library of Congress Cataloging-in-Publication Data

NBER-East Asia Seminar on Economics (13th : 2002 : Melbourne, Vic.)
Growth and productivity in East Asia / edited by Takatoshi Ito and Andrew K. Rose.
p. cm. — (NBER–East Asia seminar on economics ; v. 13)
"Contains papers from the 13th annual East Asian Seminar on Economics, which took place on June 20-22 [2002], in Melbourne, Australia"—Intro.
Sponsored by the National Bureau of Economics Research ... [et al.].
ISBN 0-226-38680-5 (cloth : alk. paper)
1. East Asia—Economic policy—Congresses. 2. East Asia—Economic conditions—Congresses. 3. Industrial productivity—East Asia—Congresses. 4. Economic development—Congresses. 5. Production (Economic theory)—Congresses. I. Ito, Takatoshi, 1950– II. Rose, Andrew, 1959– III. National Bureau of Economic Research. IV. Title. V. NBER–East Asia seminar on economics (Series) ; v. 13.

HC460.5.N38 2002
338.95—dc22 2004041254

⊗ The paper used in this publication meets the minimum requirements of the American National Standard for Information Sciences—Permanence of Paper for Printed Library Materials, ANSI Z39.48-1992.

Relation of the Directors to the Work and Publications of the National Bureau of Economic Research

1. The object of the NBER is to ascertain and present to the economics profession, and to the public more generally, important economic facts and their interpretation in a scientific manner without policy recommendations. The Board of Directors is charged with the responsibility of ensuring that the work of the NBER is carried on in strict conformity with this object.

2. The President shall establish an internal review process to ensure that book manuscripts proposed for publication DO NOT contain policy recommendations. This shall apply both to the proceedings of conferences and to manuscripts by a single author or by one or more coauthors but shall not apply to authors of comments at NBER conferences who are not NBER affiliates.

3. No book manuscript reporting research shall be published by the NBER until the President has sent to each member of the Board a notice that a manuscript is recommended for publication and that in the President's opinion it is suitable for publication in accordance with the above principles of the NBER. Such notification will include a table of contents and an abstract or summary of the manuscript's content, a list of contributors if applicable, and a response form for use by Directors who desire a copy of the manuscript for review. Each manuscript shall contain a summary drawing attention to the nature and treatment of the problem studied and the main conclusions reached.

4. No volume shall be published until forty-five days have elapsed from the above notification of intention to publish it. During this period a copy shall be sent to any Director requesting it, and if any Director objects to publication on the grounds that the manuscript contains policy recommendations, the objection will be presented to the author(s) or editor(s). In case of dispute, all members of the Board shall be notified, and the President shall appoint an ad hoc committee of the Board to decide the matter; thirty days additional shall be granted for this purpose.

5. The President shall present annually to the Board a report describing the internal manuscript review process, any objections made by Directors before publication or by anyone after publication, any disputes about such matters, and how they were handled.

6. Publications of the NBER issued for informational purposes concerning the work of the Bureau, or issued to inform the public of the activities at the Bureau, including but not limited to the NBER Digest and Reporter, shall be consistent with the object stated in paragraph 1. They shall contain a specific disclaimer noting that they have not passed through the review procedures required in this resolution. The Executive Committee of the Board is charged with the review of all such publications from time to time.

7. NBER working papers and manuscripts distributed on the Bureau's web site are not deemed to be publications for the purpose of this resolution, but they shall be consistent with the object stated in paragraph 1. Working papers shall contain a specific disclaimer noting that they have not passed through the review procedures required in this resolution. The NBER's web site shall contain a similar disclaimer. The President shall establish an internal review process to ensure that the working papers and the web site do not contain policy recommendations, and shall report annually to the Board on this process and any concerns raised in connection with it.

8. Unless otherwise determined by the Board or exempted by the terms of paragraphs 6 and 7, a copy of this resolution shall be printed in each NBER publication as described in paragraph 2 above.

This volume is dedicated to the memory of Richard H. Snape, who passed away in the fall of 2002, shortly after the Melbourne conference on which this volume is based.

Contents

Acknowledgments xiii

Introduction 1
Takatoshi Ito and Andrew K. Rose

PART I. MACRO PRODUCTIVITY

1. **Ideas and Education: Level or Growth Effects and Their Implications for Australia** 9
Steve Dowrick
Comment: John Leahy
Comment: Andrew K. Rose

2. **Australia's 1990s Productivity Surge and Its Determinants** 41
Dean Parham
Comment: Chin Hee Hahn
Comment: Francis T. Lui

3. **Institutions, Volatility, and Crises** 71
Daron Acemoglu, Simon Johnson, and James Robinson
Comment: Steve Dowrick
Comment: Dipinder S. Randhawa

4. **GATT/WTO Accession and Productivity** 109
David D. Li and Changqi Wu
Comment: Simon Johnson
Comment: Epictetus E. Patalinghug

5. The Contribution of FDI Flows to Domestic Investment in Capacity, and Vice Versa 149
Assaf Razin
Comment: Kyoji Fukao
Comment: Dean Parham

PART II. MICRO PRODUCTIVITY

6. Sectoral Productivity and Economic Growth in Japan, 1970–98: An Empirical Analysis Based on the JIP Database 177
Kyoji Fukao, Tomohiko Inui,
Hiroki Kawai, and Tsutomu Miyagawa
Comment: Peter Drysdale
Comment: Keiko Ito

7. Foreign Ownership and Productivity in the Indonesian Automobile Industry: Evidence from Establishment Data for 1990–99 229
Keiko Ito
Comment: Muhammad Chatib Basri
Comment: Francis T. Lui

8. Productivity Growth and R&D Expenditure in Taiwan's Manufacturing Firms 277
Jiann-Chyuan Wang and Kuen-Hung Tsai
Comment: Tsutomu Miyagawa
Comment: Jungho Yoo

9. Bankruptcy Policy Reform and Total Factor Productivity Dynamics in Korea: Evidence from Microdata 297
Youngjae Lim and Chin Hee Hahn
Comment: Chong-Hyun Nam
Comment: Epictetus E. Patalinghug

10. Information Technology and Firm Performance in Korea 327
Jong-Il Kim
Comment: Chong-Hyun Nam
Comment: Dipinder S. Randhawa

11. **How Important Is Discrete Adjustment in Aggregate Fluctuations?** 351
Andrew Caplin and John Leahy
Comment: Jong-Il Kim
Comment: Assaf Razin

Contributors 377
Author Index 381
Subject Index 385

Acknowledgments

EASE is sponsored by the National Bureau of Economic Research (NBER) in Cambridge, Massachusetts; the Productivity Commission of Australia; the Korea Development Institute (KDI) in Seoul; the Chung-Hua Institution for Economic Research in Taipei; the Tokyo Center for Economic Research; and the Hong Kong University of Science and Technology (HKUST). We thank all our sponsors, but especially the Productivity Commission of Australia and the NBER, for making EASE-13 possible. Finally, we acknowledge our debt to Anne Krueger, one of the founders of EASE, whose responsibilities to the IMF and the global economy have unfortunately precluded her continued participation in the seminar.

Takatoshi Ito
University of Tokyo and NBER

Andrew K. Rose
UC Berkeley and NBER

Introduction

Takatoshi Ito and Andrew K. Rose

This volume contains papers from the thirteenth annual East Asian Seminar on Economics, which took place on June 20–22 in Melbourne, Australia. We are grateful to the local sponsor, the Australian Productivity Commission, an appropriate choice considering the topic of conference, productivity.

The productivity of a country as a whole is one of the most important determinants of its quality of life, and the rate of productivity growth is one of the most important long-run issues studied by economists. Countries with highly productive citizens tend to have high life expectancy and literacy rates, low rates of mortality and disease, lots of freedom, ample education and leisure, and considerable purchasing power. Studying the determinants of productivity levels and how they vary across countries and industries is thus an important task for economists, and one that was much discussed in EASE-13. But growth rates matter too. In just the same way that small differences between rates of interest matter a lot over long periods of time, tiny differences in sustained growth rates can accumulate quickly to make a large difference in income levels. Hence it is important for economists to study productivity growth rates and how they vary across time and countries, even if only by small amounts. Appropriately, a number of the conference papers are concerned with studying productivity growth.

Growth theory was pioneered by Robert Solow in the mid-1950s. There

Takatoshi Ito is a professor at the Research Center for Advanced Science and Technology, University of Tokyo, and a research associate of the National Bureau of Economic Research.

Andrew K. Rose is the Bernard T. Rocca Jr. Professor of International Trade at the Haas School of Business, University of California–Berkeley, director of its Clausen Center for International Business and Policy, and a research associate of the National Bureau of Economic Research.

were then many papers dedicated to explaining what determines growth and what kind of technological innovation is most likely to explain the long-run movement of macroeconomic economic variables, including the capital-labor ratio and the real wage rates. Growth accounting was a statistical exercise to attribute economic growth into contributions from capital (machines, plants, with quality being adjusted) and labor (employment, hours, with education being adjusted). What is not explained by these contributions was called total factor productivity (TFP). In many estimates, TFP growth was very high for economies that were growing exceptionally fast (like Japan from the mid-1950s to mid-1970s). A standard criticism is that productivities are assumed in theory to be exogenous and measured in empirical research to be residuals.

Then, there was a substantial hiatus in the study of economic growth and productivity between the late 1960s and the late 1980s. At that point a series of influential theoretical pieces appeared, the most important being those by Paul Romer, Paul Krugman, Robert Lucas, and others. The "new" growth theory was distinguished from the "old" theory in that productivity growth was generated by economic activities themselves, thus being "endogenous." (See EASE-4 for new growth theory applied to East Asian macroeconomic experiences.) Somewhat afterward, the discussion turned toward investigations of the empirics of productivity and growth; initially this work was largely macroeconomic in nature (the work by Robert Barro comes to mind quickly). After an initial round of seemingly strong results concerning the nature of economic growth conducted from cross-country regression exercises (e.g., work by Barro, Mankiw, Romer, and Weil among others), a flood of contradictory and confusing research results followed. As a result, the work in this area has become increasingly microeconomic in nature.

Many of the papers in EASE-13 continue this trend and are both empirical and microeconomic. However, we have striven to present a wide-ranging array of work on the area, and accordingly we include a number of theoretical and/or macroeconomic pieces below.

The first paper is a lucid summary by Steve Dowrick of recent developments in macroeconomic theory concerning the determinants of long-run growth and productivity change. The dust has only recently settled on the debate between those who believe in neoclassical growth models of the sort pioneered by Robert Solow, and advocates of endogenous growth (Romer and colleagues). In endogenous growth models, high rates of productivity and growth can continue indefinitely because of investments in research and development, which yield a continuing stream of inventions. The roles of education and human capital in generating productivity growth though ideas are accordingly large, and the survey by Dowrick is apposite. After providing a clear survey of the theoretical and empirical issues, he applies the results to Australia. He arrives at the startling conclusion that Australia's long-run productivity growth rate could rise by as much as a third of a percentage point annually in return for a relatively small one-year investment in schooling and knowledge creation.

Dean Parham picks up the issue of Australian productivity growth in his paper. He focuses on the 1990s, a period that is not only recent but also unusually interesting in that TFP growth picked up by over one percentage point annually. A number of alternative hypotheses have been advanced to explain this important acceleration in productivity growth, and Parham's paper is in essence a horse race between them. The explanations include (1) the wide-ranging policy reforms initiated somewhat earlier; (2) the general improvement in the quality of labor (of exactly the sort discussed and recommended by Dowrick); and (3) the somewhat notorious effect of information technology (IT). Throughout, Parham is careful to use as a benchmark of comparison the "new economy" experience of the United States during approximately the same period. (He dismisses the possibility of external shocks, given the strength and duration of the boom.)

The results are strikingly clear for an empirical economics paper, especially for an empirical project in the productivity literature: Australia's policymakers are to be congratulated for their far-sighted microeconomic reforms. Parham comes to this conclusion as a residual explanation; it is the only one that cannot be easily rejected. One would be happier with more direct evidence. Still, there is simply no evidence of sufficiently large changes in either workforce skills or IT to plausibly account for the substantial change in TFP growth. Moreover, the American productivity boom followed the Australian boom, further reducing the likelihood of an IT-driven "new economy" productivity surge in Australia. Parham's results are obviously significant for policymakers. They also have an intriguing political-economy aspect, which is worthy of further work. Parham's view is that the lags to the productivity benefits of reforms are long, at least compared to the length of electoral cycles; but reforms usually also bear a short-run political cost.

Parham's lags from policy reform to macroeconomic benefit are in the order of years, perhaps even a decade. But the consequences of *institutions* can be even longer-lived, as the fascinating paper by Daron Acemoglu, Simon Johnson, and James Robinson shows. In an interesting and influential series of studies, these authors have shown that the propensity of European colonists to establish solid macroeconomic institutions in a colony depended inversely on the difficulty of colonizing. In countries close to the equator that were (and still are) riddled by tropical disease, European powers chose—or were forced—not to encourage migration. Instead they simply set up institutions to extract resources from the populace for Northern enrichment. In more temperate climates with lower population densities (such as North America, South Africa, and the Antipodes), European powers instead established institutions with solid property and political rights to induce mass migration. The consequences of these differing institutions are large and persist for hundreds of years. In particular, Acemoglu, Johnson, and Robinson show that weak institutions (such as few political constraints on the executive) are associated with substantially higher macroeconomic volatility. For instance, output is more volatile in countries with weak institutions, even controlling for a number of alternative factors. This instability is also manifest in a number of other dimensions, including the prevalence of currency, banking, and political crises. Good news for Australia but, given the persistence of institutions, a crucial area for further work for Africa and Latin America.

David D. Li and Changi Wu share the same sweeping interest in macroeconomic phenomena and institutions, while also pursuing a novel empirical strategy. They are interested in assessing the impact of accession to the World Trade Organization (WTO) and its predecessor the General Agreement on Tariffs and Trade (GATT). These institutions are widely considered to be one of the three legs of the postwar multilateral international economic system (the others being the International Monetary Fund [IMF] and the World Bank). Li and Wu's focus on the WTO is intrinsically important, given the alleged (but disputed) importance of openness for productivity and growth. It is also an issue of topical import, given the fury that surrounds the entire globalization debate. Li and Wu use a large sample of macroeconomic data covering almost 100 developing countries between 1960 and 1998. Some 60 of these countries acceded to the GATT/WTO during the period. One might expect that entry into the multilateral trade system should bring substantial benefits in the form of increased productivity levels and/or growth rates, as well as increased openness to trade, foreign direct investment (FDI), faster growth, and increased investment. Yet the results are anything but clear. Even using an event-study methodology that focuses attention on the periods surrounding GATT/WTO accessions, Li and Wu are forced to split their sample in order to tease out positive results. Although they find do find some effects of GATT/WTO accession, these are nor particularly large, and they vary substantially with country characteristics. We hope this fascinatingly weak result will inspire others to pursue the topic further.

Assaf Razin is also concerned with the impact of external phenomena on the domestic economy. He focuses on information advantages that foreign managers may have that encourage FDI. As he notes, much FDI does not involve any (substantial) capital flow. His microeconomic model instead focuses on the role of FDI in "cream-skimming" high-productivity investments that result from the informational advantage that foreign managers have. He derives a rich set of predictions that show that FDI should behave differently from loans or portfolio capital flows, which are plagued by traditional principal-agent problems. What is especially notable about his work is the fact that he actually takes the model to the data, constructing a "gravity" model of capital flows, which he uses to test predictions about FDI and portfolio flows. Razin finds that, consistent with his model, FDI has a larger effect on both investment and output than either loans or portfolio flows. That is, FDI investors seem to raise both the quantity and the quality of investment productivity.

Many of the interesting consequences of productivity growth are macroeconomic. Nevertheless, it is often difficult to determine the causes of productivity without peering into the microeconomic data that lie underneath the aggregates. A number of the contributors to EASE-13 exploit data sets that make up in depth what they lack in scope. Happily, sometimes no substantial trade-off at all is required, as in the paper on sectoral productivity by Kyoji Fukao, Tomohiko Inui, Hiroki Kawai, and Tsutomu Miyagawa. This article is a first peek at a remarkable new database, which covers eighty-four Japanese sectors over the past thirty years. One of the best features of this data set is that it covers a large number of sectors outside manufacturing. Another is that it includes extremely detailed information on the type of inputs—for instance, separating IT from other capital. Fukao et al. have a number of findings; for instance, they document that reallocation of resources across sectors in the 1990s actually lowered TFP growth. But the real importance of their paper is in presenting the new data set to the world. It is hard to overstate the potential value of this resource (especially given the ongoing Japanese slump), and we look forward to more work in this vein.

Similar painstaking efforts were made by Keiko Ito, who analyzed foreign ownership of productivity in the Indonesian automobile industry. Using the establishment data, Ito calculates the TFP growth rate for multinational corporations (MNCs). In the literature and casual observations, MNCs are considered to be superior to local firms in managerial resources. Ito's paper empirically studies the difference in productivity between MNCs and locally owned establishments. Results show that both MNCs and local establishments experienced increasing returns to scale in the 1990s. The scale effect is found to be higher for foreign establishments. Surprisingly, TFP growth rates were negative for both local and MNC establishments. Among the TFP growth, the scale effect and the capital utilization effects were important, while technological change effect was very small. It is important to understand why the Indonesian automobile industry remains relatively inefficient. Ito suggests that too much protection is the culprit.

An example of the sort of careful painstaking empirical work that represents real progress in the area is the paper by Jiann-Chyuan Wang and Kuen-Hung Tsai. The authors collect data for over 130 Taiwanese firms and use them to examine the impact of research and development (R&D) on productivity. There are limitations to their data set; the firms are all large, publicly traded, manufacturing firms, and the data set only extends back to 1994. Such are often the handicaps associated with disaggregated data sets. Yet the results are provocative. When Wang and Tsai split their sample of firms into high-tech and conventional, they find a dramatically higher impact of R&D on productivity in the high-tech sample. Perhaps even more intriguing is their rejection of Schumpeter's much-quoted (but little tested!) hypothesis that larger firms benefit more from R&D.

A well-governed economy encourages the efficient use of resources and discourages inefficient firms; it should smile on the good and frown on the bad. While much public policy discussion centers on the barriers to *entry* of new firms, it is also important to understand barriers to *exit* of failing firms. Plants that used resources inefficiently but were not shut down were a major reason for the low level of productivity of the former centrally planned economies. Since legal barriers to exit are probably the most important obstacles, it is accordingly important to understand the effects of bankruptcy law. Youngjae Lim and Chin Hee Hahn do exactly that, taking full advantage of the change in Korean law that followed Korea's financial crisis of late 1997. They develop an extensive microeconomic data set. They use data at both the firm level (which is needed to discuss bankruptcy issues) and at the plant level (to examine the effects on productivity through resource reallocation). Reassuringly, they find that the post-crisis improvement in bankruptcy law has improved performance in the sense that productivity problems *before* bankruptcy are less persistent.

Jong-Il Kim's paper analyzes the effects of IT investments in Korea. Results based on firm-level data show that IT investments enhance productivity. IT capital is valued more highly in the financial market than the book value. He concludes that part of contribution from IT capital to production is not measured in traditional growth accounting.

Finally, Andrew Caplin and John Leahy built a model of discrete investment using an Ss framework and compare that to a representative agent model with continuous investment. Often IT investment needs a large fixed cost. The result of the paper shows that under some conditions, both models are observationally equivalent. Since investment is associated with much productivity and real economic growth, this paper shows that the results from two disparate streams of modeling can be combined easily (under certain circumstances), thereby simplifying the modeling of underlying sources of growth.

I

Macro Productivity

1

Ideas and Education
Level or Growth Effects and Their Implications for Australia

Steve Dowrick

Introduction

The importance of human capital for economic growth was highlighted in much of the "new growth theory" that came to prominence in the late 1980s and early 1990s. The neoclassical growth model, formalized three decades earlier, had focused on the accumulation of machinery and equipment and emphasized the feature of diminishing returns—which implied that such investment would not be able to drive long-run growth. The new generation of studies switched attention to the accumulation of human capital and the possibility that returns to investment in education, training, and research may not suffer from diminishing returns.

There is an important distinction between embodied and disembodied human capital. Human capital in the form of abilities and skills is embodied inasmuch as it lives and dies with particular people. We invest in human capital not only through formal education and training programs but also through experience on the job and through domestic and social interaction. The time and effort devoted to parenting, for example, represents an enormous investment in the human capital of the next generation.

The accumulation of abilities contributes both to psychic rewards and to marketed economic activity. Whereas the value of the former is hard to measure, there are relatively straightforward ways for us to measure the latter. Economists are only just beginning to address seriously the task of

Steve Dowrick is professor of economics and ARC Senior Research Fellow in the School of Economics, Australian National University.

The author thanks Creina Day and Shebnem Pollack for research assistance and acknowledges the Melbourne Institute for assistance in preparing the background papers for their 2002 Economic and Social Outlook Conference, and acknowledges the Australian Research Council for financial assistance.

evaluating nonmarket activities such as domestic labor—see, for example, Folbre and Nelson (2000) and Apps and Rees (2001). I focus in this paper on market-related returns to human capital because we do not yet have internationally standardized valuations of nonmarket activities.

The most extensively documented feature of embodied human capital is the relationship between education and wages. Studies of earnings in advanced capitalist economies typically find that each extra year of schooling raises earnings by 5 to 10 percent. These findings are confirmed by Australian studies such as those by Miller, Mulvey, and Martin (1995), who analyze earnings of twins and find that the return to a year of education lies between 4.5 percent and 8.3 percent, and Preston (1997) who reports high rates of return to advanced educational qualifications. The results of Miller, Mulvey, and Martin are particularly interesting because they control for the influences of genetic and domestic background to identify the direct contribution of education—following studies by Ashenfelter and Krueger (1994) and Ashenfelter and Rouse (1997, 1998) that estimate U.S. rates of return between 9 and 16 percent.

This evidence leads us to expect that, if the average educational attainment of the working-age Australian population were to rise by one year, real gross domestic product (GDP) should rise by up to 8 percent. This increase in the level of GDP will, typically, take place gradually. An increase in the length of schooling of teenagers will only increase the average educational experience of the adult population as the new, better-educated cohorts enter the workforce, replacing older cohorts. We expect the transition to last four decades, if people enter the labor force aged twenty and exit at an age of about sixty. If this is so, the annual growth rate of GDP will be 0.2 percentage points above trend during the transition period, resulting in an overall 8 percent increase, after which time the growth rate will revert to trend—with, perhaps, some lagged adjustment to the stock of physical capital. In this sense, changes in educational investment are predicted to have *growth effects* in the short run (albeit a short run of forty years), but only *level effects* in the long run.

This is the conventional approach, which treats human capital as an investment good in much the same way as a farmer might consider investing in tractors. There are, however, features of human capital that can give it a much more important role in economic development. This is particularly true when we turn our attention to disembodied human capital, the realm of knowledge and ideas that do not live and die with their inventors but can be transmitted freely between people and carried forward over generations.

A crucial economic attribute of disembodied human capital, highlighted in recent models of endogenous growth, is that ideas are both nonrival and cumulative. Nonrivalry implies that once the idea of using electronic circuits to carry out binary computations has been announced, people can simultaneously use this idea to develop a wide range of applications. One person's use of the idea does not prevent another person from using it at the same time. Moreover, ideas are cumulative: The idea of electronic computing has lead to the idea of quantum computing, which may in turn lead to yet further ideas.

Analysis of these attributes of nonrivalry and cumulative feedback has led growth theorists to speculate that investment in the generation of ideas can be the engine of long-run growth. The nonrivalry of knowledge also leads us to expect market failure. When others reap the benefits of someone's new ideas, market forces alone are unlikely to generate the optimal level of investment in knowledge—implying a need for government subsidy.

If the generation of disembodied human capital—ideas/technology—is the engine of growth, we should expect to find that embodied human capital—skills and abilities—also affect long-run growth. Ideas do not reproduce themselves without the input of highly skilled researchers. Perhaps of equal importance, the more skilled the workforce, the better it is able to absorb, implement, and adapt the new ideas emanating from the research and development (R&D) sector. To the extent that technological change is endogenous, we expect educational attainment to have long-run growth effects in addition to the conventional prediction of level effects.

In the following sections I review and evaluate evidence from recent theoretical and econometric studies relating economic growth to investment in both embodied and disembodied human capital. I restrict my attention on the empirical front to the relatively well-documented areas of investment in formal schooling and R&D, noting that this omits potentially important areas of investment in health and in informal education and training that takes place within the family and within the workplace.

1.1 Rethinking Economic Growth: The Role of Knowledge

Knowledge is fundamental to economic progress. Our material standard of living would be reduced to unrecognizable levels if we were to suffer collective amnesia—forgetting that a circular shape reduces friction, not remembering how to read and write, losing all knowledge of electrodynamics. All economic activities depend on institutions that encourage the preservation, transmission, and development of knowledge.

This seems blindingly obvious. Yet for several recent decades, the economic analysis of growth was dominated by an approach that sidelined the role of knowledge. Economists concentrated on the accumulation of objects rather than the accumulation of ideas.

The object-oriented approach to economic growth was formalized in 1956 by two economists operating at opposite ends of the globe: Robert Solow at MIT in Cambridge and Trevor Swan at ANU in Canberra. Their neoclassical growth models were formulated independently but in broadly the same way, leading to similar conclusions. Accumulation of capital—machinery, buildings, equipment, and the like—is the engine of growth in the short run. Policies that increase the share of resources going to investment will raise the productive capacity of the economy. But as the growth of the capital stock outpaces the limited resources of land and labor, the impact of each successive unit of investment is diminished. However large the boost to the investment rate, growth will eventually revert to some fixed rate determined by exogenous technological progress.

This implication of the neoclassical growth model is illustrated in figure 1.1. A boost to investment at time T_0 raises the rate of growth (the slope of the logarithmic output line) from the solid line A to the dashed line B. Ultimately, however, growth reverts to the exogenous rate, where line B becomes parallel to line A, albeit with output and incomes at a higher level than would have obtained at the lower investment rate. Tax incentives, or other policies that influence investment, affect only the level of output, not the long-run rate of growth.

The key to this conclusion is the assumption of diminishing returns to capital accumulation. Underlying this notion is the idea of capital as a collection of similar objects. A self-employed dressmaker who purchases his first sewing machine will register a large increase in annual output. Purchase of a second machine will reduce the amount of downtime when the first machine is under repair, but the consequent addition to annual output is relatively small. A third machine would probably be redundant. This assumption about diminishing returns is typically captured in growth models by postulating an aggregate production function of Cobb-Douglas

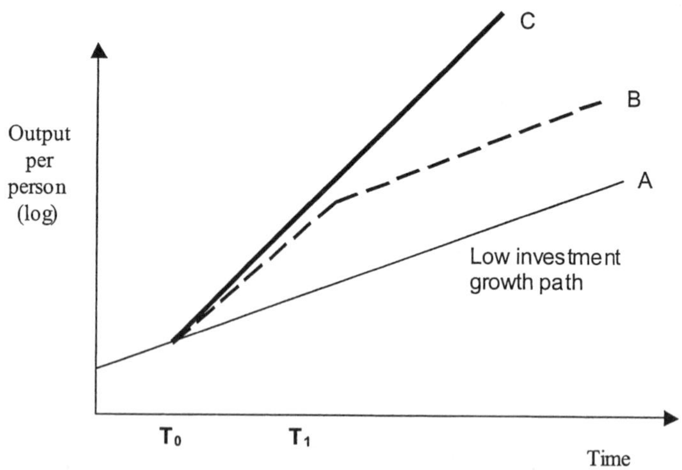

Fig. 1.1 The impact of increased investment in the neoclassical and endogenous growth models

form exhibiting constant returns to scale, where output per unit of labor at time t, y_t, is related to the net capital stock per unit of labor, k_t, as:

$$y_t = A_t(k_t)^\alpha \tag{1}$$

The elasticity of output with respect to capital, represented by the parameter α, is assumed to be less than unity. The parameter A_t represents the level of technology at time t, sometimes referred to as total factor productivity.

The marginal product of capital is

$$\frac{\partial y_t}{\partial k_t} = \frac{\alpha A_t}{k_t^{1-\alpha}}, \tag{2}$$

which, given $\alpha < 1$, diminishes toward zero as capital intensity increases.

1.1.1 The Revolution in Growth Theory: Endogenous Growth

This way of thinking about economic growth was challenged in a series of papers, starting with Paul Romer in 1986, heralded as "the new growth theory" or "endogenous growth theory."[1] A prominent feature of this new wave of economic models—indeed, their defining feature—is that policy intervention and the nature of institutions can influence the long-run growth rate of the economy.

In terms of figure 1.1, the new models suggest that policy or institutional change, instituted at time T_0, could permanently alter the slope of the growth path, as illustrated by the dotted path C.

There are various technical features of these models that make it feasible for the long-run growth rate to be determined endogenously—that is, determined by economic behavior that is analyzed within the model. One possibility arises where the degree of substitutability between capital and labor is sufficiently high that returns to the accumulation of capital do not diminish to zero.[2] We can imagine that this might be the case in some manufacturing processes where human labor is readily replaced by robots, or in the delivery of some financial services such as ATM banking. But it is not clear that this robotic model of growth is applicable to all sectors of the economy.

More interesting, to my mind at least, are models of endogenous growth that build on the economic properties of complementarity, dynamic feedback, and nonrivalry in investment. These are the properties that distin-

1. The key papers are Paul M. Romer (1986, 1990), Lucas (1988), Rebelo (1991), and Aghion and Howitt (1992). Paul Romer (1993) acknowledges the intellectual debt due to Adam Smith, Joseph Schumpeter, Arthur Lewis, and others. Further important contributions, analyzing specialization, have come from Australian economists: Yang and Borland (1991), Borland and Yang (1992), and Shi and Yang (1995).

2. This possibility was canvassed by the Australian economist John Pitchford (1960), who illustrated his argument using a constant elasticity of substitution production function.

guish the accumulation of ideas and skills from the accumulation of objects. It is worthwhile considering each of them in turn.

1.1.2 Complementarity of Investment

Complementarity arises when your investment increases the return (monetary and/or psychic) to my investment. This may occur when we invest in activities that exhibit network externalities. Learning to play chess, to speak Esperanto, or to read and write becomes much more rewarding for me if others invest in the same skills. Complementarity is not exclusive to investment in human capital; the benefits I get from investing in a telephone line and a fax machine are also enhanced when others do the same. But complementarity is probably more pervasive in the accumulation of skills than in the accumulation of objects. Indeed, such complementarity is an essential ingredient of the development of "social capital."

Complementarity is a feature of the endogenous growth model of Lucas (1988), where the productivity of any worker is enhanced not only by his or her individual level of skill but also by the average skill level among their fellow workers. This implies that the economic analysis of external effects is relevant to growth. Although my productivity depends in part on your human capital, I cannot expect you to take that into account when you decide how much education and training to undertake—and vice versa. So if we make individual decisions about the time and money we spend on education and training, we are likely to underinvest. It follows, from Lucas's analysis of such externalities, that there may be an important role for government to play. Subsidizing education will improve economic welfare in the sense that everyone will be better off as a result of an increase in human capital.[3]

1.1.3 Dynamic Feedback

These education externalities are not, however, sufficient in themselves to drive long-run growth. In Lucas's model, the rate of output growth is still limited by diminishing returns to the accumulation of both physical and human capital. He endogenizes growth by appealing to another feature of education: dynamic feedback. As we learn more, it becomes easier to acquire further knowledge and skills. An obvious example is reading. Once we have learned this skill, the acquisition of further information and skills is facilitated through book learning.

This view of dynamic feedback can be represented by a function expressing the change in the level of human capital in some representative

3. This is not the only reason for subsidizing education. Given that many parents are constrained in financing their children's education, there are both equity and efficiency reasons for public support.

household as a function of the amount of adult labor time, L_h, that is devoted to education (of self or of children) and the current level of human capital per person, h_t.

$$\frac{dh_t}{dt} = \phi \cdot L_h \cdot h_t^{\gamma} \tag{3}$$

The extent of dynamic feedback is captured by the value of the exponential parameter γ. A value of zero implies that there is no feedback. Aggregate output per person, y, now depends on both physical and human capital per person:

$$y_t = A(k_t)^{\alpha}(h_t)^{\beta}, \tag{4}$$

where we maintain the assumption of diminishing returns by restricting α, $\beta < 1$.

Endogenous growth is made feasible by the existence of positive feedback in the second sector of this economy, the education sector. To demonstrate this, take logarithms of equation (4), differentiate with respect to time and substitute equation (3) to derive the growth rate of output per worker:

$$\frac{dy_t}{dt} \cdot \frac{1}{y_t} = \alpha \frac{dk_t}{dt} \cdot \frac{1}{k_t} + \beta \frac{dh_t}{dt} \cdot \frac{1}{h_t} = \alpha \frac{dk_t}{dt} \cdot \frac{1}{k_t} + \beta \frac{\phi L_h}{h_t^{1-\gamma}} \tag{5}$$

Whether or not the accumulation of human capital can drive long-run growth is determined by the final term in this equation. With no positive feedback (i.e., if $\gamma = 0$), this term diminishes to zero as the level of human capital, h_t, increases over time. (This is exactly what happens to the physical capital term, as a given investment rate leads to slower and slower proportional growth in the stock.) But if there is sufficiently high feedback in human capital accumulation (i.e., if $\gamma = 1$), the final term in equation (5) is a positive constant. That is to say, the long-run growth rate is positive. Moreover, it is increasing in the amount of labor time that is devoted to education.

Given sufficient dynamic feedback, public subsidy of education and training can increase long-run growth. In the presence of positive externalities, or other sources of market failure, such policy will also increase economic welfare.

1.1.4 Embodied or Disembodied Human Capital

Is it reasonable, however, to suppose that the feedback effect is sufficiently strong to make education the engine of long-run growth? Note that even if the feedback parameter is close to unity—say, $\gamma = 0.9$—the long-run rate of growth in equation (5) will diminish to zero as the level of human capital increases. Stable long-run growth requires a parameter value of unity. It also requires that there be no limit to the accumulation of human capital. Human capacities to think, organize, and remember are, however, usually presumed to be finite. Moreover, our skills and abilities die with us and have to be replaced in every successive generation.[4]

In addressing the problem of limits to human capabilities, Paul M. Romer (1990) emphasizes the distinction between the skills and abilities that are embodied in individual humans, and disembodied knowledge. He focuses on the properties of the latter category, the world of ideas and research, supposing that there is sufficient dynamic feedback in the research sector to generate endogenous growth and that the scope for developing new ideas is limitless.

In Romer's model, it is the number of people engaged in research and development that drives long-run growth. His mathematical representation of the generation of new ideas (or blueprints for new products) is similar to that of Lucas's educational sector:

$$\frac{dA_t}{dt} = \phi L_A A_t, \tag{6}$$

where A_t represents the number of productive ideas that have been realized at time t in history, and the differential, dA/dt, is the current output of new ideas from the research sector. L_A represents the amount of human capital, or the number of researchers, devoted to innovation.

Crucially, Romer assumes that the rate of innovation is directly proportional to the extant stock of knowledge. This is the "standing on shoulders" hypothesis of knowledge accumulation, so labelled by Charles Jones (1998), in reference to Isaac Newton's disclaimer: "If I have seen farther than others, it is because I was standing on the shoulders of giants."

In the accumulation of disembodied ideas, rather than embodied skills, it is indeed plausible to suppose that the level of current output might be directly proportional to the size of the stock. The more ideas and theorems that we have to draw on, the easier it is to generate new ones. Moreover, ideas do not necessarily disappear when their developer dies: They can typically be recorded and transmitted at minimal cost.

Implicit in Romer's formulation of research output is the idea that there is an evenly distributed and infinite universe of potential ideas waiting to be discovered. Thus, a given amount of research effort will produce a predictable number of new ideas. A more realistic approach, allowing the discovery rate to fluctuate, is summarized by Aghion and Howitt (1998) in their discussion of general-purpose technologies stemming from innovations such as the steam engine, the electric dynamo, and the computer.

4. Lucas (1988) asserts that his model of endogenous growth can be sustained across generations if a child's initial endowment of human capital is proportional to the level already attained by the adults—but, unless Lysenko was correct, the genetic transmission of acquired human capital is unlikely.

1.1.5 Nonrivalry of Ideas

As well as hypothesizing dynamic feedback in the generation of new ideas, Romer emphasizes that ideas have another significant economic property, *nonrivalry*. Objects are usually rival, meaning that if you are using something, I cannot use it at the same time. But this is not true of ideas. Once the binomial theorem has been published, your use of it does not in any way interfere with my use of it.

Of course, people can try to stop others from making use of patented ideas. But the *excludability* of ideas depends on the actions of people supported by institutions of laws and property rights, rather than nonrivalry, which is an inherent feature of ideas.

Romer makes use of this distinction by assuming that ideas are fully excludable in their application to the production of goods. For example, a researcher can acquire full patent protection for the design of a new drug; it can only be manufactured if royalties are paid. On the other hand, she has no protection against other researchers who can reverse engineer her ideas and come up with their own different but improved drug design. Indeed, when the original researcher files her patent, she has to describe her idea, thereby providing her rivals with a free input into their subsequent research.

Romer's hypothesis that ideas are nonrival and nonexcludable in the research process has important implications for public policy. Researchers may reap the benefits from the direct application of their ideas, but they do not receive monetary reward from others who "stand on their shoulders." Left to the market, there will be an undersupply of research effort. Public intervention is required to subsidize research, hence to stimulate growth, up to the socially optimum level.

Other aspects of knowledge accumulation are analysed by Aghion and Howitt (1992, 1998), who emphasize the Schumpeterian notion of "creative destruction." Patent rights may bestow monopoly power on the producer of a particular generation of an innovative good, but they cannot prevent the development by a rival of the next generation of goods that are superior in quality and/or price. The creation of the improved version destroys the flow of profits to the previous monopolist. Unbridled competition in such a market can lead to too much research being carried out, where the research is concerned with marginal quality improvements rather than new products and processes. Nevertheless, such research is still capable of driving long-run economic growth.

1.2 The Cambridge Counterrevolution

The intellectual euphoria of endogenous growth theory was challenged by a group of economists, mostly connected with or based in Cambridge,

Massachusetts, who chose to stand behind (or on the shoulders of) Nobel laureate Robert Solow of the Massachusetts Institute of Technology.

Solow (1994) himself is critical of the knife-edge assumption required to generate stable long-run growth in the models of Romer and Lucas. His point is that these models require the dynamic feedback parameter in the education/research sector to be exactly equal to unity. If we look back to Lucas's model, where the growth rate of the economy is determined by equation (5), we can see that a value of 0.9 for the parameter γ will, eventually, reduce growth to zero: The final term of that equation has $h_t^{1-\gamma}$ in the denominator, which drives the term to zero as human capital, h_t, rises if γ is less than one. Stable long-run growth requires that the parameter be exactly one.

Romer (1994) has argued that this knife-edge property can be overcome in a more complex model. More damaging to the endogenous growth cause, however, has been the empirical work of another Cambridge (Harvard)–based economist, Greg Mankiw. In a much-cited paper—Mankiw, Romer, and Weil (1992)—he and his coauthors do not tackle the endogenous growth modelers head-on. Rather, they steal the ball of human capital from the endogenous growth scrum and use it to reconstruct the 1956 Solow model.

Their "augmented Solow model" includes human capital as a third factor in the aggregate production function, alongside capital and unskilled labor. They investigate the relationship between steady-state levels of output and the three inputs, using secondary-school enrollment rates as a proxy for the rate of investment in human capital. They conclude that the factors are of approximately equal importance—that is, that the elasticity of output with respect to each factor is approximately one-third—and that together they account for 80 percent of the observed variation in 1985 income levels across some ninety-eight nations.

This was a neat sidestep, rather than a direct hit on endogenous growth theory. There was no attempt to directly confront the two models with a discriminating statistical test, but the 1956 model was effectively rehabilitated—even though the econometric evidence is likely to be flawed due to the endogeneity of the explanatory variables. Moreover, this was only half-time in the comeback match. In an equally influential second half, the Mankiw, Romer, and Weil (1992) paper provided a clever reinterpretation of an empirical regularity. Studies of postwar economic growth had typically reported a conditional convergence effect. These studies ran regression models of the form

$$(7) \qquad (\ln y_{iT} - \ln y_{i0}) = \alpha_0 + \beta \ln y_{i0} + \mathbf{g}\mathbf{X}_i + \varepsilon_i,$$

where the dependent variable is the growth rate of y, output per capita (or per worker), over a period of T years. $\mathbf{X}_i$ represents a vector of additional explanatory variables. "Conditional convergence" is said to exist if the regression parameter, β, is negative—a lower starting value for y is associated with a higher subsequent rate of growth, conditional on the **X** variables that explain differences in rates of growth.

Previous authors[5] had interpreted conditional convergence as evidence that technological spillovers from the most advanced economies enabled less advanced economies to imitate and thus enjoy relatively fast productivity growth. The Mankiw-Romer-Weil reinterpretation of such evidence, echoed by their Harvard colleagues Robert Barro and Jeffrey Sachs,[6] involves treating the **X** variables as determinants of the neoclassical steady state, rather than the long-run growth rate. They then interpret the initial income variable ($\ln y_0$) as a measure of distance from steady state and the β-coefficient as a measure of the speed of convergence to steady state.

This reinterpretation of the evidence in favor of the neoclassical model has been complemented by the more direct approach of MIT graduate Charles Jones.[7] He highlights the fact that endogenous growth models based on the accumulation of knowledge, such as Romer's model, typically suggest that the rate of growth should be an increasing function of the resources devoted to R&D.[8] He cites evidence from the United States that contradicts this prediction: "Since 1950, the fraction of the labour force engaged in formal R&D has increased by almost a factor of three. Despite these changes, average growth rates . . . are no higher today than they were from 1870 to 1929" Jones (1998, 157).

Jones also criticizes some of the key assumptions underpinning the knowledge-based models of endogenous growth. In particular, he suggests that knowledge creation may become more difficult over time as the easy ideas are discovered first, leaving subsequent researchers with a pool that has been "fished out." He also suggests that researchers may often duplicate each other's efforts, "stepping on toes" rather than "standing on shoulders."

These critiques of endogenous growth theory seem to imply that policies aimed at increasing investment in education and/or research will not be successful in raising the rate of economic growth for a sustained length of time. I will argue in the next section of the paper that this is not necessarily the case.

1.3 Reconciling Conflicting Theories of Growth

A crucial difference between the neoclassical and new growth theories concerns the question of whether the long-run rate of growth of the econ-

5. For example, Abramovitz (1986) and Dowrick and Nguyen (1989).
6. See Barro and Lee (1994) and Sachs and Warner (1997).
7. See Jones (1995a,b).
8. However, Aghion and Howitt (1998) show that their Schumpeterian model of endogenous innovation can be adapted to eliminate the scale effect.

omy is some exogenous constant or whether it can be influenced by public policy. Put another way, the question is whether policies and institutions that influence the rate of accumulation of physical and/or human capital have long-run effects on the *level* of economic activity or on its *rate of growth.* For purposes of practical policy making, however, this distinction may be relatively unimportant—if the long run never arrives. Looking back to figure 1.1, if economies are subject to shocks of sufficient magnitude and frequency, it may be difficult, if not impossible, to tell whether the long-run growth path really looks like path B or path C. In the short run—between time T_0 when the first major shock occurs and some time T_1 when another such event occurs—the paths may be virtually indistinguishable.

The evidence of the neoclassical revivalists can be interpreted to support this view. Mankiw, Romer, and Weil (1992), Barro and Sala-i-Martin (1995), and Sachs and Warner (1997) all report growth regression evidence suggesting that the rate of convergence toward steady state is of the order of 2 percentage points per year, implying that it will take more than thirty years for a country to halve the gap between its current income and the steady-state level.[9] Within a half-life of several decades, we must surely expect that there will be changes in investment rates and changes in the rate of technological progress such that the neoclassical economy is rarely able to get close to steady state.

A useful way to think of this problem is to consider the specification of the Error Correction Model (ECM). The ECM is commonly used to decompose macroeconomic time series into cyclical and long-run components and to test for long-run cointegrating relationships. A typical regression is of the form

$$(\ln y_t - \ln y_{t-1}) = \alpha\{\mathbf{X}_t - \mathbf{X}_{t-1}\} + \lambda[\ln y_{t-1} - \beta\mathbf{Z}_{t-1}] + \varepsilon_t, \tag{8}$$

where y represents real output and the dependent variable is the growth rate of output. The explanatory variables are segregated. The **X** variables, which influence short-run movements, are entered in first differences. The **Z** factors are entered as lagged variables, along with the lagged value of output, y_{t-1}. For analysis of the long-run path, the first differences are set to zero, yielding the long-run path for output as a function of the **Z** variables:

$$\ln y_{T^*} = \beta\mathbf{Z}_{T^*} \tag{9}$$

9. Subsequent studies on panel data have estimated higher speeds of convergence: In particular, Islam (1995) and Lee, Pesaran, and Smith (1997) estimate annual convergence rates up to 9 percent and 30 percent respectively. But Dowrick and Rogers (2002) show that these studies confound the effects of neoclassical convergence—due to diminishing returns to investment—with the effects of international technology diffusion. Separating out these effects, they find that the half-life of neoclassical convergence is more than fifteen years.

This very general empirical specification is consistent with both exogenous growth and endogenous growth models. If the **Z** vector contains a time trend, *T*, the regression coefficient on *T* is an estimate of the exogenous rate of technological progress—as in the neoclassical model. However, the **Z** vector may equally well contain the time trend interacted with another variable, such as the level of human capital. If so, the coefficient on this term captures the impact of human capital on the long-run growth rate of the economy—as predicted by some endogenous growth models.

In the ECM framework, the sign of the regression coefficient λ indicates whether output converges to the long-run path. The square brackets in equation (8) capture last period's deviation from the long-run path. The negative value of λ indicates the proportion of last period's "error" that is "corrected" in the current period.

A typical time series study that is trying to identify breaks in trend growth, using thirty to forty annual observations, might find a half-life for the business cycle of two to three years.[10] In this context, the "trend" growth is approximated by the average growth rate over one or two decades, averaging out fluctuations over three or four business cycles. But if convergence to the neoclassical steady-state growth path has a half-life of thirty years, this time scale is clearly insufficient to capture the underlying long-run rate of growth. Rather, we are identifying changes in the slope of the transitional growth path.

This supposition is confirmed by the recent study of Jones (2001). He adopts a modified growth accounting approach to analyze the last fifty years of U.S. growth. He finds that only one-fifth of the actual growth rate of labor productivity (averaging 2.0 percent per year) has been attributable to exogenous technical change. The remaining four-fifths of growth (1.6 percent per year) is attributable to continued growth in education and research intensity. In his terms, "Transition dynamics associated with educational attainment and the growth in research intensity account for 80 percent of growth" (p. 23).

Jones's conclusion is couched in the language of the neoclassical approach. Sustained growth above steady-state levels can only be transitional and is driven by sustained (but ultimately bounded) growth in the share of GDP going to investment in human capital. An alternative interpretation of the same evidence might claim that increased investment in human capital has raised the long-run endogenous rate of growth.

Evidence that reconciles the two approaches to understanding growth comes from Benhabib and Spiegel (1994), who carry out econometric esti-

10. A pooled time series cross-section study by Lee, Pesaran, and Smith (1997), allowing for heterogeneity in country-specific time trends, has estimated convergence in the Solow-Swan model to have a half-life of 2.5 years. I interpret this as a failure to distinguish the speed of transition to steady state from the fluctuations of the business cycle.

mation on various models to explain variation in twenty-year growth rates (1965–85) on a cross section of seventy-eight countries. In their preferred model, technological progress is the sum of two components: an exogenous component, as in the neoclassical model, and a semi-endogenous component, related to the rate of absorption of technology from the technological leading country, captured by an interactive term between the productivity gap and the level of human capital. Their preferred model draws on the analysis of Nelson and Phelps (1966).

They report that the interactive term is statistically significant, supporting the idea that there is an endogenous component to technological progress. At the same time, they estimate an output elasticity close to 0.5 for physical capital, suggesting diminishing returns to investment and a slow rate of convergence toward the steady-state capital stock.

Broadly similar results are reported by Dowrick and Rogers (2002). Our study differs from that of Benhabib and Spiegel (1994) in that we carry out the analysis on a panel of growth data. This enables us to test for country-specific effects. We also use an instrumental variable estimator to control for reverse causation between growth and the explanatory variables. Country-specific effects, which we interpret as endogenous components of technical progress, are found to be important. We confirm the finding that the level of human capital facilitates technological catch-up, especially among the middle-income and richer countries.

These models combine features of the neoclassical theory with the new growth theory. Changes in the rate of physical investment have, ultimately, only level effects; however, within a time frame of one or two decades this is indistinguishable from a growth effect. At the same time, countries have different rates of technological progress with an endogenous component, dependent on the stock of human capital and the allocation of resources to research, and a semi-endogenous component, dependent on the rate of technological change at the frontier and on the country's ability to absorb ideas from abroad.

1.4 Evidence on Education and Growth

Some of the earliest studies that investigated the link between education and economic growth were conducted by Mankiw, Romer, and Weil (1992) and Barro (1991). They examined variations in school enrollment rates, using a single cross section of both the industrialized and the less-developed countries. Both studies concluded that schooling has a significantly positive impact on the rate of growth of real GDP. They interpreted this as evidence of changes to (short-run) transitional growth paths. Barro and Sala-i-Martin (1995) also investigated the impact of educational expenditures by governments, finding that they have a strong positive impact. Using instrumental variable techniques to control for simultaneous causation, their regressions suggest that the annual rate of return on public education is of the order of 20 percent.[11]

A series of subsequent studies made use of panel data, examining changes over time in both education and growth. Several of these panel studies—including Benhabib and Spiegel (1994), Islam (1995) and Caselli, Esquivel, and Lefort (1996)—failed to detect any significant relationship between the rate of increase of educational capital and the rate of economic growth. They suggested that the positive findings of the earlier cross-section studies were due to omitted variable bias, failing to control for country-specific effects.

More recently, a third generation of studies has suggested a number of reasons why the negative findings of previous panel studies might have been biased. Pritchett (2001) has argued that poor policies and institutions have hampered growth in many of the least developed economies, directing skilled labor into relatively unproductive activities, hence disrupting the statistical relationship between education and growth in samples that include less-developed economies. Krueger and Lindahl (2001) suggest that the problem of unobserved variation in educational quality is exacerbated in panel data. Taking data quality into account, they show that increases in the stock of schooling do improve short-run economic growth. Hanushek and Kimko (2000) confirm that direct measures of labor force quality, from international mathematics and science test scores, are strongly related to growth. Temple (2001) finds that growth effects are positive but nonlinear. These nonlinear effects may be missed by studies that impose linearity.

Overall, it seems that studies that pool the least and the most developed economies do not find consistent and robust relationships between education and growth. For evaluation of Australian policy, it is probably more useful to examine studies that are restricted to Organization for Economic Cooperation and Development (OECD) economies.

Mankiw, Romer, and Weil (1992) estimate the determinants of countries' steady-state income levels as a function of investment in both physical and human capital. For their cross section of OECD countries, they estimate an elasticity of 0.76 between steady-state output and the proportion

11. Barro and Sala-i-Martin (1995) report an increasing marginal effect on growth of years of schooling, but this may be due to a lack of variation in the data on primary enrollments. More surprising is their finding that positive growth effects are confined to male education. On the other hand, a study by Caselli, Esquivel, and Lefort (1996) uses a more sophisticated panel estimation technique (general method of moments) and reverses the result—it is female secondary education rather than male education that promotes growth. This finding is confirmed by Knowles, Lorgelly, and Owen (2002). These contradictory results probably reflect strong colinearity between female education, male education, and other measures of development, such as life expectancy and fertility, which are included in the regressions. Moreover, where many women are involved in domestic rather than market economic activity, the educational enhancement of their contribution to economic welfare may not be picked up directly by standard measures of GDP.

Table 1.1 Predicted Increase in the Level of Output for an Additional Year of Schooling in the Adult Population of an OECD Country

Study	Level Effect (%)
Bassanini and Scarpetta (2002)	6
Mankiw, Romer, and Weil (1992)	6–15

of the workforce enrolled in secondary school. Translating the elasticity into the marginal impact of an additional year of schooling in OECD countries (where average schooling varies between five and twelve years), this implies that steady-state real GDP increases in a range of 6 to 15 percent, with an estimated 8 percent increase for a country like Australia with average schooling of ten years.

Bassanini and Scarpetta (2002) analyze panel data, using annual data for twenty-one OECD countries from 1971 to 1998. They use a pooled mean group estimator, which allows for cross-country variations in short-run coefficients, but they test for and impose homogeneity on long-run coefficients. Their most reliable estimates suggest that the return to an additional year of schooling is a 6 percent increase in steady-state output. Table 1.1 summarizes these results.

These macroeconomic estimates refer to that part of the social returns to schooling that is captured in GDP. It appears that these estimates are close in magnitude to microeconomic estimates of private returns to the education of individuals. This implies that the external effects of education are relatively small, at least in the context of the *level* effects of education.

These conclusions must be modified, however, in the light of a series of empirical studies that have been inspired by the hypothesis of Nelson and Phelps (1966) that human capital may influence the rate of introduction of new technologies. Benhabib and Spiegel (1994), for example, compare models that treat human capital as a direct input into production with models treating human capital as an intermediate input into the acquisition of skills and/or knowledge. The former implies a relationship between output growth and educational growth, whereas the latter implies a relationship between output growth and the average stock of human capital per worker. Their econometric evidence favours the latter model. A more educated workforce can more readily identify, adapt, and implement new ideas—whether the ideas are generated domestically or overseas.

This finding, that education levels affect long-run technological progress, is confirmed by Frantzen (2000), who analyzes the growth of total factor productivity (TFP) between 1961 and 1991 in the business sectors of twenty-one OECD countries. It is also confirmed by Dowrick and Rogers (2002), who investigate the rate of technological convergence between 1970 and 1990 for a wide sample of fifty-one countries and for a sample of thirty-five relatively rich countries.

Table 1.2 **Predicted Increase in Long-Run Economic Growth in Australia Due to an Additional Year of Schooling in the Adult Population**

Study	Growth Effect (percentage points)
Benhabib and Spiegel (1994)	0.3
Frantzen (2000)	0.8
Dowrick and Rogers (2002)	0.2–0.5[a]

[a]The lower of these estimates is derived using the coefficient reported in table 2 in Dowrick and Rogers (2002) using the full sample of countries. The higher estimate is from the coefficients in table 3, using the thirty-five-country sample of relatively rich economies with better data quality.

These studies share a common regression specification of the general form

$$\text{(10)} \qquad \text{TFP growth in country } i = \alpha S_i + \beta S_i f(\text{pr}_i) + \ldots,$$

where S_i is the average years of schooling in the adult population, and pr_i is the ratio of productivity in the technologically leading country relative to country *i*.

The first regression coefficient, α, captures the impact of schooling on domestic innovation. The second regression coefficient, β, captures the impact of schooling on the absorption of technological spillovers from the technologically leading country.

All three studies find that the level of schooling is a statistically significant determinant of growth. The predicted effect of an additional year of schooling in the adult population on the annual rate of growth of TFP is $\alpha + \beta f(\text{pr}_i)$. Considering the case of Australia, where the U.S. productivity ratio is approximately 1.5, we compare the predicted growth effects of schooling in table 1.2.

Even the lowest of these estimates predicts a highly significant boost to annual economic growth, one-fifth of a percentage point, for every additional year of schooling.

1.4.1 Australia's Educational Attainment Report

In the light of these estimates, it is of interest to draw up a report card on Australia's record of educational attainment. The data we use are taken from Barro and Lee (2001), who have revised and updated their previous estimates of the average years of schooling in the population aged twenty-five and over. Figure 1.2 shows the time path of this measure for Australia and selected OECD countries.

Forty years ago, Australian adults averaged 9.4 years of schooling, a level of attainment that not only was significantly above that of the other countries illustrated, but was surpassed only by New Zealand out of the 100 countries covered by Barro and Lee. By the year 2000, Australia's av-

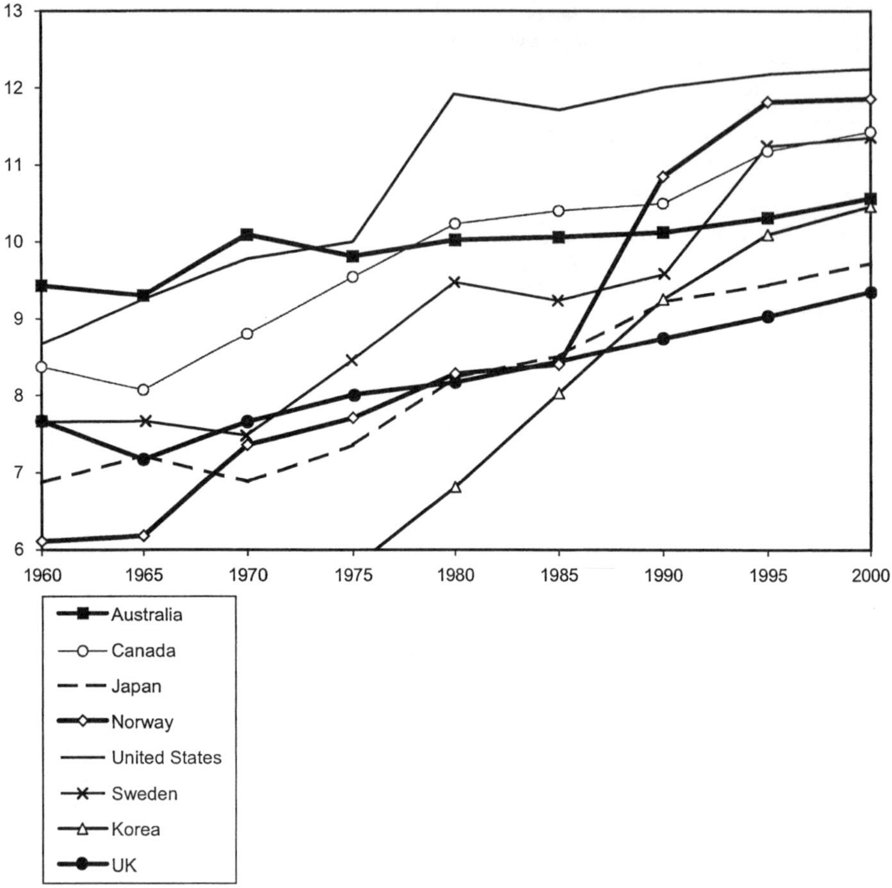

Fig. 1.2 Average years of schooling in the adult population
Source: Barro and Lee (2001).

erage schooling level had climbed to 10.6 years. Attainment rose faster, however, in all of our comparator countries, with the result that Australia has slipped below the United States, Norway, Sweden, and Canada, is only fractionally higher than Korea, and is only slightly higher than Japan.

Of course, the average of years of schooling is an imperfect measure of skills and abilities, since educational quality varies across countries and over time, and because it ignores the abilities acquired through experience and workplace training. In the mid-1990s, twenty countries participated in the OECD's International Adult Literacy Survey. This survey provides a direct comparison of work-related skills, including measures of literacy and numeracy. Figure 1.3 presents a scatter plot that demonstrates that, on either measure, Australian adults rate close to the OECD average.

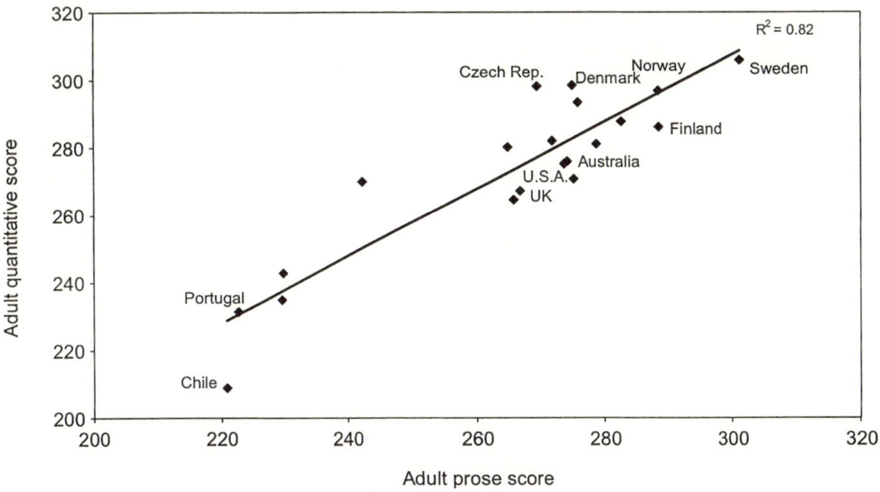

Fig. 1.3 Quantitative and verbal skills
Source: Barro and Lee (2001).

The Third International Maths and Science Study, conducted in 1994 and 1995, confirms Australia's average performance. On measures of seventh-grade proficiency in math and science, Australian school students ranked fifteenth and twelfth respectively out of the thirty-seven country scores reported by Barro and Lee (2001).

These international comparisons suggest that Australia's educational report card should be marked "Started well, but slacked off. Substantial room for improvement."

1.5 The Contribution of Research and Development to Economic Growth

I have already discussed the attributes of knowledge that make it significantly different from the accumulation of items of physical capital. These special attributes are nonrivalry and dynamic feedback. Once a new idea has been generated, it can be used simultaneously and costlessly in many different processes. Furthermore, the idea can serve as an example and inspiration for further research.

These are the attributes of knowledge that give it the potential to drive long-run growth. But the properties of nonrivalry and feedback also suggest that the market may fail to allocate sufficient resources to knowledge generation because individuals have difficulty in establishing and enforcing property rights over their new ideas: Some of the benefits of an innovation are likely to accrue to others. When the private return to innovation is less than the social return, governments need to subsidize R&D.

Paul M. Romer (1993) has argued that while governments should fund fundamental research, it may well be appropriate for self-funding industry associations to fund development and applied research—using governments only to enforce the collection of agreed contributions.[12] Weder and Grubel (1993) expand this point in their discussion of the "Coasean" institutions that operate in various countries to internalize knowledge spillovers and promote technical progress. In particular, they cite the occurrence of three types: (1) industry associations such as the Japanese *keiretsu* or Swiss Verbande; (2) conglomerate corporations, including multinational enterprises; and (3) geographic clustering of industries, such as Silicon Valley or the Northern Italian networks. They point particularly to the Swiss and Japanese examples, where voluntary associations, supported by public policy, encourage long-run relationships between vertically related firms and encourage joint ventures and cooperation including joint research and training schemes.

Expenditures on R&D typically constitute, for advanced economies, only a few percent of GDP—perhaps one-tenth of the expenditure devoted to investment in physical equipment and structures. In a standard growth accounting framework, variations in research effort will, therefore, explain very little of the differences in growth rates between countries. But the point of much of the new growth theory is precisely that if knowledge spillovers are substantial, and if knowledge exhibits dynamic feedback effects, then even small changes in the resources devoted to the production of knowledge may result in substantial changes in economic growth. This point is made by Grossman and Helpman (1991), who calibrate their model to match the U.S. growth experience. They predict that, while business investment constitutes around 10 percent of GDP, investment in R&D—the engine of growth—need comprise as little as 1.6 percent to generate economic growth of 2.5 percent per year.

Lichtenberg and Siegel (1991) surveyed some fifteen previous studies into R&D investment by U.S. firms and industries, reporting real private rates of return averaging 25 percent. Their own econometric study of two thousand U.S. firms revealed a 30 percent rate of return on company-funded R&D, a "productivity premium" on basic research, and a 7 percent return on federally funded company research. These estimates of private rates of return on company-funded R&D are very high, given that investment in physical capital might be expected to earn a return closer to 10 percent. The higher rate of return on research reflects, presumably, a large premium for risk and problems in diversifying or pooling such risk.

Nadiri (1993) confirms that private returns to R&D are particularly high in his review of the literature: "[N]et rates of return on own R&D of 20% to 30% at the firm level and 10% to 30% at the industry level are reasonable sets of estimates." He goes on to examine spillovers to other industries and

12. Australian agricultural research has long been funded on this basis.

concludes that "The spillover effects of R&D are often much larger than the effect of own R&D at the industry level. . . . [S]ocial rates of return often vary from 20% to over 100% with an average somewhere close to 50%" (pp. 34–35).

A subsequent paper by Lichtenberg (1992) is one of the first attempts at studying the cross-country evidence on the impact of R&D expenditures on both the level and the rate of growth of real GDP. Using a sample of seventy-four countries, his growth regressions, using the neoclassical framework, reveal that returns to R&D are approximately double the returns to physical investment—a result that is broadly consistent with estimates from the microeconomic studies of firms and industries.

Coe and Helpman (1995) try to quantify the magnitude of international R&D spillovers. They seek to explain variations in the annual growth of TFP for twenty-one OECD countries, plus Israel, over the period 1970–90. Their econometric analysis finds that the stock of knowledge in one country, measured by cumulated historical R&D expenditures, raises productivity in foreign countries with which they trade. It is not clear exactly why the extent of technology transfer should depend on the magnitude of trade with a technologically advanced economy, although their empirical findings appear to be quite robust and have been confirmed by subsequent studies. One plausible explanation stems from the observation by Eaton and Kortum (2001) that the high R&D economies are also the major world exporters of capital goods. The general trade variable used by Coe and Helpman may be acting as a proxy for the import of high-tech capital goods for which the producers are unable to expropriate all of the rents.

Frantzen (2000) has extended the Coe and Helpman approach and provides us with estimates of rates of return on domestic R&D as well as estimating the strength of international technological spillovers. He finds that the following regression has strong statistical significance on a sample of twenty-one OECD countries:

The annual growth rate of TFP in the business sector, 1961 − 1991 = 0.59

× (gross expenditure on own R&D)/(business-sector GDP) + 1.52

× SUM[(research intensity in country *i*) · (import share from country *i*)]

The first regression coefficient is an estimate of the national (social) rate of return to R&D—capturing not only the productivity benefits that accrue to the firms which make the investments but also the spillover benefits that accrue to firms in the same or related industries. The second regression coefficient captures the spillover benefit that a country can gain from research carried out by a trading partner. This benefit is proportional to the share of imports from that country in GDP—perhaps reflecting the embodied technological improvements in imported capital equipment.

It is instructive to compare Frantzen's estimates with other estimates of

Table 1.3 Estimated Rates of Return on R&D Expenditures

Study and Sample	Rates of Return (%) Private Returns	Social Returns	Cross-Country Spillovers
Lichtenberg and Siegel (1991)			
Survey of fifteen previous studies of U.S. firms and industries	25		
2000 U.S. firms	30		
Nadiri (1993)			
Survey of fifty U.S. and other studies at firm and industry level	20–30	50	
Lichtenberg and van Pottelsberghe de la Potterie (1996)			
GDP growth across OECD countries		51–63	
Frantzen (2000)			
Business-sector TFP growth across OECD countries		59	45[a]

[a]if the imports-GDP ratio equals 0.3.

returns to R&D expenditures. A summary is provided in table 1.3. Interestingly, he estimates a 59 percent social rate of return on national R&D expenditures, which is close to the average figure suggested by Nadiri's review of firm- and industry-level studies. It is also close to the results of Lichtenberg and van Pottelsberghe de la Potterie (1996), who estimate that the social rate of return on domestic R&D is 51 percent in the large Group of Seven (G7) economies but 63 percent in six smaller European countries.

All of these estimates lie substantially above the various estimates of private rates of return, implying that there are very significant spillover effects between the firms and industries within a national economy.

The implication for Australia of the benchmark Frantzen estimate can be calculated as follows. Our gross annual R&D expenditure (public and private combined) of around ten billion dollars amounts to 1.5 percent of total GDP, or approximately 2 percent of business-sector value added. An additional billion dollars' annual expenditure on R&D, representing one-fifth of 1 percent of value added, is predicted to increase the annual growth rate by just over one-tenth of a percentage point.

What would happen if the countries from which Australia imports capital goods were each to increase their research intensity by 0.2 percentage points (the same rise as in the example for Australia)? If we multiply the regression coefficient on foreign R&D by Australia's total share of imports in GDP, which is 30 percent, we find that technology spillovers are predicted to increase Australian growth by just over one-tenth of a percentage point. In other words, domestic R&D and spillovers from foreign R&D are of roughly equal importance for productivity growth.

1.5.1 Australia's Investment in Research and Development

Compared with the leading industrial economies of the OECD, Australia invests less of its resources into R&D—and a lesser proportion of that investment is carried out within the business sector. In figure 1.4 we see that the share of GDP devoted to R&D in Australia has been growing over the past few decades, from under 1 percent to around 1.5 percent. Our research intensity is, however, still well below that achieved by major industrial economies such as Japan, the United States, and Germany, where the R&D ratio has averaged 2.5 percent over the past twenty years. On the other hand, Australian R&D intensity is close to or above that of Canada and New Zealand, countries with comparably large rural sectors. R&D intensity dipped after peaking at 1.7 percent in 1996. This is attributable in the first instance to a fall in R&D within the business sector of the Australian economy, which was driven in part by the reduction in the tax concession for R&D.

Even at its peak, the Australian business sector's contribution to R&D has been comparatively low. In figure 1.5 we see that the proportion of total R&D that is carried out in the business sector had been rising from 1981 up to 1995, from 25 percent to 51 percent, but then fell to 45 percent by 1998. In the economies that are illustrated in figure 1.6, with the exception of Australia and New Zealand, well over half of national R&D was carried out by the business sector.

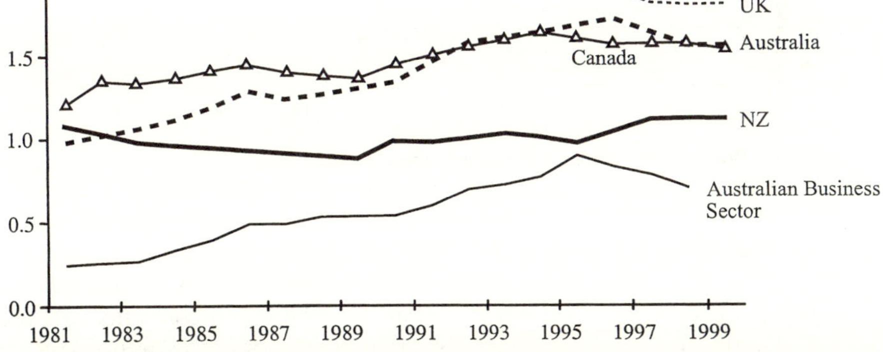

Fig. 1.4 Gross expenditure on R&D as % of GDP, 1981–99
Source: OECD R&D database.

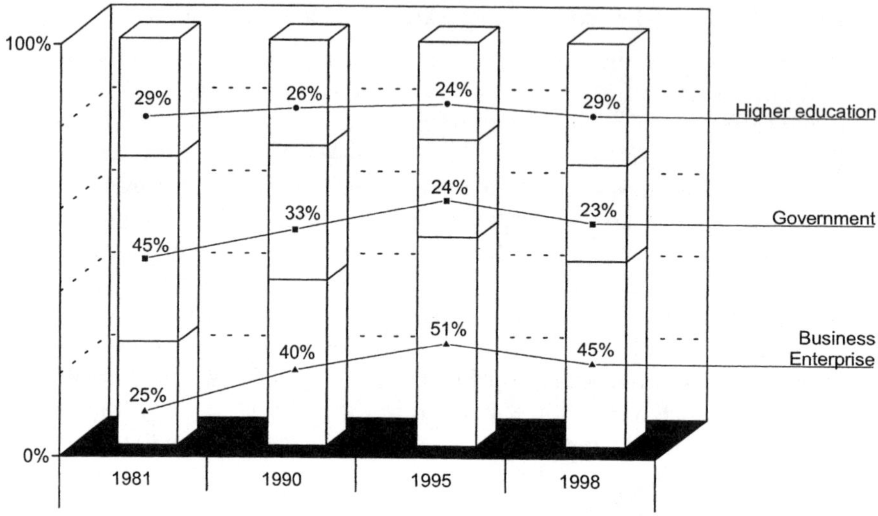

Fig. 1.5 Sectoral composition of Australian R&D

Note: The residual category is the share of private nonprofit R&D.

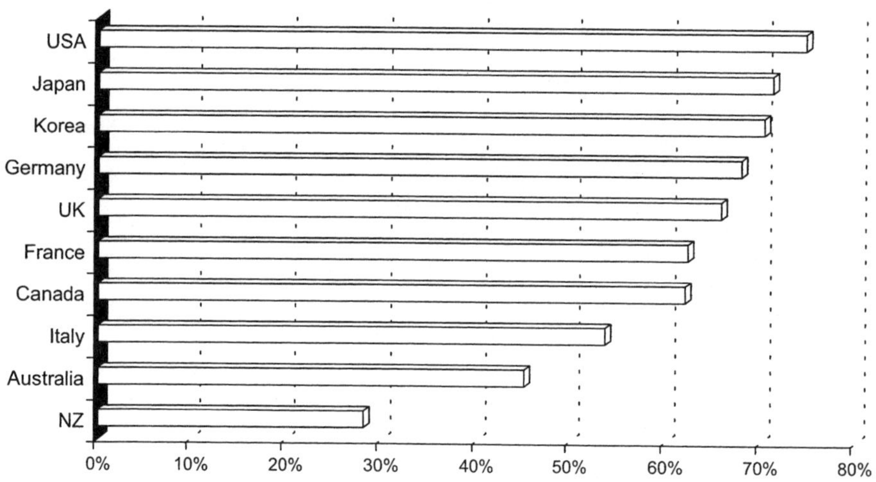

Fig. 1.6 Business enterprise R&D as a share of total (1988)

Source: OECD R&D database.

An interesting perspective on Australian performance on a broader measure of "investment in knowledge" comes from OECD (2001), which aggregates expenditures on R&D, higher education, and computer software. On this measure, Australia ranks fourteenth out of the twenty-four countries surveyed. In terms of the rate of growth of knowledge investment over the 1990s, Australia ranks tenth.

1.6 Conclusions

The neoclassical revival in growth theory has had the paradoxical effect of reinforcing one of the major points of the endogenous growth revolution. The driving force of economic growth is investment in human capital—skills and ideas—rather than investment in machines and buildings. The academic debate will no doubt continue over whether government policies that affect the rate of investment have any influence on the long-run, as well as the short-run, rate of growth of the economy. For practical purposes, however, if the "short run" involves a transition period of several decades, this debate may be strictly academic—in the pejorative sense of the word. Policies that affect investment, particularly in embodied or disembodied human capital, can have a sustained impact on economic growth.

A review of empirical studies on sources of economic growth confirms these claims: Both education and R&D are important sources of growth. In the mid-1990s, a number of studies were published claiming that there was no systematic relationship between changes in national educational attainment and changes in economic growth. Subsequent studies have, however, established that this lack of correlation was due to a mix of factors: poor institutional performance in some less-developed economies, and a failure to account for international variation in educational quality. Once we account for these factors, the evidence suggests returns to education that are consistent with microeconomic evidence on individual earnings. An increase of one year of schooling in the average educational attainment in the workforce, for example, can be expected to increase the long-run level of output by around 8 percent in a typical OECD country.

These are estimates of the *level* effects of education. A one-off increase in attainment will produce a one-off rise (albeit spread over time) in the level of GDP per capita. There is mounting evidence, however, that there are also substantial dynamic or *growth* effects, which are linked to a country's ability to implement new technologies. This evidence suggests that Australia would do well to increase its educational levels to match the OECD leaders: the United States and Scandinavia.

One of the concerns of current public debate is that the aging of the Australian population over the next fifty years will overtax (literally and metaphorically) the working-age population. From the perspective of growth theory, however, there may not be so much to fear. The aging of the demographic structure is being driven by the revolution in female education and workforce opportunities. For the generation born in the 1930s, only one-third of girls and one-half of boys completed high school. For the current generation, over 70 percent of boys and close to 80 percent of girls are completing year twelve. The past fifty years have also witnessed the end of legally enforced discrimination against women in the workforce—in the form of the marriage bar and legalized wage discrimination. These huge improvements in female education and workforce opportunities have been major factors in the fall in fertility, which is the driving force behind the changing age structure of the population.

The very factor that is causing the aging of the population, the revolution in women's education, gives us reason to expect continued strong growth of the Australian economy. The average educational attainment of the workforce will continue to rise for the next three decades as historical increases in school enrollments work their way through the adult population. These effects will be enhanced should educational enrollment continue to rise—particularly if the educational participation and achievement of Australia's young men rises to meet the levels of young women.

The evidence on the benefits of innovation is clear. A wide range of studies finds that private rates of return on R&D expenditures are very high, and that social rates of return—taking account of intranational spillovers of knowledge—are even higher.

We can summarize the potential productivity benefits for Australia of increased investment in education and research by using relatively conservative benchmark estimates, based on the large number of studies that have been summarized in this paper. Taking education first, an increase of 0.8 in the average years of schooling of the labor force would take us to 11.4 years, the average of the levels of attainment in North America and Scandinavia. The effect on the Australian economy would be an increase of one-third of a percentage point in the annual growth rate—coming both through human capital deepening and more rapid adoption of new technologies.[13]

Turning to investment in R&D, it is probably unrealistic to suppose that Australia will match the research intensity of the world leaders such as the United States or Germany. Adopting a more realistic role model, France, would require that an extra 0.6 percent of GDP be devoted to R&D—taking research intensity from 1.6 percent to 2.2 percent. Using a conservative estimate of the social rate of return,[14] the impact on the Australian economy would be an increase of one-quarter of a percentage point in the annual rate of productivity growth.

To sum up, positive prospects for continuing strong productivity growth will be enhanced if Australia emulates the higher rates of investment in knowledge—both in education and in R&D—that we observe in the leading OECD economies. An increasingly well-educated (albeit shrinking)

13. From table 1.1, the conservative estimate of the level effect is 0.8×6 percent = 0.048, which is equivalent to 0.0012 per year over forty years. From table 1.2, a conservative estimate of dynamic effect is $0.8 \times 0.003 = 0.0024$ per year. The two effects sum to 0.0036, or 0.36 percentage points per year.

14. Assuming the social rate of return is 0.4, which is substantially below the estimates summarized in table 3.

workforce, operating in an economy that continues to be open to trade in goods and ideas, will be well placed to identify, introduce, and manage the new technologies that will emerge over the next few decades.

References

Abramovitz, Moses. 1986. Catching up, forging ahead, and falling behind. *Journal of Economic History* 46:385–406.

Aghion, Philippe, and Peter Howitt. 1992. A model of growth through creative destruction. *Econometrica* 60 (March): 323–51.

———. 1998. *Endogenous growth theory.* Cambridge, Mass.: MIT Press.

Apps, Patricia, and Ray Rees. 2001. Household production, full consumption and the costs of children. *Labour Economics* 8 (6): 621–48.

Ashenfelter, Orley, and Alan B. Krueger. 1994. Estimates of the economic returns to schooling from a new sample of twins. *American Economic Review* 84 (5): 1157–73.

Ashenfelter, Orley, and Cecilia Rouse. 1997. Income, schooling, and ability: Evidence from a new sample of identical twins. NBER Working Paper no. 5688. Cambridge, Mass.: National Bureau of Economic Research, July.

———. 1998. Income, schooling, and ability: Evidence from a new sample of identical twins. *Quarterly Journal of Economics* 113 (1): 253–84.

Barro, Robert J. 1991. Economic growth in a cross section of countries. *Quarterly Journal of Economics* 106 (2): 407–43.

Barro, Robert J., and Jong-Wha Lee. 1994. Sources of economic growth. *Carnegie Rochester Conference Series on Public Policy* 40 (0): 1–46.

———. 2001. International data on educational attainment: Updates and implications. *Oxford Economic Papers* 53 (3): 541–63.

Barro, Robert J., and Xavier Sala-i-Martin. 1995. *Economic growth.* New York: McGraw-Hill.

Bassanini, Andrea, and Stefano Scarpetta. 2002. Does human capital matter for growth in OECD countries? A pooled mean-group approach. *Economics Letters* 74:399–405.

Benhabib, Jess, and Mark Spiegel. 1994. The role of human capital in economic development: Evidence from aggregate cross-country data. *Journal of Monetary Economics* 34 (2): 143–73.

Borland, Jeff, and Xiaokai Yang. 1992. Specialization and a new approach to economic organization and growth. *American Economic Review* 82 (2): 386–91.

Caselli, Francesco, Gerardo Esquivel, and Fernando Lefort. 1996. Reopening the convergence debate: A new look at cross-country growth empirics. *Journal of Economic Growth* 1 (September): 363–89.

Coe, David T., and Elhanan Helpman. 1995. International R&D spillovers. *European Economic Review* 39 (5): 859–87.

Dowrick, Steve, and Duc Tho Nguyen. 1989. OECD comparative economic growth 1950–85: Catch-up and convergence. *American Economic Review* 79 (5): 1010–30.

Dowrick, Steve, and Mark Rogers. 2002. Classical and technological convergence: Beyond the Solow-Swan growth model. *Oxford Economic Papers* 54:369–385.

Eaton, Jonathan, and Samuel Kortum. 2001. Trade in capital goods. NBER Working Paper no. 8070. Cambridge, Mass.: National Bureau of Economic Research, January.

Folbre, Nancy, and Julie A. Nelson. 2000. For love or money—or both? *Journal of Economic Perspectives* 14 (4): 123–40.

Frantzen, Dirk. 2000. R&D, human capital and international technology spillovers: A cross-country analysis. *Scandinavian Journal of Economics* 102 (1): 57–75.

Grossman, Gene M., and Elhanan Helpman. 1991. Trade, knowledge spillovers, and growth. *European Economic Review* 35:517–26.

Hanushek, Eric A., and Dennis D. Kimko. 2000. Schooling, labor-force quality, and the growth of nations. *American Economic Review* 90 (5): 1184–208.

Islam, Nazrul. 1995. Growth empirics: A panel data approach. *The Quarterly Journal of Economics* 110 (443): 1127–70.

Jones, Charles I. 1995a. R&D-based models of economic growth. *Journal of Political Economy* 103 (4): 759–84.

———. 1995b. Time series tests of endogenous growth models. *Quarterly Journal of Economics* 110 (2): 495–525.

———. 1998. *Introduction to economic growth.* New York: W. W. Norton.

———. 2001. *Sources of U.S. economic growth in a world of ideas. American Economic Review* 92 (1): 220–239.

Jones, Charles I., and John C. Williams. 2000. Too much of a good thing? The economics of investment in R&D. *Journal of Economic Growth* 5 (1): 65–85.

Knowles, Stephen, Paula K. Lorgelly, and P. Dorian Owen. 2002. Are educational gender gaps a brake on economic development? Some cross-country empirical evidence. *Oxford Economic Papers* 54:118–49.

Krueger, Alan B., and Mikael Lindahl. 2001. Education for growth: Why and for whom? *Journal of Economic Literature* 39:1101–36.

Lee, Kevin, M. Hashem Pesaran, and Ron Smith. 1997. Growth and convergence in a multi-country empirical stochastic Solow model. *Journal of Applied Econometrics* 12:357–92.

Lichtenberg, Frank R. 1992. R&D investment and international productivity differences. NBER Working Paper no. 4161. Cambridge, Mass.: National Bureau of Economic Research.

Lichtenberg, Frank R., and Donald Siegel. 1991. The impact of R&D investment on productivity: New evidence using linked R&D-LRD data. *Economic Inquiry* 29 (April): 203–28.

Lichtenberg, Frank, and Bruno van Pottelsberghe de la Potterie. 1996. International R&D spillovers: A re-examination. NBER Working Paper no. 5668. Cambridge, Mass.: National Bureau of Economic Research, July.

Lucas, Robert E., Jr. 1988. On the mechanics of economic development. *Journal of Monetary Economics* 22 (1): 3–42.

Mankiw, N. Gregory, David Romer, and David N. Weil. 1992. A contribution to the empirics of economic growth. *Quarterly Journal of Economics* 107 (2): 407–37.

Miller, Paul W., Charles Mulvey, and Nick Martin. 1995. What do twins studies reveal about the economic returns to education? A comparison of Australian and U.S. findings. *American Economic Review* 85 (3): 586–99.

Nadiri, M. Ishaq. 1993. Innovations and technological spillovers. NBER Working Paper no. 4423. Cambridge, Mass.: National Bureau of Economic Research.

Nelson, Richard R., and Edmund S. Phelps. 1966. Investment in humans, technological diffusion, and economic growth. *The American Economic Review* 56 (1/2): 69–75.

Organization for Economic Cooperation and Development (OECD). 2001. *STI Scoreboard.* Paris: Author.

Pitchford, John. 1960. Growth and the elasticity of factor substitution. *Economic Record* 36 (December): 491–504.
Preston, Alison. 1997. Where are we now with human capital theory in Australia? *The Economic Record* 73 (220): 51–78.
Rebelo, Sergio. 1991. Long-run policy analysis and long-run growth. *Journal of Political Economy* 99 (3): 500–21.
Romer, Paul. 1993. Idea gaps and object gaps in economic development. *Journal of Monetary Economics* 32 (3): 543–73.
Romer, Paul M. 1986. Increasing returns and long-run growth. *Journal of Political Economy* 94 (5): 1002–37.
———. 1990. Endogenous technological change. *Journal of Political Economy* 98 (5): S71–S102.
———. 1993. Implementing a national technology strategy with self-organizing industry investment boards. *Brookings Papers on Economic Activity, Microeconomics:* 345–90.
———. 1994. The origins of endogenous growth. *Journal of Economic Perspectives* 8 (1): 3–22.
Sachs, Jeffrey D., and Andrew M. Warner. 1997. Fundamental sources of long-run growth. *American Economic Review* 87 (2): 184–88.
Shi, Heling L., and Xiaokai K. Yang. 1995. A new theory of industrialization. *Journal of Comparative Economics* 20 (2): 171–89.
Solow, Robert M. 1994. Perspectives on growth theory. *Journal of Economic Perspectives* 8 (1): 45–54.
Temple, Jonathan R. W. 2001. Generalizations that aren't? Evidence on education and growth. *European Economic Review* 45 (4–6): 905–18.
Weder, Rolf, and Herbert G. Grubel. 1993. The new growth theory and Coasean economics: Institutions to capture externalities. *Weltwirtschaftliches Archiv:* 488–513.
Yang, Xiaokai, and Jeff Borland. 1991. A microeconomic mechanism for economic growth. *Journal of Political Economy* 99 (31): 460–82.

Comment John Leahy

This paper provides a nice survey of the literature on knowledge and growth. At the heart of the discussion is the contrasting role played by knowledge in traditional growth theory and in the "new" growth theory.

In the traditional theory, as reformulated in the 1990s, knowledge is embodied in human capital. As its name suggests, human capital is just another form of capital. Human capital, like physical capital, is accumulated through investment, in this case investment in education. Like physical capital, it is subject to diminishing returns; given the supplies of the other factors, each additional unit of education adds a bit less to aggregate production. Modeling knowledge in this way does very little to alter the im-

John Leahy is professor of economics at New York University and a research associate of the National Bureau of Economic Research.

plications of traditional growth models, namely that accumulation of factors is subject to diminishing returns and does little to raise growth in the long run.

New growth theory makes two challenges to the traditional theory. First, by assuming constant returns to accumulable factors, it challenges the assumption that growth is exogenous in the long run. Second, by reinterpreting knowledge as ideas rather than human capital, it opens the door for the modeling of a number of interesting externalities.

While much has been made of the first challenge, I agree with Dowrick that the important contribution of the new growth literature lies in the reinterpretation of the role of knowledge and the novel externalities that arise. Endogenous growth depends on functional form assumptions that are convenient mathematically but for which we have no empirical evidence. We have no idea what would happen if suddenly the world found itself with twice the physical capital and twice the human capital, since this event has not yet happened.

The interpretation of knowledge as ideas has several implications that are relevant for public policy. First, ideas, unlike human capital, are nonrival. Absent legal restrictions, the fact that one person has an idea does not prevent others from having or using the same idea. The social returns to developing a new idea may therefore exceed the private return. The optimal government response may be to subsidize research. On the other hand, new ways of doing things tend to replace old ways of doing things. This creative destruction may mean that social returns are actually lower than private returns. Innovators do not take into consideration the losses to others that their innovations create. In such a case, the optimal government response would be to tax innovation.

The important question for public policymakers regards the size of these effects. The paper does a good job of surveying the empirical literature. Current studies tend to find large spillovers. Education in one country appears to raise productivity at home and abroad. The returns to R&D appear great, but the social returns appear greater still. These results appear to justify large subsidies to education and research and development.

At this point, I believe that the author could have been a bit more skeptical. I have severe doubts concerning both the magnitude and the interpretation of these results. As concerns interpretation, it is very difficult to identify a causal link between education and growth, let alone external effects of education within a country or the spillovers onto other countries. Not only may causality be reversed—with growth providing the resources for greater education—but countries with the foresight to educate their population probably get a lot of other things right as well. They may be more stable or have lower discount rates or better tax policy. They may subsidize other activities related to knowledge creation. They may have social systems that reward effort at all levels. It is very difficult to identify the effect of an exogenous shift in human capital induced by a government subsidy to education. Most studies do not even attempt to use instrumental variables, probably because there are few valid instruments.

The other problem is that some of the estimated effects are implausibly large. Most of the R&D studies cited in the paper find private rates of return in the neighborhood of 25 percent. This raises the question "Why are private agents not doing more R&D?" Firms appear to be leaving a lot of money on the table. Maybe, however, these returns are overstated and government-subsidized or -funded projects would yield substantially less. One possibility is that these estimates capture average rather than marginal rates of return. For example, economic research is valuable, but would doubling the money spent on economic research double the output of economic knowledge? Probably not. Another possibility is survivorship bias. We may not measure correctly all of the money spent on projects that don't pan out. Firms that fail are often dropped from the sample. In the end, the 7 percent return cited on federally funded R&D makes one wonder if policies would yield such amazing results.

In my mind, generating convincing estimates of the size of the externalities emphasized by the new growth literature remains one of the more important tasks facing growth economics.

Comment Andrew K. Rose

Steve Dowrick has given us a long, thorough, but focused survey of education and growth. He gives a fine summary of the theoretical literature that has obsessed much of the macroeconomics profession for the 1990s and concludes that the issue of whether growth is better modeled as being endogenous or exogenous may not actually be that relevant in practice. More important to my mind, he has also provided a number of estimates from both the micro- and macroeconomic literatures on the effects of education on output, and he concludes that they are large, even for an advanced OECD country like Australia. He believes there are large externalities and that the case for government intervention is secure. I agree with most of what he says, which seems reasonable in both the small and the large.

My personal view is that a survey like this should always focus precisely on a well-defined question. In this case, Dowrick is interested in answers to the question "What is the return to an additional year of education?" This creates a convenient taxonomy to organize the empirical estimates from

Andrew K. Rose is B.T. Rocca Professor of Economic Analysis and Policy at the Haas School of Business, University of California–Berkeley, and a research associate of the National Bureau of Economic Research.

the literature. It is divided into micro- and macroeconomic estimates at three levels: (1) the returns to the individual; (2) the returns to the nation, which may well be higher if there are externalities; and (3) the returns to the world, which may be higher still if there are foreign externalities. Of course, there is also the possibility of negative externalities, and Dowrick considers the costs of extra education which also play into the analysis.

In future work like this, I would like to see more emphasis placed on the externalities themselves. How much do we really know from quantifiable microeconomic evidence on the existence of large positive externalities? Since this is where the real case for policy intervention lies, I personally would feel more confident if I could cite a number of reliable studies that present strong evidence of positive externalities.

The reason I would find this is reassuring lies in the magnitudes of the returns to education cited. Almost all the returns to education and R&D are high—huge, in fact. It makes me feel that I've personally underinvested! More generally, the returns are so high that they strain plausibility. Lots of education is wasted, and much R&D might well be unproductive—is it all being taken into account? Let me put it another way. The returns are so large that the question of the paper's title is almost irrelevant, since the issue of levels versus growth rate effects is a sideshow if the returns are so high. So is concern for underinvestment in education, if the personal returns are as high as cited.

I also believe there is a lot of scope in this area for a comprehensive meta-analysis. This is the increasingly accepted way to conduct a quantitative survey. The author chooses a coefficient of interest that has been estimated in a number of papers—for instance, the value of a marginal year of education. Each paper contributes a single observation of this underlying variable, and the resulting vector of estimates is treated as the dependent variable. The characteristics of the studies are treated as the regressors. Meta-analysis like this might enable us to understand the sources of variation in the estimates of the returns to education, and enable us to handle them with more confidence.

2 Australia's 1990s Productivity Surge and Its Determinants

Dean Parham

2.1 Introduction

Australia's growth performance since the early 1990s has been exceptional. Over the last ten years, annual gross domestic product (GDP) growth averaged just under 4 percent—a performance not seen since the 1960s and early 1970s. Strong growth even persisted in the midst of the 1997 Asian financial crisis and the 2001 global downturn.

A surge in productivity growth has underpinned Australia's good performance. After showing its weakest rate in the 1980s, Australia's productivity growth accelerated by a little over 1 percentage point to new highs in the 1990s—labor productivity growth at an average 3.2 percent a year and multifactor productivity (MFP) growth at 1.8 percent a year.

The much-improved performance has stimulated a search for reasons. A few commentators have disputed the significance of the evidence of a productivity surge by speculating about the influence of recovery from the early 1990s recession and measurement error.[1] But the length and strength

Dean Parham is assistant commissioner at the Productivity Commission, Australia.

This paper partly draws on and updates previous work undertaken with colleagues Paul Roberts and Haishun Sun (Parham, Roberts, and Sun 2001). Paula Barnes, Paul Roberts, and Tracey Horsfall assisted with the preparation of the paper. Richard Snape made comments on a previous draft. Helpful comments from discussants at the seminar and the editors and referees of the volume of proceedings are gratefully acknowledged. Any remaining errors are mine. The views expressed do not necessarily reflect the views of the Productivity Commission.

1. To account for an acceleration in productivity growth any measurement error would have to have worsened (if an overestimation) or diminished (if an underestimation). The latter is more possible in that estimation of productivity in some service industries may have improved. On the other hand, many OECD countries have similarly improved and harmonized aspects of estimation, without generating estimates of productivity acceleration anywhere near the strength of Australia's.

of the productivity resurgence—controlling for cyclical influences—demand some "structural" explanations. Most attention has focused on three candidates:

- a shift in the production frontier due to the introduction of new technology—specifically information and communications technologies (ICTs);
- a shift toward the frontier through efficiency improvements stimulated by a set of microeconomic policy reforms—"catch-up" gains from firms moving toward best practice and from resources shifting to where they can be used more productively;
- an increase in average education attainment and skills that would increase human capital deepening and promote productivity through the absorption and development of technologies and efficient business practices.

This paper concentrates on the first possible explanation, particularly since there has been worldwide interest in ICTs as a source of productivity growth. A comparison with U.S. experience, using a growth accounting framework, provides the basis for assessing the contribution of ICTs to Australia's aggregate productivity acceleration. Productivity growth and the ICT contributions to it are sensitive to cyclical effects. This study is distinguished from others by the attention paid to selection of periods that minimize cyclical effects. The paper also draws on other empirical work to briefly assess other possible explanations.

2.2 An Overview of Australia's Productivity Performance

Australia's recent productivity performance needs to be set in a broad historical and international context to highlight some of the developments that should be covered in a comprehensive explanation of the 1990s surge.

2.2.1 A Broad Sweep across Countries and the Decades

Australia's rate of productivity growth was comparatively low over most of the twentieth century. At the beginning of the century, Australia had one of the highest levels of labor productivity in the world (Maddison 2001), reflecting a relative abundance of natural resources per hour worked. Governments subsequently traded this high productivity position for nation building as, with widespread popular support, they encouraged population growth, diversification of the economic base, and redistribution of income through a set of policies that (perhaps unintentionally) held growth in productivity in check.

Nevertheless, Australia still enjoyed a relatively high ranking at the start of the postwar era. In 1950, Australia's GDP per hour was 81 percent of

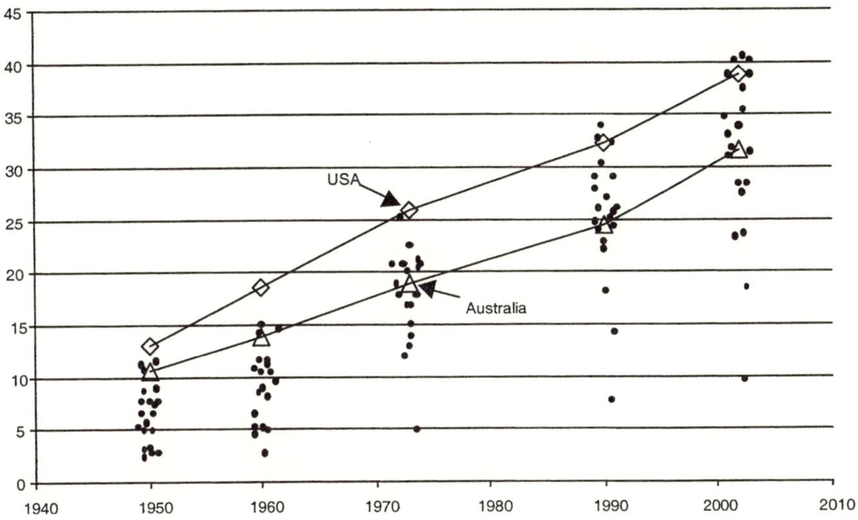

Fig. 2.1 Labor productivity in OECD countries, 1950, 1960, 1973, 1990, and 2001: GDP per hour (US$ at purchasing power parity)

Source: Data from University of Groningen and The Conference Board, GGDC Total Economy Database, 2003; http://www.eco.rug.nl/ggdc, accessed 25 July 2003.

the productivity leader—the United States—and it ranked fourth among a group of twenty-two developed or high-income countries (figure 2.1[2] and table 2.1).

The next four decades were a period of catch-up to the leader and convergence in productivity levels. European countries, in particular, started to catch up and in some cases overtook the United States (figure 2.1).

Australia did not participate in this "convergence club." Many countries also overtook Australia as it slipped further behind the United States in the 1950s and then merely maintained its position relative to the United States until 1990. Australia's ranking slipped to sixteen by 1990.

A string of policy reviews in the 1960s, 1970s, and 1980s attributed this relatively poor performance to highly regulated product, capital, and labor markets and the inefficient provision of economic infrastructure (energy, water, transport, communications), which was dominated by government-owned enterprises operating without clear commercial imperative or performance regulation.

As a consequence of relatively poor productivity growth, Australia's ranking on the international league table of GDP per capita also dropped—from five in 1950 to sixteen in 1990 (table 2.1).

2. Figure 2.1 shows productivity levels in twenty-two OECD countries in 1950, 1960, 1973, 1990, and 2001. Some observations are offset from the reference year on the chart to avoid overwriting.

Table 2.1 **Australia's Rankings on Productivity, Average Income, and Labor Utilization Levels among Twenty-Two OECD Countries**

	1950	1960	1973	1990	2002
GDP per hour					
Australia's rank	4	5	12	16	16
% of U.S. level	81	75	73	76	83
GDP per capita					
Australia's rank	5	8	10	16	8
% of U.S. level	78	78	76	73	78
Labor utilization					
Australia's rank	15	16	6	6	7
% of U.S. level	96	104	104	96	96

Source: See figure 2.1.

Note: Labor utilization is the number of hours worked per head of total population. It explains the difference between GDP per hour and GDP per capita.

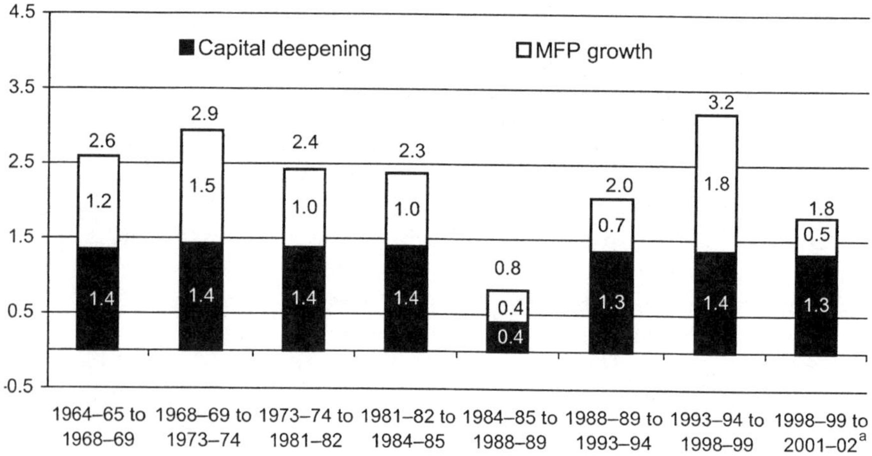

Fig. 2.2 Growth in labor productivity over productivity cycles and contributions from capital deepening and multifactor productivity, 1964–65 to 2001–02: average annual rates of growth (percent)

Source: Australian Bureau of Statistics (ABS) 5204.0 and Productivity Commission estimates.

Note: Productivity cycles are the intervals between productivity peaks, as identified by the ABS. [a]Incomplete cycle.

2.2.2 The Productivity Surge in the 1990s

Figure 2.2 shows the rates of labor productivity growth over productivity cycles in the market sector of the Australian economy. Measurement over productivity cycles—from productivity peak to productivity peak—neutralizes the spurious influence of the business cycle. The latest period, 1998–99 to 2001–02, is not a complete cycle. Since productivity growth over this period cannot be taken confidently to be an underlying

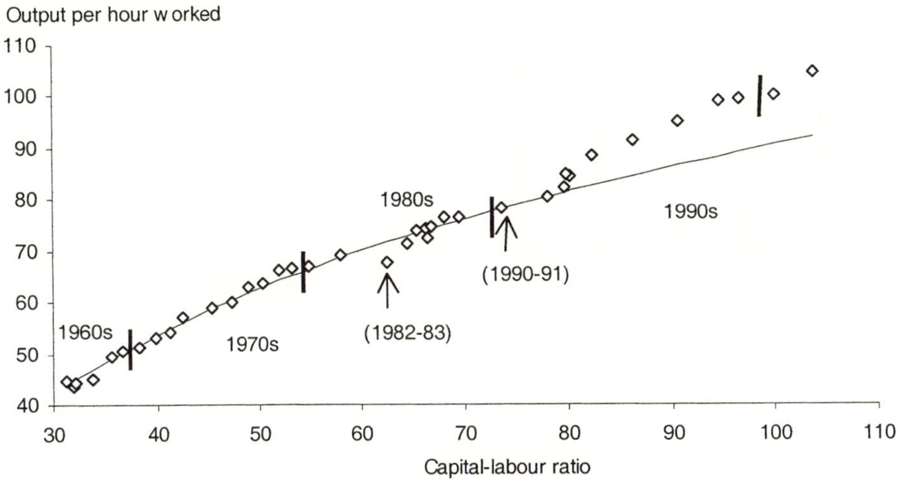

Fig. 2.3 Australia's growth path, 1964–65 to 2001–02 (indexes 2001–01 = 100)
Source: ABS 5204.0.
Note: The years in brackets correspond to troughs in the business cycle.

rate, attention is focused on the most recent completed cycle, 1993–94 to 1998–99.

The figure shows that Australia's productivity growth rebounded in the 1990s, with underlying rates reaching record highs. The record 3.2 percent annual average labor productivity growth in the 1993–94 to 1998–99 cycle compares with an average of 2.0 percent in the previous cycle and 1.7 percent over the cycles from 1981–82 to 1993–94.

MFP growth was the major contributor to improved labor productivity growth. With the rate of capital deepening stable at around 1.4 percent a year, better MFP growth has accounted for all of the acceleration in Australia's underlying labor productivity growth (fig. 2.2). Record MFP growth of 1.8 percent a year accounted for around two-thirds of labor productivity growth in the 1990s cycle. MFP accelerated from 0.7 percent a year—the average over both the previous cycle and the three cycles between 1981–82 and 1993–94.

The start of the surge cannot be pinpointed with precision because of recession-related effects. Figure 2.3 suggests that the Australian economy took a new growth path, based on higher MFP growth, in the early 1990s, by 1993.[3] Even without precision, it would appear that Australia's

3. Figure 2.3 plots paired observations of the capital-labor ratio and labor productivity levels. Because of the general tendency of capital deepening, the observations line up in chronological order. Shifts from one observation to another can be attributed to combinations of capital deepening and MFP growth. If the relative importance of MFP growth increases, as happened in the 1990s, the observations follow a steeper gradient. See Parham (1999) for more details on growth path analysis.

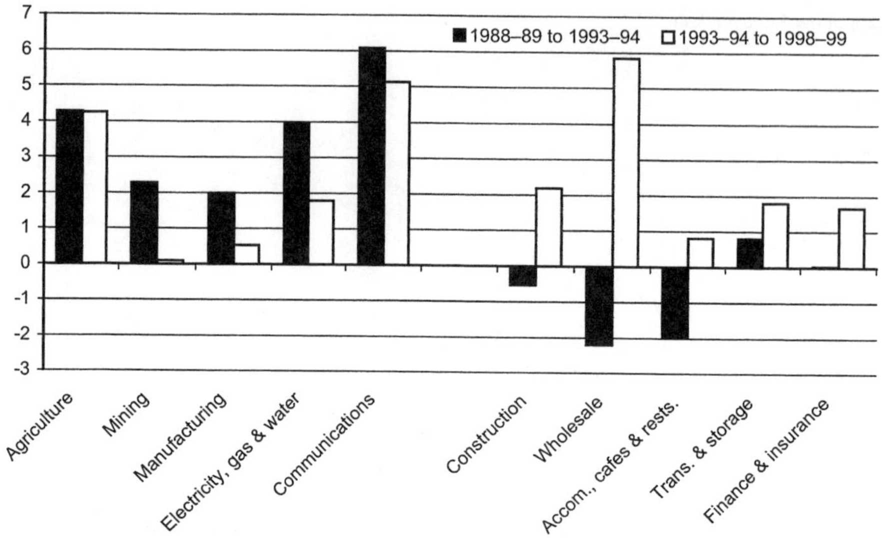

Fig. 2.4 MFP growth in selected industries over the last two aggregate productivity cycles: average annual rates of growth (percent)

Source: Productivity Commission estimates based on unpublished ABS data.

productivity surge predated the uplift in U.S. productivity growth from 1995.

Strong productivity growth in the 1990s fuelled relatively strong growth in average incomes and raised Australia's GDP per capita ranking to 8 by 2002 (table 2.1). Australia's level of GDP per head had recovered from 73 percent of the U.S. level in 1990 to regain its very long-term position at around 78 percent by 2001.

In summary, Australia's productivity and average income growth were relatively poor when there was a worldwide productivity boom in the catch-up and convergence era of the postwar period. Australia only started to catch up on the United States during the 1990s—a period of mixed performance across countries. U.S. productivity accelerated, contributing to a breakdown in convergence across OECD countries.[4] Australia not only kept pace with, but exceeded, the U.S. acceleration to record one of the highest accelerations in the Organization for Economic Cooperation and Development (OECD) area (OECD 2001a).

The 1990s brought an important change in the industry sources of aggregate productivity growth. Figure 2.4 presents MFP growth rates in industry sectors over the past two aggregate productivity cycles. Some cau-

4. Catch-up and convergence stalled in the 1990s as U.S. productivity accelerated relative to most other countries (Australia being one notable exception). Convergence actually broke down in the second half of the 1990s, when the U.S. productivity acceleration was strongest (OECD 2001a; McGuckin and van Ark 2002).

tion about the precision of industry estimates is appropriate, particularly in view of the value added method of estimation, which has been used in the absence of data to support a KLEMS approach.[5]

In the 1988–89 to 1993–94 cycle, there was relatively strong productivity growth in the "traditional" contributors to aggregate productivity growth—agriculture, mining, and manufacturing (left-hand side of fig. 2.4). Two other strong performers—communication services and electricity, gas, and water—joined these traditional sectors in this cycle. Their improved performance stemmed from the major efficiencies (e.g., better investment decisions and reductions in excess manning) achieved in government enterprises, as well as technological advances in some activities.

While productivity growth remained relatively strong in most of these industries in the 1990s cycle (mining and manufacturing being exceptions), all these industries experienced a deceleration compared with the previous cycle. On these estimates, none made a contribution to the productivity surge from 1993–94.

A new set of service industries emerged in the 1990s. The standout performer was wholesale trade. Other service industries—for example, construction and finance and insurance—also increased their rate of productivity growth significantly. Because of their relative size, wholesale trade, construction, and finance and insurance made the most substantial contributions to the aggregate acceleration (table 2.2).

2.2.3 Key Features of the Productivity Surge

This sketch of Australia's productivity performance has highlighted the following key developments that need to be explained:

- From an international perspective, Australia's productivity growth switched from being relatively slow over at least four decades to become relatively fast in the 1990s.
- The acceleration in labor productivity growth came through improved efficiency (MFP growth) rather than increased capital deepening.
- The 1990s surge in MFP growth originated in a new set of service industries, in particular wholesale trade, construction, and finance and insurance.

The absence of a worldwide productivity boom, the relative strength of Australia's productivity acceleration, and its starting point in the early 1990s suggest that some specifically Australian factors must form at least an important part of the explanation.

The contribution of ICTs is now assessed. There was an ICT boom in the 1990s in a number of countries, including Australia.

5. The differences in value added and KLEMS approaches are discussed by, for example, Gullickson and Harper (1999).

Table 2.2 **Industry Contributions to the Acceleration in Market-Sector Multifactor Productivity (MFP)**

	MFP Acceleration (% per annum)	Output Share (%)	Contribution (percentage points)
Agriculture	0.0	6	0.0
Mining	–2.2	8	–0.3
Manufacturing	–1.5	22	–0.5
Electricity, gas, and water	–2.2	5	–0.2
Construction	2.7	9	0.4
Wholesale trade	8.0	9	1.1
Retail trade	0.7	9	0.1
Accommodation, cafes, and restaurants	2.8	3	0.1
Transport and storage	1.0	9	0.1
Communications	–1.0	5	–0.1
Finance and insurance	1.7	11	0.3
Cultural and recreational services	–1.7	3	–0.1
Market sector	1.1	100	1.1

Source: Productivity Commission estimates based on ABS data.

Notes: MFP acceleration is the change in growth from the period 1988–89 to 1993–94 to the period 1993–94 to 1998–99. Output shares are calculated from estimates of current price value added for 1993–94.

2.3 The Role of ICTs in Australia's Productivity Surge

Many consider ICTs to be the major productivity-enhancing technological advance of the 1990s. Advances in ICTs have brought widespread and, in some cases, quite fundamental changes to businesses and households. ICTs have been linked to labor productivity growth through three avenues.

Increases in capital deepening. Labor productivity can rise as a result of higher capital use per unit of labor, as firms invest in more ICTs (where measurement of ICT volumes takes into account increases in quality). Many analysts have noted this mechanism affords ICTs no special qualities. As they have become cheaper, firms have substituted ICTs for labor and other forms of capital—as could happen for many other inputs.

Productivity gains in ICT production. Producers' ability to manufacture much more powerful ICT equipment, with relatively little increase in inputs, generates substantial MFP gains. If the gains are of sufficient magnitude and production is on sufficient scale, they can show up as contributions to aggregate MFP growth.

Productivity gains in ICT-using industries. This is the more controversial source of ICT-related productivity gains. It requires that use of ICTs generate MFP gains. On the one hand, "new economy" enthusiasts have pointed to MFP gains from such sources as increasing returns from ICT use and spillovers from network economies. On the other hand, skeptics have either denied or found little evidence to support the existence of MFP gains from use.

Australia cannot access productivity gains from ICT production. The ICT equipment production sector is not of sufficient size to generate productivity gains of national significance.

However, Australia has become a high ICT user. In 2000, Australia ranked third (behind the United States and Finland) among OECD countries on expenditure on ICTs as a proportion of non-residential investment—a marked step up from its 1980 ranking (OECD 2002). Investment in ICTs became a sizable proportion of total investment in Australia from the mid-1980s. Since then, the growth of investment has been very strong, especially in the second half of the 1990s, when investment in hardware grew by 35 percent a year and software investment by 20 percent a year in real terms.

As an importer of ICTs, Australia has benefited from a sizable terms-of-trade gain through the rapidly declining prices of ICTs. Strong international competition has meant that MFP gains in production have been passed on to purchasers. The Australian Treasury (Treasury 2002) stated that ICT prices have fallen in domestic currency terms by 9.5 percent a year and raised the terms of trade by 0.3 percent a year between 1985 and 2001. Since 1995, ICT prices have fallen by nearly 15 percent a year and raised the terms of trade by 0.75 percent a year.

2.3.1 Aggregate Growth Accounting[6]

A conventional productivity growth accounting exercise is now used to assess the influence of ICTs on Australia's productivity performance. A comparison with the United States is used to infer the likely contribution of ICTs to Australia's aggregate productivity growth.

The estimates of Australian labor productivity growth and the growth accounting contribution to it are based on national accounts data constructed by the Australian Bureau of Statistics (ABS). In keeping with modern practice, the ABS uses hedonic (or constant-quality) price deflators to estimate real volumes of ICTs produced and purchased. Hedonic prices have not been specifically generated for Australia. The ABS uses the U.S. price deflator for hardware, adjusted for exchange rate movements and a time lag, and a price deflator for software that shows a nominal 6 percent a year decline. The U.S. and Australian deflators are shown in figure 2.5.

There has been a string of U.S. studies of ICT contributions to productivity growth. For brevity, however, this paper focuses on comparisons with the United States, based on Bureau of Labor Statistics (BLS) data. Using BLS data brings two advantages:

6. The growth accounting presented in this section is updated from Parham, Roberts, and Sun (2001).

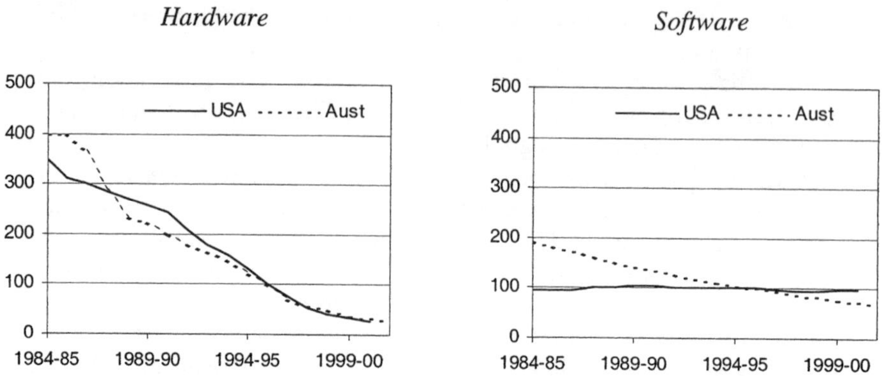

Fig. 2.5 ICT hardware and software price indexes, United States and Australia (index 1995–96 = 100)

Source: Unpublished ABS data and Bureau of Labor Statistics (BLS) data.

- The ABS models its methods closely on BLS methods, and this enhances comparability.[7]
- Access to the BLS data set assists flexibility in choosing periods for comparison.

A capital services measure of capital input is used and labor input is measured by hours worked. U.S. studies also include a labor composition or "quality" component, but this component cannot be estimated on a comparable basis or for the entire period for Australia. Consequently, this component is added back into the U.S. MFP growth estimates presented hereafter to assist comparability with Australian estimates.[8]

There was a big step up in contributions from ICT capital deepening from 1995 in the United States and Australia (fig. 2.6). The timing and strength of the ICT capital-deepening contributions in the two countries are remarkably close. This suggests that there have been similar rates of increase in ICT use in the two countries and supports the validity of using the United States as a comparator for the assessment of the impacts of ICT use in Australia.

Our work at the Productivity Commission has paid particular attention to selection of periods that identify underlying rates of productivity

7. Nevertheless, there are a few differences of note. Australian data cover information technology (IT), without communications equipment, whereas U.S. data cover ICTs. The U.S. estimates used here cover the private business sector, whereas Australian estimates cover the market sector. The main difference between the two is that the ABS-defined market sector excludes property and business services.

8. This does, of course, assist comparability, but in a conceptually inferior way. It would be preferable to factor out labor composition effects in Australia in order to draw comparisons with the United States. The practical significance of this issue rests on whether compositional effects would have been greatly different in the two countries. Unpublished ABS work (see section 2.4.1) suggests that compositional effects in Australia over the 1980s and 1990s would not be greatly dissimilar to those in the United States.

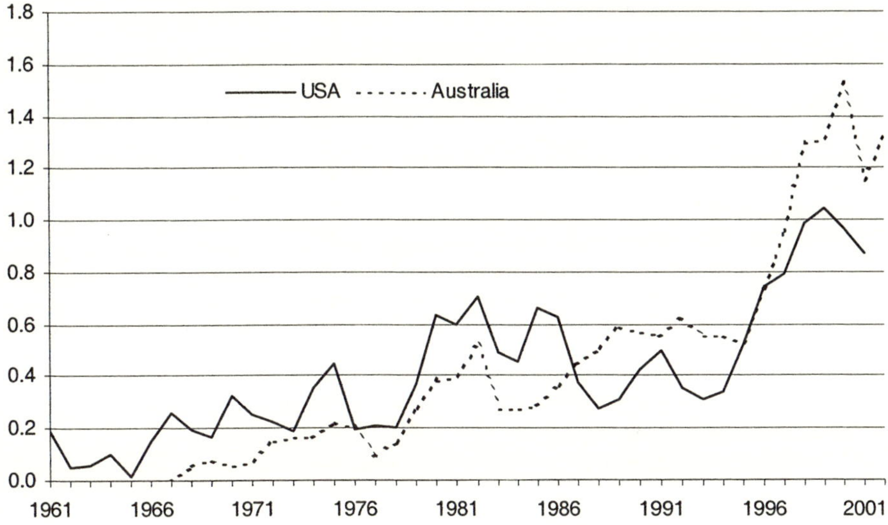

Fig. 2.6 Contributions of ICT capital deepening to labor productivity growth in the United States and Australia, 1961 to 2002 (percentage points)

Source: Productivity Commission estimates based on unpublished ABS data (to 2001–02) and BLS data (to 2001).

Note: For Australia, years refer to twelve months ending 30 June.

growth. Focus on underlying trends, rather than pre- and post-1995 rates of growth, presents a departure from nearly all other previous Australian and U.S. studies.

It is not surprising that most studies have used 1995 as the dividing year between periods for comparison of productivity growth and ICT contributions to it—for example, accounting for productivity growth in the second half of the 1990s (1995–99) compared with the first half (1990–95).[9] The 1995 year corresponds to the takeoff point in more rapid advances in ICT technology, declines in ICT prices, growth in investment in ICTs, and, as just seen, growth in ICT capital deepening. Using 1995 as a break point between periods therefore highlights the ICT takeoff and its effects.

But using 1995 as the break point creates problems in identifying and accounting for underlying rates of productivity growth. U.S. labor productivity was in a trough in 1995, at a point below trend (fig. 2.7).[10] Esti-

9. Major examples of studies using pre- and post-1995 periods are Oliner and Sichel (2000), Gordon (2000), Jorgenson and Stiroh (2000), and CEA (2001). Gordon, however, does make a cyclical adjustment. Simon and Wardrop (2001) is an Australian example.

10. A Hodrick-Prescott filter is used to form the trend series presented in figure 2.7. This does not clearly identify the Australian peaks as being above trend. However, the ABS uses an eleven-period Henderson moving average to identify a trend series and (the same) productivity peaks in official productivity estimates.

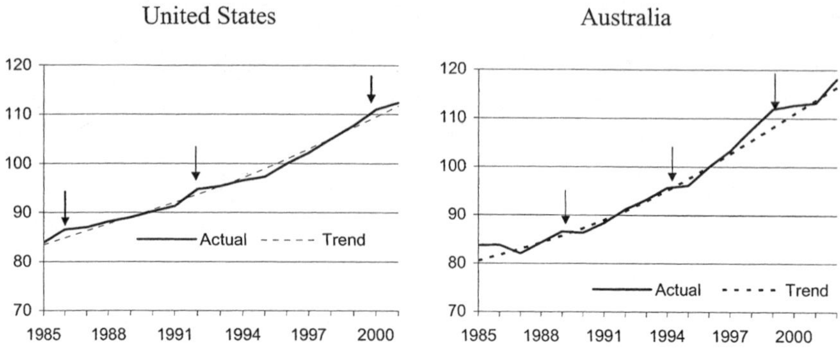

Fig. 2.7 Identifying peaks in U.S. and Australian labor productivity (index 1996 = 100)

Source: Unpublished ABS data (to 2001–02) and BLS data (to 2001).

Note: For Australia, years refer to twelve months ending 30 June.

mates of average growth from 1995 to the end of the 1990s are from a trough to a peak and therefore overstate the underlying rate of labor productivity growth. Moreover, the size of the estimated labor productivity acceleration is quite sensitive to minor variations in period selection around 1995 (Parham, Roberts, and Sun 2001).

Issues with the break point and sensitivity can be set aside by analyzing contributions to *trend* rates of productivity growth. The ABS method of estimating productivity growth over productivity cycles—from productivity peak to productivity peak—is one way of measuring underlying rates of growth. Adopting this method puts the prime focus on accelerations in underlying rates of productivity growth.

The contributions to labor productivity growth over productivity cycles are shown for the United States in figure 2.8 and for Australia in figure 2.9. The 1990s cycle for the United States is from 1992 to 2000 and for Australia from 1993–94 to 1998–99. Contributions to the labor productivity *accelerations* in the 1990s cycle (compared with the previous cycle) in both countries are presented in table 2.3. Contributions to the labor productivity accelerations from the first to the second half of the 1990s are shown for purely comparative purposes in table 2.4. The estimated labor productivity acceleration is lower according to the productivity cycle method, compared with the pre- and post-1995 method. In particular, the U.S. acceleration is still significant but a much less spectacular 0.5 of a percentage point (table 2.3), compared with 1.1 percentage points (table 2.4).

There are several important similarities in the U.S. and Australian results:

- The ICTs have made strong capital-deepening contributions. The ICT capital-deepening contribution has increased steadily from the 1960s

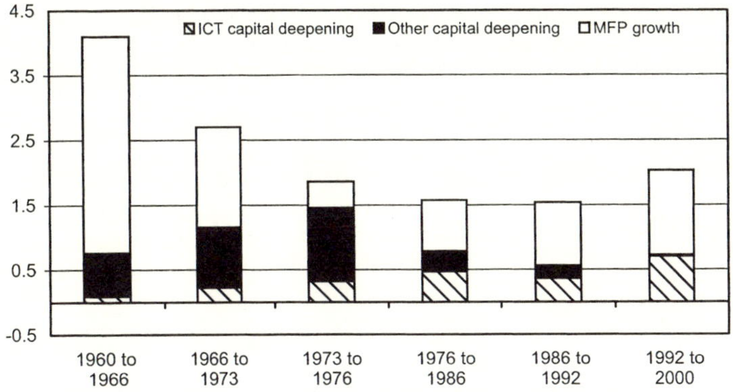

Fig. 2.8 Contributions to U.S. labor productivity growth over productivity cycles, 1960 to 2000 (percent per year)

Source: Productivity Commission estimates based on BLS data.

Note: MFP growth includes the labor composition (quality) contribution.

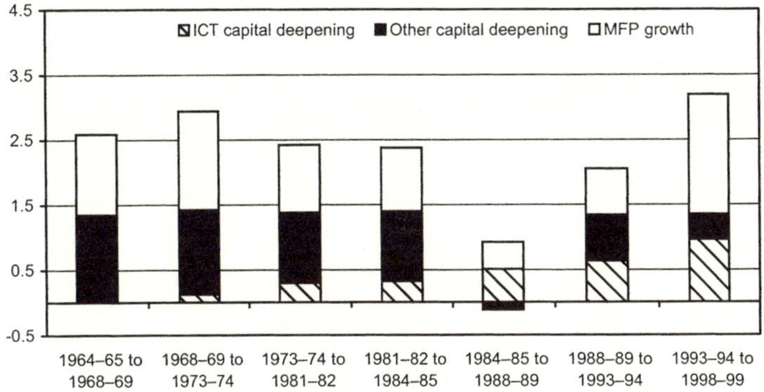

Fig. 2.9 Contributions to Australian labor productivity growth over productivity cycles, 1964–65 to 1998–99 (percent per year)

Source: Productivity Commission estimates based on unpublished ABS data.

in both countries (figs. 2.8 and 2.9). ICT capital deepening accounted for around a third of labor productivity growth in both countries in their respective 1990s cycles. ICT capital deepening made the same contribution (0.3 of a percentage point) to the 1990s labor productivity *accelerations* in both countries (table 2.3).[11]

- However, there has been little or no increase in the overall rate of capital deepening in either country, especially in Australia (table 2.3). Much or all of the increased use of ICTs (per hour worked) in the

11. The slightly lower contribution in the United States was due to stronger labor input growth rather than weaker ICT capital growth.

Table 2.3 **Contributions to Labor Productivity Accelerations in the 1990s Productivity Cycle in the United States and Australia (percentage points)**

	United States	Australia
Labor productivity acceleration	0.5	1.2
Capital deepening	0.2	0.0
ICT capital	0.3	0.3
Hardware	0.3	0.4
Software	0.1	–0.1
Other	0.0	
Other capital	–0.2	–0.3
MFP contribution	0.3	1.1

Notes: United States column shows growth in 1992 to 2000 less growth in 1986 to 1992. Australia column shows growth in 1993–94 to 1998–99 less growth in 1988–89 to 1993–94.

Table 2.4 **Contributions to Productivity Accelerations from 1990–95 to 1995–2000 in the United States and Australia (percentage points)**

	United States	Australia
Labor productivity acceleration	1.1	1.1
Capital-deepening contribution	0.6	0.4
ICT	0.5	0.5
Other	0.1	–0.1
MFP contribution	0.5	0.6

Note: For Australia, years refer to twelve months ending 30 June.

1990s has been offset by slower growth in use of other forms of capital (per hour worked). This result contrasts with that found in most other studies of the United States (exemplified by the results in table 2.4), which have found that ICTs have contributed to a marked increase in the rate of substitution of capital for labor.

- Growth in MFP accounted for over half the labor productivity growth in the 1990s cycle in both countries. Faster MFP growth accounts for most of the 1990s labor productivity *accelerations* in both countries—entirely so in Australia's case.

The main difference between the U.S. and Australian results lies in the strength of the productivity accelerations. The acceleration in underlying labor productivity growth in Australia, at 1.2 percentage points, is more than twice that in the United States (table 2.2). With similar capital-deepening contributions, the chief explanation for the difference lies in the much stronger MFP acceleration in Australia (1.1 percentage points) than in the United States (0.3 of a percentage point).

The stronger productivity acceleration in Australia suggests that the

Australian economy benefited from one or both of two factors: bigger gains from the use of ICTs and/or more gains from non-ICT factors. In either case, it does not necessarily mean—and generally it is highly unlikely—that productivity levels in Australia have moved ahead of U.S. levels. Rather, as the background in section 2.2 suggests, it is likely that Australia had more scope to improve from a lower base and has caught up on at least some of the superior U.S. levels.

It seems reasonable to assume, consistent with the U.S. leadership in productivity and ICTs, that the U.S. estimates establish the upper limit of 0.3 of a percentage point on the productivity acceleration that can be associated specifically with ICT production and use.[12] Studies such as that by Oliner and Sichel (2000) have attributed around 0.3 of a percentage point of aggregate MFP growth acceleration to ICT production, although the acceleration was calculated pre- and post-1995 and may therefore overstate the contribution to the acceleration in trend productivity growth.[13] The acceleration over productivity cycles would be less—perhaps half or one- or two-tenths of a percentage point.

Even if the more favorable view of the importance of ICTs is taken from the comparison between the first and second halves of the 1990s, table 2.3 suggests that the maximum acceleration due to production and use of ICTs is 0.6 of a percentage point (the MFP acceleration in the United States). Taking the contribution of ICT production to be around 0.3 of a percentage point, as calculated by Oliner and Sichel, means that the ICT use component is a maximum of 0.3 of a percentage point.

The estimate of one- or two-tenths of a percentage point from ICT use in the United States is devoid of any catch-up effects, since the United States is at the frontier. This estimate therefore indicates the extent of spillover productivity gains associated with ICT use. In Australia, they would be in addition to any catch-up effects.

The estimated magnitude fits well with other econometrically based evidence. Bean (2000) used a cross-country regression as a basis to calculate that Australia's rate of ICT uptake would have contributed 0.12 percentage points to annual productivity growth. Gretton, Gali, and Parham (2002) constructed an aggregate contribution of 0.14 percentage points from the formal analysis of firm-level data.

12. This implicitly assumes that no other contributors to productivity growth, such as technological change unrelated to ICTs, have accelerated in the United States. Using the United States as a benchmark for Australia also implicitly assumes that there are no important differences in industry composition between the two economies.

13. There has been some overstatement of the productivity acceleration apportioned to ICT production. Productivity improvements have been calculated by the dual method of measuring price declines and attributing them entirely to productivity improvements. However, some of the price declines have been due to declining profit margins (see, for example, Aizcorbe 2002).

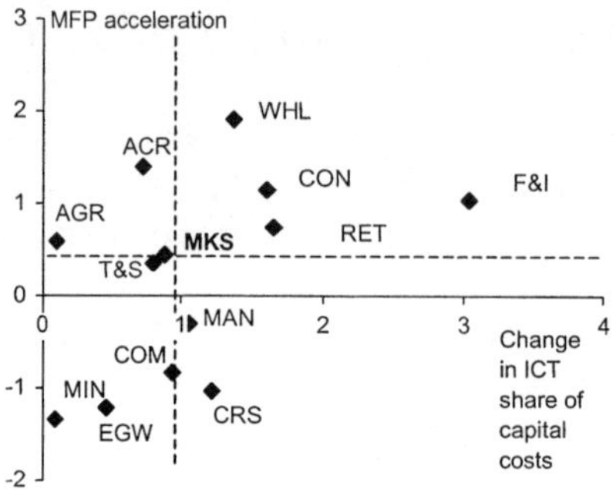

ACR	Accommodation, cafes & restaurants
AGR	Agriculture
COM	Communication services
CON	Construction
CRS	Cultural & recreational services
EGW	Electricity, gas & water
F&I	Finance & insurance
MAN	Manufacturing
MIN	Mining
MKS	Market sector
RET	Retail trade
T&S	Transport & storage
WHL	Wholesale trade

Fig. 2.10 Change in industry ICT use and productivity growth in Australian industries over the 1990s (percentage points)

Source: Productivity Commission estimates based on unpublished ABS data.

Note: The productivity acceleration is calculated as the change in *trend* MFP growth between financial years 1990–95 and 1995–2000.

2.3.2 An Industry Perspective

While the evidence to date suggests that MFP gains associated with ICTs at the aggregate level are significant but not spectacular, there is evidence of stronger links in some industries. In some countries, including the United States, Japan, Korea, Finland, and Ireland, there are opportunities for very substantial productivity gains in the manufacture of ICTs.

There also appear to be stronger links associated with the *use* of ICTs in certain industries. Several studies of the United States have found evidence of productivity acceleration in the 1990s in wholesale trade; retail trade; finance, insurance, and real estate (especially in financial intermediation); and business services. These have also been characterized as intensive users of ICTs (Stiroh 2001; Nordhaus 2001; Centre for the Study of Living Standards [CSLS] 2000; Council of Economic Advisors [CEA] 2001; Pilat and Lee 2001).

As noted in section 2.2, a similar set of industries emerged in the 1990s as major contributors to Australia's productivity surge. The pattern of increased ICT usage and MFP acceleration across Australian industries is displayed in figure 2.10.[14] Finance and insurance, wholesale trade, retail trade, and construction had above-average increases in ICT use and had

14. The use of *trend* rates of productivity growth and different periods explains the differences in industry productivity accelerations show in figures 2.4 and 2.10.

above-average MFP accelerations. Unfortunately, the equivalent industry data are not available from BLS sources to replicate this chart for the United States.

The coincidence of industries with increases in ICT use and productivity accelerations in the United States and Australia provides some circumstantial evidence for a link between ICT use and productivity growth at an industry level—concentrated in distribution, financial intermediation, and business services (although Australian productivity data on the last industry are not available). There may also be ICT-productivity links at the firm level in other industries that, because of interfirm differences in these and other factors, do not translate as readily into industry or aggregate trends (see Brynjolfsson and Hitt 2000). But figure 2.10 also suggests that the productivity accelerations in some Australian industries were unrelated to ICT use (and equally that increases in ICT use in some industries were not associated with MFP accelerations).

The relationship between ICT use and productivity growth is complex rather than immediate and direct. ICTs are often viewed as general-purpose technologies that require time to bring to their full potential and enable productivity gains by providing a platform for other innovations in products and processes (see, for example, Brynjolfsson and Hitt 2000 and Bresnahan, Brynjolfsson, and Hitt 2002).

The Australian evidence supports the view that it is changes in products and processes, enabled at least in part by ICTs, that generate productivity gains.[15] The finance and insurance industry has been restructured to operate much more through ICTs (for example, ATM, Internet, and phone banking) than through traditional face-to-face contacts, leading to a restructuring of branch operations. Many new products (for example, financial derivatives) are now on offer.

An earlier study by Productivity Commission staff (Johnston et al. 2000) also found that ICTs played a part in the restructuring of wholesaling activities. Wholesalers were able to use bar-code and scanning technology and inventory management systems as part of the process of transforming wholesaling from a storage-based to a fast flow-through operation.

The complexity of the relationships between ICT use and productivity performance reinforces the importance of taking an industry or firm point of view. Productivity gains depend on the different actions that different firms take. A firm focus helps to identify the importance of lags between uptake of ICTs and productivity gain and the significance of complementary innovations in products and processes. The significance of ICTs and

15. If the ICT hedonic price deflators are measured correctly, advances in ICTs are measured as embodied improvements. The MFP gains associated with ICT use, for example through firm reorganization, can then be considered as disembodied improvements that are nevertheless captured by the users. In some cases, lower transactions costs in business exchanges could be a spillover benefit of expanding ICT networks.

complementarities has been confirmed in Productivity Commission work for an international project, coordinated by the OECD, to explore the links between ICT use and performance at the firm level (Gretton, Gali, and Parham 2002). Productivity-enhancing complementarities between ICTs, skills, and business restructuring were found in an analysis of an Australian longitudinal micro data set.

The main conclusion from the aforementioned growth accounting is that the rapid uptake of ICTs has had important but comparatively small influence on aggregate productivity growth in Australia. It appears to account for, at most, one- or two-tenths of a percentage point of Australia's 1.1 percentage point MFP acceleration. On the other hand, ICTs have had more marked productivity effects in individual firms and industries. It would appear that ICTs provide at least partial explanation for the acceleration in the new set of service industries—particularly finance and insurance, construction, and wholesale trade.

However, the mere availability of new ICT technologies does not explain why Australian businesses adopted them with such vigor from the mid-1980s and put them to such productive use in the 1990s. After all, Australia's prior history was generally one of relatively slow adoption of advanced technologies. And although new ICTs have been available worldwide, many other advanced countries have not been as quick or productive on the uptake. A probable explanation for this conundrum is provided later.

2.4 Other Explanations

The conclusion that ICTs have only contributed a relatively small part of the acceleration leaves the vast bulk of Australia's improved performance unexplained—an unsatisfactory point on which to finish this paper. This section briefly draws on other work to at least consider other possible explanations.

2.4.1 Education and Skills

Steve Dowrick has reminded us of the importance of skills in the workforce as a source of growth, both directly as an "embodied" labor input and indirectly in fostering absorption and further development of technology (see Dowrick 2002a,b and chap. 1 in this volume). He has highlighted the increase in school retention rates and labor force participation of females over the past ten to fifteen years. Basing his conclusions on a review of the empirical literature, Dowrick finds that raising Australia's average years of schooling by 0.8 could raise Australia's annual rate of productivity growth by a third of a percentage point through direct and indirect means.

Whereas Dowrick casts his analysis in a long-term framework (given the time required for the flow of educational attainments to affect the average across the stock of employment), it is nevertheless of considerable interest to see if higher skills could have played a part in Australia's 1990s productivity surge. The information presented in Dowrick's papers shows that Australia (along with New Zealand) had the highest average schooling across countries in 1960, but average attainment grew faster in comparator countries over the next four decades, so that Australia slipped significantly in position by 2000. Nevertheless, the increase in average schooling in Australia was higher in the 1990s than in the 1980s.

Productivity Commission colleagues Barnes and Kennard (2002) have added more information. They examined preliminary ABS research that takes account of changes in workforce composition in the construction of a "quality-adjusted" labor input series. This series reflects changes in the labor inputs of groups identified by gender, educational attainment, and potential workforce experience. Taking into account workforce experience, the growth in skills was faster in the 1980s than in 1990s.

Barnes and Kennard's work suggests that there has not been a human capital accumulation effect on 1990s MFP growth. The relative increase in skills in the 1980s, accounted for the order of 0.3 of a percentage point of average annual MFP growth. But the skill contribution *decelerated* to around 0.05 of a percentage point from 1993–94. The direct contribution of skills to the 1990s productivity acceleration is *negative* on these numbers.

However, indirect effects, where education and skills assist the development and absorption of technology, could still be important. Links to the absorption of ICTs is a particular case in point, and, as noted above, complementarities between skills and ICT use have been empirically confirmed. On the other hand, there is a gap in the ability of education and skill levels to explain the broad sweep of Australia's productivity performance. When Australia's average years of schooling was above other countries around the 1960s and early 1970s, the rate of productivity catch-up was relatively poor. After a period of relatively slow growth in attainment and when Australia's average schooling had fallen below other countries, the rate of productivity catch-up was relatively high. Without undermining the general importance of education and skills, this suggests that other factors were acting as the main constraint on productivity growth in earlier decades and as the main facilitators of productivity growth in the 1990s. It is also difficult to explain the industry sources of the productivity acceleration in terms of education and skills—perhaps not so much in financial intermediation, but certainly in wholesale trade.

2.4.2 Policy Reforms

By the 1980s, Australia's continued slippage on the international league table of average income, combined with pessimism about the future, galvanized community support for governments to take policy action to address structural weaknesses in the Australian economy. Key objectives were to raise growth in productivity and living standards.

Policy reforms, which have been introduced progressively since the mid-1980s, have included deregulation of access to finance, floating the currency, marked reductions in barriers to trade and foreign direct investment, commercialization (and some privatization) of government business enterprises, strengthening domestic competition, and increasing labor market flexibility.

Policy reforms were designed to improve productivity performance by

- sharpening incentives to be more productive, chiefly by strengthening competition from domestic and overseas sources;
- opening the economy to trade, investment, technologies, and know-how developed overseas;
- providing greater flexibility (for example, less regulatory restriction, more flexible labor markets) to adjust production processes and firm organization to improve productivity.

It may be a matter of logic that, if previous policy frameworks were holding productivity growth in check, reform of those frameworks would allow productivity to accelerate. But empirical evidence is needed to confirm the importance of reforms.

A number of analysts, calling on a range of empirical and other evidence, have found that microeconomic policy reforms have played a major role in Australia's productivity surge (see, for example, Productivity Commission [PC] 1999; Bean 2000; Dowrick 2000; Forsyth 2000; OECD 2001b). Macroeconomic policies have also been framed in ways that have helped to maintain stability in output growth.

However, it is difficult to put a particular order of magnitude on the influence of policy reforms on productivity growth. Formal analysis is not straightforward, particularly since it is difficult to construct a measure of policy reform at the aggregate level that accurately quantifies the timing, breadth, and intensity of reforms. By definition, reforms have operated at the micro level through a mixture of industry measures (e.g., deregulation, commercialization of government enterprises), sectoral measures (e.g., phased reductions in tariffs on manufactures) and general measures (e.g., deregulation of access to finance and the introduction of enterprise flexibility into workplace bargaining). Furthermore, it is difficult to specify a structure of lags between implementation of reforms (which was often graduated) and production response.

Despite these difficulties, Salgado (2000) found a positive link between structural reforms and aggregate productivity growth. On his estimates, reforms contributed between 0.5 and 0.9 of a percentage point at the aggregate level. Empirical support is also found in detailed industry and firm case studies (see, for example, PC 1999). For example, the links between policy reforms and strong productivity responses in government business enterprises (see section 2.2) can be firmly established. And there are evident links between reforms and trends in proximate determinants of productivity growth, such as openness to trade and investment, industry specialization (including intra-industry trade), uptake of advanced technologies, business R&D, and rates of innovation (PC 1999).

The influence of policy reforms can explain the developments in the Australian economy outlined in section 2.2. It can explain improvements in efficiency (MFP growth rather than capital deepening). Reforms were intended to realize catch-up gains by forcing and enabling businesses to improve technical efficiency (moving toward best practice), reduce or close inefficient operations, and adopt a more innovative, market-driven culture. Delayed success in catch-up, facilitated by policy reforms, can explain Australia's transition from an international laggard to a front-runner in productivity growth. It would also provide a "home-grown" or Australian-specific explanation for the productivity success in the 1990s.

Reforms could also help to explain the emergence of rapid and innovative use of ICTs in the 1990s. With stronger competitive incentive, businesses became more alert to the opportunities that new technologies provide and, with greater flexibility, became better able to put them to productive use.

But can the introduction of policy reforms explain the industry sources of the productivity acceleration? The incidence of reforms is clear in areas such as electricity, gas and water, and parts of communications services and transport and storage, following reforms to the operations of government enterprises. Financial intermediation has also been subject to far-reaching reforms over many years. But what about the standout performer, wholesale trade?

Johnston et al. (2000) found that reforms were acting as underlying drivers and facilitators of productivity gains in wholesaling. It was not so much that wholesaling became much more ICT intensive or that new "breakthrough" technologies became available. It was more that the competitive incentives to be productive became stronger and that new flexibilities became open to businesses to use ICTs as part of a more general process of restructuring and transformation. For example, the motor vehicle industry was looking for efficiencies all along the "value chain," including in distribution, to meet the increased competition from cheaper imports entering under lower border protection. Distribution has increasingly involved streamlined delivery of imported products and more customized products from local producers building fewer models at fewer production plants. Another contributor in some areas of wholesaling was the reform of industrial relations processes that allowed greater labor flexibility through the introduction of split shifts and reduced the rigidity of job demarcations.

A plausible explanation for the productivity gains in wholesaling is that, under increased competitive pressure, businesses rationalized production facilities and took advantage of more efficient transport and information systems to reconfigure their distribution processes. They greatly reduced costs of storage and handling in the process. The large productivity gains in wholesaling were passed on, with profit margins declining in the 1990s (Parham et al. 2000).

2.5 Conclusions

Australia's labor productivity and MFP growth reached record highs in the 1990s. An acceleration of over 1 percentage point shifted Australia from being a laggard to being a front-runner on productivity growth among OECD countries. Higher labor productivity growth in the 1990s came from improved efficiency rather than capital deepening. A new set of service industries, particularly wholesale trade, construction, and finance and insurance, appears to be at the heart of the productivity acceleration.

Taking into account the historical and international trends, it seems clear that the Australian economy has embarked on a process of catch-up, much delayed in comparison with many other high-income countries. Australia has not been favored in comparison to other countries by some new technology, a change in the structure of industries, a leap forward in the skills of the workforce, or any other obvious structural factor. It seems that there has been a general improvement in efficiency of resource use that has narrowed, but not eliminated, the productivity gap with many other advanced economies.[16]

This paper has concentrated on the role that ICTs may have played in Australia's productivity surge. Australia is a high user but low producer of ICTs. As an importer of ICTs it has benefited from terms-of-trade effects as ICT prices have declined. Australian businesses have also used ICTs in "smart" ways—taking advantage of the product and process innovations that ICTs enable. These have been a source of productivity gain for firms. And ICTs have played a role in the service industries contributing to the acceleration in aggregate productivity.

However, the overall contribution of ICTs to higher aggregate productivity growth in terms of frontier shifts has been relatively small. Comparison with the United States suggests that use of ICTs could only account for one- or two-tenths of a percentage point of the underlying productivity acceleration. This result is lower than that found in previous U.S. and Aus-

16. A remaining productivity gap at the aggregate level is evident in the data presented in section 2.2. Research at the Groningen Growth and Development Centre on sectoral comparisons (van Ark and Timmer 2002) suggests that Australia has slipped further behind U.S. labor productivity levels in two areas of strong U.S. growth—manufacturing (where Australia remains at around 40 percent of U.S. levels) and wholesale and retail trade (around 50 percent of U.S. levels). In transport and communications, however, Australia has moved further ahead of the United States since 1980 and is now about 150 percent of the U.S. level.

tralian studies, which have overstated the contribution of ICTs to productivity growth by failing to control for cyclical influences.

An increase in educational attainment and skills may also have contributed in some small measure to Australia's productivity surge. The timing of human capital accumulation—faster in the 1980s than the 1990s—and the extent of the increase—slower in Australia than in other countries—do not sit well with Australia's historically and internationally strong productivity surge in the 1990s. There would appear to be only a weak link between skills and the industry sources of productivity growth—particularly in wholesaling.

Nevertheless, education and skills could still have some indirect influence through absorption of technology. The uptake and productive use of ICTs is a particular case in point. (The productivity impacts of skills and ICTs would therefore not be additive.)

There is theoretical and empirical support for policy reforms playing a substantial role in Australia's productivity surge through catch-up gains in efficiency. Nevertheless, further empirical evidence would help to bolster this conclusion. Policy reforms also provide plausible explanation for Australia's shift from laggard to front-runner and the industry sources of the productivity acceleration.

Rather than being "alternative" explanations, reforms ICTs and skills can be seen as complementary. In a more competitive, open, and flexible business environment, Australian businesses were forced and enabled to restructure in order to catch up. They also became more alert to opportunities that new technologies, such as ICTs, could provide, and either these businesses incorporated them into their restructuring moves or new firms emerged to take the new opportunities. That is, reforms played a part in driving the uptake of ICTs and in enabling them to be used productively. The right amount and mix of education and skills also assisted the use of ICTs and the identification and implementation of ways to take advantage of what the new technologies could offer.

References

Aizcorbe, A. 2002. Why are semiconductor prices falling so fast? Industry estimates and implications for productivity measurement. Washington, D.C.: Federal Reserve Board. Mimeograph.

Barnes, P., and S. Kennard. 2002. Skill and Australia's productivity surge. Productivity Commission Staff Research Paper. Canberra, Australia: Productivity Commission.

Bean, C. 2000. The Australian economic "miracle": A view from the north. In *The Australian economy in the 1990s,* ed. D. Gruen and S. Shrestha, 73–114. Sydney: Reserve Bank of Australia.

Bresnahan, T., E. Brynjolfsson, and L. Hitt. 2002. Information technology, workplace organization, and the demand for skilled labor: Firm-level evidence. *Quarterly Journal of Economics* 117 (February): 339–76.

Brynjolfsson, E., and L. Hitt. 2000. Beyond computation: Information technology, organizational transformation, and business performance. *Journal of Economic Perspectives* 14 (4): 23–48.

Centre for the Study of Living Standards (CSLS). 2000. Trend productivity and the new economy. Paper prepared for the Economic Policy Institute. Ottawa, Canada: September.

Council of Economic Advisors (CEA). 2001. *Economic report of the president.* Washington, D.C.: GPO.

Dowrick, S. 2000. The resurgence of Australian productivity growth in the 1990s: Miracle or mirage? Paper presented to the 29th Annual Conference of Economists. 4 July, Queensland, Australia.

———. 2002a. The contribution of innovation and education to economic growth. Paper presented at Melbourne Institute Economic and Social Outlook Conference, Towards Opportunity and Prosperity. 4–5 April, Melbourne, Australia.

———. 2002b. Growth prospects for Australia: Lessons from the revolution and counter-revolution in the theory of economic growth. Paper presented at Melbourne Institute Economic and Social Outlook Conference, Towards Opportunity and Prosperity. 4–5 April, Melbourne, Australia.

Forsyth, P. 2000. Microeconomic policies and structural change. In *The Australian economy in the 1990s,* ed. D. Gruen and S. Shrestha, 235–67. Sydney: Reserve Bank of Australia.

Gordon, R. 2000. Does the "new economy" measure up to the great inventions of the past? *Journal of Economic Perspectives* 14 (4): 49–74.

Gretton, P., J. Gali, and D. Parham. 2002. Uptake and impacts of the ICTs in the Australian economy: Evidence from aggregate, sectoral, and firm levels. Paper presented at the OECD Workshop on ICT and Business Performance Conference. 9 December, Paris.

Gullickson, W., and M. Harper. 1999. Possible measurement bias in aggregate productivity growth. *Monthly Labor Review* 122 (2): 47–67.

Johnston, A., D. Porter, T. Cobbold, and R. Dollamore. 2000. Productivity in Australia's wholesale and retail trade. Productivity Commission Staff Research Paper. Canberra, Australia: AusInfo.

Jorgenson, D., and K. Stiroh. 2000. Raising the speed limit: US economic growth in the information age. *Brookings Papers on Economic Activity,* Issue no. 1:125–211. Washington, D.C.: Brookings Institution.

Maddison, A. 2001. *The world economy: A millennial perspective.* Paris: OECD Development Center.

McGuckin, R., and B. van Ark. 2002. Performance 2001: Productivity, employment, and income in the world's economies. Conference Board Research Report no. R-1313-02-RR. New York: Conference Board.

Nordhaus, W. 2001. Productivity growth and the new economy. NBER Working Paper no. 8096. Cambridge, Mass.: National Bureau of Economic Research, January.

Organization for Economic Cooperation and Development (OECD). 2001a. The new economy: Beyond the hype. Paris: OECD.

———. 2001b. *OECD economic surveys: Australia.* Paris: OECD.

———. 2002. *Measuring the information economy.* Paris: OECD.

Oliner, S., and D. Sichel. 2000. The resurgence of growth in the late 1990s: Is information technology the story? *Journal of Economic Perspectives* 14 (4): 3–22.

Parham, D. 1999. The New Economy? A New Look at Australia's Productivity Performance, Productivity Commission Staff Research Paper. Canberra, Australia: AusInfo, May.

Parham, D., P. Barnes, P. Roberts, and S. Kennett. 2000. Distribution of the economic gains of the 1990s. Productivity Commission Staff Research Paper. Canberra, Australia: AusInfo, November.

Parham, D., P. Roberts, and H. Sun. 2001. Information technology and Australia's productivity surge. Productivity Commission Staff Research Paper. Canberra, Australia: AusInfo.

Pilat, D., and F. Lee. 2001. Productivity growth in ICT-producing and ICT-using industries: A source of growth differentials in the OECD? Science, Technology, and Industry Working Paper no. 2001/4. Paris: OECD.

Productivity Commission (PC). 1999. *Microeconomic reforms and Australian productivity: Exploring the links.* Commission Research Paper. Canberra, Australia: AusInfo, November.

Salgado, R. 2000. Australia: Productivity growth and structural reform. In *Australia: Selected issues and statistical appendix,* IMF Country Staff Report 00/24, 3–35. Washington, D.C.: International Monetary Fund.

Simon, J., and S. Wardrop. 2001. Australian use of information technology and its contribution to growth. Paper prepared for the Conference of Economists. September, Perth, Australia.

Stiroh, K. 2001. Information technology and the US productivity revival: What do the industry data say? Federal Reserve Board of New York. Mimeograph.

Treasury (Commonwealth). 2002. *Budget papers, statement 4: Australia's terms of trade—Stronger and less volatile.* Canberra, Australia: AGPS.

van Ark, B., and M. Timmer. 2002. Industry productivity comparisons. *De Economist* 150 (1): 95–109.

Comment Chin Hee Hahn

This paper addresses the question why the pace of productivity growth in Australia accelerated in the 1990s. As possible explanations this paper considers three factors: micro policy reforms in various areas since the mid-1980s, upgrading of labor skills, and the increasing use of ICTs. I think this is a very important question, especially in the following sense. In the growth literature, there have been debates over whether the variations in income levels or growth rates are driven by variations in total factor productivity growth (TFPG) or by variations in the pace of input accumulation. Theoretically, this debate has its root in the debates over whether the neoclassical growth theory or the endogenous growth theory is the more appropriate framework to explain the observed cross-country differences in growth rates. One of the main claims from the neoclassical side came from Mankiw, Romer, and Weil (1992), who show that, once the cross-

Chin Hee Hahn is a research fellow at the Korea Development Institute.

country differences in human capital are taken into account, the cross-country income levels (or growth rates) are mostly explained by the differences in input accumulation. However, there seems to be growing evidence that it is the differences in TFPG, rather than the differences in the pace of input accumulation, that drives the diverse growth outcome. Klenow and Rodriguez-Clare (1998), Easterly et al. (1993), and Rodrik (1999) are examples along this line. One of the main implications from these studies seems to be that in order to explain the variations (both cross-sectional and over time within a country) in growth rates of output, we have to look at policy or institutional factors that can explain the variations in TFPG. I think this paper asks exactly this question: what the determinants are behind Australia's productivity surge in the 1990s.

I think this paper provides very interesting facts, relying on growth accounting methodology, on the patterns of Australia's productivity growth, together with the role of ICT investments, which could be summarized as follows. First, it is carefully documented that Australia experienced acceleration in the growth rate of labor and total factor productivity in the 1990s. Second, the acceleration in the labor productivity growth is predominantly accounted for by the acceleration in the pace of TFPG, not in the pace of input accumulation. The pace of input accumulation has been clearly stable over time. Third, the acceleration in TFPG in the 1990s has been concentrated in several service-sector industries, such as wholesale trade, transport and storage, and finance and insurance, which usually use ICT intensively. Fourth, ICT capital deepening occurred while other conventional capital accumulation slowed down, making the pace of total capital accumulation stable over the decades. I think these facts provided by this paper provide the basis for any future research efforts that aim to explain the patterns of Australian productivity growth in the 1990s. If we accept these facts, then I think any serious set of explanations for the productivity surge in Australia in 1990s should be able to explain these facts altogether. I think the author is rightly going this way.

Methodologically, the author uses standard tools in the literature and pays special attention to the business-cycle effects, so that the empirical facts provided in this paper seems to be quite reliable.

Relying on the growth accounting, elimination of candidate explanations, and comparison with the benchmark case of the United States, the author claims that micro policy reforms in the 1980s account for most of the productivity surge by about 1 percentage point (annual average) in the 1990s and that the ICT factor accounts for only a small part (at most 0.3 of a percentage point). The paper further emphasizes the importance of earlier policy reforms by claiming that increased market competition coming from the reforms induced the economic agents to use ICTs more intensively and efficiently.

Overall, the facts provided in this paper are interesting. However, although the author's emphasis on earlier policy reform as the main driving force behind the productivity surge in the 1990s is quite reasonable, I think the author's way of supporting this argument seems to be vulnerable to some criticisms, which I think substantially undermines the validity of his argument.

First, there seems to be some discrepancies between the author's initial question and what the author actually does in his paper. The question he raises is what the major factors are, among the three competing hypotheses, behind the productivity surge. However, what the author does seems to be, mainly, to answer how much of the acceleration in labor productivity growth in the 1990s is accounted for by the ICT investments. If one uses the growth accounting methodology alone, one cannot expect to distinguish between the three competing hypotheses he suggested, especially between the policy reform story and the ICT story. I think that's why the author tries to use the approach of "elimination" of a story that is relatively easily quantifiable—in this case the ICT story. However, even if we believe his argument that the ICT (and labor skill) story explains at best a small fraction of the acceleration in TFPG, that does not mean that all of the remaining TFPG surge is attributable to earlier policy reforms. That is, there may be other factors that have not been considered in the paper from the start.

Second, the paper would be more coherent if it were clear about whether the labor productivity or total factor productivity should be focused along the discussion. Since the author starts out his paper by providing facts on TFPG, I think the following discussion should be the one that tries to explain the TFPG surge, not the labor productivity surge. The growth accounting methodology he uses in his main analysis alone cannot be used to explain the TFPG surge; it is merely a methodology that further decomposes input accumulation into conventional capital and ICT capital.

Third, since the author does not deal with spillovers from ICT use, it seems to be premature to conclude that ICT is not a main factor in Australia's productivity surge. Rather, the fact that industries with rapid pickup in TFPG in the 1990s were the industries using ICT intensively suggests that the opposite might be true (although I still do not believe that this is the very plausible story). Also, the author's claim that the TFPG gain from ICT in Australia cannot exceed the gain found in the United States is not very convincing. The size of network externalities associated with ICT use might be different across countries.

So here are my suggestions. First, cross-industry variation in changes of TFPG might be worthwhile to examine. The fact that industries that experienced a productivity surge in the 1990s were mostly nontradable service industries seems to be worth paying attention to. This fact seems to imply that it might be worthwhile to look at, for example, whether there have been significant changes in terms of trade, which affected the domestic demand component of GDP disproportionately. Second, since the wholesale trade industry is a large industry for most economies and it experienced the most rapid acceleration in TFPG in the 1990s, it might be worthwhile to narrow down on discussing why that industry's TFPG accelerated. Third, if it is practically difficult to provide convincing evidence on the role of reforms in enhancing productivity, then it might be desirable to change the organization of the paper by strengthening the description of the empirical facts and by discussing briefly the possible reasons at the later part of the paper.

References

Easterly, William, Michael Kremer, Lant Pritchett, and Larry Summers. 1993. Good policy or good luck? Country growth performance and temporary shocks. *Journal of Monetary Economics* 32:459–483.

Klenow, Peter J., and Andres Rodriguez-Clare. 1998. The neoclassical revival in growth economics: Has it gone too far? In *NBER macroeconomics annual 1997,* ed. Ben S. Bernanke and Julio J. Rotemberg, 73–103. Cambridge: MIT Press.

Mankiw, N. Gregory, David Romer, and David N. Weil. 1992. A contribution to the empirics of economic growth. *Quarterly Journal of Economics* 107 (2): 407–437.

Rodrik, Dani. 1999. Where did all the growth go? External shocks, social conflict, and growth collapses. *Journal of Economic Growth* 4:385–412.

Comment Francis T. Lui

Dean Parham has tried to show in his paper that labor productivity has experienced a marked increase in Australia from the early 1990s to the late 1990s. Moreover, a significant portion of the increase is due to the acceleration of multifactor productivity (MFP) growth in this period. In the United States, during the same period, acceleration in MFP growth is estimated to be 0.6 percent, while that in Australia is 1 percent. The main question posed is why there is such a difference in acceleration of MFP growth rates.

The paper attributes this to a package of policy reforms in Australia. These reforms are generally aimed at enhancing competition and the flexibility for firms to make adjustments. Although economic theory tells us that they may indeed raise productivity, are we really sure that productivity acceleration in the sample period is driven by them? The paper attempts to eliminate a number of alternative possibilities. The arguments given are plausible, but they should not stop us from identifying other explanations.

First, if we look at the data cited seriously, the difference between the

Francis T. Lui is professor of economics and director of the Center for Economic Development, Hong Kong University of Science and Technology.

United States and Australia is not very big. A difference of 0.4 percentage points per year amounts only to a total of about 2 percentage points during the entire sample period. With such a small difference, are we begging the question too much? Could this 2 percent be due to simple measurement errors? We need data from a longer sample period to rule out this possibility.

Second, the measurement of MFP growth in the United States may also be biased. Even though education has been taken into account in arriving at the MFP measures, it is unclear whether the *quality* aspect of education has been fully considered. It is fairly well established that the quality of U.S. schooling in the 1970s and 1980s, as measured by SAT scores and reading and mathematics skills, was declining. This means that if only the *quantity* side of education, such as the number of years of schooling, is taken into account, the estimate for the MFP growth in the United States will be lower than the true value.

Third, the reforms in Australia can introduce more competitive pressure in the market. This could result in MFP growth eventually, but this may take a long time to achieve. The reforms can also raise capacity utilization, which may be confused with improvement in MFP growth.

Fourth, the speeds of technology spillovers and market penetration may be different in the United States and Australia. The fact that software prices in Australia decline much faster than those in the United States indicates this possibility, which, in fact, is not an uncommon phenomenon at all. For example, as in Australia, the manufacturing sector of information and communication technology (ICT) products in Hong Kong is small. But the market penetration rate of mobile phones there is deeper than that of the United States.

Fifth, much of the acceleration is driven by wholesale trade, cafes, and restaurants. But these all exhibit negative growth in MFP in the *previous* period. Is the growth acceleration due to the elimination of inefficiencies in these sectors, or just recovery from business cycles? These sectors are all consumption related. Is it possible that people have revised their anticipated permanent income because of greater optimism? In this scenario, the MFP growth may not necessarily be related to the reforms.

Another contending hypothesis is that every factor contributes a little bit to the overall change in the measured MFP. The possible strong linkage between policy reforms and MFP growth may need a longer sample period to establish. Alternatively, if there were more case studies of how these reforms have affected various industries, then the conclusions in the paper would be on firmer ground.

3 Institutions, Volatility, and Crises

Daron Acemoglu, Simon Johnson, and James Robinson

3.1 Introduction

There is a growing consensus among economists that differences in institutions, in particular the enforcement of property rights, rule of law, and constraints placed on politicians and elites, have a first-order effect on long-run economic development (see, among others, North and Thomas 1973; Jones 1981; North 1981; Olson 1982). Recent empirical findings support this notion. There is a strong correlation between institutions and economic and financial development (e.g., Knack and Keefer 1995; Mauro 1995; La Porta et al. 1998; and Hall and Jones 1999), especially when we look at the historically determined differences in institutions (e.g., Acemoglu, Johnson, and Robinson 2001, 2002).

In this paper and a companion paper, Acemoglu et al. (2003), we argue that institutions also have a first-order effect on short- and medium-run economic instability. We document that societies that have weak institutions for historical reasons have suffered substantially more output volatil-

Daron Acemoglu is professor of economics at the Massachusetts Institute of Technology (MIT) and a research associate of the National Bureau of Economic Research. Simon Johnson is the Ronald A. Kurtz Associate Professor at the Sloan School of Management, Massachusetts Institute of Technology, and a faculty research fellow of the National Bureau of Economic Research. James Robinson is professor of political science and economics at the University of California–Berkeley.

For helpful comments, we thank our discussants, Steve Dowrick and Dipinder Randhawa, and the editors, Takatoshi Ito and Andrew Rose. For comments on related work we thank Stijn Claessens, Alessandra Fogli, Tatiana Nenova, Sebastián Mazzuca, Ragnar Torvik, seminar participants at New York University and MIT, and attendees at the Asian Institute for Corporate Governance's Second Asian Corporate Governance Conference, the Carnegie-Rochester Public Policy 2002 conference, and the World Bank Financial Globalization conference for their suggestions.

ity and experienced more severe output, exchange rate, banking, and political crises over the past thirty years. The link we document between the historically determined component of institutions and economic instability calls for a quite different view of medium-run macroeconomic volatility, and for more work to understand the relationship between institutions and volatility. This paper is therefore meant more as a progress report to encourage others to investigate these issues.

To isolate the historically determined (and plausibly exogenous) component of differences in institutions, we build on Acemoglu, Johnson, and Robinson (2001, 2002). These papers focus on countries that were colonized by European powers. This is an attractive sample for understanding the role of institutions in economic development because the intervention of Europeans, setting up very different institutions in various parts of the globe, is the closest we have to a natural social experiment in the creation of institutions.[1]

In Acemoglu, Johnson, and Robinson (2001) we documented that different colonization strategies and different institutions set up by Europeans had radically different implications for economic development. Places prospered when Europeans set up institutions that protected private property rights, enforced the rule of law, and placed tight constraints on politicians and powerful elites. In contrast, areas where Europeans established new extractive institutions, or took over existing ones, stagnated or grew only slowly. We demonstrated the effect of historical institutions on economic development by exploiting variation in the feasibility of large-scale settlements by Europeans. Where the disease environment was favorable for Europeans to settle, Europeans settled in large numbers and developed institutions very similar to, or even substantially better than, institutions in Europe. These settler colonies, such as the United States, Canada, Australia, or New Zealand, have grown steadily over the past 200 years, especially taking advantage of the opportunity to industrialize. In many other colonies—for example, in sub-Saharan Africa, South Asia, and Central America—Europeans faced high or very high mortality rates, and settlement was not feasible. In these areas, the colonizers were much more likely to develop extractive institutions, used mostly to exploit the native population for the benefit of a few rich Europeans, and these institutions have often proved incompatible with sustained rapid growth.

Based on this argument, we used the mortality rates faced by European settlers as an instrument for institutional development and current institutions. Figure 3.1 shows the reduced-form relationship between income per capita (our measure of long-term development) today and mortality rates

1. There may also be differences in the institutional development of colonized and noncolonized countries (e.g., Japan and Thailand), but this is harder to analyze and not part of this paper.

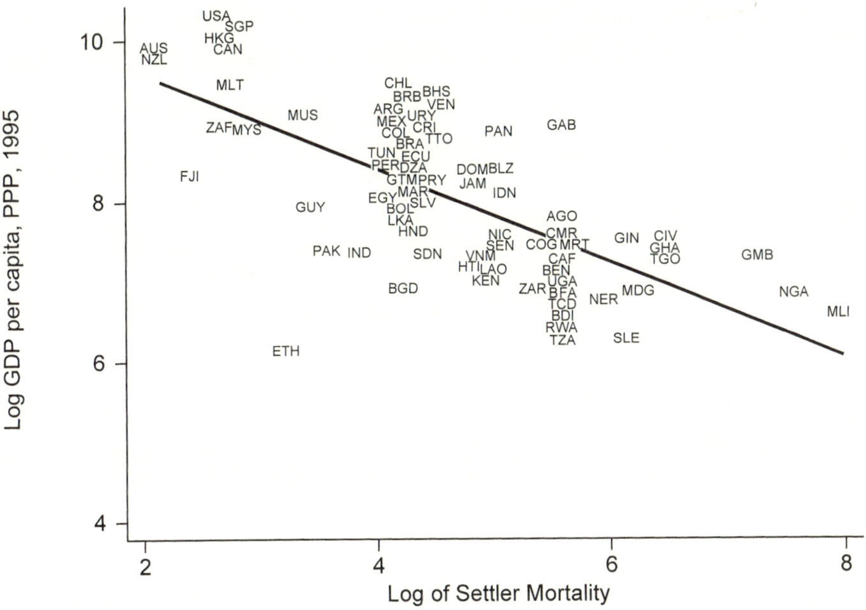

Fig. 3.1 Settler mortality and income today

faced by settlers (log of the mortality rates per annum per 1,000 settlers, where each person who dies is replaced) more than 150 years ago. There is a strong and robust relationship. Places where Europeans faced much higher mortality rates are significantly poorer today. In Acemoglu, Johnson, and Robinson (2001) we documented that the relationship between income per capita today and settler mortality in the past most likely works through institutional development, does not reflect the effect of diseases on the local population, and is not caused by other omitted characteristics that are correlated with the mortality rates faced by settlers.

The current paper highlights a surprisingly strong relationship between these mortality rates and various measures of instability and crises during the past thirty to forty years. As in Acemoglu, Johnson, and Robinson (2001), our interpretation is that this relationship reflects the effect of historically determined institutions (more specifically, institutions shaped by differential European colonization strategies and settlement patterns) on instability. In other words, not only did societies that inherited extractive institutions from their colonial past fail to take advantage of development opportunities over the long run, but their recent medium-run experience has been characterized by frequent crises and substantial instability.

Figures 3.2, 3.3, and 3.4 show the relationship between our (log) settler mortality measure and various measures of volatility since 1970. Figure 3.2 shows the relationship between the standard deviation of gross domestic

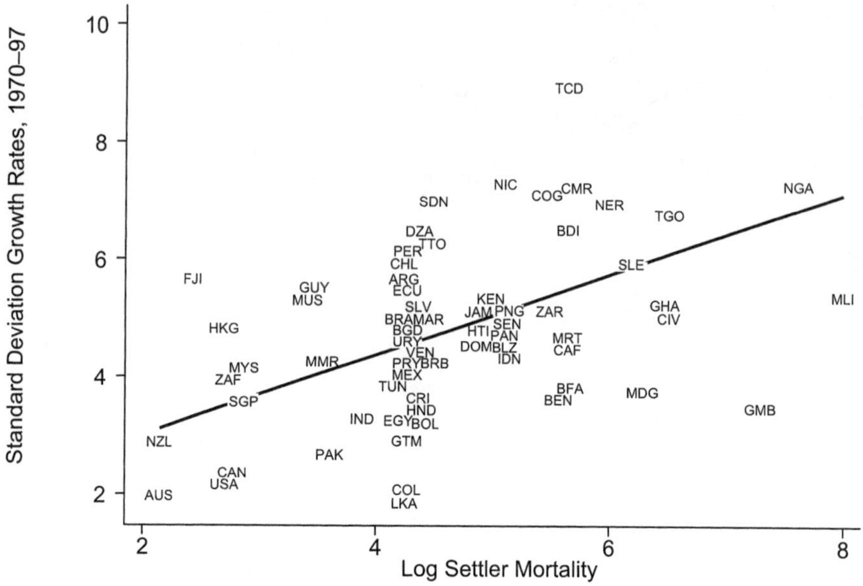

Fig. 3.2 Volatility of output against log settler mortality

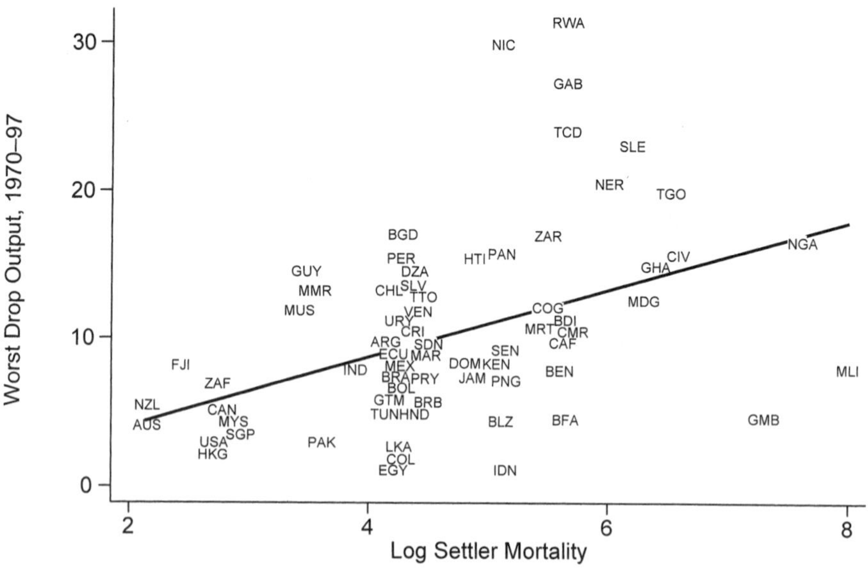

Fig. 3.3 Worst output drop against log settler mortality

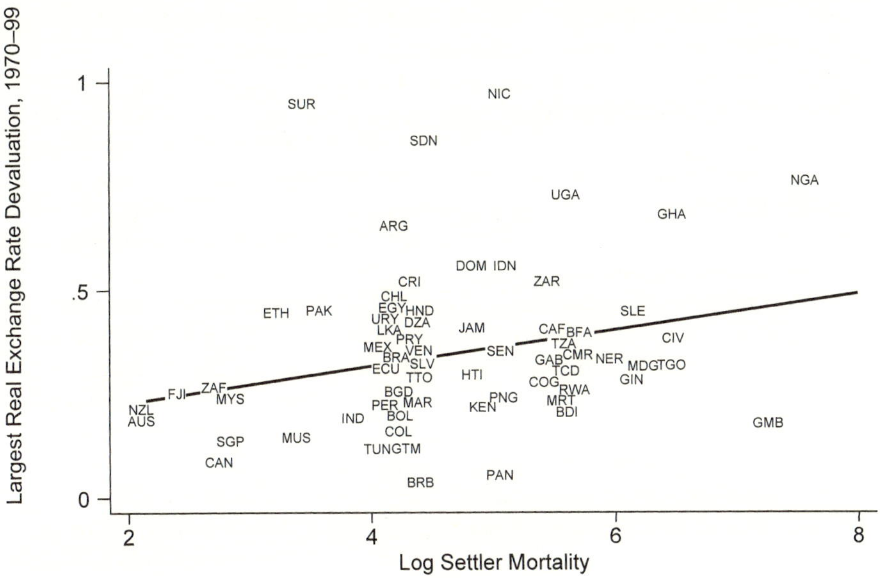

Fig. 3.4 Largest real exchange rate depreciation against log settler mortality

product (GDP) growth between 1970 and 1997 and settler mortality.[2] Figure 3.3 depicts the relationship between the largest output drop during the same period (as a measure of severity of crises) and settler mortality. Figure 3.4 presents the largest real exchange rate depreciation against settler mortality as a way of showing the relationship between balance-of-payment crises and our measure of historical institutions. These figures document that there is a strong relationship between this historical variable and the propensity of these societies to experience output volatility, severe output collapses, and balance-of-payment crises. We will show later that there is also a strong robust positive relationship between log settler mortality and the incidence of banking and political crises.[3]

Our argument is that these reduced-form relationships reflect the effect of institutions on economic instability. Societies with weak institutions not

2. We drop two outliers, Gabon and Rwanda, from this figure to make the pattern clearer. This does not change the relationship, and these countries are included in the regression analysis that follows.

3. The reduced-form coefficients on log settler mortality in the regressions corresponding to figures 3.1, 3.2, and 3.3 are 0.66 (standard error 0.18, R^2 0.19, 67 observations) using output volatility, 2.3 (standard error 0.6, R^2 0.19, 68 observations) using worst output drop, and 0.038 (standard error 0.021, R^2 0.05, 66 observations) using largest real exchange rate depreciation. In addition, we report results for banking crises and political crises. The regression of a dummy for a systemic banking crisis on log settler mortality gives a coefficient of 0.15 and the standard error is 0.062, with 37 observations and an R^2 of 0.15. The regression of a dummy for political crisis on log settler mortality gives a coefficient 0.15, and the standard error is 0.039, with 80 observations and an R^2 of 0.17.

only fail to take advantage of economic opportunities but also experience significant political struggles and associated economic instability. In the rest of the paper, we build the case that the relationship between settler mortality and instability indeed reflects the causal effect of institutions on economic and political instability. We also show that this relationship is robust to the inclusion of various controls for other potential determinants of instability. The same relationship also holds if we restrict the sample to just countries above median world income or to just former British colonies.

Our results suggest that there is a first-order effect of institutions on economic and political instability. In short, institutional weaknesses not only cause slow growth over long periods of time (e.g., 50–100 years) but are also associated with higher volatility and instability over 20- to 40-year periods. Although there are natural and intuitive reasons to expect such a relationship between institutions and instability, the precise mechanisms are not clear. A great deal more research is needed on the theoretical and empirical relationship between institutional weaknesses and instability.

In a related work, Acemoglu et al. (2003) show that the results reported here for output volatility and worst drop in output are robust to including a wide range of alternative measures of institutions and macroeconomic variables. They also present evidence that institutions determine macroeconomic policies such as government consumption and the extent of real exchange rate overvaluation, and that these distortionary macroeconomic policies have little effect on volatility once the direct effect of underlying institutions is taken into account.

The rest of the paper is organized as follows. The next section motivates the use of settler mortality as an instrument for the historically determined component of institutions. It also describes the settler mortality variable and shows the relationship between settler mortality and current institutions. Section 3.3 documents the relationship between various measures of instability and the historically determined component of institutions. It also documents that these relationships are robust to the inclusion of the obvious control variables. Section 3.4 concludes.

3.2 Historical Determinants of Institutions in Former European Colonies

3.2.1 Settler Mortality as an Instrumental Variable

The set of former European colonies provides an attractive sample for isolating the historically determined component of institutions, since the institutions in almost all former colonies have been heavily influenced by their colonial experience (see La Porta et al., 1998, and Acemoglu, Johnson, and Robinson, 2001, for more detailed discussions). Specifically, many important dimensions of institutions in former colonies were shaped by the strategy of colonization.

In Acemoglu, Johnson, and Robinson (2001, 2002), we contrasted institutions of private property, which place effective constraints on elites and rulers and do protect the property rights of a broad segment of society, and extractive institutions, which fail to impose constraints on elites and politicians and do not provide secure property rights for the majority of the population. We argued that institutions of private property were more likely to arise when Europeans settled in large numbers and set up institutions protecting economic and political rights for themselves. The "neo-Europes"—the United States, Canada, Australia, and New Zealand—are perhaps the best examples of European settlement associated with the development of good institutions. In contrast, extractive institutions emerged when Europeans pursued a strategy of extracting various types of resources from the colonies without settling and without developing participatory institutions. Note that we are not arguing that institutions are immutable and unchanging over time. Rather our historical analysis suggests that institutions persist: that is, although institutions do change over time, the initial colonial form of these institutions continues to have some effect for at least several hundred years.

This reasoning suggests that in places where the disease environment was not favorable to European health and settlement Europeans could not settle, and the cards were stacked against the development of institutions of private property. Based on this reasoning, we use measures of mortality rates experienced by early actual and potential European settlers in the colonies as an instrument for historical and current institutions in these countries. Schematically, the reasoning underlying this instrumentation strategy is

(potential) settler mortality	→ settlements	→ early institutions	→ current institutions	→ current performance

Based on this reasoning, we use data on the mortality rates of soldiers, bishops, and sailors stationed in the colonies between the seventeenth and nineteenth centuries (Curtin 1989, 1998; Gutierrez 1986). These give a good indication of the mortality rates faced by settlers. Europeans were well informed about these mortality rates at the time, even though they did not know how to control the diseases that caused these high mortality rates, especially yellow fever and malaria (see Acemoglu, Johnson, and Robinson, 2001, for more detail).[4]

An important issue is of course the validity of the exclusion restriction presumed by this instrumentation strategy—that is, whether the mortality rates faced by the settlers between the seventeenth and nineteenth centuries could actually have an effect on current outcomes through another channel. Our instrument would not be valid, for example, if there were a

4. The differences in mortality rates were large (see appendix table A2 in Acemoglu, Johnson, and Robinson 2001). For a settlement size maintained through replacement of 1,000 Europeans before 1850, the annual mortality rates ranged from 8.55 in New Zealand (lower than in Europe at that time) to 49 in India, 130 in Jamaica, and around 500 in West Africa.

strong correlation between European mortality rates over 150 years ago and the health of the current population or climate, and if current health and climate affects current economic outcomes. However, the majority of European deaths in the colonies were caused by malaria and yellow fever. Although these diseases were fatal to Europeans, who had no immunity, they had much less effect on indigenous adults, who had developed various types of immunities. These diseases are therefore unlikely to be the reason why many countries in Africa and Asia are poor today.

This notion is supported by the mortality rates of local people in high–settler mortality areas, which were comparable to the mortality rates of British troops serving in Britain or in healthier colonies. Moreover, yellow fever is essentially eradicated today, so this component of the mortality rates faced by Europeans more than 150 years ago should not have a direct effect on income or other outcomes today. To substantiate the validity of our instrumentation approach, in Acemoglu, Johnson, and Robinson (2001) we showed that the results are robust to controlling for climate, humidity, other geographic variables, and current health conditions, and that we obtain very similar results by exploiting only differences in European mortality due to yellow fever. On the basis of these findings, we take mortality rates of European settlers between the seventeenth and nineteenth centuries as an instrument for current institutions in the former colonies.

3.2.2 Measuring Contemporary Institutions

What are the institutions that matter? In our empirical analysis here, we use an institutional variable for which we have data for a broad cross section of countries at the beginning of the sample: constraints placed on the executive, as measured in the Polity IV data set based on the work of Robert Gurr. For every independent country, the Polity IV data set reports a qualitative score, between 1 and 7, measuring the extent of constitutional limits on the exercise of arbitrary power by the executive. This "constraint on the executive" variable is conceptually attractive because it measures institutional and other constraints that are placed on presidents and dictators (or monarchies).

Theoretically, we expect a society where elites and politicians are effectively constrained to experience less infighting between various groups to take control of the state, and to pursue more sustainable policies (see Acemoglu et al. 2003). Nevertheless, constraint on the executive is only one measure of institutions, and it is quite possible that a country might have adequate constraints on the executive, but suffer from corruption or weak property rights for other reasons. More generally, the relevant institutions are a cluster of social arrangements that include constitutional and social limits on politicians' and elites' power, the rule of law, provisions for mediating social cleavages, strong property rights enforcement, a minimum amount of equal opportunity, and the like. This cluster determines whether agents with investment opportunities will undertake these investments,

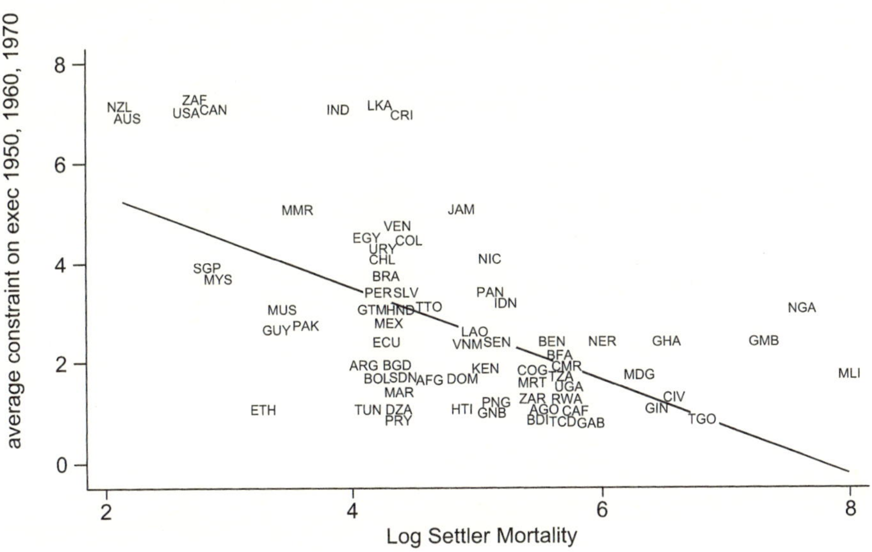

Fig. 3.5 Average constraint on executive (1950, 1960, 1970) versus log settler mortality

whether there will be significant swings in the political and social environment leading to crises, and whether politicians will be induced to pursue unsustainable policies in order to remain in power in the face of deep social cleavages. Therefore, we prefer to be relatively loose on what the fundamental institutional problems are, and instead we try to isolate the historically determined component of these institutional differences.

Figure 3.5 shows the first-stage relationship between our constraint on the executive variable (average value for 1950, 1960, and 1970) and the log of European settler mortality in annualized deaths per thousand mean strength. This measure reports the death rate among 1,000 soldiers per year where each death is replaced with a new soldier and was the standard measure in the army records from which much of our information comes. We use logs rather than levels, because otherwise some of the African observations are extreme outliers. The figure shows a strong relationship between the measure of institutions used in this paper and settler mortality more than 150 years ago. Our interpretation is that this reflects the causal effect of colonial policies on current institutions, and hence it can serve as a useful source of variation for identifying the effect of institutions on macroeconomic outcomes.

3.2.3 Institutions and Economic Outcomes

We now briefly examine the relationship between the historically determined component of institutions and current per capita income and recent growth rates. The first column in panel A of table 3.1 replicates our main

Table 3.1 **Income, Growth, and Institutions**

	Ex-Colonies Sample (1)	Ex-Colonies above Median World Income (2)	Ex-Colonies without Africa (3)	Ex-Colonies Sample (4)	Ex-Colonies above Median World Income (5)	Ex-Colonies without Africa (6)
	A. Dependent Variable is Log GDP per Capita in 1995					
Two-stage least squares						
Average protection against expropriation, 1985–95	0.96	0.50	0.56			
	(0.17)	(0.08)	(0.10)			
Initial constraint on executive				0.62	0.46	0.57
				(0.11)	(0.16)	(0.18)
First stage for measure of institutions						
Log settler mortality	–0.58	–1.10	–1.21	–0.91	–1.15	–1.25
	(0.13)	(0.26)	(0.24)	(0.16)	(0.36)	(0.35)
R^2	0.24	0.44	0.41	0.34	0.33	0.29
No. of observations	64	25	37	68	23	35

	(7)	(8)	(9)	(10)	(11)	(12)
	B. Dependent Variable is Average Annual Growth of GDP per Capita, 1970–97					
Two-stage least squares						
Initial constraint on executive	0.75	0.50	0.50	1.57	0.98	1.05
	(0.22)	(0.32)	(0.31)	(0.71)	(0.60)	(0.58)
Log GDP per capita in 1970				–1.58	–2.04	–1.42
				(1.00)	(2.46)	(0.81)
First stage for measure of institutions						
Log settler mortality	–0.95	–1.35	–1.31	–0.54	–0.97	–0.98
	(0.16)	(0.32)	(0.35)	(0.20)	(0.35)	(0.40)
Log GDP per capita in 1970				0.84	1.21	0.63
				(0.27)	(0.56)	(0.39)
R^2	0.37	0.44	0.30	0.45	0.53	0.35
No. of observations	63	25	35	61	25	34

Notes: Standard errors are in parentheses. All regressions are cross-sectional with one observation per country. In panel A the dependent variable is the level of log GDP per capita in 1995, and in panel B it is the average annual growth rate of GDP per capita from 1970 to 1997; both are from the World Bank. The independent variable in columns (1), (2), and (3) of panel A is average protection against expropriation risk, 1985–95, from Political Risk Services, as used in Acemoglu, Johnson, and Robinson (2001); a higher score indicates more protection. In all other columns the independent variable, initial constraint on executive, is average constraint on executive in 1950, 1960, and 1970, which is an average of the Polity score in each year; countries that are still colonies in a particular year are assigned a score of 1. In both panels the measure of institutions is instrumented using log settler mortality before 1850 (where mortality is per 1,000 per annum with replacement). The ex-colonies sample includes all former colonies of European powers for which Acemoglu, Johnson, and Robinson (2001) report data. Alternative samples are ex-colonies above median world per capita income in 1970, as measured by Summers-Heston and reported in Barro and Lee (1993) but excluding Gabon and ex-colonies without any African countries. For more detailed data definitions and sources see table 3A.2.

regression from Acemoglu, Johnson, and Robinson (2001), which looks at the effect of institutional differences on (log) income per capita today. Our two-stage least squares (2SLS) estimate of the effect of institutions on income per capita is relatively precisely estimated and large. For example, it implies that improving Nigeria's institutions to the level of Chile could lead to a sevenfold increase in Nigeria's income (Chile currently has per capita income more than eleven times that of Nigeria).[5]

The lower part of panel A shows the first-stage relationship between institutions and log of potential European settler mortality. In Acemoglu, Johnson, and Robinson (2001), we used average protection against expropriation risk between 1985 and 1995 as our measure of institutions. We do not focus on this measure in the current paper, since we prefer a measure that refers to the beginning of our sample period (i.e., 1970), and the protection against expropriation variable is not available for the 1960s and 1970s. Column (4) replicates the same regression as column (1) with the "constraint on the executive" variable that we use throughout this paper. The first-stage relationship for this regression is shown in figure 3.5. Mortality rates faced by early European settlers explain over 25 percent of the variation in this measure of current institutions.

Columns (7) and (10) turn to a regression of the average growth rate between 1970 and 1997 on constraint on the executive before 1970, again instrumented by log settler mortality (with or without controlling for initial income). We express growth rates in percentage points (e.g., 2 percent rather than 0.02) to save on decimal points; see table 3A.3 for summary statistics. Column (7) shows a statistically significant relationship, indicating faster growth since 1970 among countries with better historically determined institutions. For example, the coefficient of 0.75 implies that a country like the United States, with a value of constraint on the executive of 7, is predicted to grow about 3 percent a year faster than a country like Nigeria, with a score of 3. The estimate of the effect of initial "constraint on the executive" on growth becomes larger when we control for initial income in column (10), but also the standard error more than triples (the coefficient is still statistically significant at the 5 percent level).[6]

It is useful to know whether the relationship between the historically determined component of institutions and economic outcomes is driven

5. Note that the comparisons of countries here and later in the text are only intended to be illustrative. They do not imply anything about the "fit" of the regression.

6. That the effect of historically determined institutions on post-1970 growth becomes weaker when we control for initial income is not surprising. Initial income (i.e., income per capita 1970) is determined largely by historical institutions, so our measure of institutions and initial income are highly correlated. In fact, much of the divergence among the former colonies took place between 1750 and 1950, when countries with good institutions took advantage of industrialization opportunities and those with extractive institutions failed to do so (see Acemoglu, Johnson, and Robinson, 2002). So our measure of institutions is as good a determinant of income level in 1970 as subsequent growth.

mainly by the contrast between rich and poor nations. Columns (2), (5), (8), and (11) report regressions for countries above the median world per capita income in 1970 (using the Summers-Heston income per capita data for that year, from Heston, Summers, and Aten 2002). In these regressions, and all those in subsequent tables that use this subsample, we drop Gabon, which is an outlier with high volatility (including Gabon in this sample does not change the results). In table 3.1, the estimates for this subsample are similar to, but lower than, those for the sample of all ex-colonies. They continue to be highly significant in income level regressions (columns [2] and [5]) but are only significant at the 10 percent level in the growth regressions (columns [8] and [11]).

Finally, columns (3), (6), (9), and (12) report regressions for ex-colonies without Africa, to show that the effect of the historically determined component of institutions on income level and growth is not driven by a contrast between African and non-African nations. In this smaller sample, the 2SLS estimate of the effect of institutions on economics outcome is again lower than that for all ex-colonies. Nevertheless, this estimate is still significant at the 5 percent level in the income level regressions and significant at the 10 percent in the growth regressions. In the subsequent analysis, we find that the results without Africa are similar to those that use former colonies above median world per capita income, so we just report the latter.[7]

3.3 Institutions and Measures of Crises

3.3.1 Identification Strategy

The economic relationship we are interested in identifying is

$$X_{c,t-1,t} = \alpha + \beta \cdot I_{c,t-1} + Z'_{c,t-1,t} \cdot \gamma + \varepsilon_{c,t-1,t}, \quad (1)$$

where $X_{c,t-1,t}$ is the outcome of interest for country c between times t and $t-1$. The five outcomes that we will look at are overall volatility (standard deviation of growth), severity of crises (worst output drop), largest real exchange rate depreciation, a dummy for banking crises, and a measure of political crises. In our baseline regressions, the time period will be from 1970 to 1997 (this choice is dictated by data availability and our desire to start the analysis at a point in time where all countries in our sample are independent nation states). We examined alternative time periods, for example starting in 1960 or 1980, and did not find any important difference in results.

7. Omitting Africa is also informative on the question of whether the length of colonial control was important. Much of Africa was under formal colonial rule only briefly. Nevertheless, it was under European influence since at least 1600 through slave trading and other interactions.

$I_{c,t-1}$ is our measure of institutions at the beginning of the sample, constructed as the average value for the constraint on the executive measure from the Polity IV data set for 1950, 1960, and 1970. In taking this average, we assign the lowest score to countries that are not yet independent (and that are therefore not in the Polity IV data set).[8] This is reasonable because in a country still under colonial control there are typically few real constraints on the power of the rulers. In addition, $Z_{c,t-1,t}$ is a set of other controls, ranging from macro variables, to financial development variables, to other determinants of economic instability, such as terms of trade shocks etc.[9]

The parameter that we are interested in identifying is β, the effect of institutions. The simplest strategy is to estimate the model in equation (1) using ordinary least squares (OLS) regression. There are two problems with this strategy: (1) Institutions are endogenous, so we may be capturing reverse causality, or the effect of some omitted characteristics (geography, culture, or other variables) on both institutions and economic outcomes; and (2) institutions are measured with error, and the variable we have does not correspond to the desired concept. In particular, although the institutions we have in mind are multidimensional, constraint on the executive only measures one of these dimensions, and that quite imperfectly.

Both of these concerns imply that OLS regressions will give results that are difficult to interpret and that do not correspond to the causal effect of institutions and policy variables on economic outcomes. Ideally, we would like to estimate equation (1) using 2SLS with a plausible instrument for institutions. This instrument should be correlated with the endogenous regressors and should be orthogonal to any other omitted characteristics and not correlated with the outcomes of interest through any channel other than their effect via the endogenous regressors (i.e., institutions).

In this paper, we pursue the strategy of instrumenting for institutions using the historically determined component of institutions, specifically from the colonial experience of former colonies, as discussed in the previous section. To the extent that the instrument is valid, it will solve the endogeneity, the omitted variables bias, and the measurement error prob-

8. We take these averages rather than simply using the 1970 value of the index, since we are interested in the long-run component of these constraints (not in the year-to-year fluctuations) and also because the Polity data set gives very high scores to a number of former colonies in 1970 that subsequently drop by a large amount. This reflects the fact that many of these countries adopted the constitution of their former colonial powers but did not really implement the constitution or introduce effective checks. Using simply the 1970 value of the constraints on the executive gives very similar results.

9. In Acemoglu et al. (2003) we report regression results with and without the log of initial income per capita. Following Barro (1991) this variable is included in most growth regressions to control for convergence effects. It is also useful to include it in regressions of volatility or crises because, as shown in Acemoglu and Zilibotti (1997), poorer countries suffer substantially more volatility. However, we find that including initial income per capita does not change our basic results, so it is omitted here. This suggests that institutions affect volatility through mechanisms other than their effect on income per capita.

lems. In particular, if the instrument is valid, we can estimate the effect of institutions on economic outcomes, the β parameters, consistently in models that exclude other potentially endogenous controls, such as the macro policy variables. In Acemoglu et al. (2003), we adopt a variety of strategies to deal with the potential endogeneity of macro policy variables. Here we simply treat all controls, including the macro variables, as exogenous. This strategy typically creates an upward bias in the effect of these controls and a potential downward bias in β, the effect of institutions on instability (see the appendix of Acemoglu, Johnson, and Robinson 2001). We therefore pursue this strategy here since it is conservative, in the sense of stacking the cards against finding a substantial role for institutions.

3.3.2 Output Volatility

Table 3.2 shows the relationship between institutions and volatility. Column (1) reports the OLS relationship between the standard deviation of output growth (measured by real GDP per capita) and our measure of institutions. This OLS relationship is shown in figure 3.6. Column (2) shows the estimated 2SLS result when we instrument for institutions using log settler mortality. These results suggest that countries with institutional problems suffer substantially more volatility. For example, the estimate of –0.79 in column (2) implies that a 1 point higher score in the institutional index translates into about a 0.79 decline in the standard deviation of growth. To get an idea of magnitudes, note that on the basis of this estimate, we should expect a country like the United States, which has an institutional score of 7, to have a standard deviation 3.16 lower than a country like Nigeria, which has an institutional score of 3.[10]

Columns (4) through (9) show that the 2SLS relationship between output volatility and institutions is robust when we include the obvious control variables. Column (4) controls for three important macroeconomic variables: log average inflation, which is the log of average annual inflation in the Consumer Price Index from 1970 to 1997, from the World Bank; government consumption, which is the average of the ratio of real government "consumption" expenditure to real GDP from 1970 to 1989, from the Barro and Lee (1993) data set; and real exchange rate overvaluation, which is an index of real overvaluation of the official exchange rate during 1970–98, constructed by Easterly and Levine (2003) using the methodology of Dollar (1992). In this case, the coefficient on institutions falls in absolute value to –0.48 but remains significant. None of the macro variables are significant.[11]

10. This gap is approximately two-thirds of the actual gap in standard deviation between the United States (7.37) and Nigeria (2.16) in the data, which is 5.21. This comparison is for illustrative purposes only and not to show the fit of the regression.

11. Acemoglu et al. (2003) look at alternative macroeconomic variables and present a larger set of specifications. The only macro variable that is typically significant is the extent of real exchange rate overvaluation.

Table 3.2 **Institutions and Output Volatility**

	Ex-Colonies Sample (1)	Ex-Colonies Sample (2)	Ex-Colonies above Median Income per Capita (3)	Ex-Colonies, Controlling for Macro Variables (4)	Ex-Colonies Controlling for Financial Development (5)	Ex-Colonies, Controlling for Terms of Trade (6)	Ex-Colonies, Controlling for Natural Resources (7)	Ex-Colonies, Controlling for Latitude (8)	Ex-Colonies, Controlling for Religion (9)	Only Former British Colonies (10)
Initial constraint on the executive	–0.55	–0.79	–1.02	–0.48	–0.76	–0.76	–0.80	–0.73	–0.90	–0.75
	(0.11)	(0.20)	(0.29)	(0.21)	(0.28)	(0.20)	(0.21)	(0.24)	(0.23)	(0.23)
p-value for macro variables				[0.25]						
Financial development					–0.005					
					(0.027)					
Terms of trade						60.00				
						(22.16)				
Natural resources							2.01			
							(2.36)			
Latitude								–1.18		
								(2.15)		
p-value for religion									[0.30]	
R^2	0.27									
No. of observations	63	63	27	44	63	60	61	63	63	21

Notes: Dependent variable is standard deviation of growth rate of real GDP per capita between 1970 and 1997. Standard errors are in parentheses. Cross-sectional regressions with one observation per country; the dependent variable is standard deviation of real GDP per capita growth rate between 1970 and 1997. Column (1) is OLS; all other columns are 2SLS using log settler mortality as an instrument for institutions. Column (3) limits the sample to former European colonies above median world income. Column (4) includes log average inflation, which is the log of average annual inflation in the Consumer Price Index from 1970 to 1997, from the World Bank; government consumption, which is the average of the ratio of real government "consumption" expenditure to real GDP from 1970 to 1989 from the Barro and Lee data set; and real exchange rate overvaluation, which is an index of real overvaluation of the official exchange rate during 1970–98, constructed by Easterly and Levine (2003) using the methodology of Dollar (1992). Column (5) includes the log of average money-GDP ratio for 1970–97, from the World Bank. Column (6) includes the standard deviation of terms-of-trade shocks in 1970–89 times export-GDP ratio in 1970, from the Barro and Lee data set. Column (7) includes the share of primary exports in GDP in 1970 from Sachs and Warner (1997). Column (8) includes the absolute normalized value of distance from the equator (i.e., a standardized measure of latitude), in which a higher value indicates that a country's capital is further from the equator. Column (9) includes the percent of the population that is Muslim, Catholic, and Protestant in 1980 (with "other" as the omitted group); from La Porta et al. (1999). Column (10) restricts the sample just to former British colonies. Initial constraint on the executive is average constraint on executive in 1950, 1960, and 1970, which is an average of the Polity score in each year; countries that are still colonies in a particular year are assigned a score of 1. We instrument for institutions using log settler mortality (where mortality is per 1,000 per annum with replacement). All regressions, other than those in columns (3) and (10), include all former colonies of European powers for which we have data. For more detailed data definitions and sources see table 3A.2.

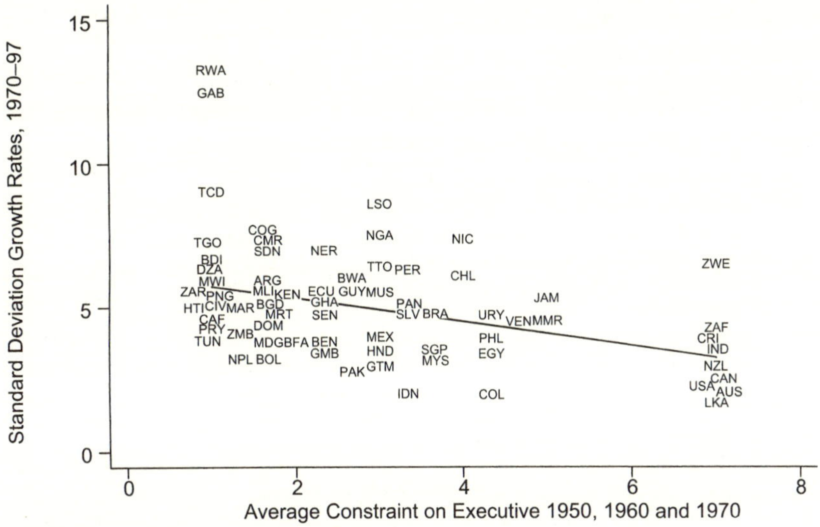

Fig. 3.6 Volatility of output against average constraint on executive

Column (5) includes the log of M2 over GDP, using averages for 1970–97 (see Easterly, Islam, and Stiglitz, 2000, for the use of this variable in this context). Many macroeconomists emphasize weak financial intermediation as a primary cause of economic volatility. We also find no strong evidence supporting this claim. The financial intermediation variables are not significant, while the institutions variable is still significant, with a coefficient of –0.76 and standard error of 0.28.

Column (6) includes the standard deviation of terms of trade shocks in 1970–89 times export-GDP ratio in 1970, from the Barro and Lee (1993) data set. This measures the openness to the economy and, in particular, its vulnerability to fluctuations in traded goods prices (e.g., this measure is higher if the country exports more primary commodities). In this column the coefficient on institutions is essentially unchanged compared with our base case: coefficient of –0.76 (standard error of 0.2). This measure of the terms of trade is also significant.

Column (7) includes the share of primary exports in GDP in 1970 from Sachs and Warner (1997). This is both a basic measure of openness and exposure to shocks and a way to control for the importance of natural resources in the economy. In this case the coefficient on institutions increases to –0.8, while the standard error is virtually unchanged at 0.21.

Column (8) includes the absolute value of latitude (distance of a country's capital from the equator). This is a standard control variable representing the potential effect of geographical factors. Here the coefficient on institutions falls slightly in absolute value to –0.73, and the standard error increases to 0.24, but institutions are still highly significant. Latitude itself is not significant.

Column (9) includes the fraction of the population that was Muslim, Catholic, and Protestant in 1980 (with "other" as the omitted group; see La Porta et al. 1999). The coefficient on institutions now increases in absolute size to –0.9, and the standard error is 0.23. The religion variables are jointly not significant.

Columns (3) and (10) look at subsamples of our ex-colonies sample. Column (3) includes only those former colonies that have above-median world income per capita. In this case, we find a larger coefficient in absolute terms (–1.02) and a somewhat higher standard error (0.29). Column (10) restricts attention to just those countries that were formerly British colonies. In this case the coefficient (–0.75) and standard error (0.23) are almost identical to those reported in column (2).

Overall these results indicate two robust findings. The first is that initial institutions are strongly correlated with subsequent output volatility. The second is that most other potential control variables are not significant determinants of volatility. This is the case even though, to stack the cards against us, we use contemporaneous values of these controls, so any endogeneity (e.g., more volatility leading to less financial development) would tend to bias the coefficients upward. The only significant determinant of volatility in table 3.2, other than institutions, is terms-of-trade shocks.

3.3.3 Worst Drop in Output

Table 3.3 presents a number of specifications that look at the impact of institutions on the severity of crises, measured by the largest output drop between 1970 and 1997. In the IV regressions, our measure of institutions—constraint on the executive—is instrumented by European settler mortality. We use the same control variables and alternative samples as in table 3.2.

Worst output drop is defined so that a larger positive number means a bigger fall in GDP per capita. The OLS coefficient on institutions, in column (1), is –1.28, and the standard error is 0.41. The OLS relationship is shown in figure 3.7. When we instrument for institutions—for example, in column (2)—the coefficient increases in absolute value to –2.27, while the standard error rises to 0.7.

The alternative specifications in table 3.3 show that institutions are robustly significant. Including the macro variables in column (4) reduces the coefficient on institutions slightly, but again the macro variables themselves are not jointly significant. Financial development (column [5]), terms of trade (column [6]), natural resource exports (column [7]), latitude (column [8]), and religion (column [9]) are all insignificant. In almost all cases the coefficient on institutions is above 2 in absolute value; the exceptions are when we control for financial development (column [5]) and when we restrict the

Table 3.3 Institutions and Worst Drop in Output

	Ex-Colonies Sample (1)	Ex-Colonies Sample (2)	Ex-Colonies above Median Income per Capita (3)	Ex-Colonies, Controlling for Macro Variables (4)	Ex-Colonies Controlling for Financial Development (5)	Ex-Colonies, Controlling for Terms of Trade (6)	Ex-Colonies, Controlling for Natural Resources (7)	Ex-Colonies, Controlling for Latitude (8)	Ex-Colonies, Controlling for Religion (9)	Only Former British Colonies (10)
Initial constraint on the executive	–1.28 (0.41)	–2.27 (0.70)	–2.70 (1.03)	–2.13 (0.87)	–1.74 (0.96)	–2.35 (0.77)	–2.35 (0.73)	–2.18 (0.87)	–2.76 (0.83)	–1.67 (0.77)
p-value for macro variables				[0.96]						
Financial development					–0.081 (0.091)					
Terms of trade						90.20 (85.39)				
Natural resources							7.18 (8.38)			
Latitude								–1.76 (7.82)		
p-value for religion									[0.18]	
R^2	0.14									
No. of observations	63	63	27	44	63	60	61	63	63	21

Notes: Dependent variable is worst drop in real GDP per capita between 1970 and 1997. Standard errors are in parentheses. Cross-sectional regressions with one observation per country; the dependent variable is worst real GDP per capita growth rate between 1970 and 1997. Column (1) is OLS; all other columns are 2SLS using log settler mortality as an instrument for institutions. Column (3) limits the sample to former European colonies above median world income. Column (4) includes log average inflation, which is the log of average annual inflation in the Consumer Price Index from 1970 to 1997, from the World Bank; government consumption, which is the average of the ratio of real government "consumption" expenditure to real GDP from 1970 to 1989 from the Barro and Lee data set; and real exchange rate overvaluation, which is an index of real overvaluation of the official exchange rate during 1970–98, constructed by Easterly and Levine (2003) using the methodology of Dollar (1992). Column (5) includes the log of average money-GDP ratio for 1970–97, from the World Bank. Column (6) includes the standard deviation of terms-of-trade shocks in 1970–89 times export-GDP ratio in 1970, from the Barro and Lee data set. Column (7) includes the share of primary exports in GDP in 1970 from Sachs and Warner (1997). Column (8) includes the absolute normalized value of distance from the equator (i.e., a standardized measure of latitude), in which a higher value indicates that a country's capital is further from the equator. Column (9) includes the percent of the population that is Muslim, Catholic, and Protestant in 1980 (with "other" as the omitted group); from La Porta et al. (1999). Column (10) restricts the sample just to former British colonies. Initial constraint on the executive is average constraint on executive in 1950, 1960, and 1970, which is an average of the Polity score in each year; countries that are still colonies in a particular year are assigned a score of 1. We instrument for institutions using log settler mortality (where mortality is per 1,000 per annum with replacement). All regressions, other than those in columns (3) and (10), include all former colonies of European powers for which we have data. For more detailed data definitions and sources see table 3A.2.

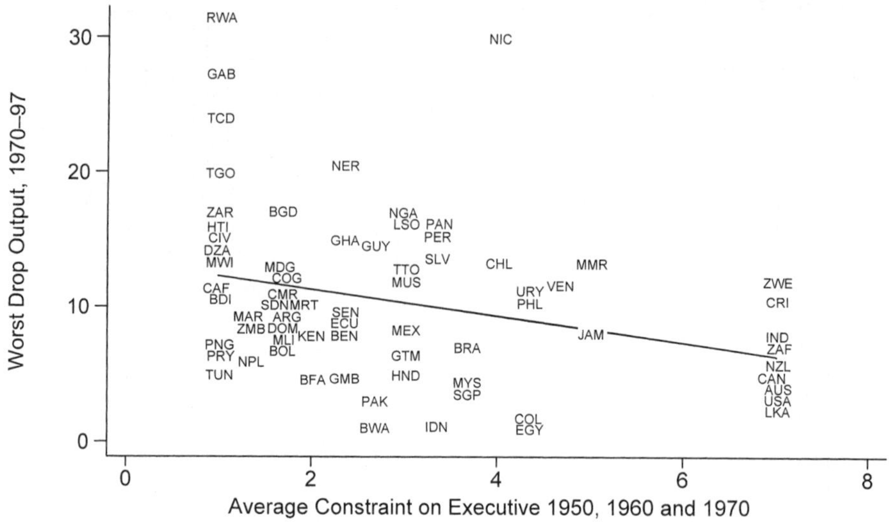

Fig. 3.7 Worst output drop, 1970–97, against average constraint on executive

sample to just former British colonies (column [10]); but even in these cases the institutions coefficient remains significant (although only at the 10 percent level in column [5]). Overall, the results are very similar to our baseline results, showing that the effect of the historically determined component of institutions on output collapses is robust and is not simply driven by some other sources of output crises that are correlated with institutions.

These results confirm the conclusion of the previous section that there appears to be a close link between institutions and economic instability, most likely not mediated primarily through the standard macroeconomic variables or through financial development or through reliance on primary exports. The baseline coefficient estimate is again very large; it suggests that between 1970 and 1999 Nigeria is likely to have experienced a worst output drop around 10 percentage points worse than that of the United States (the actual difference in worst output drop is 13 percentage points).

3.3.4 Exchange Rate Crises

Are institutions also related to exchange rate and balance-of-payments crises? To answer this question, we use change in the real exchange rate as a rough but reasonable measure of severity for exchange rate and balance-of-payments crises.[12]

In table 3.4 we look at the largest annual change in real exchange rate

12. Note that we use changes in the real exchange rate because in some instances a large nominal depreciation simply matches high steady inflation and is not associated with a crisis. See Pivovarsky and Thaicharoen (2002) for a related analysis of exchange rate crises.

Table 3.4 **Institutions and Largest Real Exchange Rate Depreciation**

	Ex-Colonies Sample (1)	Ex-Colonies Sample (2)	Ex-Colonies above Median Income per Capita (3)	Ex-Colonies, Controlling for Macro Variables (4)	Ex-Colonies Controlling for Financial Development (5)	Ex-Colonies, Controlling for Terms of Trade (6)	Ex-Colonies, Controlling for Natural Resources (7)	Ex-Colonies, Controlling for Latitude (8)	Ex-Colonies, Controlling for Religion (9)	Only Former British Colonies (10)
Initial constraint on the executive	–0.009	–0.048	–0.057	–0.050	–0.042	–0.060	–0.051	–0.054	–0.055	–0.083
	(0.013)	(0.024)	(0.034)	(0.033)	(0.030)	(0.028)	(0.024)	(0.030)	(0.027)	(0.038)
p-value for macro variables				[0.29]						
Financial development					–0.002					
					(0.003)					
Terms of trade						–3.70				
						(2.81)				
Natural resources							0.07			
							(0.30)			
Latitude								0.10		
								(0.25)		
p-value for religion									[0.71]	
R^2	0.01									
No. of observations	62	62	24	44	59	59	59	62	62	20

Notes: Dependent variable is largest real exchange rate depreciation, 1970–99. Standard errors are in parentheses. Cross-sectional regressions with one observation per country; the dependent variable is largest depreciation in real exchange rate between 1970 and 1997, using the index constructed by Easterly and Levine (2003) based on the methodology of Dollar (1992). Column (1) is OLS; all other columns are 2SLS using log settler mortality as an instrument for institutions. Column (3) limits the sample to former European colonies above median world income. Column (4) includes log average inflation, which is the log of average annual inflation in the Consumer Price Index from 1970 to 1997, from the World Bank; government consumption, which is the average of the ratio of real government "consumption" expenditure to real GDP from 1970 to 1989 from the Barro and Lee data set; and real exchange rate overvaluation, which is an index of real overvaluation of the official exchange rate during 1970–98, constructed by Easterly and Levine (2003) using the methodology of Dollar (1992). Column (5) includes the log of average money-GDP ratio for 1970–97, from the World Bank. Column (6) includes the standard deviation of terms-of-trade shocks in 1970–89 times export-GDP ratio in 1970, from the Barro and Lee data set. Column (7) includes the share of primary exports in GDP in 1970 from Sachs and Warner (1997). Column (8) includes the absolute normalized value of distance from the equator (i.e., a standardized measure of latitude), in which a higher value indicates that a country's capital is further from the equator. Column (9) includes the percent of the population that is Muslim, Catholic, and Protestant in 1980 (with "other" as the omitted group); from La Porta et al. (1999). Column (10) restricts the sample just to former British colonies. Initial constraint on the executive is average constraint on executive in 1950, 1960, and 1970, which is an average of the Polity score in each year; countries that are still colonies in a particular year are assigned a score of 1. We instrument for institutions using log settler mortality (where mortality is per 1,000 per annum with replacement). All regressions, other than those in columns (3) and (10), include all former colonies of European powers for which we have data. For more detailed data definitions and sources see table 3A.2.

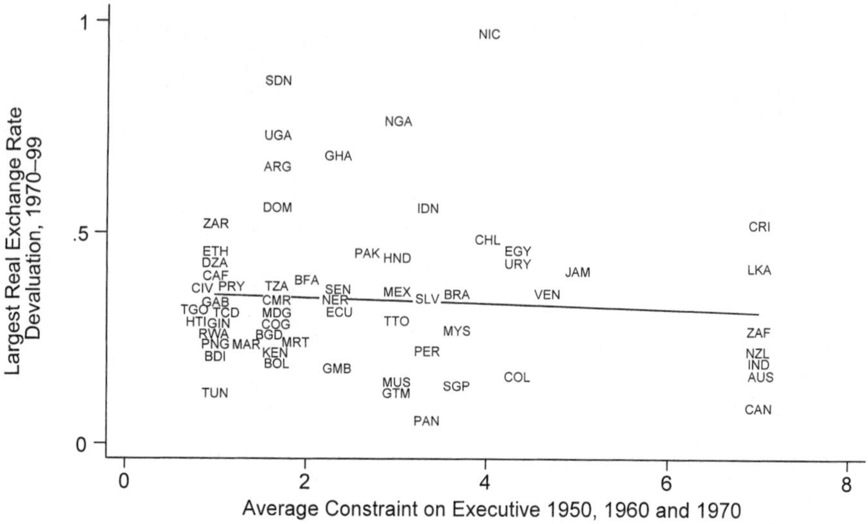

Fig. 3.8 Largest real depreciation against average constraint on executive

over the period 1970–99 using the index of the real exchange rate constructed by David Dollar (1992) and updated by Easterly and Levine (2003). The advantage of this measure is that it allows provides comparable data for almost all countries.[13]

Our dependent variable is expressed as a decimal, with a higher positive number indicating a larger real depreciation. We are comparing the "worst" (i.e., largest) real depreciation experience of countries. Figure 3.8 shows the OLS relationship. Countries with better institutions experienced a lower absolute value (i.e., less bad) "worst" real depreciation over this period. The OLS coefficient on institutions in column (1), –0.009, indicates that countries with a 1 point better score in terms of institutions have a lower (in absolute value) "worst depreciation" by 0.9 percentage points.

When we instrument for institutions using log settler mortality, the coefficient on institutions increases in absolute size to –0.048 (with the standard error rising to 0.024). The coefficient estimate implies that over a thirty-year period Nigeria's worst exchange rate depreciation (i.e., arguably part of its worst balance-of-payments crisis) would be 20 percentage points higher than that of Canada—the actual difference was nearly 70 percentage points.

This large coefficient on institutions is confirmed in the alternative spec-

13. The real exchange rate is computed by Easterly and Levine (2003) as the average amount that domestic prices in U.S. dollars are higher than international prices in U.S. dollars. We omit the United States when we use maximum real devaluation as the dependent variable. However, the United States is included when we use the average real exchange rate overvaluation as a right-hand-side variable.

ifications of table 3.4 (with the same structure of columns as tables 3.2 and 3.3). The coefficient on institutions is always at least –0.04 and is as large as –0.083 (for the British colonies only in column [10]) and is significant in all columns, except in columns (3), (4), and (5), where we respectively limit the sample to countries above median world income, control for the macro variables, and control for financial development. None of the control variables are significant in any specification we have investigated.

3.3.5 Banking Crises

Table 3.5 reports results using an indicator of "systemic" banking crises as the dependent variable. Our main data source is Barth, Caprio, and Levine (2002), who report data on banking systems, including an indicator of banking crises for ninety-two countries. However, they do not distinguish between large and small crises. For example, in their data the United States' savings and loans crisis is coded as a crisis, even though it involved a relatively small part of the financial system. To create a variable measuring "systemic crisis" we use information from Boyd, Kwak, and Smith (2002), who code whether there was a systemic or nonsystemic banking crisis for a smaller set of countries.[14]

We have data on banking crises only for 44 former colonies in total, with 25 countries suffering systemic banking crises over this time period. Out of this 44, we also do not have data on institutions or settler mortality for an additional 8. Most of the missing countries are relatively poor countries in Africa. Therefore, these results on banking crises should be seen as quite tentative, mostly as suggesting a promising line for future research.

Column (1) shows an OLS coefficient on institutions of –0.1, with a standard error of 0.04.[15] When we instrument for institutions using settler mortality, the coefficient increases in absolute size to –0.15 and the standard error rises to 0.07. This implies that the 4-point difference in institutional scores of Nigeria and the United States should translate into 0.6 difference in the probability of a systemic banking crisis, which is again a very large effect.

The coefficient on institutions is significant in all our alternative specifications, with the exception of column (5), where we control for financial development. The only control variables that are significant are the macro variables, which are jointly significant at the 10 percent level in column (4).

Looking just at the twenty countries that are above median world per capita income and for which we have data (column [3]) suggests a stronger

14. More specifically, we treat all the Barth, Caprio, and Levine (2002) crises as systemic unless Boyd, Kwak, and Smith (2002) indicate otherwise. As a result, Canada, India, and the United States are reclassified from 1 to 0.

15. We are estimating a linear probability model using OLS and IV. Such linear probability models are consistent with both OLS and IV, and, as argued by Angrist (2001), they are conceptually appealing, especially with IV.

Table 3.5 **Institutions and Banking Crises**

	Ex-Colonies Sample (1)	Ex-Colonies Sample (2)	Ex-Colonies above Median Income per Capita (3)	Ex-Colonies, Controlling for Macro Variables (4)	Ex-Colonies Controlling for Financial Development (5)	Ex-Colonies, Controlling for Terms of Trade (6)	Ex-Colonies, Controlling for Natural Resources (7)	Ex-Colonies, Controlling for Latitude (8)	Ex-Colonies, Controlling for Religion (9)	Only Former British Colonies (10)
Initial constraint on the executive	–0.10	–0.15	–0.31	–0.20	–0.08	–0.15	–0.16	–0.16	–0.16	–0.19
	(0.04)	(0.07)	(0.09)	(0.09)	(0.11)	(0.08)	(0.07)	(0.10)	(0.10)	(0.09)
p-value for macro variables				[0.08]						
Financial development					–0.010					
					(0.010)					
Terms of trade						–0.17				
						(13.02)				
Natural resources							–0.92			
							(0.77)			
Latitude								0.07		
								(0.81)		
p-value for religion									[0.95]	
R^2	0.16									
No. of observations	36	36	20	30	35	35	35	36	36	17

Notes: Dependent variable is dummy for systemic banking crises between 1970 and 2000. Standard errors are in parentheses. Cross-sectional regressions with one observation per country; the dependent variable is dummy variable for systemic banking crisis from Levine et al., modified using coding in Boyd et al. Column (1) is OLS; all other columns are 2SLS using log settler mortality as an instrument for institutions. Column (3) limits the sample to former European colonies above median world income. Column (4) includes log average inflation, which is the log of average annual inflation in the Consumer Price Index from 1970 to 1997, from the World Bank; government consumption, which is the average of the ratio of real government "consumption" expenditure to real GDP from 1970 to 1989 from the Barro and Lee data set; and real exchange rate overvaluation, which is an index of real overvaluation of the official exchange rate during 1970–98, constructed by Easterly and Levine (2003) using the methodology of Dollar (1992). Column (5) includes the log of average money-GDP ratio for 1970–97, from the World Bank. Column (6) includes the standard deviation of terms-of-trade shocks in 1970–89 times export-GDP ratio in 1970, from the Barro and Lee data set. Column (7) includes the share of primary exports in GDP in 1970 from Sachs and Warner (1997). Column (8) includes the absolute normalized value of distance from the equator (i.e., a standardized measure of latitude), in which a higher value indicates that a country's capital is further from the equator. Column (9) includes the percent of the population that is Muslim, Catholic, and Protestant in 1980 (with "other" as the omitted group); from La Porta et al. (1999). Column (10) restricts the sample just to former British colonies. Initial constraint on the executive is average constraint on executive in 1950, 1960, and 1970, which is an average of the Polity score in each year; countries that are still colonies in a particular year are assigned a score of 1. We instrument for institutions using log settler mortality (where mortality is per 1,000 per annum with replacement). All regressions, other than those in columns (3) and (10), include all former colonies of European powers for which we have data. For more detailed data definitions and sources see table 3A.2.

relationship than for the sample as a whole: a coefficient of –0.31 and a standard error of 0.09. This suggests the possibility that institutions and income need to be above some threshold level before systemic banking crises occur. Given current data limitations, however, we regard this result with some caution. Nevertheless, the results in table 3.5 are quite consistent with what we find using more comprehensive data on output and exchange rates: Worse institutions lead to greater economic instability and crises.

3.3.6 Political Crises

Changes in power in institutionally weak societies may lead to economic instability, and institutional weaknesses encourage power struggles and increase the likelihood of major shifts in power. This subsection investigates whether major political crises are more likely when institutions are weak.

To measure political crises we use the data set of the State Failure Task Force (1998), which indicates periods of "state failures": that is, major political crises, such as civil wars, revolutions, and violent fighting between different factions. We supplement this data with information on revolutions from the Barro and Lee (1993) data set. We code a country as having had a political failure if it had either a state failure according to the State Failure Task Force (1998) or a revolution or both between 1960 and 1998. Of the 72 former colonies for which we have data, 56 had a political crisis defined in this way.

As with our analysis of banking crisis, we emphasize the need for further research on the issue of who exactly has had what kind of political crisis. We do not yet know how best to aggregate and compare these crises. Nevertheless, table 3.6 provides a preliminary look at the relationship between a dummy for "political failure" and initial constraint on the executive, instrumented by log settler mortality. Again, the robust if crude result is that countries with weak institutions at the beginning of the sample were more likely to suffer political failures of some kind over the past thirty to forty years.

Column (1) of table 3.6 shows an OLS estimate of –0.09 on institutions, with a standard error of 0.02. As with the previous tables, the absolute value of the effect of institutions increases when we instrument using log settler mortality. In column (2), for example, the coefficient on institutions is –0.14 (standard error of 0.04), and in column (10), for just former British colonies, the coefficient is –0.16 (standard error of 0.07). This implies, for example, an approximately 0.56 difference in the probability of a political crisis between Nigeria and the United States.

The least significant result for institutions is again in column (5), when we control for financial development—the coefficient on institutions is significant at the 10 percent level. Again, financial development itself is not significant. None of the other control variables in table 3.6 are significant, apart from the macro policy variables (column [4]), which are jointly

Table 3.6 **Institutions and Political Crises**

	Ex-Colonies Sample (1)	Ex-Colonies Sample (2)	Ex-Colonies above Median Income per Capita (3)	Ex-Colonies, Controlling for Macro Variables (4)	Ex-Colonies Controlling for Financial Development (5)	Ex-Colonies, Controlling for Terms of Trade (6)	Ex-Colonies, Controlling for Natural Resources (7)	Ex-Colonies, Controlling for Latitude (8)	Ex-Colonies, Controlling for Religion (9)	Only Former British Colonies (10)
Initial constraint on the executive	–0.09	–0.14	–0.11	–0.15	–0.10	–0.15	–0.15	–0.13	–0.14	–0.16
	(0.02)	(0.04)	(0.06)	(0.06)	(0.06)	(0.05)	(0.04)	(0.05)	(0.05)	(0.07)
p-value for macro variables				[0.02]						
Financial development					–0.008					
					(0.006)					
Terms of trade						–3.88				
						(5.17)				
Natural resources							0.04			
							(0.48)			
Latitude								–0.21		
								(0.47)		
p-value for religion									[0.49]	
R^2	0.16									
No. of observations	72	72	30	45	64	63	63	72	72	23

Notes: Dependent variable is dummy for political crisis between 1960 and 2000. Standard errors are in parentheses. Cross-sectional regressions with one observation per country; the dependent variable is dummy variable for political crisis between 1960 and 1997 from the State Failures data set, supplemented by revolution coding from Barro and Lee data set. Column (1) is OLS; all other columns are 2SLS using log settler mortality as an instrument for institutions. Column (3) limits the sample to former European colonies above median world income. Column (4) includes log average inflation, which is the log of average annual inflation in the Consumer Price Index from 1970 to 1997, from the World Bank; government consumption, which is the average of the ratio of real government "consumption" expenditure to real GDP from 1970 to 1989 from the Barro and Lee data set; and real exchange rate overvaluation, which is an index of real overvaluation of the official exchange rate during 1970–98, constructed by Easterly and Levine (2003) using the methodology of Dollar (1992). Column (5) includes the log of average money-GDP ratio for 1970–97, from the World Bank. Column (6) includes the standard deviation of terms-of-trade shocks in 1970–89 times export-GDP ratio in 1970, from the Barro and Lee data set. Column (7) includes the share of primary exports in GDP in 1970 from Sachs and Warner (1997). Column (8) includes the absolute normalized value of distance from the equation (i.e., a standardized measure of latitude), in which a higher value indicates that a country's capital is further from the equator. Column (9) includes the percent of the population that is Muslim, Catholic, and Protestant in 1980 (with "other" as the omitted group); from La Porta et al. (1999). Column (10) restricts the sample just to former British colonies. Initial constraint on the executive is average constraint on executive in 1950, 1960, and 1970, which is an average of the Polity score in each year; countries that are still colonies in a particular year are assigned a score of 1. We instrument for institutions using log settler mortality (where mortality is per 1,000 per annum with replacement). All regressions, other than those in columns (3) and (10), include all former colonies of European powers for which we have data. For more detailed data definitions and sources see table 3A.2.

significant at the 5 percent level. Taken separately, government consumption and the overvaluation of the real exchange rate are significant: More government consumption is associated with greater probability of a political crisis, and a more appreciated real exchange rate is associated with a lower probability of a political crisis.

As with our analysis of banking crises, we regard these results for political crises as suggestive but very preliminary. We need more work that looks carefully at the determinants and effects of different kinds of crises. Nevertheless, table 3.6 suggests that political crises are in some way intimately tied to the process through which relatively weak institutions generate greater economic instability.

3.4 Conclusion

Taken together, the results presented in this paper suggest an important link between institutions and economic (and most likely political) instability. The historically determined component of institutions has a first-order effect on volatility, severity of economic crises, exchange rate crises, systemic banking crises, and political crises. This effect is robust to including the obvious control variables and to restricting the sample to just countries above median world income or just former British colonies. Our interpretation is that institutional differences across countries are a fundamental determinant of economic and political instability. However, a great deal more research is needed before we fully understand exactly how, when, and why institutions cause instability.

Appendix

Table 3A.1 Country Abbreviations

Country's full name:	Abbreviation used in figures:	Country's full name:	Abbreviation used in figures:
Argentina	ARG	Côte d'Ivoire	CIV
Australia	AUS	Cameroon	CMR
Burundi	BDI	Congo, Rep.	COG
Burkina Faso	BFA	Colombia	COL
Bangladesh	BGD	Costa Rica	CRI
Bolivia	BOL	Dominican Republic	DOM
Brazil	BRA	Algeria	DZA
Botswana	BWA	Ecuador	ECU
Central African Republic	CAF	Egypt, Arab Rep.	EGY
Canada	CAN	Ethiopia	ETH
Chile	CHL	Gabon	GAB

(*continued*)

Table 3A.1 (continued)

Country's full name:	Abbreviation used in figures:	Country's full name:	Abbreviation used in figures:
Ghana	GHA	Pakistan	PAK
Guinea	GIN	Panama	PAN
Gambia, The	GMB	Peru	PER
Guatemala	GTM	Philippines, The	PHL
Honduras	HND	Papua New Guinea	PNG
Haiti	HTI	Paraguay	PRY
Indonesia	IDN	Rwanda	RWA
India	IND	Sudan	SDN
Jamaica	JAM	Senegal	SEN
Kenya	KEN	Singapore	SGP
Sri Lanka	LKA	El Salvador	SLV
Lesotho	LSO	Chad	TCD
Morocco	MAR	Togo	TGO
Madagascar	MDG	Trinidad and Tobago	TTO
Mexico	MEX	Tunisia	TUN
Mozambique	MOZ	Tanzania	TZA
Mauritania	MRT	Uganda	UGA
Mauritius	MUS	Uruguay	URY
Malawi	MWI	United States	USA
Malaysia	MYS	Venezuela, RB	VEN
Niger	NER	South Africa	ZAF
Nigeria	NGA	Congo, Dem. Rep.	ZAR
Nicaragua	NIC	Zambia	ZMB
Nepal	NPL	Zimbabwe	ZWE
New Zealand	NZL		

Table 3A.2 Variable Definitions and Sources

Variable	Definition	Source
Log GDP per capita (PPP) in 1995	Logarithm of GDP per capita, on PPP basis, in 1995	World Bank, World Development Indicators, CD-Rom, 1999 (data on Suriname are from the 2000 version of this same source)
Log GDP per capita in 1970	Logarithm of real GDP per capita (1980 international prices) from Summers Heston data set v.4.0	Barro-Lee data set; used in Barro and Lee (1993) and available from the NBER website: www.nber.org
Growth rate of GDP per capita, 1970–97	Annual GDP growth rate minus annual population growth rate	World Bank, World Development Indicators, CD-Rom, 1999
Standard deviation of growth, 1970–97	Standard deviation of GDP per capita growth rate	Calculated from the growth rate of GDP per capita; from the World Bank, World Development Indicators, CD-Rom, 1999
Worst output drop, 1970–97	Worst annual GDP per capita growth rate (Sign has been changed so that a negative growth rate is a positive "output drop.")	Calculated from the Growth Rate of GDP per capita; from the World Bank, World Development Indicators, CD-Rom, 1999
Constraint on executive in 1950, 1960, and 1970	A seven-category scale, from 1 to 7, with a higher score indicating more constraints. Score of 1 indicates unlimited authority; score of 3 indicates slight to moderate limitations; score of 5 indicates substantial limitations; score of 7 indicates executive parity or subordination. Scores of 2, 4, and 6 indicate intermediate values.	Polity IV data set, downloaded from Inter-University Consortium for Political and Social Research; variable described in Gurr (1997)
Average protection against expropriation risk, 1985–95	Risk of expropriation of private foreign investment by government, from 0 to 10, where a higher score means less risk. We calculated the mean value for the scores in all years from 1985 to 1995.	Data set obtained directly from Political Risk Services, September 1999. These data were previously used by Knack and Keefer (1995) and were organized in electronic form by the IRIS Center (University of Maryland). The original compilers of this data are Political Risk Services.

(*continued*)

Table 3A.2 (continued)

Variable	Definition	Source
Money/GDP	Log of average money-GDP ratio for 1970–97 (and subperiods where specified)	World Bank, World Development Indicators, CD-Rom, 1999
Standard deviation of terms-of-trade shocks	Standard deviation of an index of terms-of-trade shock, 1970–89	Barro-Lee (1993) data set; available from NBER website
Export/GDP	Ratio of exports to GDP in 1970	Barro-Lee data set
Share of primary exports in GDP	Exports of commodities divided by GDP in 1970	Sachs-Warner data set, available on the Web; used in Sachs and Warner (1997)
Banking crisis	Dummy equal to one if there was a banking crisis that was systemic	Barth, Caprio, and Levine (2002), supplemented by Boyd, Kwak, and Smith (2002)
Revolution	Dummy equal to one if there was at least one revolution from 1960 to 1984	Barro-Lee data set
State failure	Dummy equal to one if there was a civil war, breakdown of social order, major ethnic conflict, or major regime transition, as defined by the State Failure Project	State Failure Task Force (1998)
Political crisis	Dummy equal to one if either the revolution dummy or the state failure dummy or both equal one	Barro-Lee data set and State Failure Task Force (1998)
Log settler mortality	Log of estimated mortality for European settlers during the early period of European colonization (before 1850). Settler mortality is calculated from the mortality rates of European-born soldiers, sailors and bishops when stationed in colonies. It measures the effects of local diseases on people without inherited or acquired immunity.	Acemoglu, Johnson, and Robinson (2001), based on Curtin (1989), Curtin (1998), and Gutierrez (1986)

Note: PPP = purchasing power parity.

Table 3A.3 Descriptive Statistics

	Ex-Colonies Sample		
	Mean Value	25th Percentile	75th Percentile
Annual growth GDP per capita, 1970–97	1.07	0.09	1.95
Standard deviation of growth (GDP per capita), 1970–97	4.68	3.44	5.69
Worst drop output (GDP per capita), 1970–97	9.03	6.05	14.23
Average constraint on the executive in 1950, 1960, and 1970	2.33	1.50	3.67

Note: For detailed sources and definitions see table 3A.2.

References

Acemoglu, Daron, Simon Johnson, and James A. Robinson. 2001. Colonial origins of comparative development: An empirical investigation. *American Economic Review* 91:1369–401.

———. 2002. Reversal of fortune: Geography and institutions in the making of the modern world income distribution. *Quarterly Journal of Economics* 117:1231–94.

Acemoglu, Daron, Simon Johnson, James A. Robinson, and Yunyong Thaicharoen. 2003. Institutional causes, macroeconomic symptoms: Volatility, crises, and growth. *Journal of Monetary Economics* 50 (1): 49–123.

Acemoglu, Daron, and Fabrizio Zilibotti. 1997. Was Prometheus unbound by chance? Risk, diversification, and growth. *Journal of Political Economy* 105: 1167–200.

Angrist, Joshua D. 2001. Estimations of limited dependent variable models with dummy endogenous regressors: Simple strategies for empirical practice. *Journal of Business and Economic Statistics* 19 (1): 2–16.

Barro, Robert J. 1991. Economic growth in a cross section of countries. *Quarterly Journal of Economics* 106:407–33.

Barro, Robert J., and Jong-Wha Lee. 1993. International comparisons of educational attainment. *Journal of Monetary Economics* 32:363–94.

Barth, James R., Gerard Caprio, Jr., and Ross Levine. 2002. Banking systems around the globe: Do regulation and ownership affect performance and stability? World Bank, Auburn University, and University of Minnesota. Unpublished manuscript.

Boyd, John H., Sungkyu Kwak, and Bruce Smith. 2002. The real output losses associated with modern banking crises, or, "the good, the bad, and the ugly." University of Minnesota and University of Texas at Austin. Manuscript, February.

Curtin, Philip D. 1989. *Death by migration: Europe's encounter with the tropical world in the 19th century.* New York: Cambridge University Press.

———. 1998. *Disease and empire: The health of European troops in the conquest of Africa.* New York: Cambridge University Press.

Dollar, David. 1992. Outward oriented developing economies really do grow more rapidly. *Economic Development and Cultural Change* 40:523–44.

Easterly, William, Roumeen Islam, and Joseph Stiglitz. 2000. Shaken and stirred:

Explaining growth volatility. In *Annual World Bank conference on development economics,* 191–211. Washington, D.C.: The World Bank. April.
Easterly, William, and Ross Levine. 2003. Tropics, germs, and crops: How endowments influence economic development. *Journal of Monetary Economics* 50 (1): 3–39.
Gurr, Ted Robert. 1997. Polity II: Political structures and regime change, 1800–1986. University of Colorado, Department of Political Science. Unpublished manuscript.
Gutierrez, Hector. 1986. La mortalité des eveques Latino-Americains aux XVIIe et XVIII siècles (Mortality of Latin American bishops in the seventeenth and eighteenth centuries). *Annales de Demographie Historique,* 29–39.
Hall, Robert E., and Charles I. Jones. 1999. Why do some countries produce so much more output per worker than others? *Quarterly Journal of Economics* 114:83–116.
Heston, Alan, Robert Summers, and Bettina Aten. 2002. *Penn World Table version 6.1.* Philadelphia: Center for International Comparisons at the University of Pennsylvania, October.
Jones, Eric L. 1981. *The European miracle: Environments, economies, and geopolitics in the history of Europe and Asia.* New York: Cambridge University Press.
Knack, Stephen, and Philip Keefer. 1995. Institutions and economic performance: Cross-country tests using alternative measures. *Economics and Politics* 7:207–27.
La Porta, Rafael, Florencio Lopez-de-Silanes, Andrei Shleifer, and Robert W. Vishny. 1998. Law and finance. *Journal of Political Economy* 106:1113–55.
———. 1999. The quality of government. *Journal of Law, Economics, and Organization* 15 (1): 222–79.
Mauro, Paolo. 1995. Corruption and growth. *Quarterly Journal of Economics* 110 (3): 681–782.
North, Douglass C. 1981. *Structure and change in economic history.* New York: W. W. Norton.
North, Douglass C., and Robert P. Thomas. 1973. *The rise of the Western world: A new economic history.* Cambridge, U.K.: Cambridge University Press.
Olson, Mancur. 1982. *The rise and decline of nations: Economic growth, stagflation, and economic rigidities.* New Haven, Conn.: Yale University Press.
Pivovarsky, Alexander, and Yunyong Thaicharoen. 2002. Institutions and the severity of currency crises. MIT, Department of Economics, and Harvard University, Kennedy School of Government. Unpublished manuscript.
Sachs, Jeffrey D., and Andrew Warner. 1997. Fundamental sources of long-run growth. *American Economic Review: Papers and Proceedings* 87 (2): 184–88.
State Failure Task Force. 1998. State Failure Task Force report: Phase II findings. Prepared by Daniel C. Esty, Jack A. Goldstone, Ted Robert Gurr, Barbara Huff, Marc Levy, Geoffrey D. Dabelko, Pamelo T. Surko, and Alan N. Unger. McLean, Va.: Science Applications International Corporation, 31 July.

Comment Steve Dowrick

This paper is part of an ongoing and important research program into the impact of current institutions on economic development. In an earlier paper, Acemoglu, Johnson, and Robinson (2001) proposed a novel solution

Steve Dowrick is professor of economics and ARC Senior Research Fellow in the School of Economics, Australian National University.

to the problem of identifying the exogenous component of institutional quality in their analysis of the determinants of the current levels of real GDP per capita in countries that had been subject to European colonization. Their instrumental variable was the mortality rate among the clergy and military at the beginning of the colonization period. Their argument is that these mortality rates were well recorded and publicized, influencing the subsequent pattern of European settlement and hence not only the nature of colonial institutions of property rights and democracy but also the nature of current institutions. Furthermore, they presented evidence that the impact of disease on the early colonizers was distinct from its impact on the indigenous population, both then and now.

Here the same approach is taken to identifying the impact of current institutions on various measures of economic volatility, including the variability of output growth, exchange rate depreciation, banking crises, and political crises.

The authors' solution to the identification problem is ingenious. It is backed up convincingly both by a well-researched historical narrative (presented in more detail in their earlier paper) and by careful statistical testing of the requirement that their instrumental variable should be orthogonal to a range of other variables that might influence their dependent variables, such as inflation and terms-of-trade shocks and latitude. Of course, one could continue to search for other variables that are correlated with settler mortality and also influence current volatility, but to my mind the authors have canvassed the most likely candidates, and their results do appear to be robust.

In fact, my only concern with the paper is that the authors have probably overstated the economic significance of their results. Although they have identified the impact of the exogenous component of institutional quality on volatility, that impact may be relatively small compared with other influences on volatility. For example, the paper compares the predicted impact of institutional quality on the difference in output growth volatility between the United States and Nigeria, finding that the difference in quality scores explains two-thirds of the difference in volatility. Examination of figure 3.2, which illustrates the scatter plot of output volatility against the instrumental variable, suggests that the authors have chosen to compare a pair of countries most favorable to their hypothesis. Nigeria and the United States are not only close to the extremes of the settler mortality variable, but also close to the linear regression line illustrated in the figure. Since settler mortality is the only instrumental variable, the predicted effect of institutional quality in the two-stage least squares (2SLS) estimation is likely to be close to the illustrated ordinary least squares (OLS) regression on the instrument. Hence, the choice of a pair of countries lying further away from the regression line—for example, comparing Indonesia with Gabon, or comparing Mali with Fiji—would probably lead to the conclusion that institutional quality differences explain relatively little of the difference in volatility.

Rather than examining the predictions of their model for an arbitrary pair of countries, the authors should compare all the predicted values of their 2SLS regression with the actual values, perhaps reporting the correlation coefficient. I suspect that they will find that their instrumented measure of institutional quality does not explain a large part of the overall variance in measures of volatility. If so, that is important to note. But it does not detract from the value of the paper in identifying an exogenous component of institutional quality and demonstrating that it has a systematic and robust impact on economic volatility.

Reference

Acemoglu, Daron, Simon Johnson, and James A. Robinson. 2001. Colonial origins of comparative development: An empirical investigation. *American Economic Review* 91 (5): 1369–401.

Comment Dipinder S. Randhawa

Simon Johnson and his coauthors (hereafter AJR) offer a remarkably lucid, creative, and cogent analysis of the origins of institutions and their links to current economic performance. This paper contends that societies that for historical reasons have weak institutions have suffered substantially more output volatility and experienced more severe output contraction, exchange rate depreciation, and banking and political crisis over the past thirty years.

It is an extension of the authors' earlier work examining differential rates of growth among former European colonies. The line of reasoning, drawing upon data on mortality rates among bishops, sailors, and soldiers from the seventeenth to the nineteenth centuries, contends that the mortality rates among the European settlers influenced the prospects for settlements. Evolving settlements in turn led to the creation of institutions. The legacy of these institutions was sustained into the postcolonial period with profound implications for economic growth (Acemoglu, Johnson, and Robinson 2001). This paper extends the analysis to look at the origins of instability and crisis in developing economies.

The focus is on countries colonized by the European powers. The authors document that different colonization strategies and different institutions set up by Europeans had radically different implications for economic development. Places prospered when Europeans "set up institu-

Dipinder S. Randhawa is a teaching fellow at the National University of Singapore Business School.

tions that protected private property rights, enforced the rule of law, and placed tight constraints on politicians and powerful elites. In contrast, areas where Europeans established new extractive institutions, or took over existing ones, stagnated or grew only slowly."

The current project constitutes a valuable addition to the literature linking institutional structures with long-term development. The logic is compelling. The stated objective is to demonstrate "the effect of historical institutions on economic development by exploiting variation in the feasibility of large-scale settlements by Europeans." Accordingly, Europeans built settlements in areas where the incidence of mortality and morbidity was low. Areas with high incidence of disease and mortality were not deemed attractive for settlement. The differential settlement patterns resulting from differences in mortality rates resulted in distinct patterns of economic activity. In areas where settlers suffered high mortality rates, the form of economic exchange was extractive. In these areas, the colonizers were much more likely to exploit the native population for the benefit of a few rich Europeans, and these institutions have proved incompatible with sustained rapid growth.

Based on this approach, AJR use mortality rates faced by European settlers as an instrumental variable for institutional development and current institutions. There is a strong and robust relationship between per capital income growth rates (as a measure of long-term development) and mortality rates. The interpretation is that this relationship reflects the effect of historically determined institutions (more specifically, institutions shaped by differential European settlement patterns) on instability. They further contend that not only did societies that inherited extractive institutions from their colonial past fail to take advantage of development opportunities over the long run, but their recent medium-run experience has been characterized by frequent crises and substantial instability.

Causality (Embedded and Explicit)

A first reading of the paper may be misleading. Although proposed as such in the text, the data at hand and a perusal of the demographics of settlements do not suggest a monotonic relationship between mortality rates and settlements—an embedded assumption, albeit not crucial to the central relationship between the development of institutions and crisis. It seems unlikely we can obtain a monotonic relationship among experiences as diverse as the Spanish expansion in Latin America, which resulted in large European settlements in the midst of high mortality rates, or the Dutch in Indonesia, where high mortality rates led to small settlements yet the small cohort of settlers remained engaged primarily in lucrative intraregional trade.

A clearer line of causality emerges from the postcolonial institutional setup and its impact on economic development and vulnerability of the economy to crisis. That there is continuity in the development and effectiveness of institutions in the pre- and postcolonial periods is widely acknowledged, but the embedded contention that these institutional characteristics are immutable over time is yet to be established. The import of this assertion, seemingly an illustration of predestination, is that postcolonial initiatives toward institutional development matter little for economic performance. It implicitly abstracts from postcolonial policy regimes and all the changes therein—where, at the very least, a number of economies transitioned from an import substitution strategy of industrialization to export orientation, often with commensurate changes in institutional structures. The measures and proxies of institutions deployed all draw upon institutional constructs of the past thirty years (contemporary institutions).

A switching regime model to ascertain whether there is a change in the colonial regime and postindependence policy regime would provide validation for implicit causality and offer a direct link between current performance and regimes established during the colonial period. At issue also are questions about the robustness of instrumental variables, including mortality rates.

The innovative use of mortality rates as an instrumental variable for settlements and institutional development during the colonial expansion is fascinating; however, its linkages with current institutions, on both the theoretical (or intuitive) and the empirical plane, are less clear. Incorporation of a control variable reflecting postindependence policy regimes may strengthen the line of causation. This assumes importance given the variability in regimes across and within (chronologically) former colonies. It leaves open an arena for subsequent research to inquire into the linkages between institutions, macroeconomic policy, and economic performance.

Proxies for Instability

The AJR paper uses five proxies for instability: output volatility, the most severe drop in output, largest exchange rate depreciation, and dummy variables for banking crises and political crises. The results are tabulated in table 3C.1. By and large, the findings lend support to the choice of the instrumental variable; nevertheless, considerable ambiguity prevails. The authors propose the framework as a blueprint to encourage other researchers to delve into the area.

Data problems on a project of this scope are substantial. A rich retinue of macroeconomic variables testifies to the robustness of the instrumental variable, especially vis-à-vis output volatility and the worst loss in output. Variation in output is an appealing measure of volatility. The choice of worst drop in output over a period in excess of twenty-five years raises a few questions. The prevailing exchange rate regime, the extent of openness of the economy, and the timing of external help or of implementation of an International Monetary Fund program have significant ramifications for

Table 3C.1 Summary of Results: 1970–97

Proxy for Instability	Variable	Result for Instrumental Variable (mortality levels)
Output volatility	Standard deviation of PCY GDP growth rate	Significant
Worst drop in output	Worst annual PCY GDP growth rate	Significant
Exchange rate	Standard deviation of terms-of-trade shocks	Significant, except when controlled for financial development and macro policy variables
Banking crisis	Binary (dummy) variable	Significant, except when controlled for financial development and macro policy variables
Political crisis	Binary (dummy) variable	Significant, except when controlled for financial development and some macro policy variables

Note: PCY = per capita income.

output loss during a crisis, as would the nature of the crisis (i.e., systemic or otherwise).

The proxy for exchange rate crisis—the magnitude of exchange rate depreciation—is likely to be impacted by all the factors previously mentioned, including openness of the economy and the nature of the exchange rate crisis.

Considering banking and political crises as binary variables may have contributed to the indecisive results—in the case of the former, a widely used measure conveying the intensity of the crisis is the cost (in terms of GDP) of rehabilitating the banking sector.

The intuition behind using measures such as "the largest drop in output" or the "percentage depreciation" is not clear. There is a large body of literature that addresses the role of policy regimes, the extent of openness of the economy, and the level of indebtedness as being the prime determinants of the intensity of the crisis.

Financial Development

The debate on what constitutes an appropriate measure of financial development and, if we do agree on the issue, what indeed a measure of financial development does reflect, is an open issue. Therein may lie the answer to the ambiguous results obtained for the two measures of crisis.

The proxy M2/GDP, a widely used measure of financial development, reflects the extent of monetization of the economy. In a broader sense, financial development is now deemed to reflect not only the efficacy of intermediation but also the screening and monitoring functions performed by markets and institutions. A single-dimensional variable may not be adequately equipped to reflect these attributes. Studies have documented strong relationships between financial liberalization and financial development—the primary motivation behind the recommendation of deregulation of the financial sector. Experiences dating back to Chile and the Southern Cone of Latin America in the late seventies and early eighties testify to the folly of blanket deregulation, in contrast to the more interventionist policy regimes among the two generations of Asian tigers, which was an essential construct underlying the Asian Miracle. Of course, some deem the same set of policies to have undone the "miracle" in 1997. Perhaps the route to take on this issue is the one sought by a number of researchers in the literature on financial crisis: that is, to seek that configuration of institutional frailties and macroeconomic vulnerabilities that give rise to financial fragility and crisis.

The debate on the speed and extent of financial liberalization remains unresolved. Positive real interest rates almost unequivocally lead to financial deepening (increasing M2/GDP). Strengthening of institutions for financial development requires a range of commensurate initiatives that researchers are yet to pin down. As the authors point out, the precise mechanisms (linking institutions with growth and instability) are not clear, and a great deal more research is needed on the theoretical and empirical relationship between institutional weaknesses and instability.

Along with its precursor (Acemoglu, Johnson, and Robinson 2001), this paper performs a stellar role in laying out a blueprint for inquiring into the origins of institutions and delineating their impact on growth and stability. One would expect a new strand of the literature tackling the range of issues addressed in this paper. To that end, the authors not only have made a valuable contribution, but will indeed have provided an impetus to research in the field.

Reference

Acemoglu, Daron, Simon Johnson, and James A. Robinson. 2001. The colonial origins of comparative development: An empirical investigation. *American Economic Review* 91:1369–1401.

4

GATT/WTO Accession and Productivity

David D. Li and Changqi Wu

4.1 Introduction

In the era of globalization, the event of an economy's accession to the World Trade Organization (WTO) invariably attracts widespread attention. The recent events of China's successful accession to the WTO and Russia's push to obtain WTO membership are just two such instances. Many developing and emerging-market countries believe that the accession to the WTO would enhance their productivity and economic prosperity. Nevertheless, the real impact of the accession to the WTO on the productivity of a developing or emerging-market economy remains unanswered.

The WTO, whose former incarnation is the General Agreement on Trade and Tariff (GATT), is an international organization with 144 economies as its members in 2002. It has played a significant role in promoting international trade and pushing for greater integration of the world economy. In GATT's forty-eight years of history until 1994, trade barriers among member economies fell significantly. Under the three main principles of "most-favored-nation status," "national treatment," and "consensus," GATT members engaged in seven rounds of negotiations. As a result,

David D. Li is associate professor of economics and associate director of the Center for Economic Development at the Hong Kong University of Science and Technology. Changqi Wu is adjunct associate professor of economics at the Hong Kong University of Science and Technology.

We would like to thank two discussants, Simon Johnson and Epictetus Patalinghug; the seminar chairs, Takatoshi Ito and Andrew Rose; and participants at the Thirteenth NBER-East Asian Seminar on Economics for their comments and suggestions. We would also like to thank David W. Fan for his excellent research assistance. The financial support of Hong Kong Research Grant Council (RGC HKUST6072/01HHKUST6227/03H) is gratefully acknowledged.

tariffs on traded manufactured goods fell from an average of 40 percent before the organization was established to less than 5 percent in the 1990s. Meanwhile, the volume of international trade has been increasing twice as fast as the output of the world since the 1950s.

The event of accession to GATT/WTO is actually an important testing case of the much more general and bigger issue of globalization, which has been controversial. We summarize that there are two broad groups of controversies about globalization. The first group of controversies is general. They are about who, if anyone, benefits from globalization. There have been econometric studies of the positive impact of trade liberalization on economic growth and development (e.g., Harrison 1996). More generally, the view of the advantage of backwardness that low-income economies ought to benefit from opening up to the world economy, as popularized by Alexander Gerschenkron's theory of the advantage of backwardness (Gerschenkron 1962), seems to be widely accepted. However, some have challenged whether openness is a by-product or measure of other more fundamental changes in the domestic economy (e.g., Rodriguez and Rodrik 2000; Kenny and Williams 2001). According to this view, "integration into the world economy" cannot "substitute for a development strategy." Furthermore, after the recent Asian financial crises, some argue that the globalization, especially hastened by improper order of sequencing, can produce a detrimental effect on developing countries (Rodrik 1997; Stiglitz 2002).

The second cluster of controversies is about particular consequences of opening up. For example, what will happen to inward foreign direct investment (FDI) once a country opens up? One often-made argument is that inward FDI will fall based on the tariff-jumping theory (Brecher and Diaz-Alejandro, 1977). That is to say, FDI is an alternative way to enter a market when export is not a feasible option under high import tariffs before a country joins GATT/WTO. Import and FDI are substitutes. The drastic reduction in import tariffs makes direct export to the target market a feasible option. After a country joins the GATT/WTO, therefore, the FDI will fall. A competing hypothesis is that FDI will increase after a country opens up. This happens because a reduction of trade barriers makes the economy more likely to become a production base to serve the world market. In turn, more FDI results in increases in intrafirm trade in intermediate goods so that the volume of international trade will also increase. Hence, FDI and exports are complements.

Accession to GATT/WTO provides a useful event study to facilitate the debates on these two sets of issues. The accession cases happen relatively quickly so that simultaneous changes in other factors are easy to control for. Also, by comparing what happened before and after the accession in an accession economy, one can control for heterogeneity across different economies. Both factors are advantages over cross-sectional studies covering many years.

We are not aware of any systematical study assessing the impact of the GATT/WTO accession across countries, although there are many country-specific studies of GATT/WTO accessions, such as Milthorp (1997); Mutti, Sampson, and Yeung (2000); and Fernandez de Cordoba and Kehoe (2000). A recent exception is Rose (2002), who finds that WTO accession did not visibly increase an economy's trade. This is surprising, given the existence of widely different theories and opinions on these issues and extensive observations of the event of GATT/WTO accession.

Apparently, the impact of the GATT/WTO accession is likely to be different on different types of economies. We therefore classify the economies in two alternative ways. The first approach is to divide the sample economy into two groups by the level of per capita GDP of 1987, the median year of our sample. We call the economies with per capita GDP over US$3,000 high-income economies and others low-income ones. This classification is motivated by Gerschenkron's theory of the advantage of backwardness. Another classification is by the institutional configuration of an economy. We are inspired by the work of La Porta et al. (1999), who argue that the origin of the economy's legal institutions is a key factor affecting economic performance. We thus divide the economies into common-law economies, continental European law economies, and formerly socialist systems. Our classification of the economies in this fashion comes from La Porta et al. (1999).

4.2 The Data Set and Methodology

In spirit, we are following the method of "event study."[1] That is, we collect data on those economies before and after they became members of GATT/WTO and study whether there are significant changes in those economies. In doing so, we also need to include in our sample countries that did not join GATT/WTO in the same period, including countries that had already been members of the GATT/WTO by the beginning of the sample year. The method of event study has been widely used in economics and finance literature. An advantage of event study over standard cross-section or time series analysis is that it enables us to concentrate on the event itself, which usually happens in a short time window with few other changes at the same time.

4.2.1 The Data Set

Our sample covers 112 economies from 1960 to 1998. The sample consists of almost all economies in the world, except those that underwent prolonged wars during the covered years, such as the Congo, Iran, Iraq, and

1. See MacKinlay (1997) for a detailed survey of event study methods applied in economics and finance.

so on, and economies that have had major boundary changes during the sample years, since we cannot find consistent economic statistics on those boundary-changing economies over time. Examples in the latter group include most of the former Soviet republics. Table 4.1 lists the names of all economies in the sample with their descriptive statistics.

The sample consists of seventy-four economies that joined GATT/WTO during the sample years and eighteen economies that had already joined GATT/WTO by 1960 and twenty that had not become members of GATT/WTO by 1998. The latter group forms a reference for us to examine the impact of GATT/WTO accessions. Also, we classify the sample economies by the level of per capita GDP in 1987. This way, we divide the sample into high-income and low-income economies. We also classify the sample economies by their legal economic systems: common law, continental European law, and socialist economic system. Table 4.2 provides summary statistics of the different types of the sample economies.

Data sources include the *World Investment Report* of the United Nations Conference on Trade and Development (UNCTAD), the *International Financial Statistics* (IFS) of the International Monetary Fund (IMF), World Development Indices (WDI) of the World Bank, and publications by GATT/WTO.

4.2.2 Economic Variables Examined

We are interested in two sets of economic indices of the accession economies. The first set of economic variables is GDP, export in constant U.S. dollars and constant local currency, the ratio of import and export to GDP, logarithm of FDI, and the ratio of FDI to GDP, respectively. These variables measure the openness of the economy. The second economic index of our concern is the growth rate of total factor productivity (TFP), which is the term in the aggregate production function besides those of capital and labor. The TFP is a measure of the overall efficiency of the economy.

4.2.3 The Duration of the Impact of the Accession

In modeling the impact of the GATT/WTO accession, we need to specify the duration of the impact. One cannot expect the accession to have a permanent impact on the *growth rate* of the economic variables of the economy while a permanent shift in the *level* of the economic variable is likely. Ideally, with a long enough time horizon in panel data, one can endogenously specify the time pattern of the impact. Unfortunately, this is not the case in the study, since we only have thirty-nine years of observation in total for a typical country, and for a typical accession economy we only have fifteen years of observation after accession.

Facing this limit, we constrain our model to the specification that the impact of the accession is within ten years. That is, starting from the

Table 4.1 Sample Economies: Characteristics, Accession Dates, and Predicted Dates of Qualification for GATT/WTO Membership

Country	Accession	Population in 1987 (in millions)	GDP per capita in 1987 (const 1995 US$)	Legal Origin: English	Legal Origin: Socialist	Legal Origin: French	Legal Origin: German	Predicted Year of Qualification
1 Albania	Sept.-2000	3.08	916		Soc			>1998
2 Algeria		23.15	1,741			Fre		1975
3 Angola	Apr.-94	10.63	443			Fre		1993
4 Antigua and Barbuda	Mar.-87	0.06	6,222	Eng				1978
5 Argentina	Oct.-67	22.91	6,030			Fre		1972
6 Bahrain	Dec.-93	0.54	9,769	Eng				1981
7 Bangladesh	Dec.-72	70.45	191	Eng				>1998
8 Barbados	Feb.-67	0.24	4,276	Eng				1961
9 Belize	Oct.-83	0.16	1,872	Eng				1981
10 Benin	Sept.-63	4.31	365			Fre		>1998
11 Bhutan		0.56	364	Eng				1981
12 Bolivia	Sept.-90	6.57	832			Fre		1974
13 Botswana	Aug.-87	1.16	2,578	Eng				1961
14 Brazil	July-48	140.45	4,352			Fre		>1998
15 Brunei Darussalam	Dec.-93	0.28	17,792	Eng				n.a.
16 Bulgaria	Dec.-96	8.36	1,409		Soc			>1998
17 Cameroon	May-63	10.55	978			Fre		>1998
18 Central African Republic	May-63	2.74	385			Fre		1967
19 Chile	Mar.-49	12.45	2,808			Fre		1986
20 China	Nov.-01	1,084.03	305		Soc			>1998
21 Colombia	Oct.-81	29.09	1,868			Fre		>1998
22 Comoros		0.4	534			Fre		1981
23 Costa Rica	Dec.-90	3.06	2,992			Fre		1966
24 Côte d'Ivoire	Dec.-63	10.62	840			Fre		1974
25 Cyprus	July-63	0.66	8,523	Eng				1976
26 Czech Republic	Apr.-93	10.33	4,651		Soc			1993
27 Djibouti	Dec.-94	0.58	877			Fre		1992
28 Dominica	Apr.-93	0.07	3,005	Eng				1978
29 Dominican Republic	May-50	6.66	1,447			Fre		1985
30 Ecuador	Jan.-96	11.7	1,564			Fre		>1998

(continued)

Table 4.1 (continued)

Country	Accession	Population in 1987 (in millions)	GDP per capita in 1987 (const 1995 US$)	Legal Origin				Predicted Year of Qualification
				English	Socialist	French	German	
31 Egypt	May-70	33.05	478			Fre		1980
32 El Salvador	May-91	5.31	1,401			Fre		1974
33 Equatorial Guinea		0.34	334			Fre		1986
34 Estonia		1.56	4,595		Soc			1993
35 Fiji	Nov.-93	0.76	2,440	Eng				1961
36 Gabon	May-63	0.87	3,797			Fre		1961
37 Gambia	Feb.-65	0.4		Eng				1967
38 Ghana	Oct.-57	13.53	338	Eng				1961
39 Greece	Mar.-50	10	10,012			Fre		1967
40 Grenada	Oct.-94	0.094	2,864	Eng				1978
41 Guatemala	Oct.-91	8.98	1,372			Fre		>1998
42 Guinea	Dec.-94	6.42	550			Fre		>1998
43 Guyana	July-66	0.66	703	Eng				1961
44 Haiti	Jan.-50	6.09	503			Fre		>1998
45 Honduras	Apr.-94	5.49	693			Fre		1975
46 Hong Kong	Apr.-86	5.52	15,021	Eng				1961
47 Hungary	Sept.-73	10.44	3,363		Soc			>1998
48 India	July-48	798.68	278	Eng				>1998
49 Indonesia	Feb.-50	168.99	649			Fre		>1998
50 Iran, Islamic Republic of		50.42	1,254			Fre		1975
51 Ireland	Dec.-67	2.9	6,838	Eng				1961
52 Israel	July-62	4.37	13,368	Eng				1961
53 Italy	May-50	56.6	16,689			Fre		1961
54 Jamaica	Dec.-63	2.35	1,577	Eng				1961
55 Jordan	Apr.-00	2.85	1,974			Fre		1977
56 Kazakhstan		15.93	2,187		Soc			>1998

57 Kenya	Feb.-64	21.31	339	Eng			1961
58 Korea, Republic of	Apr.-67	29.9	1,673			Ger	1967
59 Kuwait	May-63	1.87	11,085		Fre		1963
60 Lebanon		3.41			Fre		1990
61 Lesotho	Jan.-88	1.64	406	Eng			1961
62 Liechtenstein	Mar.-94	. . .	. . .			Ger	n.a.
63 Macao	Nov.-91	0.38	14,223		Fre		1987
64 Maldives	Apr.-83	0.17	. . .	Eng			1986
65 Mali	Jan.-93	9.16	251		Fre		>1998
66 Malta	Nov.-64	0.35	5,765		Fre		1961
67 Mauritania	Sept.-63	1.86	454		Fre		1973
68 Mauritius	Sept.-70	0.83	1,190		Fre		1961
69 Mexico	Aug.-86	77.02	3,051		Fre		1996
70 Micronesia, Fed. Sts.		0.09		Eng			n.a.
71 Mongolia	Jan.-97	2.33	437	Soc			>1998
72 Morocco	June-87	22.6	1,186		Fre		>1998
73 Mozambique	July-92	14.69	134		Fre		1993
74 Namibia	Sept.-92	1.42	2,087	Eng			1981
75 New Zealand	July-48	3.32	15,600	Eng			1987
76 Nicaragua	May-50	3.58	572		Fre		1974
77 Oman	Nov.-00	1.49	5,185		Fre		1969
78 Pakistan	July-48	99.95	410	Eng			1980
79 Panama	Sept.-97	2.72	3,123		Fre		1981
80 Papua New Guinea	Dec.-94	4.2	1,136	Eng			1962
81 Paraguay	Jan.-94	4.71	1,827		Fre		1987
82 Peru	Oct.-51	20.34	2,639		Fre		>1998
83 The Philippines	Dec.-79	47.31	1,132		Fre		1993
84 Portugal	May-62	9.99	8,352		Fre		1965
85 Puerto Rico		3.44	9,187		Fre		1961
86 Romania	Nov.-71	20.47		Soc			>1998

(*continued*)

Table 4.1 (continued)

Country	Accession	Population in 1987 (in millions)	GDP per capita in 1987 (const 1995 US$)	Legal Origin				Predicted Year of Qualification
				English	Socialist	French	German	
87 Saudi Arabia		13.72	6,988	Eng				1961
88 Senegal	Sept.-63	6.74	572			Fre		1974
89 Seychelles		0.07	5,146			Fre		1977
90 Singapore	Aug.-73	2.19	7,302	Eng				1966
91 Slovak Republic	Apr.-93	5.32	3,082		Soc			1993
92 Slovenia	Oct.-94	1.99	9,053		Soc			1992
93 Solomon Islands	Dec.-94	0.37	833	Eng				1981
94 South Africa	June-48	32.93	4,145	Eng				1961
95 Spain	Aug.-63	38.61	12,391			Fre		1964
96 Sri Lanka	July-48	16.36	540	Eng				1961
97 St. Kitts and Nevis	Mar.-94	0.041	5,401	Eng				1978
98 Suriname	Mar.-78	0.37	718			Fre		1971
99 Swaziland, Kingdom of	Feb.-93	0.85	1,411	Eng				1971
100 Thailand	Nov.-82	48.63	1,200	Eng				1968
101 The Kyrgyz Republic	Dec.-98	4.8	833		Soc			>1998
102 Togo	Mar.-64	3.21	367			Fre		1970
103 Tonga		0.09	1,510	Eng				1982
104 Trinidad and Tobago	Oct.-62	1.2	4,287	Eng				1961
105 Tunisia	Aug.-90	8.16	1,823			Fre		1975
106 Turkey	Oct.-51	52.57	2,473			Fre		1997
107 Turkmenistan		3.4	1,983		Soc			>1998
108 United Arab Emirates	Mar.-94	2.29	17,646	Eng				1974
109 Uruguay	Dec.-53	3.04	4,832			Fre		1976
110 Venezuela	Aug.-90	19.5	3,350			Fre		1974
111 Zambia	Feb.-82	6.12	565	Eng				1961
112 Zimbabwe	July-48	8.89	621	Eng				1976

Table 4.2 Summary of Various Subgroups of the Sample

	Accession Economies before 1951	Accession Economies within 1951–1998	Accession Economies after 1998	Nonmembers
Average population in 1987 (in millions)	97.5	11.2	273	8.3
Average per capita GDP in 1987 (in 1995 US$)	4,187.6	3,734.6	2,095.0	2,985.3
Average import/GDP ratio in 1987 (%)	22.1	45.2	29.5	43.58
Average export/GDP ratio in 1987 (%)	20	40.5	28.1	31.9
No. of economies of common law origin	6	31	0	4
No. of former Socialist systems	8	39	2	7
No. of economies of continental European legal origin	0	8	2	3

Note: There are two countries (Korea and Liechtenstein) that belong to the German legal system. Therefore, the total number of countries in this table is 110.

accession year, the growth rate of the economic variables of our concern may have a constant upward shift in each year. After the tenth year, there is no change in the growth rate. We also repeated all the estimation procedures by using eight and twelve years as the alternative time span of impact, and the results are very similar. This gives us confidence that ten years is a good approximation of the duration of the accession effect on an economy.

4.2.4 The Classification of Economies

We classify the economies in two alternative ways in order to examine potentially different effects of the GATT/WTO accessions. The two classifications are most likely to be relevant to explaining an economy's response to its GATT/WTO accession. The first classification is by per capita GDP. We follow the World Bank classification and use the economies' per capita GDP in 1987 to divide all the sample economies into high-income and medium- or low-income economies. The dividing per capita GDP level is 3,000 constant U.S. dollars in 1987. In principle, we can also have more refined classification by further dividing the economies with per capita income below US$3,000 into medium- and low-income groups. However, there is a data constraint that prevents us from estimating models with such refined classifications: We do not have many low-income economies that joined GATT/WTO during the sample years.

The second classification is by initial social economic institutions. We have three categories: economies that originated from common-law legal institutions, from continental European legal institutions, and from socialist systems, respectively. The classification is borrowed from La Porta et al. (1999). In theory, one can further divide the continental European law countries into the French type, the German type, and the Scandinavian type. Again, the data set does not contain enough economies to allow us to go into such detailed classification. In the study, we group French, German, and Scandinavian economies into the category of continental European legal origin.

4.2.5 Dealing with the Endogeneity Issue of GATT/WTO Accessions

Our objective is to study the impact of the event of the accession to GATT/WTO on the accession economy. To achieve that goal, we must deal with the question of endogeneity. That is, it is likely that economies did not or were not selected randomly to join GATT/WTO, and by the time an economy was able to access to GATT/WTO, its economic performance already began to be different from its past and from those non–GATT/WTO members. This is a classical sample selection problem. In other words, when we see an economy's performance improved after its GATT/WTO accession, was the improvement due to the action of the accession and subsequent policy and institutional changes? Or was it due to the fact that the economy in question had reached a new plateau of economic development and openness, enabling it to have better economic performance than before, which was certified by existing members of GATT/WTO in approving it to be a new member?

This is a critical and often pesky issue in similar empirical studies. We take two alternative methods to deal with the sample selection problem. The first method is due to Heckman and Hotz (1989). The idea is that if an economy, indexed by i, is chosen in year t to be a member of GATT/WTO, i must already have been intrinsically different by year t, which enables existing members of GATT/WTO to award membership to country i in year t. Although we obviously cannot measure how intrinsically different i had become by year t, we can generate a variable called the selection variable as a regressor in the regressions to capture this effect. The selection variable takes on the value 0 before year $t-2$ and then the values of 1, 2, 3, 4, . . . for the subsequent years of $t-2$, $t-1$, $t+1$, . . . , respectively. The estimated coefficients of the selection variable tell us how intrinsically different an accession economy is starting from two years before the accession. For instance, in a regression of log(GDP), if the coefficient of the selection variable is 0.02 and statistically significant, then this tells us that, on average, those economies that joined GATT/WTO began to perform differently two years before the accession. Their GDP level was 2 percent higher each year two years before the actual accession year until one year after the accession year. This hypothetical finding would imply that the GATT/WTO accession mechanism selected those economies that had an initial jump in GDP to be new members. In the same regression, the WTO dummy that takes on nonzero values after the year of accession is left to capture the actual accession effect that we are interested in.

Why did we choose the $t-2$ to t time window for the selection variable? The answer is that we also experimented with alternative configurations, including $t-5$, or $t-4$, or $t-3$ to $t+1$, or $t+2$. The findings are qualitatively similar, so we only report the $t-2$ to t results.

The other approach that we adopted to deal with the endogeneity issue of GATT/WTO accessions is to explicitly model the endogenous selection effect. We model the endogenous selection effect as one that starts to exist when an economy is perceived to be qualified and acceptable to be a member of GATT/WTO. Let us call this the qualification date. Note that the qualification date and the actual accession date, in principle, are different and separated by noneconomic and random factors, such as political and diplomatic disputes. The qualification date may be earlier than the actual accession date, since political issues may delay accession negotiations; for example, the midair collision of military aircraft in the South China Sea in 2001 significantly slowed down China's scheduled accession negotiations with the United States. Similarly, the qualification date may be later than the accession date in cases of premature accessions, when some existing members of GATT desired earlier acceptance of a nonmember economy for political considerations. Examples include Hungary in the 1970s, when it was still a socialist economy but was relatively politically friendly to the West and therefore was eagerly accepted by Western members of the GATT.

The strategy for us to implement the foregoing idea consists of two steps. First, we try to explain econometrically when an economy is qualified to be a member of WTO. To do this, we run a probit regression explaining the event of GATT/WTO accession. The implicit assumption is that the actual date of accession and the qualification date are separated by random noise. The independent variables are lagged per capita income, import-GDP, export-GDP, and legal origin. Second, we use the fitted probit regression to predict when an economy is qualified to be a member of the WTO. We then use this estimated qualification date to generate a selection dummy variable for use in our main regressions in order to isolate and capture the selection effect. The selection dummy is 0 before the qualification date and is 1, 2, 3, . . . , afterward. That is, we model that after an economy is qualified to be a member of GATT/WTO, it might be on a growth path different from the variable of our concern.

Note that the actual accession effect, which is our main concern, rather than the selection effect, by definition only starts to take place upon the actual accession of an economy to GATT/WTO. Thus, in regression, we can use the accession dummy as an independent variable to capture this effect.

4.2.6 The Econometric Models

We estimate two sets of econometric models. The first one is to examine the impact of accession on individual economic variables of the economy such as GDP, capital stock, import and export, and FDI. Let x_{it} be the one of the variables previously mentioned, and the first set of regressions are as follows:

$$(1)\quad \log(x_{it}) = \alpha_i + \sum_{j=1}^{J} (\beta_j T_t + \gamma_j \text{Selection}_{it} + \delta_j \text{WTO}_{it}) j\text{Dummy}_{it} + \varepsilon_{it},$$

where α_i is a country-specific scale factor, which allows different countries to have different initial levels of economic variable x; that is, it is the fixed effects coefficient. j is an index of the type of the economy (e.g., high income or low income; common law, continental law, or formerly socialist economy). β_j is type J economy's normal growth rate of variable x. T_t is time trend, equaling to 1, 2, . . . , for the years of 1960, 1961, respectively. γ_j is the coefficient capturing the endogenous selection effect of GATT/WTO accessions. Selection_{it} is a variable to index the selection effect. There are two alternative methods to valuate Selection_{it}, corresponding to the two alternative methods explained above. WTO_{it} is the timer of the actual accession: It equals to 1, 2, . . . , 10, for the first, second, . . . , tenth year of accession, and it remains at the level of 10 after the tenth year of accession. Finally, we assume that the error term ε_{it} is independent across country (indexed by i) but might be correlated across time (indexed by t).

As explained, we use two alternative measures of the variable Selection_{it}. The first method comes from Heckman and Hotz (1989) and lets Selection_{it} be equal to 0 until three years before the accession, when it becomes 1, 2, 3 for the three years right before the accession. After the accession, Selection_{it} stays at 3. δ_j is the coefficient of the actual accession impact, which is our main concern. Figure 4.1 illustrates the valuation of Selection_{it} in this method together with the WTO_{it} variable.

The alternative valuation of Selection_{it} is the following. Let $\text{ACC}_{it} = 0$ or $\text{ACC}_{it} = 1$ depending on our prediction of whether country i is already a member of GATT/WTO by year t. The prediction is based on a fitted probit regression of GATT/WTO membership on one-year lagged per capita income, import-GDP, export-GDP, and legal origin. As for Selection_{it}, it is 0 if $\text{ACC}_{it} = 0$ and it is 1, 2, 3, . . . , respectively, after the first year in which $\text{ACC}_{it} = 1$.

The economic interpretation of model (1) is that for a type J economy, the economic variable x has a steady-state growth rate of β_i, and after the accession, within ten years, the growth rate further changes by δ_j. γ_j captures the effect on the economy when the economy is selected or qualified to be a member of GATT/WTO.

The second set of regressions that we estimate are for discovering the im-

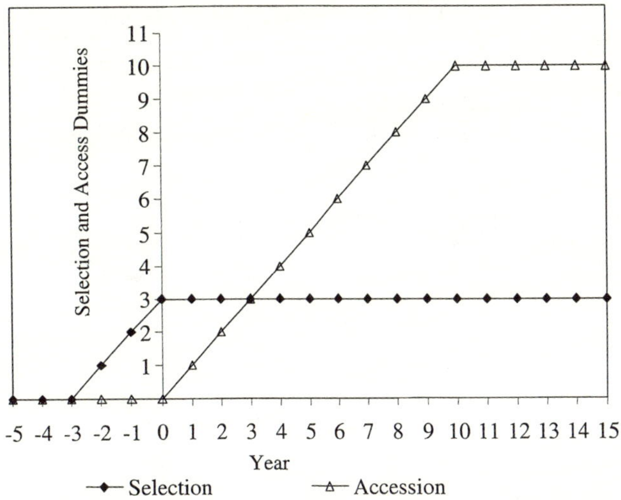

Fig. 4.1 The selection effect and the accession effect
Note: Year 0 stands for the accession year.

pact of the GATT/WTO on productivity changes in the economy. The model is as follows:

$$(2)\quad \log(\text{GDP}_{it}) = \alpha_i + \sum_{j=1}^{J}(\beta_j T_t + \gamma_j \text{Selection}_{it} + \delta_j \text{WTO}_{it})\, j\text{Dummy}_{it} + \beta_{\text{Import}}\left(\frac{\text{Import}}{\text{GDP}}\right)_{it} + \beta_{\text{Export}}\left(\frac{\text{Export}}{\text{GDP}}\right)_{it} + \beta_{\text{FDI}}\left(\frac{\text{FDI}}{\text{GDP}}\right)_{it} + \sum_{q=\text{LowIncome}}^{\text{HighIncome}}[\beta_{qK}\log(\text{Capital}_{it}) + \beta_{qL}\log(\text{Labor}_{it})]\, q\text{Dummy}_{it} + \varepsilon_{it},$$

where α_i is a country-specific coefficient capturing initial productivity differences among countries (i.e., the fixed effects coefficient). β_{Import}, β_{Export}, and β_{FDI} are the coefficients measuring the potential influence of openness on the economy's productivity. γ_j and δ_j are parameters to capture the selection and the accession impact, respectively, similar to model (1). β_{qK} and β_{qL} are the elasticity coefficients of capital and labor, respectively, for income group q. q indexes either high-income or low-income countries, since high-income and low-income economies may adopt different production technology. That is, we allow the possibility that the capital and labor elasticities vary across different types of economies. All other variables and parameters are the same as or similar to those in equation (1).

Table 4.3 A Probit Regression of GATT/WTO Membership

Independent Variable	WTO/GATT Membership (Yes = 1) (panel data probit with random effect)
One Year Lagged Per Capita GDP	0.00014***
	(12.79)
One Year Lagged Import/GDP	0.023***
	(8.87)
One Year Lagged Export/GDP	0.0080***
	(2.89)
Continental Law Origin Dummy	–0.50***
	(–5.03)
Socialist Origin Dummy	–1.48***
	(–5.08)
Intercept	–0.64***
	(–5.39)
Wald Chi-Square(5)	419.83
No. of observations	3,254

Note: T-statistics are in parentheses.
***Significant at the 1 percent level.
**Significant at the 5 percent level.
*Significant at the 10 percent level.

4.3 The Findings

4.3.1 Predictions of the Qualification for GATT/WTO Membership

Table 4.3 reports the estimation results of the probit regression of the GATT/WTO membership. The dependent variable is whether country *i* had already become a member of GATT/WTO by year *t* with 1 corresponding to yes and 0 to no, respectively. This is to be used to predict which economies would be qualified to be members of GATT/WTO at various years, which, in turn, is used to capture the selection effect of the GATT/WTO accessions. As expected, it shows that an economy's GDP per capita is a significant predictor of its GATT/WTO membership. So is the extent of the economy's openness as measured by import-GDP, export-GDP, and FDI-GDP. Meanwhile, other things being equal, economies with common-law origins are more likely to be members of GATT/WTO than those with continental-law origins and socialist economies. This is perhaps because economies with common-law origins are more credibly adaptable to externally imposed regulations of GATT/WTO.

Based on the estimation results, we predict which economies would begin to be qualified as members of GATT/WTO, and by which year. Tables 4.4 to 4.6 give the predictions. Among the 18 economies that were already GATT members before 1960, we predicted that 13 of them would have

Table 4.4 **The Actual and Predicted Accession Years for Economies that Had Been Members of GATT by 1960**

Country	Accession Year	Predicted Accession Year
Predicted to be Members of GATT/GATT (13 economies)		
South Africa	June 1948	<1960
New Zealand	July 1948	1987
Pakistan	July 1948	1980
Sri Lanka	July 1948	<1960
Zimbabwe	July 1948	1976
Chile	March 1949	1986
Greece	March 1950	1967
Dominican Republic	May 1950	1985
Italy	May 1950	<1960
Nicaragua	May 1950	1974
Turkey	October 1951	1997
Uruguay	December 1953	1976
Ghana	October 1957	<1960
Predicted Not to be Members of GATT/WTO before 1998 (5 economies)		
Brazil	July 1948	n.a.
India	July 1948	n.a.
Haiti	January 1950	n.a.
Indonesia	February 1950	n.a.
Peru	October 1951	n.a.

joined GATT either before 1960 or during 1960–98. Out of the 18 economies, 5 were predicted not to have joined GATT/WTO by 1998. For the 74 economies that joined GATT/WTO between 1960 and 1998, 45 economies were predicted to have joined before the actual accession year; 15 were predicted to have joined after the actual date; and 14 were predicted to have never accessed in the 1960–98 window. Finally, for the 20 economies that had not joined GATT/WTO by 1998, we predicted that 11 of them would have joined by 1998 and 5 otherwise (for 4 other economies, we do not have available data to make the predictions).

4.3.2 Impact on Import, Export, and Foreign Direct Investment

Tables 4.7 to 4.10 report results of regressions of various measures of import. As dependent variable, the regressions use three alternative measures of imports: import in constant U.S. dollars, import in constant local currency, and the ratio of import to GDP (both are in constant local currency and the ratio is in percentage). Note that the ratio of import to GDP is often regarded as a measure of openness of the economy.

Looking at the regressions with income dummies as reported in tables 4.7 and 4.8, one can easily find a consistent pattern. That is, after accession,

Table 4.5 **The Actual and Predicted Accession Years for Economies that Joined GATT/WTO during 1960–1998**

Country	Accession Year	Predicted Accession Year
Economies Whose Predicted Accession was Earlier than Actual Accession (45 economies)		
Angola	April 1994	1993
Antigua and Barbuda	March 1987	1978
Bahrain	December 1993	1981
Barbados	February 1967	<1960
Belize	October 1983	1981
Bolivia	September 1990	1974
Botswana	August 1987	<1960
Costa Rica	December 1990	1966
Czech Republic	April 1993	1993
Djibouti	December 1994	1992
Dominica	April 1993	1978
El Salvador	May 1991	1974
Fiji	November 1993	<1960
Gabon	May 1963	<1960
Grenada	October 1994	1978
Guyana	July 1966	<1960
Honduras	April 1994	1975
Hong Kong	April 1986	1961
Ireland	December 1967	<1960
Israel	July 1962	<1960
Jamaica	December 1963	<1960
Kenya	February 1964	<1960
Korea, Republic of	April 1967	1967
Kuwait	May 1963	1963
Lesotho	January 1988	<1960
Macao	November 1991	1987
Malta	November 1964	<1960
Mauritius	September 1970	<1960
Namibia	September 1992	1981
Panama	September 1997	1981
Papua New Guinea	December 1994	1962
Paraguay	January 1994	1987
St. Kitts and Nevis	March 1994	1978
Singapore	August 1973	1966
Slovak Republic	April 1993	1993
Slovenia	October 1994	1992
Solomon Islands	December 1994	1981
Suriname	March 1978	1971
Swaziland, Kingdom of	February 1993	1971
Thailand	November 1982	1968
Trinidad and Tobago	October 1962	<1960
Tunisia	August 1990	1975
United Arab Emirates	March 1994	1974
Venezuela	August 1990	1974
Zambia	February 1982	<1960

Table 4.5 (continued)

Country	Accession Year	Predicted Accession Year
Economies Whose Predicted Accession was Later than Actual Accession (15 economies)		
Argentina	October 1967	1972
Central African Republic	May 1963	1967
Côte d'Ivoire	December 1963	1974
Cyprus	July 1963	1976
Egypt	May 1970	1980
Gambia	February 1965	1967
Maldives	April 1983	1986
Mauritania	September 1963	1973
Mexico	August 1986	1996
Mozambique	July 1992	1993
The Philippines	December 1979	1993
Portugal	May 1962	1965
Senegal	September 1963	1974
Spain	August 1963	1964
Togo	March 1964	1970
Economies that Are Predicted Not to Join GATT/WTO by 1998 (14 economies)		
Bangladesh	December 1972	n.a.
Benin	September 1963	n.a.
Bulgaria	December 1996	n.a.
Cameroon	May 1963	n.a.
Colombia	October 1981	n.a.
Ecuador	January 1996	n.a.
Guatemala	October 1991	n.a.
Guinea	December 1994	n.a.
Hungary	September 1973	n.a.
The Kyrgyz Republic	December 1998	n.a.
Mali	January 1993	n.a.
Mongolia	January 1997	n.a.
Morocco	June 1987	n.a.
Romania	November 1971	n.a.

high-income economies had statistically significant increases in the growth rate of import and in the ratio of import to GDP. The increases were also economically significant: The increase in the growth rate of import is around 5 percent per year and from 0.79 percent to 1.04 percent per year in the percentage of import-GDP. In contrast, the findings about low-income economies are mixed. Table 4.7 shows no statistically significant results on the selection and accession effects for low-income economies. Table 4.8 shows negative coefficients of the selection effect but positive ones for the accession effect.

Tables 4.9 and 4.10 show a general pattern of the impact of GATT/WTO accessions on economies of different legal institutions. Continental-law economies showed statistically and economically significant increases in

Table 4.6 **The Actual and Predicted Accession Years for Economies that Had Not Been Members of GATT/WTO by 1998**

Country	Accession Year	Predicted Accession Year
	Predicted to Join during 1960–1998 (12 economies)	
Algeria	n.a.	1975
Bhutan	n.a.	1981
Comoros	n.a.	1981
Equatorial Guinea	n.a.	1986
Estonia	n.a.	1993
Jordan	April 2000	1977
Lebanon	n.a.	1990
Oman	November 2000	1969
Puerto Rico	n.a.	1961
Saudi Arabia	n.a.	1961
Seychelles	n.a.	1977
Tonga	n.a.	1982
	Predicted Not to Join by 1998 (4 economies)	
Albania	September 2000	n.a.
China	November 2001	n.a.
Kazakhstan	n.a.	n.a.
Turkmenistan	n.a.	n.a.

Table 4.7 **Regressions of Measures of Import with Income Dummies Using the Heckman and Hotz (1989) Method to Control for Selection Endogeneity**

	Dependent Variable		
	Log(Import) (U.S.$)	Log(Import) (local constant currency)	Import/GDP (%)
Year · HighIncome	0.052***	0.055***	0.12***
	(31.28)	(33.36)	(2.81)
Year · LowIncome	0.039***	0.038***	0.47***
	(35.70)	(34.60)	(16.06)
Selection · HighIncome	0.024	0.012	2.47***
	(1.19)	(0.60)	(4.95)
Selection · LowIncome	0.0018	0.0062	–0.28
	(0.15)	(0.53)	(–0.89)
Accession · HighIncome	0.050***	0.046***	0.79***
	(7.56)	(7.36)	(5.04)
Accession · LowIncome	0.0057	0.0053	–0.057
	(1.28)	(1.20)	(–0.48)
Intercept	–63.61***	–62.80***	657.04***
	(–35.12)	(–34.62)	(–13.99)
R^2	0.646	0.636	0.163
No. of observations	2,855	3,067	3,398

Notes: *T*-statistics are in parentheses. HighIncome = 1 if in 1987 the GDP/Population > U.S.$3,000; otherwise, LowIncome = 1. Selection = 0 until two years before GATT/WTO accession; Selection = 1, 2, 3, 3, 3, . . . thereafter.

***Significant at the 1 percent level.

Table 4.8 **Regressions of Measures of Import with Income Dummies Using Predicted GATT/WTO Membership to Control for Selection Endogeneity**

	Dependent Variable		
	Log(Import) (U.S.$)	Log(Import) (local constant currency)	Import/GDP (%)
Year · HighIncome	0.041***	0.042***	0.083
	(14.19)	(14.25)	(0.93)
Year · LowIncome	0.050***	0.049***	0.48***
	(36.00)	(35.19)	(12.58)
Selection · HighIncome	0.016***	0.018***	0.081
	(4.78)	(5.31)	(0.84)
Selection · LowIncome	–0.02***	–0.02***	–0.039
	(–11.16)	(–11.11)	(–0.79)
Accession · HighIncome	0.050***	0.044***	1.04***
	(8.27)	(7.66)	(7.00)
Accession · LowIncome	0.0094**	0.0097**	–0.080
	(2.30)	(2.36)	(–0.70)
Intercept	–72.14***	–69.26***	650.50***
	(–28.25)	(–26.26)	(–8.39)
R^2	0.664	0.653	0.157
No. of observations	2,855	3,067	3,398

Notes: T-statistics are in parentheses. HighIncome = 1 if in 1987 the GDP/Population > U.S.$3,000; otherwise, LowIncome = 1. Selection = 0 before predicted GATT/WTO accession; Selection = 1, 2, 3, 4, . . . thereafter.

***Significant at the 1 percent level.

**Significant at the 5 percent level.

all three measures of import. The increase in the growth rate of import was around 3 percent per year and from 0.25 percent to 0.28 percent in the percentage of import to GDP. Common-law economies also had significant increase in import but mostly in the ratio of import to GDP. The increase in the import/GDP percentage was 0.25 percent or .037 percent, depending on the configuration of the regressions. As for the socialist economies, we found that the accession effect was *negative* in the ratio of import to GDP ratio, although the selection effect was positive. A robust result is the decrease around 1 percent or 1.5 percent per year after the accession in the percentage of import-GDP.

Tables 4.11 to 4.14 report regressions of the impact of GATT/WTO accessions on export. The regressions are of three alternative measures of export: export in constant U.S. dollars, export in constant local currency, and export-GDP, respectively. Similar to import-GDP, the ratio of export to GDP is often regarded as a measure of dependence of the economy on foreign markets as well as international competitiveness.

Table 4.9 **Regressions Measures of Import with Legal Origin Dummies Using the Heckman and Hotz (1989) Method to Control for Selection Endogeneity**

	Dependent Variable		
	Log(Import) (U.S.$)	Log(Import) (local constant currency)	Import/GDP (%)
Year · CommonLaw	0.039***	0.042***	0.41***
	(22.48)	(23.90)	(9.58)
Year · ContinentalLaw	0.044***	0.043***	0.32***
	(34.69)	(34.18)	(10.69)
Year · Socialist	0.058***	0.058***	0.67***
	(8.12)	(8.02)	(4.36)
Selection · CommonLaw	0.037**	0.029	0.89**
	(2.06)	(1.62)	(2.13)
Selection · ContinentalLaw	–0.017	–0.019	–0.11
	(–1.14)	(–1.29)	(–0.30)
Selection · Socialist	–0.32***	–0.32***	2.58**
	(–6.65)	(–6.57)	(2.30)
Accession · CommonLaw	0.0045	0.00025	0.27*
	(0.69)	(0.004)	(1.74)
Accession · ContinentalLaw	0.028***	0.029***	0.25**
	(5.18)	(5.76)	(1.96)
Accession · Socialist	–0.0040	–0.0040	–0.97*
	(–0.18)	(–0.18)	(–1.85)
Intercept	–61.99***	–60.93***	–690.84***
	(–30.41)	(–30.02)	(–14.21)
R^2	0.576	0.564	0.151
No. of observations	2,855	3,067	3,398

Notes: T-statistics are in parentheses. Selection = 0 until two years before GATT/WTO accession; Selection = 1, 2, 3, 3, 3, . . . thereafter.

***Significant at the 1 percent level.

**Significant at the 5 percent level.

*Significant at the 10 percent level.

From tables 4.11 and 4.12, we can see that the high-income economies had significant increases in the growth rate of export (3 percent to 5 percent per year) and in export-GDP (1.2 percent to 1.5 percent per year) due to the accession effect. Low-income economies also experienced increases in the growth rate of export, but the magnitude of increase, around 1 percent per year, is significantly smaller than that of the high-income counterparts. Moreover, there is some evidence (in one regression) that low-income economies experienced slight decreases (0.2 percent a year) in the ratio of export to GDP (table 4.12).

The results in tables 4.13 and 4.14 show that those continental-law economies enjoyed positive and significant accession effects in export. The growth of export increased by around 1 to 2 percent per year due to

Table 4.10 Regressions of Measures of Import with Legal Origin Dummies Using Predicted GATT/WTO Membership to Control for Selection Endogeneity

	Dependent Variable		
	Log(Import) (U.S.$)	Log(Import) (local constant currency)	Import/GDP (%)
Year · CommonLaw	0.051***	0.052***	0.34***
	(13.73)	(13.68)	(2.88)
Year · ContinentalLaw	0.046***	0.045***	0.42***
	(28.49)	(27.85)	(10.84)
Year · Socialist	0.046***	0.046***	0.80***
	(6.65)	(6.57)	(5.45)
Selection · CommonLaw	–0.013***	–0.011***	0.11
	(–3.24)	(–2.70)	(0.94)
Selection · ContinentalLaw	–0.0059***	–0.0050**	–0.22***
	(–2.59)	(–2.25)	(–4.04)
Selection · Socialist	0.093***	0.093***	2.44***
	(2.77)	(2.74)	(2.87)
Accession · CommonLaw	0.011*	0.0054	0.37**
	(1.75)	(0.86)	(2.48)
Accession · ContinentalLaw	0.026***	0.028***	0.28***
	(5.15)	(5.75)	(2.37)
Accession · Socialist	–0.042*	–0.042*	–1.49***
	(–1.81)	(–1.79)	(2.65)
Intercept	–71.47***	–68.75***	–770.57***
	(–22.00)	(–20.96)	(–8.07)
R^2	0.572	0.560	0.155
No. of observations	2,855	3,067	3,398

Notes: T-statistics are in parentheses. Selection = 0 until two years before GATT/WTO accession; Selection = 1, 2, 3, 4, . . . , thereafter.

***Significant at the 1 percent level.

**Significant at the 5 percent level.

*Significant at the 10 percent level.

accession, and the export-GDP ratio increased by about 0.2 percent per year. The common-law economies showed mixed signs in changes in the growth rate of export but significant increases in export-GDP (around 0.5 percent to 0.7 percent per year). However, the socialist economies actually experienced decreases in export-GDP due to the accession effect in the magnitude of 0.7 percent to 0.9 percent per year, although the accession did seem to have chosen the faster-growing socialist economies in export.

Tables 4.15 to 4.18 list regressions of two alternative measures of FDI: log(FDI) and FDI-GDP ratio. Tables 4.15 and 4.16 are about the impact of GATT/WTO accession on high- and low-income economies. They show

Table 4.11 **Regressions of Measures of Export with Income Dummies Using the Heckman and Hotz (1989) Method to Control for Selection Endogeneity**

	Dependent Variable		
	Log(Import) (U.S.$)	Log(Import) (local constant currency)	Import/GDP (%)
Year · HighIncome	0.059***	0.059***	0.029
	(35.88)	(37.37)	(0.82)
Year · LowIncome	0.042***	0.042**	0.29***
	(39.35)	(39.35)	(11.71)
Selection · HighIncome	0.087***	0.10***	3.02***
	(4.37)	(5.28)	(7.23)
Selection · LowIncome	0.024***	0.026**	0.52**
	(2.06)	(2.28)	(1.98)
Accession · HighIncome	0.044***	0.033***	1.20***
	(6.90)	(5.62)	(8.96)
Accession · LowIncome	0.0090**	0.0087**	–0.20**
	(2.07)	(2.07)	(–1.98)
Intercept	–71.79***	–70.19***	–369.82***
	(–40.59)	(–40.41)	(–9.27)
R^2	0.705	0.697	0.161
No. of observations	2,859	3,070	3,402

Notes: See table 4.7.

***Significant at the 1 percent level.

**Significant at the 5 percent level.

Table 4.12 **Regressions of Measures of Export with Income Dummies Using Predicted GATT/WTO Membership to Control for Selection Endogeneity**

	Dependent Variable		
	Log(Import) (U.S.$)	Log(Import) (local constant currency)	Import/GDP (%)
Year · HighIncome	0.062***	0.063***	0.012
	(21.45)	(22.30)	(0.16)
Year · LowIncome	0.050***	0.050***	0.31***
	(36.52)	(36.64)	(9.62)
Selection · HighIncome	–0.0030	–0.0052	0.072
	(–0.90)	(–1.61)	(0.87)
Selection · LowIncome	–0.014***	-0.014***	–0.013
	(–7.83)	(7.93)	(–0.30)
Accession · HighIncome	0.054***	0.045***	1.51***
	(9.13)	(8.04)	(11.85)
Accession · LowIncome	0.014***	0.014***	–0.13
	(3.47)	(3.54)	(–1.36)
Intercept	–85.03***	–84.47***	–388.69***
	(–33.44)	(–32.79)	(–5.87)
R^2	0.709	0.700	0.147
No. of observations	2,859	3,070	3,402

Notes: See table 4.8.

***Significant at the 1 percent level.

Table 4.13 Regressions of Measures of Export with Legal Origin Dummies Using the Heckman and Hotz (1989) Method to Control for Selection Endogeneity

	Dependent Variable		
	Log(Import) (U.S.$)	Log(Import) (local constant currency)	Import/GDP (%)
Year · CommonLaw	0.045***	0.046***	0.24***
	(25.03)	(26.47)	(6.41)
Year · ContinentalLaw	0.047***	0.046***	0.18***
	(36.67)	(37.09)	(7.28)
Year · Socialist	0.064***	0.064***	0.44***
	(8.75)	(8.89)	(3.31)
Selection · CommonLaw	0.085***	0.081***	1.95***
	(4.66)	(4.53)	(5.49)
Selection · ContinentalLaw	–0.0024	0.0076	0.017
	(–0.16)	(0.53)	(0.06)
Selection · Socialist	–0.28***	–0.28***	4.23***
	(–5.59)	(–5.68)	(4.42)
Accession · CommonLaw	0.000095	–0.0019	0.51***
	(0.01)	(–0.29)	(3.87)
Accession · ContinentalLaw	0.027***	0.023***	0.20*
	(5.03)	(4.59)	(1.82)
Accession · Socialist	0.0017	0.0017	–0.77*
	(0.08)	(0.08)	(–1.72)
Intercept	–70.23***	–68.13***	–394.12***
	(–33.90)	(–33.94)	(–9.49)
R^2	0.617	0.613	0.138
No. of observations	2,859	3,070	3,402

Notes: See table 4.9.
***Significant at the 1 percent level.
*Significant at the 10 percent level.

that both the high-income group and the low-income group had statistically significant and positive increases in log(FDI) due to the accession effect, while the high-income group saw much bigger increases than the low-income group (12 to 13 percent vs. 7 to 9 percent per year). Moreover, there is no strong evidence that the FDI-GDP ratio significantly increased due to the accession effect for both income groups (only one out of four regressions shows statistically positive changes).

One robust finding across regressions in tables 4.17 and 4.18 is that the continental-law economies had drastic upward shifts (around 15 or 16 percent) in log(FDI) due to accession. There is weak evidence that the common-law economies had a higher FDI-GDP ratio due to the accession effect. The former socialist economies did not show any significant changes in either log(FDI) or FDI-GDP due to accession.

Table 4.14 **Regressions of Measures of Export with Legal Origin Dummies Using Predicted GATT/WTO Membership to Control for Selection Endogeneity**

	Dependent Variable		
	Log(Import) (U.S.$)	Log(Import) (local constant currency)	Import/GDP (%)
Year · CommonLaw	0.062***	0.062***	0.093
	(16.31)	(16.66)	(0.92)
Year · ContinentalLaw	0.049***	0.049***	0.27***
	(30.00)	(31.03)	(8.21)
Year · Socialist	0.053***	0.053***	0.63***
	(7.53)	(7.65)	(4.97)
Selection · CommonLaw	–0.018***	–0.017***	0.23**
	(–4.39)	(–4.25)	(2.18)
Selection · ContinentalLaw	–0.0052**	–0.0065***	–0.18***
	(–2.23)	(–2.94)	(–3.94)
Selection · Socialist	0.038	0.038	1.04
	(1.11)	(1.12)	(1.42)
Accession · CommonLaw	0.013**	0.010*	0.73***
	(2.01)	(1.65)	(5.73)
Accession · ContinentalLaw	0.028***	0.025***	0.24**
	(5.33)	(5.15)	(2.31)
Accession · Socialist	–0.020	–0.020	–0.89*
	(–0.85)	(–0.86)	(–1.84)
Intercept	–83.62***	–82.16***	–416.40***
	(–25.32)	(–25.36)	(–5.08)
R^2	0.613	0.610	0.131
No. of observations	2,859	3,070	3,402

Notes: See table 4.10.
***Significant at the 1 percent level.
**Significant at the 5 percent level.
*Significant at the 10 percent level.

4.3.3 Impact on Gross Domestic Product Growth

Tables 4.19 and 4.20 report the regression results on the impact of accession on the growth rate of GDP, using the Heckman and Hotz (1989) method and the predicted accession approach to control for the selection effect. The two tables show consistent results. Classified by income level, economies with high per capita income experienced positive and statistically significant increase in their GDP growth after the accession. The impact was around 1.5 percent and 1.6 percent increase in the GDP growth rate per year for the ten years after accession. For low-income countries, we cannot find any statistically significant changes in GDP growth after GATT/WTO accession. The two tables also show conflicting evidence on the selection effect for low-income economies. For the high-income group,

Table 4.15 **Regressions of Measuures of FDI with Income Dummies Using the Heckman and Hotz (1989) Method to Control for Selection Endogeneity**

	Dependent Variable	
	Log(FDI) (U.S.$)	FDI/GDP (%)
Year · HighIncome	0.096***	0.074***
	(15.70)	(3.46)
Year · LowIncome	0.080***	0.099***
	(18.70)	(6.81)
Selection · HighIncome	0.043	0.33
	(0.47)	(1.09)
Selection · LowIncome	0.057	0.20
	(1.44)	(1.42)
Accession · HighIncome	0.12***	0.068
	(3.63)	(0.61)
Accession · LowIncome	0.077***	0.091
	(4.19)	(1.49)
Intercept	–151.69***	–180.26***
	(–21.82)	(–7.61)
R^2	0.367	0.0546
No. of observations	2,132	2,606

Notes: See table 4.7.

***Significant at the 1 percent level.

Table 4.16 **Regressions of Measures of FDI on Income Dummies Using Predicted GATT/WTO Membership to Control for Selection Endogeneity**

	Dependent Variable	
	Log(FDI) (U.S.$)	FDI/GDP (%)
Year · HighIncome	0.096***	0.15***
	(6.21)	(2.97)
Year · LowIncome	0.097***	0.063***
	(15.15)	(2.94)
Selection · HighIncome	0.0047	–0.089
	(0.03)	(–1.62)
Selection · LowIncome	–0.023***	0.069***
	(–2.92)	(2.61)
Accession · HighIncome	0.13***	0.053
	(4.10)	(0.48)
Accession · LowIncome	0.090***	0.12**
	(5.28)	(2.11)
Intercept	–174.06***	–176.89***
	(–13.60)	(–4.18)
R^2	0.369	0.0570
No. of observations	2,132	2,606

Notes: See table 4.8.

***Significant at the 1 percent level.

**Significant at the 5 percent level.

Table 4.17 **Regressions of Measures of FDI with Legal Origin Dummies Using the Heckman and Hotz (1989) Method to Control for Selection Endogeneity**

	Dependent Variable	
	Log(FDI) (U.S.$)	FDI/GDP (%)
Year · CommonLaw	0.10***	0.11***
	(17.49)	(5.22)
Year · ContinentalLaw	0.071***	0.074***
	(16.27)	(4.85)
Year · Socialist	0.27***	0.25***
	(7.09)	(3.82)
Selection · CommonLaw	–0.015	0.45**
	(–0.25)	(2.25)
Selection · ContinentalLaw	0.032	0.11
	(0.68)	(0.64)
Selection · Socialist	0.18	0.19
	(1.09)	(0.40)
Accession · CommonLaw	0.0084	0.094
	(0.34)	(1.16)
Accession · ContinentalLaw	0.15***	0.072
	(7.04)	(0.92)
Accession · Socialist	–0.094	–0.14
	(–0.86)	(–0.66)
Intercept	–167.22***	–191.62***
	(–21.62)	(7.98)
R^2	0.374	0.060
No. of observations	2,132	2,606

Notes: See table 4.9.
***Significant at the 1 percent level.
**Significant at the 5 percent level.

table 4.20 shows a positive selection effect: that is, high-income economies qualified for GATT/WTO membership had a 1.1 percent increase in GDP growth, besides an 1.5 percent to 1.6 percent increase in GDP growth after the actual accession.

As for the differences among economies of different legal institutions in responding to GATT/WTO accessions, table 4.20 shows that the common-law economies in the sample experienced, on average, a 1 percent increase in GDP growth after their accession to GATT/WTO, while socialist economies had a decrease of about 2 percent in GDP growth. Both are statistically significant. However, the same pattern is not present in table 4.19, which is based on the Hechman and Hotz (1989) method and controlling for endogeneity of the accessions. One may summarize that there is some evidence that the common-law economies' growth rate benefited from

Table 4.18 **Regressions of Measures of FDI with Legal Origin Dummies Using Predicted GATT/WTO Membership to Control for Selection Endogeneity**

	Dependent Variable	
	Log(FDI) (U.S.$)	FDI/GDP (%)
Year · CommonLaw	0.17***	0.055
	(9.88)	(1.09)
Year · ContinentalLaw	0.073***	0.062***
	(11.07)	(2.63)
Year · Socialist	0.29***	0.26***
	(8.06)	(4.07)
Selection · CommonLaw	–0.081***	0.076
	(–4.20)	(1.38)
Selection · ContinentalLaw	–0.0016	0.023
	(–0.19)	(0.78)
Selection · Socialist	–0.18	0.35
	(–1.24)	(1.12)
Accession · CommonLaw	0.028	0.154**
	(1.18)	(2.02)
Accession · ContinentalLaw	0.16***	0.10
	(8.10)	(1.42)
Accession · Socialist	0.080	–0.21
	(0.48)	(–0.96)
Intercept	–219.06***	–143.76***
	(–14.80)	(–3.16)
R^2	0.379	0.059
No. of observations	2,132	2,606

Notes: See table 4.10.

***Significant at the 1 percent level.

**Significant at the 5 percent level.

GATT/WTO accession but that the socialist economies actually suffered in GDP growth.

4.3.4 Impact on Total Factor Productivity

Tables 4.21 to 4.24 list results of a set of production function regressions. The purpose is to study how the accessions affected the economies' TFP, which is the residual term in an economy's aggregate production function. Regressions in tables 4.21 and 4.22 use dummies for per capita income. Those in tables 4.23 and 4.24 use dummies for the economies' legal institutions.

The first regressions of tables 4.21 and 4.22 indicate that the high-income economies did experience a statistically significant increase in TFP growth in the amount of 1 percent per year due to the accession effect, while there

Table 4.19 **Regressions on Log(GDP) Using the Heckman and Hotz (1989) Method to Control for Selection Endogeneity**

	Log(GDP)		Log(GDP)
Year · HighIncome	0.039***	Year · CommonLaw	0.040***
	(45.99)		(43.70)
Year · LowIncome	0.038***	Year · ContinentalLaw	0.037***
	(59.32)		(54.47)
Selection · HighIncome	0.011	Year · Socialist	0.039***
	(1.12)		(14.71)
Selection · LowIncome	0.013*	Selection · CommonLaw	0.051***
	(1.88)		(5.58)
Accession · HighIncome	0.016***	Selection · ContinentalLaw	–0.013
	(4.75)		(–1.55)
Accession · LowIncome	–0.0024	Selection · Socialist	–0.099
	(–0.92)		(–4.46)
Intercept	–51.40***	Accession · CommonLaw	0.0045
	(–50.97)		(1.28)
		Accession · Continetal	0.0016
			(0.55)
		Accession · Socialist	–0.013
			(–1.21)
		Intercept	–50.54***
			(–47.53)
R^2	0.757	R^2	0.735
No. of observations	3,647	No. of observations	3,647

Notes: See table 4.7.
***Significant at the 1 percent level.
*Significant at the 10 percent level.

is some evidence (the first regression in table 4.22 but not in table 4.21) that the low-income economies' TFP growth also increased by 0.5 percent per year. More interestingly, in the regressions where we control for the indirect effects of accession via import, export, and FDI, the net effects of accession on TFP growth for low-income economies are statistically significant and positive (1 percent per year) and slightly negative for high-income economies. This shows that the low-income economies did benefit in terms of higher economic efficiency through the intangible influences of accession to GATT/WTO (rather than through the tangible changes in import, export, and FDI).

From tables 4.23 and 4.24, we can see that there is weak evidence that both the common-law economy group and the continental-law group experienced positive accession effects in TFP growth. The magnitude of TFP increase per year due to GATT/WTO accessions is around 0.5 percent. It is weak rather than strong evidence because some regressions have statistically significant TFP increase but others have insignificant results. Perhaps a more interesting finding is that the socialist accession economies

Table 4.20 **Regressions of Log(GDP) Using Predicted GATT/WTO Membership to Control for Selection Endogeneity**

	Log(GDP)		Log(GDP)
Year · HighIncome	0.032***	Year · CommonLaw	0.040***
	(19.81)		(21.99)
Year · LowIncome	0.040***	Year · ContinentalLaw	0.040***
	(49.85)		(44.04)
Selection · HighIncome	0.011	Year · Socialist	0.036***
	(5.85)		(14.08)
Selection · LowIncome	–0.044***	Selection · CommonLaw	0.029
	(–3.97)		(1.43)
Accession · HighIncome	0.016***	Selection · ContinentalLaw	–0.0069***
	(5.18)		(–5.45)
Accession · LowIncome	–0.0046	Selection · Socialist	–0.044**
	(–0.92)		(–2.54)
Intercept	–49.39***	Accession · CommonLaw	0.010***
	(–32.69)		(3.06)
		Accession · Contineta	0.0011
			(0.40)
		Accession · Socialist	–0.021**
			(–2.13)
		Intercept	–53.03***
			(–47.53)
R^2	0.760	R^2	0.733
No. of observations	3,647	No. of observations	3,647

Notes: See table 4.8.
***Significant at the 1 percent level.
**Significant at the 5 percent level.

had no positive increases in TFP due to the accession effect. In fact, after separating the indirect effects via import, export, and FDI, we find that the direct effect of accession on TFP growth was about –1.1 percent per year.

4.3.5 Summary and Interpretation of the Findings

Overall, the findings of our regressions can be summarized in two parts.

First, in terms of engaging more international trade and attracting more FDI, both the high-income and low-income groups made significant progress, with the high-income group having much more gains than the other group. In this regard, both the common-law country group and the continental-law group saw significant increase, while the former socialist economies had either insignificant or mixed changes due to the accessions.

Second, with regard to changes in the growth rate of the economywide TFP, the high-income group and the common-law as well as continental-law economies saw significant increases due to their accessions to GATT/WTO. The low-income group and the former socialist economies had ei-

Table 4.21 Production Function Regressions with Income Dummies Using the Heckman and Hotz (1989) Method to Control for Selection Endogeneity

	Dependent Variable	
	Log(GDP)	Log(GDP)
Year · HighIncome	0.023***	0.0082***
	(21.19)	(6.26)
Year · LowIncome	0.0065***	0.0031*
	(3.98)	(1.87)
Log(Capital) · HighIncome	0.59***	0.588***
	(30.00)	(20.91)
Log(Capital) · LowIncome	0.58***	0.60***
	(35.85)	(42.29)
Log(Labor) · HighIncome	0.022	0.40***
	(0.58)	(7.28)
Log(Labor) · LowIncome	0.66***	0.43***
	(11.28)	(7.60)
Selection · HighIncome	0.0023	–0.046***
	(0.26)	(–3.69)
Selection · LowIncome	–0.0070	–0.0031
	(–1.28)	(–0.69)
Accession · HighIncome	0.010***	–0.0063*
	(3.53)	(–1.71)
Accession · LowIncome	0.0033	0.010***
	(1.61)	(5.43)
Import/GDP		–0.0033***
		(–8.74)
Export/GDP		0.0061***
		(14.36)
FDI/GDP		–0.00026
		(–0.37)
Intercept	–20.24***	–5.76***
	(–11.95)	(–3.17)
R^2	0.865	0.867
No. of observations	3,377	2,304

Notes: See table 4.7.
***Significant at the 1 percent level.
*Significant at the 10 percent level.

ther insignificant or even slightly negative changes in their productivity due to the accessions.

The findings lend themselves to easy interpretations. Economic backwardness, as indexed by low per capita income, did not seem to be an important positive factor enabling an economy to benefit from joining GATT/WTO. Initial economic institutions before joining international organizations are shown to be much more important. Economies with proper initial economic institutions are positioned to benefit most from

Table 4.22 **Production Function Regressions with Income Dummies Using Predicted GATT/WTO Membership to Control for Selection Endogeneity**

	Dependent Variable	
	Log(GDP)	Log(GDP)
Year · HighIncome	0.020***	0.00037*
	(13.23)	(1.81)
Year · LowIncome	0.0071***	0.0031*
	(4.38)	(1.89)
Log(Capital) · HighIncome	0.59***	0.61***
	(29.91)	(22.54)
Log(Capital) · LowIncome	0.58***	0.60***
	(36.30)	(41.71)
Log(Labor) · HighIncome	0.019	0.32***
	(0.52)	(6.35)
Log(Labor) · LowIncome	0.75***	0.44***
	(12.77)	(7.49)
Selection · HighIncome	0.0042***	0.0056***
	(2.93)	(3.06)
Selection · LowIncome	–0.0068***	–0.00066
	(–7.84)	(–0.75)
Accession · HighIncome	0.010***	–0.0077**
	(3.89)	(–2.14)
Accession · LowIncome	0.0046**	0.010***
	(2.35)	(5.35)
Import/GDP		–0.0033***
		(–8.70)
Export/GDP		0.0060***
		(14.03)
FDI/GDP		–0.00019
		(–0.27)
Intercept	–19.86***	–3.26
	(–10.84)	(–1.59)
R^2	0.868	0.867
No. of observations	3,377	2,304

Notes: See table 4.8.

***Significant at the 1 percent level.

**Significant at the 5 percent level.

*Significant at the 10 percent level.

joining GATT/WTO. Countries with inefficient institutions such as the socialist economic system were found to benefit little, if not negatively, from the accession.

4.4 Concluding Remarks

In the spirit of event study, we put together a large panel data set with over 112 economies covering the years from 1960 to 1998. Seventy-four of

Table 4.23 Production Function Regressions with Legal Origin Dummies Using the Heckman and Hotz (1989) Method to Control for Selection Endogeneity

	Dependent Variable	
	Log(GDP)	Log(GDP)
Year · CommonLaw	0.018***	0.0091***
	(17.26)	(7.82)
Year · ContinentalLaw	0.019***	0.0052***
	(50.61)	(4.79)
Year · Socialist	0.0092***	0.0092***
	(4.32)	(4.28)
Log(Capital) · HighIncome	0.69***	0.65***
	(35.58)	(25.08)
Log(Capital) · LowIncome	0.69***	0.65***
	(35.58)	(25.08)
Log(Labor) · HighIncome	0.57***	0.59***
	(33.80)	(41.30)
Log(Labor) · LowIncome	0.21***	0.34***
	(5.89)	(8.37)
Selection · CommonLaw	0.026***	0.027***
	(3.43)	(3.54)
Selection · ContinentalLaw	–0.022***	–0.0091*
	(–3.51)	(–1.71)
Selection · Socialist	–0.070***	–0.099***
	(–3.91)	(–6.45)
Accession · CommonLaw	0.0042	0.0041
	(1.53)	(1.49)
Accession · ContinentalLaw	0.0041*	0.0064***
	(1.83)	(2.67)
Accession · Socialist	0.0040	–0.011*
	(0.50)	(–1.65)
Import/GDP		–0.0031***
		(–8.45)
Export/GDP		0.0055***
		(13.13)
FDI/GDP		–0.00041
		(–0.60)
Intercept	–28.96***	–8.93***
	(–21.96)	(–6.15)
R^2	0.862	0.872
No. of observations	3,377	2,304

Notes: See table 4.9.

***Significant at the 1 percent level.

*Significant at the 10 percent level.

Table 4.24 **Production Function Regressions with Legal Origin Dummies Using Predicted GATT/WTO Membership to Control for Selection Endogeneity**

	Dependent Variable	
	Log(GDP)	Log(GDP)
Year · CommonLaw	0.026***	0.019***
	(16.75)	(9.31)
Year · ContinentalLaw	0.022***	0.0039***
	(19.64)	(3.15)
Year · Socialist	0.0078***	0.0054**
	(3.75)	(2.54)
Log(Capital) · HighIncome	0.71***	0.65***
	(36.36)	(25.37)
Log(Capital) · LowIncome	0.58***	0.60***
	(34.79)	(41.76)
Log(Labor) · HighIncome	0.074**	0.33***
	(1.97)	(6.22)
Log(Labor) · LowIncome	0.18***	0.35***
	(4.86)	(8.76)
Selection · CommonLaw	–0.0087***	–0.011***
	(–5.62)	(–5.57)
Selection · ContinentalLaw	–0.0050***	0.00074
	(–5.16)	(0.80)
Selection · Socialist	–0.042***	–0.0032***
	(–3.34)	(–0.32)
Accession · CommonLaw	0.0095***	0.0068***
	(3.72)	(2.65)
Accession · ContinentalLaw	0.0020	0.0049**
	(0.97)	(2.19)
Accession · Socialist	–0.0029	–0.014*
	(–0.38)	(–1.93)
Import/GDP		–0.0033***
		(–8.98)
Export/GDP		0.0055***
		(13.08)
FDI/GDP		–0.00017
		(–0.25)
Intercept	–36.85***	–13.64***
	(–21.86)	(–7.05)
R^2	0.863	0.870
No. of observations	3,377	2,304

Notes: See table 4.10.

***Significant at the 1 percent level.

**Significant at the 5 percent level.

*Significant at the 10 percent level.

them became members of GATT/WTO during the sample period. We study the changes in GDP growth, capital stock, import, export, FDI, and TFP of the accession economies around the year of joining GATT/WTO, using the rest of economies as references. We allow the possibility that different types of economies responded differently around the event. The classifications of the type of the economies are by per capita income and by initial economic institutions.

The findings indicate that the economy group with per capita income higher than US$3,000 (in 1987) benefited much more than the lower-income group. Countries of common-law origin benefited much more than those of continental-law origin. The former socialist economies had little gain associated with the accession. These findings cast serious doubt on the commonly received belief that backwardness in economic development is an advantage of economic growth. Instead, the findings provide evidence that having proper initial economic institutions is important for economic development via globalization for a developing economy.

References

Brecher, Richard, and Carlos Diaz-Alejandro. 1977. Tariffs, foreign capital, and immiserizing growth. *Journal of International Economics* 7 (2): 317–22.

Fernandez de Cordoba, Gonzalo, and Timothy J. Kehoe. 2000. Capital flows and real exchange rate fluctuations following Spain's entry into the European community. *Journal of International Economics* 51 (1): 49–78.

Gerschenkron, Alexander. 1962. *Economic backwardness in historic perspective.* Cambridge, Mass.: Harvard University Press.

Harrison, Ann. 1996. Openness and growth: A time-series, cross-country analysis for developing countries. *Journal of Development Economics* 48:419–47.

Heckman, James, and V. Joseph Hotz. 1989. Choosing among alternative nonexperimental methods for estimating the impact of social programs: The case of manpower training. *Journal of the American Statistical Association* 84:862–80.

Kenny, Charles, and David Williams. 2001. What do we know about economic growth? Or, why don't we know very much? *World Development* 29 (1): 1–22.

La Porta, Rafael, Florencio Lopez-de-Silanes, Andrei Shleifer, and Robert Vishny. 1999. The quality of government. *Journal of Law and Economics and Organization* 154 (1): 222–79.

MacKinlay, Graig. 1997. Event studies in economics and finance. *Journal of Economic Literature* 35 (1): 13–39.

Milthorp, Peter. 1997. Integration of former Soviet Union economies in transition into the World Trade Organization. *Economics of Transition* 5 (1): 215–23.

Mutti, Jack, Rachelle Sampson, and Bernard Yeung. 2000. The effects of the Uruguay Round: Empirical evidence from US industry. *Contemporary Economic Policy* 18 (1): 59–86.

Nelson, Richard R., and Bhaven N. Sampat. 2001. Making sense of institutions as a factor shaping economic performance. *Journal of Economic Behavior & Organization* 44 (1): 31–54.

Rodriguez, Francisco, and Dani Rodrik. 2000. Trade policy and economic growth: A skeptic's guide to the cross-national evidence. Harvard University, Kennedy School of Government. Working Paper.
Rodrik, Dani. 1997. Has globalization gone too far? Washington, D.C.: Institute for International Economics, March. Mimeograph.
Rose, Andrew K. 2002. Do we really know that WTO increases trade? NBER Working Paper no. 9273. Cambridge, Mass.: National Bureau of Economic Research.
Stiglitz, Joseph E. 2002. *Globalization and its discontents.* New York: W. W. Norton.

Comment Simon Johnson

The authors have selected an excellent topic. Does joining the WTO help or hurt economic growth? There are some interesting rival hypotheses. For example, perhaps foreign direct investment will decline after a country joins the WTO, as firms no longer have an incentive to engage in "tariff wall jumping." More generally, there may be two forms of WTO accession: those that genuinely promote more trade and growth, and those that primarily benefit a controlling elite by facilitating greater expropriation of one form or another. It is also theoretically possible that WTO accession might lead to more or less political instability.

This paper offers an appealing event-study-type methodology to study accession. Looking at a window of (–5, +10) and using annual data and country fixed effects for all countries that joined GATT/WTO since 1960 is surely a sensible way to proceed. It is also attractive to start with simple measures and then add more complex indicators of performance. Dividing countries into low, middle, and high income is reasonable, although it does prompt the reader to wonder about deeper underlying causes of per capita income levels (e.g., is this the result of institutions or geographical conditions or something else that might cause an important omitted variable problem?) Examining the effect of initial institutions is also an important step.

The authors' findings are thought-provoking, and they have done us a great service by pulling together an invaluable data set (table 4.1 will be widely cited). I'm sure they (and others) will subject their results to a great deal more in the form of robustness checks, particularly looking at the effects of institutions. Examining five-year average values or decade averages (before and after) would be appealing. We also need more detail on when exactly negotiations began, in order to think about alternative "win-

Simon Johnson is the Ronald A. Kurtz Associate Professor at the Sloan School of Management, Massachusetts Institute of Technology, and a faculty research fellow of the National Bureau of Economic Research.

dows." Given the work by Dani Rodrik and Bill Easterly on the slowdown of growth in developing countries, we particularly need to see various alternative controls for time effects (Rodrik 1999; Easterly 2001).

Looking forward to the research that will build on this paper, researchers must get to grips with the mechanism through which WTO accession brings economic benefits. Reducing tariffs and nontariff barriers may have direct positive effects. It could also be the case that accession is a form of commitment by local elites not to engage in some forms of expropriation. This appears to be an important role of European Union (EU) accession in Eastern Europe—political elites in Hungary and Poland, for example, are much more constrained than their counterparts in Belarus and Ukraine, because breaking with the EU accession process would have large political and economic costs. But how general is this effect?

Future research could use the method of Rajan and Zingales (1998), or perhaps the recent alternative proposal of Fisman and Love (2002), to look more at which sectors grow faster and slower with WTO accession. To what extent do the sectoral effects vary with income level or institutions? Is there any indication that the rich and powerful within countries gain disproportionately?

The main worry with this kind of study is of course identification. Perhaps it is the case that countries join the WTO when they were going to grow anyway. The authors again take an important step in their analysis of selection, but in the next round of research, we should look for situations in which the trade regime is in some sense exogenous—that is, the effect of joining the WTO is well identified. Alternatively, we need an instrumental variable that both is correlated with trade liberalization and can be excluded from the main regression. Studies of trade and financial liberalization currently lack such instruments.

The emerging conventional wisdom on liberalizations seems to be some form of the new "Columbia School" view. There are differences in the views of Bhagwati, Sachs, Stiglitz, and Rodrik (formerly at Columbia) on this issue, but all warn strongly against financial liberalization, particularly as it may lead to vulnerability to panics and speculative attacks (Bhagwati 1998; Radelet and Sachs 1998; Sachs and Warner 1997; Stiglitz 2002; Rodrik 1997). At the same time, at least three of these four remain broadly sympathetic to trade liberalization. The next generation of research will hopefully test these ideas directly and with properly identified regressions.

Some of the historical evidence should make us cautious about expecting all trade liberalizations to have positive effects. The rapid growth of external trade in Europe after 1500 was associated with very different economic and political changes in different places. In Northwest Europe the growth of trade led to broad-based economic progress, contributing to the conditions that made the Industrial Revolution possible. In Spain and Portugal, the growth of trade strengthened absolutist monarchs as they captured important new cash revenues. And in Eastern Europe the evidence suggests that growing trade may have contributed to the so-called "second serfdom." Who wins and who loses from the growth of trade may depend a great deal on the precise nature of initial institutions and the distribution of power within society.

References

Bhagwati, Jagdish N. 1998. The capital myth. *Foreign Affairs* 77 (3): 7–12.

Easterly, William. 2001. The lost decades: The developing countries' stagnation in spite of policy reform. *Journal of Economic Growth* 9:135–57.

Fisman, Raymond, and Inessa Love. 2002. Patterns of industrial development revisited: The role of finance. Columbia University and The World Bank. Unpublished manuscript.

Radelet, Steven, and Jeffrey D. Sachs. 1998. The East Asian financial crisis: Diagnosis, remedies, prospects. *Brookings Papers on Economic Activity,* Issue no. 1: 1–90.

Rajan, Raghuram, and Luigi Zingales. 1998. Financial dependence and growth. *American Economic Review* 88:559–86.

Rodrik, Dani. 1997. Has globalization gone too far? Washington, D.C.: Institute for International Economics, March.

———. 1999. Where did all the growth go? External Shocks, Social Conflict, and Growth Collapses. *Journal of Economic Growth* 4 (4): 385–412.

Sachs, Jeffrey D., and Andrew Warner. 1997. Fundamental sources of long-run growth. *American Economic Review* 87 (2): 184–88.

Stiglitz, Joseph E. 2002. *Globalization and its discontents.* New York: W. W. Norton.

Comment

Epictetus E. Patalinghug

Introduction

The study by Li and Wu attempts to assess the impact of the GATT/WTO accession on the domestic economy. It adopts the event-study method to assess the impact of the WTO on the domestic economy. The authors used this method in two ways: (1) to assess the impact of the accession on each of the economic variables (e.g., GDP, capital formation, import, export, and FDI), and (2) to assess the impact of the accession on the economywide productivity. The following discussion provides comments on the link between the WTO accession and market access. It likewise dis-

Epictetus E. Patalinghug is professor of economics and management in the College of Business Administration, University of the Philippines.

cusses the logic of the regression results vis-à-vis the assumed hypothesis. And it concludes with suggestions on improving the style of the paper.

WTO Accession and Market Access

The objective of assessing the impact of the GATT/WTO accession on the domestic economy is a desirable one. However, the assumption that accession is identical with market access, as well as with the reduction in tariff and nontariff barriers, is not. The hypothesis of the study that GATT/WTO accession usually means better market access for foreign investors and therefore stimulates the inflow of FDI is most probably inappropriate. In reality, WTO accession in many countries may not be identical with market access or tariff reduction several years after accession. Several countries negotiate the magnitude, extent, and timing of their market access or tariff-reduction commitments before accession. Consider the case of two WTO member countries: the Philippines and Thailand. The Philippines was accepted into GATT in 1979 and Thailand in 1982. But until very recently trade in motor vehicles, cement, sugar, and rice (among other commodities) between the two countries is still hampered by relatively high tariff rates.

Special and differential treatment (SND) for developing countries is acknowledged as an integral part of WTO negotiations and WTO rules. The Agreement on Agriculture provided SND to developing countries in the form of (1) lesser reduction commitments on market access, export subsidies, and domestic support; (2) longer time frames for implementation of commitments; (3) greater market access in developed countries; and (4) exemption from reduction commitments (e.g., investment subsidies, agricultural input subsidies, subsidies to reduce marketing cost of agricultural products, etc.). This aspect of WTO negotiation implies that accession is not identical with market access.

In some instances, trade patterns are not very sensitive to changes in tariff rates. The volume of intra–Association of Southeast Asian Nations (ASEAN) trade has not increased beyond the 17–23 percent range after the gradual implementation of the ASEAN Free Trade Area (AFTA) tariff rates. Singapore accounts for most of the intra-ASEAN trade (Austria and Avila 2001; Teh 1993). On the contrary, the volume of trade between individual ASEAN countries and the United States or Japan (e.g., Singapore–United States trade or Thailand-Japan trade) is much larger than any bilateral intra-ASEAN trade. This pattern continues even if WTO tariff rates are relatively higher than AFTA tariff rates.

Regression Results

The regression results on the impact of the accessions on the growth rate of GDP indicate that high-income economies experienced a positive impact of about a 1.5 percent to 1.6 percent increase in the GDP growth rate per year for ten years after accession, while no significant increase was observed for low-income economies after accession. Similarly, high-income countries experienced significant increases in growth of capital, growth of import, growth of export, growth of FDI, and growth of total factor productivity as compared to low-income countries. Based on these findings, the authors conclude that the advantage of backwardness as hypothesized by Gerschenkron does not apply in this case; rather, they assert that what is more important are the initial economic institutions before joining GATT/WTO. The authors' empirical findings are consistent with the growing perception of less-developed country (LDC) members of WTO that the 1995 WTO agreements were disadvantageous to them. These findings provide support to LDCs' attempt to eliminate or prohibit in the WTO Agreement on Agriculture the practice of twenty-five developed countries of continuing to provide export subsidies. This is the biggest contributor to unfair trade in agriculture.

One conclusion from the authors' findings is that trade liberalization due to WTO accession has a varying impact on each country (low-income country vs. high-income country, or common-law country vs. socialist country). Some studies suggested that trade-GDP ratios fall as per capita income rises, while other studies showed that export-promoting economies exhibited a rise in trade-GDP ratios as per capita incomes grew rapidly. Among the GATT/WTO member countries, export-promoting countries may emerge as more successful compared to import-substituting countries (Bhagwati 1988). Although WTO accession can be interpreted as accelerating the momentum for a freer world trading system, this study's findings support the view that trade-GDP ratio increases as per capita income rises. But its most revealing finding is that WTO accession is not an opportunity to level the playing field. On the contrary, it favors high-income economies that are initially endowed with good economic institutions.

Selection Endogeneity

In addressing the issue of selection endogeneity, the authors employed two measures of the selection variable: one using the Heckman-Hotz method, and the other using the estimated qualification date that is predicted by fitting a probit regression method. In analyzing its findings, the authors conveniently cite the estimates from either measure, whichever is significant or sensible. Since the impact of the economic variables on accession does not change significantly by using either of the two alternative approaches to control for the selection effect, the paper would be reduced to a manageable length if it simply presented the regression estimates using the Heckman-Hotz method. In its present form, more than 50 percent of the paper consists of tables from alternative regression runs, whose inclusion in the paper has marginal contribution in the analysis of its findings.

Conclusion

Nevertheless, this paper is a pioneering effort at assessing the impact of GATT/WTO accession across countries.

References

Austria, Myrna, and John Lawrence Avila. 2001. Looking beyond AFTA: Prospects and challenges for inter-regional trade. *Philippine Journal of Development* 28 (2): 143–66.

Bhagwati, Jagdish. 1988. Export-promoting trade strategy: Issues and evidence. *World Bank Research Observer* 3 (1): 27–57.

Teh, Robert. 1993. Implementing the CEPT mechanism and Philippine trade and resource flows. In *The ASEAN free trade area,* ed. Mario Lamberte, 21–38. Manila: Philippine Economic Society.

5

The Contribution of FDI Flows to Domestic Investment in Capacity, and Vice Versa

Assaf Razin

5.1 Introduction

The term "foreign direct investment" (FDI) usually brings to mind a significant contribution of FDI to domestic investment and to capital inflows. However, there has been a lot of skepticism concerning the contribution of FDI to these engines of growth. As noted by Froot (1991), FDI (the purchase by a domestic resident of a controlling stake in a foreign company) actually requires neither capital flows nor investment in capacity. Conceptually, FDI is an extension of corporate control over international boundaries. Froot put it succinctly: "When Japanese-owned Bridgestone takes control over the US firm Firestone, capital need not flow into the US. US domestic lenders can largely finance the equity purchase. Any borrowing by Bridgestone from foreign-based third parties also does not qualify as FDI (although it would count as an inflow of portfolio capital into the US). And, of course, in such acquisition there is no investment expenditure; merely an international transfer in the title of corporate assets." Does this example capture the essence of FDI in emerging economies?

The answer we provide in this paper, based on a new theory and new empirical evidence, is that FDI flows do play an important role in the skimming of high-productivity investment projects and thereby contribute significantly to domestic investment in both the quantity and the quality dimensions.

Assaf Razin is Mario Henrique Simonsen Professor of Public Economics at Tel Aviv University, Friedman Professor of International Economics at Cornell University, and a research associate of the National Bureau of Economic Research.

5.2 Old and New Theories

Theories of FDI can essentially be divided into two categories: micro (industrial organization) theories and macro finance (cost of capital) theories. The early literature that explains FDI in microeconomic terms focuses on market imperfections and on the desire of multinational enterprises to expand their market power (see Caves 1971). Subsequent literature centered more on firm-specific advantages, owing to product superiority or cost advantages that stemmed from economies of scale, multiplant economies and advanced technology, or superior marketing and distribution (see Helpman 1984). According to this view, multinationals find it cheaper to expand directly in a foreign country, rather than through trade, in cases where the advantages associated with cost or product are based on internal, indivisible assets based on knowledge and technology. Alternative explanations for FDI have focused on regulatory restrictions, including tariffs and quotas, that either encourage or discourage cross-border acquisitions, depending on whether one considers horizontal or vertical integrations.

Studies examining the macroeconomic effects of exchange rate on FDI focused on the positive effects of an exchange rate depreciation of the host country on FDI inflows, because it lowers the cost of production and investment in the host countries, raising the profitability of FDI. The wealth effect is another channel through which a depreciation of the real exchange rate could raise FDI. A depreciation of the real exchange rate, by raising the relative wealth of foreign firms, could make it easier for those firms to use retained profits to finance investment abroad and to post a collateral in borrowing from domestic lenders in the host country capital market (see Froot 1991 and Razin and Sadka 2003). There is also a large literature on different forms of spillovers from inward investors in the form of new technologies, new ideas, and capital accumulation on the growth of output in the domestic economy (see Blomström, Kokko, and Globerman 2001).

What is the essential difference between portfolio investment and FDI investment from the point of view of corporate governance?

Management under portfolio equity ownership may be plagued by a free-rider problem. Under dispersed ownership, if an individual shareholder does something to improve the quality of management, the benefits will also accrue to all other shareholders (see Hart 2000). In contrast, the FDI investor, who is endowed with management skills and gains control of the firm, has better incentives to pursue proper monitoring of management and will be in a better position to micromanage the firm. Furthermore, based on possessing "intangible capital" in his or her source country, the FDI investor can apply more efficient management standards in the host country compared to domestic investors. Thus, the unique advantage to

FDI, which has only recently been explored, is the potential for superior micromanagement, based on the specialization in niches of industry. Important issues with FDI from this standpoint are (1) what the salient characteristics are of the free-FDI-flows equilibrium, when FDI investors take control over domestic firms; (2) what constitutes the gains from FDI flows to the host economy, given that the foreign investors appropriate the private rewards resulting from their superior management skills; and (3) whether or not the free-FDI-flows regime is more efficient than free-portfolio-flows regime.

In an integrated capital market, with full information, all forms of capital flows (FDI, loans, and portfolio equity and debt) are indistinguishable. In the presence of incomplete information, these flows are significantly different from one another. In Razin and Sadka (2002), we developed a stylized model of FDI in the presence of imperfect information with respect to the firm's productivity.

We formalized the unique advantage of FDI investment over other types of investment in a stylized model. Suppose that initially all firms are still owned by original (domestic) uninformed owners, and suppose that the productivity shock is purely idiosyncratic. At the beginning of the first period, when investment decisions are made, firms are still uninformed about the productivity shock (the productivity level of the specific firm that they own). It will be revealed only in the second period, when output from new capital becomes public knowledge. In order to make new investment the firm must first incur a fixed setup cost. As the firms are all ex ante identical, if they have to make the investment decision based on this level of information, they will all invest *the same,* in accordance with the expected level of the productivity factor. Assume now that at this stage, before the productivity factor is known, foreign direct investors step in. Upon acquiring and effectively managing the firm, the FDI investor can better monitor the productivity of the firm than his or her domestic investor counterpart. He or she can thus fine-tune the level of capital stock more closely to the value of the productivity factor. Anticipating this fine-tuned investment schedule, the value of the firm to the *potential* FDI investor is *larger* than the reservation value to the original owner and the corresponding bid value to potential domestic investors. Therefore, FDI investors will outbid domestic investors for the firms in the domestic industry. Competition among potential FDI investors will drive the price up close to the price that reflects the upgraded management of the firm. The initial domestic owners will gain the rent, which is equal to difference between the FDI investor's shadow price and the initial owner's reservation price.

If the competition between potential FDI investors is *perfect,* all the benefits from the superior FDI management skills accrue to the host economy, leaving the FDI investors with a return on their investment just equalling the world rate of interest. The gains to the host economy from FDI inflows can in this case be classified into two categories. First, there are the conventional gains that stem from opening the economy to the new flow of capital, thereby allowing a more efficient *intertemporal* allocation of consumption (e.g., via consumption smoothing). Second, there are the intrinsic gains associated with the superior micromanagement by FDI investors. The entire gain of the FDI investors is captured by the domestic economy because of assumed perfect competition among these investors over the domestic firms. If, however, there is imperfect competition among FDI investors, the gains will split between them and the host country.

The economic gains from FDI, relative to portfolio inflows, lie only in the *efficiency of investment,* since in both cases there are consumption-smoothing effects and the same world interest rate (r) prevails in the host country in both the FDI-flows regime and the portfolio-flows regime. In other words, the gains from FDI, in comparison to portfolio flows, do not include the traditional gains from opening up the domestic capital market to foreign capital inflows because these traditional gains are also present in the portfolio-flows regime. Razin and Sadka (2002) were able also to show that, under some plausible conditions on the form of the production function, the *size* of the aggregate stock of capital is larger under FDI than under portfolio equity flows.

5.3 The Evidence[1]

Like its theoretical counterpart, empirical work has tended to focus either on underlying factors to explain the location of FDI flows across countries or on explaining the cyclical behaviour of FDI flows using macroeconomic variables and assessing the contribution of FDI flows to investment and growth.

To what extent is there empirical support for such claims of the significant impact of FDI on domestic investment?

5.3.1 Previous Literature

A comprehensive study by Bosworth and Collins (1999) provides evidence concerning the effect of capital inflows on domestic investment for fifty-eight developing countries during 1978–95. The authors distinguish among three types of inflows: FDI, portfolio investment, and other financial flows (primarily bank loans). Bosworth and Collins find that an increase of a dollar in capital inflows is associated with an increase in domestic investment of about fifty cents. (Both capital inflows and domestic

1. See Borensztein, DeGregorio, and Lee (1998) and Bosworth and Collins (1999) for a similar panel data analysis.

investment are expressed as percentages of gross domestic product [GDP]). This result, however, masks significant differences among different types of inflows. Foreign direct investment appears to bring about close to a one-for-one increase in domestic investment; there is virtually no discernible relationship between portfolio inflows and investment (little or no impact), and the impact of loans falls between those of the other two. These results hold both for the fifty-eight-country sample and for a subset of eighteen emerging markets (see fig. 5.1).

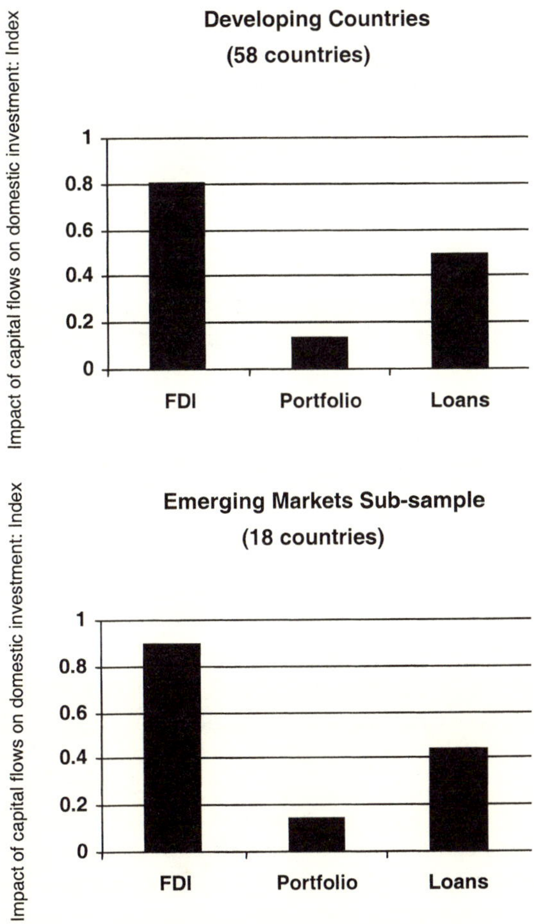

Fig. 5.1 Estimated impact of capital flows on domestic investment

Source: Loungani and Razin (2001), based on Bosworth and Collins (1999).

Note: The height of the bar represents the estimated impact of $1 of the indicated capital flow on domestic investment.

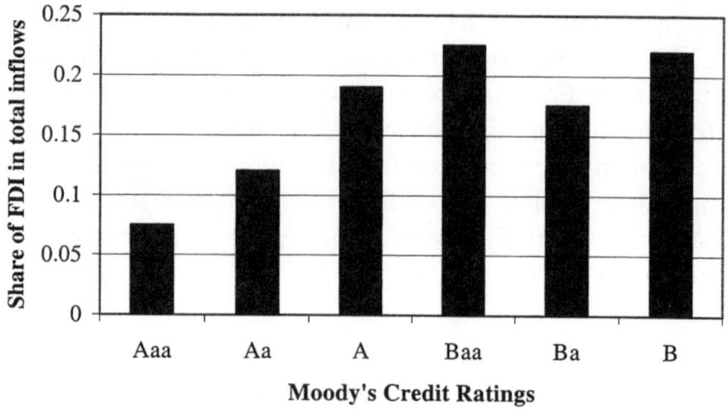

Fig. 5.2 FDI's share in total inflows is higher in countries with weaker credit ratings
Source: Albuquerque (2003).

An additional (striking) feature of FDI flows that was noted in previous literature is that the share of FDI in total inflows is higher in riskier countries, as measured either by countries' credit ratings for sovereign (government) debt or other indicators of country risk (see fig. 5.2). There is also some evidence that the FDI share is higher in countries where the quality of corporate governance institutions is lower. What can explain these seemingly paradoxical findings? One explanation is that FDI is more likely, compared with other forms of capital flows, to take place in countries with missing or inefficient markets. In such settings, foreign investors will prefer to operate directly instead of relying on local financial markets, suppliers, or legal arrangements.

5.3.2 Determinants of Foreign Direct Investment Flows: A Gravity Model

Razin, Rubinstein, and Sadka (2003) employ a gravity model of bilateral FDI and portfolio capital flows in order to explain determinants of the mobility of financial capital across countries. The authors estimate jointly a participation equation (the decision whether to export FDI at all) and a gravity equation (the decision how much FDI exports to make). They find that the error terms in these two equations are negatively and significantly correlated. The negative correlation suggests that the source countries with relatively low set up costs of FDI investment are also those with high marginal productivity of capital. These findings are summarized in table 5.1.

In Mody, Razin, and Sadka (2002) we interpret the industry specialization measure in the source country as an indication of a comparative advantage to the potential foreign direct investors in eliciting good invest-

Table 5.1 **Determinants of FDI in a Gravity Equation and Selection Equation**

	Gravity	Selection
Host GDP per capita	0.762	0.264
	(0.054)	(0.030)
Source GDP per capita	0.002	1.928
	(0.207)	(0.073)
Common language	1.209	0.024
	(0.085)	(0.049)
Average years of schooling (host)	0.087	0.000
	(0.023)	(0.014)
Average years of schooling (source)	0.295	0.058
	(0.025)	(0.015)
rho	–0.585	–0.585
	(0.077)	(0.077)
No. of observations	9,848	9,843

Source: Razin, Rubinstein, and Sadka (2003).

Notes: Maximum livelihood estimation: FDI (real US$) from source to destination country (1981–98, three-year averages). Numbers in parentheses are standard errors.

ment opportunities in the destination country, relative to domestic investors in the host country. This advantage may stem, for example, from the ability of FDI investors to apply better industry-specific micromanagement standards. To capture this element we assume a lower cost of cream skimming (of high-productivity firms) on the part of foreign direct investors. The second category of variables underscores the role of information as a determinant of FDI inflows. As banks are the main providers of debt capital in emerging markets, and they usually conduct rigorous scrutiny of the creditworthiness of their debtors, we conjecture that, ceteris paribus, firms with high debt-equity ratio tend to be more transparent. In this case, the advantage of FDI investors in their cream-skimming skills (that is, the selection of high-productivity firms) is less pronounced and therefore FDI inflows are less abundant.

5.4 Capital Inflows, Investment in Capacity, and Growth: Panel Data

5.4.1 Empirical Framework for the Panel-Data Analysis

In this subsection I describe the econometric approach for the estimation of the interactions between domestic investment, FDI flows, international loans, and international portfolio investment. The sample consists of sixty-four developing countries, including Israel,[2] in the period 1976 to

2. This section draws on Hecht, Razin, and Shinar (2003).

1997 (twenty-two years in total; see appendix A). All the variables but the dummies are expressed in terms of GDP percentages. The source of data is the World Development Indicators (WDI) database (see appendix A). The system of equations is given by

1. $I = \beta_{i1j} + \beta_{i2}I(-1) + \beta_{i3}\text{DY} + \beta_{i4}\text{DY}(-1) + \beta_{i5}\text{FDI} + \beta_{i6}P + \beta_{i7}L + \beta_{i8}G$

2. $\text{FDI} = \beta_{f1j} + \beta_{f2}\text{FDI}(-1) + \beta_{f3}I + \beta_{f4}\text{DY} + \beta_{f5}\text{DY}(-1) + \beta_{f6}\text{Res2}$

3. $L = \beta_{l1j} + \beta_{l2}L(-1) + \beta_{l3}I + \beta_{l4}\text{DY} + \beta_{l5}\text{DY}(-1)$

4. $P = \beta_{p1j} + \beta_{p2}P(-1) + \beta_{p3}I + \beta_{p4}\text{DY} + \beta_{p5}\text{DY}(-1) + \beta_{p6}\text{Res1}$,

where

I = gross domestic investment (% of GDP)
FDI = foreign direct investment (% of GDP)
L = bank loans (% of GDP)
P = portfolio investment flows (% of GDP)
DY = annual percentage growth rate of GDP
G = general government consumption (% of GDP)
Res1 = multiple exchange rates (single exchange rate = 0; more than one = 1)
Res2 = restrictions on current account transactions (no controls = 0; controls = 1)
j = country index, j = 01, 02, 03, . . . , 64

The four-equation system has four endogenous variables: I, FDI, P, and L as dependent variables and observations. Every equation also includes, as an explanatory variable, the dependent variable lagged one period. The exogenous variables used for identification are government expenditure (G), a dummy variable for multiple exchange rates (Res1), a dummy variable for restrictions on current account transactions (Res2), and lagged dependent variables.

Table 5.2 describes the interactions among the endogenous and the exogenous variables in the four-equation system.

Two versions are estimated: ordinary least squares (OLS) regressions, as a benchmark, and two-stage least squares (TSLS) regressions with a country-specific effect. To avoid nonstationarity of the residuals in the four-equation system, we introduce lagged dependent variables on the right-hand side of the equation system.

5.4.2 Domestic Investment: Findings

Tables 5.3 through 5.6 present the estimation results, and we discuss them equation by equation.

Table 5.2 **Expected Interactions among Endogenous and Exogenous Variables**

	Endogenous Variables				Exogenous Variables								
	FDI	*P*	*L*	*I*	*I*(–1)	FDI(–1)	*P*(–1)	*L*(–1)	DY	DY(–1)	*G*	Res2	Res1
I	+	+	+	+				+	+	+			
FDI				+		+			+	+			+
P				+			+		+	+			+
L				+				+	+	+			

Table 5.3 **Determinants of Domestic Investment in Capacity**

	OLS	TSLS
Foreign direct investment, FDI	0.16	0.23
	(5.2)	(6.8)
Loan inflows, *L*	–0.06	0.12
	(–2.2)	(3.0)
Portfolio inflows, *P*	0.03	0.18
	(0.3)	(2.0)
Lagged domestic investment, *I*(–1)	0.87	0.66
	(96.1)	(51.2)
Output growth, DY	0.15	0.15
	(10.4)	(10.9)
Lagged output growth, DY(–1)	0.06	0.06
	(3.8)	(4.4)
Government expenditure, *G*	0.03	0.01
	(2.3)	(0.5)
Long-run effect of FDI on *I*	0.94	0.68
Long-run effect of *L* on *I*	–0.35	0.35
Long-run effect of *P* on *I*	0.18	0.53
R^2 adjusted	0.40	0.53

Notes: Estimated using Eviews software. *I*(–1), FDI, *P*, *L*, and *G* are in terms of ratio to GDP; *t*-values appear in parentheses.

We start with table 5.3, which describes the effects of capital inflows on domestic investment.

The coefficient of FDI is significant in the OLS and TSLS regressions. Long-run FDI effect on domestic investment is 0.94 in the OLS regression and 0.68 in the TSLS regression. Thus, potential for an upward bias in the OLS estimation procedure appears to be validated. Indeed the effect of FDI on domestic investment is smaller in TSLS regressions. The loan coefficient is significant and positive in both the OLS and the TSLS regressions, at a similar magnitude. However, the long-run coefficient (adjusted

Table 5.4 **Determinants of FDI Inflows**

	OLS	TSLS
Domestic investment, *I*	0.03	0.07
	(3.0)	(5.0)
Lagged foreign direct investment, FDI(–1)	0.60	0.50
	(19.6)	(16.0)
Output growth, DY	0.01	0.02
	(0.10)	(1.6)
Lagged output growth, DY(–1)	–0.01	0.02
	(–0.1)	(1.3)
Dummy for capital controls, Res2 (no controls = 0; controls = 1)	–0.03	–0.02
	(–2.1)	(–1.2)
Long-run effect of *I* on FDI	0.08	0.14
R^2 adjusted	0.13	0.29

Notes: FDI and *I* are in terms of ratio to GDP; *t*-values appear in parentheses.

for the lag structure of the regression) moves up from –0.35 in the TSLS regression. The coefficient of the portfolio-investment variable is not significant in the OLS regression and becomes significant in the TSLS regression. Interestingly, the long-run effect of FDI on domestic investment, 0.68, exceeds the corresponding effect of portfolio investment, 0.53, which in turn exceeds the effect of loans, 0.35.

Foreign Direct Investment Inflows

Table 5.4 describes the effect of domestic investment on FDI inflows, allowing for the effects of a group of other traditional variables, such as growth and capital controls.

The coefficient of domestic investment is positive and significant in both the OLS and the TSLS regression. The long-run effect in the OLS (0.08) is smaller than in the TSLS (0.14).

Loan Inflows

Table 5.5 describes the effect of domestic investment on loan inflows, allowing for the effect of growth. The coefficient of domestic investment is negative and nonsignificant in the OLS but positive and significant in the TSLS regression. The long-run effect moves up from –0.03 in the OLS regression to 0.08 in the TSLS regression.

Portfolio Inflows

Table 5.6 describes the effect of domestic investment on portfolio investment inflows. The explanatory power of the regression is poor, however, and most of the right-hand-side variables have nonsignificant coefficients.

Table 5.5 Determinants of Loans Inflows

	OLS	TSLS
Domestic investment, I	–0.01	0.04
	(1.4)	(3.0)
Lagged L, $L(-1)$	0.66	0.50
	(22.9)	(16.7)
Output growth, DY	0.01	–0.001
	(0.8)	(–0.05)
Lagged output growth, DY(–1)	0.02	–0.0002
	(1.2)	(–0.02)
Long-run effect of I on L	–0.03	0.08
R^2 adjusted	0.24	0.25

Notes: $L(-1)$ and I are in terms of ratio to GDP; t-values appear in parentheses.

Table 5.6 Determinants of Portfolio Investment Inflows

	OLS	TSLS
Domestic investment, I	0.004	0.01
	(0.5)	(0.7)
Lagged portfolio investment, $P(-1)$	0.46	0.40
	(4.8)	(4.8)
Output growth, DY	0.001	–0.001
	(0.2)	(–0.1)
Lagged output growth, DY(–1)	0.007	0.004
	(0.5)	(0.3)
Dummy for multiple exchange rates, Res1 (one exchange rate = 0; more than one = 1)	–0.001	–0.002
	(–0.6)	(–0.9)
Long-run effect of I on portfolio investment flows	0.007	0.017
R^2 adjusted	0.03	0.13

Notes: $P(-1)$ and I are in terms of ratio to GDP; t-values appear in parentheses.

The regression analysis effectively flashes out an autocorrelation process of the portfolio investment flows.

5.4.3 The Contribution of Capital Inflows to Output Growth: Findings

In this section we estimate the contribution of FDI, loans, and portfolio investment to output growths. Similarly to the empirical framework in the first subsection of section 5.3.3, the system of equations is given by

1. $\mathrm{DY} = \beta_{i1j} + \beta_{i2}\mathrm{DY}(-1) + \beta_{i3}I + \beta_{i4}I(-1) + \beta_{i5}\mathrm{FDI} + \beta_{i6}P + \beta_{i7}L + \beta_{i8}G + \beta_{i9}\mathrm{Log(GDP)}$

2. $\mathrm{FDI} = \beta_{f1j} + \beta_{f2}\mathrm{FDI}(-1) + \beta_{f3}\mathrm{DY} + \beta_{f4}I + \beta_{f5}I(-1) + \beta_{f6}\mathrm{Res2} + \beta_{f7}\mathrm{Log(GDP)}$

3. $L = \beta_{l1j} + \beta_{l2}L(-1) + \beta_{l3}\mathrm{DY} + \beta_{l4}I + \beta_{l5}I(-1) + \beta_{l6}\mathrm{Log(GDP)}$

Table 5.7 **Expected Interactions between Endogenous and Exogenous Variables**

	Endogenous Variables				Exogenous Variables									
	FDI	*P*	*L*	DY	DY(–1)	FDI(–1)	*P*(–1)	*L*(–1)	Log(GDP)	*I*	*I*(–1)	*G*	Res2	Res1
I	+	+	+		+				+	+	+	+		
FDI				+		+			+	+	+		+	
P				+			+		+	+	+			+
L				+				+	+	+	+			

4. $$P = \beta_{p1j} + \beta_{p2}P(-1) + \beta_{p3}\text{DY} + \beta_{p4}I + \beta_{p5}I(-1) + \beta_{p6}\text{Res1} + \beta_{p7}\text{Log(GDP)},$$

where

G = general government consumption (% of GDP)
FDI = foreign direct investment (% of GDP)
L = bank loans (% of GDP)
P = portfolio investment flows (% of GDP)
I = gross domestic investment (% of GDP)
DY = annual percentage growth rate of GDP
Res1 = multiple exchange rates (single exchange rate = 0; more than one = 1)
Res2 = restrictions on current account transactions (no controls = 0; controls = 1)
Log (GDP) = natural logarithm of GDP
j = country index, j = 01, 02, 03, . . . , 64

Table 5.7 describes the interactions among the endogenous and the exogenous variable in the four-equation system.

Output Growth

Table 5.8 describes the effects of capital inflows on growth. The coefficient of FDI is significant in the OLS and TSLS regressions. Long-run FDI effect on output growth is 0.1 in the OLS regression and 0.23 in the TSLS regression. The effect of FDI on output growth is smaller in TSLS regressions. Thus, potential for a downward bias in the OLS estimation procedure appears to be demonstrated. The long-run coefficient in the TSLS regression is 0.23.

The loan coefficient and the portfolio coefficient are not significant in the OLS and the TSLS regressions. However, the long-run coefficient of portfolio flows exceeds 0.1.

Foreign Direct Investment Inflows

Table 5.9 describes the effect of output growth on FDI inflows, allowing for the effects of a group of other control variables, such as domestic investment and capital controls.

Table 5.8 **Determinants of Growth**

	OLS	TSLS
Foreign direct investment, FDI	0.09	0.20
	(3.0)	(5.0)
Loan inflows, *L*	0.01	0.02
	(0.2)	(0.4)
Portfolio inflows, *P*	0.05	0.10
	(0.6)	(1.0)
Lagged output growth, DY(–1)	0.12	0.12
	(7.6)	(6.9)
Domestic investment, *I*	0.27	0.24
	(14.4)	(11.4)
Lagged domestic investment, *I*(–1)	–0.22	–0.18
	(–12.1)	(–9.1)
Government expenditure, *G*	–0.19	–0.19
	(–8.4)	(–7.9)
Log(GDP)	–0.01	–0.004
	(–3.3)	(–1.45)
Long-run effect of FDI on DY	0.1	0.23
Long-run effect of *L* on DY	0.01	0.02
Long-run effect of *P* on DY	0.06	0.11
R^2 adjusted	0.04	0.1

Notes: *I*(–1), FDI, *P*, *L*, and *G* are in terms of ratio to GDP; *t*-values appear in parentheses.

Table 5.9 **Determinants of FDI Inflows**

	OLS	TSLS
Output growth, DY	0.02	0.05
	(1.3)	(2.2)
Lagged foreign direct investment, FDI(–1)	0.45	0.49
	(13.4)	(13.4)
Domestic investment, *I*	0.07	0.08
	(3.8)	(3.7)
Lagged domestic investment, *I*(–1)	–0.01	–0.01
	(–0.5)	(–0.4)
Dummy for capital controls, Res2	–0.002	–0.002
(no controls = 0; controls = 1)	(–0.1)	(–0.8)
Log(GDP)	0.01	0.01
	(3.5)	(3.0)
Long-run effect of DY on FDI	0.04	0.05
R^2 adjusted	0.26	0.3

Notes: FDI and *I* are in terms of ratio to GDP; *t*-values appear in parentheses.

The coefficient of output growth is positive and significant in the TSLS regression. The long-run effect is 0.05.

Loan Inflows

Table 5.10 describes the effect of output growth on loans inflows, allowing for the effect of domestic investment. The coefficient of output growth is nonsignificant in both the regressions.

Portfolio Inflows

Table 5.11 describes the effect of output growth on portfolio investment inflows. The explanatory power of the regression is poor, however, and most of the right-hand-side variables have nonsignificant coefficients. The

Table 5.10 Determinants of Loans Inflows

	OLS	TSLS
Output growth, DY	–0.005	–0.005
	(–0.3)	(–0.2)
Lagged *L*, *L*(–1)	0.49	0.49
	(14.2)	(14.0)
Domestic investment, *I*	0.06	0.07
	(3.2)	(3.4)
Lagged domestic investment, *I*(–1)	–0.03	–0.04
	(–1.5)	(–1.8)
Log(GDP)	–0.01	–0.01
	(–2.8)	(–2.3)
Long-run effect of *I* on *L*	–0.01	–0.01
R^2 adjusted	0.27	0.27

Notes: *L*(–1) and *I* are in terms of ratio to GDP; *t*-values appear in parentheses.

Table 5.11 Determinants of Portfolio Investment Inflows

	OLS	TSLS
Output growth, DY	–0.0004	0.003
	(–0.025)	(0.12)
Lagged portfolio investment, *P*(–1)	0.37	0.37
	(3.9)	(3.9)
Domestic investment, *I*	0.003	0.001
	(0.2)	(0.05)
Lagged domestic investment, *I*(–1)	0.01	0.01
	(0.3)	(0.4)
Dummy for multiple exchange rates, Res1	–0.002	–0.002
(one exchange rate = 0; more than one = 1)	(–0.72)	(–0.6)
Long-run effect of *I* on Port	0	0
R^2 adjusted	0.15	0.15

Notes: *P*(–1) and *I* are in terms of ratio to GDP; *t*-values appear in parentheses.

regression analysis effectively flashes out an autocorrelation process of the portfolio investment flows.

Summary

We now summarize the main findings of the panel data analysis concerning interactions between capital inflows and investment in capacity (or growth):

1. Foreign direct investment flows have a larger (independent) effect on domestic investment in capacity (or growth) than loan inflows or foreign-portfolio inflows.
2. Domestic investment in capacity (or output growth) has more pronounced effects on FDI inflows than on either loan inflows or foreign-portfolio inflows.

5.5 Conclusion

Kindleberger (1969) suggests that in order to think about FDI we must ask not why capital might flow into a country, but rather why some particular asset would be worth more under foreign than under domestic control. In this chapter I discuss empirical implications of a new theory of FDI, which captures a unique feature: hands-on management standards that enable investors to react in real time to the changing economic environment surrounding the investors. Equipped with superior managerial skills, foreign direct investors are able to outbid portfolio investors for the top productivity firms in a particular industry in which they have specialized in the source country. Consequently, FDI investors would make investment both larger and higher quality than the domestic investors. The theory can explain both two-way FDI flows among developed countries and one-way FDI flows from developed to developing countries. Gains to the host country from FDI stem from the informational value of FDI.

Main predictions of the theory are consistent with evidence from panel data: Larger FDI coefficients in the domestic-investment and output-growth regressions relative to the portfolio equity and international loans inflow coefficients reflect a unique role for FDI in the domestic investment and growth process.

Does this mean that the chapter brings out a case for subsidizing either domestic investment in capacity (because it brings in more FDI) or FDI (because it helps domestic investment in capacity and growth)?

A cautionary word based on the Irish case is in order. One can argue, convincingly, that the heavy subsidization of FDI inflows in Ireland in the past two decades resulted in impressive GDP growth rates but with less pronounced effect on the well-being of Irish residents, as crudely measured by the Irish gross national product growth rates. Thus, gains to the host country are not fully captured by the increase in domestic investment in capacity, to which FDI inflows give rise.

Appendix A

List of Sixty-Four Countries in HRS Estimation

Algeria
Argentina
Bangladesh
Belize
Benin
Bolivia
Botswana
Brazil
Burkina Faso
Burundi
Cameroon
Central African Republic
Chad
Chile
Colombia
Congo, Republic of the
Costa Rica
Côte d'Ivoire
Dominica
Ecuador
Egypt, Arab Republic of
Gabon
The Gambia
Ghana
Grenada
Guatemala
Guyana
India
Indonesia
Israel
Jamaica
Jordan
Kenya
Korea, Republic of
Lesotho
Malawi
Malaysia
Mali
Mauritania
Mauritius
Mexico
Morocco
Nepal
Niger
Nigeria
Pakistan
Papua New Guinea
Peru
The Philippines
Rwanda
Senegal
Sierra Leone
South Africa
Sri Lanka
St. Vincent and the Grenadines
Swaziland
Syrian Arab Republic
Thailand
Togo
Trinidad and Tobago
Tunisia
Uruguay
Zambia
Zimbabwe

Sources of Data

The principal source of data is the World Bank WDI 2000 CD-ROM.
Capital control data were taken from IMF publications.
A few missing data items regarding loans for Israel were taken from the Bank of Israel resources.

Appendix B

Definitions of Series

Terms of trade: (DTT) adjustment (constant LCU) (NY.TTF.GNFS.KN). The terms-of-trade effect equals capacity to import less exports of goods and services in constant prices. Data are in constant local currency. The change is calculated as the difference from one year to the other.

Public spending on education: (ED3), total (% of GNP, UNESCO) (SE.XPD.TOTL.GN.ZS). Public expenditure on education (total) is the percentage of GNP accounted for by public spending on public education plus subsidies to private education at the primary, secondary, and tertiary levels. For more information, see WDI table 2.9.

GDP per capita: (CY), PPP (current international $) (NY.GDP.PCAP.PP.CD). GDP per capita based on purchasing power parity (PPP). GDP PPP is gross domestic product converted to international dollars using PPP rates. An international dollar has the same purchasing power over GDP as the U.S. dollar in the United States. Data are in current international dollars. For more information, see WDI tables 1.1, 4.11, and 4.12. For the estimation we used the logarithm of CY.

Foreign direct investment: (FDI), net inflows (% of GDP) (BX.KLT.DINV.DT.GD.ZS). Foreign direct investment is net inflows of investment to acquire a lasting management interest (10 percent or more of voting stock) in an enterprise operating in an economy other than that of the investor. It is the sum of equity capital, reinvestment of earnings, other long-term capital, and short-term capital as shown in the balance of payments. For more information, see WDI table 5.1.

General government consumption: (*G*) (% of GDP) (NE.CON.GOVT.ZS). General government consumption includes all current spending for purchases of goods and services (including wages and salaries). It also includes most expenditures on national defense and security but excludes government military expenditures that are part of government capital formation. For more information, see WDI table 4.9.

Gross domestic investment: (*I*) (% of GDP) (NE.GDI.TOTL.ZS). Gross domestic investment consists of outlays on additions to the fixed assets of the economy plus net changes in the level of inventories. Fixed assets include land improvements (fences, ditches, drains, and so on); plant, machinery, and equipment purchases; and the construction of roads, railways, and the like, including commercial and industrial buildings, offices, schools, hospitals, and private residential dwellings. Inventories are stocks of goods held by firms to meet temporary or unexpected fluctuations in production or sales. For more information, see WDI tables 1.4 and 4.9.

GDP growth: (DY) (annual %) (NY.GDP.MKTP.KD.ZG). Annual percentage growth rate of GDP at market prices based on constant local currency. Aggregates are based on constant 1995 U.S. dollars. For more information, see WDI tables 4.1 and 4.2.

Portfolio investment: (*P*), excluding LCFAR (BoP, current US$) (BN.KLT.PTXL.CD). Portfolio investment excluding liabilities constituting foreign authorities' reserves covers transactions in equity securities and debt securities. Data are in current U.S. dollars. This series was divided in the matching GDP to get the portfolio investment as a share of GDP.

Bank and trade-trade lending: (*L*) (PPG + PNG) (NFL, current US$) (DT.NFL.PCBO.CD). Bank and trade-related lending covers commercial bank lending and other private credits. Data are in current U.S. dollars. For more information, see WDI table 6.7. This series was divided in the matching GDP to get the loans flows as a share of GDP.

Total financial flows: (TLY64F) is the sum of FDI, *total portfolio* flows

(PLY64), and *total loans* (OLY64), where flows are divided by GDP. Data include sixty-four developing countries.

Capital controls: Data on capital controls for all IMF member countries, years 1966–97. Dummy takes the value 1 when a restriction is in place, and 0 otherwise.

1. Multiple exchange rates (Res1)
2. Restrictions on current account transactions (Res2)
3. Restrictions on capital account transactions (Res3)
4. Surrender of export proceeds (Res4)

References

Albuquerque, Rui. 2003. The composition of capital flows: Risk sharing through foreign direct investment. *Journal of International Economics* 61:353–83.

Blomström, Magnus, Ari Kokko, and Steven Globerman. 2001. The determinants of host country spillovers from foreign direct investment: A review and synthesis of the literature. In *Inward investment, technological change and growth: The impact of multinational corporations on the U.K. economy,* ed. N. Pain, 34–65. New York: Palgrave Press.

Borensztein, Eduardo, Jose De Gregorio, and Jong-Wha Lee. 1998. How does foreign direct investment affect growth? *Journal of International Economics* 45:115–35.

Bosworth, Barry P., and Susan M. Collins. 1999. Capital flows to developing economies: Implications for saving and investment. *Brookings Papers on Economic Activity,* Issue no. 1:143–69.

Caves, Richard E. 1971. International corporations: The industrial economics of foreign investment. *Economica* 38:1–27.

Froot, Kenneth A. 1991. Japanese foreign direct investment. In *US-Japan economic forum,* ed. Martin Feldstein and Yoshi Kosai. Cambridge, Mass.: National Bureau of Economic Research and Japan Center for Economic Growth.

Hart, Oliver. 2000. Financial contracting. *Journal of Economic Literature* 39 (4): 1079–110.

Hecht, Joel, Assaf Razin, and Nitsan Shinar. 2003. Interactions between capital flows and investment. Foreign Exchange Activity Department working paper. Jerusalem: Bank of Israel, February.

Helpman, Elhanan. 1984. A simple theory of international trade with multinational corporations. *Journal of Political Economy* 92:451–71.

Kindleberger, Charles P. 1969. *American business abroad: Six lectures on direct investment.* New Haven, Conn.: Yale University Press.

Loungani, Prakash, and Assaf Razin. 2001. How beneficial is foreign direct investment for developing countries? *Finance and Development* 38 (2): 6–10.

Mody, Ashoka, Assaf Razin, and Efraim Sadka. 2002. The role of information in driving FDI: Theory and evidence. NBER Working Paper no. 9255. Cambridge, Mass.: National Bureau of Economic Research.

Razin, Assaf, and Efraim Sadka. 2002. *Labor, capital, and finance: International flows.* New York: Cambridge University Press.

———. 2003. Gains from FDI inflows with incomplete information. *Economics Letters* 78 (1): 71–77.

Razin, Assaf, Yona Rubinstein, and Efraim Sadka. 2003. Which countries export FDI, and how much. NBER Working Paper no. 10145. Cambridge, Mass.: National Bureau of Economic Research.

Comment Kyoji Fukao

Assaf Razin's paper proposes an interesting new theory of foreign direct investment (FDI). The new theory is based on the following two assumptions:

1. Some foreign investors can get information on the optimal investment level of local firms at a lower fixed cost than firms in the host country.
2. A potential buyer needs to acquire the local firm in order to apply its technology.

According to Razin, FDI is the result of informational advantages of foreign firms. In contrast with this, the standard theory regards FDI as international movements of intangible assets, such as the stock of technological knowledge or marketing know-how.[1] Foreign firms conduct direct investment because they can carry out production at a lower cost or have better marketing skills. Since international mergers and acquisitions (M&As) have increased substantially in the last decade and asymmetric information issues seem to play an important role in M&A processes, Razin's new theory is very timely and provides a useful contribution to the study on international M&As.

I have three comments. My first comment is on the applicability of the new theory to "green field" investments. Although cross-border M&As have rapidly increased especially in the case of FDI among developed economies, the majority of direct investments into developing economies are still of the "green field" type. Table 5C.1 shows the share of M&A-type investments in total FDI flows in each region during the period from 1997 to 1999. According to this table, in the case of FDI inflows into developing Asia, only 21 percent of total FDI consisted of M&As. In Razin's paper the new theory is applied to the empirical study based on data of total FDI flows. I think that the author had better elaborate on the applicability of his new theory to green field investments.

My second comment concerns the identification problem. In the empirical part of the paper, the author provides several interesting pieces of evi-

Kyoji Fukao is professor of economics at the Institute of Economic Research, Hitotsubashi University, and a fellow at the Research Institute of Economy, Trade and Industry.

1. On the standard theory of FDI, see Caves (1982) and Dunning (1977).

Table 5C.1 **Cross-Border M&As as a Percentage of FDI Inflows, 1997–99**

	%
United States	78
Western Europe	79
Latin America	59
Central and Eastern Europe	34
Developing Asia	21
Developing countries total	30

Source: UNCTAD, *World Investment Report 2000,* 2000.

dence that are consistent with the prediction of the theory: Compared with portfolio investment, inward FDI has a larger positive effect on domestic investment and economic growth in the host country. Although such findings are interesting, the "evidence" provided does not prove the validity of the new theory since we can also explain these phenomena using the standard theory. According to the standard theory, FDI will increase the stock of intangible assets, such as technological knowledge or marketing know-how in the host country, which will enhance domestic investment and economic growth. I hope that in future the author provides us with some new implications and tests by which we can empirically distinguish the new theory from the standard theory.

My last comment is on the relationship between a parent company and its affiliates abroad. In East Asian manufacturing industry, there exist close linkages and coordination between parents and their affiliates. Production processes are commonly fragmented within an enterprise group, and unskilled labor–intensive processes are located in developing countries such as China.[2] Multinationals engage in FDI in developing East Asia not to make profits from their superior knowledge on investment timing but to establish efficient global production networks by combining their advanced technologies with developing countries' cheap labor.

To sum up my comments, Razin's paper gives us important new insights on FDI, especially on M&As, but it seems that we cannot directly apply his theory to efficiency-seeking green field–type FDI in manufacturing industries, which is the dominant form of FDI in East Asia.

References

Caves, Richard E. 1982. *Multinational enterprise and economic analysis.* Cambridge, U.K.: Cambridge University Press.

Dunning, John H. 1977. Trade, location of economic activity, and the multinational enterprise: A search for an eclectic approach. In *The international allo-*

2. On Japanese firms' intra–firm-group fragmentation of production processes, see Kimura (2001).

cation of economic activity, ed. B. Ohlin, P. O. Hesselborn, and P. M. Wijkman, 395–418. London: Macmillan.

Kimura, Fukunari. 2001. Fragmentation, internalization, and inter-firm linkages: Evidence from the micro data of Japanese manufacturing firms. In *Global production and trade in East Asia,* ed. Leonard K. Cheng and Henryk Kiezkowski, 129–52. Boston: Kluwer Academic.

Comment Dean Parham

Assaf Razin's paper is now rather different from the one he presented at EASE-13. I have adapted my comments by generalizing my original remarks and adding a few more that are specifically directed at the paper as it now stands. My remarks have been informed in part by material provided in a recent study of foreign direct investment by the Productivity Commission (2002).

Foreign direct investment (FDI) is an important issue. It has been growing faster than world GDP, especially since the late 1990s (fig. 5C.1). The author's work investigates "commercial" motivations for FDI, which are becoming more important in a world of fewer barriers to investment flows and growing maturity of financial markets and institutions. The relative importance of commercial motives was illustrated in a recent survey of Australian firms engaging in outward FDI (figs. 5C.2 and 5C.3).

The paper also distinguishes between FDI, portfolio investment, and loans. It recognizes that free-rider problems induce different behavior on the part of FDI and portfolio investors. Foreign direct investment is seen to promote growth through a higher amount and more efficient allocation of investment. Some prima facie support for this proposition lies in the improvement (or lessened deterioration) in capital productivity growth in Australia that has coincided with increased inward FDI in the 1980s and 1990s (fig. 5C.4).

The examination of FDI, portfolio, and loan flows and their effects on domestic investment flows—all in a simultaneous framework—is the main novel feature of the paper. I will make a few comments about the theoretical motivation in the paper before looking at the empirical results.

Theoretical Motivation

Necessary preconditions for FDI are commonly thought to include the following factors:

- The foreign firm has some firm-specific assets (e.g., proprietary technology, know-how) that it wishes to use to advantage.

Dean Parham is assistant commissioner at the Productivity Commission, Australia.

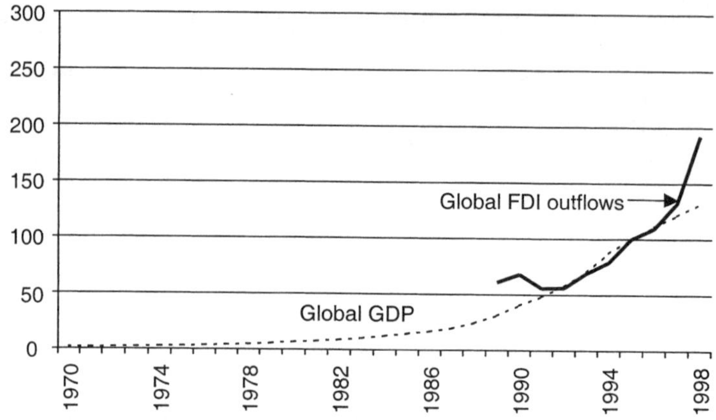

Fig. 5C.1 Global trends in outward FDI flows and GDP (index 1995 = 100)
Source: Productivity Commission (2002).

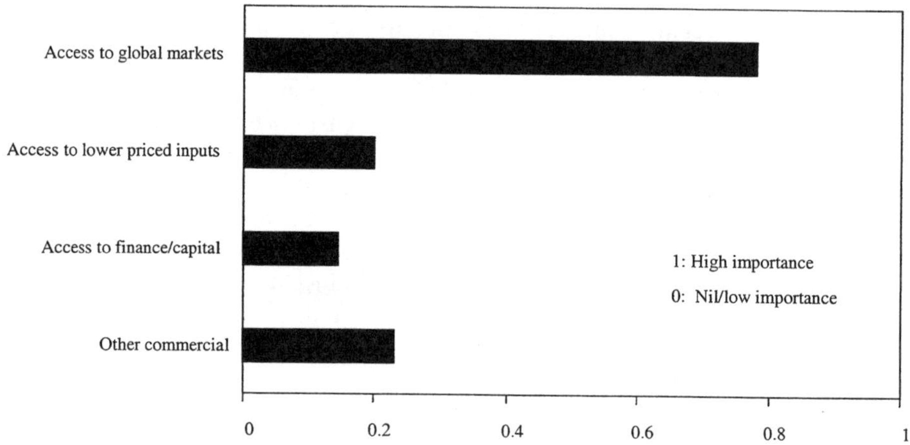

Fig. 5C.2 Commercial motives for offshore production
Source: Productivity Commission (2002).

- There are net locational advantages for the foreign firm in the host country (e.g., access to large markets, lower costs).[1]
- There are advantages in internalizing operations (through a branch operation) rather than relying on markets to exchange goods and services between foreign and local firms. For example, there may be difficulties in specifying requirements between foreign and local firms by means of contracts—a problem that may be intensified with the growth in "knowledge-intensive" production processes.

1. Advantages, such as lower transportation costs, need to outweigh disadvantages of perhaps less local knowledge, and so on.

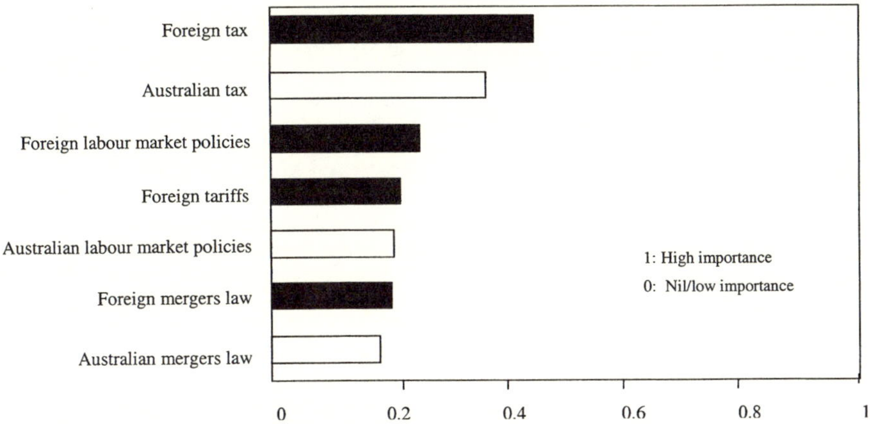

Fig. 5C.3 Government influences on offshore production
Source: Productivity Commission (2002).

The paper identifies an advantage to the foreign firm in the form of superior micromanagement. This most clearly fits with the first of the aforementioned motivations. But it has more to do with management skill than proprietary technology. It confers an advantage on FDI that is not available to portfolio investment.

The theoretical specification appears to invoke some simplifications. The foreign-firm advantage, in the form of better micromanagement, can be available to all foreign firms. Foreign firms are able to compete away the gains from their advantage. But the advantage is available to no domestic firm. This seems to require a production factor that can jump everywhere, except over country borders (or, more specifically, the border to the one country considered as a target).

Domestic firms appear to be homogeneous with respect to productivity performance (and inferior management). In practice, foreign firms are likely to decide on

- whether to establish a local branch presence (with brand name) or take over a local firm; and,
- if they decide on a takeover, whether to take over high-performing or underperforming firms, depending on expectations of productivity (or profit) *growth* across the range of firms.

The foreign-firm advantage can be competed away and captured by the domestic economy in the form of higher takeover prices. The advantage of foreigners is reflected in bid prices. If the advantage is not firm specific, foreign firms would have to build expectations about other foreign firms' bids into their own bids. This is where the competition appears to take place—in the bids. With perfect competition between foreign FDI bidders, the

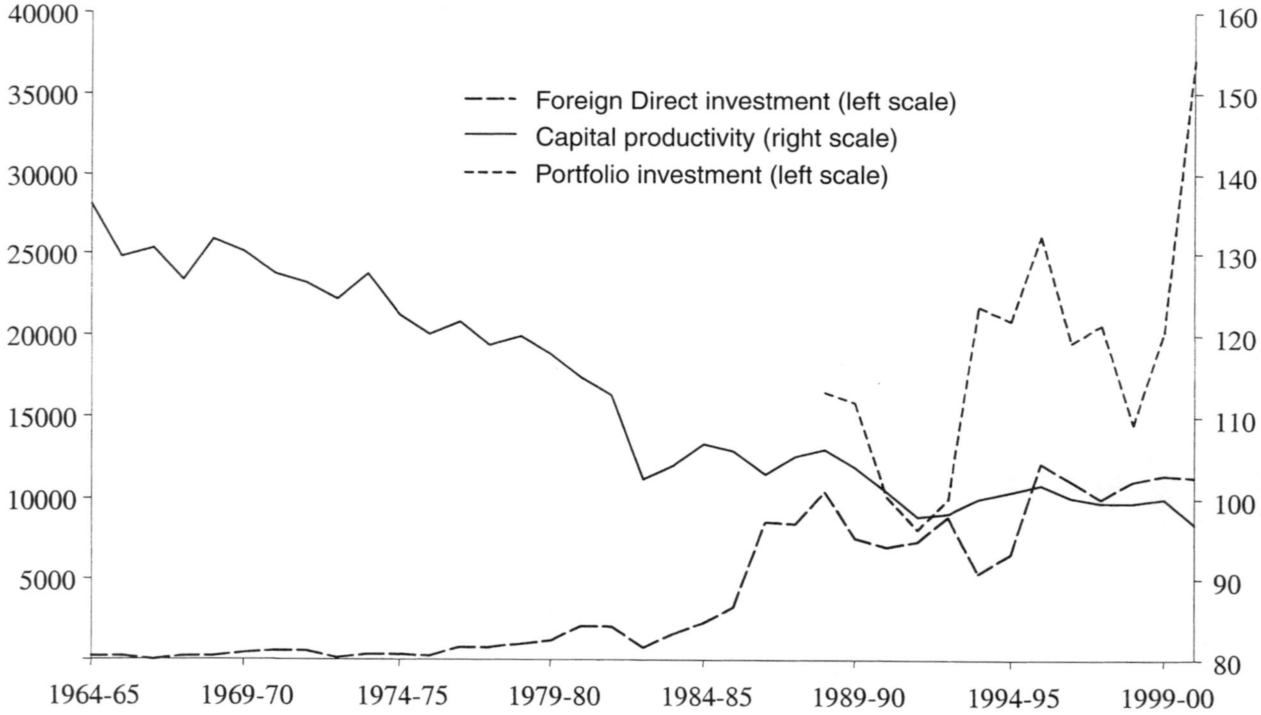

Fig. 5C.4 FDI, portfolio investment, and capital productivity in Australia ($m, left scale, index 1999–2000 = 100, right scale)

gains from the management advantage are fully transferred to the domestic economy.

A richer model might involve foreign firms with firm-specific advantages, such as proprietary technology, seeking out a suitable target from local firms with a range of productivity or profit performances, and choosing one that is expected to deliver the strongest productivity or profit growth. If the extent of the "advantage" is specific to the combination of domestic firm and foreign firm, the takeover could include an underperforming domestic firm. The foreign firm would also get a semipermanent advantage that could not be competed away by other foreign or domestic firms and not necessarily "the cream." They would still "add cream" to the local economy because they bring technology and raise performance.

Finally, the model seems to predict a *level* effect on investment, efficiency, and GDP as foreign firms exploit the extent of their advantage. Canadian evidence, at least, tends to suggest that inward FDI has important *growth* effects (Baldwin and Dhaliwal 2001).

Empirical Results

One general comment—and this is probably common to a lot of work in this area—is that there does not seem to be a tight nexus between the theory and the empirics. Perhaps I missed something, but it is not immediately obvious to me how the empirical model necessarily provides a test of the micromanagement advantage of foreign firms. I wonder whether other advantages (such as proprietary technology) and motivations could be consistent with the empirical model used.

As noted, the capital flows are analyzed in a simultaneous framework. A key finding is the confirmation that these flows have positive effects on domestic investment. Long-run effects from two-stage least squares estimation put the FDI effect (0.68) at double the loan effect (0.35) with the portfolio effect (0.53) in between. Compared with the Bosworth and Collins (1999) results, the FDI effect is a little weaker, the portfolio effect is much stronger (there is no discernible effect in Bosworth and Collins), and the loan effect is a little stronger. Some further exploration of the reasons for these differences—be they in the simultaneous specification (Bosworth and Collins found the different types of flows to be unrelated) or equation specification or other reasons—might help interpretation.

It is also interesting to note that the different types of capital flows are all found to have positive effects on growth. As might be expected, FDI is found to have a stronger effect.

References

Baldwin, John R., and Naginder Dhaliwal. 2001. Heterogeneity in labour productivity growth in manufacturing: Differences between domestic and foreign-

controlled establishments. In *Productivity growth in Canada,* 61–75. Ottawa: Statistics Canada.
Bosworth, Barry P., and Susan M. Collins. 1999. Capital flows to developing economies: Implications for saving and investment. *Brookings Papers on Economic Activity,* Issue no. 1:143–69.
Productivity Commission. 2002. Offshore investment by Australian firms: Survey evidence. Commission Research Paper. Canberra, Australia: AusInfo.

II

Micro Productivity

6

Sectoral Productivity and Economic Growth in Japan, 1970–98
An Empirical Analysis Based on the JIP Database

Kyoji Fukao, Tomohiko Inui, Hiroki Kawai, and Tsutomu Miyagawa

6.1 Introduction

Following the collapse of the so-called bubble economy, Japan's economy has entered a phase of unprecedentedly low growth. Looking for the causes of this stagnation, economists have mainly focused on demand-side factors, such as the deficiency of effective demand, the damaged balance sheets of Japanese firms, and the bad loan problems. Although the necessity of structural reforms and deregulations has also been stressed, rigorous empirical analyses of the supply-side were scarce.

From the viewpoint of growth accounting, Japan's low economic growth in the 1990s can be explained by the following three factors. The first factor is a slowdown of the labor supply caused by structural changes, such as population aging and a reduction of the work week. The second factor is a slowdown of total factor productivity (TFP) growth. The third factor is a lack of effective demand and deflation. Many economists agree on the importance of the first factor. But they are not unanimous in their view on the signifi-

Kyoji Fukao is professor of economics at the Institute of Economic Research, Hitotsubashi University, and a fellow at the Research Institute of Economy, Trade, and Industry. Tomohiko Inui is professor of economics at Nihon University. Hiroki Kawai is associate professor of economics at Keio University and a fellow at the Research Institute of Economy, Trade, and Industry. Tsutomu Miyagawa is professor of economics at Gakushuin University.

The JIP Database was compiled as part of the Economic and Social Research Institute, Cabinet Office, Government of Japan (ESRI) research project "Japan's Potential Growth." The authors are grateful to Kazuyoshi Nakata (ESRI), Naoki Okumura (ESRI), and the other members of the project for their coordination. The previous version of this paper was presented at the NBER Thirteenth Annual East Asian Seminar on Economics. The authors are grateful for the comments by Takatoshi Ito, Andrew Rose, Peter Drysdale, Keiko Ito, other conference participants, and two anonymous referees, one from the NBER and the other from the University of Chicago Press.

cance of the other two factors, which are the subject of continuing controversy. Based on a growth accounting of the Japanese economy, Hayashi and Prescott (2002) argue that the economic stagnation in Japan in recent years can be explained by the first and second factors, while the demand factor, in their view, does not play an important role. In contrast, M. Fukao (2003) and Yoshikawa (2003) hold that the scarcity of demand is the most important cause of the present stagnation. They also point out the possibility that the recent slowdown of Japan's TFP growth is caused by the decline of capacity utilization and labor hoarding as a result of the recession.

In spite of the importance of the issue, Japan's TFP growth has not been well studied in recent years. For example, the growth accounting by Hayashi and Prescott (2002) is not very sophisticated in the sense that they did not take account of the quality of labor and capacity utilization. They treated the slowdown of TFP growth as exogenous and did not try to address important questions, such as why the TFP growth rate has declined and in what sector in particular TFP growth slowed down.

In this paper we conduct a detailed analysis of Japan's TFP growth by making use of the Japan Industrial Productivity Database (the JIP Database), which we have recently completed.[1] We try to answer the following questions:

1. After the quality of labor and the capacity utilization have been taken account of, how much of the slowdown of Japan's economic growth in the 1990s can be attributed to the decline in TFP growth?
2. In what sectors is TFP growth particularly low?
3. What structural factors seem to have contributed to recent changes in sectoral TFP growth?

The paper is organized as follows: In the succeeding section, we conduct growth accounting at macro level. In the analysis we will take account of the quality of labor and capacity utilization. We also compare our results with preceding studies on this issue, such as Hayashi and Prescott (2002) and Jorgenson and Motohashi (2003). In section 6.3, we analyze sectoral TFP growth. We show that in the 1990s, TFP growth slowed down in the manufacturing sectors but accelerated in several service sectors. In section

1. The JIP Database has been compiled by us (the four authors of this paper), several economists at ESRI, and graduate students from Keio, Hitotsubashi, Tsukuba, and other universities as part of an ESRI research project. The result of this project is reported in K. Fukao, Miyagawa et al. (2003). The database contains annual information on eighty-four sectors, including forty-nine nonmanufacturing sectors, from 1970 to 1998. These sectors cover the whole Japanese economy. The database includes detailed information on factor inputs, annual nominal and real input-output tables, and some additional statistics, such as research and development (R&D) stock, capacity utilization rate, Japan's international trade statistics by trade partner, inward and outward FDI, and so on at the detailed sectoral level. An Excel file version (in Japanese) of the JIP Database is available at <http://www.esri.go.jp/en/archive/bun/abstract/bun170index-e.html>.

6.4, we examine possible structural factors that have contributed to recent changes in sectoral TFP growth by reviewing recent researches on sectoral productivity. In section 6.5, we will summarize our main results.

6.2 Supply-Side Causes of Japan's Stagnation: An Analysis at the Macro Level

In the succeeding subsection, we conduct growth accounting at the macro level using the JIP Database. We also compare our results with preceding studies on this issue.

6.2.1 Growth Accounting at the Macro Level

We begin by explaining our methodology of macro growth accounting. Let us assume that a macro production function at time t can be expressed as the following function of capital input K_t, labor input L_t, and an index of the technology level T_t.

$$(1) \qquad Y_t = F(K_t, L_t, T_t),$$

where Y_t denotes real GDP at time t. We assume constant returns to scale. The capital input K_t is derived by an aggregation of several types of assets, structures, and equipment. The labor input L_t is an aggregate of the number of workers cross-classified by sex, age, and educational attainment. The construction of these input aggregates is described in appendix A.

Additionally, we assume that the macro production function has a translog functional form. We also assume that because of the cost-minimizing behavior of firms, the marginal product of each production factor is equal to its cost share.

$$\frac{\partial \ln F}{\partial \ln K} = \frac{\partial F}{\partial K}\frac{K}{Y} = \frac{w_K}{p}\frac{K}{Y} = s_K,$$
$$\frac{\partial \ln F}{\partial \ln L} = \frac{\partial F}{\partial L}\frac{L}{Y} = \frac{w_L}{p}\frac{L}{Y} = s_L,$$

where w_K/p and w_L/p denote real service price of capital and real wage rate.

By differentiating the production function (1) over time, we get

$$d \ln Y_t = \bar{s}_{Kt}\, d \ln K_t + \bar{s}_{Lt}\, d \ln L_t + d \ln A_t,$$

where $d \ln Y_t$, $d \ln K_t$, and $d \ln L_t$ denote $\ln Y_t - \ln Y_{t-1}$, $\ln K_t - \ln K_{t-1}$, and $\ln L_t - \ln L_{t-1}$ respectively.

And

$$\bar{s}_{Kt} = \frac{(s_{Kt} + s_{Kt-1})}{2}$$

denotes the average of cost share of capital at time $t - 1$ and time t.

Similarly,

$$\bar{s}_{Ljt} = \frac{(s_{Lt} + s_{Lt-1})}{2}$$

denotes the average of the cost share of labor at time $t - 1$ and time t. The last term on the right-hand side of equation (2), $d \ln A_t$, denotes the contribution of technology improvement $\ln T_t - \ln T_{t-1}$ to the increase in production at the macro level.

$$d \ln A_t = \frac{\partial \ln F}{\partial \ln T} d \ln T_t$$

$d \ln A_t$ is usually called TFP growth. It is difficult to measure and observe the states of technology T, but we can derive the contribution of technological change to production in the following way.

$$(3) \qquad d \ln A_t = d \ln Y_t - (\bar{s}_{Kt} d \ln K_t + \bar{s}_{Lt} d \ln L_t)$$

Subtracting the growth rate of the working age population $d \ln N_t$ from both sides of equation (2), we obtain our basic equation for growth accounting.[2]

$$(4) \quad d \ln Y_t - d \ln N_t = \bar{s}_{Kt}(d \ln K_t - d \ln N_t) + \bar{s}_{Lt}(d \ln \mathrm{MH}_t - d \ln N_t) + \bar{s}_{Lt}(d \ln L_t - d \ln \mathrm{MH}_t) + d \ln A_t,$$

where $d \ln \mathrm{MH}_t$ denotes the growth rate of man-hours worked. The left-hand side of equation (4) denotes real gross domestic product (GDP) growth per working-age population. The four terms on the right-hand side denote the contribution of capital deepening, the contribution of the increase of man-hour input per working-age population, the contribution of the improvement of labor quality,[3] and the contribution of TFP growth respectively.

Panel A of table 6.1 summarizes the result of our growth accounting. Following Hayashi and Prescott (2002), we divided our data into three subperiods, 1973–83, 1983–91, and 1991–98. 1973 is the year of the first oil shock, and 1983 is when recovery from the second oil shock began. This period was followed by the boom of the "bubble economy," which lasted until 1991. Finally, the years from 1991 to 1998 represent the period of economic stagnation. Panel B of table 6.1 shows the growth rate of each production factor in each of the three periods. By comparing panel A and panel B we can derive the cost share of each factor. For example, the average cost share of capital in 1991–98 was 0.33 (=0.96/2.88).

2. The working-age population is defined as persons aged fifteen to sixty-four. We obtained the data from Prime Minister's Office (various years) and Ministry of Public Management, Home Affairs, Posts and Telecommunications (2002).

3. In appendix A we explain the definition of the labor quality index and the labor input index of the JIP Database.

Table 6.1 **Sources of Economic Growth: 1973–1998 (annual rate %)**

	Growth Rate of Real GDP (a) = (c) + (b)	Growth Rate of Working Age Population (b)	Growth Rate of (Real GDP/ Working Age Population) (c)	Growth Rate of TFP (d) = (c) – (e) – (f)	Contribution of Growth of (Real Capital/ Working Age Population) (e)	Subtotal (f) = (g) + (h)	Contribution of Growth of (Labor Input/Working Age Population): Contribution of Growth of (Manhour Input/ Working Age Population) (g)	Contribution of Growth of (Labor Input/Working Age Population): Contribution of Improvement of Labor Quality (h)
	A. Growth Accounting without Adjustment of Capacity Utilization Rates							
1973–83	3.56	0.88	2.68	–0.27	1.83	1.12	0.46	0.65
1983–91	3.94	0.84	3.09	0.54	1.47	1.08	0.62	0.46
1991–98	1.25	0.06	1.19	0.11	0.96	0.12	–0.10	0.21

	Growth Rate of (Real Capital/ Working Age Population)	Growth Rate of (Manhour Input/Working Age Population)	Growth Rate of Labor Quality Index
	B. Growth Rates of Factor Inputs		
1973–83	6.35	0.65	0.92
1983–91	4.31	0.95	0.70
1991–98	2.88	–0.14	0.32

Note: Working age population is defined as persons aged 15–64.

According to the JIP Database, real GDP growth declined from 3.94 percent of 1983–91 to 1.25 percent of 1991–98. This decline of 2.69 percentage-points can be decomposed into the following factors:

- slowdown of the growth of the working-age population: 0.79 percentage points
- slowdown of TFP growth: 0.43 percentage points
- slowdown of the growth of capital stock per working-age person: 0.51 percentage points
- slowdown of the growth of man-hour per working-age person: 0.72 percentage points
- slowdown of the improvement of labor quality: 0.25 percentage points

All these changes contributed to the decline in Japan's economic growth in the period from 1991 to 1998. From a theoretical viewpoint, these changes can be grouped—as argued in section 6.1—into the following three major factors.

First, structural changes—such as the aging of the population and the reduction of the work week—have slowed down the labor input growth. The growth rate of labor quality also declined. According to the Solow-type neoclassical growth model (Solow 1956), the decline in the working-age population growth rate by 0.79 percentage points and the 0.25 percentage-point slowdown in labor quality have reduced Japan's balanced growth rate by 1.04 percentage points.

Second, the TFP growth rate declined by 0.43 percentage points. According to the neoclassical growth model, the decline in TFP growth will also reduce the equilibrium growth rate of the real capital stock in balanced growth. If we assume a Cobb-Douglas production function with a capital share of one third, a 0.43 percentage-point decline in TFP growth will cause a 0.65 percentage-point (=0.43 + 0.43/3) decline in the balanced growth rate.

Third, Japan was trapped in deflation in the 1990s. Probably, demand factors such as the increasing unemployment and the stagnation of private investment have contributed to the decline in economic growth. It seems that a substantial part of the 0.72 percentage-point decline in the contribution of the growth of man-hours per working-age person and the 0.51 percentage-point decline in the contribution of capital deepening were caused by demand-side factors.

Table 6.2 compares the result of the growth accounting of the U.S. economy by Jorgenson, Ho, and Stiroh (2002) with our result on Japan.[4] Fol-

4. We should note that there are many differences in concepts and estimation procedures of variables between Jorgenson, Ho, and Stiroh (2002) and the JIP Database. For example, consumer durables and computer software are not included in capital in the JIP Database. The JIP Database is based on 1968 System of National Accounts (SNA), whereas Jorgenson, Ho, and Stiroh (2002) is based on 1993 SNA.

Table 6.2 **Sources of Economic Growth: United States-Japan Comparison (annual rate; %)**

	Real GDP Growth (a)	Manhour Growth (b)	Labor Productivity (GDP/Manhour) Growth (c) = (a) – (b)	TFP Growth (d) = (c) – (e) – (f)	Contribution of Labor Quality Growth (e)	Subtotal (f) = (g) + (h)	Contribution of Capital Services/Manhour Growth: Contribution of IT Capital (g)	Contribution of Capital Services/Manhour Growth: Contribution of Non-IT Capital (h)
A. The Result of Growth Accounting for the US Economy: 1973–2000								
1973–95	2.78	1.44	1.33	0.26	0.27	0.80	0.37	0.43
1995–2000	4.07	1.99	2.07	0.62	0.21	1.24	0.87	0.37
B. The Result of Growth Accounting for the Japanese Economy: 1973–1998								
1973–83	3.56	1.53	2.03	–0.30	0.65	1.68	0.16	1.52
1983–91	3.94	1.79	2.15	0.40	0.46	1.29	0.37	0.92
1991–98	1.25	–0.08	1.34	0.03	0.21	1.10	0.33	0.76
1995–98							0.52	0.63

Sources: Information pertaining to U.S. economy from Jorgenson et al. (2002). Information pertaining to Japanese economy from JIP Database.

lowing Jorgenson et al., we have treated information technology (IT) capital and non-IT capital as different factor inputs.[5] Compared with the United States, Japan's TFP growth and labor input growth were significantly lower in the 1990s. On the other hand, there was no large gap in the contribution of labor quality growth and capital deepening. Like the United States, Japan has experienced a rapid increase in the contribution of IT capital deepening in the latter half of the 1990s.

To sum up our Japan–United States comparison, it is confirmed that the three factors—the structural decline in labor input growth, the slowdown in TFP growth, and the scarcity of demand—caused Japan's "lost decade."

6.2.2 Growth Accounting with Adjustment of Capacity Utilization

As Burnside, Eichenbaum, and Rebelo (1995) and Basu (1996) have shown, there is a risk of underestimating (overestimating) TFP growth, if we do not take account of a decline (an increase) in the capacity utilization rate. Since the capacity utilization rate in Japan seems to have declined under the continuous stagnation of the 1990s, we may have overestimated the decline of the TFP growth in the previous section. In this section we examine this issue. We also compare our results with those of Hayashi and Prescott (2002).

The JIP Database contains sectoral capacity utilization rates, which are based on the Ministry of Economy, Trade, and Industry (METI) Index of Operating Ratio in the case of the manufacturing and mining sectors and on the intermediate input-capital ratio and the Bank of Japan (BOJ) Excess Capacity D.I. (Diffusion Index) in the case of the other sectors.[6] We used these data for the adjustment of TFP growth. Figure 6.1 shows the average capacity utilization rate of the manufacturing and primary sectors and that of other sectors. The average capacity utilization rate of the manufacturing and primary sectors has declined by 9.5 percentage points from 1991 to 1998. In the case of the other sectors, the decline was negligible (0.5 percentage points). The decline of the average capacity utilization rate of the macro economy was relatively small (2.4 percentage points).

In order to adjust for this change of the capacity utilization rate, we estimated Japan's TFP growth using the following growth accounting equation.[7]

5. Because of this difference, the estimated TFP growth in table 6.2 is slightly different from the TFP growth in table 6.1.

6. For more detail on estimation procedures of the sectoral capacity utilization rate, see appendix A.

7. When the capital stock is not fully utilized, the marginal productivity of capital might be different from the cost of capital. In the following growth accounting we did not take account of this possibility. As Morrison (1993) has shown, we can tackle this issue more rigorously by estimating the variable cost function. Using microdata from Japanese manufacturing firms, K. Fukao and Kwon (2003) estimated variable cost functions and made adjustments of capacity utilization and scale economies. They found that the rate of technological progress, which is defined as a downward shift of the variable cost function, declined from 1994 to 1998 in many manufacturing sectors.

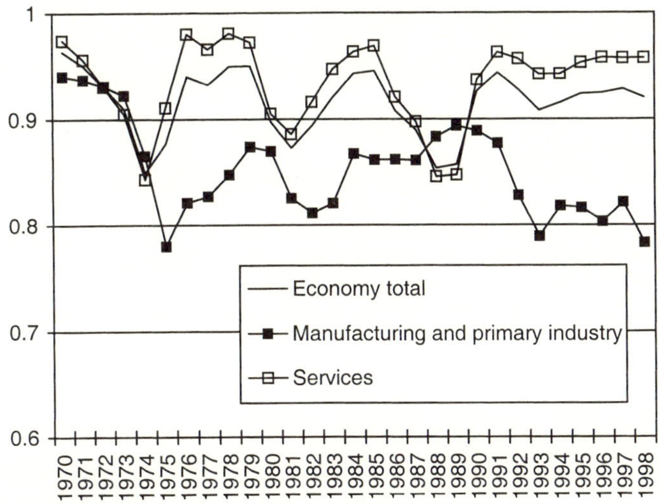

Fig. 6.1 Movement of capacity utilization rate: 1970–1998
Source: JIP Database.

Table 6.3 Growth Accounting with Adjustment of Capacity Utilization: 1973–1998 (annual rate; %)

	Growth Rate of (Real GDP/Working Age Population) (a)	Growth Rate of TFP (b) = (a) – (c) – (d)	Contribution of Growth of (Real Capital · Capacity Utilization Rate/ Working Age Population) (c)	Contribution of Growth of (Labor Input/Working Age Population) (d)
1973–83	2.68	–0.30	1.87	1.12
1983–91	3.09	0.43	1.58	1.08
1991–98	1.19	0.23	0.84	0.12

$$d \ln A_t = d \ln Y_t - [\bar{s}_{Kt}\, d \ln\left(\sum_j Z_{j,t} K_{j,t}\right) + \bar{s}_{Lt}\, d \ln L_t], \tag{5}$$

where $Z_{j,t}$ and $K_{j,t}$ denotes the capacity utilization rate and real capital input in sector *j*.

Table 6.3 shows the result of this growth accounting. According to the new growth accounting with adjustment of capacity utilization, the decline in TFP growth for the period 1983–91 to the 1991–98 period is 0.20 percentage points, which is 0.23 percentage points smaller than the corresponding result without the adjustment (table 6.1). This difference derives from the fact that the capacity utilization rate was at its peak in 1991. Without the adjustment of capacity utilization, the TFP growth before (after) 1991 is overestimated (underestimated).

Table 6.4 The Result of Growth Accounting: 1973–1998 (annual rate; %)

	Growth Rate of (Real GNP/ Working Age Population) (a)	Growth Rate of TFP (b) = (a) – (c) – (d)	Contribution of Growth of (Real Capital/Working Age Population) (c)	Contribution of Growth of (Manhour/Working Age Population) (d)
1960–73	7.2	4.1	4.1	–1.0
1973–83	2.2	0.5	2.1	–0.4
1983–91	3.6	2.4	1.4	–0.3
1991–2000	0.5	0.2	1.1	–0.8

Source: Hayashi and Prescott (2002).
Note: Working age population is defined as persons aged 20–69.

6.2.3 Comparison between Preceding Researches and Our Results

Let us compare our result with preceding growth accounting studies of the Japanese economy. Table 6.4 shows the result of Hayashi and Prescott (2002). Similar to ours, their result shows that the decline in Japan's economic growth is jointly caused by a slowdown of TFP growth, a slowdown of capital accumulation, and a decline in labor input. But compared with our result, their estimated decline in capital and labor inputs is much more moderate, and as a result their estimated decline in TFP growth (2.2 percentage-point decline) is much larger.

Probably we can explain this difference by the following factors.

First, Hayashi and Prescott do not take account of changes in the quality of labor. As panel B of table 6.1 shows, the improvement of labor quality has slowed down in recent years. They overestimate the decline in TFP growth by neglecting changes in labor quality.

Second, they do not take account of changes in capacity utilization. This factor also contributed their overestimation of the decline in TFP growth.

Third, in their growth accounting they use real gross national product (GNP), not GDP as an output measure. And they include Japan's net external assets in the capital stock. In GNP statistics, the rate of return to domestic capital is in gross term and includes capital depreciation. On the other hand, the rate of return to Japan's external assets is recorded in net term. Therefore, the appropriate capital cost of net external assets for growth accounting is usually smaller than the cost of capital located in Japan. Hayashi and Prescott (2002) did not take account of this difference and assumed that the cost share of capital was constant over time. Since Japan accumulated a huge amount of net external assets in the 1990s,[8] Hayashi and Prescott seems to have overestimated the cost share of capital

8. From the end of 1991 to the end of 1998, Japan accumulated net external assets of 71.7 trillion yen (*Annual Report of National Accounts 2001,* Economic and Social Research Institute, Cabinet Office, Government of Japan).

in the 1990s, the contribution of capital deepening in the 1990s, and, as a result, the decline in Japan's TFP growth from the 1980s to the 1990s.

Another important study is that by Jorgenson and Motohashi (2003). They found that Japan's TFP growth rate declined from 0.96 percent in 1975–90 to 0.61 percent in 1990–95 but accelerated to 1.04 percent during 1995–2000. This optimistic result is mainly based on their assumption on the deflator of IT products.[9] They assumed that the relative price of IT products compared with non-IT products in Japan has declined in a similar way as in the United States. They used their own IT product deflator, which is calculated as ([U.S. IT product price]/[U.S. non-IT product price]) · (Japan's non-IT product price) instead of Japan's official statistics. Since the relative price of IT products declined more drastically in the United States than in Japan, this procedure raises their estimation of the GDP growth rate and the TFP growth rate.[10]

Jorgenson and Motohashi adopt this procedure because they believe that quality improvements of IT products are not sufficiently taken into account in the case of Japan's price statistics.[11] Although they raised an important question, it seems to be brave to directly apply U.S. relative prices to Japan. We need a more rigorous analysis of the international price gap and the size of a hypothetical price decline, which is equivalent to the actual quality improvement of IT products.

6.3 Sectoral Productivity Growth in Japan

In the previous section we saw that the decline of Japan's TFP growth in the 1990s was not large when we make adjustments of the capacity utilization. In this section, we analyze Japan's TFP growth over the last three decades at a detailed sectoral level, which was almost impossible before the compilation of the JIP Database.[12]

6.3.1 TFP Growth at the Three-Digit Industry Level

First, let us explain our methodology. For the growth accounting of eighty-four sectors we use the following equation:

9. There are many other differences of estimation procedures between our study and Jorgenson and Motohashi's (2003). They explicitly treat land as a production factor, but we neglected land input. The inclusion of land lowers the cost share of other inputs. This difference makes their estimate of TFP growth higher than ours. They also include consumer durables and computer software in capital input, which we did not.

10. The lower price of IT products means larger IT investment. This factor reduces the estimate of the TFP growth rate.

11. Colecchia and Schreyer (2002) adopted similar approach in their comparative analysis of Organization for Economic Cooperation and Development (OECD) countries.

12. Probably the Keio Database (KDB) is the best-known database on Japan's sectoral productivity. The database covers forty-two sectors (including twenty nonmanufacturing sectors). Compared with the KDB, the JIP Database contains information on a detailed sectoral basis, especially in the case of nonmanufacturing sectors. In order to obtain access to the KDB, scholars need to get permission from Keio University.

$$(6)\quad d\ln A_{j,t} = d\ln Q_{j,t} - (\bar{s}_{K,j,t}\, d\ln Z_{j,t}K_{j,t} + \bar{s}_{L,j,t}\, d\ln L_{j,t} + \bar{s}_{M,j,t}\, d\ln M_{j,t}),$$

where $d\ln A_{j,t}$ denotes the TFP growth rate from time $t-1$ to t in sector j, while $d\ln Q_{j,t}$ denotes the growth rate of real gross output. $K_{j,t}$, $L_{j,t}$, and $M_{j,t}$ denote the capital, labor, and real intermediate input in sector j at time t. $M_{j,t}$ is a composite index of eighty-four commodities and services, which is based on the annual real input-output (IO) tables of the JIP Database. $Z_{j,t}$ denotes the capacity utilization rate. s_{Kt}, s_{Lt}, and s_{Mt} with upper bars denote the average of cost share of the capital, labor, and intermediate input in sector j at time $t-1$ and time t. In a similar way as in table 6.3, we made adjustments of changes in capacity utilization here.

As Domar (1961) has shown, the contribution of TFP growth in each sector to macro TFP growth is given by that sector's TFP growth rate multiplied by the Domar weight.[13] Table 6.5 shows each industry's TFP growth and its contribution to the macro TFP growth rate for the three subperiods.[14] This result is summarized in figures 6.2 and 6.3 at the two-digit industry level. The correspondence between the three-digit JIP classification and our two-digit classification is reported in table 6.5.

According to our result, the slowdown of TFP growth mainly occurred in the manufacturing sector. The manufacturing sector's contribution to macro TFP growth declined from 0.74 percentage points in 1983–91 to –0.03 percentage points in 1991–98.[15] On the other hand, TFP growth in the nonmanufacturing sectors has accelerated in the 1990s. The nonmanufacturing sectors' contribution to macro TFP growth has increased

13. In ordinary growth accounting at the macro level, real value added is used as a measure of output. In the case of sectoral growth accounting, real gross output is usually used as a measure of output. Because of this conceptual difference, the simple weighted average of sectoral TFP growth is not equal to macro TFP growth. Domar (1961) has shown that to equalize these, we need to weight these by using each industry's gross output divided by the value added of the whole economy.

14. In table 6.5, each industry's contribution for period (T, T') is calculated as a chain index:

$$\sum_{t=T+1}^{T'} \frac{DW_{j,t} + DW_{j,t-1}}{2}[d\ln Q_{j,t} - (\bar{s}_{K,j,t}d\ln Z_{j,t}K_{j,t} + \bar{s}_{L,j,t}d\ln L_{j,t} + \bar{s}_{M,j,t}d\ln M_{j,t})],$$

where $DW_{j,t}$ denotes the Domar weight for industry j in period t. On the other hand, in the case of our macro growth accounting in table 6.3, we directly compare factor inputs at the beginning and the end period.

$$(\ln Y_{T'} - \ln Y_T) - \left\{\frac{s_{K,T'} + s_{K,T}}{2}\left(\ln\left(\sum_j Z_{j,T'}K_{j,T'}\right) - \ln\left(\sum_j Z_{j,T}K_{j,T}\right)\right) + \frac{s_{L,T'} + s_{L,T}}{2}(\ln L_{T'} - \ln L_T)\right\}$$

Because of this difference, the total of all industries' contribution to macro TFP growth in table 6.5 is not identical with the result in table 6.3.

15. Based on growth accounting at the two-digit industry level, Nishimura et al. (2002) concluded that there was a decline in the rate of technical progress in the 1990s in Japan, and this decline occurred in both manufacturing and nonmanufacturing industries.

Table 6.5 Sources of Japan's TFP Growth by Industry: 1973–1998 (annual rate; %)

JIP Industry Code	Industry Name (two digit classification)	TFP Growth (a)			Industry Contributions to Macro TFP Growth (Domar weight) · (a)		
		1973–83	1983–91	1991–98	1973–83	1983–91	1991–98
1 Rice, wheat production	Agriculture, forestry, and fishery	–3.570	–1.418	–3.034	–0.070	–0.020	–0.020
2 Other cultivation and seed planting	Agriculture, forestry, and fishery	0.865	–2.267	–0.122	0.016	–0.034	–0.001
3 Livestock, poultry	Agriculture, forestry, and fishery	2.066	1.830	0.821	0.030	0.019	0.007
4 Veterinary, farming services	Agriculture, forestry, and fishery	–1.974	–0.497	–1.821	–0.004	–0.001	–0.002
5 Forestry	Agriculture, forestry, and fishery	–0.422	–0.931	2.769	–0.008	–0.004	0.009
6 Marine products	Agriculture, forestry, and fishery	0.728	0.136	0.379	0.006	–0.001	0.003
7 Coal, lignite mining	Mining	–5.699	–1.211	–3.425	–0.009	–0.002	–0.001
8 Metal mining	Mining	–0.489	7.249	–9.659	0.000	0.002	0.000
9 Crude oil, natural gas exploration	Mining	–6.924	4.206	–4.385	–0.003	0.001	–0.001
10 Quarry, gravel extraction, other mining	Mining	1.896	0.116	0.046	0.015	0.000	0.000
11 Livestock products	Food processing	–0.452	0.142	0.112	–0.009	0.000	0.001
12 Processed marine products	Food processing	3.407	–4.024	0.014	0.040	–0.061	0.000
13 Rice polishing, flour milling	Food processing	–1.075	–2.787	1.073	–0.022	–0.028	0.011
14 Other foods	Food processing	0.090	0.005	–0.356	0.009	–0.005	–0.011
15 Beverages	Food processing	–0.503	–0.012	–0.113	–0.007	–0.002	–0.001
16 Tobacco	Food processing	0.905	6.678	–6.131	0.003	0.021	–0.019
17 Silk	Textile, apparel and leather products	3.053	0.106	0.084	0.024	0.000	0.000
18 Spinning	Textile, apparel and leather products	1.638	0.782	–1.529	0.004	0.001	–0.001
19 Fabrics and other textile products	Textile, apparel and leather products	0.732	–1.267	–0.286	0.016	–0.024	–0.003
20 Apparel and accessories	Textile, apparel and leather products	–2.083	2.339	–0.439	–0.053	0.043	–0.007
21 Lumber and wood products	Wood, paper and printing	4.068	–0.865	–0.047	0.114	–0.010	0.000
22 Furniture	Wood, paper and printing	1.123	–0.135	–0.855	0.014	–0.001	–0.008
23 Pulp, paper, paper products	Wood, paper and printing	0.362	0.505	0.253	0.009	0.013	0.005

(continued)

Table 6.5 (continued)

JIP Industry Code	Industry Name (two digit classification)	TFP Growth (a)			Industry Contributions to Macro TFP Growth (Domar weight) · (a)		
		1973–83	1983–91	1991–98	1973–83	1983–91	1991–98
24 Publishing and printing	Wood, paper and printing	0.685	–0.819	–0.537	0.020	–0.022	–0.013
25 Leather and leather products	Textile, apparel and leather products	0.685	0.766	–0.154	0.002	0.003	–0.001
26 Rubber products	Chemicals	0.137	2.856	–1.582	0.001	0.025	–0.012
27 Basic chemicals	Chemicals	0.447	1.023	0.874	0.017	0.035	0.024
28 Chemical fibers	Chemicals	3.343	0.250	–0.106	0.014	0.000	0.000
29 Other chemicals	Chemicals	1.972	2.256	0.256	0.063	0.071	0.008
30 Petroleum products	Petroleum and coal products	–0.053	2.061	–1.326	0.021	0.039	–0.012
31 Coal products	Petroleum and coal products	0.494	0.707	–1.351	0.009	0.003	–0.003
32 Stone, clay & glass products	Other manufacturing	0.239	0.577	0.689	0.004	0.015	0.015
33 Steel manufacturing	Metal	–0.368	2.926	0.548	–0.001	0.061	0.005
34 Other steel	Metal	–1.133	0.437	–0.299	–0.116	0.019	–0.010
35 Non-ferrous metals	Metal	0.834	0.643	1.201	0.014	0.017	0.017
36 Metal products	Metal	1.068	–0.844	–0.222	0.030	–0.032	–0.006
37 General machinery equipment	General and precision machinery	1.767	0.778	–0.897	0.167	0.075	–0.081
38 Electrical machinery	Electronic and electric equipment	0.091	–0.229	0.190	0.000	–0.003	0.001
39 Equipment and supplies for household use	Electronic and electric equipment	1.730	3.235	–0.334	0.070	0.132	–0.014
40 Other electrical machinery	Electronic and electric equipment	3.079	4.427	1.714	0.105	0.304	0.130
41 Motor vehicles	Transportation equipment	0.624	0.104	–0.170	0.052	0.009	–0.013
42 Ships	Transportation equipment	0.481	1.828	–2.512	0.018	0.018	–0.007
43 Other transportation equipment	Transportation equipment	0.637	–0.538	–0.785	0.008	–0.005	–0.006
44 Precision machinery & equipment	General and precision machinery	1.788	1.787	–0.195	0.024	0.021	–0.004
45 Other manufacturing	Other manufacturing	–0.095	0.273	–0.302	–0.009	0.010	–0.011
46 Construction	Construction and civil engineering	–1.691	0.899	–1.999	–0.248	0.110	–0.221
47 Civil engineering	Construction and civil engineering	0.048	0.885	–0.814	0.013	0.061	–0.067

48 Electricity	Electric, gas, and water supply	–1.824	1.399	–0.136	–0.060	0.041	–0.003
49 Gas, heat supply	Electric, gas, and water supply	–0.619	2.706	0.991	–0.002	0.012	0.005
50 Waterworks	Electric, gas, and water supply	–1.329	0.719	–1.841	–0.010	0.003	–0.011
51 Water supply for industrial use	Electric, gas, and water supply	–1.346	–0.209	–1.850	0.000	0.000	–0.001
52 Waste disposal	Electric, gas, and water supply	–9.904	0.178	–4.630	–0.038	0.003	–0.019
53 Wholesale	Wholesale and retail	3.091	–3.450	3.137	0.360	–0.426	0.390
54 Retail	Wholesale and retail	–1.737	–0.147	0.069	–0.169	–0.028	0.007
55 Finance	Finance, insurance, and real estate	–0.684	3.129	0.015	–0.026	0.173	0.000
56 Insurance	Finance, insurance, and real estate	3.123	2.361	3.574	0.054	0.055	0.065
57 Real estate	Finance, insurance, and real estate	–3.923	–4.634	–0.472	–0.120	–0.155	–0.017
58 Housing	Imputed housing rent	–3.621	0.434	1.559	–0.260	0.031	0.139
59 Railway	Transport	–0.137	–0.134	–4.035	–0.008	–0.006	–0.055
60 Road transportation	Transport	–0.382	–0.633	–1.631	–0.015	–0.027	–0.068
61 Water transportation	Transport	–2.079	–1.198	–1.125	–0.057	–0.013	–0.014
62 Air transportation	Transport	–2.257	1.112	1.804	–0.010	0.007	0.010
63 Other transportation, packing	Transport	0.260	–0.882	–2.003	0.001	–0.010	–0.019
64 Telegraph, telephone	Communication and broadcasting	–0.723	3.465	6.481	–0.016	0.062	0.137
65 Mail	Communication and broadcasting	–5.717	5.370	–2.653	–0.021	0.021	–0.011
66 Education (private, nonprofit)	Public services, general government, and misc. sectors	–1.480	1.146	1.570	–0.014	0.014	0.021
67 Research	Public services, general government, and misc. sectors	3.861	2.027	3.762	0.006	0.005	0.010
68 Medical, hygiene (private)	Public services, general government, and misc. sectors	3.004	–1.565	–1.851	0.099	–0.060	–0.074
69 Other public services	Public services, general government, and misc. sectors	–2.582	0.711	–0.598	–0.020	–0.013	–0.002
70 Advertising	Business services	3.001	0.783	–2.361	0.029	0.011	–0.030
71 Rental of office equipment and goods	Business services	2.080	–11.249	1.367	0.023	–0.183	0.035
72 Other services for businesses	Business services	–4.500	3.091	–0.390	–0.175	0.169	–0.031
73 Entertainment	Private services	–2.826	–1.170	–1.681	–0.061	–0.036	–0.045

(*continued*)

Table 6.5 (continued)

JIP Industry Code	Industry Name (two digit classification)	TFP Growth (a)			Industry Contributions to Macro TFP Growth (Domar weight) · (a)		
		1973–83	1983–91	1991–98	1973–83	1983–91	1991–98
74 Broadcasting	Communication and broadcasting	–0.126	–2.800	0.284	–0.002	–0.014	0.001
75 Restaurants	Private services	0.197	–0.675	1.136	0.010	–0.033	0.057
76 Inns	Private services	–0.542	–2.686	1.992	–0.008	–0.038	0.027
77 Laundry, hair-cutting, public bath	Private services	–3.787	2.719	–0.489	–0.036	0.031	–0.005
78 Other services for individuals	Private services	–1.658	4.421	–0.733	–0.015	0.047	–0.009
79 Education (public)	Public services, general government, and misc. sectors	–3.205	1.076	–0.255	–0.119	0.040	–0.010
80 Medical, hygiene (public)	Public services, general government, and misc. sectors	2.197	–1.891	–0.156	0.025	–0.022	–0.006
81 Public administration	Public services, general government, and misc. sectors	–1.000	–1.574	0.440	–0.073	–0.107	0.034
82 Medical, hygiene (nonprofit)	Public services, general government, and misc. sectors	2.179	–0.652	–1.156	0.017	–0.007	–0.016
83 Others (nonprofit)	Public services, general government, and misc. sectors	0.911	–1.449	2.314	0.010	–0.018	0.031
84 Activities not elsewhere classified	Public services, general government, and misc. sectors	n.a.	n.a.	n.a.	0.000	0.000	0.000
Manufacturing subtotal					0.655	0.743	–0.028
Total					–0.307	0.403	0.197

Note: n.a. = not available.

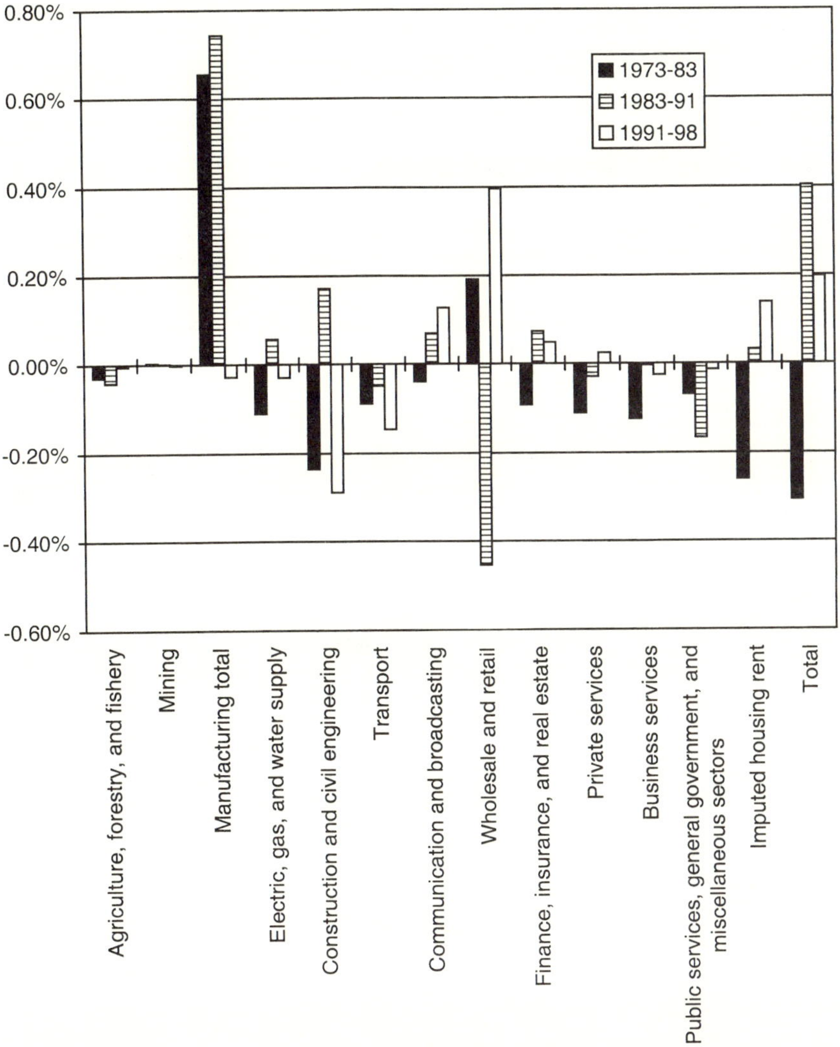

Fig. 6.2 Industry contributions to aggregate TFP growth

from –0.34 percentage points in 1983–91 to 0.22 percentage points in 1991–98.[16]

16. Cabinet Office (2002) obtains results opposite to ours. Based on growth accounting at the two-digit industry level, the study concluded that TFP growth in the manufacturing sector did not substantially decline in 1990s. Moreover, the sharp decline of TFP growth in the nonmanufacturing sector contributed to the slowdown in macro TFP growth in the 1990s. Probably the following three factors are responsible for the difference between the results of the Cabinet Office study and ours. First, the Cabinet Office study uses value added as a mea-

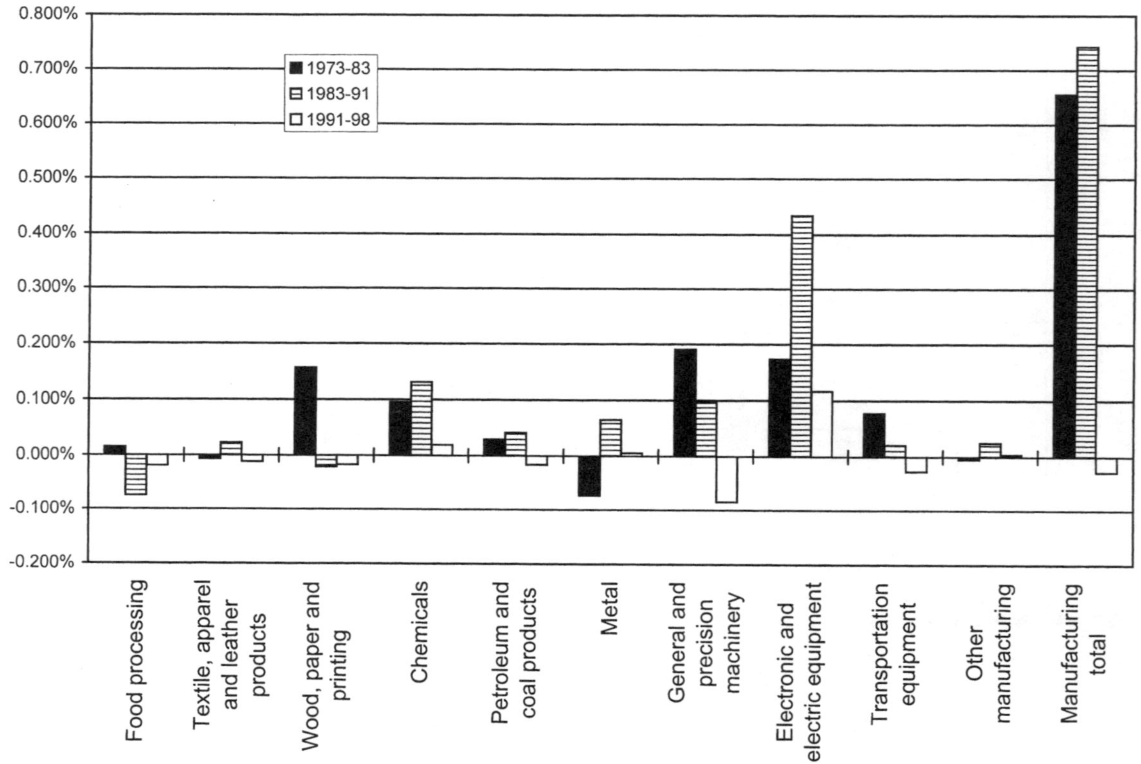

Fig. 6.3 Industry contributions to aggregate TFP growth: Manufacturing industry

6.4 Possible Structural Factors behind the Recent Change in Sectoral TFP Growth

What structural factors contributed to the recent change in the sectoral TFP growth pattern? In this subsection, we examine this issue by reviewing our recent researches on sectoral productivity.

6.4.1 Deregulation and the Acceleration of TFP Growth in the Nonmanufacturing Sector

First, let us consider the acceleration of TFP growth in the nonmanufacturing sector. Probably the most important source of this change is deregulation. The following is a list of major deregulation policies implemented in the 1990s.[17]

Commerce: Revision of the Large-Scale Retail Store Law (1992)
Telecommunication: Privatization of Nippon Telegraph and Telephone Corporation (NTT, 1985), introduction of the competition principles in all market areas (1985), liberalization of public-leased-public interconnections (1996), abolition of foreign capital regulations (excluding NTT and Kokusai Denshin Denwa Corporation [KDD]), complete privatization of KDD (1998)
Finance and insurance: Approval of mail-order sales business of insurance products (1996), partial liberalization of brokerage commission in security trade (1998), initiation of over-the-counter sales of investment trust funds by banks (1998)
Transportation: Change from the license system to the permission system and abolishment of requirement for fare revision permission in truck industry (1990), approval for individual assessment on fares cheaper than the average cost price in the taxi industry (1993), introduction of a flexible airline fare system (1996), and abolishment of double and triple tracking standards in domestic aviation (1997)
Electric utility: Relaxation of restrictions on electric power wholesaling (1995)
Employment placement: Expansion of occupations (mainly nonmanufac-

sure of output, whereas we used gross output. As Baily (1986) has shown, TFP growth based on gross output is usually different from TFP growth based on value added. Second, the Cabinet Office study takes account neither of changes in capacity utilization in nonmanufacturing sectors nor of changes in the quality of labor. Third, in order to evaluate each factor's contribution to output growth, the Cabinet Office study uses that factor's distribution share, whereas we used cost share. In the 1990s, the distribution share of labor was higher than the cost share of labor, and labor input in the manufacturing sectors declined more drastically than in nonmanufacturing sectors. Because of this difference, the Cabinet Office study arrives at a higher TFP growth in the manufacturing sector than we do.

17. This list is mainly based on Statistics and Research Bureau, Bank of Japan (1999) and Ministry of Foreign Affairs, Government of Japan (1999).

Table 6.6 Frequency Measure of Deregulation: 1970, 1980, 1990, and 1998

	1970	1980	1990	1998
Manufacturing	0.811	0.811	0.785	0.765
Electricity, gas, and water supply	0.340	0.345	0.341	0.426
Construction	0.667	0.667	0.750	0.750
Transport	0.315	0.329	0.343	0.453
Communication	0.503	0.495	0.735	0.795
Wholesale and retail trade	0.251	0.331	0.397	0.540
Finance, insurance, and real estate	0.301	0.341	0.500	0.635
Other services	0.560	0.571	0.588	0.599

Source: Nakanishi and Inui (2003).

turing occupations) to be covered by fee-charging employment placement agencies (1990, 1997)

These deregulations increased new entries, including mergers and acquisitions of Japanese firms by foreign firms, and more price competition in the non-manufacturing sector, where market competition was relatively limited compared with the manufacturing sector.[18]

Using the JIP Database, Nakanishi and Inui (2003) have tested whether Japan's deregulations have contributed to TFP growth. For this study they prepared a panel data set of a sectoral deregulation index for sixty-eight industries and for every five-year period from 1970 onward. This index is a frequency measure. A value of industry i and year t denotes the percentage of regulations abolished by year t in relation to the total number of regulations that existed in the starting year 1970.[19] The chronology of Japan's deregulation is taken from Sumitomo-Life Research Institute (1999) and Ministry of Public Management, Home Affairs, Posts and Telecommunications (2000). Table 6.6 shows their deregulation index at a relatively aggregated level. We can see that the manufacturing sector was not regulated even in 1970, whereas deregulation in the nonmanufacturing sector accelerated in the 1990s. The increase in the deregulation index was particularly large—more than 20 percentage points—in communication, wholesale and retail trade, and finance, insurance, and retail from 1980 to 1998. This finding is consistent with our result of rapid TFP growth in these industries.

The main results of Nakanishi and Inui's regression analysis are reported in table 6.7. The dependent variable is each industry's TFP growth. As explanatory variables they used the deregulation index, the growth rate of R&D stock, the growth rate of IT stock, the spillover effect of IT capi-

18. On this issue, see Sumitomo-Life Research Institute (1999) and Ministry of Foreign Affairs, Government of Japan (1999).

19. In the case of industries where there was no regulation in 1970, the deregulation index is set to one.

Table 6.7 Result on Determinants of Sectoral TFP Growth (fixed effect modal)

Explanatory Variables	Coefficients	*t*-statistics
Growth rate of deregulation index	0.071	2.314
Growth rate of own R&D stock	0.010	1.506
Growth rate of IT capital	–0.002	–0.199
Spillover effect of the growth of IT capital in other industries	0.000	0.000
Subsidiaries paid by the government/production of that industry	0.001	0.972
Time trend	–0.001	–2.499

Source: Nakanishi and Inui (2003).

Notes: Dependant variable is sectoral TFP growth. Number of observations = 340. Adjusted $R^2 = 0.080$.

tal growth in other industries, the subsidiaries-production ratio, and a time trend. They pooled data for sixty-eight industries for every five-year period from 1980 to 1998 and estimated a fixed effects model. They found that the increase in the deregulation index has a significant positive effect on that industry's TFP growth.

We have seen that in the 1990s substantial deregulations were accomplished in the nonmanufacturing industries, especially in communication, wholesale and retail trade, and finance, insurance, and real estate, and this change seems to have contributed to the acceleration of TFP growth in these industries. But we should also note that compared with other developed countries Japan's TFP growth in the nonmanufacturing sector is still quite low.

Table 6.8 compares the TFP growth rates during the 1990s in major service sectors in Japan, Australia, and the United States.[20] Total factor productivity growth rates in Australia are taken from McLachlan, Clark, and Monday (2002). Total factor productivity growth rates in the United States are taken from Yoshikawa and Matsumoto (2001). In these studies value added is used as a measure of output. For this international comparison we calculated Japan's value added based TFP growth rate of the service industries from the JIP Database. Compared with Australia, Japan's TFP growth rate in the 1990s was lower in six out of nine industries. Compared with the United States, Japan's TFP growth rate in the 1990s was lower in five out of eight industries. And in the case of average of service industries, Japan's TFP growth is still lower than that of the other countries.

The most developed economies have experienced a shift in the production structure from manufacturing to services. Hence, in order to maintain

20. We should note that a rigorous international comparison of the TFP growth is very difficult, because of the difference in the calculation methods, the industrial classification, and the periods of estimation.

Table 6.8 International Comparison of (Value Added Based) TFP Growth (annual rate; %)

Source	Australia (1993–200)	United States (1990~1999)	Japan 1990~1998)
Electricity, gas and water	1.6	1.0	–0.1
Construction	1.1	–0.7	–3.8
Wholesale	5.2	3.6	5.1
Retail	1.1	2.0	0.4
Restaurants	0.3	n.a.	1.6
Transportation	1.8	2.3	–3.0
Communication	4.0	2.4	6.0
Finance and insurance	1.2	1.5	1.8
Entertainment	–3.7	0.5	–4.5
Service sector average	2.2	1.8	0.9

Sources: Information for Australia from McLachlan, Clark, and Monday (2002). Information for the United States from Yoshikawa and Matsumoto (2001). Information for Japan from JIP Database.

Note: The average value of the TFP growth rate in the service sector is the weighted average of the industries' TFP growth rates in the table. Each industry's value added in Japan is used as a weight.

the pace of TFP growth in the economy as a whole, an acceleration of TFP growth in the service industries is very important.

6.4.2 Decomposition Analysis of TFP Growth in the Manufacturing Sector

Next let us consider the slowdown of TFP growth in the manufacturing sector.

As Baily, Hulten, and Campbell (1992) and Foster, Haltiwanger, and Krizan (1998) have shown in their productivity decomposition analysis, the start-up of productive establishments and the closure of unproductive establishments substantially contributed to U.S. TFP growth. As figure 6.4 shows, the start-up rate (number of newly opened establishments/number of all establishments) and the closure rate in Japan are about one-half of the corresponding values for the United States in the 1980s. Moreover, the gap has widened in the 1990s. In particular, the start-up rate in Japan's manufacturing sector has declined to about 2 percent in recent years. Probably this factor has contributed to the slowdown in TFP growth in Japan's manufacturing sector.

Using firm-level data from the Ministry of International Trade and Industry's Kigyo Katsudo Kihon Chosa (Basic Survey on Business Activities by Enterprises), K. Fukao and Kwon (2003) studied this issue.[21] Adopting

21. Using the same microdata, Nishimura, Nakajima, and Kiyota (2003) studied the productivity of exiting firms and conducted a productivity decomposition based on the method used by Griliches and Regev (1995) and Aw, Chen, and Roberts (2001). They were the first to point out that the average TFP level of exiting firms is higher than that of staying firms in some industries.

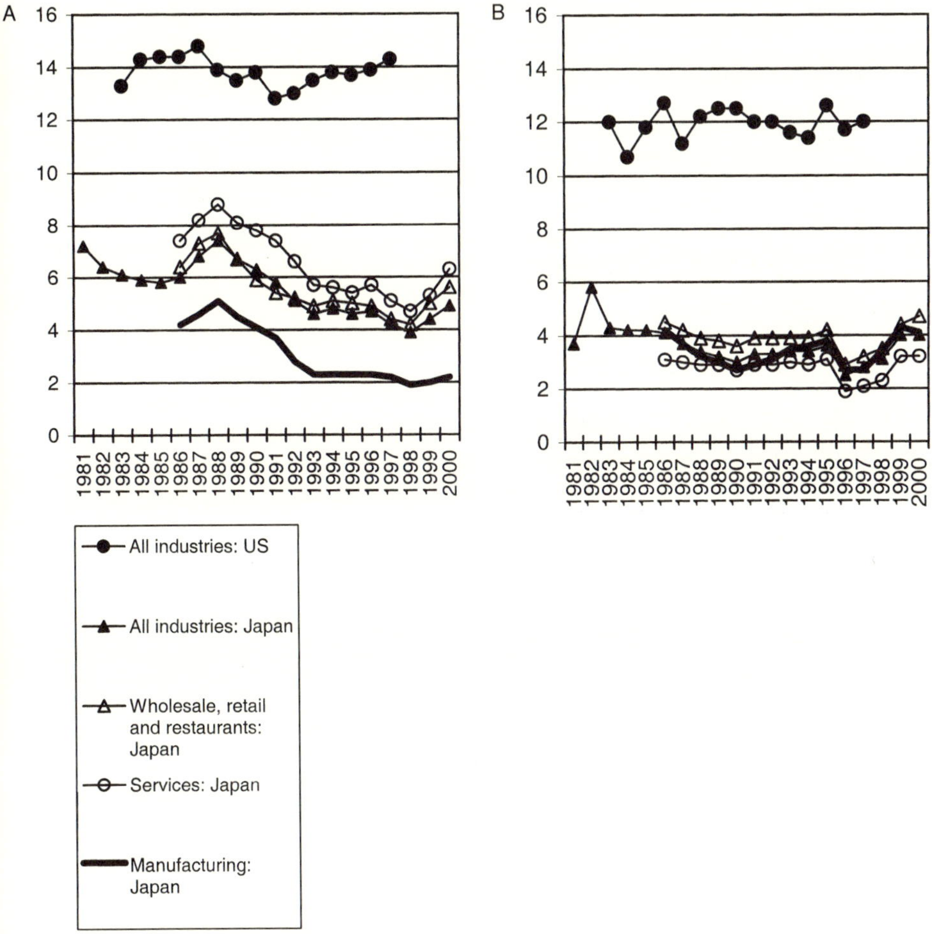

Fig. 6.4 Start-up and closure rate of establishments: Japan–United States comparison: *A*, start-up rate (%); *B*, closure rate (%)

Sources: Small Business Administration, U.S. Government (1998), Small and Medium Enterprise Agency, Ministry of Industry, Trade and Industry, Japanese Government (2001), and Study Group on "Industry Hollowing-Out" and Tariff Policy, Ministry of Finance, Japan (2002).

Note: Both the U.S. and the Japanese data are based on statistics of employment insurance program.

the methodology used by Baily, Hulten, and Campbell (1992) and Foster, Haltiwanger, and Krizan (1998), they decomposed the manufacturing sector's TFP growth of the 1994–98 period into the following five factors.[22]

22. We should note that K. Fukao and Kwon's (2003) decomposition is based on firm-level data whereas the preceding researches in the United States are based on establishment-level data.

Within effect: $\sum_{i \in s} \theta_{it-\tau} \Delta \ln TFP_{it}$,

Between effect: $\sum_{i \in s} \Delta\theta_{it}(\ln TFP_{it-\tau} - \overline{\ln TFP_{t-\tau}})$,

Covariance effect: $\sum_{i \in s} \Delta\theta_{it} \Delta \ln TFP_{it}$,

Entry effect: $\sum_{i \in N} \theta_{it}(\ln TFP_{it} - \overline{\ln TFP_{t-\tau}})$ and

Exit effect: $\sum_{i \in X} \theta_{it-\tau}(\overline{\ln TFP_{t-\tau}} - \ln TFP_{it-\tau})$,

where θ_{it} denotes firm i's sales share in year t. TFP_{it} denotes firm i's TFP level in year t.[23] TFP_t with an upper bar denotes the industry average TFP level. N is the set of newly entered firms and X the set of exited firms.

Fukao and Kwon's (2003) decomposition result is reported in tables 6.9 and 6.10.[24] Following preceding studies, they conducted a decomposition for the upturn period (1994–96) and for the downturn period (1996–98) separately. Table 6.11 compares their results with those of preceding studies for the United States and South Korea.

Their major findings are as follows.

1. The exit effect of the whole manufacturing sector in 1996–98 was negative and substantially contributed to the decline in TFP growth in the manufacturing sector. The negative exit effect means that the average TFP level of exiting firms is higher than that of staying firms.
2. The entry effect was positive both in the upturn and the downturn period. But as a result of the low entry rate, the size of the entry effect was not large.
3. The redistribution effect—that is, the share effect plus the covariance effect—was positive but relatively small in comparison with the United States.
4. The within effect (i.e., the effect of TFP growth within staying firms) was the largest factor among all the effects, and this effect changed procyclically.

The foregoing results seem to indicate that the promotion of new entries and making both the exit process and the reallocation process of resources more efficient are very important for an acceleration of TFP growth in Japan's manufacturing sector. These factors, moreover, are closely related

23. Because of the limitation of the data they could not take account of the change in labor quality in their TFP analysis. Probably because of this difference, their estimate of TFP growth is higher than our results in sections 6.2 and 6.3. They also assume that working hours and the capacity utilization rate at each firm are identical with those of the industry average. They divide the manufacturing firm data into fifty-eight sets of different industries and evaluate each firm's relative TFP level in relation to the industry average.

24. Switch-in and switch-out effect in table 6.9 and 6.10 denote contribution of the firms that moved from one industry to another industry to the industry average of TFP level.

Table 6.9 Decomposition of Sectoral TFP Growth: Upturn Period, 1994–1996 (growth in two years)

	Within Effect (a)	Between Effect (b)	Covariance Effect (c)	Total Effect among Stayers (d) = (a) + (b) + (c)	Entry Effect (e)	Exit Effect (f)	Switch-in Effect (g)	Switch-out Effect (h)	Net-entry Effect (i) = (e) + (f) + (g) + (h)	Industry Total (j) = (d) + (i)
Livestock products	–.006	–0.002	0.001	–0.007	–0.003	–0.001	–0.001	0.003	–0.002	–0.010
Seafood processing	0.011	0.002	0.001	0.014	0.010	–0.007	0.009	0.002	0.014	0.028
Manufacture of flour and grain mills products	0.030	0.003	–0.004	0.030	0.010	–0.013	–0.001	0.000	–0.003	0.027
Manufacture of miscellaneous food and related products	0.098	0.002	–0.012	0.088	0.014	–0.001	0.002	–0.003	0.013	0.100
Soft drinks, carbonated water, alcoholic beverages, tea and tobacco manufactures	0.003	0.001	0.000	0.004	0.001	–0.003	0.000	0.000	–0.001	0.003
Prepared animal foods and organic fertilizers	–0.049	–0.003	0.003	–0.049	–0.009	–0.001	–0.007	0.004	–0.013	–0.062
Silk reeling plants and spinning mills	–0.071	0.008	0.007	–0.056	–0.026	0.001	0.012	–0.013	–0.026	–0.081
Woven fabric and knitting mills	0.060	–0.003	0.009	0.066	0.009	–0.015	0.007	0.004	0.004	0.070
Dyed and finished textiles	–0.190	–0.001	0.001	–0.189	–0.027	0.009	–0.003	–0.010	–0.031	–0.220
Miscellaneous textile mill products	0.072	–0.001	0.005	0.075	0.022	0.004	0.017	–0.004	0.039	0.114
Apparel	0.041	0.000	–0.004	0.037	0.042	–0.002	0.000	0.002	0.042	0.079
Manufacture of miscellaneous textile apparel and accessories	0.066	–0.005	0.000	0.061	0.024	–0.012	0.027	–0.004	0.035	0.096
Sawing, planning mills and plywood products	0.010	0.010	0.021	0.042	0.000	0.005	0.000	0.000	0.005	0.047
Miscellaneous manufacture of wood products	0.023	0.006	0.004	0.033	0.023	–0.014	0.047	0.043	0.099	0.133
Manufacture of furniture and fixture	0.146	–0.001	0.005	0.150	0.047	0.000	0.002	–0.004	0.045	0.196
Pulp and paper	0.016	0.001	0.000	0.017	0.003	–0.003	0.003	–0.001	0.002	0.018
Coated and glazed paper	0.032	–0.005	0.020	0.047	0.011	0.007	–0.002	0.002	0.018	0.065
Newspaper industries	0.021	–0.002	0.005	0.024	0.010	–0.001	0.002	0.001	0.012	0.036
Publishing industries	0.031	–0.002	0.002	0.032	0.005	0.000	0.002	0.002	0.008	0.040
Publishing and allied industries	0.043	–0.008	–0.001	0.034	0.013	0.003	0.001	0.001	0.018	0.052

(*continued*)

Table 6.9 (continued)

	Within Effect (a)	Between Effect (b)	Covariance Effect (c)	Total Effect among Stayers (d) = (a) + (b) + (c)	Entry Effect (e)	Exit Effect (f)	Switch-in Effect (g)	Switch-out Effect (h)	Net-entry Effect (i) = (e) + (f) + (g) + (h)	Industry Total (j) = (d) + (i)
Industrial inorganic chemicals	0.059	–0.092	0.009	0.066	0.021	0.005	0.016	–0.007	0.034	0.100
Industrial organic chemicals	0.023	0.001	–0.002	0.022	0.017	0.000	0.000	0.003	0.020	0.042
Chemical fiber	–0.001	0.000	0.000	–0.001	–0.004	0.006	–0.003	0.000	0.000	–0.001
Oil and fat products, soaps, synthetic detergents, surface-active agents and paints	–0.015	0.003	0.005	–0.008	–0.008	–0.006	–0.001	0.002	–0.012	–0.020
Drugs and medicines	0.055	0.000	0.000	0.055	0.017	–0.007	0.001	0.000	0.011	0.066
Miscellaneous chemical and allied products	–0.061	–0.006	0.004	–0.063	–0.006	0.010	–0.009	0.002	–0.003	–0.066
Petroleum refining	0.004	0.000	0.000	0.004	0.000	–0.002	0.000	0.000	–0.003	0.002
Miscellaneous chemical and allied products	0.101	0.017	–0.054	0.064	0.000	–0.058	0.008	0.009	–0.041	0.023
Manufacture of plastic products	0.025	0.000	0.004	0.029	0.010	0.002	0.001	–0.003	0.010	0.038
Tires and inner tubes	–0.001	–0.001	0.000	–0.001	0.000	0.010	–0.001	–0.001	0.008	0.007
Miscellaneous rubber products	0.006	–0.004	0.002	0.005	–0.004	–0.003	–0.002	0.000	–0.008	–0.004
Manufacture of leather tanning, leather products and fur skins	0.104	–0.006	0.044	0.142	0.056	0.003	0.000	–0.008	0.051	0.193
Glass and its products	0.009	0.001	0.005	0.016	–0.003	–0.003	0.000	0.002	–0.004	0.012
Cement and its products	0.017	–0.004	0.005	0.018	0.009	–0.004	0.005	–0.001	0.009	0.027
Miscellaneous ceramic, stone and clay products	0.036	–0.002	–0.002	0.031	0.002	0.003	0.000	0.000	0.006	0.037
Pig iron and steel	0.012	–0.001	0.000	0.012	0.002	0.000	0.000	–0.004	–0.002	0.010
Miscellaneous iron and steel	0.055	–0.008	0.015	0.062	0.010	–0.001	0.009	0.005	0.023	0.085
Smelting and refining of non-ferrous metals	0.027	–0.008	–0.001	0.018	0.003	0.004	0.003	–0.003	0.006	0.025
Miscellaneous non-ferrous processing metal products	0.042	–0.001	0.010	0.051	0.013	–0.002	0.005	0.002	0.018	0.069
Fabricated constructional and architectural metal products	0.036	–0.001	0.000	0.035	0.008	–0.003	0.007	–0.006	0.006	0.042

Miscellaneous fabricated metal products	0.027	–0.002	0.003	0.028	0.004	–0.004	0.015	0.002	0.018	0.046
Metal working machinery	0.145	–0.023	0.028	0.151	0.028	0.008	0.032	–0.037	0.031	0.182
Special industry machinery	0.036	–0.001	0.001	0.036	0.004	–0.001	0.013	0.000	0.015	0.051
Office, service industry and household machines	0.018	0.001	0.002	0.021	0.008	0.006	0.002	–0.006	0.009	0.030
Miscellaneous machinery and machine parts	0.023	–0.002	0.003	0.023	0.009	–0.001	0.004	0.001	0.013	0.037
Industrial electric apparatuses	0.006	–0.003	0.002	0.005	0.000	0.003	–0.002	–0.001	0.000	0.005
Household electric appliances	0.012	0.005	0.016	0.033	0.005	–0.001	0.004	0.009	0.017	0.050
Communication equipment and related products	–0.001	0.000	0.005	0.003	0.000	–0.003	0.002	0.002	0.002	0.005
Electronic data processing machines and electronic equipment	0.005	0.001	–0.001	0.005	0.001	0.003	–0.001	–0.001	0.002	0.007
Electronic communication equipment and related products	0.076	0.000	0.002	0.078	0.010	0.002	0.015	0.001	0.027	0.106
Miscellaneous electrical machinery equipment and supplies	–0.025	0.002	0.004	–0.018	–0.006	–0.002	–0.010	0.006	–0.012	–0.030
Motor vehicles, parts and accessories	0.007	–0.001	0.002	0.008	0.000	0.000	0.000	0.000	–0.001	0.007
Miscellaneous transportation equipment	0.011	–0.001	0.006	0.016	0.000	0.002	–0.002	–0.005	0.012	
Medical instruments and apparatuses	0.068	–0.004	0.008	0.072	0.034	0.007	0.006	–0.008	0.039	0.111
Optical instruments and lenses	0.046	–0.016	0.016	0.046	0.010	–0.033	–0.006	–0.004	–0.033	0.013
Watches, clocks, clockwork-operated devices and parts	–0.048	0.008	–0.017	–0.057	–0.006	0.012	–0.007	0.000	–0.001	–0.058
Miscellaneous precision instrument	0.073	–0.006	0.001	0.068	0.026	–0.002	0.004	–0.001	0.027	0.095
Miscellaneous manufacturing industries	0.007	–0.002	0.000	0.005	0.009	0.004	0.014	0.013	0.040	0.045
Weighted average of all the industries	0.029	–0.001	0.003	0.030	0.008	–0.002	0.006	0.002	0.014	0.044
Share of each factor in industry's TFP growth	0.65	–0.03	0.06	0.68	0.17	–0.04	0.14	0.04	0.32	1.00

Table 6.10 **Decomposition of Sector TFP Growth: Downturn Period, 1996–1998 (growth in two years)**

	Within Effect (a)	Between Effect (b)	Covariance Effect (c)	Total Effect among Stayers (d) = (a) + (b) + (c)	Entry Effect (e)	Exit Effect (f)	Switch-in Effect (g)	Switch-out Effect (h)	Net-entry Effect (i) = (e) + (f) + (g) + (h)	Industry Total (j) = (d) + (i)
Livestock products	–0.008	–0.002	0.001	–0.008	–0.006	0.001	–0.002	0.002	–0.005	–0.014
Seafood processing	0.016	–0.004	0.005	0.017	0.013	–0.009	0.000	–0.003	0.001	0.018
Manufacture of flour and grain mills products	0.032	0.003	0.000	0.035	0.051	–0.006	0.000	0.001	0.045	0.080
Manufacture of miscellaneous food and related products	0.000	0.001	0.003	0.004	0.009	–0.004	0.002	–0.001	0.007	0.011
Soft drinks, carbonated water, alcoholic beverages, tea and tobacco manufactures	–0.001	0.000	0.000	–0.001	–0.001	0.001	–0.001	0.000	–0.001	–0.001
Prepared animal foods and organic fertilizers	–0.013	–0.013	0.002	–0.013	–0.006	0.003	–0.004	0.005	–0.002	–0.015
Silk reeling plants and spinning mills	–0.040	0.003	0.013	–0.024	–0.015	0.027	0.032	–0.002	0.042	0.017
Woven fabric and knitting mills	–0.033	–0.002	0.003	–0.032	0.000	0.000	0.002	–0.005	–0.004	–0.036
Dyed and finished textiles	–0.002	–0.002	0.019	0.015	–0.002	–0.019	0.000	0.004	–0.017	–0.003
Miscellaneous textile mill products	–0.057	–0.001	0.011	–0.047	–0.026	–0.002	–0.008	–0.003	–0.039	–0.086
Apparel	–0.033	0.007	–0.007	–0.034	0.006	–0.015	–0.001	–0.002	–0.012	–0.046
Manufacture of miscellaneous textile apparel and accessories	–0.059	0.000	–0.007	–0.065	–0.013	0.001	0.008	0.006	0.001	–0.064
Sawing, planning mills and plywood products	–0.069	0.001	0.007	–0.061	–0.023	0.008	–0.013	–0.003	–0.031	–0.092
Miscellaneous manufacture of wood products	–0.015	–0.016	0.004	–0.027	–0.027	–0.015	–0.014	0.008	–0.049	–0.076
Manufacture of furniture and fixture	–0.049	–0.001	0.007	–0.043	–0.024	–0.006	–0.004	0.002	–0.032	–0.075
Pulp and paper	0.000	0.001	0.002	0.003	–0.004	0.004	0.003	–0.003	0.000	0.003
Coated and glazed paper	–0.021	–0.003	0.005	–0.019	–0.015	0.006	0.000	–0.001	–0.010	–0.029
Newspaper industries	–0.030	–0.001	0.003	–0.028	0.009	–0.005	–0.002	0.000	0.002	–0.026
Publishing industries	–0.026	–0.004	0.003	–0.026	0.000	–0.001	0.000	0.001	0.000	–0.026
Publishing and allied industries	–0.019	–0.001	0.003	–0.016	0.007	–0.001	–0.001	–0.001	0.004	–0.012
Industrial inorganic chemicals	0.036	0.003	0.004	0.043	0.004	0.002	0.003	–0.004	0.004	0.047

Industrial organic chemicals	0.012	–0.001	0.001	0.013	0.010	–0.009	0.003	–0.001	0.003	0.016
Chemical fiber	0.000	–0.002	0.000	–0.002	0.000	0.000	–0.003	0.003	0.000	–0.002
Oil and fat products, soaps, synthetic detergents, surface-active agents and paints	–0.008	0.001	0.003	–0.005	0.001	0.000	–0.001	–0.001	0.000	–0.005
Drugs and medicines	0.005	0.000	0.001	0.006	0.002	–0.013	0.001	0.000	–0.010	–0.004
Miscellaneous chemical and allied products	0.004	–0.001	0.007	0.010	0.002	0.009	0.001	0.007	0.018	0.028
Petroleum refining	0.001	–0.002	0.003	0.003	0.002	0.000	0.000	0.000	0.002	0.004
Miscellaneous chemical and allied products	0.015	–0.003	0.003	0.016	0.008	–0.002	0.006	0.008	0.019	0.035
Manufacture of plastic products	–0.038	0.002	0.005	–0.036	0.000	–0.001	–0.003	0.001	–0.003	–0.039
Tires and inner tubes	0.00	0.001	0.000	0.001	0.000	0.000	0.000	0.000	0.000	0.001
Miscellaneous rubber products	–0.048	0.002	–0.003	–0.048	–0.003	0.007	–0.001	0.003	0.006	–0.042
Manufacture of leather tanning, leather products and fur skins	–0.072	–0.006	0.011	–0.067	–0.016	–0.004	0.001	–0.001	–0.021	–0.088
Glass and its products	–0.011	0.002	0.005	–0.004	0.001	0.003	0.001	0.003	0.008	0.004
Cement and its products	0.011	–0.006	0.007	0.012	0.009	–0.013	–0.003	–0.001	–0.008	0.004
Miscellaneous ceramic, stone and clay products	0.013	0.003	0.012	0.029	0.013	–0.005	0.006	0.005	0.018	0.047
Pig iron and steel	–0.003	0.000	0.002	–0.001	0.004	–0.003	0.001	–0.001	0.001	0.000
Miscellaneous iron and steel	–0.034	0.002	0.000	–0.033	–0.006	–0.002	–0.007	0.002	–0.013	–0.046
Smelting and refining of non-ferrous metals	–0.008	0.00	–0.001	–0.009	–0.002	0.003	0.006	–0.016	–0.009	–0.017
Miscellaneous non-ferrous processing metal products	0.018	0.000	0.000	0.018	0.008	–0.005	0.009	–0.003	0.009	0.027
Fabricated constructional and architectural metal products	–0.033	0.001	–0.003	–0.034	0.003	–0.005	–0.002	–0.003	–0.007	–0.041
Miscellaneous fabricated metal products	–0.009	–0.001	0.004	–0.006	0.003	0.004	–0.001	–0.012	–0.006	–0.012
Metal working machinery	–0.004	–0.007	0.012	0.001	0.000	–0.010	0.006	–0.003	–0.007	–0.006
Special industry machinery	–0.023	0.000	0.005	–0.018	0.001	–0.003	–0.004	–0.002	–0.009	–0.026
Office, service industry and household machines	–0.015	–0.003	0.007	–0.012	0.004	–0.009	–0.003	0.000	–0.007	–0.019

(*continued*)

Table 6.10 (continued)

	Within Effect (a)	Between Effect (b)	Covariance Effect (c)	Total Effect among Stayers (d) = (a) + (b) + (c)	Entry Effect (e)	Exit Effect (f)	Switch-in Effect (g)	Switch-out Effect (h)	Net-entry Effect (i) = (e) + (f) + (g) + (h)	Industry Total (j) = (d) + (i)
Miscellaneous machinery and machine parts	–0.004	0.001	0.003	0.000	0.001	–0.005	–0.001	0.001	–0.004	–0.004
Industrial electric apparatuses	–0.021	–0.001	0.002	–0.019	–0.005	–0.001	–0.001	0.002	–0.005	–0.025
Household electric appliances	0.023	–0.003	0.003	0.023	0.017	–0.010	0.017	0.002	0.027	0.050
Communication equipment and related products	0.010	–0.005	0.000	0.006	0.002	0.001	0.001	0.001	0.005	0.010
Electronic data processing machines and electronic equipment	–0.001	0.000	0.002	0.001	0.003	–0.003	0.001	0.000	0.001	0.002
Electronic communication equipment and related products	0.021	–0.009	0.010	0.022	0.010	–0.013	0.003	–0.002	–0.002	0.020
Miscellaneous electrical machinery equipment and supplies	0.047	–0.011	0.014	0.050	0.000	0.001	0.010	0.002	0.013	0.063
Motor vehicles, parts and accessories	–0.009	0.000	0.002	–0.007	0.000	–0.001	0.000	0.000	–0.001	–0.008
Miscellaneous transportation equipment	–0.004	–0.006	0.012	0.002	0.000	–0.002	–0.012	–0.003	–0.016	–0.014
Medical instruments and apparatuses	–0.055	0.003	0.007	–0.044	–0.009	–0.018	–0.004	0.000	–0.031	–0.076
Optical instruments and lenses	–0.032	0.004	0.020	–0.007	0.004	–0.008	–0.007	0.010	–0.001	–0.008
Watches, clocks, clockwork-operated devices and parts	–0.016	–0.003	0.009	–0.009	0.009	0.010	–0.004	0.010	0.025	0.015
Miscellaneous precision instrument	–0.073	–0.004	0.009	–0.067	–0.007	–0.004	–0.004	0.000	–0.015	–0.083
Miscellaneous manufacturing industries	–0.010	–0.005	0.008	–0.008	0.011	–0.007	–0.005	–0.005	–0.006	–0.014
Weighted average of all the industries	–0.008	–0.002	0.004	–0.005	0.002	–0.003	0.000	–0.001	–0.002	–0.007
Share of each factor in industry's TFP growth	1.17	0.22	–0.62	0.77	–0.31	0.46	0.00	0.08	0.23	1.00

Table 6.11 **Comparison of Productivity Decompositions between Japan, the United States, and Korea**

Source	Country	Unit of Analysis	Period	TFP Growth Total (%) (a) = (b) + (c) + (f)	Contribution of Each Effect: Within Effect (b)	Redistribution Effect Subtotal (c) = (d) + (e)	Share Effect (d)	Covariance Effect (e)	Net Entry Effect Subtotal (f) = (g) + (h)	Entry Effect (g)	Exit Effect (h)
Downturn											
Hahn (2000)	South Korea	Establishment	1995–98	4.7	–0.09	1.79			3.06		
					(–0.02)	(0.38)			(0.65)		
Baily, Hulten, and Campbell (1992)	U.S.	Establishment	1977–82	2.4	–1.10	2.54			0.96		
					(–0.46)	(1.06)			(0.40)		
Foster, Haltiwanger, and Krizan (1998)	U.S.	Establishment	1977–82	2.7	–0.24	2.24	–0.89	3.13	0.68		
					(–0.09)	(0.83)	(–0.33)	(1.16)	(0.25)		
Fukao and Kwon (2003)	Japan	Firm	1996–98 (fiscal year)	–0.7	–0.80	0.27	–0.15	0.42	–0.16	0.21	–0.37
					(1.17)	(–0.40)	(0.22)	(–0.62)	(0.23)	(–0.31)	(0.54)
Upturn											
Hahn (2000)	South Korea	Establishment	1990–95	23.0	13.11	–0.69			10.58		
					(0.57)	(–0.03)			(0.46)		
Baily, Hulten, and Campbell (1992)	U.S.	Establishment	1982–87	15.6	13.57	3.12			–1.09		
					(0.87)	(0.20)			(–0.07)		
Foster, Haltiwanger, and Krizan (1998)	U.S.	Establishment	1982–87	7.3	3.80	2.41	–1.31	3.72	1.02		
					(0.52)	(0.33)	(–0.18)	(0.51)	(0.14)		
Fukao and Kwon (2003)	Japan	Firm	1994–96 (fiscal year)	4.4	2.87	0.13	–0.13	0.26	1.08	1.36	0.00
					(0.65)	(0.03)	(–0.03)	(0.06)	(0.24)	(0.31)	0.00

Notes: The entry and exit effect of K. Fukao and Kwon (2003) includes switch-in and switch-out effect respectively. Values in parentheses denote share of each effect in total TFP growth.

with the allocation of funds through the financial system. Therefore, the problems in Japan's banking system are likely to have contributed to the slowdown of Japan's TFP growth, and their solution forms an integral part of any attempt to raising the TFP growth rate.[25]

6.5 Conclusions

Using the newly compiled data and the Japan Industrial Productivity (JIP) Database, we analyzed Japan's sectoral TFP growth in recent years. Let us summarize our main results.

1. After taking account of the quality of labor and the capacity utilization rate, we found the decline in TFP growth at the macro level from the 1980s to the 1990s not to be so great. The decline in TFP growth from the 1983–91 period to the 1991–98 period is 0.20 percentage points. Hayashi and Prescott (2002) seem to have overestimated the size of the TFP growth decline.
2. On the other hand, there was a substantial change in the pattern of sectoral TFP growth. The slowdown in TFP growth mainly occurred in the manufacturing sector. The manufacturing sector's contribution to macro TFP growth declined from 0.74 percentage points in 1983–91 to –0.03percentage points in 1991– 98. In contrast, TFP growth in the nonmanufacturing sectors accelerated during the 1990s. Nonmanufacturing sectors' contribution to macro TFP growth increased from –0.34 percentage points in 1983–91 to 0.22 percentage points in 1991–98.
3. In the 1990s, substantial deregulations were accomplished in nonmanufacturing industries, especially in communication, wholesale and retail trade, and finance, insurance, and real estate, and this change seems to have contributed to the acceleration of TFP growth in these industries. But we should also note that, compared with other developed countries, Japan's TFP growth in the nonmanufacturing sector is still quite low.
4. Regarding the manufacturing sector in the 1990s, the following three factors seems to have contributed to the low level of TFP growth. First, new entries were very limited. Second, the exit effect was negative; that is, the average TFP level of exiting firms was higher than that of staying firms. Third, the reallocation effect of resources was small.

25. Using regression analysis based on cross-industry data, K. Fukao and Kwon (2003) found that there is a significant negative correlation between the exit effect and that industry's average liability-asset ratio. That is, in industries where the liability-asset ratio is high, the exit effect tends to be negative.

Appendix A
Data Sources and Estimation Methods of the JIP Database

In this appendix we briefly explain how the JIP Database is compiled.

Estimation of Real Net Capital Stock by Industry and by Capital Goods

To construct real net capital stock by industry and by capital goods, we begin by estimating the net capital stock in 1970 as a benchmark. For the capital stock from 1971 to 1998, we used the perpetual inventory method, making use of the series for annual capital formation by industry and by capital goods and applying a constant depreciation rate for each type of fixed capital stock.

All real series are valued at 1990 prices. Our database consists of eighty-four industries based on the SNA input-output data published by ESRI. As for capital goods, we arrange thirty-seven capital goods in our database based on the commodity flow data in ESRI of the Japanese government. We name our own industry and capital goods classification as in the JIP classification. Our capital stock database covers not only the private sector but also the public enterprise sector and the government service sector. In addition, it includes residential stocks.

Estimation of Benchmark Capital Stock Data (for 1970)

We construct the benchmark stock by industry and by capital goods based on the National Wealth Survey of 1970. We transform the original data in the following four processes.

First, the statistics in the National Wealth Survey of 1970 are compiled in terms of firms and organizations. On the other hand, the sectoral statistics in the Fixed Capital Formation Matrix, which we used as the most basic statistics for our estimation of capital formation series, are compiled in terms of production activities. In order to make adjustments for this difference in the two statistics, we transformed the original data of the National Wealth Survey of 1970 into activity-based data by making use of the information on the distribution of each asset among sectors, which is available in the Fixed Capital Formation Matrix of 1970.

Second, the sectoral classification in the National Wealth Survey of 1970 is rougher than the JIP industry classification. Therefore, we construct the benchmark stock data that correspond to the JIP industry classification by using the production data in the input-output table for 1970 or the employee data in the Establishment Census of 1969 and 1972.

Third, the original data in the National Wealth Survey of 1970 are nominal values. Using price deflators for capital goods in the commodity flow statistics in ESRI, we converted the nominal values into values at 1990 price.

Fourth, in the National Wealth Survey of 1970, the statistics on public sectors are for the end of the fiscal year of 1970. Using data on investment flows, we converted the statistics to a calendar year basis.

Estimation of the Capital Formation Series

We estimate the capital formation series from 1970 to 1998 by industry and by capital goods. Classifications of industry and capital goods are based on the JIP classifications. We construct the capital formation series by the following three steps: We estimate (1) the capital formation series by industry, (2) the capital formation series by capital goods, and (3) the fixed capital formation matrix every year based on capital formation data constructed in steps (1) and (2). In the following subsections, we will explain each estimation method in detail.

Estimation of Capital Formation Series by Industry

In the manufacturing sector, we compile the annual series of the capital formation using the Census of Manufacturing. In the nonmanufacturing sector, we construct the data by examining statistics in each industry or closing accounts of public enterprises. These statistics are based on sample surveys and do not cover all establishments in each industry.

Next, using data from the Fixed Capital Formation Matrix, which is more reliable but only available every five years, we adjusted the above annual series of capital formation.

Estimation of the Capital Formation Series by Capital Goods

Basically, we compiled the capital formation series by making use of the commodity flow data of ESRI. The commodity flow data are arranged in an eight-digit classification system. We rearrange these data into the JIP capital goods classification.

The commodity flow data do not include data on construction and buildings, which are classified in the JIP capital goods classification nos. 32–37. We estimate the capital formation series for these capital goods using mainly the statistics published by the Ministry of Land Infrastructure and Transport. Finally, using the Fixed Capital Formation Matrix, we adjusted the foregoing capital formation series by industry.

We should note that our database does not cover capital formation of intangible assets, because it is based on 68SNA.

Estimation of the Annual Series of Fixed Capital Formation Matrix

As we have explained, we obtained annual capital formation data by industry or by capital goods. However, we do not have a fixed capital formation matrix for nonbenchmark years. We estimated the fixed capital formation matrix for the intermediate years by the RAS method.

Construction of Real Net Capital Stock for 1970–98

The fixed capital formation estimated in section 6.2 is expressed in nominal terms. We convert the series in nominal terms into 1990 prices by using deflators in the commodity flow data of ESRI.

Next, we accumulate capital stock from the benchmark stock in 1970 by the perpetual inventory method. Using this method, we have to consider depreciation. We assume a constant depreciation rate for each capital good. We use the depreciation rate adopted by the U.S. Bureau of Economic Analysis.

Estimation of Information Technology Capital Stock

Information technology capital goods consist of two types: tangible assets (hardware) and intangible assets (software). Our definition of IT capital goods is similar to that used by the Bureau of Economic Analysis of the U.S. government. Tangible IT assets include office machines, computers, computer peripherals, communications equipment, optical instruments, and medical instruments.[26]

In the National Accounts of Japan, only order-made software investment is estimated by making use of the Survey on Specified Service Industries. In countries like the United States, the United Kingdom, and Australia, GDP statistics cover in-house software and general application software as well as order-made software. Making use of the Survey on Information Processing and the Survey on Specified Service Industries, we estimated software investment in Japan in a fashion that is comparable to that of the United States, the United Kingdom, and Australia.

Aggregate IT investment including software investment in Japan increased by 12.4 percent per annum from 1970 to 1998 (fig. 6A.1), exceeding the average growth rate of total investment (3.2 percent). The ratio of IT investment to total investment increased from 2.8 percent in 1970 to 31.4 percent in 1998.

However, it did not increase uniformly like U.S. IT investment. In the early 1990s, its growth stagnated. Probably the stagnation was caused by the following two factors. First, investment in tangible IT assets except

26. Recently, many researchers have focused on the effects of IT investment on productivity growth. In the United States, Jorgenson and Stiroh (2000b) and Jorgenson (2001) showed that IT-related capital deepening contributed to the high economic growth rate in the late 1990s in the United States. Van Ark and Timmer (2000) examined output in IT industries and IT investment in developed and Asian countries. Miyagawa, Itoh, and Harada (2002) studied the effects of IT investment on Japan's economic growth using a sectoral database that is at a more aggregated level than the JIP Database.

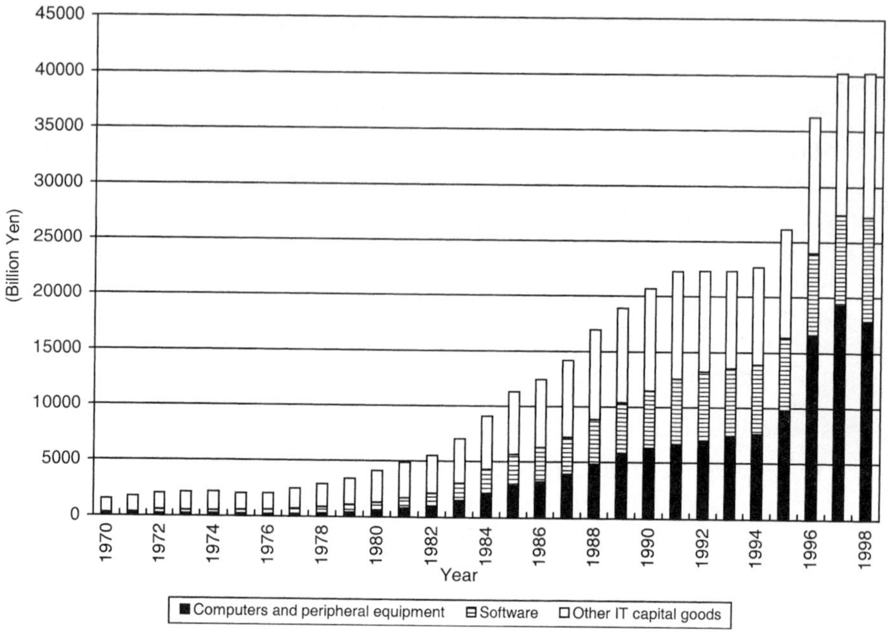

Fig. 6A.1 Aggregate IT investment in Japan (in 1990 prices)

computers and computer peripherals was strongly affected by business cycles. Second, investment in in-house software did not increase in the early 1990s, because Japanese firms had reduced costly in-house software and made an effort to increase outsourcing or utilize more standardized software since the bubble collapsed.

The IT capital stock also increased rapidly. In 1970, the IT capital stock at 1990 prices was only 5.6 trillion yen. In 1998, it reached 136 trillion yen. It grew at 11.4 percent per annum over this twenty-eight-year period. The real growth rate was similar to the nominal growth rate until 1990. However, the price fall in tangible IT capital goods contributed to the real growth of IT capital stock in the 1990s.

Estimation of Labor Input by Industry and Type of Labor

Data Description

Our measures of labor input in the JIP Database are constructed by combining the value estimates from the input-output table matrices and data from several labor force surveys. We constructed a detailed data set of the number of workers N_{ljt}, hours worked H_{ljt}, and the hourly wage W_{ljt} (l = type of worker, j = sector, t = year).

We divide the workforce cross-classified by sex, age, and educational attainment.

- Sex (2): Male, female
- Age (15): 15–19, 20–24, 25–29, 30–34, 35–39, 40–44, 45–49, 50–54, 55–59, 60–64, 65–69, 70–74, 75–79, 80–84, 85–
- Education (4): Junior high school, high school, college, university or more
- Status (2): Employed, self-employed
- Sectors (84): JIP classification
- Year: 1970–2000

Estimation of N_{ljt}, H_{ljt}, and W_{ljt}, Cross-Classified by Industry and Employment Status

First of all, we estimate the number of workers, hours worked, and hourly wages cross-classified only by industry and employment status for each year. We combine several data sources, such as the Population Census, Labor Force Survey, Manufacturing Census, Monthly Labor Survey, Basic Survey on Wage Structure, and others. Those estimates are adjusted to equal the sum of workers and income for employee with the estimates of the input-output table and the System of National Accounts. The opportunity cost of self-employed and family workers should be estimated. There are several alternative methods. We estimate it based on the ratio of marginal productivity between self-employed and employed workers, which is derived from fitted values of the production function.

Estimation of N_{kjt}, H_{kjt}, and W_{kjt}, Cross-Classified by More Detailed Category of Workers

The next step is to disaggregate our previous estimates to more detailed types of workers (gender, age, educational attainment). The estimation of the number of workers is based mainly on the Population Census. However, Japan's census statistics do not report the detailed tables cross-classified. We estimate it from several related tables based on some assumptions.

The hours worked and hourly wages are estimated using the Basic Survey on Wage Structure and Monthly Labor Survey. These data are based mainly on the Monthly Labor Survey, whose coverage is wider and more reliable. The information from the Basic Survey on Wage Structure is used only as the difference ratios from average. We derived the wage rates of the self-employed from an estimation result of the production function.

Estimation of the Sectoral Labor Input

The final step of our estimation of labor input is to estimate the Divisia index of price, quantity, and quality for each sector. The total annual manhour input of category l workers in industry j at time t is defined as the product of the number of workers and the average annual hours per worker:

$$\mathrm{MH}_{ljt} = N_{kjt} H_{kjt}$$

We define the growth of total real labor input in industry j at time t as a weighted average of the growth rates of man-hour input of all the categories.

$$d \ln L_{jt} = \sum_{l} \bar{v}^{L}_{ljt}\, d \ln \mathrm{MH}_{ljt},$$

where v^L_{ljt} with an upper bar denotes the average of the compensation shares of time $t-1$, v^L_{ljt-1} and the compensation shares of time t, v^L_{ljt}. v^L_{ljt} is defined by

$$v^L_{ljt} = \frac{w_{ljt}\mathrm{MH}_{ljt}}{\sum_l w_{ljt}\mathrm{MH}_{ljt}}$$

We made some adjustment on MH_{jt} and w_{ljt} so that the total cost over all categories of workers in each industry is equal to the total value of labor compensation in that industry as given by the input-output table of the JIP Database.

We may now define an index of "quality of sectoral labor input," or index of compositional change, as the ratio of labor input to working hours:

$$d \ln Q_{jt} = d \ln L_{jt} - \ln \mathrm{MH}_{jt},$$

where MH_{jt} is defined by

$$\mathrm{MH}_{jt} = \sum_{l} N_{kjt} H_{kjt}.$$

A rising Q_{jt} means that the percentage of the higher-paid categories in the workforce has increased in industry j over time.

Estimation of Annual Input-Output Tables

Data Sources

Every five years, the relatively reliable linked input-output (IO) table is available. Therefore we chose the years 1970, 1975, 1980, 1985, 1990, 1995, and the final year 1998 as our benchmark years. Major data sources for our annual IO tables for the benchmark years are

1970–1975–1980: linked input-output tables, Management and Coordination Agency;

1980–1985–1990: linked input-output tables, Management and Coordination Agency;

1985–1990–1995: linked input-output tables, Management and Coordination Agency; and

1998: extended input-output tables, Research and Statistics Department, Economic and Industry Policy Bureau, Ministry of Economy, Trade and Industry.

For other years we used METI's extended IO tables for every year.

Compilation Process

Among the aforementioned IO tables, there are some differences in the rule of compilation and concepts. We adjusted these differences. The lease industry's physical capital, which is rented to other industries, is treated as capital input in the lease industry. The cost of R&D in each sector is included in the production cost of that industry. The JIP Database is based on the 1968 SNA. Therefore, software investment is not included in investment. And depreciation of government capital is not included in the consumption expenditure of the government.

Next, we constructed converters to make adjustments for changes in industry classifications over time and aggregated the IO data into our eighty-four sectors.

We compiled IO tables in real terms (1990 prices) in the following way. 1970–1975–1980 IO tables contain real IO tables at 1980 prices. Similarly, 1980–1985–1990 IO tables contain real IO tables at 1980 prices. We linked these two real IO tables at year 1980. The second and the third IO statistics are linked at year 1990. The third and the fourth IO statistics are linked at year 1995.

The real values in linked IO tables are created by using price statistics such as the wholesale price index and the business service price index of the Bank of Japan in a way similar to the real values in the SNA statistics. Therefore, real values of output and intermediate input and implicit deflators in the JIP Database have basically similar characteristics as the corresponding SNA statistics except for the treatment of the base year. Japan's long-term SNA statistics are based on a price vector of a single year. In the case of the JIP Database, real values and implicit deflators are created by linking real values of different base years.

Estimation of the Supplementary Tables

In the JIP Database we have also estimated the following supplementary tables.

1. Trade Statistics by Industry and Trade Partner Country: 1980, 1985, 1990, 1995, and 2000. Using the supplementary converter table of the input-output tables of the Management and Coordination Agency, we converted the trade statistics of the Harmonized Commodity Description and Coding System (HS) nine-digit level, which are available at http://www

.customs.go.jp, into 302 manufacturing sectors, which are classified by economic activities. Using the linked input-output tables of the Management and Coordination Agency and wholesale price statistics of the Bank of Japan, we also calculated the trade statistics in constant 1990 prices.

2. *Inward- and outward-direct investment and service trade statistics by industry.* The data are based on Ito and Fukao (2003).

3. *Statistics on Japan's industrial structure: advertisement-sales ratio, land input per worker, Herfindahl index, top-four-firm concentration rate, share of firms belonging to vertical and horizontal* keiretsu *firms, and so on.* The data are based on Ito and Fukao (2003).

4. *Sectoral Capacity Utilization Rate.* For manufacturing and mining industries after 1973, we used the *Index of Operating Ratio,* Ministry of Economy, Trade and Industry, which is available at http://www.meti.go.jp/english/statistics. For other industries before 1991 and manufacturing and mining industries before 1972, we employed the following estimation procedure. Following Burnside, Eichenbaum, and Rebelo (1995) and Basu (1996), we assumed that the capacity utilization rate is closely correlated with the intermediate input-capital ratio. Following the "Wharton method," we lineally linked peak values of the intermediate input-capital ratio in each boom period and treated these interpolated values as the intermediate input-capital ratio at full capacity. Further, we used (actual intermediate input-capital ratio)/(intermediate input-capital ratio at full capacity) as our capacity utilization rate.

In the case of the period after 1991, the Japanese economy stayed in stagnation and many firms answered to *The Short-Term Economic Survey of Enterprises in Japan (Tankan)* of the Bank of Japan that they had excess capacity even at Japan's official business cycle peaks of May 1997 and October 2000.[27] It seems inappropriate to assume that the capacity utilization rate was close to one around these peaks. Therefore we did not adopt the Wharton-type method for the period from 1991. For the nonmanufacturing and nonmining sectors in this period we estimated the capacity utilization rate using the Diffusion Index of Excess Capacity (Excess Capacity D.I.), which is reported in The Short-Term Economic Survey of Enterprises in Japan (Tankan).[28] We used the following procedures. First, we estimated a model in which METI's Index of Operating Ratio is the dependent variable and BOJ's Excess Capacity D.I. is a time trend, and industry dummies are the explanatory variables, using seasonally adjusted quarterly panel data of 112 quarters and twelve manufacturing sectors for which both METI's Index of Operating Ratio and the BOJ's Excess Capacity D.I. are available. Second, we calculated a theoretical value of the capacity utilization rate for each

27. Official peak dates are available in *Business Cycle Reference Dates,* Economic and Social Research Institute, Cabinet Office, Government of Japan (http://www.esri.cao.go.jp/).

28. The data are available at http://www.boj.or.jp.en/.

nonmanufacturing sector by substituting this sector's Excess Capacity D.I. in the estimated equation. Third, we linked this theoretical value for the period of 1991–98 with the capacity utilization rate for the period of 1970–91, which is derived by the Wharton-type method.[29]

5. Sectoral R&D Stock and R&D Stock Cost Data. Data on sectoral R&D investment flows and a breakdown of investment costs are available in the Survey of Research and Development of the Management and Coordination Agency. Using these data and price statistics, we estimated the sectoral R&D stock in 1990 prices and R&D stock cost by the perpetual inventory method. We used the sectoral R&D stock depreciation rate estimated by the Science and Technology Agency (1985).

References

Aw, Bee Yan, Xiaomin Chen, and Mark J. Roberts. 2001. Firm-level evidence on productivity differentials and turnover in Taiwanese manufacturing. *Journal of Development Economics* 66 (1): 51–86.

Baily, Martin Neil. 1986. Productivity growth and materials use in the U.S. manufacturing. *Quarterly Journal of Economics* 101:185–95.

Baily, Martin Neil, Charles Hulten, and David Campbell. 1992. Productivity dynamics in manufacturing plants. *Brookings Papers on Economics Activity, Microeconomics:* 187–249.

Basu, Susanto. 1996. Pro-cyclical productivity: Increasing returns or cyclical utilization? *The Quarterly Journal of Economics* 111:719–51.

Burnside, Craig, Martin Eichenbaum, and Sergio Rebelo. 1995. Capital utilization and returns to scale. In *NBER Macroeconomics Annual,* ed. Stanley Fischer and Julio J. Rotemberg (67–123). Cambridge: MIT Press.

Cabinet Office, Government of Japan. 2002. *Annual report on the Japanese economy and public finance 2001–2002: No gains without reforms II.* Tokyo: Cabinet Office, Government of Japan.

Colecchia, Alessandra, and Paul Schreyer. 2002. ICT investment and economic growth in the 1990s: Is the United States a unique case? A comparative study of nine OECD countries. *Review of Economic Dynamics* 5 (2): 408–42.

Domar, Evsey. 1961. On the measurement of technological change. *Economic Journal* 71 (284): 709–29.

Foster, Lucia, John Haltiwanger, and C. J. Krizan. 1998. Aggregate productivity growth: Lessons from microeconomic evidence. NBER Working Paper no. 6803. Cambridge, Mass.: National Bureau of Economic Research.

Fukao, Kyoji, and Hyeog Ug Kwon. 2003. Nippon no seisansei to keizai seicho (The productivity and the economic growth of Japan: Empirical analysis based on industry-level and firm-level data). Paper presented at semi-annual conference of Japan Economic Association. 14 June, Oita, Japan.

Fukao, Kyoji, Tsutomu Miyagawa, Hiroki Kawai, Tomohiko Inui, Gaku Kimei

29. In the case of agriculture, education, medical services, and other public services, the BOJ's excess capacity D.I. is not available. We adopted the Wharton-type method in the case of these industries even for the period after 1991.

(yue xi ming), Yoshinobu Okumoto, Katsuhiko Nakamura, Masahide Hayashida, Kazuyoshi Nakata, Takehiro Hashikawa, et al. 2003. Sangyo betsu seisansei to keizai seicho: 1970–98 (Sectoral productivity and economic growth: 1970–98). *Keizai Bunseki*, no. 180:1–446. Tokyo: Economic and Social Research Institute, Cabinet Office, Government of Japan.

Fukao, Mitsuhiro. 2003. Choki fukyo no shuin wa juyo fusoku ni aru (The major cause of the long recession is the lack of demand). In *Ushinawareta Junen no Shinin wa Nanika (What is the Real Cause of the Lost Decade?)*, ed. Kikuo Iwata and Tsutomu Miyagawa, 17–20. Tokyo: Toyo Keizai Shinpo Sha.

Griliches, Zvi, and Haim Regev. 1995. Productivity and firm turnover in Israeli industry: 1979–1988. *Journal of Econometrics* 65 (1): 175–203.

Hahn, Chin-Hee. 2000. Entry, exit, and aggregate productivity growth: Micro evidence on Korean manufacturing. OECD Economics Department Working Paper, no. 272. Paris: Organization for Economic Cooperation and Development.

Hayashi, Fumio, and Edward C. Prescott. 2002. The 1990s in Japan: A lost decade. *Review of Economic Dynamics* 5 (1): 206–35.

Ito, Keiko, and Kyoji Fukao. 2003. Foreign direct investment in Japan: Empirical analysis based on establishment and enterprise census. In *Japan's Economic Recovery: Commercial Policy, Monetary Policy, and Corporate Governance,* ed. Robert M. Stern, 163–214. Cheltenham, U.K.: Edward Elgar.

Jorgenson, Dale W. 2001. Information technology and the US economy. *American Economic Review* 91:1–32.

Jorgenson, Dale W., Mun S. Ho, and Kevin J. Stiroh. 2002. Growth in U.S. industries and investments in information technology and higher education. Paper prepared for NBER/CRIW conference on measurement of capital in the new economy. 26–27 April, Washington, D.C.

Jorgenson, Dale W., and Kazuyuki Motohashi. 2003. The role of information technology in economy: Comparison between Japan and the United States. Paper prepared for RIETI/KEIO conference on Japanese economy: "Leading East Asia in the 21st Century?" 30 May, Tokyo, Japan.

Jorgenson, Dale W., and Kevin J. Stiroh. 2000a. Industry-level productivity and competitiveness between Canada and the United States. *AEA Papers and Proceedings* 90 (2): 161–67.

Jorgenson, Dale W., and Kevin J. Stiroh. 2000b. Raising the speed limit: US economic growth in the information age. *Brookings Papers on Economic Activity, Macroeconomics:* 125–211.

McLachlan, Rosalie, Colin Clark, and Ian Monday. 2002. Australia's service sector: A study in diversity. Productivity Commission Staff Research Paper. Canberra, Australia: Productivity Commission.

Ministry of Foreign Affairs, Government of Japan. 1999. Japan's approach to deregulation to the present. Tokyo: Ministry of Foreign Affairs, Government of Japan. Available at [http://www.mofa.go.jp/j_info/japan/regulate/approach9904.html]. July 10, 2003.

Ministry of Public Management, Home Affairs, Posts and Telecommunications, Government of Japan. 2000. *2000nen kisei kanwa hakusyo (White paper on deregulation 2000)*. Tokyo: Ministry of Public Management, Home Affairs, Posts and Telecommunications, Government of Japan.

———. 2002. *Nippon no tokei (Japan's statistics)*. Tokyo: Statistics Bureau, Ministry of Public Management, Home Affairs, Posts and Telecommunications, Government of Japan.

Miyagawa, Tsutomu, Yukiko Ito, and Nobuyuki Harada. 2002. Does the IT revolution contribute to Japanese economic growth? JCER Discussion Paper Series no. 75. Tokyo: Japan Center for Economic Research.

Morrison, Catherine J. 1993. *A microeconomic approach to the measurement of economic performance: Productivity growth, capacity utilization, and related performance indicators.* New York: Springer-Verlag.

Nakanishi, Yasuo, and Tomohiko Inui. 2003. Sabis sangyo no seisansei to kenkyukaihatu, IT, kisei (Productivity in the service sector and R&D, IT investment, and regulations). In *Sangyo kudoka to Nippon keizai (The hollowing-out phenomenon and the Japanese economy),* ed. Tsutomu Miyagawa, 93–105. Tokyo: Japan Center for Economic Research.

Nishimura, Kiyohiko G., Takanobu Nakajima, and Kozo Kiyota. 2003. Ushinawareta 90-nendai, Nippon no sangyo ni naniga okotta noka: Kigyo no sannyu-taishutsu to zen yoso seisansei (The lost 1990s, what happened in Japanese industry? Firms' entry-exit and total factor productivity). RIETI Discussion Paper Series no. 03-J-002. Tokyo: Research Institute of Economy, Trade and Industry.

Nishimura, Kiyohiko G., Kazunori Minetaki, Masato Shirai, and Futoshi Kurokawa. 2002. Effects of information technology and aging work force on labor demand and technological progress in Japanese industries: 1980–1998. CITJE Discussion Paper Series no. F-145. Tokyo: Center for International Research on the Japanese Economy, Faculty of Economics, University of Tokyo.

Prime Minister's Office. Various years. *Nippon no suikei jinko (Japan's estimated population).* Tokyo: Statistics Bureau, Prime Minister's Office, Government of Japan.

Science and Technology Agency. 1985. *Kagaku gijutsu hakusho 1985 (Annual report on the promotion of science and technology 1985).* Tokyo: Science and Technology Agency, Government of Japan.

Small and Medium Enterprise Agency, Ministry of Industry, Trade and Industry, Japanese Government. 2001. *2001 white paper on small and medium enterprises in Japan.* Tokyo: Ministry of Industry, Trade and Industry, Japanese Government. Available at [http://www.chusho.meti.go.jp/sme_english/index.html].

Small Business Administration, U.S. Government. 1998. *The state of small business: A report of the president.* Washington, D.C.: Small Business Administration, U.S. Government.

Solow, Robert M. 1956. A contribution to the theory of economic growth. *Quarterly Journal of Economics* 70:65–94.

Statistics and Research Bureau, Bank of Japan. 1999. 90-nendai ni okeru hiseizogyo no shueki teimei no haikei ni tsuite (On the background of low profitability of nonmanufacturing sector in the 1990s). *Nippon ginko chosa geppo (Bank of Japan monthly research report).* Tokyo: Bank of Japan, February.

Study Group on "Industry Hollowing-out" and Tariff Policy, Ministry of Finance, Japanese Government. 2002. *Chairperson's report.* Tokyo: Ministry of Finance, Japanese Government.

Sumitomo-Life Research Institute. 1999. *Kisei kanwa no keizai kouka (Economic effect of deregulations).* Tokyo: Toyo Keizai Shinpo Sha.

van Ark, Bart, and Marcel P. Timmer. 2000. Asia's productivity performance and potential at the turn of the century: An international perspective. Groningen Growth and Development Centre. Mimeograph, March.

Yoshikawa, Hiroshi. 2003. Hayashi ronbun eno komento: Sugitaru wa nao oyobazaru ga gotoshi!? (Comment on Hayashi paper: Too much is as bad as too little!?). In *Ushinawareta junen no shinin wa nanika (What is the real cause of the lost decade),* ed. Kikuo Iwata and Tsutomu Miyagawa, 21–24. Tokyo: Toyo Keizai Shinpo Sha.

Yoshikawa, Hiroshi, and Kazuyuki Matsumoto. 2001. 1990-nendai no nichibei keizai: Souron (Japan and the U.S. economy in the 1990s: General remarks). *Fi-*

nancial Review 58:1–17. Tokyo: Policy Research Institute, Ministry of Finance, Government of Japan.

Comment Peter Drysdale

This is an important report on work in progress on the huge and substantial job of putting together a big new database (the Japan Industrial Productivity [JIP] Database) that includes detailed information on factor inputs, annual input-output data, price deflators, and R&D, trade, and FDI data at a sectoral level for the Japanese economy.

The objective is to provide a sectoral account of the impact of IT investment and R&D expenditure on TFP growth.

Most studies of these relationships are aggregative. Aggregative studies provide useful first insights but are open to many interpretations. Detailed sectoral study of TFP growth and its causes, or the influences upon it, are theoretically and practically more soundly based and valuable in the understanding of policy issues and the foundation of policy strategies.

The Japan team is to be congratulated on the first large step in their work. One hopes that the database that has been assembled can be made widely available so that its richness can be exploited by researchers everywhere in trying to understand the performance of the Japanese economy.

This is an important issue. The malaise of the Japanese economy over the last decade is alternatively attributed to macro policy failure and micro or productivity failure. Understanding the character and importance of the latter requires, first, accurate measures of it and, second, rigorous analysis of the influences upon it. Only then can policy settings and priorities be got right.

This study confirms the general view that TFP growth mirrors output growth in Japan and that it has been a relatively unimportant element in output growth over the last three decades, but that its relative importance increased in the 1990s, when it accounted for 0.2 percent (or one-third) of the average 0.6 percent growth in that decade. It is not reassuring that growth performance in this decade would have been worse but for TFP growth, perhaps, but, as the paper suggests, it would have been.

The more important point the paper makes is that aggregate TFP performance masks wide differences in TFP performance across sectors.

The paper does not draw out the reasons for these variations, or speculate upon them in a way that might be subject to empirical testing, as freely as it might. This is perhaps the next phase of this project.

Peter Drysdale is professor of economics at the Asia Pacific School of Economics and Government, Australian National University.

But a casual review of the data and results is suggestive.

The results suggest that among the sectors that have performed well are those that have been subject to deregulation and privatization (transportation, telecommunications in the 1980s, and finance in the 1990s) and that those that are consistently strong performers are those that are more open and subject to the intense competitive forces in the international marketplace (such as manufacturing, the most consistently positive performer).

TFP performance is also associated with price change (deflation) with significant variation across sectors.

The paper makes some curious observations about the effects of the sectoral distribution of TFP growth on the macro economy that can only be understood in the context of popular commentary about "hollowing out" in Japan. In discussing the hollowing-out phenomenon, defined as a declining share of manufacturing output relative to services sector output, the paper observes hollowing out between 1980 and 1998. What is this supposed to imply? The increased importance of the service sector is typically associated with increased specialization and efficiency in the provision of a range of service inputs, as well as increased consumption of service outputs, as incomes rise and economies become more sophisticated. Hollowing out is normally associated in Japan with the relocation of increasingly high-cost (labor-intensive) activities offshore. The connection is that they are the flip side (or part of the flip side) of the same structural change. But the connection is incomplete.

This leads the paper to hypothesize that the cause of declining TFP performance is the shift from high-performing manufacturing to low-performing services. At best this is simply a tautologous argument. At worst it is based on a profound analytical misconception and it is wrong. The best way to make this point is simply to ask, what about Australia or the United States, two economies that are more service-sector-oriented than Japan yet enjoyed strong productivity growth through the 1990s, when Japan's productivity performance was unimpressive?

The paper tries to establish its point by observing, at length, that the "reallocation effect" was negative in the 1990s. Indeed it was. But why in Japan and not in Australia, where the same sectoral shifts have been more pronounced?

The argument in the paper is "neo-physiocratic"—it represents the back-to-manufacturing movement (as distinct from the back-to-agriculture movement). This is a serious flaw in thinking about the issues raised in the paper.

The important question is what slows productivity growth in the services sectors. Regulatory systems and closedness, both of which affect the appreciation of R&D and new technologies, are obvious answers.

The paper does explore the impact of IT investment (even though within the wrong conceptual framework) on productivity performance. The correlation between IT investment and productivity performance is high and positive. There are strong capital-deepening effects of IT investment, but there appear to be weak network effects in Japan. Exploration of significant associations across sectoral performance would seem an obvious and necessary extension of the analysis.

The work of this paper is incomplete. But the study is highly prospective. The careful and detailed analysis of the impact of IT and R&D investments on sectoral performance that has been made possible by this project will be extremely valuable to policymakers. There are more conclusions in the paper in fact than have been drawn out and highlighted. One also hopes that the main conclusions can be simplified and made interpretable to a wider public audience, because wide understanding of the relationships will be crucial to successful policy change.

Comment Keiko Ito

This is a broad-ranging, analytically and empirically strong paper, which investigates the causes of Japan's economic stagnation in the 1990s. The study is based on a newly constructed comprehensive data set, combining macro-, sectoral-, and micro-level analyses. The authors first discuss Japan's productivity growth at the macro level, referring to various empirical results presented in preceding papers that have been hotly debated in Japan. The first issue of contention addressed is whether Japan's economic slowdown in the 1990s is attributable to a decline in total factor productivity (TFP) growth. Contrary to the controversial result obtained by Hayashi and Prescott (2002), the paper finds that the TFP growth slowdown in the 1990s was much more moderate than stipulated by these two authors. The second issue is in what sectors TFP growth has been high or low. The authors find that the slowdown in TFP growth mainly occurred in the manufacturing sector, while TFP growth in the nonmanufacturing sectors accelerated in the 1990s. Finally, they consider some possible structural factors that may have affected sectoral TFP growth. According to their discussion, progress in deregulation may have contributed to the acceleration of TFP growth in some nonmanufacturing sectors, while the exit of firms with a higher TFP level as well as limited new entries may have contributed to the low TFP growth in manufacturing.

Interestingly, their results are not consistent with preceding studies for the first and second points of contention. In the following list, I point out some conspicuous differences between their estimation and that of previ-

Keiko Ito is a research assistant professor at the International Centre for the Study of East Asian Development (ICSEAD) in Kitayushu, Japan.

ous studies, which are definitely noteworthy and an important contribution of this paper:

1. The analyses are based on very comprehensive data on capital stock including IT (information technology) and R&D (research and development) capital stock at a detailed industry level.
2. The data include detailed information for the forty-nine nonmanufacturing sectors that will enable us to conduct in-depth and broad studies on the nonmanufacturing sectors as well.
3. In their growth accounting, they take account of labor quality and the capital utilization ratio. The former particularly affects their estimate of the TFP level and its growth rate.

Now I will go into some specific comments on each section. In section 6.2, the authors conduct a macro-level growth accounting and investigate the sources of the Japan's economic growth. Several other researchers have tried to examine this issue, and the estimated TFP growth rate obtained in each paper varies remarkably. As is well known, the weakest point of TFP estimation is that every TFP study offers a different estimate of TFP. As an example, here are some of the macro TFP studies in the 1990s and their estimated TFP growth rates for Japan:

- Hayashi and Prescott (2002): 1983–91 2.4 percent; 1991–98 0.2 percent. Note: using GNP data as value added and including Japan's net external assets in the capital stock.
- Jorgenson and Motohashi (2003): 1975–90 1.01 percent; 1990–95 0.74 percent; 1995–2000 1.13 percent. Note: adopting "internationally harmonized prices" calculated based on the U.S. price deflators for IT products and treating land as a production factor.
- Nakajima et al. (2002): 1985–89 –1.55 percent; 1990–94 –0.87 percent; 1995–99 0.06 percent. Note: The TFP growth rate is estimated by the output and input price changes.
- Miyagawa (2003): 1981–90 1.63 percent; 1991–95 0.56 percent; 1996–99 1.18 percent.
- Fukao et al. (this paper): 1983–91 0.54 percent; 1991–98 0.11 percent. Note: labor quality adjusted.

Given the differences in data and methodologies of TFP calculation,[1] I think that a substantial part of the difference between this study and others probably comes from the treatment of labor input. As can be seen in figure 6C.1, the estimated TFP levels were greatly lowered when labor quality was adjusted. As widely recognized, TFP levels that are calculated as "residuals" become smaller as inputs are calculated more rigorously and

1. The authors provide a detailed explanation of and critical comments on these differences in this paper. I mostly agree with their description.

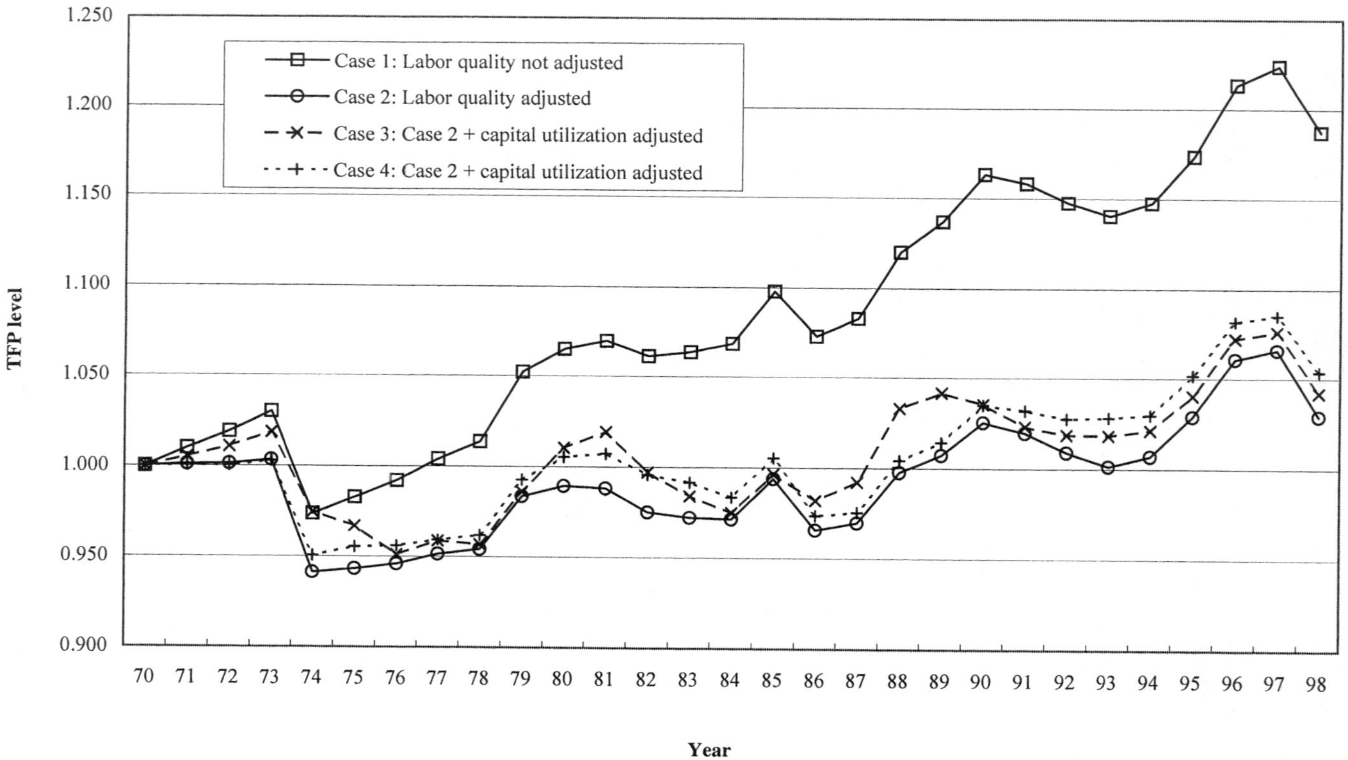

Fig. 6C.1 Trends of macro TFP level (1970 = 1.000)

Source: Fukao et al. (2003), figure 6-1-2, p. 385.

Note: In case 3, capital utilization ratio is calculated from trends of intermediate inputs. In case 4, capital utilization ratio is calculated from trends of output.

precisely. Therefore, given that the authors use the very carefully constructed data set and try to measure factor inputs as precisely as possible, their result seems to be quite convincing, and I appreciate their great contribution, which provides us with evidence that the slowdown of TFP growth was much smaller than estimated by Hayashi and Prescott. However, at the same time, the much smaller slowdown in the TFP growth rate only seems to be a logical conclusion of the much lower TFP levels they obtain. To be honest, the wildly differing results make me wonder about the empirical meaning of TFP. Many readers would also be puzzled by the various TFP growth rates presented previously.

As I already mentioned, whether or not labor quality was controlled greatly affected the TFP estimates, and I think that the labor quality adjustment should be one of the most crucial issues when we evaluate productivity growth in Japan. Their labor quality index is constructed following Jorgenson and Griliches's studies, and the methodology is theoretically and methodologically reasonable under the neoclassical framework. Although I would like to leave an in-depth discussion of labor market issues to labor economists, I would at least like to point out some issues of contention here. These include (1) whether wages reasonably reflect labor quality or productivity, (2) whether differences in educational attainment can be equated with differences in skill levels, (3) whether age differences are proportional to differences in working experience and skills, and so on.

In section 6.3, the authors analyze TFP growth rates by industry, and the detailed industry analysis on nonmanufacturing sectors is particularly interesting. They conclude that the manufacturing sector's contribution to macro TFP growth declined in the 1990s while that of the nonmanufacturing sector accelerated. However, this result is contrary to that of Nakajima et al. (2002) and Cabinet Office (2002). As the authors insist, this paper employs a more careful estimation methodology, and this result may be more reliable. According to their detailed description of the JIP Database construction process, which is reported in Fukao et al. (2003), the definition and price deflators of service output used in this paper seem to follow those used in Cabinet Office (2002) in principle. Therefore, again, I think a substantial part of the difference between the authors' result and that of Cabinet Office probably comes from the labor quality adjustment.[2] Nevertheless, this result seems to be reasonable, and I mostly agree with the authors that TFP growth accelerated in the nonmanufacturing sectors in the 1990s as a consequence of deregulation. Referring to Fukao et al. (2003), however, we should note that the TFP level of the services sector in the 1990s is lower than that in 1970, while the TFP level of the manufacturing sector in

2. Nakajima et al. (2002) use different data and employ a different approach in order to obtain more up-to-date results.

the 1990s is much higher than that in 1970. The widely observed fact in industrialized countries that productivity growth slows down as the share of the service sector in GDP expands implies an urgent need for an accurate measure of output and productivity in the service sector. As has been argued for a long time, measurement difficulties in service-sector output still present an important problem, which we empirical economists must continue to tackle.

In section 6.4, the authors try to interpret the estimated TFP growth, focusing on the deregulation process in the services sector and on the entry–exit behavior of firms in the manufacturing sector. As I already mentioned, I support the authors' view that the deregulation measures are probably the most important source of the observed TFP growth in the services sector. Although they refer to results by Nakanishi and Inui (2003) as empirical evidence on this issue, such studies are very limited, and a sufficient amount of empirical evidence has not been collected to evaluate the effects of deregulation on productivity growth. Further research on this issue would be desirable.

The authors' last analysis is to decompose TFP growth in the manufacturing sector and to investigate how much the entry and exit behavior of firms contributed to TFP growth. Their result is roughly consistent with that of Nishimura, Nakajima, and Kiyota (2003) and reveals that new entries are very limited in Japan and that the average TFP level of exiting firms was higher than that of staying firms. As argued by Nishimura et al., this might imply that natural selection mechanism in the market collapses or malfunctions. Moreover, as the authors mention, this might be related to the problems in Japan's banking system. The TFP decomposition analysis based on firm-level data is interesting in the sense that their result bring out these potential problems. However, as Nishimura et al. describe, we should note data constraints and the drawbacks of the firm-level data of the Ministry of Economy, Trade, and Industry's Basic Survey on Business Activities by Enterprises, which both Nishimura et al. and the authors use for their analyses. In the data set, we cannot accurately determine whether a firm really exited or was merged or acquired, or was dropped from the data set because of other statistical problems. Moreover, given the short time period of the analysis (1994–98), the decomposition result might only have captured a temporary shock or phenomenon.

Last but not least, and despite these criticisms, I would like to confirm again the tremendous contribution of this paper. Their newly constructed database will be extremely helpful for both academics and policymakers who are engaged in research on the Japanese economy and in pursuit of a solution for the economic problems of Japan. Moreover, this paper provides many interesting and insightful findings that should inspire many researchers to greater efforts to find a solution to the serious economic problems we are currently facing. In addition, the paper highlights the vulnerability of TFP estimation to data quality and variable definitions. To what extent do the TFP growth estimates reflect real productivity growth? May it not, to a large part, be reflecting improvements in the quality of the statistics at our disposal? Although the theoretical foundation of TFP estimation is already well established, we may need to develop a new or more sophisticated practical approach to its empirical estimation or to consider an alternative measure for productivity. However, I greatly appreciate the authors' earnest effort to accumulate more and more accurate facts based on carefully collected data sets in pursuit of more convincing policy recommendations.

References

Cabinet Office, Government of Japan. 2002. *Annual report on the Japanese economy and public finance 2001–2002: No gains without reforms II.* Tokyo: Cabinet Office, Government of Japan, November.

Fukao, Kyoji, Tsutomu Miyagawa, Hiroki Kawai, Tomohiko Inui, Ximing Yue, Yoshinobu Okumoto, Masakatsu Nakamura, Masahide Hayashida, Kazuyoshi Nakata, Kensho Hashikawa, et al. 2003. Sangyobetsu seisansei to keizai seicho: 1970–98 nen (Sectoral productivity and economic growth in Japan: 1970–98). Keizai Bunseki [Economic Analysis] no. 170. Tokyo: Economic and Social Research Institute, Cabinet Office, Government of Japan, June.

Hayashi, Fumio, and Edward C. Prescott. 2002. The 1990s in Japan: A lost decade. *Review of Economic Dynamics* 5 (1): 205–35.

Jorgenson, Dale W., and Kazuyuki Motohashi. 2003. Economic growth of Japan and the United States in the information age. RIETI Discussion Paper Series 03-E-015. Tokyo: Research Institute of Economy, Trade, and Industry, July.

Miyagawa, Tsutomu. 2003. Ushinawareta 10 nen to sangyo kozo no tenkan: Naze atarashii seicho sangyo ga umarenainoka (The lost decade and transformation of industrial structure: Why do not prospective growing industries emerge?). In *Ushinawareta 10 nen no shinin wa nanika (What is the real cause of the lost decade?),* ed. Kikuo Iwata and Tsutomu Miyagawa, 39–61. Tokyo: Toyo Keizai Shinpo-sha.

Nakajima, Takanobu, Munehisa Kasuya, Yumi Saita, and Tomoki Tanemura. 2002. Sekuta-betsu seisansei henka no bunseki to kozo henka no kensho (Empirical analysis of sectoral productivity growth and structural change). Working Paper no. 01-14. Tokyo: Research and Statistics Department, Bank of Japan, January.

Nakanishi, Yasuo, and Tomohiko Inui. 2003. Sabis sangyo no seisansei to kenkyukaihatsu, IT, kisei (Productivity in the service sector and R&D, IT investment and regulations). In *Sangyo kudoka to Nippon keizai (The hollowing-out phenomenon and the Japanese economy),* ed. Tsutomu Miyagawa. Tokyo: Japan Center for Economic Research.

Nishimura, Kiyohiko, Takanobu Nakajima, and Kozo Kiyota. 2003. Ushinawareta 1990 nendai, nihon sangyo ni nani ga okottanoka: Kigyo no sannyu taishutsu to zenyoso seisansei (What happened to Japanese industries in the lost 1990s? Analysis of firms' entry/exit and total factor productivity). RIETI Discussion Paper Series 03-J-002. Tokyo: Research Institute of Economy, Trade, and Industry, January.

7

Foreign Ownership and Productivity in the Indonesian Automobile Industry
Evidence from Establishment Data for 1990–99

Keiko Ito

7.1 Introduction

Many a developing country's government has attempted to utilize foreign direct investment (FDI) in its industrialization and technology development efforts. In the traditional theory of multinational corporations (MNCs), FDI by MNCs is regarded as the movement of managerial resources (in other words, the intangible assets related to technological knowledge in production and marketing as well as managerial know-how). A large body of literature on MNCs suggests that MNCs are more productive than local companies because of the advantages embodied in their managerial resources (e.g., Dunning 1988; Caves 1996; Markusen 1991). Moreover, the entry of MNCs may also affect overall productivity levels by bringing new ideas or increasing the level of competition in the market. This suggests that a larger presence of MNCs may play an important role in increasing productivity levels in the host country as higher-productivity foreign-owned production replaces lower-productivity domestic production.

Taking these hypothesized roles of MNCs as their point of departure, many researchers have investigated productivity gaps between MNCs and local firms, and technology transfer from MNCs to local firms, by conducting descriptive analyses based on interviews and questionnaires or calculating various productivity measures. Using establishment-level data, many studies report that foreign-owned establishments are more efficient

Keiko Ito is a research assistant professor at the International Centre for the Study of East Asian Development (ICSEAD) in Kitakyushu, Japan.

Helpful comments were provided by the editors and the discussants, M. Chatib Basri and Francis T. Lui. The author owes special thanks to Dr. Sadayuki Takii at ICSEAD for help with the compilation of the data. The views expressed in this paper are those of the author and do not necessarily reflect those of the Institute.

than local ones, suggesting that foreign ownership seems to be an important determinant of productivity in manufacturing in some countries.[1] On the other hand, there are some studies that found the difference between foreign and local plants not to be pervasive—for example, in Canada and Thailand.[2] Therefore, in light of the findings of previous studies, the so-called "ownership advantage" in the theory of MNCs has not always been corroborated, and MNCs do not always exploit firm-specific advantages in terms of productivity.

There are thus two empirical questions that I seek to shed light on in this paper. First, are foreign plants more productive than local plants, as MNC theory predicts? Second, if so, what are the determinants of the productivity of plants? Even though many previous studies have tried to answer these questions, comprehensive empirical evidence offering conclusive answers—particularly regarding the second question—is very limited.

This paper examines these issues in as much detail as possible, using the establishment-level data provided by Indonesia's Badan Pusat Statistik (BPS or Statistics Indonesia), taking the Indonesian automobile industry as a case. Most automobile firms in Indonesia were established by major Indonesian conglomerates as a joint venture or under a licensing agreement with foreign (principally Japanese) automakers. Despite government efforts to foster the industry for more than thirty years through high degrees of protection and intense policy intervention, the Indonesian automobile sector still remains in its infancy (Okamoto and Sjöholm 2000; Aswicahyono, Basri, and Hill 2000). Although it is difficult to directly test the effect of policy or institutional factors on plant productivity due to data constraints, this paper aims at evaluating the quantitative plant performance as well as investigating the industry characteristics using the establishment-level data.

Given the dominant position of foreign—principally Japanese-affiliated—

1. For example, in their study on the British manufacturing sector, Griffith and Simpson (2001) suggest that foreign-owned establishments have significantly higher labor productivity than those under domestic ownership. Doms and Jensen (1998), using U.S. plant-level data, found that U.S. multinational plants had the highest labor productivity, foreign-owned establishments had the second highest labor productivity, and U.S.-owned nonmultinational plants had the lowest. Using Indonesian establishment-level data, Blomström and Sjöholm (1999), Sjöholm (1999), Takii and Ramstetter (2000), and Takii (2002) all found that foreign establishments showed a higher productivity than local ones. In addition, Aitken and Harrison (1999) also found that in Venezuela plant productivity is positively correlated with foreign participation.

2. In Globerman, Ries, and Vertinsky's (1994) study using Canadian plant-level data, although foreign-owned plants were found to have a higher labor productivity, the differences disappear after size, capital intensity, and the share of nonproduction workers are controlled for. Ramstetter (2001b) compares average labor productivity between groups of foreign MNCs and local plants in Thai manufacturing, using establishment-level data for 1996 and 1998. He found that the vast majority of comparisons revealed that differences between local and foreign plants were statistically insignificant. His other studies also found no strong evidence suggesting that foreign establishments enjoy systematically higher productivity levels than local ones in Thailand (Ramstetter 1999, 2001a).

automakers in the Indonesian market, it might be expected that foreign-affiliated automobile manufacturers and auto parts suppliers should have been at the forefront of the development of the automobile industry in Indonesia. However, Okamoto and Sjöholm (2000), examining productivity performance and its dynamics in the Indonesian automobile industry between 1990 to 1995, concluded that productivity of the overall industry did not improve during that period, although foreign establishments tended to show a better performance than local ones. Rather, all the productivity measures (i.e., gross output per employee, value added per employee, and TFP) decreased from 1990 to 1995. Although their analysis is limited to a simple comparison of descriptive statistics between 1990 and 1995 or between local and foreign establishments, their results imply that the spillover effect of foreign MNCs does not seem to have been strong.

The productivity differentials between local and foreign plants in the automobile industry have been investigated in other countries as well. Okamoto (1999) analyzed the impact of Japanese FDI on the productivity of the U.S. auto parts industry using establishment-level data. She calculated the relative TFP index for each establishment and found that Japanese-affiliated plants were less productive than their U.S. counterparts in 1992. Griffith (1999) estimated the production function of the U.K. automobile industry, using data on individual establishments located in the United Kingdom over the period from 1980 to 1992. Her results suggest that foreign-owned establishments in this industry have significantly higher levels of output per worker (more than twice as high as domestic-owned establishments). However, these differences can be almost entirely explained by differences in input levels. That is, foreign plants invest more in physical capital, use a higher level of intermediate inputs, and pay their workers higher wages. Ito (2004) investigated the efficiency gap between foreign and local establishments and the determinants of productivity in the Thai automobile industry, using establishment-level data in 1996 and 1998. Mainly relying on the 1996 data, I calculated various partial productivity measures such as output per employee, value added per employee, capital per employee, output per capital, inventory ratios, price-cost margins, and so on, as well as the relative TFP index. In the simple comparison of those productivity measures between foreign and local establishments, foreign establishments were found to exhibit significantly higher labor productivity, capital-labor ratios, and higher wages. However, the capital productivity was significantly lower for foreign establishments than for local ones in the motor vehicle bodies and the motor vehicle parts industries. The results of the regression analyses are analogous to Griffith's results and provided no strong evidence that foreign establishments enjoy higher productivity after controlling for factor intensities. Moreover, there was no evidence that foreign plants achieved higher TFP because of their advantages in managerial resources. Therefore, the results of Griffith and Ito raised the question why domestically owned establishments were not investing in capital and/or paying their workers the same wages as foreign-owned establishments.

The aforementioned study by Okamoto and Sjöholm (2000) suggested that in the Indonesian automobile industry foreign-owned establishments tended to display higher productivity than local ones. Taking Okamoto and Sjöholm's findings and methodology as its point of departure, this paper pursues this line of enquiry further by using data for a much longer period and examines in detail the determinants of productivity and its growth by conducting regression analyses and a cost function estimation as well as a simple comparison of descriptive statistics as employed by Okamoto and Sjöholm. To this end, given the deficiencies in the BPS's establishment-level data,[3] various productivity measures will be calculated and analyzed in order to obtain robust results. First, various characteristics of automobile establishments are examined by calculating some partial productivity measures such as average variable cost and labor productivity, and other descriptive statistics. Second, by conducting ordinary least squares (OLS) regressions, determinants of the partial productivity and TFP are investigated. Third, the cost structure is examined by using the cost function framework. Finally, the growth of TFP is calculated based on the estimated cost function, and the contribution of different sources to TFP growth rate are investigated.

The remainder of the paper is organized as follows. Section 7.2 provides an overview of the development of the Indonesian automobile industry and discusses industrial organization aspects of the industry. In section 7.3, using establishment-level data, various partial productivity measures are calculated and compared in time series and between local and foreign establishments. A statistical examination of the difference between the two groups is also conducted. Section 7.4 describes the econometric model of the cost function estimation and states the methodology for the decomposition of TFP growth. Then a summary of the primary results obtained from the model estimation is presented. The final section offers some concluding remarks.

7.2 Overview of the Indonesian Automobile Industry

7.2.1 Development of the Indonesian Automobile Industry

In Indonesia, as in many other developing countries, the automobile industry is viewed as the leading edge of industrialization and skilled job cre-

3. The BPS microdata have a number of deficiencies related to nonreporting and apparently incorrect entries. For example, there were a number of apparent mistakes in the information on foreign ownership shares (e.g., foreign ownership shares of 100 percent for all but one or two random years and shares of 0 in the other years), which I corrected. Probably most problematic are the data on capital stock for each establishment. We should be cautious in using capital stock data, because their reliability is doubtful.

ation, as well as a fundamental source of positive spillovers. The Indonesian government has been nurturing the industry within the country since the late 1960s.[4] As in other Asian or Latin American countries, foreign automakers have been playing an important role in the development of the local automobile industry. Since the "new order" government assumed power in 1968, the automobile industry has received special treatment through local content rules, entry barriers, and foreign ownership restrictions (Hill 1996; Aswicahyono, Anas, and Rizal 2000). An import ban on completely built-up (CBU) cars was introduced in 1971 and remained in force until 1993, when it was replaced by tariffs ranging from 175 to 275 percent. In 1977, the government introduced a deletion program that required assemblers to use locally produced components. However, the program, which was intended to provide an opportunity for supporting industry to develop, turned out to be unsuccessful, probably due to a lack of technological capabilities of local producers, high profits required by distributors, the small production scale owing to market fragmentation, and the presence of foreign principals that kept their local agents as distributors rather than full manufacturers (Aswicahyono, Anas, and Rizal 2000). Moreover, the government used a licensing system that limited production of certain functional components such as transmissions and brake systems to one or two companies in order to ensure a minimum production scale. The system, however, not only hindered competition within the parts industry, but also led to cost increases due to small-lot production over a wide variety of products, since the one or two licensed companies were compelled to produce multiple parts under multiple brands (Takayasu, Ishizaki, and Mori 1996). As a result, although Indonesia is the second largest automobile market in the Association of Southeast Asian Nations (ASEAN)–4 countries (as of 1995), the number of auto parts manufacturers lags far behind that in Thailand (table 7.1). However, quite a few foreign auto parts suppliers (most of them Japanese) have established an affiliate in Indonesia due to the local content requirements and have been supplying major parts to automobile assemblers. The liberalization of the licensing system in 1993 and the expansion of automobile production in response to market growth in the early 1990s have brought an accelerating influx of both local and foreign parts manufacturers.[5] As in the other

4. The automobile industry is considered strategic for the following reasons: First, it supplies equipment used to meet the transportation requirement of the public; second, it creates employment opportunities in that sector and facilitates the introduction of high technology into its own and other markets; and third, it generates income for the government from import duties and taxes (Aswicahyono, Anas, and Rizal 2000).

5. The government implemented a number of deregulation packages in the 1990s. In 1993, the deletion program was replaced by an incentive program. The latter, designed to promote local parts, provided incentives to parts suppliers in the form of lower import duties on imported components, subcomponents, semifinished parts, and raw materials based on the extent of local content achieved. In 1995, the remaining components of commercial vehicles that had reached a local value-added ratio of 40 percent and of passenger cars that had reached a local value-added ratio of 60 percent were exempted from import duties. The 1995

Table 7.1 Structure of the Automobile Parts Industry in ASEAN Countries (as of January 1998)

Year	Indonesia Units	Indonesia Shares (%)	Thailand Units	Thailand Shares (%)	Malaysia Units	Malaysia Shares (%)	The Philippines Units	The Philippines Shares (%)	ASEAN-4 Units	ASEAN-4 Share (%)
	Total Number of Parts Manufacturers									
1998	150–200		750–800		200–250		150–200		1,300–1,500	
	Japanese Affiliates or Subsidiaries									
1998	82	(46.9)	209	(27.0)	61	(27.1)	54	(30.9)	406	(30.0)
	U.S. and European Affiliates or Subsidiaries									
1998	7	(4.0)	21	(2.7)	19	(8.4)	5	(2.9)	406	(4.0)

Source: Poapongsakorn and Wangdee (2000), table 2.

ASEAN-4 countries, most of the automobiles sold in Indonesia are made by Japanese automakers (table 7.2).

Figure 7.1 shows the development of automobile production since the 1960s. Despite the protection by the government, automobile production stagnated until the late 1980s. However, the industry displayed impressive growth from the early 1990s just until the financial crisis. The crisis heavily affected the industry: Automobile production dropped by about 85 percent from 389,000 units to 57,000. Although automobile production rapidly recovered from 1999 to 2000, the number of cars produced in 2000 remained below precrisis levels.

In terms of value added, the contribution of the automobile industry to the manufacturing sector increased more than threefold, from 1.6 percent in 1975 to 5.3 percent in 1990, although this subsequently declined to 4.6 percent in 1996. The share of the automobile industry in total manufacturing employment, however, remained at only 1.4–1.5 percent throughout this period. Despite the rigorous protection and state intervention, the size and significance of the Indonesian automobile industry is still quite small compared with Thailand, where the contribution of the automobile industry to the manufacturing sector reached about 15 percent in terms of value added and 4.7 percent in terms of employment in 1996 (Aswicahyono, Anas, and Rizal 2000; Ramstetter 2001a; Ito 2004).

deregulation package also removed restrictions on investments in the automobile industry for the production of new cars. Although deregulation packages suggested a shift in the government's policy paradigm from protectionism toward a market-oriented approach, the Soeharto Administration later launched the National Car Project, which contradicted the earlier market-oriented posture. However, following the International Monetary Fund (IMF) reform program in 1998 after the crisis, the government agreed that it would discontinue the granting of special tax, customs, and credit privileges to the National Car Project (Aswicahyono, Anas, and Rizal 2000).

Table 7.2 Automobile Markets in ASEAN Countries

	Indonesia		Thailand		Malaysia		The Philippines		ASEAN-4	
Year	Units	Shares (%)	Units	Shares (%)	Units	Shares (%)	Units	Shares (%)	Units	Shares (%)
					ASEAN Market Sales[a]					
1995	384,449	(27.7)	571,580	(36.9)	285,792	(4.1)	128,162	n.a.	1,369,983	n.a.
1996	337,399	(27.4)	589,126	(31.1)	364,789	(43.1)	162,095	n.a.	1,453,409	n.a.
1997	392,185	(30.6)	363,156	(22.8)	404,837	(41.6)	144,434	n.a.	1,304,612	n.a.
1998	167,234	n.a.	201,055	n.a.	198,787	(115.7)	86,751	n.a.	653,837	n.a.
1999	93,814	n.a.	218,330	n.a.	288,547	n.a.	74,415	n.a.	675,106	n.a.
					Sales by Japanese Manufacturers[b]					
1995	365,520	(95.1)	514,704	(90.0)	83,393	(29.2)	111,808	(87.2)	1,075,425	(78.5)
					Sales by U.S. and European Manufacturers[b]					
1995	17,137	(4.5)	46,322	(8.1)	21,706	(7.6)	1,127	(0.9)	86,292	(6.3)

Sources: Takayasu et al. (1996), tables 3, 8, 13, 17; Nikkan Jidosha Shinbun-sha (2000), *Jidosha Sangyo Handbook 2001* (Handbook of Automobile Industry 2001).

[a]Import shares in parentheses.

[b]Market shares in parentheses.

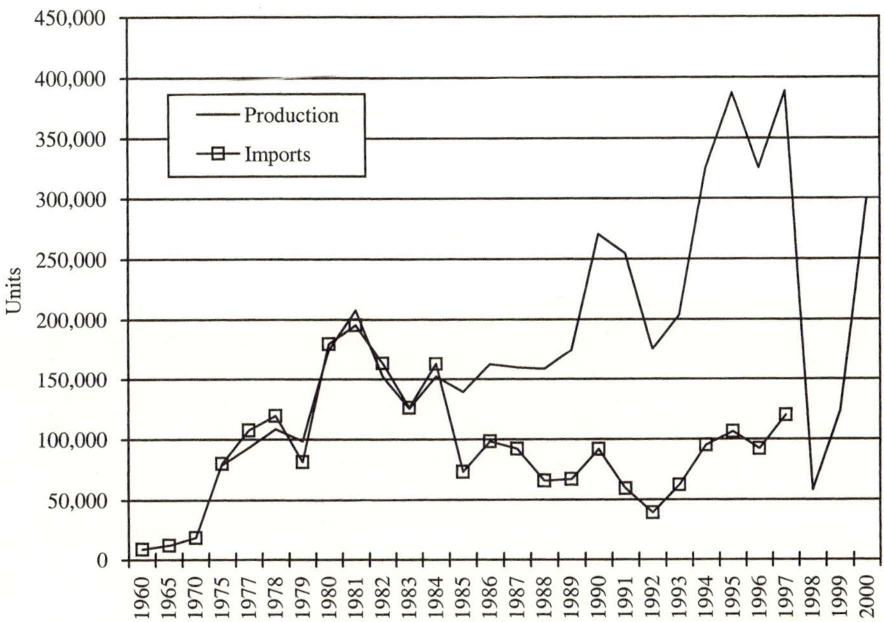

Fig. 7.1 Motor vehicle production and imports in Indonesia

Source: Nikkan Jidosha Shinbun-sha (various years).

7.2.2 Ownership and Market Structure

In the Indonesian automobile industry, foreign (particularly Japanese) firms have always been dominant players in the assembly and component sectors, except for the small-scale replacement parts segment—a pattern not untypical in developing countries. Tables 7.4 and 7.5 provide a detailed picture of the major automobile assemblers in Indonesia. Most major automobile manufacturing companies are joint ventures between local conglomerates and Japanese, European, or U.S. automakers established with the aim of gaining access to world-class technology. In 1995, there were fourteen major automobile assemblers (table 7.3). As shown in tables 7.3 and 7.4, all the assemblers rely on foreign partners, although the modalities of MNC entry have varied, depending on the regulatory environment and foreign partners' preferences.[6] Until recently, however, foreign partners were rarely able to acquire majority ownership. Another key feature of ownership patterns is a small number of local joint venture participants. The Astra group owns three manufacturers, Indomobil (Salim) group owns four, Krama Yudha group owns two, and so on. This characteristic derives in part from the highly regulated environment, in which the government virtually selected the major domestic business groups that were to participate in the industry (Aswicahyono, Basri, and Hill 2000). As a result, the Astra group holds a market share of over 50 percent, and the sum of the market shares of the three major groups (Astra, Indomobil, and Krama Yudha) reaches about 90 percent. Moreover, some assemblers produce more than one foreign brand name. Aswicahyono, Basri, and Hill point out that this feature prevents some foreign partners from having durable and close relationships with the local partner and making a major commitment to upgrading the technological capabilities of the local firm.

The Astra group, which laid its business foundations in the manufacturing of automobiles and machinery, holds a number of firms producing automobile components. According to a directory of automobile parts manufacturers (FOURIN 2000), there were 158 such automobile companies in Indonesia in the late 1990s. Out of the 158, 76 were Japanese-affiliated firms and 23 were under the control of the Astra group. Out of the 76 Japanese-affiliated firms, 15 were joint ventures with Astra group firms. Sato (1996) provides comprehensive and very detailed information on the Astra group and shows the high degree of the Astra group's vertical integration from body and general components to core components. According to her research, the Astra group is the only automaker that procures all

6. See Aswicahyono, Basri, and Hill (2000) for details. Entry to the components sector has generally been less restrictive, and in technologically less demanding segments there are some domestically owned firms that do not have formal tie-ups with foreign firms (Aswicahyono, Basri, and Hill 2000).

Table 7.3 **Major Automobile Manufacturers in Indonesia, 1995**

Group	Market Share (%)	Ethnic Group of Local Shareholders	Local Firm	Started Operation (date of establishment)	Foreign Partner: Joint Venture	Foreign Partner: Contract
(1) Astra	54.5	Government + Chinese	(a) Toyota Astra Motor	1972 (Apr. 1971)	Toyota (49%)	
			(b) Gaya Motor	(1955)		Daihatsu, Isuzu, Nissan, BMW, Ford, Peugeot
			(c) Pantja Motor	1974		Isuzu, Nissan
(2) Indomobil (Salim)	20.9	Chinese	(a) Indomobil Suzuki International	1991 (Mar. 1990)	Suzuki (49%)	
			(b) Ismac	1973 (Oct. 1971)		Nissan Chrysler
			(c) National Assemblers	1974 (Oct. 1971)		Mazda, Volvo, Hino
			(d) GM Buana Indonesia		GM (60%)	
(3) Krama Yudha	19.5	Pribumi[a]	(a) Krama Yudha Kesuma Motor	1981 (1970)		Mitsubishi
			(b) Krama Yudha Ratu Motor	1973 (Jun. 1973)		Mitsubishi
(4) Imora	1.3	Chinese	Prospect Motor	1975 (Jun. 1973)		Honda
(5) Bimantara	2.3	Pribumi[a] (Soeharto's son)	(a) German Motor	(1970)	Mercedes Benz (35%)	
			(b) Tricitra Karya	1995		Hyundai
(6) Starsauto	n.a.		Starsauto Dinamika	1995		Daewoo
(7) Humpus	0.0	Pribumi[a] (Soeharto's son)	Kia-Timor Motors		Kia (35%)	

Sources: Aswicahyono, Basri, and Hill (2000), table 3, pp. 220–21; Nomura (1996), table I-5, pp. 96–99.

[a]Pribumi is an Indonesian term referring to indigenous groups.

Table 7.4 Major Automobile Manufacturers in Indonesia, 1998

Group	Market Share (%)	Ethnic Group of Local Shareholders	Local Firm	Started Operation (date of establishment)	Foreign Partner: Joint Venture	Foreign Partner: Contract
(1) Astra	50.6	Government + Chinese	(a) Toyota Astra Motor	1972 (Apr. 1971)	Toyota (49%)	
			(b) Gaya Motor	(1955)		Isuzu, BMW, Ford, Peugeot
			(c) Pantja Motor	1974	Isuzu (12.5%)	
			(d) Astra Daihatsu Motor	(1992)	Daihatsu (40%)	
			(e) Astra Nissan Diesel Indonesia	1996	Nissan Diesel (12.5%)	
(2) Indomobil (Salim)	21.0	Chinese	(a) Indomobil Suzuki International	1991 (Mar. 1990)	Suzuki (49%)	
			(b) Ismac Nissan Manufacturing	1996 (1973)	Nissan (35%)	Audi, Volvo, Ssangyong
			(c) Ismac	1973 (Oct. 1971)		Mazda, Volvo, VW, Audi, Nissan, Chrysler
			(d) Hino Automobil Indonesia	Suspended	Hino (39%)	
(3) Krama Yudha	18.1	Pribumi[a]	(a) Krama Yudha Kesuma Motor	1981 (1970)	MKM (Mitsubishi Krama Yudha Motors & Mfg.) (99%)	
			(b) Krama Yudha Ratu Motor	1975 (Jun. 1973)		Mitsubishi

(4) Imora	1.8	Chinese	Honda Prospect Motor	(1992)	Honda Group (49%)	
(5) Bimantara	1.0	Pribumi[a] (Soeharto's son)	(a) Tricitra Karya	1995	Hyundai, Ford	
			(b) Bimantara Hyundai Indonesia	1999 (planned)	Hyundai (50%)	
(6) Starsauto	0.2		Starsauto Dinamika	1995		Daewoo
(7) Humpus	5.0	Pribumi[a] (Soeharto's son)	Kia-Timor Nasional	1998 (planned)	Hyundai (30%)	
(8) Mercedes-Benz Group Indonesia	1.3	Europe	Mercedes-Benz Group Indonesia	(1970)	DaimlerChrysler (95%)	
(9) GM	1.1	U.S.A.	GM Buana Indonesia	1994	GM (100%) *wholly owned by GM in 1997	

Sources: Aswicahyono, Basri, and Hill (2000), table 3, pp. 220–221; Nomura (1996), table I-5, pp. 96–99; FOURIN (2000).

[a]Pribumi is an Indonesian term referring to indigenous groups.

six functional components such as engines, chassis frames, brakes, and transmissions, within the group.[7]

After the 1997 Asian economic crisis, local partners' financial difficulties as well as sweeping liberalization allowed foreign investors to increase their ownership or newly acquire shares in Indonesian automobile firms, as can be seen in table 7.4. However, the Astra group still keeps the leading position in the Indonesian automobile industry.

7.3 Microdata and Productivity Measurement

7.3.1 The Data

The data used in this study are establishment-level unbalanced panel data for the period from 1990 to 1999 provided by Indonesia's BPS for the motor vehicle industry (BPS various years-a).[8] The data set provides information for each establishment on detailed industry classification, geographical location, type of ownership, starting year of commercial production, output, value added, materials and energy used, number of workers, wages, inventory, book value of fixed assets, and so on. Although each establishment is labeled by the same identification code for every year, the name of the establishment is not provided by the BPS. Moreover, for reasons of confidentiality, it is not allowed to expose the raw data or indexes for an establishment and to match the establishment data with other corporate data sources.[9] This study performs a thorough analysis of plant productivity at the five-digit Indonesian Standard Industrial Classification (ISIC) industry level: that is, motor vehicles (automobile assemblers, ISIC 38431/34100), motor vehicle bodies (automobile body suppliers, 38432/34200), and motor vehicle components and apparatuses (automobile parts suppliers, 38433/34300).[10] Table 7.5 shows the number of establishments,

7. With regards to these functional components, the government used a licensing system, as mentioned previously in this section. In this situation, the Astra group secured licenses for all items because Astra was in a favorable position to secure the limited licenses (Sato 1996).

8. The establishment-level data were collected for the Industrial Survey conducted annually by the BPS. Covered in the survey are large and medium establishments (i.e., all establishments employing twenty workers or more). The response rate of the annual survey is around 75–85 percent—for example, 85 percent, 84.47 percent, and 75.35 percent for the years 1991, 1995, and 1999, respectively.

9. Indeed, it is extremely difficult to identify the name of the establishment by matching it with the *Manufacturing Industry Directory* provided by the BPS, for the following reasons: (1) The directory only includes categories such as detailed industry, geographical location, and number of workers, but does not include other information such as starting year of operation and fixed assets; (2) many establishments agglomerate in some particular regions or subregions, which makes it difficult to use the location information as a key criterion; (3) information on the number of workers, which often varies in a short period, is not a good criterion particularly for medium or small establishments.

10. The ISIC was changed beginning with the 1998 survey. For the motor vehicles industry, for example, the ISIC code had been 38431 before 1998 but was changed to 34100 in 1998.

Table 7.5 **Industry Definitions by Five-Digit Indonesia Standard Industrial Classification and Employment, Output, and Value Added, by Industry**

	Motor Vehicles (38431/34100)[a]		
	1990	1995	1999
No. of Establishments (in which foreign-owned establishments)			
BPS	10	14	13
	(2)	(5)	(8)
This sample	7	7	5
	(2)	(3)	(3)
No. of Persons Engaged (share of which accounted for by foreign-owned establishments)			
BPS	7,642	14,181	10,533
This sample	5,675	7,626	5,437
	D	(75.7%)	(85.0%)
Value of Gross Output (unit: millions of rupiahs) (share of which accounted for by foreign-owned establishments)			
BPS	1,812,352	4,573,780	3,434,349
This sample	1,190,773	2,911,686	3,101,157
	D	(81.7%)	(98.1%)
Value Added at Market Prices (unit: millions of rupiahs) (share of which accounted for by foreign-owned establishments)			
BPS	854,399	2,160,723	1,741,803
This sample	663,256	1,527,761	1,537,402
	D	(92.2%)	(96.9%)
Main Country of the Investors of Foreign-Owned Establishments (this sample)			
Japan	1	1	2
United States	0	1	0
Germany	0	0	0
Korea	0	0	0
Others	1	1	1
Unknown	0	0	0
Foreign Ownership Share of Foreign-Owned Establishments (this sample)			
Distribution (%)			
0 < & <30	0	0	0
30 =< & < 50	1	2	2
50 =< & <70	1	1	0
70 =< & <90	0	0	1
90 =< & <100	0	0	0
100	0	0	0
Range (%)			
Minimum share	49	49	49
Maximum share	57	60	70

(*continued*)

Table 7.5 (continued)

	Motor Vehicle Bodies (38432/34200)[a]		
	1990	1995	1999
No. of establishments (in which foreign-owned establishments)			
BPS	118	124	81
	(7)	(2)	(1)
This sample	54	60	39
	(0)	(0)	(1)
No. of Persons Engaged (share of which accounted for by foreign-owned establishments)			
BPS	18,824	17,831	7,381
This sample	8,792	9,723	4,483
	n.a.	n.a.	D
Value of Gross Output (unit: millions of rupiahs) (share of which accounted for by foreign-owned establishments)			
BPS	340,133	429,871	293,416
This sample	104,444	179,785	144,216
	n.a.	n.a.	D
Value Added at Market Prices (unit: millions of rupiahs) (share of which accounted for by foreign-owned establishments)			
BPS	151,402	160,594	188,572
This sample	41,846	57,991	105,865
	n.a.	n.a.	D
Main Country of the Investors of Foreign-Owned Establishments (this sample)			
Japan	0	0	0
United States	0	0	0
Germany	0	0	0
Korea	0	0	0
Others	0	0	0
Unknown	0	0	1
Foreign Ownership Share of Foreign-Owned Establishments (this sample)			
Distribution (%)			
0 < & <30	0	0	0
30 =< & < 50	0	0	1
50 =< & <70	0	0	0
70 =< & <90	0	0	0
90 =< & <100	0	0	0
100	0	0	0
Range (%)			
Minimum share	n.a.	n.a.	60
Maximum share	n.a.	n.a.	60

Table 7.5 (continued)

	Motor Vehicle Component and Apparatus (38433/34300)[a]		
	1990	1995	1999
No. of establishments (in which foreign-owned establishments)			
BPS	68	121	150
	(8)	(16)	(41)
This sample	34	44	75
	(6)	(8)	(17)
No. of Persons Engaged (share of which accounted for by foreign-owned establishments)			
BPS	11,622	29,185	23,755
This sample	8,247	16,318	15,950
	(27.4%)	(26.4%)	(38.2%)
Value of Gross Output (unit: millions of rupiahs) (share of which accounted for by foreign-owned establishments)			
BPS	988,156	3,531,507	5,049,558
This sample	687,163	2,543,486	3,583,401
	(62.9%)	(51.0%)	(65.4%)
Value Added at Market Prices (unit: millions of rupiahs) (share of which accounted for by foreign-owned establishments)			
BPS	329,198	1,014,521	2,478,389
This sample	274,140	765,440	1,695,000
	(63.1%)	(68.6%)	(67.1%)
Main Country of the Investors of Foreign-Owned Establishments (this sample)			
Japan	4	6	7
United States	0	0	0
Germany	0	0	1
Korea	0	0	1
Others	0	0	0
Unknown	2	2	8
Foreign Ownership Share of Foreign-Owned Establishments (this sample)			
Distribution (%)			
0 < & <30	1	1	0
30 =< & <50	1	1	1
50 =< & <70	4	5	4
70 =< & <90	0	1	5
90 =< & <100	0	0	3
100	0	0	4
Range (%)			
Minimum share	25	25	40
Maximum share	65	70	100

Sources: Author's calculations based on BPS establishment-level data (various years-a).

Notes: BPS figures are calculated from the raw data set provided by the BPS. "This sample" figures are calculated from the data set compiled for my analyses in this paper. n.a. = not available.

[a]Industrial classification code for BPS, *Statistik Industri* (various years-d). The industry code was changed in 1998. D = suppressed to avoid disclosure of data of individual establishments.

employment, output, and value added in each five-digit industry in 1990, 1995, and 1999. Because many observations in the raw data provided by the BPS do not contain sufficient information or because there are not contiguous time series observations for many establishments, such deficient observations were excluded from the sample used for the productivity analysis in this paper. The number of establishments included in the final compilation by the BPS, *Statistik Industri* (BPS, various years-d) is ten, for example, in the motor vehicles industry (38431/34100) for the year 1990, which is shown in the row labeled "BPS" in table 7.5. However, after the unreliable observations have been eliminated, the sample used in this study contains seven establishments for motor vehicles in 1990 shown in the next row in table 7.5, labeled "This sample." While "foreign-owned establishments" in this study are defined as those where the foreign ownership share is more than zero, in the present sample the foreign ownership share in fact exceeded 25 percent in all cases. In terms of gross output and value added, the share of foreign-owned establishments is extremely high at more than 80 percent in the motor vehicles industry and 50–70 percent in the motor vehicle component industry. However, in terms of the number of establishments and employment, the foreign share is relatively small. As for the nationality of foreign establishments, it was found that the majority of foreign-owned establishments were Japanese-affiliated ones. The table also shows that quite a few establishments newly entered the Indonesian automobile industry during the sample period, particularly in the motor vehicle component industry after 1995. As mentioned in the previous section, this trend is attributable to the economic boom in Indonesia and neighboring ASEAN countries in the early 1990s, the introduction of the incentive program, and the liberalization of the licensing system in 1993.[11]

Table 7.6 shows a set of descriptive statistics on the sampled establishments by detailed industry in 1990, 1995, and 1999.[12] The table shows that the different indicators move quite differently over time in each of the three sectors, which might in part be due to heterogeneity among the establishments and to the small sample size, particularly in the motor vehicles in-

11. Table 7A.1 summarizes the entry and exit flows in the data set compiled for the analysis in this paper.

12. The statistics for the overall motor vehicle industry (at the four-digit ISIC level or the two-digit level in the new ISIC) are presented in table 7A.2. The upper panel of table 7A.2 gives the simple mean of each variable for all the sampled establishments, while the bottom panel of table 7A.2 gives the simple mean only for the large establishments in the sample. Table 7A.2 shows that employment, output, and value added per establishment increased in the period from 1990 to 1995 but then decreased from 1995 to 1999 in real terms. Capital stock and wages, however, increased in the period from 1990 to 1999 in real terms. Moreover, regarding productivity measures, average variable cost and value added per employee deteriorated during the period from 1990 to 1995 but recovered during 1995 to 1999. Output per employee improved from 1990 to 1999. These productivity measures indicate that the average productivity increased from 1995 to 1999 in real terms despite the 1997 financial crisis and the succeeding economic disorder.

Table 7.6 **Descriptive Statistics of the Sample of Establishments, by Detailed Industry (simple average)**

	Motor Vehicles (38431/34100)		
	1990	1995	1999
No. of observations	7	7	5
Herfindahl index	0.828	0.659	0.949
No. of employees	811	1,089	1,087
Output per establishment[a]	217,000	357,000	275,000
Value added per establishment[a]	146,000	220,000	184,000
Capital stock per establishment[a]	11,100	52,400	68,500
Years in operation	18.4	23.4	18.6
Productivity measures			
Average variable cost[b]	0.40	0.50	0.58
Output per employee[a]	108.9	225.1	83.7
Value added per employee[a]	70.6	85.4	57.6
TFP (in logarithm)	3.5	3.0	2.6
Inventory ratios (%)			
Total inventory	n.a.	23.1	21.4
Final goods inventory	n.a.	10.6	11.6
Work-in-process inventory	n.a.	1.3	3.6
Raw materials inventory	n.a.	11.9	9.5
Other indicators			
Capital-labor ratio[a]	17.8	52.5	66.9
Share of nonproduction workers (%)	24.3	27.5	33.5
Production worker wages[c]	4,479	6,749	4,699
Nonproduction worker wages[c]	8,893	11,235	6,868
Price-cost margin (%)[d]	58.6	50.5	34.9
Export share in output (%)	0.0	0.0	20.0
Import ratio (%)	44.6	27.7	39.6
	Motor Vehicle Bodies (38432/34200)		
	1990	1995	1999
No. of observations	54	60	39
Herfindahl index	0.088	0.089	0.381
No. of employees	163	162	115
Output per establishment[a]	2,441	2,540	1,580
Value added per establishment[a]	1,127	970	1,215
Capital stock per establishment[a]	1,455	2,355	3,226
Years in operation	9.8	14.7	15.6
Productivity measures			
Average variable cost[b]	0.73	0.72	0.64
Output per employee[a]	14.6	14.1	7.9
Value added per employee[a]	5.9	5.6	4.9
TFP (in logarithm)	2.7	2.5	2.3

(*continued*)

Table 7.6 (continued)

	Motor Vehicle Bodies (38432/34200)		
	1990	1995	1999
Inventory ratios (%)			
Total inventory	n.a.	20.5	33.3
Final goods inventory	n.a.	2.2	5.1
Work-in-process inventory	n.a.	8.1	12.4
Raw materials inventory	n.a.	14.0	20.6
Other indicators			
Capital-labor ratio[a]	26.7	27.9	34.3
Share of nonproduction workers (%)	14.1	19.1	24.0
Production worker wages[c]	1,763	1,883	1,454
Nonproduction worker wages[c]	3,749	2,839	3,210
Price-cost margin (%)[d]	26.5	27.7	30.2
Export share in output (%)	1.1	0.8	0.0
Import ratio (%)	5.8	3.5	5.7
	Motor Vehicle Component and Apparatus (38433/34300)		
	1990	1995	1999
No. of observations	34	44	75
Herfindahl index	0.175	0.174	0.087
No. of employees	243	371	213
Output per establishment[a]	25,600	49,600	21,300
Value added per establishment[a]	14,000	16,100	13,200
Capital stock per establishment[a]	6,507	10,500	17,600
Years in operation	9.4	13.2	10.7
Productivity measures			
Average variable cost[b]	0.54	0.64	0.61
Output per employee[a]	87.2	85.1	82.0
Value added per employee[a]	43.6	25.2	54.1
TFP (in logarithm)	2.6	2.4	2.2
Inventory ratios (%)			
Total inventory	n.a.	27.4	33.2
Final goods inventory	n.a.	8.2	7.2
Work-in-process inventory	n.a.	4.0	4.5
Raw materials inventory	n.a.	16.3	24.9
Other indicators			
Capital-labor ratio[a]	24.8	24.7	88.4
Share of nonproduction workers (%)	21.3	18.9	19.9
Production worker wages[c]	2,707	2,966	3,286
Nonproduction worker wages[c]	7,200	8,655	18,083
Price-cost margin (%)[d]	44.4	39.5	32.9
Export share in output (%)	0.0	4.0	9.6
Import ratio (%)	42.9	47.7	40.0

Source: Author's calculations based on BPS establishment-level data (various years-a).

Notes: Some of the observations were not included because of missing values or recording mistakes. n.a. = not available.

[a]In 1993 millions of rupiahs. For price deflators, see appendix A.

[b]Average variable cost is defined as the sum of labor and intermediate input costs divided by output.

[c]In 1993 1,000 rupiahs. For price deflators, see appendix A.

[d]Price-cost margin is defined as (value added – wages paid)/output.

dustry. For example, in the motor vehicles industry, labor productivity measured by output per employee in real terms increased from 1990 to 1995 but decreased from 1995 to 1999, whereas it decreased throughout the entire period in the motor vehicle bodies and the motor vehicle component industries. Production worker wages, on the other hand, first increased but then decreased in the motor vehicles and the motor vehicle bodies industries, but rose in both periods in the motor vehicle component industry. In contrast, uniform movements for all three industries could be observed for output, which grew from 1990 to 1995 but then shrank, and for capital stock per establishment, which increased throughout the period. TFP, finally, deteriorated throughout the period from 1990 to 1999.[13]

Comparing the various statistics across industries, the table presents many interesting observations: The Herfindahl index measured by output share of each establishment is extremely high in the motor vehicles industry, implying a high concentration in this industry. The average price-cost margin is also high, particularly in the motor vehicles industry, which again suggests a lack of competition in the industry. It should be noted, however, that the price-cost margin diminishes in 1999 in the motor vehicles and the motor vehicle component industries. This trend might reflect the demand contraction after the crisis, although the price-cost margins nevertheless remain at quite a high level.[14] The shares of nonproduction workers as well as wages are both higher in the motor vehicles industry than in other industries, which might be a reflection of the fact that motor vehicle assembler establishments are owned by a large company. Total inventory ratios are high at around 20–30 percent in every industry, and import ratios are also high in the motor vehicles and the motor vehicle component industries. Another notable observation is that the export share in output goes up remarkably in the motor vehicles and the motor vehicle component industries during this period.

7.3.2 Productivity Differences between Foreign and Local Establishments

Table 7.7 compares a set of descriptive statistics of foreign and local establishments by detailed industry.[15] The first two columns give the mean

13. Following Baily, Hulten, and Campbell (1992) and Okamoto (1999), TFP of the *i*th establishment in each industry for year t is defined as follows: $\ln \text{TFP}_{it} = \ln Y_{it} - \alpha_L \ln L_{it} - \alpha_K \ln K_{it} - \alpha_M \ln M_{it}$, where Y_{it} is real gross output, and L_{it}, K_{it}, and M_{it} are labor, capital, and intermediate inputs for the *i*th establishment in year t. α_L, α_K, and α_M are factor income shares of labor, capital, and intermediate inputs, averaged over industries and years of the period from 1990 to 1999.

14. Average price-cost margins are in the range from 26 percent to 59 percent in table 7.6. These figures seem to be high compared with those in Thailand and Japan. The price-cost margins are around 25 percent in the Thai automobile industry and around 20 percent in the Japanese automobile industry (Ito 2001, 2004).

15. Table 7A.3 presents a comparison between large foreign and large local establishments in the overall motor vehicle industry. Given that most local establishments are much smaller in size than foreign ones, it appears more meaningful to compare productivity measures between establishments of similar size. The table shows that the size of establishments measured

Table 7.7 Descriptive Statistics of the Sample of Establishments by Ownership in the Motor Vehicle Industries, by Detailed Industry (simple average)

	Motor Vehicles (38431/34100)											
	1990–96 pooled		1990		1995		1999		Ratio of Foreign to Domestic			
	DO	FO	DO	FO	DO	FO	DO	FO	1990–96	1990	1995	1999
No. of observations	31	19	5	2	4	3	2	3				
No. of employees	426	1,843***	407	1,821	464	1,923	409	1,540	4.3	4.5	4.1	3.8
Output per establishment[a]	80,457	504,258***	24,144	699,903	114,633	679,119	13,381	449,704	6.3	29.0	5.9	33.6
Value added per establishment[a]	27,502	345,394**	14,230	477,003	29,185	475,109	11,139	299,881	12.6	33.6	16.3	27.0
Capital stock per establishment[a]	10,083	70,312***	7,228	20,753	16,941	99,631	11,668	106,417	7.0	2.9	5.9	9.1
Years in operation	21.6	18.2	19.2	16.5	26.0	20.0	16.0	20.3	0.8	0.9	0.8	1.3
Average variable cost[b]	0.61	0.52	0.42	0.35	0.52	0.47	0.56	0.59	0.9	0.8	0.9	1.1
Output per employee[a]	177.4	149.7	57.5	237.3	265.3	171.5	20.5	125.9	0.8	4.1	0.6	6.1
Value added per employee[a]	59.4	90.0	33.6	162.9	63.3	115.0	16.9	84.8	1.5	4.8	1.8	5.0
TFP (in logarithm)	3.3	3.3	3.4	3.9	2.8	3.2	2.5	2.6	1.0	1.1	1.2	1.1
Total inventory (%)[c]	26.1	39.3	n.a.	n.a.	13.8	35.5	46.6	4.5	1.5	n.a.	1.4	0.1
Final goods inventory (%)[c]	3.7	6.1	n.a.	n.a.	0.6	23.9	28.8	0.1	1.6	n.a.	2.6	0.0
Work-in-process inventory (%)[c]	13.5	3.1	n.a.	n.a.	0.9	1.9	8.3	0.5	0.2	n.a.	40.8	0.1
Raw materials inventory (%)[c]	54.7	20.3	n.a.	n.a.	0.1	10.7	17.9	3.9	0.4	n.a.	2.2	0.2
Capital-labor ratio[a]	25.5	43.2	20.1	12.3	39.0	70.4	28.6	92.5	1.7	0.6	1.8	3.2
Share of nonproduction workers (%)	26.6	27.1	27.1	17.3	23.6	32.8	31.1	35.0	1.0	0.6	1.4	1.1
Production worker wages[d]	4,852	6,417	4,082	5,469	6,223	7,449	4,198	5,033	1.3	1.3	1.2	1.2
Nonproduction worker wages[d]	9,692	11,125	7,399	12,627	9,545	13,489	3,889	8,854	1.1	1.7	1.4	2.3
Price-cost margin (%)[e]	45.8	48.5	56.8	63.2	48.4	53.1	43.7	29.0	1.1	1.1	1.1	0.7
Export share in output (%)	0.0	3.8	0.0	0.0	0.0	0.0	0.0	33.3	n.a.	n.a.	n.a.	n.a.
Import ratio (%)	31.7	52.3*	42.9	48.8	18.3	40.1	0.0	66.1	1.6	1.1	2.2	n.a.

	Motor Vehicle Bodies (38432/34200)											
No. of observations	416	0	54	0	60	0	38	1				
No. of employees	164	n.a.	163	n.a.	162	n.a.	80	1,445	n.a.	n.a.	n.a.	18.1
Output per establishment[a]	2,588	n.a.	2,441	n.a.	2,540	n.a.	650	36,916	n.a.	n.a.	n.a.	56.8
Value added per establishment[a]	1,159	n.a.	1,127	n.a.	970	n.a.	398	32,266	n.a.	n.a.	n.a.	81.2
Capital stock per establishment[a]	1,827	n.a.	1,455	n.a.	2,355	n.a.	2,628	25,946	n.a.	n.a.	n.a.	9.9
Years in operation	12.5	n.a.	9.8	n.a.	14.7	n.a.	15.4	23.0	n.a.	n.a.	n.a.	1.5
Average variable cost[b]	0.72	n.a.	0.73	n.a.	0.72	n.a.	0.66	0.15	n.a.	n.a.	n.a.	0.2
Output per employee[a]	14.7	n.a.	14.6	n.a.	14.1	n.a.	7.4	25.5	n.a.	n.a.	n.a.	3.5
Value added per employee[a]	6.7	n.a.	5.9	n.a.	5.6	n.a.	4.4	22.3	n.a.	n.a.	n.a.	5.1
TFP (in logarithm)	2.6	n.a.	2.7	n.a.	2.5	n.a.	2.3	3.3	n.a.	n.a.	n.a.	1.5
Total inventory (%)[c]	19.8	n.a.	n.a.	n.a.	20.5	n.a.	32.7	55.6	n.a.	n.a.	n.a.	1.7
Final goods inventory (%)[c]	1.5	n.a.	n.a.	n.a.	2.2	n.a.	5.0	10.0	n.a.	n.a.	n.a.	2.0
Work-in-process inventory (%)[c]	3.7	n.a.	n.a.	n.a.	8.1	n.a.	11.9	30.9	n.a.	n.a.	n.a.	2.6
Raw materials inventory (%)[c]	13.5	n.a.	n.a.	n.a.	14.0	n.a.	20.7	17.2	n.a.	n.a.	n.a.	0.8
Capital-labor ratio[a]	27.2	n.a.	26.7	n.a.	27.9	n.a.	34.7	18.0	n.a.	n.a.	n.a.	0.5
Share of nonproduction workers (%)	18.3	n.a.	14.1	n.a.	19.1	n.a.	23.9	27.2	n.a.	n.a.	n.a.	1.1
Production worker wages[d]	1,954	n.a.	1,763	n.a.	1,883	n.a.	1,480	473	n.a.	n.a.	n.a.	0.3
Nonproduction worker wages[d]	3,413	n.a.	3,749	n.a.	2,839	n.a.	3,278	750	n.a.	n.a.	n.a.	0.2
Price-cost margin (%)[e]	29.4	n.a.	26.5	n.a.	27.7	n.a.	28.7	85.2	n.a.	n.a.	n.a.	3.0
Export share in output (%)	0.6	n.a.	1.1	n.a.	0.8	n.a.	0.0	0.0	n.a.	n.a.	n.a.	n.a.
Import ratio (%)	4.1	n.a.	5.8	n.a.	3.5	n.a.	5.8	0.0	n.a.	n.a.	n.a.	0.0
	Motor Vehicle Component and Apparatus (38433/34300)											
No. of observations	255	55	28	6	36	8	58	17				
No. of employees	255	452***	214	377	334	539	170	358*	1.8	1.8	1.6	2.1
Output per establishment[a]	18,456	99,905***	11,407	92,067	29,636	139,366	9,497	61,520**	5.4	8.1	4.7	6.5
Value added per establishment[a]	6,820	48,892***	6,797	47,806	6,371	59,967	6,091	37,433**	7.2	7.0	9.4	6.1
Capital stock per establishment[a]	8,724	22,625***	5,450	11,439	9,013	17,345	12,786	34,077**	2.6	2.1	1.9	2.7
Years in operation	11.1	10.8	9.5	9.2	13.3	12.9	11.4	8.2	1.0	1.0	1.0	0.7
Average variable cost[b]	0.63	0.51**	0.55	0.46	0.66	0.55	0.57	0.74	0.8	0.8	0.8	1.3

(*continued*)

Table 7.7 (continued)

	Motor Vehicle Component and Apparatus (38433/34300)											
	1990–96 pooled		1990		1995		1999		Ratio of Foreign to Domestic			
	DO	FO	DO	FO	DO	FO	DO	FO	1990–96	1990	1995	1999
Output per employee[a]	61.0	152.2***	69.1	172.1	66.6	168.5	42.8	215.7*	2.5	2.5	2.5	5.0
Value added per employee[a]	24.6	71.8***	33.1	92.7	16.3	65.4	27.4	145.4*	2.9	2.8	4.0	5.3
TFP (in logarithm)	2.3	3.0***	2.5	3.2**	2.3	3.1*	2.1	2.4	1.3	1.3	1.3	1.1
Total inventory (%)[c]	20.4	24.0	n.a.	n.a.	27.9	24.9	41.1	10.2**	1.2	n.a.	0.9	0.2
Final goods inventory (%)[c]	4.6	4.4	n.a.	n.a.	9.0	4.7	8.9	2.3***	1.0	n.a.	0.5	0.3
Work-in-process inventory (%)[c]	2.6	1.0***	n.a.	n.a.	3.7	5.4	5.6	1.1**	0.4	n.a.	1.5	0.2
Raw materials inventory (%)[c]	11.7	13.8	n.a.	n.a.	15.5	19.8	31.1	6.8	1.2	n.a.	1.3	0.2
Capital-labor ratio[a]	35.2	52.9	25.0	24.3	24.2	26.9	63.1	174.7*	1.5	1.0	1.1	2.8
Share of nonproduction workers (%)	20.3	24.1*	20.6	24.5	18.2	21.6	18.8	23.7	1.2	1.2	1.2	1.3
Production worker wages[d]	2,499	4,680***	2,245	4,864**	2,448	5,299**	1,930	7,912**	1.9	2.2	2.2	4.1
Nonproduction worker wages[d]	6,789	10,497***	5,825	13,617*	8,632	8,757	8,104	49,782	1.5	2.3	1.0	6.1
Price-cost margin (%)[e]	38.6	48.3**	43.2	49.9	37.9	46.9	38.6	47.7	1.3	1.2	1.2	1.2
Export share in output (%)	3.7	3.0	0.0	0.2	4.9	0.0**	5.0	25.3*	n.a.	n.a.	n.a.	5.1
Import ratio (%)	40.6	65.9***	38.1	65.4	43.8	65.4	32.2	64.6***	1.6	1.7	1.5	2.0

Source: Author's calculations based on BPS establishment-level data (various years-a).

Notes: Some of the observations were not included because of missing values or recording mistakes. The *t*-tests are performed based on the assumption of unequal variances. n.a. = not available; DO = domestic-owned; FO = foreign-owned.

[a]In 1993 millions of rupiahs. For price deflators, see appendix A.

[b]Average variable cost is defined as the sum of labor and intermediate input costs divided by output.

[c]Inventory data are not available for 1990 and 1991.

[d]In 1993 1,000 rupiahs. For price deflators, see appendix A.

[e]Price-cost margin is defined as (value added – wages paid)/output.

***Significant at the 1 percent level.

**Significant at the 5 percent level.

*Significant at the 10 percent level.

values for domestic and foreign-owned establishments for years before the financial crisis (i.e., from 1990 to 1996). In addition, the local-foreign comparisons are conducted for the years 1990, 1995, and 1999. *T*-tests are also performed to examine the statistical difference between the domestic and the foreign-owned establishments. The four columns from the right show the ratio of foreign- to domestic-owned establishments.

Table 7.7 indicates that foreign establishments tend to be larger than local ones in terms of employment, output, value added, and capital stock. Wages and labor productivity, measured by output per employee, value added per employee, and TFP, are significantly higher for foreign establishments in the motor vehicle component industry. However, these differences are not statistically significant in the motor vehicles industry, which again might be due in part to heterogeneity among the establishments and to the small sample size. One interesting observation is that inventory ratios tend to be higher for foreign establishments but are lower in 1999 in the motor vehicles and the motor vehicle component industries (statistically significant in the latter). The import ratios tend to be much higher for foreign establishments in the motor vehicles and the motor vehicle component industries, and they are statistically significant in some cases. In addition, the capital-labor ratio and the share of nonproduction workers are higher for foreign establishments in many cases, but the difference is not statistically significant.

7.3.3 Comparing Productivity Trajectories

The last thing to be done in this section is to compare the productivity trajectories of foreign and local establishments, controlling for industry-wide time effects as well as observable plant-specific productivity determinants like age and size. Four productivity proxies are used here: average variable cost (AVC), output per employee in real terms (LAB), value added per employee in real terms (VALAB), and total factor productivity (TFP). Average variable cost is defined as the sum of labor and intermediate input costs divided by output in real terms. To purge these productivity measures of industrywide time effects and observable plant-specific characteristics, each is expressed in logarithms and regressed on time dummies (D_{jt}, specific to year *t* and the *j*th five-digit ISIC industry), age of the establishment (AGE), age of the establishment squared, size of the establishment (SIZE), and size of the establishment squared. Both age and size are measured in logarithms. Establishment size is measured by employment and normalized on mean industry employment.[16] In addition, interaction terms of age

by output, value added, and capital stock is generally larger for foreign establishments, and that wages, labor productivity, the capital-labor ratio, and the import ratio tend to be higher for foreign establishments.

16. It might be preferable to use capital stock data instead as the size variable. However, given the poor reliability of capital stock data, we used employment data as a proxy for the size variable.

variables and the dummy variable for foreign establishments (FOR) are included in order to see the marginal difference of the age effects between local and foreign establishments. The following equations are estimated:

$$(1)\quad \ln(\text{PRODUCTIVITY}) = \sum_{j=1}^{J}\sum_{t=1}^{T} \gamma_{jt} D_{jt} + \beta_1 \ln(\text{AGE}_{it}) + \beta_2[\ln(\text{AGE}_{it})]^2 + \beta_3 \ln(\text{SIZE}_{it}) + \beta_4[\ln(\text{SIZE}_{it})]^2 + \varepsilon_{it}$$

$$(2)\quad \ln(\text{PRODUCTIVITY}) = \sum_{j=1}^{J}\sum_{t=1}^{T} \gamma'_{jt} D_{jt} + \beta'_1 \ln(\text{AGE}_{it}) + \beta'_2[\ln(\text{AGE}_{it})]^2 + \beta'_3\text{FOR}_{it} \cdot \ln(\text{AGE}_{it}) + \beta'_4\text{FOR}_{it} \cdot [\ln(\text{AGE}_{it})]^2 + \beta'_5 \ln(\text{SIZE}_{it}) + \beta'_6 [\ln(\text{SIZE}_{it})]^2 \beta'_7\text{FOR}_{it} + \varepsilon'_{it}$$

with PRODUCTIVITY = AVC, LAB, VALAB, and TFP.

The residuals from the regressions using equation (1) are then used as the indexes of deviation from time- and industry-specific productivity norms. In order to see whether the productivity difference between foreign and local establishments is significant or not, the dummy variable for foreign establishments (FOR) is added in equation (2).

Table 7.8 presents the regression results of the equations. The scale effects are strongly significant in all equations. Labor productivity measures (output per employee and value added per employee) and TFP improve with age, but the marginal difference of the age effects between local and foreign establishments is not statistically significant. In labor productivity equations (4) and (6), the coefficients on the dummy variable for foreign establishments (FOR) are positive and significant, suggesting that foreign establishments enjoy higher labor productivity than local ones. However, in TFP equation (8), the coefficient on the dummy variable for foreign establishments (FOR) is negative and not significant.[17]

Using the residuals of equations (1), (3), (5), and (7) in table 7.8, unweighted average trajectories for residuals of average variable cost, output per employee, value added per employee, and TFP are calculated and presented by plant ownership type in figure 7.2. In panel A through panel D, foreign-owned establishments are shown to be substantially and consistently more efficient than local ones. Although the gap in labor productivity (output per employee and value added per employee) between local and

17. An extremely large assembler establishment in terms of both employment and output is included in the data set. When conducting regression analyses without this outlier establishment, the results were almost identical. However, the coefficient on the dummy variable, FOR, became insignificant for the equation of value added per employee, although the coefficient on FOR for the equation of output per employee remained positive at the 10 percent significance level.

Table 7.8 **Determinants of Productivity (ordinary least squares regressions)**

	Dependent Variable			
	ln(average variable cost)		ln(real output per employee)	
	(1)	(2)	(3)	(4)
ln(AGE)	0.006	0.042	0.498*	0.761***
	(0.05)	(0.32)	(1.87)	(2.76)
(ln(AGE))^2	0.007	–0.003	–0.158**	–0.211***
	(0.23)	(–0.11)	(–2.60)	(–3.43)
FOR · ln(AGE)		–0.877		–0.763
		(–1.56)		(–0.89)
FOR · (ln(AGE))^2		0.221		0.212
		(1.61)		(0.94)
ln(SIZE)	–0.080***	–0.065***	0.390***	0.296***
	(–4.32)	(–4.21)	(10.06)	(8.76)
(ln(SIZE))^2	–0.003	–0.004	–0.082***	–0.090***
	(–0.32)	(–0.47)	(–3.90)	(–5.06)
FOR		0.470		1.593**
		(0.88)		(2.24)
No. of observations	1,134	1,134	1,134	1,134
F	4.88***	4.82***	18.76***	20.21***
Adj. R^2	0.118	0.145	0.327	0.378
	ln(real value added per employee)		ln(Total Factor Productivity)	
	(5)	(6)	(7)	(8)
ln(AGE)	0.274	0.529*	0.275*	0.228
	(1.05)	(1.95)	(1.91)	(1.51)
(ln(AGE))^2	–0.117**	–0.165***	–0.082***	–0.074**
	(–1.99)	(–2.76)	(–2.60)	(–2.27)
FOR · ln(AGE)		–0.458		0.561
		(–0.55)		(1.05)
FOR · (ln(AGE))^2		0.109		–0.096
		(0.50)		(–0.71)
ln(SIZE)	0.385***	0.302***	0.166***	0.135***
	(10.13)	(9.20)	(8.26)	(7.90)
(ln(SIZE))^2	–0.078***	–0.082***	–0.015	–0.019*
	(–3.78)	(–4.64)	(–1.35)	(–1.94)
FOR		1.427**		–0.363
		(2.06)		(–0.76)
No. of observations	1,124	1,124	1,125	1,125
F	23.74***	24.38***	11.56***	11.23***
Adj. R^2	0.382	0.430	0.246	0.275

Source: Author's calculations.

Notes: The numbers in parentheses are *t*-statistics based on White's robust standard errors (White 1980). All equations include interaction of year dummies with industry dummies.

***Significant at the 1 percent level.

**Significant at the 5 percent level.

*Significant at the 10 percent level.

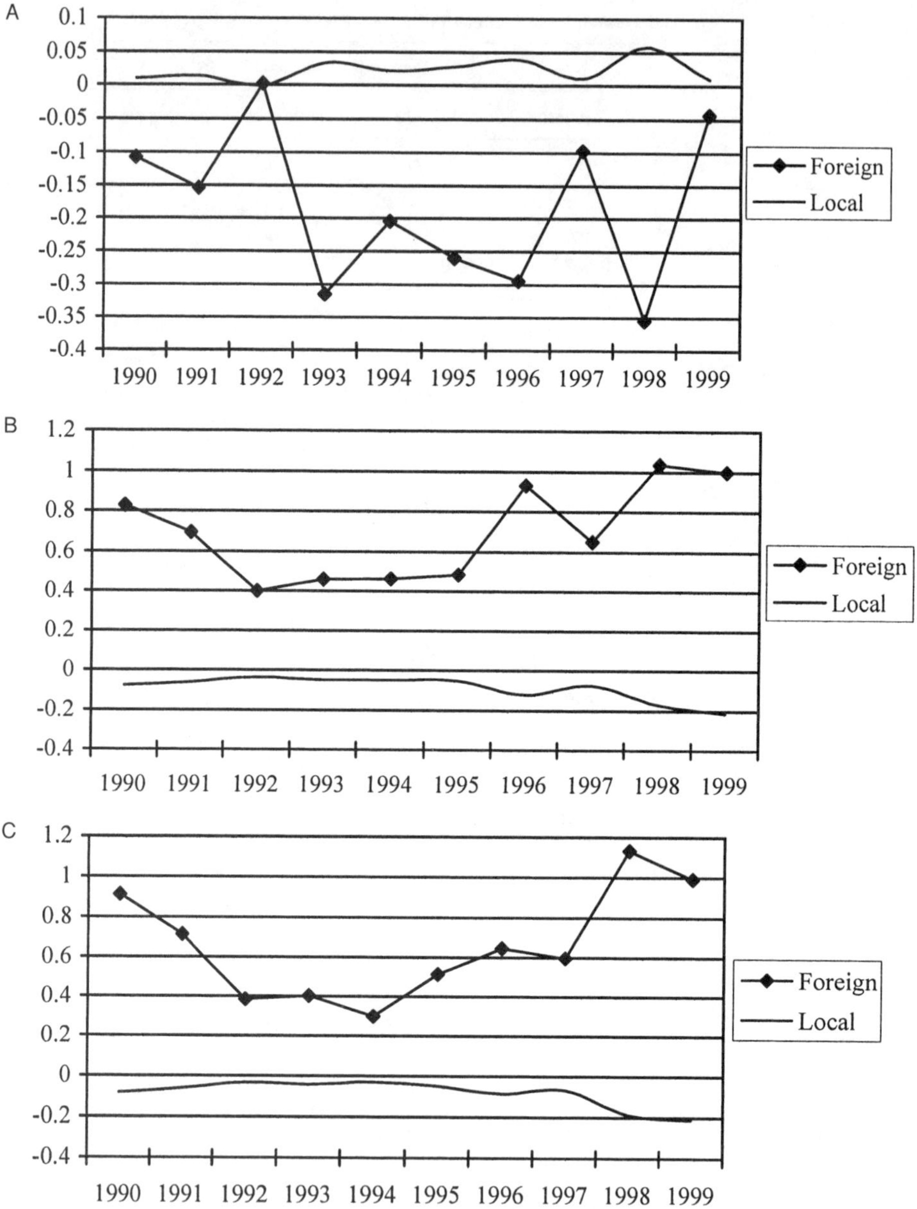

Fig. 7.2 Path of productivity residuals (purged of time, age, and size effects): *A*, path of average variable cost residuals (from eq. [1] in table 7.8); *B*, path of average labor productivity residuals (measured as output per employee, from eq. [3] in table 7.8); *C*, path of average labor productivity residuals (measured as value added per employee, from eq. [5] in table 7.8); *D*, path of average total factor productivity residuals (from eq. [7] in table 7.8).

Source: Author's calculations based on equations (1), (3), (5), and (7) in table 7.8.

D

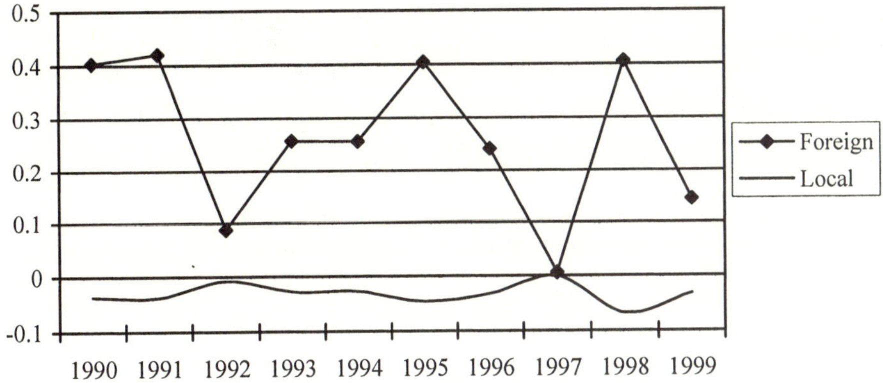

Fig. 7.2 (cont.)

foreign establishments seems to be smaller around 1992 to 1995, it becomes larger from 1996 onward. The trajectories of the average variable cost residuals and TFP residuals fluctuate during the period, and there is no clear trend for both foreign and local establishments.

7.4 Total Factor Productivity Growth and Its Decomposition

7.4.1 The Model Specification

So far, the various productivity measures show that foreign-owned establishments tend to be larger in size and show higher productivity than local ones. In terms of labor productivity, the difference between local and foreign establishments is statistically significant. Although the average TFP level tended to be higher for foreign-owned establishment, the gap in TFP levels between local and foreign establishments became insignificant after industrywide time effects and observable plant-specific characteristics such as age and size were controlled for. In this section, in order to investigate the determinants of productivity growth, the cost function framework is employed to analyze the source of TFP growth as well as the cost elasticities for foreign and local establishments. Moreover, the cost function framework is advantageous because it can endogenize the impact of capital utilization.[18] Although the establishment-level data are available for up to 1999, the cost function analysis relies on the 1990–96 data since the after-crisis data are not very appropriate for the cost function analysis.[19]

18. There is no information on the number of hours worked in the database. Although the survey asks the percentage of actual production to production capacity during the year, the quality of the capacity utilization data is too poor to be used for the analysis.

19. For the after-crisis period, it would be very difficult to separate the effect of economies of scale from the effect of low demand. With this regard, the author thanks Francis T. Lui and an anonymous referee for their comments.

Following Fuss and Waverman (1992), Nadiri and Nandi (1999), Kawai (2000), and so on, the variable cost function in the translog form is specified for the purpose of estimation. Since physical capital stock is considered as a quasi-fixed input in the short run, the variable cost function is given by[20]

$$(3)\quad \log \mathrm{VC}_t = (a_0 + df_0 \cdot \mathrm{FOR} + a_T \cdot T) + a_L \cdot \log\left(\frac{P_{Lt}}{P_{Mt}}\right) + a_Y \cdot \log Y_t$$
$$+ a_K \cdot \log K_t + (a_L + df_L \cdot \mathrm{FOR}) \cdot \log\left(\frac{P_{Lt}}{P_{Mt}}\right)$$
$$+ (a_Y + df_Y \cdot \mathrm{FOR} \cdot \log Y_t + (a_K + df_K \cdot \mathrm{FOR}) \cdot \log K_t$$
$$+ a_{LT} \cdot \log\left(\frac{P_{Lt}}{P_{Mt}}\right) \cdot T + a_{YT} \cdot \log Y_t \cdot T + a_{KT} \cdot \log K_t \cdot T$$
$$+ \frac{1}{2} a_{LL} \cdot \left(\log\left(\frac{P_{Lt}}{P_{Mt}}\right)\right)^2 + a_{YL} \cdot Y_t \cdot \log\left(\frac{P_{Lt}}{P_{Mt}}\right)$$
$$+ a_{KL} \cdot K_t \cdot \log\left(\frac{P_{Lt}}{P_{Mt}}\right) + \frac{1}{2} a_{YY} \cdot (\log Y_t)^2$$
$$+ a_{YK} \cdot \log Y_t \cdot \log K_t + \frac{1}{2} a_{KK} \cdot (\log K_t)^2 + \frac{1}{2} a_{TT} \cdot T^2$$

In the foregoing equation, the following regularity conditions are imposed:

$$(4)\qquad a_L + a_M = 1$$
$$a_{LL} + a_{LM} = a_{ML} + a_{MM} = 0$$
$$a_{KL} + a_{KM} = a_{YL} + a_{YM} = 0$$

The definitions of the variables in equation (3) are as follows. The two variable factors are labor and materials. The average wage rate is normalized by the material's price (P_{Lt}/P_{Mt}), and the variable cost (VC_t) is in real terms. Output and physical capital stock are denoted by Y_t and K_t, respectively. Intercept and slope dummy variables are used to capture the difference in production technology between foreign and local establishments. A dummy variable, FOR, takes zero for local establishments and 1 for foreign ones. An index of time (T) represents disembodied technological change. Subscript t is used to represent time.

Taking derivatives with respect to the natural logarithm of labor and material prices (P_{Lt}, P_{Mt}), and using Shephard's lemma, one obtains the labor share function as

$$(5)\qquad S_{Lt} = a_L + df_L \cdot \mathrm{FOR} + a_{LT} \cdot T + a_{LL} \cdot \log\left(\frac{P_{Lt}}{P_{Mt}}\right) + a_{LY} \cdot \log Y_t$$
$$+ a_{KL} \cdot \log K_t$$

20. A subscript i, which represents plant i, is omitted in the following equations for simplicity.

The variable cost function (3) and the labor share function (5) are jointly estimated by using the time series and cross-section establishment-level data from 1990–96. A maximum likelihood method is employed. Several elasticities are derived as follows:

$$\text{(6)}\quad \varepsilon_{Yt} = a_Y + a_{YT}\cdot T + a_{LY}\cdot \log\left(\frac{P_{Lt}}{P_{Mt}}\right) + a_{YK}\cdot \log K_t + a_{YY}\cdot \log Y_t + df_Y\cdot \text{FOR}$$

$$\varepsilon_{Kt} = a_K + a_{KT}\cdot T + a_{KL}\cdot \log\left(\frac{P_{Lt}}{P_{Mt}}\right) + a_{KK}\cdot \log K_t + a_{YK}\cdot \log Y_t + df_K\cdot \text{FOR}$$

$$\varepsilon_{Tt} = a_T + a_{LT}\cdot \log\left(\frac{P_{Lt}}{P_{Mt}}\right) + a_{KT}\cdot \log K_t + a_{YT}\cdot \log Y_t + a_{TT}\cdot T$$

Moreover, the calculated TFP growth rate can be decomposed into several factors by applying formula (7).[21]

$$\text{(7)}\quad \log\frac{\text{TFP}_t}{\text{TFP}_{t-1}} = \frac{1}{2}\left[\left(1-\frac{\text{VC}_t}{\text{TC}_t}\varepsilon_{Yt}\right)+\left(1-\frac{\text{VC}_{t-1}}{\text{TC}_{t-1}}\varepsilon_{Yt-1}\right)\right]\log\frac{Y_t}{Y_{t-1}} - \frac{1}{2}\left\{\left[1+\frac{\text{VC}_t}{\text{TC}_t}(\varepsilon_{Kt}-1)\right]+\left[1+\frac{\text{VC}_{t-1}}{\text{TC}_{t-1}}(\varepsilon_{Kt-1}-1)\right]\right\} \cdot\log\frac{K_t}{K_{t-1}} - \frac{1}{2}\left[\frac{\text{VC}_t}{\text{TC}_t}\varepsilon_{Tt}+\frac{\text{VC}_t}{\text{TC}_{t-1}}\varepsilon_{Tt-1}\right]\frac{\dot{T}}{T},$$

where TC_t represents total cost. The first term on the right-hand side of equation (7) indicates the contribution from the change in output. The second term represents the contribution from capacity expansion, reflecting the difference in the marginal conditions between the short-run and the long-run equilibrium. That is, in the short-run equilibrium, the shadow price of capital ($-\partial\text{VC}_t/\partial K_t$) is likely to differ from the long-run rental price of capital (P_{Kt}) due to the adjustment cost. If the quasi-fixed input, physical capital, was at the optimal level, then $\partial\text{VC}_t/\partial K_t = -P_{Kt}$ and $\varepsilon_{Kt} = -P_{Kt}K_t/\text{VC}_t$. Using these relationships and the definition of total cost and variable cost, $\text{TC}_t = \text{VC}_t + P_{Kt}K_t$, the second term on the right-hand side of equation (7), is cancelled out when physical capital is at the optimal level. Therefore, the effect represented by the second term can be interpreted as a capital utilization effect. The third term indicates the contribution from technological progress.

By using this decomposition, we can interpret the TFP growth from both supply-side and demand-side aspects. On the supply side, economies of scale arise if average cost falls as output rises, and they may be a char-

21. For details on the decomposition formula, see appendix B.

Table 7.9 Estimation Results

Parameter	Variable Cost Function Estimate	Standard Error	z
A0	–16.760	37.023	–0.45
AT	0.420	0.791	0.53
AL	0.450	0.293	1.53
AY	0.717	0.535	1.34
AK	–0.284	0.518	–0.55
ALT	0.005	0.003	1.51
AYT	–0.004	0.006	–0.74
AKT	0.006	0.006	1.11
ALL	0.083	0.010	8.1***
AYL	–0.097	0.005	–18.61***
AKL	0.039	0.005	8.21***
AYY	0.083	0.012	6.69***
AYK	–0.024	0.009	–2.72***
AKK	–0.007	0.009	–0.74
ATT	–0.005	0.008	–0.57
DF (intercept dummy)	–0.054	0.642	–0.08
DFL (Slope dummy with labor)	0.138	0.023	6.02***
DFY (Slope dummy with output)	–0.186	0.043	–4.29***
DFK (Slope dummy with capital stock)	0.144	0.047	3.1***
No. of observations	744		
R^2	0.9449		
R^2 for labor share function	0.333		

Source: Author's calculations.
***Significant at the 1 percent level.

acteristic of the technology. However, at the same time, sufficient demand size is a necessary condition for an increase in output. Therefore, the scale effect (the first term on the right-hand side of equation [7]) captures both supply-side and demand-side factors. On the other hand, the capacity utilization effect (the second term) captures the effect from a change in demand in the short run.

7.4.2 The Data and Estimation Results

Data on output and physical capital stock are expressed in real terms, deflated by the wholesale price index (1993 = 100).[22] The price of labor for each establishment was calculated by dividing the total payroll by the number of workers. The price of materials was calculated for each establishment as a weighted average of the wholesale price index for imported manufacturing raw materials and the wholesale price index for manufac-

22. For details, see appendix A.

Table 7.10 **Variable Cost Elasticities (1990–1996 average)**

	Output (E_{Yt})	Capital (E_{Kt})	Time (E_{Tt})	Scale Effect ($1/E_{Yt}$)
All establishments	0.890	–0.022	0.011	1.124
Foreign establishments	0.813	0.057	0.019	1.229
Local establishments	0.898	–0.030	0.011	1.114

Source: Author's calculation based on estimation results in table 7.9.

Table 7.11 **Decomposition of Average Annual TFP Growth Rate, 1990–1996 (%)**

	Scale Effect	Capital Effect	Technological Change Effect	TFP
All establishments	0.117	–1.511	–0.011	–1.405
Foreign establishments	–0.441	–3.257	–0.018	–3.717
Local establishments	–0.468	–1.506	–0.010	–1.984

Source: Author's calculation based on estimation results in table 7.9.

turing raw materials. The expenditures on imported materials and domestically produced raw materials are used as a weight. Estimates of the coefficients of the variable cost function (3) are presented in table 7.9, and the derived elasticities based on the average value of each variable are presented in table 7.10. The important characteristics of the cost side of the industry are summarized below.

The variable cost elasticities of output (E_{Yt}) are shown in the first column, and the scale effect, which is defined as the inverse of E_{Yt}, is shown in the last column of table 7.10. The results show a relatively high cost elasticity of output for local establishments. On average, a 1 percent increase in output causes an increase of 0.81 percent in the variable cost for foreign establishments and an increase of 0.90 percent in the variable cost for local establishments. The scale effect presented in the last column indicates that both foreign and local establishments experienced increasing returns to scale during the period from 1990 to 1996. The scale effect is relatively higher for foreign establishments.

The elasticity of variable cost with respect to increases in physical capital stock (E_{Kt}) is shown in the second column of table 7.10. The negative values for E_{Kt} indicate that variable costs decline with increases in the levels of the quasi-fixed input. The capital elasticity for all establishments on average is negative over the period from 1990 to 1996. It should be noted that the capital elasticity is positive for foreign establishments, suggesting that capital utilization is extremely inefficient in foreign establishments.

Average TFP growth rates and their decomposition are shown in table 7.11. The TFP growth rate for each year is estimated using equation (7).

The average annual TFP growth rate remained very low and negative for both local and foreign establishments. A substantial negative capital effect is observed particularly for foreign establishments. This might be a reflection of the fact that many establishments invested in machinery and equipment or other fixed capital in the early 1990s based on the expectation of continuing growth in the Indonesian automobile market. In addition, quite a few foreign and local establishments were newly established in the mid-1990s, which also may have contributed to the negative capital effect on TFP growth. On average, compared with local establishments, foreign establishments had a lower TFP growth rate over the 1990–96 period. As a result, the average TFP growth rate over the period is –3.7 percent for foreign establishments and –2.0 percent for local establishments, suggesting that both foreign and local establishments experienced substantial negative TFP growth on average.

It should be noted that the greatest part of the TFP growth rate is explained by the scale and the capital effects, and that the technological change effect is negligible over the sample period for both foreign and local establishments.

7.5 Concluding Remarks

According to economic theory, manufacturing plants owned by multinational corporations are considered to be more productive than local ones because of their advantages in managerial resources. This paper empirically studies the difference in productivity between foreign-owned and local establishments and tries to uncover the sources of productivity growth for both foreign and local establishments. Given drawbacks in establishment-level data of developing countries like Indonesia, this paper calculates various productivity measures in order to make the analyses as thorough as possible and obtain robust and comprehensive results.

Consistent with previous empirical studies, the results of this paper suggest that foreign establishments tend to be larger in size, enjoy higher labor productivity, and pay higher wages than local ones. Moreover, foreign establishments tend to show a higher import ratio than local ones. As for the export share in output, this was negligibly small before the financial crisis, but more recently foreign establishments increased the export share rapidly. The results of the regression analysis of the determinants of productivity measures show that foreign establishments achieved significantly higher labor productivity than local ones (table 7.8). However, a comparison of TFP levels for foreign and local establishments reveals no significant evidence that foreign plants do in fact enjoy higher TFP that could be attributed to their ownership-specific advantages, as economic theory would suggest. Furthermore, the results instead indicate that the scale effect is an important determinant of productivity levels. The cost function analysis in this paper enables us to calculate the variable cost elasticities and find out the difference in cost structures between foreign and local establishments. Moreover, using the estimated variable cost function, the different sources of TFP growth are investigated. It is found that both foreign and local establishments experienced increasing returns to scale, and that the scale effect is relatively higher for foreign establishments. The results also show the existence of excess capacity. In particular, capital utilization is extremely inefficient in foreign establishments. The results of the decomposition of TFP growth suggest that the average annual TFP growth rate remained very low or negative for both local and foreign establishments even before the financial crisis. In addition, the greatest part of the TFP growth rate is explained by the scale effect and the capital utilization effect, while the technological change effect is negligible for both foreign and local establishments. This suggests that demand-side factors are rather important for productivity growth in Indonesia. According to Rhys (1998), the minimum efficient scale is about 250,000 units per year for automobile assembly and about one million units per year for the casting of engine blocks and pressing of panel parts. In Indonesia, however, even the largest assembler plant only assembles at most about 75,000 automobiles per year, which is much lower than the production scale of a major Japanese assembly plant (approximately 600,000 units per year) or a major Thai assembly plant (approximately 150,000 units per year).[23]

On the other hand, according to economic theory, the inefficiency of capital utilization may be the result of the fragmented small market and noncompetitive reasons that affect market power (Tirole 1988). As argued in section 7.2, although there are more than ten automobile assemblers in Indonesia, a small number of conglomerates own more than one assembly firm and produce more than one brand name. Moreover, one conglomerate, the Astra group, commands a market share of more than 50 percent and controls a large number of affiliated auto parts suppliers. The high average price-cost margins also imply that there is little competition in the Indonesian automobile market. Therefore, an important reason for the poor overall performance of both foreign and local establishments seems to have been the highly concentrated structure of the industry and the lack of competition.

The results of this paper strongly confirm that production scale and capital utilization are extremely important determinants of productivity and that technological change is negligible for both foreign and local establish-

23. The information on units of cars assembled in a year was taken from various yearbooks of the automobile market and interviews by the author.

ments. They therefore clearly demonstrate the importance of sufficient market scale and competition if efficiency is to be improved.

As Okamoto and Sjöholm (2000) argue, the government interventions may have created an environment in which weak competition allows inefficient establishments to stay in the industry. Sufficiently large demand and sufficient technological capabilities are essential to the development of the automobile industry; otherwise, the industry will remain in its infancy stage. Although the Indonesian government has introduced some deregulation packages since the early 1990s, the liberalization policy seemed to lack a rigorous discipline or strategy: The government also launched the national car project in 1996, to which it granted special privileges. However, following the IMF instructions after the 1997 crisis, they scrapped the privileges to the national car project and began to implement various liberalization policies. In 1999, the government abandoned the incentive system, which it had introduced in 1993 to foster the auto parts industry, liberalized the imports of CBU cars, and lowered import tariffs. Moreover, the government sold its shares in PT of Astra International to a Singaporean company in 2000.[24] It is difficult to evaluate the effects of the liberalization policy on plant productivity in the automobile industry, as the analysis in this paper is limited to the short period from 1990 to 1999 and plant productivity was heavily affected by the large demand shock after the crisis. Nevertheless, some indexes seem to provide a positive sign for the future prospects of productivity growth. For example, in the motor vehicle component industry, average variable cost and value added per employee improved from 1995 to 1999, and the export share in output rapidly increased during the period. At the same time, the Herfindahl index decreased substantially, suggesting an intensification of competition in the motor vehicle component industry (table 7.6). In order to judge whether the liberalization packages are successful and whether the intensified competition in both the domestic and the overseas markets contributes to productivity improvements, further studies are required, in which case the introduction of a cross-country comparative perspective should be helpful.

Appendix A

Data Description

The value of plant output is measured as the sum of the total value of production and revenues from manufacturing services. The value of output is

24. PT is an abbreviation of Indonesian words, *perséroan terbatas,* referring to limited companies.

deflated by the wholesale price index of manufactured commodities defined at the three-digit ISIC industry level.

In my analysis, each producer uses three inputs in production: labor, capital, and intermediate materials. Labor input is measured as the number of production and other workers. Total payments to labor are measured as total salaries to both groups and are deflated by the general consumer price index.

Capital input is estimated as the book value of fixed assets, including buildings, machinery and equipment, vehicles, and other fixed capital. To control for price-level changes in new capital goods, using the 1993 book values as the basis, I deflate the changes in each plant's book values between the years by the wholesale price indexes for capital goods. By adjusting these deflated changes to the 1993 book values, I scale the book values of capital goods at each year to the 1993 basis. The change in the book value of buildings is deflated by the wholesale price index of residential and nonresidential buildings. The changes in the book values of machinery and equipment, vehicles, and other fixed capital are deflated by the wholesale price index of capital goods. In addition, it should be noted that some missing values of fixed assets are linearly interpolated or extrapolated by the author, using the number of employees for the establishment as an explanatory variable.

Material input includes raw materials and fuel used by the plant. Expenditures on domestically produced raw materials are deflated by the wholesale price index for manufacturing raw materials, and expenditures on imported raw materials are deflated by the wholesale price index for imported manufacturing raw materials. Fuel expenditures are deflated by the consumer price index for fuel, electricity, and water (unfortunately, the wholesale price index for fuel is not available).

The wholesale price indexes are taken from the BPS, *Monthly Statistical Bulletin: Economic Indicators* (various years-b). The consumer price indexes are taken from the BPS, *Statistical Yearbook of Indonesia* (various years-c).

In order to obtain the total cost for each establishment, the rental rate of physical capital is calculated as $w_{kt} = p_{Kt} \cdot (r_t + \delta_K)$, where r_t is the real rate of return in year t, δ_K is the depreciation rate of capital, and p_{Kt} is the price deflator for capital investment in year t. I used the interest rates for investment at commercial banks, obtained from the Bank Indonesia, *Indonesian Financial Statistics* (various years). The depreciation rate was assumed at an arbitrary 10 percent.

Table 7A.1 Entry and Exit Flows in the Data Set

No. of Establishments (in which foreign-owned establishments)	1990–1995		1995–1997		1997–1999	
Motor Vehicles (38431/34100)[a]						
Continuing	7	(3)	4	(2)	5	(3)
Newly entered	0	(0)	2	(1)	0	(0)
In which newly established	0	(0)	1	(0)	0	(0)
Exit	0	(0)	3	(1)	1	(0)
Motor Vehicle Bodies (38432/34200)[a]						
Continuing	50	(0)	47	(0)	38	(1)
Newly entered	9	(0)	9	(0)	1	(0)
In which newly established	5	(0)	7	(0)	0	(0)
Exit	4	(0)	12	(0)	18	(0)
Motor Vehicle Component and Apparatus (38433/34300)[a]						
Continuing	33	(6)	37	(7)	62	(10)
Newly entered	10	(2)	29	(4)	13	(7)
In which newly established	6	(1)	22	(4)	13	(7)
Exit	1	(0)	6	(2)	4	(1)

Source: Author's calculations based on BPS establishment-level data (various years-a).

Notes: Ownership information for exiting establishments is based on the foreign ownership share in the initial year in the period, while for operating and newly entered establishments it is based on the foreign ownership share in the last year of the period.

[a]Industrial classification code for BPS, *Statistik Industri* (various years-d). The industry code was changed in 1998.

Table 7A.2 Descriptive Statistics of the Sample of Establishments (simple average)

	Motor Vehicles Total (3843/34), Full Sample		
	1990	1995	1999
No. of establishments	95	111	119
No. of employees per establishment	239	303	217
Output per establishment[a]	26,600	43,500	25,500
Value added per establishment[a]	16,500	20,800	16,500
Capital stock per establishment[a]	3,973	8,749	15,000
Years in operation	10.3	14.7	12.6
Productivity measures			
Average variable cost[b]	0.64	0.67	0.62
Output per employee[a]	47.5	55.5	57.8
Value added per employee[a]	24.2	18.4	38.1
Capital-labor ratio[a]	25.4	28.1	69.8
Share of nonproduction workers (%)	17.4	19.6	21.8
Inventory ratios (%)			
Total inventory	n.a.	23.4	32.6
Final goods inventory	n.a.	5.1	6.7
Work-in-process inventory	n.a.	6.0	7.2
Raw materials inventory	n.a.	14.8	22.6

Table 7A.2 (continued)

	Motor Vehicles Total (3843/34), Full Sample		
	1990	1995	1999
Other indicators			
Production worker wages[c]	2,301	2,619	2,745
Nonproduction worker wages[c]	5,416	5,726	12,717
Price-cost margin (%)[d]	35.2	33.8	32.1
Export share in output (%)	0.7	2.0	6.9
Import ratio (%)	22.0	22.5	28.5

	Motor Vehicles Total (3843/34), Large Establishments		
	1990	1995	1999
No. of establishments	48	56	60
No. of employees per establishment	407	539	369
Output per establishment[a]	52,000	85,800	50,200
Value added per establishment[a]	32,300	41,000	32,400
Capital stock per establishment[a]	6,349	15,900	27,800
Years in operation	10.5	14.1	12.7
Productivity measures			
Average variable cost[b]	0.55	0.62	0.54
Output per employee[a]	84.2	101.9	107.7
Value added per employee[a]	43.9	32.8	71.6
Capital-labor ratio[a]	18.6	27.1	111.4
Share of nonproduction workers (%)	20.4	21.6	22.7
Inventory ratios (%)			
Total inventory	n.a.	24.5	28.5
Final goods inventory	n.a.	8.0	4.3
Work-in-process inventory	n.a.	3.8	3.4
Raw materials inventory	n.a.	13.6	24.4
Other indicators			
Production worker wages[c]	3,118	3,769	3,996
Nonproduction worker wages[c]	7,863	8,816	21,732
Price-cost margin (%)[d]	43.0	38.5	37.3
Export share in output (%)	0.0	4.0	13.7
Import ratio (%)	36.7	37.7	46.3

Source: Author's calculations based on BPS establishment-level data (various years-a).

Notes: Some of the observations were not included because of missing values or recording mistakes. n.a. = not available. "Large establishments" are defined as the largest 50 percent of establishments sorted by output each year.

[a]In 1993 millions of rupiahs. For price deflators, see appendix A.

[b]Average variable cost is defined as the sum of labor and intermediate input costs divided by output.

[c]In 1993 1,000 rupiahs. For price deflators, see appendix A.

[d]Price-cost margin is defined as (value added – wages paid)/output.

Table 7A.3 **Descriptive Statistics of the Sample of Establishments by Ownership in the Motor Vehicle Industries (simple average)**

	Motor Vehicles Total (3843/34), Large Establishments											
	1990–96 pooled		1990		1995		1999		Ratio of Foreign to Domestic			
	DO	FO	DO	FO	DO	FO	DO	FO	1990–96	1990	1995	1999
No. of observations	317	74	40	8	45	11	39	21				
No. of employees	385	809***	341	738	447	916	256	579*	2.1	1.8	1.6	2.1
Output per establishment[a]	25,507	203,725***	13,637	244,026	36,706	286,572	14,836	115,803	8.0	8.1	4.7	6.5
Value added per establishment[a]	9,412	125,021***	7,779	155,106	8,736	173,188	9,660	74,679	13.3	7.0	9.4	6.1
Capital stock per establishment[a]	8,005	34,869***	4,865	13,768	10,085	39,787	19,073	44,024*	4.4	2.1	1.9	2.7
Years in operation	11.7	12.7	10.4	11.0	14.0	14.8	13.7	10.7	1.1	1.0	1.0	0.7
Average variable cost[b]	0.62	0.51***	0.57	0.43	0.65	0.53	0.46	0.69	0.8	0.7	0.8	1.5
Output per employee[a]	75.0	151.5***	63.4	188.4*	85.4	169.3	61.3	193.8*	2.0	2.5	2.5	5.0
Value added per employee[a]	29.3	76.5***	30.6	110.3*	21.6	78.9	39.7	130.9*	2.6	2.8	4.0	5.3
Capital-labor ratio[a]	23.2	50.4**	18.1	21.3	24.3	38.8	87.7	155.5	2.2	1.0	1.1	2.8
Share of nonproduction workers (%)	22.2	24.8	20.0	22.7	20.9	24.7	21.2	25.5	1.1	1.2	1.2	1.3
Total inventory (%)[c]	22.1	27.8	n.a.	n.a.	18.5	16.7	14.8	11.6	1.3	n.a.	0.9	0.8
Final goods inventory (%)[c]	3.7	4.8	n.a.	n.a.	4.0	3.8	2.6	2.4	1.3	n.a.	1.0	0.9
Work-in-process inventory (%)[c]	4.0	4.1	n.a.	n.a.	2.4	0.8**	2.7	1.0**	1.0	n.a.	0.3	0.4
Raw materials inventory (%)[c]	15.2	18.7	n.a.	n.a.	10.1	7.8	17.0	6.9	1.2	n.a.	0.8	0.4
Production worker wages[d]	3,212	5,126***	2,739	5,015**	3,252	5,885*	2,300	7,146**	1.6	2.2	2.2	4.1
Nonproduction worker wages[d]	7,669	10,658***	6,761	13,369**	8,515	10,047	11,033	41,600	1.4	2.3	1.0	6.1
Export share in output (%)	3.3	3.2	0.0	0.1	5.0	0.0**	7.4	25.2*	n.a.	n.a.	n.a.	5.1
Import ratio (%)	32.1	62.4***	31.7	61.3*	32.6	58.5*	37.7	61.7**	1.9	1.7	1.5	2.0

Source: Author's calculations based on BPS establishment-level data (various years-a).

Notes: Some of the observations were not included because of missing values or recording mistakes. The t-tests are performed based on the assumption of unequal variances. n.a. = not available; DO = domestic-owned; FO = foreign-owned. "Large establishments" are defined as the largest 50 percent of establishments sorted by output each year.

[a]In 1993 millions of rupiahs. For price deflators, see appendix A.

[b]Average variable cost is defined as the sum of labor and intermediate input costs divided by output.

[c]Inventory data are not available for 1990 and 1991.

[d]In 1993 1,000 rupiahs. For price deflators, see appendix A.

***Significant at the 1 percent level.

**Significant at the 5 percent level.

*Significant at the 10 percent level.

Appendix B
Total Factor Productivity Decomposition Formula

The TFP decomposition formula is derived as follows. When physical capital stock (K_t) is considered as a quasi-fixed input in the short run, the variable cost (VC_t) function is given by

$$\text{(B1)} \qquad \mathrm{VC}_t = h(P_{Lt}, P_{Mt}, K_t, Y_t, t),$$

where P_{Lt} and P_{Kt} are the factor prices of labor and of intermediate inputs, and Y_t denotes output.

Taking the total derivative with respect to time t, we get

$$\text{(B2)} \qquad \frac{d\mathrm{VC}_t}{dt} = \sum_{f=L,M} \frac{\partial h}{\partial P_{ft}} \frac{dP_{ft}}{dt} + \frac{\partial h}{\partial K_t} \frac{dK_t}{dt} + \frac{\partial h}{\partial Y_t} \frac{dY_t}{dt} + \frac{1}{\mathrm{VC}_t} \frac{\partial h}{\partial t}$$

Using $\varepsilon_{Kt} = \partial \ln \mathrm{VC}_t / \partial \ln K_t$, $\varepsilon_{Y_t} = \partial \ln \mathrm{VC}_t / \partial \ln Y_t$ and applying Shephard's lemma, equation (B2) becomes

$$\text{(B3)} \qquad \frac{d \ln \mathrm{VC}_t}{dt} = \frac{\mathrm{TC}_t}{\mathrm{VC}_t} \sum_{f=L,M} s_{ft} \frac{d \ln P_{ft}}{dt} + \varepsilon_{Kt} \frac{d \ln K_t}{dt} + \varepsilon_{Yt} \frac{d \ln Y_t}{dt} + \frac{1}{\mathrm{VC}_t} \frac{\partial h}{\partial t},$$

where $s_{ft} = P_{ft} X_{ft} / \mathrm{TC}_t$.

On the other hand, since the variable cost is defined as $\mathrm{VC}_t = \Sigma_{f=L,M} P_{ft} X_{ft}$, taking the total derivative of this definition equation yields

$$\text{(B4)} \qquad \frac{d \ln \mathrm{VC}_t}{dt} = \frac{\mathrm{TC}_t}{\mathrm{VC}_t} \sum_{f=L,M} s_{ft} \frac{d \ln X_{ft}}{dt} + \frac{\mathrm{TC}_t}{\mathrm{VC}_t} \sum_{f=L,M} s_{ft} \frac{d \ln P_{ft}}{dt}$$

Subtracting the common terms from equations (B3) and (B4), and applying the Törnqvist index–type approximation, we obtain

$$\text{(B5)} \qquad \frac{1}{2}\left(\frac{\mathrm{VC}_t}{\mathrm{TC}_t}\varepsilon_{Kt} + \frac{\mathrm{VC}_{t-1}}{\mathrm{TC}_{t-1}}\varepsilon_{Kt-1}\right)\ln \frac{K_t}{K_{t-1}} + \frac{1}{2}\left(\frac{\mathrm{VC}_t}{\mathrm{TC}_t}\varepsilon_{Y_t} + \frac{\mathrm{VC}_{t-1}}{\mathrm{TC}_{t-1}}\varepsilon_{Yt-1}\right)$$

$$\cdot \ln \frac{Y_t}{Y_{t-1}} + \frac{1}{2}\left(\frac{1}{\mathrm{TC}_t}\frac{\partial \mathrm{VC}_t}{\partial t} + \frac{1}{\mathrm{TC}_{t-1}}\frac{\partial \mathrm{VC}_{t-1}}{\partial t}\right)$$

$$= \frac{1}{2} \sum_{i=L,M} (s_{it} + s_{it-1}) \ln \frac{X_{it}}{X_{it-1}}$$

On the other hand, the definition of TFP growth rate is given by

$$\text{(B6)} \qquad \ln \frac{\mathrm{TFP}_t}{\mathrm{TFP}_{t-1}} = \ln \frac{Y_t}{Y_{t-1}} - \frac{1}{2} \sum_{f=L,K,M} (s_{ft} + s_{ft-1}) \ln \frac{X_{ft}}{X_{ft-1}}$$

From the definition of the TFP growth rate (B6) and equation (B5), the TFP growth decomposition formula is derived as equation (7) in section 7.4.

References

Aitken, Brian J., and Ann E. Harrison. 1999. Do domestic firms benefit from direct foreign investment? Evidence from Venezuela. *American Economic Review* 89 (3): 605–18.

Aswicahyono, Haryo, Titik Anas, and Jose Rizal. 2000. The Indonesian automotive industry. *ASEAN Automotive Report.* Retrieved from [www.asean-auto.org/Indonesia.pdf]. 3 May 2002.

Aswicahyono, Haryo, M. Chatib Basri, and Hal Hill. 2000. How not to industrialise? Indonesia's automotive industry. *Bulletin of Indonesian Economic Studies* 36 (1): 209–41.

Badan Pusat Statistik or Statistics Indonesia (BPS). Various years-a. Diskettes and CD-ROMs containing establishment-level data from *Statistik Industri* (Industrial Statistics): Raw data for 1990–1999. Jakarta: Badan Pusat Statistik.

———. Various years-b. *Monthly statistical bulletin: Economic indicators.* Jakarta: Badan Pusat Statistik.

———. Various years-c. *Statistical yearbook of Indonesia.* Jakarta: Badan Pusat Statistik.

———. Various years-d. *Statistik industri: Besar dan sedang* (Industrial statistics: Large and medium manufacturing statistics). Jakarta: Badan Pusat Statistik.

Baily, Martin Neil, Charles Hulten, and David Campbell. 1992. Productivity dynamics in manufacturing plants. *Brookings Papers on Economic Activity, Microeconomics:* 187–267.

Bank Indonesia. Various years. *Indonesian financial statistics.* Jakarta: Bank Indonesia.

Blomström, Magnus, and Fredrik Sjöholm. 1999. Technology transfer and spillovers: Does local participation with multinationals matter? *European Economic Review* 43:915–23.

Caves, Richard E. 1996. *Multinational enterprise and economic analysis.* 2nd ed. Cambridge: Cambridge University Press.

Doms, Mark E., and J. Bradford Jensen. 1998. Comparing wages, skills, and productivity between domestically and foreign-owned manufacturing establishments in the United States. In *Geography and ownership as bases for economic accounting,* NBER Studies in Income and Wealth, Vol. 59, ed. Robert E. Baldwin, Robert E. Lipsey, and J. David Richardson, 235–55. Chicago: University of Chicago Press.

Dunning, John H. 1988. *Explaining international production.* London: Unwin Hyman.

FOURIN. 2000. *2000 Asean Taiwan jidosha buhin sangyo* (Directory of the automobile parts industry in ASEAN and Taiwan 2000). Nagoya: FOURIN.

Fuss, Mevyn A., and Leonard Waverman. 1992. *Costs and productivity in automobile production: The challenge of Japanese efficiency.* Cambridge, U.K.: Cambridge University Press.

Globerman, Steven, John C. Ries, and Ilan Vertinsky. 1994. The economic performance of foreign affiliates in Canada. *Canadian Journal of Economics* 27 (1): 143–56.

Griffith, Rachel. 1999. Productivity and foreign ownership in the UK car industry. Working Paper Series no. W99/11. London: The Institute for Fiscal Studies.

Griffith, Rachel, and Helen Simpson. 2001. Characteristics of foreign-owned firms in British manufacturing. Working Paper no. 01/10. London: The Institute for Fiscal Studies.

Hill, Hal. 1996. Indonesia's industrial policy and performance: "Orthodoxy" vindicated. *Economic Development and Cultural Change* 45 (1): 147–74.

Ito, Keiko. 2001. Plant productivity, *keiretsu,* and agglomeration in the Japanese automobile industry: An empirical analysis based on micro-data of *Census of Manufactures 1981–1996.* Hitotsubashi University. Mimeograph.

———. 2004. Foreign ownership and plant productivity in the Thai automobile industry in 1996 and 1998: A conditional quantile analysis. Forthcoming in the *Journal of Asian Economics* 15 (2).

Kawai, Hiroki. 2000. Japan. In *Pacific economic outlook structure project: Productivity growth and industrial structure in the Pacific region: Background papers,* ed. Pacific Economic Cooperation Council (PECC), 197–229. Osaka, Japan: Japan Committee for Pacific Economic Outlook, Kansai Economic Research Center.

Markusen, James R. 1991. The theory of the multinational enterprise: A common analytical framework. In *Direct foreign investment in Asia's developing economies and structural change in the Asia-Pacific region,* ed. Eric D. Ramstetter, 11–32. Boulder, Colo.: Westview Press.

Nadiri, M. Ishaq, and Banani Nandi. 1999. Technical change, markup, divestiture, and productivity growth in the U.S. telecommunications industry. *Review of Economics and Statistics* 81 (3): 488–98.

Nikkan Jidosha Shinbun-sha. Various years. *Jidosha sangyo handbook* (Handbook of automobile industry). Tokyo: Nikkan Jidosha Shinbun-sha.

Nomura, Toshiro. 1996. Indonesia no kokuminsha keikaku to Humpus Kia no jidosha shijo sannyu (The national car project and entry of Humpus and Kia into the automobile market in Indonesia). *Shokei Ronso* 46:81–154.

Okamoto, Yumiko. 1999. Multinationals, production efficiency, and spillover effects: The case of the U.S. auto parts industry. *Weltwirtschaftliches Archiv* 135: 241–60.

Okamoto, Yumiko, and Fredrik Sjöholm. 2000. Productivity in the Indonesian automotive industry. *ASEAN Economic Bulletin* 17 (1): 60–73.

Poapongsakorn, Nipon, and Chayanit Wangdee. 2000. The impact of technological change and corporate reorganization in the ASEAN automobile industry. *ASEAN Automotive Report.* Retrieved from [www.asean-auto.org]. 3 May 2002.

Ramstetter, Eric D. 1999. Comparisons of foreign multinationals and local firms in Asian manufacturing over time. *Asian Economic Journal* 13 (2): 163–203.

———. 2001a. Labor productivity in foreign multinationals and local plants in Thai manufacturing, 1996 and 1998. Working Paper Series Vol. 2001-13. Kitakyushu, Japan: The International Centre for the Study of East Asian Economic Development.

———. 2001b. Labor productivity in local plants and foreign multinationals by nationality in Thai manufacturing, 1996 and 1998. Working Paper Series Vol. 2001-31. Kitakyushu, Japan: The International Centre for the Study of East Asian Economic Development.

Rhys, Garel. 1998. The motor industry. In *Applied economics,* ed. Brian J. Atkinson, Frank Liversey, and Bob Hilward, 250–72. Basingstoke, U.K.: Macmillan Business.

Sato, Yuri. 1996. The Astra group: A pioneer of management modernization in Indonesia. *Developing Economies* 34 (3): 247–80.

Sjöholm, Fredrik. 1999. Technology gap, competition, and spillovers from direct foreign investment: Evidence from establishment data. *Journal of Development Studies* 36 (1): 53–73.

Takayasu, Kenichi, Yukiko Ishizaki, and Minako Mori. 1996. The imminent advent of the age of global competition for the automobile industry in Southeast

Asia. *RIM Pacific Business and Industries* 3 (33): 2–48. Tokyo: Center for Pacific Business Studies, Sakura Institute of Research.
Takii, Sadayuki. 2002. Productivity differentials between local and foreign plants in Indonesian manufacturing, 1995. Working Paper Series Vol. 2002-02. Kitakyushu, Japan: The International Centre for the Study of East Asian Development.
Takii, Sadayuki, and Eric D. Ramstetter. 2000. Foreign multinationals in Indonesian manufacturing 1985–1998: Shares, relative size, and relative labor productivity. Working Paper Series Vol. 2000-18. Kitakyushu, Japan: The International Centre for the Study of East Asian Development.
Tirole, Jean. 1988. *Theory of industrial organization.* Cambridge: MIT Press.
White, Halbert. 1980. A heteroskedasticity-consistent covariance matrix estimator and a direct test for heteroskedasticity. *Econometrica* 48:813–38.

Comment Muhammad Chatib Basri

This is an excellent paper and valuable reading. It addresses the issues of the relationship between foreign ownership and productivity. In particular, this paper addresses two questions: First, are foreign plants more productive than local plants, as the MNC theory predicts? Second, if so, what are the determinants of the plants' productivity? This paper also focuses on the establishment data during 1990–99. Consistent with the previous study, this paper shows that foreign establishments tend to be larger in size, enjoy high labor productivity, and pay higher wages than the local ones. In addition, this paper suggests that foreign establishments have a significantly higher productivity than local ones (as presented in table 7.5). In terms of total factor productivity, this paper shows that scale effect and capital utilization are important determinants of productivity level, whereas technological change is negligible. One of the important contributions made by this paper is a comprehensive and in-depth study of the productivity of the Indonesian automotive industry. The results produced by Ito should be regarded as the best indicative given the short time period from 1990 to 1999.

The result on productivity is consistent with previous studies by Okamoto and Sjöholm (2000), among others (Aswicahyono, Basri, and Hill 2000), that argue that protective policy during the period before the economic crisis led to weak competition and allowed inefficient establishments to survive. This is particularly true as suggested by a comparative indicator, the Asian automotive industry in 1995. In terms of sales, production, and exports, Indonesia lagged behind other Asian countries, with the exception of the Philippines. In terms of makers, Indonesia, as well as China and the Philippines, experienced problems in market segmentation.

Muhammad Chatib Basri is associate director for research at the Institute for Economic and Social Research, Faculty of Economics, University of Indonesia.

This can be seen from the comparison between production and number of makers. With 388,000 production units in Indonesia, there were thirteen makers. The average maker produced around 30,000 units, which was very low, particularly compared with South Korea's 525,000 units (Aswicahyono, Basri, and Hill 2000).

As pointed out by Basri (2001), from the 1970s until the end of the 1980s, the structure of local ownership in the automotive industry was dominated by a patrimonialist patronage. The ambitious nationalist policy to develop Indonesia's domestic automotive industry resulted in a high level of trade protection through nontariff barriers, tariffs, and local content schemes. Furthermore, this policy created rents that attracted rent seekers into the industry. The Indonesian automotive industry is a classic example of an infant industry that failed to grow. In Indonesia the automotive industry is something coined an old baby or a permanent infant industry.

On the ownership issue there are several important characteristics to observe. First, major groups produce more than one brand name, often with little apparent synergy in the production activities of these groups. For example, one group produces Mercedes Benz and Hyundai. Second, until recently, foreign partners were rarely able to obtain majority ownership (Aswicahyono, Basri, and Hill 2000). It is therefore not surprising that some joint-venture partners are reluctant to make a major commitment with the local firms, such as upgrading technological capabilities. These characteristics help to explain why there was little spillover from the foreign to the local firms.

Now I will go into specific comments.

Ownership is a tricky empirical concept in Indonesia, and it is hard to distinguish various ownerships in Indonesia. In addition, foreign presence is apparent in various ways, some of which unrelated to equity investment—for example, licensing (Aswicahyono and Hill 2002). Unfortunately Ito says little about the definition of foreign ownership in her paper, and how to treat joint ventures, which play an important role in the pattern of ownerships in Indonesia.

With regard to the ownership concept, it is important to observe whether the productivity differences are due to the productivity aspects (efficiency, technological change, etc.) or to differences in treatment for foreign and local establishments. This is particularly important for the case of Indonesia, as pointed out by Aswicahyono, Basri, and Hill (2000), as the modalities of MNC entry have varied depending on the regulatory environment and foreign partners' preference.

On the descriptive analysis it is interesting to compare the results in table 7.6 with table 7A.1. Some figures—including output per employee, value added per employee, and average variable cost—in table 7.6 are inconsistent with table 7A.1. I believe these inconsistencies appear due to aggregation and price deflator problems. As I understand that the Indonesian wholesale price index is not available for five-digit ISIC, there is a possibility of underestimating or overestimating the value while aggregating some variables in real terms.

The other interesting figures are export share in output. Ito shows that export share increased significantly and accounted for 20 percent of the output in the motor vehicles industry (table 7A.1). Although this figure is consistent with the export figures (the value of export in 1999 had almost doubled compared to 1995 for vehicles [SITC 781-3] and had more than doubled for components [SITC 784]), we should interpret these figures carefully. In 1998–99 producers shifted toward the export market due to the collapse of domestic demand, whereas at the same time the total output dropped due to the economic crisis. As a result, the ratio of export share to output significantly increased, but it had less to do with increasing productivity in export.

Ito employs three productivity proxies: average cost, output per employee in real terms, and value added per employee. There is a little problem in calculating with these proxies, particularly the average cost. Average cost is very sensitive with price deflators. Unfortunately the wholesale price index is available only up to four-digit ISIC; thus, we cannot distinguish the price deflator for motor vehicles assembly and components, which obviously have different prices. Aswicahyono, Basri, and Hill (2000) assert that share of foreign ownership (in terms of value added or employment) is higher in motor vehicle assembly than in components or body manufacture. Thus, if we employ the single wholesale price index for the overall auto industry, there is a possibility that the average cost is understated for foreign establishments and overstated for local establishments.

In obtaining the total cost of each establishment, the rental rate of physical capital is estimated as $w_{kt} = p_{Kt} \cdot (r_t + \delta_K)$. Ito uses the interest rate for investment at commercial banks. This is particularly true for perfect competition markets (theoretically in a perfect competition we expect that $\text{MP}_k = r$). However, if the market is not perfect, which is the case of the Indonesian capital market, we cannot assume that MP_k is equal to r. Perhaps it is more useful to calculate r_t as follows:

$$\text{VA} = wL + rK,$$

$$r = \frac{(\text{VZ} - wL)}{K},$$

then from this obtain the real rate of return.

On the determinants of productivity, Ito shows that scale effect (proxy by size) is strongly significant in all equations. Although this is consistent with the hypothesis, nevertheless I wonder whether the author has checked the possibility of endogeneity problem. In these equations, size is proxied by labor, whereas all the productivity measures are also determined by labor. Thus there is a possibility of nonrandom selection problems, and that is why sizes are strongly significant for all equations.

Ito's findings show that the greatest part of TFP growth is explained by the scale effect and capital effect, whereas the role of technological change is negligible. These are very important results and support previous studies that indicate that the performance of the Indonesian automotive industry is poor. The change of TFP mainly took place due to the demand-side or policy variable rather than the supply-side or productivity variable of the automotive industry. The significant drop in scale effect in 1991–92 has more to do with the liquidity squeeze implemented by the Indonesian government in 1991 than with the productivity factors. The similar explanation applies for the case of 1997–98. The significant drop of TFP was mainly driven by the economic crisis. As a response to the rupiah's plunge in August 1997, the government raised interest rates drastically. Bank Indonesia Certificate (SBI) rates, which were only 11.2 percent in August 1997, rose significantly to 43 percent in March 1998. Before the crisis, most vehicles were purchased not in cash but on credit, from banks as well as automotive producers' multifinance operation. Thus to interpret these findings it is very important to understand the economic policy underlying the change of scale effects, which in many cases have less to do with the supply side or change in economies of scale or productivity.

The formula in equation (7) should be treated carefully for the short-run case where capital is fixed in the short run. The decline in output will have a larger impact on the decline in scale effect in the short run rather than in the long run. Thus, we need a careful interpretation for TFP growth for the short run, since the decline in the scale effect is likely to be caused by rigidity rather than by an economies of scale problem.

This paper offers a lot of potential to draw out policy implications, for instance, the importance of sufficient market scale and competition for the purpose of efficiency improvement. What is missing in the conclusion is the question of what the brief picture of the way ahead is, considering that there is a significant reduction in trade protection and large exchange rate protection due to the deep rupiah depreciation. Ito argues that weak competition led to economic efficiency. With regard to the economic liberalization that has taken place in Indonesia, the appropriate question to raise is whether or not the productivity of the auto industry will improve in the future.

These comments and suggestions do not detract from the overall summary judgment that this paper is worth reading and offers an important contribution for the study of the automotive industry in Indonesia.

References

Aswicahyono, H. H., M. C. Basri, and H. Hill. 2000. How not to industrialize? Indonesia's automotive industry. *Bulletin of Indonesian Economic Studies* 36 (1): 209–41.

Aswicahyono, H. H., and H. Hill. 2002. Perspiration vs. inspiration. *The Journal of Development Studies* 38 (3): 138–63.
Basri, M. C. 2001. *The political economy of manufacturing protection in Indonesia: 1975–1995.* Ph.D. diss. Australian National University, Canberra, Australia.
Okamoto, Y., and F. Sjöholm. 2000. Productivity in the Indonesian automotive industry. *ASEAN Economic Bulletin* 17 (1): 60–73.

Comment Francis T. Lui

Keiko Ito has a carefully written paper that is both solid and stimulating. Its empirical findings have important policy implications. Using data from the Indonesian automobile industry from 1990 to 1999, the paper sheds light on the following questions.

First, do multinational corporations (MNCs) possess an "ownership advantage" (i.e., do the superior management resources they have enable them to attain higher productivity). Second, has the productivity of local automobile plants in Indonesia been helped by any possible spillover effects of the MNCs? Third, what are the effects of protectionist policies on the productivity growth rates of both local and foreign establishments in the Indonesian auto industry?

A key finding of the paper is that there is no real ownership advantage in the Indonesian automobile industry. If one uses partial productivity measures, foreign establishments may appear to be superior. However, once the more appropriate measure, total factor productivity (TFP), is used, and if other variables such as the size of establishments are controlled for, then there is no evidence showing that foreign plants outperform local ones. Given this result, it is not surprising that local plants have not enjoyed any productivity spillovers from foreign establishments. Indeed, estimated TFP growth is negative during the sample period of 1990–99 for both foreign and local establishments.

Why does ownership advantage fail to operate in Indonesia? Ito's paper tries to decompose TFP growth into the scale effect, capital effect, and technological change. It is found that there has been very little technological change in both local and foreign establishments, but the scale of the plants plays an important role. This reminds us that technological change, or the Solow residual, may just be a measure of ignorance. After properly controlling for most of the appropriate factors, this residual should remain constant.

One can of course attribute the negative results in the paper to Indonesia's protectionist policies. To a large extent, this may be well justified.

Francis T. Lui is professor of economics and director of the Center for Economic Development, Hong Kong University of Science and Technology.

However, one can also turn the empirical evidence around and argue for the need for "proper" protection. Since size is important, and foreign enterprises do not exert positive externalities, the Indonesian policies of imposing a bar on completely built-up cars from 1971 to 1993 and an import tariff of up to 275 percent in 1993 may be viewed as attempts to increase the size of domestic automobile production and therefore appropriate. One can argue that the protectionist policies have not been stringent enough. Perhaps foreign automobile makers should not be allowed to operate at all, even in the production of auto parts. Had this been done, local establishments might have been able to exploit the scale effect further. I would like to see how Ito could rule out this possibility.

Another possibility is that the auto industry in Indonesia remains an infant industry. It can be argued that the productive capabilities of the local plants are so low that they cannot benefit from any superior management skills or technology that foreign enterprises may have.

Given more time to develop in the future, local plants may be able to learn more effectively.

These hypotheses presuppose that any of the positive spillover effects possibly coming from the MNCs cannot offset the loss in productivity of the local plants due to the reduction in scale economy. But are MNCs really doing that badly in their productivity? The empirical results may also be interpreted in the following way. First, there has been negative TFP growth in these foreign enterprises. Second, the negative growth is due mainly to the fact that their sizes are not big enough. Third, the scale effect has motivated them to invest in making themselves larger. Fourth, this may lead to underutilization of capacity in the short run.

If we believe in this interpretation, we can argue that the real problem is not on the supply side, but rather on the demand side. Because of the low level of economic development, motorization is not significant in Indonesia. The very size of the market must have limited the capability of the automobile industry to exploit the scale effect. Foreign enterprises might have anticipated that the situation would improve in the future, and therefore they were willing to invest heavily. The apparent inefficiencies in the beginning could be considered as part of the costs of long-term investments. However, the unanticipated Asian Financial Crisis has dramatically reduced the size of the market, at least temporarily. As a result, scale economy cannot be exploited. Moreover, foreign enterprises also find that they have overinvested in their capacities. The evidence based on the 1990–99 sample period probably cannot tell the complete story. In the future, if the Indonesian economy keeps on growing, perhaps foreign enterprises will be able to reap their harvests. However, if scale and capital effects dominate the changes in TFP, it is doubtful whether local companies will be able to benefit a lot, even in the long run.

The foregoing discussion does not imply that the current protectionist policy in Indonesia has not done too much damage. One example showing the dramatic negative effect of protectionism is the automobile industry in China. Before the 1980s, it was difficult to see foreign-made cars running in China. As late as the mid-1980s, some of the auto plants in China were still struggling with producing backward and obsolete Soviet models. In more recent years, protectionism has not disappeared, but it has been diminished significantly. The import tariff is still substantial, but at least imported cars can be seen anywhere in the country. There are also joint ventures that appear to be doing well. For example, Volkswagen has a joint venture with the government of Shanghai. The latter imposes another form of protectionist policy of requiring all the taxis there to use Volkswagen cars only. This may create deadweight loss, but TFP growth of the joint venture may be positive.

Finally, the paper would be easier to follow if the appendix also contained some details on how certain technical equations can be derived.

8

Productivity Growth and R&D Expenditure in Taiwan's Manufacturing Firms

Jiann-Chyuan Wang and Kuen-Hung Tsai

8.1 Introduction

Ever since the 1960s, research and development (R&D) investment has been regarded as an important factor in the improvement of productivity levels. The rationale is that knowledge, which can be created and accumulated through the R&D efforts of a firm or industry, will subsequently become available to product innovations or to the production process (Mansfield 1965, 1969), and as a result nationwide economic development is promoted; indeed, the advanced countries have invested significant expenditure on R&D activities based upon this rationale.[1]

Two notable issues have been explored, the first of which is the extent to which R&D influences productivity, while the second is concerned with the rates of return provided by R&D. Numerous studies have attempted to estimate the marginal product of R&D capital or the rates of return on R&D investment (see, for example, Griliches 1980, 1994; Scherer 1983, 1993; Griliches and Lichtenberg 1984; Goto and Suzuki 1989). Based upon several different levels of data aggregation, or different types of estimation model, these studies demonstrate that the output elasticity of R&D lies between 0.06 and 0.14, while the rates of return on privately financed R&D investment are between 20 percent and 50 percent. However, these studies have continually failed to produce consistent results, with some even fail-

Jiann-Chyuan Wang is a research fellow at the Chung-Hua Institution for Economic Research. Kuen-Hung Tsai is an assistant professor in the Department of Shipping and Transportation Management at National Taiwan Ocean University.

We would like to thank Tsutomu Miyagawa, Jungho Yoo, and two anonymous referees for their insightful suggestions and comments.

1. For example, the average annual rates of R&D expenditure in the United States and Japan, relative to GDP, are around 2.64 percent and 3.04 percent, respectively (NSC 2001).

ing to determine the contribution of R&D to productivity growth (Link 1981; Griliches and Lichtenberg 1984).

A substantial amount of R&D expenditure is invested annually in Taiwan's manufacturing sector. According to data reported by the National Science Council (NSC) (2001), the average share of R&D expenditure within the manufacturing sector accounts for over 95 percent of domestic R&D expenditure; however, the resultant growth in total factor productivity (TFP), the impact of R&D on productivity growth, and the rate of return on R&D expenditure have seldom been seriously examined at firm level. This study sets out, therefore, to estimate firm productivity growth based upon panel data for a sample of 136 firms for the period 1994–2000. The aims of the study are to determine to what degree R&D influences productivity, to further estimate the rates of return on R&D investment within manufacturing firms, and to analyze the differences in productivity growth and the rates of return on R&D investment between industries. Finally, we will test the famous Schumpeterian hypothesis, that the returns on R&D are an increasing function of firm size.

Following this introduction, the remainder of this paper is organized as follows. In the next section we undertake a review of previous studies in this area, followed by an introduction to the methodology adopted in this study, including both the model and the data resources employed in the estimations. Some basic statistics and the results of our estimations and tests are presented and interpreted in the penultimate section. We conclude with some remarks on our findings in the final section, where we also offer some suggestions for further research.

8.2 Literature Review

In any general examination of previous studies, there are two main considerations: The first is the level of data aggregation, and the second is the type of estimation model used. At firm level, Griliches and Mairesse (1984, 1998) and Cuneo and Mairesse (1984) used time series data to estimate the contribution of R&D based on the production function model. They found that the approximate output elasticity of R&D capital lies between 0.06 and 0.10. In a cross-sectional study, Griliches (1995) further demonstrated that the output elasticity of R&D stock was around 0.09–0.14. Adopting the model of R&D intensity, Clark and Griliches (1984), Griliches (1986), and Lichtenberg and Siegel (1991) showed that in U.S. manufacturing firms, the rates of return on R&D were between 10 percent and 39 percent. Goto and Suzuki (1989) further concluded that the rates of return on R&D investment in Japanese manufacturing industries tended to be around 40 percent, and Wakelin (2001) demonstrated that the rates of return on R&D capital were around 27 percent in U.K. manufacturing firms. However, in an earlier study, Link (1983) found that the R&D

coefficient in U.S. manufacturing industries in the 1970s failed to achieve statistical significance.

At industry level, most researchers adopt an R&D intensity model. Terleckyj (1974), Griliches and Lichtenberg (1984), Scherer (1993), and Griliches (1994) each found that the rates of return on privately financed R&D investment were between 20 percent and 50 percent in U.S. manufacturing industries, whereas Goto and Suzuki (1989) showed that the estimated R&D rates of return in Japanese manufacturing industries were around 26 percent. Furthermore, van Meijl (1997), Vuori (1997), and Hanel (2000) found that the rates of return on R&D investment within manufacturing industries in France, Finland, and Canada were around 19 percent, 14 percent, and 34 percent, respectively. It should be noted, however, that Scherer (1983) concluded that the impact of R&D on productivity was insignificant.

There are two points worth noting from any examination of the previous studies. First of all, most of the empirical findings demonstrate that R&D investment does have a significant effect on productivity growth or value added, but we should also keep in mind that such a general summary of prior empirical studies may be overoptimistic because of the "file drawer" problem: that is, the likelihood that studies supporting the null hypothesis (no significant results) will be rejected and therefore buried away in file drawers (Rosenthal 1979; Begg and Berlin 1988).

Second, estimations with the R&D intensity model often neglect the obsolescence of R&D. Most of the previous studies have substituted R&D expenditure for increments in R&D capital in order to avoid the difficult task of measuring R&D capital; however, such a substitution not only neglects the reduction in the effective appropriation of knowledge but also overestimates the net rates of return on R&D (see, for example, Wakelin 2001; Hanel 2000; Lichtenberg and Siegel 1991; Griliches and Lichtenberg 1984).

8.3 Methodology

8.3.1 The Model

In common with most analyses of the contribution to productivity growth from R&D (see, for example, Griliches 1986; Goto and Suzuki 1989; Lichtenberg and Siegel 1991; Hanel 2000; Wakelin 2001), the model adopted for this study is the extended Cobb-Douglas production function model:[2]

2. One could of course consider more complicated functional forms, such as the translog or constant elasticity of substitution (CES) functions, but we use the Cobb-Douglas function based on most empirical studies and on some exploratory computations.

$$Q_{it} = Ae^{\lambda t} L_{it}^{\alpha} K_{it}^{1-\alpha} R_{it}^{\gamma} e^{\varepsilon_{it}}, \tag{1}$$

where Q, L, K, and R respectively represent value added (or sales), labor, physical capital, and R&D capital. The R&D capital is a measurement of the stock of knowledge possessed by a firm at a given point in time; λ is the rate of disembodied technical change; A is a constant; and constant returns to scale have been assumed with respect to the conventional factors (L and K). The parameters, α and γ, are the output elasticity of labor and R&D capital.

By taking logarithms of the variables, equation (1) can be expressed in log form:[3]

$$(q - k)_{it} = a + \lambda t + \alpha(\ell - k)_{it} + \gamma r_{it} + \nu_{it}, \tag{2}$$

where the variables in lower case (q, l, k, and r) are the respective logarithms of value added, labor, and physical and R&D capital, and ν_{it} is the error term in the equation. Equation (2) is the model employed to estimate the impact of R&D on productivity growth. Based upon the estimate of γ in equation (2) and the definition of R&D output elasticity, the rates of return on R&D investment can be easily estimated across firms and over periods. Furthermore, to test the Schumpeterian hypothesis, another equation, as follows, is considered:

$$(q - k)_{it} = a + \lambda t + a(l - k)_{it} + \gamma r_{it} + \gamma_s s_{it} + e_{it}, \tag{3}$$

where the variable s is the logarithm of the product of R&D capital by assets, γ_s is the coefficient linking the relationship between the firm size and the impact of R&D on productivity, and e_{it} is the error term in equation (3).

Two points are worth noting relating to the disturbance terms, ν_{it} and e_{it}. First, in addition to the inputs listed in the model, some unobservable factors, such as managerial capabilities, also have considerable impacts on the creation of a firm's value added (Wernerfelt 1984; Barney 1991; Peteraf, 1993). These factors will vary across firms; thus, the variances of ν_{it} and e_{it} are heteroskedastic. In other words, the variance derived from some unobservable factors is viewed as an error component of ν_{it} and e_{it}.

Second, within our data set, each firm is observed at several points during each year, and some factors omitted from equations (2) and (3) may be correlated across periods. After accounting for this possibility, it seems reasonable to model the data as having serial correlation. Since the empir-

3. By taking logs differentiated with respect to time and imposing the equality of rates of return on R&D across firms, or over periods, we can rewrite equation (1) as a linear function of R&D intensity: $(dQ/Q - dK/K)_{it} = \lambda + \alpha(dL/L - dK/K)_{it} + \rho(dR/Q)_{it} + e_{it}$, where $\rho = dQ/dR$, representing the increment in value added generated by a unit increase in R&D resource θ years earlier. With the newly expressed model, we would obviously estimate ρ directly; however, we have not pursued such an alternative model here since this model presupposes that the rate of obsolescence of R&D capital is zero and assumes that the rates of return on R&D investment are equal across firms and over periods.

Table 8.1 **Growth Rate of Major Variables and R&D-Sales Ratio**

Industry	N	Labor	Capital	Value Added	GRS	RS
Food	11	0.03	6.31	5.35	–0.007	0.85 (0.29)
Chemicals	30	0.19	7.68	2.73	0.035	1.61 (2.00)
Textiles	31	–0.52	8.06	5.20	–0.004	0.49 (0.51)
Machinery	12	–1.25	6.58	9.70	0.003	1.59 (0.98)
Metals	9	0.41	1.93	1.02	–0.027	0.66 (0.29)
Electronic equipment	43	5.72	18.85	22.53	0.052	3.79 (2.35)
Total	136	1.65	10.71	10.67	0.021	1.68 (2.44)

Notes: N = the number of firms; GRS = the growth rates of R&D to sales ratio; RS = the R&D to sales ratio in year 2000. Figures in parentheses are standard deviations.

ical literature is overwhelmingly dominated by the autoregression with first-order serial correlation (AR [1]) model (Greene 1993), the disturbance process with an AR (1) form is assumed in our model. To summarize, these two problems will be considered in the estimations since they could result in biased or inefficient estimates.

8.3.2 The Data and Variables

The examination of related issues is based on a longitudinal data set that includes a sample of 156 large firms stratified from the Taiwan Stock Exchange (TSE). As a result of a number of missing observations on R&D expenditure and questionable data on other variables, we have limited the sample to 136 firms. These samples are fully balanced over the seven-year period, 1994–2000.

The sample covers most R&D-performing manufacturing industries, including food (11 firms), textiles (31 firms), chemicals (30 firms), metals (9 firms), machinery (12 firms), and electronic equipment (43 firms).[4] Since the number of firms within each of these industries is too small to work with separately, we classify the sample into two groups: high-tech firms within the electronic equipment industry (32 percent), and other industrial firms (68 percent).[5] Through this method of classification, in addition to alleviating the problem of heterogeneity, we can also explore the difference in R&D effect on productivity growth between the high-tech sector and other manufacturing firms.

Table 8.1 provides some general information on the samples and variables, in the form of descriptive statistics, with columns (3) to (6) respectively representing labor growth rates, physical capital, value added, and R&D-sales ratio (R&D intensity) across each sector for the period 1994–

4. Electronic equipment includes computers and peripherals, integrated circuits (IC), telecommunications, and other electronics.

5. Here we divide the sample into two because R&D expenditure is the indicator most widely used in identifying high-tech organizations or industries (Baruch 1997).

2000. The figures in the last column of table 8.1 represent R&D intensity for each industry in 2000.

Based on the figures provided in table 8.1, there are a number of interesting observations to be made. First of all, the growth rates of labor and physical capital in the electronic equipment industry are, to a great extent, higher than in other industries. Second, the average growth rate of the R&D-sales ratio is much more rapid in high-tech firms than in other firms. Moreover, the R&D intensity in high-tech firms is much higher than in other firms; for example, in 2000, the average ratio of R&D to sales in electronic equipment was around two to five times that of other firms. Third, there is much more rapid growth in both R&D intensity and value added in high-tech firms. In summary, the statistics provided in table 8.1 suggest substantially noticeable development of the electronic equipment industry in Taiwan.

While noting the descriptive statistics provided in table 8.1, it is worth keeping in mind that although our sample firms are so-called large manufacturing firms, firm size differs significantly. During the observed periods, for all industries, all of the variation coefficients of the variables are large; for example, in 2000, the respective variation coefficients of labor and fixed assets in the electronic equipment industry were around 137 percent and 60 percent. These figures show that to a large degree, the dispersion of firm size is high.

In addition to output (value added), labor, and physical capital, another major variable in the estimation model is R&D capital, which has been viewed as a measurement of the current state of technical knowledge, determined, in part, by current and past R&D expenditure (Griliches 1979). In other words, an increase in R&D capital in period t reflects not only the R&D expenditure of period t but also previous R&D expenditure that bears fruit during the period. There is some sort of distributed lag structure that connects past R&D expenditure to a current increase in technical knowledge, and ideally one would like to estimate the lag structure from the data. Unfortunately, it is difficult to obtain the information required to determine the lag structure; thus, we simply use the average lag.

With the simplification of R&D impact lag structure (average lag), the measurement of firm R&D capital is often expressed as $R_t = E_{t-\theta} + (1 - \delta)R_{t-1}$ (following Griliches 1980; Goto and Suzuki 1989; and Odagiri and Kinukawa 1997), where E is a deflated measure of R&D, θ is the average lag, and δ is the rate of obsolescence of R&D capital.[6] The equation leads to R&D expenditure in period $t - \theta$ becoming R&D capital in period t. Assuming that the growth rate of R&D capital is equal to the growth rate of

6. Other forms of lag structure, such as geometrically declining weights, could be assumed; however, various constructed lag measures and different initial conditions make little difference to the results (Griliches and Mairesse 1984).

E, the R&D capital of the original period is obtained as $R_0 = E_{1-\theta}/(g + \delta)$, where g is the growth rate of E.

Following the approach of Goto and Suzuki (1989), we use the average lag θ, based on simplifying evidence. Patents are a good indicator of benefit creation (Bound, Griliches, and Jaffe 1984; Pakes and Griliches 1984; Griliches 1998), and according to Lin and Lee (1996) and Tsai (1997), R&D investment has a significant impact on patents two years later. Moreover, a simulation study indicated that the lag length of the effect of R&D expenditure on productivity growth lies between one and three years (Xu, Wang, and Tsai 1998). These findings suggest that the average lag in Taiwan is around two years. Pakes and Schankerman (1984) also demonstrated that the R&D lag for the chemicals, machinery, and electronics industries is around two years; therefore, we set the average lag length as 2 ($\theta = 2$) to measure R&D capital.[7]

The depreciation rate (δ) reflects the replacement of old knowledge with new knowledge, or the reduction in the effective appropriation of knowledge. As suggested by Goto and Suzuki (1989), we examine the length of time taken by firms' patents to generate revenue in order to estimate the rate of obsolescence of R&D capital. We use the inverse of the length of time to measure the rate of obsolescence of R&D capital, with the firms investigated being the sample used in our analysis. Among these firms, the average rates of obsolescence were around 14.5 percent in general machinery, 6.2 percent in food, 12.4 percent in chemicals, 7.2 percent in textiles, 6.5 percent in metals, and 20.4 percent in electronic equipment.[8]

As suggested in Griliches and Mairesse (1984) and undertaken by Goto and Suzuki (1989), we measure output (Q) by value added, deflated by the wholesale price index rather than by sales. Another consideration is that one element of the observations on non–energy intermediate materials or energy input is unavailable. Labor (L) is measured simply by the total number of employees because there is no available information on the labor working hours of firms. Note that R&D manpower is deducted from labor since R&D manpower is evaluated as R&D expenditure. Our measure of physical capital (K) is total fixed gross assets; however, fixed gross assets in firms' financial statements are measured by nominal value (book value).

7. Lagged R&D expenditure is used in many studies, but there is no general agreement on the correct lag length. Hall and Mairesse (1995) pointed to the stability of firm R&D expenditure in the United States and Germany and to the insensitivity of the results to the choice of lag.

8. Odagiri and Kinukawa (1997) estimated the rate of obsolescence of R&D capital in four Japanese industries: electrical machinery, transportation machinery, general machinery, and chemicals. The respective rates of obsolescence were 13.9 percent, 11.3 percent, 7.2 percent, and 9.2 percent. Goto and Suzuki (1989) also demonstrated that the respective rates of obsolescence of R&D capital in seven Japanese industries were 24.6 percent (precision machinery), 14.5 percent (communications equipment), 14.2 percent (transportation equipment), 6 percent (food), 7.2 percent (general machinery), 7.2 percent (stone, clay, and glass) and 7.5 percent (nonferrous metals).

We use the gross fixed capital price index from *The Trends in Multi-Factor Productivity,* published by the Directorate-General of Budget, Accounting, and Statistics (DGBAS; 2001) to deflate total fixed gross assets.

Not only is the composition of R&D expenditure little known, but the available data concerning real R&D expenditure are also bedeviled by the lack of a suitable price index for R&D inputs. In view of the inherent difficulties, most of the previous studies have adopted the same means used by U.S. government officials: that is, the use of the gross domestic product (GDP) index to deflate R&D expenditure. However, based on the GDP deflator, the rate of increase of R&D expenditure is usually overestimated. Here we construct the deflator index to deflate R&D expenditure as in Mansfield, Romeo, and Switzer (1983).[9]

8.4 The Results

Since the analyzed sample is a panel data set, a random effects model is assumed in our analysis.[10] A number of different models based upon equation (2) are estimated using the feasible generalized least squared (FGLS) method.[11] The estimates of the production function with and without year dummy variables (with year dummies as opposed to a time trend) are listed separately in tables 8.2 and 8.3. Note that tables 8.2 and 8.3 also provide the estimates of the product term of R&D capital by assets for all firms as well as separately for high-tech and other firms. The estimates, denoted by γ_s, of the product of R&D stock by assets are used to test the Schumpeterian hypothesis.

The comparisons of table 8.2 and table 8.3 clearly show that using year dummy variables instead of a linear trend makes little difference to the estimates of the whole sample. The estimate of R&D capital elasticity (γ), lying between 0.18 and 0.20, is significant at the 1 percent level, with the results showing that R&D has a significant impact on productivity growth.

Since the sample comprised firms engaging in R&D in rather diverse industries, it was also of interest to investigate the differences between sectors. When the sample is split into two categories, the estimates for the two

9. Although we used the GDP deflator of each industry to deflate R&D expenditure and then constructed R&D capital, such an alternative construction makes little difference to the estimates.

10. Equation (2) can be treated as a fixed or random effects panel model. Since the chi-square tests, suggested by Hausman (1978), coming from different models based upon equation (2) show that the exploratory variables are most likely uncorrelated with the individual effects, a random effects panel model is assumed in this study.

11. Before estimating the model, in order to test the assumption of constant returns to scale with respect to the conventional factors, we rewrite equation (2) as $(q - k)_t = a + \lambda_t + \alpha(l - k)_{it} + \omega k_{it} + \gamma r_{it} + v_{it}$, where $\omega = \alpha + \beta - 1$. If ω is significantly different from zero, the constant returns to scale for labor and physical capital can then be rejected. Here the estimate of ω is approximately 0.021 ($t = 0.96$, $P > 0.05$), which indicates that the assumption is not rejected at the 5 percent significance level.

Table 8.2 **Production Function Estimates, Excluding Year Dummies**

Regressions	α	γ	λ	γ_s	R^2	MSE
All firms (N = 136)						
(1)	0.485***	0.187***	0.037**		0.352	0.167
	(0.071)	(0.031)	(0.015)			
(2)	0.467***	0.184***	0.037**	0.004	0.354	0.168
	(0.079)	(0.032)	(0.015)	(0.007)		
High-tech firms (N = 43)						
(3)	0.305***	0.297***	0.125***		0.468	0.190
	(0.115)	(0.073)	(0.032)			
(4)	0.325***	0.299***	0.125***	–0.003	0.468	0.191
	(0.130)	(0.074)	(0.033)	(0.017)		
Other firms (N = 93)						
(5)	0.674***	0.055	0.021		0.326	0.133
	(0.087)	(0.037)	(0.016)			
(6)	0.613***	0.049	0.021	0.017*	0.333	0.133
	(0.094)	(0.037)	(0.016)	(0.010)		

Note: Figures in parentheses are estimated standard errors.
***Significant at the 1 percent level.
**Significant at the 5 percent level.
*Significant at the 10 percent level.

Table 8.3 **Production Function Estimates, Including Year Dummies**

Regressions	α	γ	γ_s	R^2	MSE
All firms (N = 136)					
(1′)	0.472***	0.199***		0.360	0.165
	(0.071)	(0.031)			
(2′)	0.459***	0.197***	0.003	0.362	0.160
	(0.079)	(0.032)	(0.007)		
High-tech firms (N = 43)					
(3′)	0.292***	0.308***		0.473	0.191
	(0.117)	(0.074)			
(4′)	0.308**	0.309***	–0.003	0.473	0.192
	(0.132)	(0.075)	(0.011)		
Other firms (N = 93)					
(5′)	0.668***	0.070*		0.346	0.129
	(0.087)	(0.037)			
(6′)	0.613***	0.064*	0.016	0.351	0.129
	(0.093)	(0.037)	(0.010)		

Note: Figures in parentheses are estimated standard errors.
***Significant at the 1 percent level.
**Significant at the 5 percent level.
*Significant at the 10 percent level.

groups are indeed rather distinct.[12] The estimate of R&D capital elasticity, at around 0.30 for high-tech firms, is much larger than for other firms. Note that the estimate of R&D output elasticity for other firms is around only 0.06, which is even insignificant in the model without year dummies. In addition, although the difference in the estimated time trend coefficients (the rate of technical progress λ) between high-tech firms and other firms is rather significant, the estimates of λ are significant in the high-tech firms ($\lambda = 0.125, p < 0.01$) but insignificant for other firms.

Given estimates of γ, the estimates of dQ/dR are calculated by multiplying the estimates of γ by the ratio of value added to the stock of R&D. The estimated average rates of return on R&D investment for the whole sample during the periods 1996–2000 were around 23 to 25 percent. Compared to the findings of previous studies—that the analytical unit is at firm level—our results are consistent with the similar estimates of 21 percent for the United States (Lichtenberg and Siegel 1991) and 27 percent for the United Kingdom (Wakelin 2001) but considerably lower than the 40 percent found in Japan (Goto and Suzuki 1989). Furthermore, the estimated rates of return on investment in R&D for each industry, for the years 1996 to 2000, are listed in table 8.4. The estimates in table 8.4 suggest that the average rates of return on R&D capital for the high-tech industry, at around 35 percent, are much larger than in other industries, at around 8 to 10 percent.

The Schumpeterian hypothesis (Schumpeter 1950) supported the belief of a greater likelihood of large firms' both undertaking research activities and achieving a measure of success. However, although Link (1981) found evidence of a systematic relationship between firm size and the impact of R&D on productivity, the empirical results of Lichtenberg and Siegel (1991) did not provide support for the Schumpeterian hypothesis. In our investigation, using total assets as a proxy for firm size, the estimates are positive for all firms, irrespective of whether the model contains year dummy variables, but insignificant at the 5 percent level.

When the sample is divided into two categories (high-tech firms and other firms), the γ_s estimates (the parameter of the product term of R&D capital by total assets) are still insignificant. Obviously, with respect to R&D impact on productivity, we are unable to determine from these findings whether different size "regimes" exist. Aside from total fixed assets, we also use sales as a proxy variable for firm size. At the 5 percent significance level, the tests of the estimates of γ_t still do not demonstrate that the impact of R&D on productivity growth is an increasing function of firm size.[13]

12. Dividing the sample into two allows for much of the heterogeneity, bringing down the sum of the square of errors (SSE) by around 12 percent (corresponding to a high F ratio of 16.05, $p < 0.01$).

13. One attribution of the statistical insignificance is that all of our sample firms are "large" firms. However, firm size among these so-called large firms differs significantly. For example, in 2000, the average amount of total fixed assets in high-tech firms was NT$15,187,200, and the standard deviation was NT$8,760,197. The coefficient of variation (the ratio of standard deviation to mean) exceeds 50 percent.

Table 8.4 **Average Rates of Return on R&D Investment (%)**

Industry	1996	1997	1998	1999	2000
Food	9.79	9.24	8.97	8.75	8.96
	(2.50)	(1.87)	(1.75)	(0.79)	(0.95)
Chemicals	8.54	8.17	7.96	7.59	7.84
	(1.36)	(1.38)	(1.93)	(1.02)	(0.89)
Textiles	9.60	9.30	8.94	8.28	8.75
	(2.37)	(2.28)	(1.11)	(1.03)	(0.95)
Machinery	8.32	8.12	8.08	7.93	8.03
	(2.12)	(1.98)	(1.16)	(1.06)	(1.14)
Metals	10.73	10.04	9.88	9.66	9.90
	(2.67)	(2.41)	(2.44)	(2.11)	(2.01)
Electronic equipment	36.84	35.97	35.31	34.99	35.12
	(4.97)	(4.47)	(4.23)	(4.11)	(3.91)

Note: Figures in parentheses are standard deviations.

Table 8.5 **Average Annual Rates of TFP Growth (%)**

Industry	1996	1997	1998	1999	2000
Food	5.14	0.54	–16.01	7.67	5.73
	(2.23)	(2.83)	(5.82)	(2.35)	(2.78)
Chemicals	2.31	–0.15	–19.63	12.50	5.46
	(2.72)	(2.39)	(3.76)	(2.80)	(1.72)
Textiles	1.24	0.04	–15.28	–6.30	7.39
	(2.11)	(2.41)	(2.71)	(2.88)	(2.39)
Machinery	4.12	0.95	–15.82	5.40	8.33
	(2.97)	(3.18)	(5.92)	(2.25)	(2.97)
Metals	2.78	0.59	–1.19	–0.60	–1.49
	(1.98)	(1.74)	(1.45)	(1.52)	(1.72)
Electronic equipment	6.39	9.08	–7.26	4.41	13.21
	(2.44)	(2.58)	(2.85)	(2.72)	(1.99)

Note: Figures in parentheses are standard deviations.

In addition, the estimates listed in tables 8.2 and 8.3 also show that the labor share (α) in high-tech firms is small. One possible explanation is that the value added in high-tech firms is created mainly through their R&D efforts, such as new product development, represented by the amount of R&D expenditure, and the input of R&D manpower is deducted from the total numbers of employees. Since the contribution from ordinary labor (the remaining employees of totality) to value added is always lower, the estimates here seem to be reasonable. The results are also consistent with the finding of 0.27 by Griliches and Mairesse (1984) in scientific firms ($N = 77$).

Based on the estimates of α for each of the two categories, and the conventional definition of TFP (TFP = $Q/L^{\alpha}K^{1-\alpha}$), we can further calculate the annual TFP growth rates for each industry. The estimates are listed in table 8.5, which shows that there was a dramatic decline in TFP growth rates in 1998, which nevertheless started to rise again after 1999.[14] The results show that the TFP growth in these industries seems to depend upon short-term fluctuations, and one obvious and possible explanation for this is the severe impact on the Taiwanese economy of the Asian financial crises between the fourth quarter of 1997 and the first quarter of 1999.

8.5 Conclusions

In this study, we have analyzed the relationship existing between output (value added), employment, physical capital, and R&D capital, based upon a complete sample of 136 large firms listed in the TSE over the period 1994–2000. Our findings suggest that R&D investment was a significant determinant of firm productivity growth during the second half of the 1990s. For the whole sample, R&D output elasticity was around 0.18; however, when the sample is divided into two categories, high-tech and other firms, we observe a statistically significant difference in R&D elasticity between the two samples. The R&D elasticity for high-tech firms is around 0.3, but only 0.07 for other firms. In addition, we find that the average rate of return on investment in high-tech firms, at around 35 percent, is larger than that estimated in other firms, at around 9 percent. Our study also demonstrates that TFP growth declined across all the selected industries in 1998 but then started to pick up again after 1999. We speculate that the slump in TFP growth rates in 1998 can be attributed, to a large extent, to the Asian financial crisis. Moreover, our empirical results do not support the Schumpeterian hypothesis, which states that the impact of R&D on productivity is an increasing function of firm size.

Nevertheless, a couple of related points need to be discussed further. First, the impact on productivity from these different types of R&D may differ markedly. In general terms, R&D work can be classified into three types: basic research, applied research, and technical development. A number of studies have found that the contribution from basic research is greater than that of either applied research or technical development (see, for example, Lichtenberg and Siegel 1991; Martin 1998; Salter and Martin 2001). However, since the proportion of R&D expenditure spent on basic research in Taiwanese manufacturing firms has been rather small, our estimations should still be valid, even though we do not take into consideration the distinction between these different types of R&D.

Second, the double-counting of capital and R&D capital may bias the estimated effects of R&D. The estimate of R&D intensity or R&D capital is not particularly accurate when certain types of expenditure are ac-

14. This trend is consistent with the calculation reported in DGBAS (2001). However, the figures listed in table 8.5 cannot be compared with overall estimates of TFP since the estimates in Taiwan are always calculated at industry level.

counted for in both R&D capital and ordinary capital (Schankerman 1981). Expenditure on R&D in Taiwan has been clearly defined as all spending attributed to R&D activities, such as labor costs, administration, maintenance, and the acquisition of equipment for R&D purposes (NSC 2001). In accordance with the Statute for Industrial Upgrading, the R&D expenditure of any firms in Taiwan applying for R&D tax credits is closely scrutinized by the tax authorities; therefore, the purchase of equipment for R&D projects has to be recorded in R&D expenses but not necessarily in fixed assets. Thus, potential double-counting of capital should have little impact on the estimated effects of R&D.

Third, capital utilization rates should be considered in this analysis.[15] In this study we have assumed that the short-term fluctuations in TFP came as a result of the Asian financial crisis. According to the findings of Wang, Hsin, and Tsai (1999), the Asian financial crisis damaged the exports of Taiwan's manufacturing industries and further reduced the utilization rates of manufacturing equipment. Thus, in order to exclude the demand shock from the Asian financial crisis, one should regard capital utilization rates as an exploratory variable in the empirical model. Unfortunately, the capital utilization rates of the sample firms cannot be determined, and the variable cannot be constructed from other variables in the current dataset.

Fourth, we have tried to separate the effects arising from interindustry differences. Our analysis covers several industries, and in order to reduce the estimated bias of R&D effects on the characteristic differences across these industries, we include industry dummies in the estimated model. However, the use of industry dummy variables brings down the sum of the square of errors (SSE) by only around 0.62 percent, corresponding to a low F ratio of 0.69 ($p > 0.05$), and since the omnibus test (F-test) is not significant at the 5 percent significant level, we ignore the impact of the industry dummy variable on the estimation.

Fifth, one may doubt that the larger R&D estimate in the high-tech firms is coming spuriously at the expense of the labor coefficient. To address this concern, alpha is fixed to labor's share in the model. This restriction does not make the estimates significantly different compared to the findings in tables 8.2 and 8.3. This robustness check confirms our finding that the R&D output elasticity in high-tech firms is significantly greater than that of other firms.

Finally, the sample period that we have observed, from 1994 to 2000, coincides with the information technology (IT) boom; therefore, the potential exists for the IT bubble to have caused a disturbance to TFP growth trends during our study period. Throughout the IT bubble period, tele-

15. We appreciate the insightful suggestions provided by Tsutomu Miyagawa and Jungho Yoo, and we have tried to use industrial utilization rates of manufacturing equipment as a proxy for firms' capacity utilization rates. Although the estimates are not significant at the 5 percent level, we consider that this insignificance is most likely the result of the use of a proxy.

communications and the Internet formed the backbone of IT investment, and although Taiwanese firms were involved in the IT boom, their Internet business was still at a rather embryonic stage and the telecommunications industry remained small, thus limiting the impact of the IT bubble.

Our study does of course have its limitations. First of all, as in the standard approach, we aggregate R&D expenditure linearly into R&D stock, ignoring the possibility that knowledge production depends nonlinearly, not only on current efforts, but also on previously accumulated outcomes. Second, the results cannot explain the time-dimensional differences of R&D performance across firms, since the time period is not yet long enough; our estimation also fails to reveal how the impacts of R&D on productivity growth are actually realized. Third, it may be worth trying to include in the estimation model a skills variable, such as the number of engineers and technicians; however, we cannot separate the effects of a skills variable because most of the firms in the sample omit many of the observations on these related variables. Fourth, we do not discuss the more general topic of simultaneous R&D decisions (simultaneity), which has recently entered into the discussion. If R&D is chosen on the basis of economic incentives, it is unlikely to be completely independent of the errors that affect the production relations that we attempt to estimate in this study. Finally, although our sample does cover 136 large manufacturing firms belonging to six industries, it clearly cannot represent all manufacturing firms; therefore, the interpretation of the findings in our study should remain conservative.

References

Barney, J. B. 1991. Firm resources and sustained competitive advantage. *Journal of Management* 17:99–120.

Baruch, Y. 1997. High technology organization: What it is, what it isn't. *International Journal of Technology Management* 13 (2): 179–95.

Begg, C. B., and J. A. Berlin. 1988. Publication bias: A problem in interpreting medical data. *Journal of the Royal Statistical Society* A151 (part 3): 419–63.

Bound, J., Z. Griliches, B. H. Hall, and A. Jaffe. 1984. Who does R&D and who patents? In *R&D, patents, and productivity,* ed. Z. Griliches, 21–54. Chicago: University of Chicago Press.

Clark, K. B., and Z. Griliches. 1984. Productivity growth and R&D at the business level: Results from the PIMS data base. In *R&D, patents, and productivity,* ed. Z. Griliches, 393–416. Chicago: University of Chicago Press.

Cuneo, P., and J. Mairesse. 1984. Productivity and R&D at firm level in French manufacturing. In *R&D, patents, and productivity,* ed. Z. Griliches, 375–92. Chicago: University of Chicago Press.

Directorate-General of Budget, Accounting, and Statistics. 2001. *Trends in multifactor productivity.* Taipei, Taiwan: Directorate-General of Budget, Accounting, and Statistics, Executive Yuan.
Goto, A., and K. Suzuki. 1989. R&D capital rate of return on R&D investment and spillover of R&D in Japanese manufacturing industries. *Review of Economics and Statistics* 71 (4): 555–64.
Greene, W. H. 1993. *Econometric analysis.* 2nd ed. Englewood Cliffs, N.J.: Prentice Hall.
Griliches, Z. 1979. Issues in assessing the contribution of research and development to productivity growth. *Bell Journal of Economics* 10 (1): 92–116.
———. 1980. R&D and productivity slowdown. *American Economic Review* 70 (1): 343–48.
———. 1986. Productivity, R&D, and basic research at firm level in the 1970s. *American Economic Review* 76 (1): 141–54.
———. 1994. Explanations of productivity growth: Is the glass half empty? *American Economic Review* 84 (1): 1–25.
———. 1995. R&D and productivity. In *Handbook of the economics of innovation and technological change,* ed. P. Stoneman, 52–89. Oxford, U.K.: Blackwell.
———. 1998. Patent statistics as economic indicators: A survey. In *R&D and productivity,* ed. Z. Griliches, 287–343. Chicago: University of Chicago Press.
Griliches, Z., and F. Lichtenberg. 1984. R&D and productivity growth at industry level: Is there still a relationship? In *R&D, patents, and productivity,* ed. Z. Griliches, 465–501. Chicago: University of Chicago Press.
Griliches, Z., and J. Mairesse. 1984. Productivity and R&D at firm level. In *R&D, patents, and productivity,* ed. Z. Griliches, 339–75. Chicago: University of Chicago Press.
Griliches, Z., and J. Mairesse. 1998. R&D and productivity growth: Comparing Japanese and US manufacturing firms. In *R&D and productivity,* ed. Z. Griliches, 187–210. Chicago: University of Chicago Press.
Hall, B. H., and J. Mairesse. 1995. Exploring the relationship between R&D and productivity in French manufacturing firms. *Journal of Econometrics* 65:263–93.
Hanel, P. 2000. R&D, inter-industry and international technology spillovers and the total factor productivity growth of manufacturing industries in Canada, 1974–1989. *Economic Systems Research* 12 (3): 345–61.
Hausman, J. A. 1978. Specification tests in econometrics. *Econometrics* 46:1251–71.
Lichtenberg, F., and D. Siegel. 1991. The impact of R&D investment on productivity: New evidence using linked R&D-LRD data. *Economic Inquiry* 29 (2): 203–29.
Lin, H. L., and X. F. Lee. 1996. The study of the relationship between patents and R&D expenditures in Taiwan: An application of non-negative integer model (in Chinese). *Economics Articles* 24 (2): 273–302.
Link, A. N. 1981. *Research and development activity in US manufacturing.* New York: Proger.
Mansfield, E. 1965. Rates of return from industrial R&D. *American Economic Review* 55 (3): 863–73.
———. 1969. Industrial research and development: Characteristics, costs, and diffusion of results. *American Economic Review* 59 (1): 65–71.
———. 1980. Basic research and productivity increase in manufacturing. *American Economic Review* 70 (3): 863–73.
Mansfield, E., A. Romeo, and L. Switzer. 1983. R&D price indexes and real R&D expenditures. *Research Policy* 12:105–12.

Martin, F. 1998. The economic impact of Canadian university R&D. *Research Policy* 27:677–87.

National Science Council (NSC). 2001. *Indicators of science and technology.* Taipei, Taiwan: National Science Council, Executive Yuan.

Odagiri, H., and S. Y. Kinukawa. 1997. Contributions of channels of inter-industry R&D spillovers: An estimation of Japanese high-tech industries. *Economic Systems Research* 9 (1): 127–42.

Pakes, A., and Z. Griliches. 1984. Patents and R&D at firm level: A first look. In *R&D, patents, and productivity,* ed. Z. Griliches, 55–72. Chicago: University of Chicago Press.

Pakes, A., and M. Schankerman. 1984. The rate of obsolescence of patents, research gestation lags, and the private rates of return to research and resources. In *R&D, patents, and productivity,* ed. Z. Griliches, 73–88. Chicago: University of Chicago Press.

Peteraf, M. A. 1993. The cornerstones of competitive advantage: A resource-based view. *Strategic Management Journal* 14:179–91.

Rosenthal, R. 1979. The "file drawer" problem and tolerance for null results. *Psychological Bulletin* 86:638–41.

Salter, A. J., and B. R. Martin. 2001. The economic benefits of publicly-funded basic research: A critical review. *Research Policy* 30:509–32.

Schankerman, M. 1981. The effects of double counting and expensing on the measured returns to R&D. *Review of Economics and Statistics* 63 (3): 454–58.

Scherer, F. M. 1983. R&D and declining productivity growth. *American Economic Review* 73 (1): 215–18.

———. 1993. Lagging productivity growth: Measurement technology and shock effect. *Empirica* 20:5–24.

Schumpeter, J. A. 1950. *Capitalism, socialism, and democracy.* 3rd ed. New York: Harper & Row.

Terleckyj, N. E. 1974. *Effects of R&D on the productivity growth of industries: An exploratory study.* Washington, D.C.: National Planning Association.

Tsai, K. H. 1997. The impact of R&D on patents in Taiwan (in Chinese). *Sun Yat Sen Management Review* 5 (2): 25–46.

van Meijl, H. 1997. Measuring inter-sectoral spillovers: French evidence. *Economic Systems Research* 9 (1): 25–46.

Vuori, S. 1997. Inter-industry technology flows and productivity in Finnish manufacturing. *Economic Systems Research* 9 (1): 67–80.

Wakelin, K. 2001. Productivity growth and R&D expenditure in UK manufacturing firms. *Research Policy* 30:1079–90.

Wang, J. C., P. H. Hsin, and K. H. Tsai. 1999. *The impact of Asian financial crisis on Taiwan's industrial competitiveness* (in Chinese). Taipei: Chung-Hua Institution for Economic Research.

Wernerfelt, B. 1984. A resource-based view of the firm. *Strategic Management Journal* 5:171–80.

Xu, T. D., J. C. Wang, and K. H. Tsai. 1998. *The impact of technology expenditures on economic development* (in Chinese). NSC Report. Taipei, Taiwan: National Science Council.

Comment Tsutomu Miyagawa

An Overview of the Paper

The paper examined effects of R&D on productivity at the firm level, for firms listed on the Taiwan Stock Exchange. It adopted a standard methodology for estimation in output elasticity of R&D capital. Following Griliches (1986), the authors assumed a Cobb-Douglas production function with total factor productivity (TFP) that depends on R&D capital and disembodied technical change. Using firm-level microdata (136 large manufacturing firms listed on the Taiwan Stock Exchange), they estimated output elasticity of R&D capital.

The main results are as follows. In all industries, the estimated elasticity was between 0.18 and 0.2, which was larger than that of previous studies. The estimated elasticity was higher in high-tech firms than in other firms. The rate of return on R&D capital was also higher in high-tech firms than in other firms.

Schumpeter asserted that large firms tend to carry out R&D expenditure actively. Tsai and Wang tried to test the Schumpeterian hypothesis. They added the product term of R&D capital by firm assets to the standard estimation and examined the parameters of the new term. However, the estimated parameters were not significant, and the Schumpeterian hypothesis was not supported. Finally, using the estimated parameters, they calculated late 1990s TFP. A rapid slowdown in TFP growth was found in the period of the Asian currency crisis.

The estimation methodology in the paper is standard, and the estimated results are reasonable. In particular, the high output elasticity and high rate of return on R&D capital in high-tech industries are very impressive. This conclusion is not found in the previous Japanese analyses about R&D expenditure. The results in the paper will stimulate Japanese research in this field.

Why Is the Rate of Return on Research and Development Capital in High-Tech Firms So High?

One of the main results Tsai and Wang included in the paper is that output elasticity and rate of return on R&D capital were higher in high-tech firms than in other firms. They noted that estimated values of output elasticity and rate of return were reasonable from the viewpoint of international comparison. However, they did not explain the reason for high-tech firms' higher rates of return on R&D capital.

To try to do this, I think the authors can examine three hypotheses. The first hypothesis is that TFP was higher in high-tech firms than in other

Tsutomu Miyagawa is professor of economics at Gakushuin University.

firms. To prove the first hypothesis, they need to show TFP growth data in high-tech firms and in other firms.

The second hypothesis is that the difference in rate of return reflects a difference in the depreciation rate of R&D capital. The rate of return they measured is gross rate of return, including depreciation rate. High-tech firms tend to hold assets that depreciate faster than assets held in other firms, due to rapid technological progress. If they compare the net rate of return of the two types of firms, they may find smaller differences.

The last hypothesis is that spillover effects are stronger in high-tech firms than in other firms. Griliches (2000) pointed out that the positive contribution of knowledge externalities has increased due to the declining cost of communication. If spillover effects dominated in high-tech industries, then γ and rate of return in high-tech firms may be overestimated. To check the significance of spillover effects, they should estimate the following production function (based on their equation [2]) including externalities.

$$(2') \qquad (q - k)_{it} = a + \lambda t + \alpha(l - k)_{it} + \gamma r_{it} + \mu R_t + \nu_{it},$$

where R_t is R&D expenditures at the industry level.

If all three hypotheses are rejected, other candidate explanations would be market imperfection or government intervention. The authors should check whether either market imperfection in Taiwan's financial market or government subsidization of high-tech firms has generated the difference in rate of return of R&D capital. I think that these tasks will become further research topics for the authors.

Other Comments

Besides the problem of rate of return, I will make two more comments on the paper. First, the authors assumed a Cobb-Douglas type production function described in equation (1). They assumed that the total of the labor share and real capital share is equal to 1 and that all value added is distributed to ordinary labor and real capital. However, R&D capital also includes labor costs for researchers, as they noted later in the paper. Although the labor cost in R&D capital should be distributed from value added, the assumption of the production function does not consider this. Thus, I propose that they also estimate a production function without the restriction that the total of the labor share and real capital share is equal to 1. In addition, it would be better that they revise footnote 10.

My second additional comment concerns the assumption that the rapid fall in the TFP growth rate was an effect of the Asian currency crisis (table 8.5). The result showed that TFP growth depended on short-term fluctuations. In my opinion, TFP should be interpreted from the supply side, although several interpretations of TFP were proposed in this conference. From this point, I recommend that the authors consider capital utilization rate in estimating parameters, in order to exclude demand shock from the short-term fluctuations of TFP.

References

Griliches, Zvi. 1986. Productivity, R&D, and basic research at firm level in the 1970s. *American Economic Review* 76 (1): 141–54.

———. 2000. *R&D, education, and productivity.* Cambridge, Mass.: Harvard University Press.

Comment Jungho Yoo

This paper estimates the elasticity of output at firm level with respect to R&D capital, utilizing data on 136 manufacturing firms in Taiwan for the 1994–2000 period. It finds that the output elasticity was around 0.18, which seems somewhat high but falls within the range of estimates in earlier, similar empirical studies conducted by others for other countries.

The authors divide the sample into high-tech and conventional firms and find the R&D elasticity of output to be around 0.3 for the high-tech firms and 0.07 for the others. This also tends to confirm the findings of earlier studies that differentiate "scientific" sectors from other sectors and obtain much higher elasticity estimates for the former and lower estimates for the latter, except that the scientific sectors referred to chemicals, drug, electrical and electronic equipment, and scientific instruments.

The paper also computes the growth rates of TFP, utilizing the estimated labor share in the Cobb-Douglas function, and finds very high growth rates. For example, in year 2000, in five industries—except for the metal industry, for which the growth rate turned out to be negative—the growth rates of TFP were all greater than 5 percent, electronic equipment registering 13.2 percent.

The paper is very much focused on what it sets out to do and achieves its purpose; that is, it confirms significant contribution made by R&D capital to productivity growth for Taiwanese manufacturing firms. It reports only what is directly related to the estimation. Some description of the Taiwanese manufacturing industries would give the readers, especially foreign readers, a better understanding of the context within which this study is conducted.

First, I would like to see some more discussion of the data themselves. For example, some discussion would help of changes in output and of cap-

Jungho Yoo is a senior fellow at the Korea Development Institute.

ital inputs over the period under study, at the aggregate and industry levels, and also of relative magnitude of R&D stock in comparison with physical capital.

Second, it seems worthwhile in a future study to try including skill variables such as share of engineers, technicians, skilled workers, and so on. Doing so produced lower estimates of the R&D elasticity in earlier, similar studies, although interpretation of this result requires caution, as it is related to the substitutability and complementarity between labor skill and R&D stock.

The third comment is not directed just to this paper but is relevant more generally to other studies as well where actual output is used in the estimation of R&D elasticity of output and indeed in the estimation of a production function. Firms do not always produce at their maximum capacity, but the capacity utilization is almost always less than 100 percent and tends to rise during a period of expansion. If a capacity utilization variable is missing in a regression that covers a period of business expansion, it will produce an upwardly biased estimate of R&D elasticity. This may indeed be a matter of some importance to this paper, since the 1994–2000 period under study coincides with the global IT boom.

9

Bankruptcy Policy Reform and Total Factor Productivity Dynamics in Korea
Evidence from Microdata

Youngjae Lim and Chin Hee Hahn

9.1 Introduction

During the onset of the Korean financial crisis in 1997, an inefficient corporate bankruptcy system had a detrimental effect on Korea's economy. Prior to the crisis, in 1996 and the first three-quarters of 1997, many large-sized firms facing bankruptcy actively sought shelter under the court-administered rehabilitation procedures. However, the inadequacies of the bankruptcy system led to poor discipline in targeting the appropriate financially distressed firms to undergo the rehabilitation procedure. Meanwhile, before the outbreak of the economic crisis, the uncertainty and delay encountered in dealing with failing firms clearly added to the distortion of the resource allocation process in Korea's economy.

In other words, the exit barriers for large firms seemed to have decreased the efficiency of resource allocation before the onset of the crisis. Prior to the crisis, Korea's corporate bankruptcy system had a tendency to work as a de facto exit barrier. For example, before the reform, producers with persistently declining productivity were more likely to be accepted in some rehabilitation procedure if they were deemed as having high social value, such as a large output or employment share in the economy.

Hence, the natural course of action for postcrisis Korea was to undertake a sweeping reform of its corporate bankruptcy system. As was the case with other structural reforms in the corporate sector, reforming Korea's bankruptcy policy was pushed forward based on the belief that new reforms were essential in preventing recurrent economic crises from plaguing the econ-

Youngjae Lim is a research fellow and head of the Corporate Affairs and Competition Policy Division at the Korea Development Institute. Chin Hee Hahn is a research fellow at the Korea Development Institute.

omy. Yet past experiences of crisis-hit countries suggest that there is a strong possibility that incomplete or weak reforms will often lead to recurrent economic crises. Despite this suggestion, to the best of our knowledge, there are few empirical studies that examine how bankruptcy reforms in postcrisis Korea affect the efficiency of resource reallocation and, ultimately, total factor productivity (TFP) growth in Korea's economy.[1]

Against this backdrop, our study aims at addressing the effects of bankruptcy policy reform by analyzing data at the firm or plant level. First, by employing firm-level panel data, the study examines how the postcrisis reforms in the bankruptcy policy affected the productivity dynamics of failing firms. The analysis focuses on bankruptcy procedures administered by the courts. These in-court settlements are necessary for failing firms faced with bankruptcy that are unsuccessful in securing an out-of-court settlement after exhausting all options. Maintaining discipline in in-court bankruptcy procedures would have far-reaching consequences on out-of-court bankruptcy procedures, since the discipline would act as an effective and credible deterrent for failing, but not yet bankrupt, firms.

We examine whether the firms accepted under the reformed court-administered rehabilitation procedures experienced less persistent problems in their prebankruptcy TFP compared to firms undergoing the same process before the reforms. We expect that, if the reform in the in-court bankruptcy procedures is successful, then only rehabilitation programs would accept firms with temporary difficulties, whereas failing firms with persistently declining productivity would be rejected. Successful reform of the corporate bankruptcy system would then imply an improvement in the efficiency of resource reallocation.

Second, to formulate an idea of how bankruptcy policy reform contributes to preventing prolonged economic stagnation, we examine how the reforms improved the efficiency of resource reallocation and, in turn, aggregate TFP growth.

Previous studies have documented that the resource reallocation process from exiting producers to entering producers explains a substantial por-

1. There are some recent studies that begin by examining the determinants of the divergent growth path of crisis-hit countries and (simply) suggest that policies such as bankruptcy policy reform are possible candidates. However, these studies do not use details of institutions at the micro level to analyze the effect of bankruptcy policy reform on the resource reallocation process of the economy. For instance, Hayashi and Prescott (2000) show that the Japanese economy's poor performance in the 1990s was due to failure to improve productivity and not the failure to accumulate inputs. Based on this finding and other evidence, they further suggest that the industrial policy of protecting failing or declining industries or firms by the Japanese government is the main culprit behind the "lost decade." Meanwhile, in a comparative study of Chile and Mexico, Bergoeing et al. (2001) show that the decade-long divergent growth paths of the two countries since the financial crisis in the early 1980s are predominantly driven by the differences in TFP growth rates. They suggest that policies such as the bankruptcy policy reform are candidates for explaining the different paths of the two countries.

tion of TFP changes at the aggregate level. Most of the studies find that exiting producers exhibit persistently declining productivity while entering producers that survive the market selection process exhibit rapidly increasing productivity (e.g., Foster, Haltiwanger, and Krizan 1998; Hahn 2000). This pattern suggests that policies that prevent the efficient reallocation of resources via entry and exit could be potentially very costly, with the cost possibly growing over time. On the contrary, bankruptcy policy reforms, which induce inefficient firms to exit with a lower cost and allocate released resources to efficient entrants or incumbents, would enhance the rate of aggregate productivity growth.

In this study, we use Korean manufacturing plant-level data to ask whether the productivity dynamics of entering and exiting producers hold in Korea. Specifically, we answer the following questions. What kinds of time profiles do the TFP numbers of exiting and entering producers exhibit? Given the pattern of productivity dynamics, how does the competitive process of entry and exit improve aggregate productivity? Can we expect the policies that improve the efficiency of resource reallocation, such as bankruptcy policy reform, to improve aggregate TFP instantaneously or over a period of time?

The outline of this study is as follows. Section 9.2 examines the effects of the postcrisis bankruptcy policy reform in Korea on the resource reallocation process using the firm-level data. In particular, we discuss the key elements in the postcrisis bankruptcy reforms and then proceed to analyze the TFP performance of failing firms entering the court-administered rehabilitation procedures before and after the reform. Section 9.3 examines the mechanism by which the reform improves the efficiency of resource reallocation or the performance of aggregate TFP. Our analysis uses plant-level panel data on the Korean manufacturing sector. Section 9.4 summarizes and concludes.

9.2 Bankruptcy Policy Reform and the Productivity Dynamics of Failing Firms

9.2.1 Corporate Bankruptcy System prior to the Economic Crisis

Exit Barriers for Large Firms

Past Korean economic growth was made possible by the growth or restructuring of existing firms rather than by the dynamic entry and exit process. During the period of development when profitable new markets were rapidly emerging, the inadequate corporate bankruptcy system did not significantly distort the resource allocation of the economy due to the ability of the economy to easily reallocate resources from declining sectors to emerging profitable sectors. Under these circumstances, through rationalization programs, the government played an active role in reallocating resources from failing firms to other existing firms. At the same time, many of the failing firms were not filing for bankruptcy procedures overseen by the courts.[2]

In particular, most small and medium-sized bankrupt firms were effectively liquidated on a nonjudicial basis. A bankrupt firm's debt was usually collected on an individual basis under the Civil Procedure Act. Most of the bankrupt firm's assets were already subject to mortgage or security, consequently leaving little for unsecured creditors. Additional procedures for the collection of debt were not necessary.[3]

For large firms, however, the too-big-to-fail argument played a part in building exit barriers in the sense that inefficient firms were often allowed to operate through some explicit or hidden subsidies from the government. Several large-sized bankrupt firms were periodically bailed out through the government's various rationalization measures, undercutting Korea's formal bankruptcy procedures.

Since the early 1990s, however, Korea's inadequate corporate bankruptcy system began to distort the economy's resource allocation, which increasingly grew until the outbreak of the financial crisis in 1997. Since the early 1990s, some failing firms began to enter court-administered bankruptcy procedures, but the bankruptcy system was often abused by controlling shareholders of the failing firms.

By enacting the Rule on Corporate Reorganization Procedure in 1992, the Supreme Court began to shift toward improving judicial bankruptcy procedures. In particular, the new rule established conditions for initiating corporate reorganization proceedings. These conditions were high social value, financial distress, and potential for rehabilitation. Interestingly, however, economic efficiency was not a condition for corporate reorganization. The new rule tended to give preference to larger failing firms for in-court corporate bankruptcy settlements, thereby creating a de facto exit barrier for large firms. For example, producers with persistently declining productivity were more likely to be accepted in one of the rehabilitation procedures if they were deemed as having high social value such as a large output or employment share in the economy.

Exit Barriers from the Controlling Shareholders of Failing Firms

Prior to the economic crisis, the controlling shareholders of large failing firms often sought to take shelter under court-administered rehabilitation

2. One technical hurdle in enforcing judicial bankruptcy procedures was the Act on Special Measures for Unpaid Loans of Financial Institutions. The act gave the Korea Asset Management Corporation (KAMCO) the authority to hold auctions of the bankrupt firm's assets before the initiation of court procedures. The act basically nullified the Corporate Reorganization Act because the auction of assets by KAMCO effectively preempted the corporate reorganization process. In 1990, the Constitutional Court declared this provision unconstitutional, paving the way for the expanded use of judicial bankruptcy procedures.

3. See Nam, Oh, and Kim (1999) for the details on the Korean bankruptcy system prior to the 1990s.

procedures. However, the inadequacies of the bankruptcy system led to poor discipline in targeting the appropriate financially distressed firms to undergo the rehabilitation procedure. This problem was particularly accentuated given the growing number of distressed firms.

The frequent abuse of the corporate reorganization procedure, highlighted by several notorious cases involving controlling shareholders of failing firms, forced the court to amend the system in 1996. In particular, the court argued for wiping out shares held by controlling shareholders responsible for a firm's failure. The introduction of the amendment in 1996 produced an unintended consequence: Controlling shareholders of failing firms pursued other means that would allow them to retain their ownership and control. Controlling shareholders found a loophole in the bankruptcy proceedings through the composition procedure, which was originally designed for small and medium-sized firms with less complex capital structures. However, before the law's revision after the crisis, the composition procedure did not contain an explicit limit on a firm's size and enabled existing management of larger firms to retain control.

As shown in table 9.1, there was a dramatic rise in bankruptcy filings for the composition procedure. The number of cases increased from nine cases in 1996 to 322 in 1997 and to 728 in 1998. In the first three-quarters of 1997, before the onset of the crisis, many large firms on the verge of financial collapse sought to file for bankruptcy under the composition procedure. Kia Motors was among the many that filed for composition procedure. This firm deserves special attention. In the case of Kia Motors, the debtor and creditors initially sought to file for different procedures: Kia, the debtor, initially filed for composition procedure, but shortly thereafter creditors decided to file for corporate reorganization. In cases where involved parties file for different proceedings, as was the case with Kia Motors, corporate reorganization overrides a composition filing. In the end, the court accepted Kia Motors' bankruptcy filing for corporate reorganization, but the

Table 9.1 **Bankruptcy Filings before and after the Crisis (unit: number of cases, %)**

Bankruptcy Procedure	1995	1996	1997	1998	1999	2000	2001	2002
Reorganization	79	52	132	148	37	32	31	19
	(76.0)	(65.8)	(26.8)	(14.9)	(9.1)	(13.2)	(12.3)	(15.3)
Composition	13	9	322	728	140	78	51	23
	(12.5)	(11.4)	(65.5)	(73.3)	(34.4)	(32.2)	(20.2)	(18.6)
Liquidation	12	18	38	117	230	132	170	82
	(11.5)	(22.8)	(7.7)	(11.8)	(56.5)	(54.6)	(67.5)	(66.1)
Total	104	79	492	993	407	242	252	124
	(100.0)	(100.0)	(100.0)	(100.0)	(100.0)	(100.0)	(100.0)	(100.0)

Source: Supreme Court of Korea (various issues).

Notes: The year 2002 covers January to October. Numbers in parentheses denote the percentage.

uncertainty and delay resulting from the inefficient bankruptcy system in dealing with large failing firms (such as Kia Motors) clearly worsened the situation of the economy.

9.2.2 Postcrisis Bankruptcy Policy Reforms

The economic crisis of 1997 placed tremendous strain on the existing corporate bankruptcy system for both in-court and out-of-court proceedings because of the soaring number and scale of bankruptcies. Table 9.1 shows that the filings for judicial bankruptcy procedures rose dramatically in 1997. The fallout from the economic crisis on the bankruptcy system was the main driving force in implementing revisions in the bankruptcy laws and procedures. In addition, the International Monetary Fund (IMF) and the International Bank for Reconstruction and Development (IBRD) required that improvements be made in the corporate bankruptcy system as a condition for the bailout package.

After the economic crisis, the Korean government implemented reform efforts to remove exit barriers along two separate lines: One involved the court-administered bankruptcy procedure, and the other included the prebankruptcy informal arrangements for corporate restructuring. Whereas the workout procedure had a significant impact on the corporate restructuring of larger failing firms, the court-administered procedures focused on the restructuring of medium-sized failing firms.

In this study, we focus on policy reform in the court-administered bankruptcy system. Except for small firms with less complex capital structures, the court-administered bankruptcy procedures would be the last resort for insolvent firms if the interested parties could not agree on the prebankruptcy informal arrangements for corporate restructuring. For prebankruptcy informal arrangements, one of the most effective disciplines should come from that of the court-administered bankruptcy procedures. In other words, during out-of-court informal settlements the incentives of interested parties would be directly affected by what they expect the outcome of the court-administered bankruptcy proceedings to be.

Bankruptcy Policy Reform in 1998: Economic Efficiency Criterion and the Removal of the Exit Barriers for Large Firms

The most crucial element in the postcrisis court-administered bankruptcy system was the court's establishment and tight enforcement of an economic efficiency criterion in selecting qualified firms for judicial bankruptcy procedures. Instead of being based on economic efficiency, the prereform system was based on high social value and prospects for rehabilitation. Presently, a comparison of a distressed firm's value as a going concern with its liquidation value is required to initiate judicial bankruptcy proceedings.

The new criterion greatly contributed to removing the de facto exit barrier placed on large firms that had existed in the in-court bankruptcy system prior to the crisis. Prior to the crisis, producers with persistently declining productivity were more likely to be accepted into a rehabilitation procedure as long as they exhibited high social value such as a large output or employment share in the economy.

The reforms initiated in 1998 represented the most dramatic change in the system since the enactment of the corporate bankruptcy laws in 1962. However, in the wake of the crisis, in an effort to quickly implement the reforms, the government was not successful in initiating a fully comprehensive revision.[4] The shortcomings of the first reforms resulted in another round of revisions in 1999. The two revisions to the bankruptcy laws significantly expanded the role of the courts in the corporate bankruptcy process. If not for the workout procedure introduced as an out-of-court settlement in 1998, the role of the courts would have been much greater.

Besides the economic efficiency criterion, the 1998 reforms attempted to speed up bankruptcy proceedings. The revisions introduced time limits for critical steps in the proceedings, such as for the decision on stay, the report of debts and equities, the approval of the reorganization plan, and other related steps. Additional changes in the 1998 revision included the following. First, the reforms established mechanisms to induce a more active role for the creditors, such as introducing a creditor's conference. Second, to enhance the court's capacity to deal with a large volume of bankruptcy cases, the court receivership committee was introduced as a special advisor to oversee the critical steps in the proceedings. Third, the process of wiping out the shares of controlling shareholders was strengthened and made more transparent. Fourth, to prevent the abuse of the composition procedure, some critical enhancements were made to the Composition Act. For example, large firms with complex capital structures were not allowed to file bankruptcy under the composition procedure. Table 9.1 shows the impact resulting from changes to the Composition Act, as the number of composition filings decreased sharply from 728 in 1998 to 140 in 1999.

Bankruptcy Policy Reform in 1999: Mandatory Liquidation System

Despite these significant revisions in 1998, there was room for further reform, as mentioned previously. To some extent, in fact, the 1999 reforms filled the gap between the initial reform proposals and what was finally passed in the 1998 revisions. While the revisions were being developed in 1999, there was an initial debate on the inclusion of an automatic stay provision for the new law. Under an automatic stay, the debtors' assets would be automatically protected from creditors seeking to secure their claims. After strong arguments were presented for both sides on the issue of automatic stay, the final compromise was to speed up the initiation of the proceedings to within a month of the filing.

4. See Koo (1998) for the details on the bankruptcy policy reform in 1998. Right after the financial crisis broke out in December 1997, the bankruptcy policy reform was made in February 1998.

Although the automatic stay provision can enhance the rehabilitation of failing firms after bankruptcy, the debtor may choose to utilize the court in order to avoid a formal default and thereby evade criminal punishment under the Illegal Check Control Act. According to the Illegal Check Control Act, the managers or controlling owners of failing firms who issued bad checks are criminally liable. The objective of the act was to overcome the informational asymmetry between debtors and creditors. Creditors faced with highly unreliable accounting information would be less willing to facilitate loans to debtors without a credible means of recourse. As a result, debtors are forced to make a credible commitment to repayment by risking incarceration in the case of default.

The new revision also facilitated an efficient transition between corporate reorganization and liquidation. After the initiation decision, the court must compare the going-concern value of the firm with its liquidation value. If the liquidation value is larger than the going-concern value, the court must declare the liquidation of the firm. Donga Construction, which was liquidated in early 2001, was the first large firm to travel down this path. The mandatory liquidation provision could be considered as a reform that contributes to enhance the efficiency of bankruptcy system.

However, the mandatory liquidation provision created an unintended consequence. The possibility of liquidation instilled fear among failing firms to a point where many attempted to avoid the judicial rehabilitation procedures. Resolving this problem in the current judicial bankruptcy system remains one of the major future policy objectives in Korea.

9.2.3 Bankruptcy Policy Reform and the Productivity Dynamics of Bankruptcy Cohorts

Firms go bankrupt due to their inability to pay their debts. A critical element in designing a corporate bankruptcy system is the ability to distinguish (or to elicit information on) whether an insolvent firm's financial distress is temporary or persistent. One method by which to resolve this issue empirically is analyzing the productivity of insolvent firms. In the study, we construct TFP measures for the firms in our data set to evaluate the performance of the corporate bankruptcy system instituted after the economic crisis. We examine a failing firm's cross-sectional distribution of corporate bankruptcy and time series productivity before and after bankruptcy filing.

Use of Bankruptcy Procedures by Chaebol Category after the Crisis

Table 9.2 shows the composition of bankruptcy procedures applied to insolvent firms by *chaebol* category from 1997 to 1999. The table demonstrates the relative share of bankruptcy procedures among insolvent firms, weighted by the size of assets. The insolvent firms in a given year include only those that went bankrupt for the first time in that year and exclude

Table 9.2 **Insolvent Firms' Procedure by the *Chaebol* Category (unit: trillion won, %)**

	1997			1998				1999			
	No Procedure	Composition	Corporate Reorganization	No Procedure	Composition	Corporate Reorganization	Workout	No Procedure	Composition	Corporate Reorganization	Workout
1–30 largest *chaebols*	0.35	0.61	9.48	0.09983	0	0	5.669	0	0	0	3.455
	(3.38)	(5.80)	(90.82)	(1.73)	(0.00)	(0.00)	(98.27)	(0.00)	(0.00)	(0.00)	(100)
31–60 largest *chaebols*	0	0	0.19	0	0	0	5.713	0	0	0	0.5862
	(0.00)	(0.00)	(100)	(0.00)	(0.00)	(0.00)	(100)	(0.00)	(0.00)	(0.00)	(100)
61–300 largest *chaebols*	3.18	7.69	12.67	0.7850	1.560	6.795	13.05	0	1.081	0.2857	14.71
	(13.51)	(32.66)	(53.84)	(3.54)	(7.03)	(30.62)	(58.81)	(0.00)	(6.73)	(1.78)	(91.50)
Small *chaebols* and	3.95	1.32	8.27	2.090	1.638	1.469	3.354	0.4627	0.9036	0.4040	25.68
independent firms	(29.16)	(9.73)	(61.11)	(24.44)	(19.16)	(17.18)	(39.22)	(1.69)	(3.29)	(1.47)	(93.55)

Source: Lim (2003).

Notes: The frequencies are weighted by the asset size. Author's calculation for all the firms in the National Information and Credit Evaluation (NICE) data. Numbers in parentheses denote the percentage.

those from other years; hence, the table gives us the incidence of new bankruptcies in the specific year. By focusing on the year cohorts, we can control for various year-specific effects and single out the relationship between the various rehabilitation settlements and the size factor over time.

Once firms are insolvent, they can enter into either court-administered or out-of-court settlements, including corporate reorganization, composition, or workout procedures. But not all firms enter into one of these rehabilitation programs; instead, some are simply left bankrupt for a prolonged period of time. Firms under these circumstances are cut off from credit, which limits them to only cash transactions.

Table 9.2 shows the relative share of different types of settlements for new *chaebol* bankruptcies from 1997 to 1999. The firms that went bankrupt in 1997 show a clear pattern. For the top thirty *chaebols,* the majority (94 percent in terms of asset size) was accepted into corporate reorganization, whereas only a fraction (6 percent in terms of asset size) was accepted into composition. On the other hand, quite a significant proportion of small-sized *chaebols* entered into the composition program. A substantial portion of the independent firms (and a less substantial portion of small *chaebols*) did not qualify for any rehabilitation program after bankruptcy.

In 1998, the government introduced an out-of-court workout procedure. Table 9.2 shows that, for large *chaebols,* the workout program was the main method of settlement. Similarly, the workout program played an important role among independent firms. By 1999, the role of the workout program had increased significantly, and most of the new bankruptcies (in terms of asset size) were handled through the out-of-court workout procedure.

Examining the Pre-Exit Productivity of Bankruptcy Cohorts

Note that one of the most significant changes in the 1998 revision was the introduction of the economic efficiency criterion. The new revision required that the courts compare the going-concern value of the firm with its liquidation value for the initiation of judicial bankruptcy proceedings. A preliminary analysis shows that the firms that filed for bankruptcy between 1998 and 2000 experienced less persistent difficulties compared to firms filing in 1997. For the firms filing bankruptcy in 1997, their productivity was lower than solvent firms several years before they entered into one of the rehabilitation programs. Rehabilitation mechanisms applied to firms under these conditions are most likely doomed to failure from the start. Rehabilitation procedures must target firms that undergo bankruptcy due to temporary setbacks and that have high potential for recovery. These characteristics are present in the 1998–2000 cohorts. The introduction of the economic efficiency criterion in 1998 appears to have affected the types of firms targeted. Note that the 1998 reform was initiated at the beginning of the year.

These hypotheses can be tested statistically in the following manner. Tables 9.3 and 9.4 show regressions of productivity on a set of dummy

Table 9.3 **Productivity Dynamics of Bankruptcy Cohorts before and after Bankruptcy Policy Reform (firms undergoing corporate reorganization or composition)**

	Dependent Variable: Productivity				
Independent Variable	For the 1996 Cohort (1)	For the 1997 Cohort (2)	For the 1998 Cohort (3)	For the 1999 Cohort (4)	For the 2000 Cohort (5)
1993	–0.0687115	–0.0820866	–0.0069199	0.0251072	0.0092007
	(0.1739958)	(0.0596231)	(0.035766)	(0.0527104)	(0.0795996)
1994	–0.0629782	–0.0815479	–0.0366698	–0.0219148	–0.0277665
	(0.1739847)	(0.0602887)	(0.0347451)	(0.0500552)	(0.0750421)
1995	–0.0588727	–0.1367584**	–0.0390412	0.0127083	–0.0821738
	(0.1739736)	(0.0588782)	(0.0339194)	(0.0474052)	(0.0711893)
1996	–0.3647536	–0.1347013**	0.0070321	0.0317036	–0.0124563
	(0.02245488)	(0.0595412)	(0.0334223)	(0.0470457)	(0.0700231)
1997	–0.2869542	–0.2780865**	–0.0574577	–0.0368554	0.0304901
	(0.2245442)	(0.063298)	(0.0356012)	(0.0460487)	(0.0689116)
1998	–0.1409918	–0.2565868**	–0.3211885**	–0.1993039**	–0.003248
	(0.1739603)	(0.0650112)	(0.0447192)	(0.0648769)	(0.0711459)
1999	–0.1321559	–0.1544865**	–0.1599611**	–0.1475066**	–0.2036022**
	(0.2245506)	(0.0700572)	(0.0466198)	(0.0722738)	(0.091783)
2000	–0.1572699	–0.1793303**	–0.1627449**	–0.2222749**	–0.3875751**
	(0.2245766)	(0.0765336)	(0.0488477)	(0.0778949)	(0.1376069)
Year dummies included	Yes	Yes	Yes	Yes	Yes
Industry dummies included	Yes	Yes	Yes	Yes	Yes
No. of observations	40,205	40,476	41,025	40,588	40,373

Notes: Numbers in parentheses are standard errors. Independent variable = dummy variable denoting a specific cohort interacted with year and industry dummy.

**Significant at the 5 percent level.

*Significant at the 10 percent level.

Table 9.4 **Profitability Performance of the Bankruptcy Cohorts before and after Bankruptcy Policy Reform (firms undergoing corporate reorganization or composition)**

	Dependent Variable: Profitability				
Independent Variable	For the 1996 Cohort (1)	For the 1997 Cohort (2)	For the 1998 Cohort (3)	For the 1999 Cohort (4)	For the 2000 Cohort (5)
1993	–5.53285	–1.053267	1.02541	–2.983965	–4.046776
	(102.5908)	(35.0131)	(20.11472)	(28.94122)	(42.627)
1994	–5.593412	–2.923504	–0.1474853	–2.976718	–1.751188
	(102.5857)	(34.5993)	(19.65527)	(27.26436)	(39.96213)
1995	–3.757859	–4.626083	–0.618984	–2.501499	–7.389917
	(102.5831)	(34.20874)	(19.36783)	(26.70296)	(38.80357)
1996	–55.05091	–5.89941	–0.7878422	–2.480486	–2.169504
	(132.4078)	(34.98389)	(19.43056)	(26.52319)	(39.95305)
1997	–109.6434	–19.09772	–3.990996	–5.698947	–1.671837
	(102.5782)	(34.97537)	(20.27411)	(26.16555)	(38.25027)
1998	–3.665419	–29.41768	–32.68748	–31.58403	–13.42344
	(102.5801)	(37.19917)	(24.80246)	(36.19649)	(41.20706)
1999	–0.8003833	–12.61717	–5.174351	–15.59426	–19.05743
	(132.4098)	(36.73676)	(22.27227)	(31.50063)	(50.03865)
2000	–10.02233	–1.937577	–0.7337271	1.431097	–4.809503
	(132.4134)	(41.18623)	(24.02397)	(35.79111)	(59.18531)
2001	36.11783	9.827578	0.1038245	9.514607	–99.89773
	(132.4123)	(41.85452)	(25.12973)	(37.65765)	(61.25584)
Year dummies included	Yes	Yes	Yes	Yes	Yes
Industry dummies included	Yes	Yes	Yes	Yes	Yes
No. of observations	52,026	52,345	53,031	52,520	52,236

Notes: Numbers in parentheses are standard errors. Independent variable = dummy variable denoting a specific cohort interacted with year and industry dummy.
**Significant at the 5 percent level.
*Significant at the 10 percent level.

variables referring to the specific year bankruptcy cohort interacted with the year dummy. Only the particular cohort and the group of solvent firms are included in each regression. Therefore, the reported coefficients are the productivity differential between the specific bankruptcy cohort and the group of solvent firms.

Table 9.3 shows that for the 1997 (corporate reorganization or composition) bankruptcy cohort, the reported coefficients are negative from 1993 to 2000 and significant from 1995 to 2000. The 1996 bankruptcy cohort shows a similar pattern, but standard errors are large due to the small sample size of the 1996 cohort. On the other hand, for the pre-exit years of the 1998–2000 bankruptcy cohorts, the coefficients are small and significantly negative only around the time of bankruptcy.

Table 9.4 shows a similar pattern of results for the profitability variable. Profitability does not show a clear pattern for the pre-exit year productivity of failing firms. A possible interpretation of this result is that some explicit or hidden subsidies given to failing firms at the pre-exit years may have worked to blur the pattern of persistently declining productivity for the bankruptcy cohorts before the reform.

As discussed in section 9.2.2, the most crucial element in the postcrisis court-administered bankruptcy system was the implementation of an economic efficiency criterion. The court established and tightly enforced an economic efficiency criterion in selecting qualified failing firms for the judicial rehabilitation procedures. One of the key criteria for all judicial bankruptcy proceedings was to conduct a comparison of the value of a distressed firm as a going concern with its liquidation value.

Instead of economic efficiency, the prereform system was based on high social value and prospects for rehabilitation. Note that the prospects for rehabilitation could vary depending on the amount of subsidies from creditors and the government. In comparison to the prereform system, the new system removed the possibilities for interested parties (for example, controlling shareholders, labor union, or local/central governments) to be in the way of a failing firm's exit. In other words, the new system contributed toward removing the de facto exit barrier that benefited large firms under the in-court bankruptcy system prior to the crisis. Under the new system, producers with persistently declining productivity were less likely to be accepted into a rehabilitation procedure regardless of whether they exhibited high social value such as a large output or employment share in the economy.

9.3 Entry, Exit, and Aggregate Productivity Growth in Korea before and after the Crisis

In the previous section, it was found that firms accepted in the court-administered rehabilitation program after the reform had less persistent problems in prebankruptcy TFP performance than firms in a similar situation before the reform. We interpret this finding as lending support to the argument that bankruptcy policy reform enhanced the efficiency of resource reallocation after the crisis.

How, then, is the bankruptcy policy reform likely to affect the aggregate TFP growth? To answer this question, we use plant-level data to examine how resource reallocation by the competitive process of entry and exit contributes to aggregate productivity growth.

Before proceeding any further, it may be helpful to provide a brief review of the relevant literature. Recently, a growing number of studies have explored the relationship between the resource reallocation process of entry and exit and aggregate TFP growth using plant- or firm-level data.[5] Most studies support the hypothesis that the process of entry and exit enhances the aggregate productivity. This phenomenon is the result of at least one of the following three effects: market selection, learning, and "shadow of death." The market selection effect is the part of the aggregate productivity gain that results from the survival of the efficient firms. The learning effect implies that surviving entrants become relatively more efficient over time. Finally, the "shadow of death" effect denotes the phenomenon that exiting plants exhibited relatively low productivity performance several years earlier.[6]

Can we expect that the same forces are at work in Korea's case? To answer this question, we will discuss what the actual patterns of plant entry and exit have been and whether the plant turnovers reflect productivity differential among plants. Our methodology is based on Hahn (2000).[7]

9.3.1 Patterns of Plant Entry and Exit in the Korean Manufacturing Industry

In Hahn (2000), there are two types of entry: birth and switch-in. Birth is defined as a plant that first appears in the data set. Switch-in occurs when a plant switches from one market to another from one period to the next. A market is defined at the five-digit industry level. A continuing plant is identified neither as birth nor as switch-in. Similarly, there are two types of exit: death and switch-out. Death is defined as a plant's disappearance from the data set in the next period, whereas switch-out occurs when a

5. For a recent survey of the empirical literature in this vein, see Tybout (1996b), Caves (1998), and Foster, Haltiwanger, and Krizan (2001).

6. With regard to the question of how much of the aggregate productivity growth is accounted for by entry and exit, however, the available evidence seems mixed. For example, Foster, Haltiwanger, and Krizan (2001) on the United States and Aw, Chen, and Roberts (2001) on Taiwan report a large role of entry and exit in aggregate productivity growth, while Baily, Hulten, and Campbell (1992) on the United States and Griliches and Regev (1995) on Israel find a minor role.

7. See Hahn (2000) for a more detailed discussion on the methodology.

Table 9.5 **Contribution of Plant Births (unit: %)**

	Under 5 Years							
	1–3		4–5		Total		Over 5 Years	
Year	Number of Plants	Current Output	Number of Plants	Current Output	Number of Plants	Current Output	Number of Plants	Current Output
1995	53.32	17.13	14.22	9.09	67.54	26.22	32.46	73.78
1996	47.60	15.36	18.68	11.11	66.29	26.46	33.71	73.54
1997	45.40	14.77	18.67	10.63	64.08	25.40	35.92	74.60
1998	39.45	12.77	18.63	8.68	58.08	21.45	41.92	78.55

Source: Hahn (2000).

Table 9.6 **Contribution of Plant Deaths (unit: %)**

	Within 5 Years							
	1–3		4–5		Total		Survive More Than 5 Years	
Year	Number of Plants	Current Output	Number of Plants	Current Output	Number of Plants	Current Output	Number of Plants	Current Output
1990	36.85	13.36	15.71	6.48	52.57	19.85	47.43	80.15
1991	37.41	14.52	17.11	7.62	54.52	22.14	45.48	77.86
1992	39.28	15.08	16.72	7.77	56.00	22.85	44.00	77.15
1993	43.71	14.92	20.23	9.13	63.93	24.05	36.07	75.95

Source: Hahn (2000).

plant moves out to another market in the next period. Under these working definitions, the actual patterns of entry and exit can be documented.

The contribution (in percent) of plant births and deaths are shown in table 9.5 and table 9.6, respectively. These statistics are in terms of output and number of plants. Specifically, table 9.5 illustrates what fraction of output or number of plants for each year is attributable to plants based on their age. Table 9.6 shows similar statistics for each year by group of plants that die within a certain time period. Overall, the numbers below suggest that plant turnover rate was quite high in the Korean manufacturing sector during the 1990–98 period.

According to table 9.5, plants less than five years of age accounted for more than 25 percent of manufacturing production, except for the crisis year of 1998. In 1998, the contribution from plants aged less than five years declined sharply to 21.5 percent. This decline is attributable not only to a fall in the birth rate but also to a rise in the closing of young plants, reflecting the severe recession. In terms of plant number, the importance of births becomes more pronounced; one- to five-year-old plants accounted for about 65 percent of the total plants for each year, except for 1998. The larger contribution of young plants in terms of plant number indicates the relatively small size of those plants.

The new plant entry rate in Korea seems to be higher than most other countries for which similar studies are available. For example, plants aged less than five years account for about 25 percent of a given year's output in Korea; 13.6 to 18.5 percent in the United States; 18.3 to 20.8 percent in Colombia; and 15.0 to 15.7 percent in Chile.[8] Comparing the entry rate of Korea and Taiwan might be useful since, even though both countries were equally dynamic countries, these countries differed vastly in their industrial structure. That is, it is well known that Korea's past economic success relied heavily on *chaebols,* while Taiwan's success depended on small and medium-sized enterprises (SMEs). If Korean *chaebols* employed a more capital-intensive production structure requiring larger sunk setup costs than SMEs in Taiwan, then it could well be conjectured that, combined with policy related exit barriers, these costs worked as an entry barrier, thus lowering the entry rate in Korea. Consistent with this hypothesis, the entry rate in Korea reported by Hahn (2000) seems to be less pronounced compared to Taiwan's. In a similar study for Taiwan, Aw, Chen, and Roberts (2001) report that one- to five-year-old firms account for approximately one-third to one-half of the production in nine Taiwanese manufacturing industries in 1991.[9] Further study is required to shed more light on this issue.

The plant death rate is also high in the Korean manufacturing industry. This fact is not surprising given the high cross-sectional correlation between the entry and exit rates reported in the literature. Although there is some variation over the years, more than half the plants, representing about 20 percent of output, cease to exist within a span of five years. In 1993, the contribution of the plants that die within five years became significantly larger, reflecting the severe economic recession in 1998. The contribution of plant deaths in terms of plant number is much larger than in terms of output, indicating that the deaths are concentrated among the smaller plants.

Plant death conditional on birth (not reported) is even higher than the unconditional death rates reported above. In terms of both plant number and output, the death rate conditional on births is much higher than the unconditional death rate, especially during the first three years of operation. Thus, new plants seem to fail easily, especially during the first three

8. The observation year varies by country. See Dunne, Roberts, and Samuelson (1988) for the United States and Roberts (1996) and Tybout (1996a) for Colombia and Chile, respectively. The U.S. figure is based on firm-level data.

9. Unfortunately, a direct comparison of the two studies could be somewhat misleading because Hahn (2000) uses plant-level data while Aw, Chen, and Roberts (2001) use firm-level data. Nevertheless, relatively high entry rate in Taiwan seems to be a robust conclusion, since entry rate measured at plant level would be higher than at firm level insofar as there are multiplant firms.

Table 9.7 **Average Productivity of Plant Groups, 1990–98**

		Entry		Exit		
Year	Continuing	Birth	Switch-In	Death	Switch-Out	Total
1990	–0.005			–0.044	–0.026	–0.016
1991	0.046	–0.031	0.041	–0.003	0.050	0.026
1992	0.061	–0.005	0.061	0.018	0.068	0.046
1993	0.087	0.030	0.096	0.051	0.101	0.072
1994	0.132	0.056	0.141	0.101	0.144	0.118
1995	0.190	0.132	0.199	0.150	0.202	0.174
1996	0.197	0.143	0.208	0.160	0.214	0.185
1997	0.239	0.177	0.252	0.182	0.245	0.218
1998	0.256	0.200	0.267			0.249

Source: Hahn (2000).
Note: Unweighted averages.

years. This fact might be due to, among other factors, the low productivity of these plants on average during the early stages of operation. This result is consistent with the theories of firm dynamics such as Jovanovic (1982) and Hopenhayn (1992). Switch-ins and switch-outs (not reported) are also frequently observed in the Korean manufacturing sector. In terms of output, they are almost as important as births or deaths. Compared with births or deaths, switch-ins or switch-outs are generally bigger in size.

9.3.2 Productivity Differential among Plant Groups at a Point in Time

Having described the plant entry and exit rates in the Korean manufacturing sector, we proceed to the issue of whether plant turnovers reflect certain patterns of productivity differential. We first examine the relationship between plant turnover patterns and plant productivity, both at a point in time and over a period of time.[10]

Table 9.7 compares the unweighted mean productivity levels of plants that exist in a given year. We split the sample into five plant groups as defined earlier. The main findings are summarized as follows. First, plants that die in a given year are, on average, less productive than surviving plants in that year. Depending on the year, failed plants (deaths) are about 3 to 6 percent less productive than continuing plants. This result is consistent with heterogeneous plant- or firm-level models that predict that market selection forces sort out low-productivity plants from high-productivity plants.

Second, new plants (births) are on average less productive than continu-

10. Plant productivity level is measured according to chained-multilateral index number approach as developed in Good (1985) and Good, Nadiri, and Sickles (1997) and employed in Aw, Chen, and Roberts (2001). For details, see Hahn (2000).

ing plants in the first year that they are observed. Furthermore, new plants are even less productive than failed ones. In fact, the productivity of a typical birth-plant is the lowest among all groups of plants in every year. Initial low productivity of birth-plants relative to continuing or failed plants is not consistent with the presence of the simple vintage effect that implies that new plants are more productive than older plants. However, the result is not necessarily contradictory to the prediction of several recent models of plant dynamics, such as Jovanovic (1982) and Hopenhayn (1992). Potential entrants who are uncertain about their productivity but hold a positive outlook on their postentry productivity performance—that is, who expect they could catch up with the incumbents in terms of productivity sooner or later—may enter despite their initially low productivity. Of course, birth-plants are also heterogeneous in terms of productivity, as will be discussed below.

The initial low productivity level of birth-plants relative to incumbents is also documented by other studies, although these studies differ from ours in data and methodologies. For example, Aw, Chen, and Roberts (2001) report that, in the case of Taiwanese manufacturing firms, entrants in 1986 are between 0.6 percent and 6.9 percent less productive than incumbent firms depending on industry. Meanwhile, table 10 in Foster, Haltiwanger, and Krizan (2001) reports that there is no statistical difference between continuing plants and entering plants in terms of multifactor productivity in 1987, based on ten-year interval analysis of plant-level data on the U.S. manufacturing sector. However, the same table illustrates that the cohort of plants that entered during the past five-year period, rather than ten-year period, show lower productivity than continuing plants in 1987.[11]

Third, switch-in or switch-out plants have higher productivity than birth- or death-plants, respectively. The productivity of switch-ins or switch-outs is roughly comparable to continuing plants on average. Higher productivity of switch-ins relative to birth-plants is consistent with the idea that having experience in a related market is beneficial. Also, the finding that switch-outs have productivity levels comparable to continuing plants seems to suggest that high productivity plants have mobility. Finally, each new cohort of births is more productive than their previous cohorts. This finding conforms well to the presumption of recent research and development–based endogenous growth models, such as Grossman and Helpman (1991), in that potential entrants gain from externalities due to previous innovation.

These findings suggest that plant turnovers, especially entry by birth and exit by death, are not random events. In other words, the productivity of

11. They report, however, that, in terms of labor productivity, entering plants have lower productivity than continuing plants even at ten-year intervals.

birth- and death-plants is more likely to be located at the lower end of the productivity distribution. In particular, the lower productivity of failed plants relative to continuing plants indicates that market selection forces are at work as predicted by theoretical models of plant or firm dynamics. Market selection of low-productivity plants from surviving high-productivity plants is a process that enhances the aggregate level of productive efficiency.

The lower productivity of new plants relative to continuing plants or even failed plants is consistent with the prediction of theoretical models and is similar to the experience of other countries. However, this finding could cast doubt on the positive role of exit and entry on the aggregate efficiency gain. Specifically, the instantaneous effect of resource reallocation by plant deaths and births on aggregate productivity growth might be very small or even negative. This result might be especially true if the resources released by failed firms are entirely reallocated to birth-firms. Is this the end of the story? The answer is no. To further elucidate this point, we now discuss the dynamic aspects of the relationship between plant turnovers and productivity. Specifically, we discuss postentry and pre-exit performance of plants by focusing on market selection, learning, and the shadow-of-death effects.

9.3.3 Postentry Performance: Market Selection and Learning

To proceed, we exploit the longitudinal aspect of the data set to examine whether market selection forces sort out low-productivity plants among birth-plants. In our sample, there are eight cohorts of births according to birth year from 1991 to 1998. Focusing on a particular birth-year cohort has the advantage of controlling for the possible age effect on survival. For example, we examine whether plants that belong to the 1991 birth cohort but die in 1993 have lower productivity at the time of death compared to the other surviving members of the birth cohort. To do so, we regress plant productivity on a set of year dummies (not reported) and a dummy variable denoting whether the plant died after birth within the sample period interacted with year dummies. Thus, the estimated coefficients denote the productivity differential between failures and survivors at the time of death. The regression results for three birth cohorts are reported in table 9.8.

The table shows that, for each birth-year cohort reported, exiting plants demonstrate significantly lower productivity than surviving plants at the time of death. Depending on the cohort year or death year, deaths are less productive than surviving plants by about 3 to 6 percent. Thus, the evidence from the Korean manufacturing sector clearly supports the presence of a market selection effect: Market forces sort out plants on the basis of productivity.

As noted by Foster, Haltiwanger, and Krizan (2001), the entry and exit

Table 9.8 Market Selection among Birth Cohorts

	Births 1991	Births 1993	Births 1995
Deaths 1992	–0.065		
	(0.005)		
Deaths 1993	–0.044		
	(0.004)		
Deaths 1994	–0.036	–0.042	
	(0.004)	(0.003)	
Deaths 1995	–0.032	–0.032	
	(0.004)	(0.003)	
Deaths 1996	–0.048	–0.030	–0.053
	(0.004)	(0.003)	(0.003)
Deaths 1997	–0.038	–0.044	–0.039
	(0.003)	(0.002)	(0.002)

Source: Hahn (2000).
Note: Numbers in parentheses are standard errors.

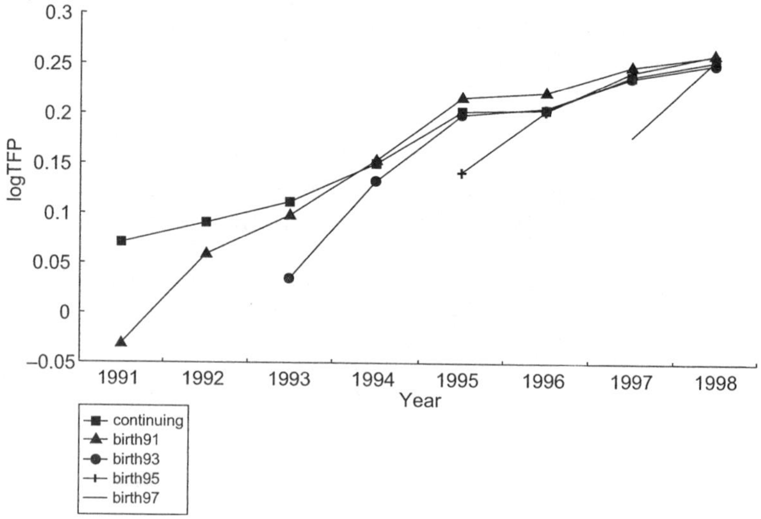

Fig. 9.1 Postentry productivity performance of surviving births: Learning
Source: Hahn (2000).

process also contributes to aggregate productivity growth through rapid learning of surviving entrants. In the Korean manufacturing sector, the learning effect is also observed. To illustrate the point, let us examine the productivity performance of the surviving members of the birth-plants relative to continuing plants. Figure 9.1 shows the average productivity of birth cohorts that survived until 1998 by birth-year compared to continuing plants in 1991 that also survived until 1998. Continuing plants increase their productivity steadily and improve their average productivity by about

23 percent during the 1991–98 period. Each birth-year cohort starts with a productivity disadvantage relative to continuing plants at the year of entry. However, every birth cohort exhibits a very rapid improvement in productivity following entry and catches up with continuing plants in terms of productivity level after several years. The initial productivity differential between birth- and continuing plants ranges from 6 to 10 percent depending on the birth-year. In the following year after entry, the productivity differential narrows to only about 0 to 3 percent. In the third year after entry, the productivity level of birth-plants is roughly the same as, or even slightly higher than, continuing plants. The 1991 birth cohort in particular, which has the longest time series, maintains a higher average productivity than continuing plants three years after entry. Thus, the results are clearly supportive of the presence of a rapid learning effect by surviving members of birth-plants, especially during the first several years after entry.

9.3.4 Pre-Exit Productivity Performance of Deaths: Shadow-of-Death Effect

In order to understand the connection between the micro process of entry and exit and the aggregate productivity growth, it would be ideal if we could examine the counterfactual phenomenon of what would have happened to the productivity performance of failed plants if they had survived. Unfortunately, this seems to be an impossible task. However, it could prove to be beneficial to examine predeath productivity performance of death-plants in order to formulate an idea of the counterfactual. The issue is whether plant deaths reflect a random or transitory event or a persistently bad productivity performance record.

Figure 9.2 shows the time series of the average productivity of plants that existed in 1990 grouped by the year of death compared to plants that survived throughout the sample period. There are two points to be noted here. First, there is a significant productivity gap not only at the time of death but also in the years preceding death between each death cohort and the group that survived until 1998, even though each death cohort experienced absolute productivity gain over time. This phenomenon suggests that plant deaths reflect underlying productivity differences that have existed for a long period of time. In other words, those differences are not just a result of a random or transitory event. To take an example from the 1997 death cohort, the productivity disadvantage relative to the surviving group is about 6.5 percent in 1997. However, the productivity differential dates back as early as 1990, when it is already as large as 3.7 percent. Similar results hold for other death cohorts. Thus, plant deaths seem to reflect not only a disadvantage in productivity at a point in time but also a persistently poor history of productivity.[12]

12. Hahn (2000) shows that these results remain largely intact when taking into account the industry composition effect.

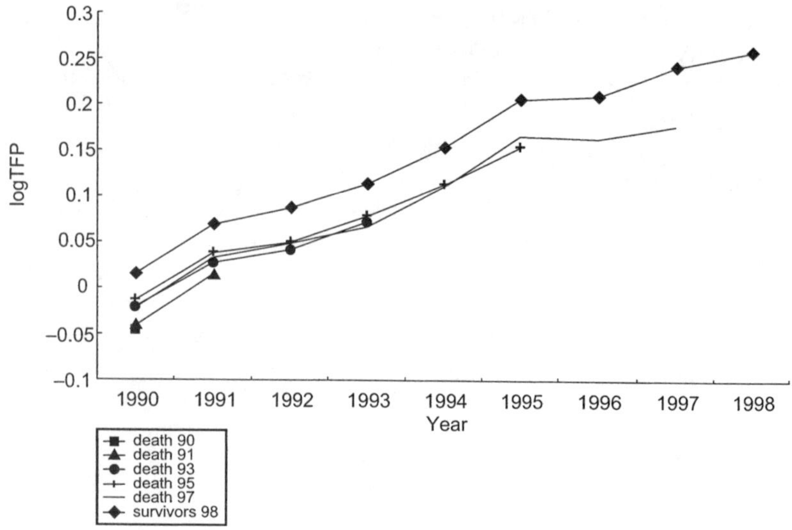

Fig. 9.2 Pre-exit productivity performance of deaths: Shadow of death
Source: Hahn (2000).

Second, the productivity differential between failed and surviving plants tends to widen, especially during the periods nearing the death year. For example, in the 1997 death cohort, the productivity differential fluctuates between 3.5 and 4.7 percent during 1990–96 period, but in 1997 it rises to 6.5 percent. Similar patterns are found for other death-year cohorts.

Thus far we have examined the predeath productivity performance of death cohorts relative to surviving groups of plants and have observed large and persistent productivity differences. The disparities often widen over time during the period near the death-year. However, such large and persistent productivity differences observed in figure 9.2 might reflect other uncontrolled factors that differ between survivors and failures, such as plant age. That is, younger plants may be less productive and suffer death more frequently than older plants. In order to control for this possible age effect on productivity and survival, we also looked at the predeath performance of plants that are born in the same year.

Figure 9.3 shows predeath productivity of a 1991 birth cohort that is further divided by the death-year compared to the 1991 births that survived until 1998. For comparison, the productivity performance of 1991 continuing plants that survived until 1998 is also shown. As expected, the persistence of productivity differential among 1991 births is somewhat less pronounced than suggested by figure 9.2. The 1991 birth-plants that die before 1998 do not demonstrate a noticeable productivity disadvantage in the early years of operation compared to the surviving group. Especially in the first year of operation (1991), there is virtually no productivity differential between surviving and failed plants.

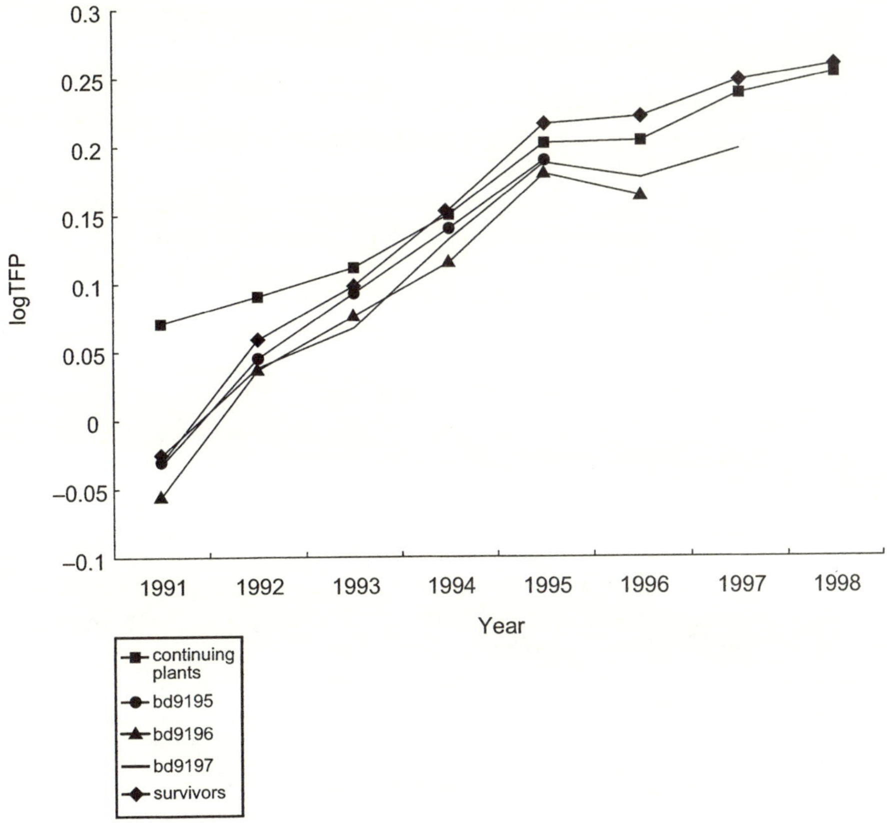

Fig. 9.3 Pre-exit productivity performance of deaths among 1991 births

However, as surviving members of 1991 births improve their productivity at a faster rate, a productivity gap begins to develop and persists over time. In addition, for each death-year cohort among the 1991 births, the productivity disadvantage relative to the continuing group becomes the largest in the last year they are observed. Thus, even if the possible age effect on productivity and survival is controlled for, plant deaths still reflect somewhat persistent productivity disadvantage that often widens during the period near death.

These findings seem to suggest that plant deaths reflect persistently poor productivity performance, which often worsens near the death year. In other words, low productivity of deaths is not just an outcome of random or transitory events.

9.3.5 Entry, Exit, and Aggregate Total Factor Productivity Growth

The empirical evidence we have presented is summarized as follows. Overall, plant deaths reflect persistently low productivity in the past. Entering plants may initially begin with a relatively low productivity level, but over time, they go through the process of market selection: The inefficient fail and the efficient survive. The surviving entrants experience rapid learning and become highly efficient over time.

This pattern of productivity dynamics suggests that the major effect of resource reallocation of entry and exit on aggregate productivity will emerge over time, even though the instantaneous gain may be small or even negative. The evidence also suggests that policies that inhibit the resource reallocation process of entry and exit of businesses are likely to be inefficient. In particular, although the cost of such policies may not appear immediately, it will materialize and grow over time in the form of forgone aggregate productivity gain. Alternatively, policies that improve the efficiency of resource reallocation, such as bankruptcy policy reform, may not improve aggregate TFP instantaneously. However, the benefits from such policies will most likely be realized over time.

9.4 Concluding Remarks

This study has found that failing firms, which are accepted in court-administered rehabilitation procedures after the bankruptcy reforms, had less persistent problems in prebankruptcy TFP performance compared to failed firms before the reforms. We interpret this finding as lending support to the argument that bankruptcy policy reform improved the efficiency of resource reallocation after the crisis.

To get an idea of how the bankruptcy policy reform affects the performance of aggregate TFP, we examined how the resource reallocation by the competitive process of entry and exit contributed to aggregate productivity growth based on evidence from plant-level data on the Korean manufacturing sector. The empirical analysis supports that, in Korea, exiting producers exhibit persistently declining productivity whereas entering producers that survive the market selection process show rapidly increasing productivity. These specific patterns of productivity dynamics suggest that policies that prevent resources from being reallocated efficiently via entry and exit could potentially be very costly, with the cost growing over time. Conversely, bankruptcy policy reform, which induces inefficient firms to exit and allocates the released resources to efficient entrants or incumbents, would contribute to increasing the rate of aggregate productivity growth.

Appendix

Data

Productivity Dynamics of Distressed Firms in Korea

Firm-Level Productivity Measure

We use detailed financial information on the firms that have external audit reports. According to the Act on External Audit of Joint-Stock Corporations, a firm with assets of seven billion won or more must issue audited financial statements. The data thus include all firms with assets of seven billion won or more. For these data, firm productivity is estimated using the chained-multilateral index number approach.

Data on Bankruptcy Filings by Distressed Firms

The information on corporate bankruptcy was gathered from various sources such as the courts, the Financial Supervisory Service, and the Bank of Korea.

Plant Productivity in Korean Manufacturing Sector

The data used for this section are from the unpublished plant-level database underlying the *Annual Report on Mining and Manufacturing Survey*. The data cover all plants with five or more employees in 580 manufacturing industries at the five-digit industry level. The data are an unbalanced panel with approximately 60,000 to 90,000 plants for each year during the 1990–98 period, so that the total number of observations is roughly 700,000. See Hahn (2000) for details in measurement of plant total productivity.

References

Aw, Bee Yan, Xiaomin Chen, and Mark J. Roberts. 2001. Firm-level evidence on productivity differentials, turnover, and exports in Taiwanese manufacturing. *Journal of Development Economics* 66 (1): 51–86.

Baily, Martin Neil, Charles Hulten, and David Campbell. 1992. Productivity dynamics in manufacturing plants. *Brookings Papers on Economic Activity, Microeconomics:* 187–267.

Bergoeing, Raphael, Patrick J. Kehoe, Timothy J. Kehoe, and Raimundo Soto. 2001. A decade lost and found: Mexico and Chile in the 1980s. Federal Reserve Bank of Minneapolis Staff Report 292. Minneapolis: Federal Reserve Bank of Minneapolis.

Caves, Richard E. 1998. Industrial organization and new findings on the turnover and mobility of firms. *Journal of Economic Literature* 37 (4): 1947–82.

Dunne, Timothy, Mark J. Roberts, and Larry Samuelson. 1988. Patterns of firm entry and exit in U.S. manufacturing industries. *RAND Journal of Economics* 19 (4): 495–515.

Foster, Lucia, John Haltiwanger, and C. J. Krizan. 2001. Aggregate productivity growth: Lessons from microeconomic evidence. In *New developments in productivity analysis,* ed. Charles Hulten, Edwin Dean, and Michael Harper, 303–63. Chicago: University of Chicago Press.

Good, David H. 1985. *The effect of deregulation on the productive efficiency and cost structure of the airline industry.* Ph.D. diss. University of Pennsylvania, Philadelphia, Pennsylvania.

Good, David H., M. Ishaq Nadiri, and Robin Sickles. 1997. Index number and factor demand approaches to the estimation of productivity. In *Handbook of applied econometrics: Microeconometrics, Vol. II,* ed. H. Pesaran and P. Schmidt, 14–80. Oxford, U.K.: Blackwell Publishers.

Griliches, Zvi, and Haim Regev. 1995. Firm productivity in Israeli industry. *Journal of Econometrics* 65:175–203.

Grossman, Gene M., and Elhanan Helpman. 1991. *Innovation and growth in the global economy.* Cambridge: MIT Press.

Hahn, Chin Hee. 2000. Entry, exit, and aggregate productivity growth: Micro evidence on Korean manufacturing. OECD Economics Department Working Paper no. 272, ECO/WKP(2000)45. Presented at the OECD workshop "The Causes of Economic Growth." 6–7 July, Paris, France. Also published as Korea Development Institute Policy Study 2000–04.

Hayashi, Fumio, and Edward C. Prescott. 2002. The 1990s in Japan: A lost decade. *Review of Economic Dynamics* 5:205–35.

Hopenhayn, Hugo A. 1992. Entry, exit, and firm dynamics in long-run equilibrium. *Econometrica* 60 (5): 1127–50.

Jovanovic, Boyan. 1982. Selection and the evolution of industry. *Econometrica* 50 (3): 649–70.

Koo, Bon Cheon. 1998. The economic analysis of corporate exit and the reform proposals (in Korean). Korea Development Institute.

Lim, Youngjae. 2003. The corporate bankruptcy system and the economic crisis. In *Economic crisis and corporate restructuring in Korea: Reforming the chaebol,* ed. S. Haggard, W. Lim, and E. Kim, 207–32. Cambridge, Mass.: Cambridge University Press.

Nam, Il Chong, Soogeun Oh, and Joon-Kyung Kim. 1999. Insolvency mechanisms in Korea. Korea Development Institute Working Paper 9918.

Roberts, Mark J. 1996. Colombia, 1977–85: Producer turnover, margins, and trade exposure. In *Industrial evolution in developing countries: Micro patterns of turnover, productivity, and market structure,* ed. Mark J. Roberts and James R. Tybout, 227–59. New York: Oxford University Press.

Supreme Court of Korea. Various issues. *Judicial yearbook.* Seoul, Korea: Ministry of Court Administration, Supreme Court of Korea.

Tybout, James R. 1996a. Chile, 1970–86: Trade liberalization and its aftermath. In *Industrial evolution in developing countries: Micro patterns of turnover, productivity, and market structure,* ed. Mark J. Roberts and James R. Tybout, 200–226. Oxford University Press.

———. 1996b. Heterogeneity and productivity growth: Assessing the evidence. In *Industrial evolution in developing countries: Micro patterns of turnover, productivity, and market structure,* ed. Mark J. Roberts and James R. Tybout, 43–72. Oxford University Press.

Comment Chong-Hyun Nam

This is a very interesting paper. First of all, I was impressed very much by the sheer size of the data set, which covers over 37,000 observations. Using this data set, the paper produces a number of powerful statistical results. I think they are not only revealing by themselves but also provide very useful information for the policymakers concerned.

I have only a couple of comments to make. My first comment is that the paper produces many invaluable statistical results in the tables and figures. And yet the paper tends to be too sketchy in interpreting and explaining those results.

The paper, for example, does not go very far in examining and evaluating the costs and benefits associated with those bankruptcy policy reforms and their consequences. The paper would gain a lot if it could try to dig into the implications of these statistical results, from the perspectives of both the firms and the government.

My second comment is that, despite a lot of data work, the paper seems to fall short of presenting a sensible bankruptcy policy reform package for Korea. If the authors ever want to come up with a sensible policy reform package, they will have to take into consideration the following two aspects very carefully.

One is that any policy reform package needs to properly reflect the sources of firm failures. In fact, firm failures can be brought on by a variety of reasons. Some may originate from shifts in comparative advantages due to changes in underlying factor compositions. Continued birth and death of the firms is then a natural consequence. For this case, only a freer entry and exit mechanism is to be desired.

Firm failures may also be caused by some unforeseen or unexpected factors such as financial or political crisis or temporary worldwide recessions induced by them. These factors are most likely to be beyond the control of individual firms, but they can drive many firms into bankruptcy that otherwise would have been healthy. Some kinds of social insurance program may be desired for this case.

Yet some failures may be purely due to lack of management talent or mismanagement on the part of owner-*cum*-managers in charge. A quick liquidation process may be desired for this kind of circumstances.

Another aspect that needs to be taken into consideration is that some firm failures may be closely related with some country-specific factors such as excessively powerful labor unions, lack of credit rating capability on the part of financial institutions, lack of transparency in related laws and regulations, or corrupted bureaucracy and unjust political influences. One

Chong-Hyun Nam is professor of economics at Korea University.

may want to uncover the importance of these factors as a cause of firm failures in the case of Korea and use it in making a policy reform package. I believe the experience of many Korean firms that suffered from these factors can provide invaluable information on this matter.

Comment Epictetus E. Patalinghug

Introduction

This study attempts (1) to examine the effect of postcrisis bankruptcy policy reform in Korea on the productivity of ailing firms, and (2) to examine how the reform would improve the performance of aggregate TFP over time. The following discussion will cover the following issues and how they are treated by the Lim-Hahn study: bankruptcy policy reforms, conceptual framework, and effect of entry and exit on productivity.

Bankruptcy Policy Reforms

The authors have adequately discussed how Korea's corporate bankruptcy system has evolved from court-administered procedures often abused by the controlling shareholders of failing firms to a court-administered system with a mandatory-liquidation provision feared by failing firms. The old system in which old bankrupt firms were periodically bailed out by the government was gradually replaced by the court-administered bankruptcy system.

The paper points out that after some restrictions were put on the composition procedure in 1998, large firms with complicated capital structures were not allowed to use this procedure. In 1997, large-sized *chaebols* preferred the corporate reorganization form of bankruptcy mechanism, and beginning in 1998 the same firms preferred the workout procedure. The authors' argument is that the rehabilitation procedure must target firms that undergo bankruptcy due to temporary setbacks and have high potential for recovery. Under this condition, bankruptcy policy reform will enhance the efficiency of resource allocation.

Conceptual Framework

The authors test the hypothesis whether there is a significant productivity difference between specific year bankruptcy cohorts and the group of solvent firms. However, the statistical tests to verify this hypothesis are not very conclusive. First, the statistical tests do not include firms that utilized

Epictetus E. Patalinghug is professor of economics and management in the College of Business Administration, University of the Philippines.

the workout procedure. Second, even among firms undergoing corporate reorganization or composition, there is no clear pattern for the pre–exit year productivity of failing firms when profitability is used as the dependent variable (table 9.4). And third, the inconclusive result in table 9.4 is casually dismissed as probably being due to some explicit or hidden subsidies given to failing firms at the pre-exit years. Nevertheless, nowhere in this paper is there a discussion or documentation (based on past studies) of the magnitude of subsidies given to failing firms.

Effect of Entry and Exit on Productivity

In section 9.3 of the paper, the authors tackle the role of the process of entry and exit on aggregate productivity growth by examining whether plant deaths reflect temporary bad luck or persistently bad productivity performance in the past. The finding of the paper is that plant deaths reflect persistently bad productivity performance. It concludes that policies that hinder the process of entry and exit could be potentially very costly.

The pace of firm learning may be related to the nature of the Korean national innovation system. The link between learning and innovation (Lundvall 1992) may provide an explanation on the pattern of plant entry and exit in Korea.

In using the chained multilateral index in estimating plant-level TFP, the paper could have decomposed TFP into two components: (1) between-plant variations, and (2) within-plant variations. Aw, Chen, and Roberts (2001) not only decomposed firm-level productivity growth into several components (continuing firms, entering firms, exiting firms, and market share contribution) but went further and documented the cross-sectional differences in TFP between exporting and nonexporting firms. The paper could have broadened its perspective of the dynamics of Korean plants by documenting the productivity differentials between domestic-oriented plants and export-oriented plants.

Conclusion

This paper is very good at describing the bankruptcy policy reform experience of South Korea. The significant difference in the types of settlement (e.g., corporate reorganization, composition program, or workout program) availed by top *chaebols* compared to small *chaebols* is revealing. The relevance of the paper to other crisis-hit developing economies (e.g., Indonesia, Malaysia, Thailand, and the Philippines) is its description of a structured bargaining game among interested parties. For instance, the Korean courts mainly oversee the process according to predetermined rules. And court-administered procedure is biased against the controlling shareholders of ailing firms. In contrast, the courts in other countries (e.g., the Philippines and Indonesia) need some tutoring on how to implement the new provisions of their bankruptcy laws. Unlike the case of South Korea, bankruptcy laws in other crisis-hit countries are still biased in favor of the controlling shareholders of ailing firms. Finally, the paper likewise reveals that the workout (or out-of-court) procedure was the main form of settlement for large-sized *chaebols* in 1998 and 1999. This experience is also popularly used by ailing corporate groups in other crisis-hit countries because it conveniently allows the introduction of noneconomic (e.g., political) factors. The paper therefore is important in explaining how the design of the bankruptcy mechanisms in the Korean experience veers away from a tendency to rehabilitate ailing firms that do not have the potential for recovery. The paper is a very good addition to the literature on bankruptcy policy reforms in crisis-hit economies.

References

Aw, Bee Yan, Xiaomin Chen, and Mark J. Roberts. 2001. Firm level evidence on productivity differentials, turnover, and exports in Taiwanese manufacturing. *Journal of Development Economics* 66 (1): 51–86.

Lundvall, Bengkt-Ake. 1992. *National systems of innovation.* London: Pinter Publishers.

10 Information Technology and Firm Performance in Korea

Jong-Il Kim

10.1 Introduction

Information technology (IT) has made a considerable contribution to the recent economic growth of Korea. Semiconductor, personal computer, and telecommunication equipments ranked first, third, and sixth in export in 2000, respectively (Annual Statistical Report of Korea). A recent Organization for Economic Cooperation and Development (OECD) report reveals that the productivity growth in Korea could be to the large extent attributable to the strength in IT manufacturing (Pilat and Lee 2001). Along with expansion of IT-manufacturing sectors in Korea, Korean firms have become more IT equipped, particularly after the economic crisis in 1997. This study tries to examine the effect of IT use on Korean firm performance in the late 1990s.[1]

The existing studies for Korean firms are not numerous due to the lack of data (Shin, Kim, and Song 1998; Kang and Song 1999; Lee 2000).[2] This study is similar to the existing studies in that it tries to find some evidence on the relationship between IT and firm performance. However, this study

Jong-Il Kim is associate professor of economics at Dongguk University.

The author thanks National Information and Credit Evaluation for providing data.

1. Information technology could be too broad to be defined in a single word. In this study, we define IT narrowly as technology related to office, accounting, and computing equipment, which affects the operation of firms most.

2. The only available source of data on firm-level IT spending is a survey done by Korea Information Society Development Institute (KISDI). It covers firms listed in the Korea Stock Exchange and provides data on IT labor and capital in 1996. Information technology capital reported in the survey includes hardware (personal computers, mainframe computers, and peripheries), software, and networking facilities (routers, server, cables, transmission equipment, and switching system). The IT labor is reported as number of IT staff and IT labor expense.

Table 10.1 Recent Trend of Information Technology Indexes in Korea

	1997	2001
Internet backbone networks	80	144
Subscribers to broadband Internet services (thousands)	14	7,810
Internet users (thousands)	1,630	24,380
Personal computers (thousands)	6,930	20,700
Telephone lines (thousands)	20,430	22,680
Mobile phones (thousands)	6,910	29,050
IT production (trillions of Korean Won)	75.5	150.3
IT value added (trillions of Korean Won)	39.1	70.2
GDP share (%)	8.6	12.9
IT export (US$ billions)	31.3	38.4
Workers in IT sector (thousands)	560	660
IT companies	9,397	17,719
IT venture companies	636	5,073

Source: Korea Ministry of Information and Communication.

Note: Broadband Internet services are XDSL, cable modem, LAN, B-WILL, and satellite Internet services. The Internet user is defined as an individual of age seven or older who regularly uses the Internet more than once a month. Workers represent waged employees.

approaches the issue to the furthest extent we can utilize the limited data. Whereas most studies analyze the period before 1997 economic crisis, this study pays attention to 1997–2000.

Table 10.1 shows how fast Korea rushed toward the information age between 1997 and 2001. The number of personal computers increased three times, and internet users rose by a factor of more than ten. Korea exceeded most developed countries in the diffusion of broadband Internet services in 2001: IT production increased about twice, pushing the IT share of the gross domestic product (GDP) to 12.9 percent. The venture company boom established many new successful IT venture companies registered in the KOSDAQ stock market.

In 1997–2000, most Korean firms introduced unprecedented reform under the pressure of economic crisis. Many workers were laid off, and many operations done internally were outsourced. Total investment declined with the severe recession after the crisis, but IT investment accelerated instead (figure 10.1). It is well known that IT reduces coordination and transaction costs and thus helps companies to adopt flexible coordination systems. The coincidence of structural reform and massive IT investment implies that IT investment could have worked as a complementary factor to the reorganization of Korean firms, a hypothesis this study explores.

Section 10.2 provides some empirical findings on the role of IT investment in firm productivity growth. First, a simple production function is estimated to compare marginal product of IT and ordinary inputs. Next, we

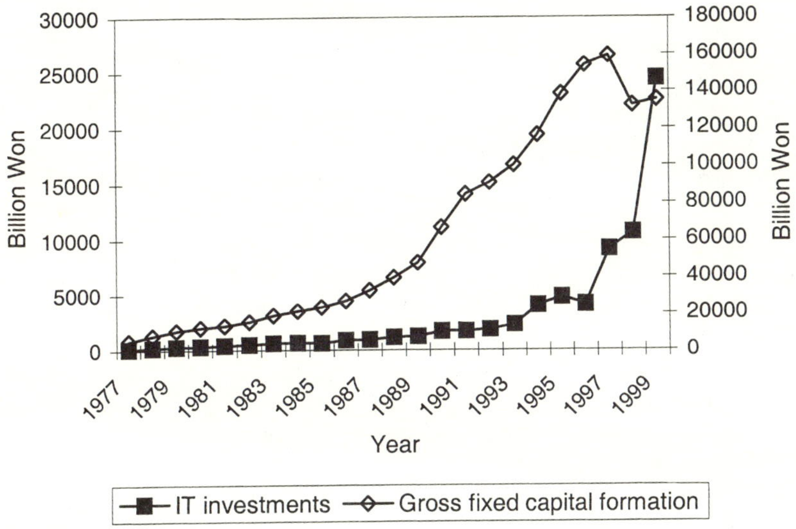

Fig. 10.1 Trends of Information Technology investment and total investment in Korea

Note: The data for the United States are obtained from the U.S. Bureau of Economic Analysis, where the IT capital is defined as computers and peripheral equipment, and office, accounting, and computing machinery. For Korea, IT investment is the 70 percent of the absorption of office, accounting, and computing machinery calculated based on the OECD STAN database. Seventy percent of absorption is assumed to be the share of investment based on the input-output table; IT investment is in constant prices.

examine the effect of IT spending on firm profitability and total factor productivity. Finally, the valuation of IT capital in the financial market is estimated. Based on the firm-level findings, section 10.3 exercises a simple experimental growth accounting to see how much contribution IT investment might have made to the recent economic growth of Korea.

10.2 Information Technology Investment and Firm Performance

10.2.1 Marginal Product of Information Technology Investment

To start with, we estimate a simple Cobb-Douglas production function to calculate the marginal product of IT investment, as much of the work in this area has done (Berndt and Morrison 1995; Brynjolfsson and Hitt 1995; Lichtenberg 1995). The production function is specified as

$$Y_i = A_i C_i^{\alpha} K_i^{\beta} L_i^{\gamma}, \tag{1}$$

where Y_i, C_i, K_i, and L_i are defined as output, IT stock, non-IT fixed capital stock, and non-IT labor of firm i, respectively. A_i, an efficiency level of firm i, cannot be specified separately for each firm due to degree of freedom since we are using only one-year cross-sectional data.[3] Instead, industry dummy variables are included in the regression to distinguish the sectoral differences.[4]

Output is defined as value added obtained from the financial statements provided by the National Information and Credit Evaluation. Non-IT fixed capital stock is obtained from the same source by subtracting IT capital stock from the fixed assets. Non-IT labor input is defined as total labor expense net of IT labor expense. Following Brynjolfsson and Hitt (1995), IT stock is defined so that it includes spending on both IT capital and labor.[5] Information technology capital is a stock variable, while IT labor expense is a flow variable. To combine the two into a single stock variable, it is assumed IT labor expense stayed at the current level for the last several years and IT labor stock depreciates fully in three years. From this, we construct the IT stock that equals the sum of IT capital stock and three times the IT labor expense.

The production function in equation (1) is estimated by the ordinary least squares method in logarithmic form. Thus the estimated coefficient reported in table 10.2 is the output elasticity. All coefficients in the regression are statistically significant at the 5 percent level, and the output elasticity of labor is 0.87—somewhat higher than 0.6–0.7, the level usually taken in the analysis.[6] Based on the estimates the marginal product of each input can be calculated. For example, the marginal product of IT stock ($\partial Y/\partial C$) is $\alpha(Y/C)$. Since the ratios of input to output are different across firms, we utilize an arithmetic mean to compute the marginal product. On the average, our sample firms operate with IT stock, non-IT capital, and labor as much as 10,197, and 52 percent of value added, respectively. The marginal product of IT stock is estimated to be 0.42, eight times higher than non-IT capital stock.

3. Since the data on IT spending are available only for 1996, a production function can be estimated by using cross-sectional data from 1996.

4. Industries are classified as fishery, mining, food and beverages, textiles, clothing, leather, wood and products, paper, printing, chemicals, petroleum, rubber and plastic products, nonmetal, basic metal, metal products, industrial machinery, office and accounting machinery, electronic goods, electrical goods, transport equipment, shipbuilding, precision and optical instruments, utilities, construction, transportation, wholesale and retail, hotels, and finance. More than 80 percent of firms in the sample belong to manufacturing. Since the financial statements do not report value added for firms in the financial sector, firms in the financial sector are not included in the analysis except for the profitability and market value analysis to be done later in this section.

5. The survey data from KISDI provide firms' IT capital stock in 1996, which includes IT assets with more than one year's durability, such as hardware, peripherals, software, and networking facilities. Therefore, the data on IT capital stock from the survey are actually IT fixed assets plus software. Since the amount of software stock is not reported separately, we use this variable as IT capital stock.

6. Since a firm's decision on whether to spend on IT may depend on its productivity, there may be a selection and a simultaneity problem. Thus, our coefficient estimates could have a negative bias on capital and a positive bias on labor. See Olley and Pakes (1996).

Table 10.2 Production Function Estimates

Variable	Parameter Estimates	
Constant	0.3617	
	(0.8661)	
IT stock (α)	0.0434**	
	(2.2410)	
Physical capital (β)	0.1057***	
	(3.6153)	
Labor expense (γ)	0.8736***	
	(21.9116)	
No. of observations	225	
R^2	0.9269	
	Ratio to Value Added	Marginal Product
IT stock	0.1024	0.4238
Physical capital	1.9727	0.0536
Labor expense	0.5209	0.4550

Note: The figures in parentheses are *t*-statistics.
***Significant at the 1 percent level.
**Significant at the 5 percent level.

Since the estimated marginal product is gross of depreciation, taxes, and other costs, we should subtract user costs (= interest rate + depreciation rate – the rate of expected capital gains) to compute the net returns. To get a rough estimate of net returns, we assume depreciation rates of IT stock and non-IT capital stock to be 0.2 and 0.05, respectively, and expected capital gains on IT stock and non-IT capital stock to be –0.15 and 0.05, respectively, following the approximation of previous studies (Lau and Tokutsu 1992; Lichtenberg 1995). Finally, we assume the interest rate in Korea to be 0.15. The net returns to IT investment are –0.08 (= 0.42 – [0.15 + 0.2 + 0.15]), and those to non-IT investment are –0.10 (= 0.05 – [0.15 + 0.05 – 0.05]). The net returns are not as different as gross returns due to the higher depreciation rate and declining price of IT stock. The result contrasts with that of Lichtenberg (1995), who reported that the net returns to IT investment in the United States are significantly positive.

10.2.2 Effects of Information Technology Investment on Profitability

Next, we examine whether IT stock improves a firm's profitability. The profitability is measured as the ratio of operating profits to total assets, and the index of IT investment is defined as IT stock per worker.[7] To control for firm-specific characteristics, we include capital intensity (per-worker total

7. Good performance in current profit or total profit may be a result of latent capital gains of assets that the firm holds. Thus it may be better to use operating profits than current or total profits.

Table 10.3 **The Effect of Information Technology Stock on Operating Profits**

Year	IT Stock	Capital Intensity	Sales Growth	Debt Ratio
1996	–0.0004	–0.0001***	0.0097**	0.0499
	(–1.7225)	(–3.2678)	(1.8407)	(0.2721)
1997	0.0000	–0.0001***	0.0406***	0.3136
	(0.0649)	(–2.7411)	(4.0173)	(1.4669)
1998	–0.0001	–0.0000	0.1604***	0.1877
	(–0.1607)	(–0.3860)	(6.5629)	(0.3022)
1999	0.0019***	–0.0000	0.0592***	–0.6575
	(3.3034)	(–1.2232)	(3.7472)	(–1.6378)
2000	0.0011	–0.0000	0.0745***	0.1066
	(1.4146)	(–0.2870)	(3.9818)	(0.1665)

Notes: The independent variable is operating profit of each year. Each regression includes constant and industry dummy variables. The figures in parentheses are *t*-statistics.

***Significant at the 1 percent level.

**Significant at the 5 percent level.

fixed assets), sales growth, the debt ratio (total debt over equity capital), and industry dummies.[8] Since profits could be influenced by short-term business fluctuation and idiosyncratic factors, we exercise the analysis for each year from 1996 to 2000.

Table 10.3 shows the empirical result. As expected, sales growth has a significant positive impact on a firm's profitability. The estimated coefficients of IT stock per worker are not significant except for 1999, and the signs of the estimates do not show any regularity. Considering the low estimates of the net returns to IT investment, it is not surprising that the IT investment does not have any significant effect on profits. Capital intensity also has a significantly negative effect in 1996 and 1997, which seems to be consistent with negative net returns to capital investment.

10.2.3 Effects of Information Technology Investment on Productivity

Next we analyze the relationship between IT investment and the productivity of firms. After taking logarithms of equation (1) and differentiating with respect to time, we get

$$y_i = a_i + \alpha c_i + \beta k_i + \gamma l_i, \tag{2}$$

where y_i, c_i, k_i, and l_i are growth rates of output, IT stock, non-IT capital stock, and non-IT labor of firm *i*, respectively. Therefore,

$$y_i - \beta k_i - \gamma l_i = a_i + \alpha c_i. \tag{3}$$

8. Analyzing a firm's profitability with the regression method is problematic due to specification problems since it does not have any structural form and is affected by many omitted factors. We choose the controls following Strassman (1990).

Table 10.4 **The Effect of IT Stock on the Growth of Firm TFP, Output, Employment, and Capital**

Period	TFP Growth	*Y* Growth	*L* Growth	*K* Growth
1996–97	0.0135**	0.0119**	–0.0039**	0.0007
	(2.3844)	(2.0440)	(–2.0357)	(0.2984)
1996–98	0.0085**	0.0067	–0.0024	–0.0014
	(3.4566)	(1.8912)	(–1.6420)	(–0.6987)
1996–99	0.0033	0.0069**	–0.0012	–0.0018
	(1.7572)	(2.8129)	(–1.0294)	(–1.1258)
1996–2000	0.0018	0.0016	–0.0008	–0.0018
	(1.3994)	(0.8604)	(–0.7326)	(–1.3698)

Notes: Each regression includes constant, industry, and R&D dummy variables. The figures in parentheses are *t*-statistics.

**Significant at the 5 percent level.

The left-hand side of equation (3) is the growth rate of total factor productivity (TFP). It depends on growth in IT stock (c_i) as well as undetected firm-specific factors (a_i). Thus, the faster IT stock accumulates, the faster TFP grows. Since we don't have time series of IT stock, we regress the conventional estimate of TFP growth on the level of IT stock defined as per-worker IT stock.[9]

To compute TFP growth, output and capital input are defined as value added and fixed assets, respectively.[10] Labor input is defined as the number of employees. The labor income share is computed as an arithmetic mean of labor expense divided by value added of firms in an industry a firm belongs to. Capital income share is one minus labor income share. Since TFP growth of a firm fluctuates along with the firm-specific business cycle in the short run, we use one-year to four-year TFP growth as dependent variables. In the regression, we include industry and research and development (R&D) dummy variables to control for the firm specific factors.[11]

Table 10.4 presents the relationship between IT stock and TFP growth. Although we cannot get statistically significant estimates for all the coefficients, figures in table 10.4 show a tendency that IT stock pays off with increase in TFP growth by augmenting the value added and saving ordinary labor and capital.[12] It is consistent with the fact that IT investment stimu-

9. Under the constant returns to scale, we get $(y_i - l_i) - \beta(k_i - l_i) = a_i + \alpha(c_i - l_i)$ from equation (3). Therefore, the TFP growth of a firm depends on per-worker IT stock.

10. Value added and fixed assets are deflated by the deflators for GDP and gross fixed capital formation obtained from National Accounts, respectively.

11. Since many firms do not have R&D expenditure, R&D effort is specified as a dummy variable that distinguishes firms with and without R&D expenditure.

12. Dewan and Min (1997) estimated a CES-translog production function to find that the IT capital was a net substitute for both ordinary capital and labor in the United States for 1988–92.

Table 10.5 **Employment and Wage Share by Worker Type in Korea (%)**

	Nonproduction Worker		Highly Skilled Nonproduction Worker		Low-Skill Nonproduction Worker	
Year	Employment	Wage	Employment	Wage	Employment	Wage
1981	35.9	51.4	9.6	21.2	26.3	30.2
1986	40.7	55	13.6	26.1	27.1	28.9
1991	49.1	57.6	13.5	22.4	35.6	35.2
1993	48.8	56.5	20.1	29.3	28.7	27.2
1996	52.3	59.9	23	32.1	29.3	27.8
1998	56.2	64.5	27.7	38.3	28.5	26.2

Source: Kim (2001).

Notes: Highly skilled nonproduction workers are managers, specialists, and engineers. Low-skilled nonproduction workers include office attendants, clerks, retail salespersons, and the like. See detailed classification in Kim (2001). The raw data are obtained from the Report on Occupational Wage Survey of the Korea Ministry of Labor.

Table 10.6 **Effect of Information Technology Investment on Up-Skilling of Labor**

Period	Employment	Wage
1981–98	2.00**	2.40**
	(3.29)	(3.32)
1981–91	0.14	0.44
	(0.82)	(1.60)
1991–98	1.86**	1.96**
	(3.06)	(2.77)

Notes: The estimates are from Kim (2001). The dependent variable is the rate of change in the proportion of sectoral highly skilled nonproduction workers. The explanatory variable is the average of 1990 and 1995 share of office, accounting, and computing machinery in total sectoral investment obtained from the input-output table. The figures in parentheses are *t*-statistics.

**Significant at the 5 percent level.

lates the up-skilling of labor and thus increases value added per unit of input in operation. Table 10.5 shows the trend of labor up-skilling in Korea. The proportion of nonproduction workers increased in terms of employment and wage in the last two decades. Among nonproduction workers, the proportion of highly skilled workers increased continuously over the period. It increased sharply from 1996 to 1998 in employment and wage. In contrast, the share of low-skilled nonproduction workers leveled off in the 1990s and declined in 1998. Recent structural reform seems to have replaced low-skilled workers with highly skilled workers. The estimated coefficients in table 10.6 show that the sectoral difference in the speed of substitution of highly skilled for low-skilled workers significantly depends on IT investment. The impact of IT investment seems to be much higher in the 1990s than in the 1980s.

This empirical result of productivity growth without profit from IT investment does not contradict economic theory. Although IT has increased productivity and created substantial value for consumers, these benefits might have not resulted in higher profitability. That is, through IT investment, firms did not gain competitive advantage but maintained competitive parity and benefits of IT investment flew into consumer surplus.[13] However, IT has radically changed the way products and services are produced, and it has accelerated the substitution of the low value–adding ordinary inputs for high value–adding IT-intensive ones. It is consistent with the finding that the estimate of gross returns to IT investment is quite high but that of net returns is actually negative. Since most firms in Korea underwent unprecedented structural reform in the late 1990s, the impact of IT could have been much more substantial.

10.2.4 Market Valuation of Information Technology Capital

The empirical findings so far imply that IT investment has higher marginal product than ordinary capital and leads to higher TFP growth. However, the increase in IT investment alone cannot incur expected gains unconditionally. Firms usually pour their valuable resources into worker reeducation and retraining, adjustment in operational routine, and rearrangement of existing facilities to exploit the new technology. The difference of IT stock among firms in a similar industry may be due to the difference in potential capability of firms to adjust themselves to IT.[14] It means that installing IT capital is not free and requires adjustment costs. However, the financial statements disregard the valuable intangible assets created through IT investment. For example, the accounting system does not consider expenditures on worker training, software, R&D, and advertisement for brand building as an investment, although they raise the potential value of a firm. Instead, they are treated as expenses. If we take the creation of intangible assets into consideration, the value of installed IT capital should exceed the acquisition price. Therefore, the installed IT capital should be valued in the stock market higher than the book value.

According to the neoclassical model, a firm maximizes the present value of profit flows, which is equal to market value of firm $V(0)$.

$$V(0) = \int_0^{\infty} u(t)\pi(t)dt, \tag{4}$$

13. See Hitt and Brynjolfsson (1996).

14. Brynjolfsson and Hitt (1996) found that the estimate of marginal products of IT capital is sensitive to how they estimate the production function. When they introduced firm-specific fixed effects in the model, the marginal product of IT capital decreased by half from the estimate without fixed effects. They concluded that half of IT's effect on firm performance may come from the firm's intrinsic capability.

where $u(t)$ is a discount factor and $\pi(t)$ is profit at time t. The profit at time t is firm's revenue minus total cost. That is,

$$\pi(t) = pF(K_1, \ldots, K_J, I_1, \ldots, I_J, L) - wL - z_1 I_1 - \ldots - z_J I_J,$$

where J types of capital stock (K) and labor (L) are combined to produce output with price p. Here, we introduce the adjustment cost of investment by specifying a production function as $F(K_1, \ldots, K_J, I_1, \ldots, I_J, L)$ (Lucas 1967). The function F, homogenous of degree one, is nondecreasing and concave in K and L, and nonincreasing and convex in I. z_j is the acquisition price of capital j, and w is wage rate. Capital stock accumulates over time through investment (I_j) net of depreciation ($\delta_j K_j$).

$$\frac{dK_j}{dt} = I_j - \delta_i K_j, \text{ for all } j = 1, 2, \ldots, J.$$

Then the Hamiltonian is set up as

$$\begin{aligned} H(K_1, \ldots, K_J, I_1, \ldots, I_J, L, t) \\ &= (pF(K_1, \ldots, K_J, I_1, \ldots, I_J, L) - wL - z_1 I_1 - \ldots - z_J I_J)u(t) \\ &+ \sum_{i=1}^{J} \lambda_i (I_i - \delta_i K_i). \end{aligned}$$

Here the Lagrangian multiplier λ_j represents the shadow value of one unit of installed capital j. Using the first-order conditions and assumptions made, the stock market value of a firm is the sum of the shadow value of various types of installed capital goods.[15] That is,

$$V(0) = \sum_{j=1}^{J} \lambda_j(0) K_j(0).$$

Here λ_j is a shadow value of capital j. If there is no adjustment cost, λ_j should be equal to unity. Thus, $(\lambda_j - 1)K_j$ is the size of adjustment costs originating from the capital investment. For the analysis, we classify a firm's asset into three types: IT fixed asset, non-IT fixed asset, and other assets. The market value of a firm is the sum of equity and debt. The equity value of a firm is calculated by multiplying the average stock price and total issue of equities in December 1996.[16] The data on IT fixed assets are taken from the Korea Information Society Development Institute (KISDI) survey (1997). Non-IT fixed asset is computed as total fixed asset net of IT fixed asset. Other assets are calculated by subtracting total fixed assets from total assets.

Table 10.7 shows the estimates of market valuation of three types of capital assets. The estimated market value of IT capital is about 6.8 in 1996, which is much higher than 1, while those of other ordinary capital assets

15. For the derivation of the market value of a firm, see the appendix.
16. December is when firms report their annual financial statements.

Table 10.7 The Market Valuation of Various Assets in 1996

Asset Type	Parameter Estimates
IT fixed capital assets	6.7617
	(6.6359)
Non-IT fixed capital assets	0.8789
	(46.1147)
Other capital assets	0.8844
	(180.0090)

Notes: Regression includes constant, industry, and R&D dummies, and advertisement as controls. The figures in parentheses are *t*-statistics.

are below 1. It means one won of IT capital asset is valued at about 6.8 won in the stock market. If the stock market is efficient, IT capital worth one won when purchased increases a firm's value about 6.8 won once installed.

The market value of IT capital goods estimated in this study for Korean firms is somewhat lower than that for the U.S. firms estimated by Brynjolfsson and Yang (1997). They found that the market value for each dollar of installed IT capital goods is on the order of ten times greater than that for each dollar of ordinary capital goods. It is noteworthy the United States has the higher estimated shadow value of IT capital stocks in spite of a longer history of IT investment. If the higher market valuation of IT capital comes only from the short-term rent during the time gap between the identification of opportunity and actual realization of investment, the estimates for Korean firms should be greater than those for the U.S. firms. The fact that we have the estimates the other way round indicates that IT investment accompanies a series of complementary investments. Higher valuation of IT capital goods in the United States implies that U.S. firms with a longer history of IT investment have better organization and more intangible assets adjusted to the IT environment.

10.3 Implications for Aggregate Economic Growth

In this section, we extend the results from the previous section to country-level productivity growth.[17] For our purpose, we utilize growth-accounting analysis, but the analysis is different from the conventional methodology. A production function is defined as in section 10.2,

$$Y = pF(K_1, K_2, I_1, I_2, L, t), \tag{5}$$

where K_1, I_1, K_2, and I_2 are IT capital stock, IT investment, non-IT capital stock, and non-IT capital investment, respectively. Here we introduce time

17. The exercise in this section is experimental since our methodology and treatment of data are too crude and simple to be considered as precise estimation.

(t) as a factor for technical progress. From the assumption that the production function is linearly homogeneous and firms maximize profits under competitive market, we get

$$pF(K_1, K_2, I_1, I_2, L, t) = pF_{K1}K_2 + pF_{k2}K_2 + pF_{I1}I_1 + pF_{I2}I_2 + pF_L L$$
$$= r_1K_2 + r_2K_2 + (z_1 - \lambda_1)I_1 + (z_2 - \lambda_2)I_2 + wL.^{18}$$

Based on the empirical findings from the previous section, we assume that the shadow value of non-IT capital stock is not different from the replacement cost ($z_2 = \lambda_2$). Then,

$$Y = r_1K_2 + r_2K_2 + (z_1 - \lambda_1)I_1 + wL.$$

Therefore,

$$Y + (\lambda_1 - z_1)I_1 = r_1K_2 + r_2K_2 + wL.$$

The term $(\lambda_1 - z_1)I_1$ is due to the discrepancy between the shadow value and acquisition price of IT investment. It originates from the intangible assets created with IT investment. The costs of creating intangible assets such as software, worker retraining, and organizational reform to exploit the IT should be, in a true sense, counted as investment. However, in the balance sheet, they belong to expenses and are not included as investment in National Accounts. Thus, the true GDP of a country should be revised as GDP (Y) plus unmeasured investment in intangible assets: $(\lambda_1 - z_1)I_1$.

Differentiating equation (5) with respect to time and dividing by Y, we get

$$\text{(6)} \qquad \frac{\dot{Y}}{Y} + (\lambda_1 - z_1)\frac{\dot{I}_1}{Y} = \frac{r_1K_1}{Y}\frac{\dot{K}_1}{K_1} + \frac{r_2K_2}{Y}\frac{\dot{K}_2}{K_2} + \frac{wL}{Y}\frac{\dot{L}}{L} + \frac{\dot{A}}{A},$$

where $\dot{A}/A = pF_t/Y = F_t/F$.[19] The left-hand side of the equation is GDP growth plus unmeasured creation of intangible assets.

Under the assumption of constant returns to scale, conventional TFP growth is calculated as

$$\text{(7)} \qquad \frac{\dot{A}}{A} = \frac{\dot{Y}}{Y} - \alpha_1\frac{\dot{K}_1}{K_1} - \alpha_2\frac{\dot{K}_2}{K_2} - (1 - \alpha_1 - \alpha_2)\frac{\dot{L}}{\mathrm{L}}.$$

This conventional growth accounting excludes the unmeasured investment of creating intangibles by imposing λ_1 equal to z_1. If we take into account unmeasured investment accompanying IT investment, TFP growth could be revised as

$$\text{(8)} \qquad \frac{\dot{A}}{A} + (\lambda_1 - z_1)\frac{\dot{I}_1}{Y} = \frac{\dot{A}}{A} + \left(\frac{\lambda_1}{z_1} - 1\right)\frac{\dot{I}_1}{I_1}\left(\frac{z_1I_1}{Y}\right).$$

Therefore, the faster IT investment accelerates and the greater the share of IT investment is in total expenditure (GDP), the greater revised TFP

18. It is from the first-order conditions in the appendix.
19. The price level, P and z_j, are fixed, and thus the variables are real in constant prices.

growth exceeds conventional one. Considering that IT investment accelerated in 1996–2000, there would have been substantial IT-induced TFP growth disregarded in the conventional growth accounting.

To apply the foregoing idea to Korean economic growth, output defined as real GDP is obtained from National Accounts. Labor is defined as total employment obtained from the statistical yearbook. For our purpose, we define IT capital goods narrowly as office, accounting, and computing machinery. National Accounts do not provide data on IT capital investment. Therefore, we estimate the IT capital investment from absorption of IT capital goods.[20] The absorption of IT capital goods is calculated by subtracting net export of office, accounting, and computing machinery obtained from the OECD structural analysis (STAN) database from gross output. Since the absorption includes consumption as well as investment, we utilize the data from gross fixed capital formation of the input-output table. The input-output table has the data on gross fixed capital formation by detailed types of capital goods and classifies computers and office machinery as separate items. Thus we compare the computed level of absorption and the amount of IT goods investment in 1990 and 1995 from the input-output table. It is found that the ratios of investment to absorption in both years are approximately 0.7. Thus, we assume 70 percent absorption of IT capital goods is spent for investment. Since the absorption is in current prices, we deflate the data by using the producer price index of office machinery. Next, non-IT fixed capital formation is obtained by subtracting IT investment from total gross fixed capital formation. Both IT and non-IT capital stock are constructed by the perpetual inventory method.[21]

Finally, we need the factor income share for each input. We start by assuming the labor income share to be 0.6, the share usually taken by many studies in economic growth. Since we distinguish IT and non-IT capital stock, we need to allocate the capital income share, 0.4, into the share of each type of capital. From the assumption that the rate of returns is equal to user cost, we get

$$(9) \quad \alpha_1 + \alpha_2 = \frac{r_1 K_1}{Y} + \frac{r_2 K_2}{Y} = \frac{(i + \delta_1 - \pi_1)K_1}{Y} + \frac{(i + \delta_2 - \pi_2)K_2}{Y} = 0.4.$$

As in the previous section, we assume δ_1, δ_2, π_1, and π_2 to be 0.2, 0.05, –0.15, and 0.05, respectively. The only unknown variable, interest rate (i), can be computed from equation (9). After solving equation (9) for interest

20. Shin, Kim, and Chung (1998) constructed IT capital stock. For our purpose, this data set is not useful. First, it includes too broad a range of items, such as electric cable, transformers, and telephones, that cannot be included in true IT investment affecting firm performance. Second, it provides data only until 1995.

21. As in section 10.2, we assume the service life of IT capital goods is five years and that of non-IT capital goods is twenty years. That is, the depreciation rates of IT and non-IT capital goods are assumed to be 0.2 and 0.05, respectively. Benchmark capital does not affect data for 1980–2000 much since we accumulate the investment from the mid-1960s.

rate, we can easily compute the income shares of IT and non-IT capital, which turn out to be 0.0108 and 0.3892, respectively.

Table 10.8 presents the result of growth accounting of Korean economic growth since 1980. The average GDP growth rates in the first row show that the Korean economy continued rapid growth until the recent crisis at over 7 percent per annum. Economic growth in 1996–2000 declined due to severe recession in 1998. The next four rows decompose the output growth by showing the growth rate attributable to each factor of growth. In the 1980s, the economic growth was attributable in the largest share to TFP growth followed by non-IT capital accumulation. In the 1990s, the contribution of non-IT capital accumulation was highest. In contrast, the contribution of IT capital stock to economic growth is not as high, since the factor share of IT capital stock is small in spite of the rapid growth of IT capital stock. It is noticeable that the accelerated IT capital accumulation in the late 1990s contributed as much as 8 percent of 1996–2000 growth, higher than in previous periods.

Now, we use equations (6) and (8) to compute the hypothetical GDP growth that includes the disregarded unmeasurable investment coming with IT investment. The empirical findings of table 10.7 show that the stock market value of IT fixed capital is about 6.8 times acquisition price in 1996. As an experimental attempt, we impose λ_1/z_1 equal to 6 for 1980–2000.[22] The hypothetical GDP growth is slightly higher than conventional measure until 1995. However, with rapid growth of IT investment, the hypothetical output growth is ostensibly higher during the period 1996–2000. If we regard the output growth due to unmeasured factors as TFP growth, the TFP growth in 1996–2000 based on hypothetical GDP is as high as 9 percent per annum.

Since the additional contribution of TFP growth in the above is attributable to IT investment, the overall contribution of IT investment is the sum of this and the contribution of physical IT capital accumulation. The overall contribution of IT investment was 8 percent of output growth in the early 1980s. It increased to more than 20 percent in the early 1990s. In the late 1990s, it contributed as much as 66 percent of economic growth. Our simple experiment indicates that the contribution of IT investment could have been quite substantial, particularly in the late 1990s.

10.4 Concluding Remarks

This study examined the effect of IT investment on Korean firm performance in 1996–2000. The overall empirical findings support the hypothe-

22. Following computation systematically depends on how we put λ_1/z_1. Since our sample firms are relatively big firms listed in the Korean Stock Exchange, the estimated shadow value of 6.76 may overestimate the unmeasureable investment.

Table 10.8 **The Role of Information Technology Investment in Korean Economic Growth**

	1981–85		1986–90		1991–95		1996–2000	
	Average Annual Growth Rate	Contribution (%)	Average Annual Growth Rate	Contribution (%)	Average Annual Growth Rate	Contribution (%)	Average Annual Growth Rate	Contribution (%)
Conventional GDP	7.525	100	9.056	100	7.188	100	4.751	100
IT fixed capital	0.216	3	0.163	2	0.211	3	0.394	8
Non-IT capital	2.313	31	3.104	34	4.019	56	2.599	55
Employment	1.079	14	2.268	25	1.455	20	0.373	8
Conventional TFP	3.917	52	3.520	39	1.503	21	1.385	29
Revised GDP	7.968	100	10.365	100	8.701	100	12.760	100
Revised TFP	4.360	55	4.829	47	3.016	35	9.394	74
IT contribution	0.659	8	1.472	14	1.724	20	8.404	66

Notes: The growth rate of revised GDP is constructed by assuming the shadow value of IT investment is six times greater than acquisition price. The growth rate of revised TFP is the growth rates of conventional TFP plus the growth rates of revised GDP minus the growth rates of conventional GDP. The IT contribution is contribution of IT fixed capital accumulation plus contribution of revised GDP minus contribution of conventional GDP.

sis that IT investment enhances productivity by increasing value added and saving ordinary capital and labor. Installed IT capital is estimated to be valued in the financial market at about 6.8 times acquisition price. It implies that IT investment accompanies the creation of intangible assets. Taking this into account, the contribution of IT investment to aggregate economic growth would be much greater than the figures provided by the conventional growth accounting.

Although this study found some evidence supporting the positive role of IT investment in enhancing firm productivity, it needs further investigation. First, some studies found that the utilization of IT in a firm is closely related with firm-specific assets such as management ability. Since the data on IT investment are available only for 1996, cross-sectional analysis done in this study could not clarify enough the relationship between IT intensity and firm-specific factors. The panel data approach would bring about fruitful results on this issue. Second, the data include firms listed in the Korea Stock Exchange only. Therefore, our sample does not cover enough firms in Korea. This may lead to biases in the results. In addition, to appreciate fully the technological differences among industries, further detailed industry classification would be needed. Finally, finding the case stories on how the adoption of IT helped the reform of Korean firms would be needed to substantiate the empirical evidence this study found.

Appendix

Market Valuation of a Firm

Many studies trying to measure intangible assets have used the stock market valuation. For example, Griliches (1981) and Hall (1999) used this approach to measure the intangible assets created from R&D expenditure. Brynjolfsson and Yang (2000) adopted this approach to the analysis of market valuation of IT capital goods.

The first-order conditions for the optimization problem in section 10.2 are as follows.

$$\frac{\partial H}{\partial \lambda_j} = \dot{K}_j = I_j - \delta_j K_j, \quad \forall j \text{ and } \forall t \qquad \frac{\partial H}{\partial K_j} = -\dot{\lambda}_j = pF_{Kj}u(t) - \lambda_j\delta_j, \quad \forall j \text{ and } \forall t$$

$$\frac{\partial H}{\partial I_j} = 0 = (pF_{Ij} - z_j)u(t) + \lambda_j, \quad \forall j \text{ and } \forall t$$

$$\frac{\partial H}{\partial L} = 0 = (pF_L - w)u(t), \quad \forall t,$$

with transversality condition $\lim_{t\to 8}\lambda(t)K(t) = 0$. Here, F_k is the partial derivative with respect to factor k. By using the first-order conditions, transversality condition, and the assumption that the production function F is homogeneous of degree one, we get

$$\begin{aligned}
\sum_{j=1}^{J} \lambda_j(0)K_j(0) &= \sum_{j=1}^{J} [\lambda_j(0)K_j(0) - \lambda_j(\infty)K_j(\infty)] \\
&= \sum_{j=1}^{J} \int_0^{\infty} (-\dot{\lambda}_j K_j - \lambda_j \dot{K}_j)dt \\
&= \sum_{j=1}^{J} \int_0^{\infty} (pF_{Kj}K_j + pF_{Ij}I_j - z_jI_j)u(t)dt \\
&= \int_0^{\infty} \left[\sum_{j=1}^{J} (pF_{Kj}K_j + pF_{Ij}I_j - z_jI_j) + pF_L L - wL \right] u(t)dt \\
&= \int_0^{\infty} [pF(K_1, \ldots, K_J, I_1, \ldots, I_J, L, t) - zI_j - wL]u(t)dt \\
&= V(0).
\end{aligned}$$

Therefore, the stock market value of a firm is the sum of shadow values of various types of capital goods. Without adjustment costs, the shadow value is close to the book value. From the first-order conditions, we note that the total cost of investing one unit of capital good, K_j, is $z_j - pF_{Ij}$, which is the sum of the acquisition (z_j) and the adjustment costs ($-pF_{Ij} > 0$). Compared with ordinary capital investment, IT investment may bring about the additional costs of building complementary intangible assets. Then total cost of investing one unit of IT capital could be much higher than that of ordinary capital.

References

Berndt, E. R., and C. J. Morrison. 1995. High-tech capital formation and economic performance in U.S. manufacturing industries: An exploratory analysis. *Journal of Econometrics* 65:9–43.

Brynjolfsson, E., and L. M. Hitt. 1995. Information technology as a factor of production: The role of differences among firms. *Journal of Economics of Innovation and New Technology* 3:183–99.

———. 1996. Paradox lost? Firm-level evidence on the returns to information systems spending. *Management Science* 42 (4): 541–58.

Brynjolfsson, E., and S. Yang. 1997. The intangible costs and benefits of computer investments: Evidence from the financial markets. Paper presented at the International Conference on Information Systems. December, Atlanta, Georgia.

Brynjolfsson, E., and S. Yang. 2000. Intangible assets and growth accounting: Evidence from computer investments. Massachusetts Institute of Technology, Sloan School of Management. Mimeograph.

Dewan, S., and C.-K. Min. 1997. The substitution of information technology for other factors of production: A firm-level analysis. *Management Science* 43 (12): 1660–75.

Griliches, Z. 1981. Market value, R&D, and patents. *Economics Letters* 7:183–87.
Hall, B. H. 1999. Innovation and market value. NBER Working Paper no. 6984. Cambridge, Mass.: National Bureau of Economic Research.
Hitt, L. M., and E. Brynjolfsson. 1996. Productivity, profit, and consumer welfare: Three different measures of information technology's value. *MIS Quarterly* (June): 121–42.
Kang, L., and J. Song. 1999. Information technology investment and productivity and performance of Korean banks (in Korean). *KyungJeHak YeonKu* 47 (6): 65–98.
Kim, J.-I. 2001. Employment structure and information technology (in Korean). In *Information and communication technology and new economy,* ed. I. W. Park, 37–75. Seoul: Korea Telecom Management Research Center.
Korea Information Society Development Institute. 1997. A survey on information technology utilization. Seoul, Korea: Korea Information Society Development Institute. Korea Ministry of Information and Communication. Korean IT statistics. [http://www.mic.go.kr/index.jsp].
Lau, L. J., and I. Tokutsu. 1992. The impact of computer technology on the aggregate productivity of the United States: An indirect approach. Stanford University, Department of Economics. Unpublished manuscript.
Lee, K. 2000. Adoption of information technology and performance of firms in the Korean textile industry (in Korean). *KukJeKyungJe Yongu* 6 (2): 145–74.
Lichtenberg, F. R. 1995. The output contributions of computer equipment and personnel: A firm-level analysis. *Journal of Economics of Innovation and New Technology* 3:201–17.
Lucas, R. E. 1967. Adjustment costs and the theory of supply. *Journal of Political Economy* 75:321–34.
Olley, G. S., and A. Pakes. 1996. The dynamics of productivity in the telecommunications equipment industry. *Econometrica* 64:1263–97.
Pilat, Dirk, and Frank C. Lee. 2001. Productivity growth in ICT-producing and ICT-using industries: A source of growth differentials in the OECD? STI Working Paper no. 2001/4. Paris: OECD.
Shin, I., H. Kim, and B. Chung. 1998. The estimation of information technology investment and capital stock in Korea (in Korean). *KukJeKyungJe Yongu* 4 (3): 1–22.
Shin, I., H. Kim, and J. Song. 1998. The use of information technology and performance of Korean firms (in Korean). *KyungJeHak Yongu* 46 (3): 253–78.
Strassman, P. A. 1990. *The business value of computers: An executive guide.* New Canaan, Conn.: Information Economics Press.

Comment Chong-Hyun Nam

This is a very interesting piece of empirical work, and I enjoyed reading it. I have only a few comments to make.

My first comment is concerned with the problem of data limitation. The empirical work in the paper is based on a very limited data set, just one-year IT (information technology) investment data for 225 micro firms for

Chong-Hyun Nam is professor of economics at Korea University.

1996. The paper shows very well how much mileage one could get out of this limited data set in analyzing the effect of IT investment on the performance of the Korean firms and of the Korean economy. But the problems with data limitation remain.

A problem with the IT investment data as used in the study is that they are based on a narrow definition of IT capital. The IT capital used here includes only office and accounting equipment and computing machinery. So it leaves out such important IT capital goods as information equipment and other IT-related electrical products. These kinds of capital goods turn out to comprise more than 25 percent of IT investment for Japan, as shown in the paper by Fukao and others (chap. 6 in this volume). I suppose, therefore, the paper may need to discuss consequential effects expected from this data problem.

Another problem with the IT data is that the paper assumes that relative IT investment share in total capital investment stays rather stable over time or increases at an annual rate of 10 percent for the sample period 1996–2000. This assumption seems to me too naive, however. Indeed, as shown in figure 10.1, the share of IT investment in total fixed capital formation increases sharply beginning in 1996 from about 2 percent to over 12 percent in 1999. So the growth rate of IT investment needs to be adjusted accordingly to make it a more realistic value, I think.

My second comment has to do with the choice of sample period for the study, namely, the 1996–2000 period. The author argues that the 1996–2000 period is likely to be a good one since drastic structural transformation was taking place along with huge IT investment in Korea for this sample period. But I am not so sure that this argument is true, because it looks to me rather difficult to separate out the effects of IT investment from the effects of other policy reforms undertaken in the same period in accounting for the sources of growth for the Korean economy.

As is well known, the 1996–2000 sample period represents one of the most turbulent periods that the Korean economy has ever experienced. This period includes, for example, the 1997 financial crisis, which quickly developed into an economic crisis in 1998, registering a minus 6.7 percent growth rate with more than a 7 percent unemployment rate for 1998.

A number of reform measures were, therefore, undertaken by the government to get the economy out of the deep economic crisis. They include, for example, the cleaning up of the ailing financial sector, accelerated privatization, improvements to labor market flexibility, and so on. At the same time, the government placed strong pressure upon the firms to reorganize, to improve their governance system and their debt structure, and to make their production lines more lean and specialized in their products.

All of these reform measures should have had tremendous impact on the efficiency of the Korean economy, and they helped the economy to get back to a 10 percent annual growth rate again by 1999. I hope the author tries to illustrate some of these policy reforms undertaken during the sample period somewhere in the paper and discusses their potential or consequential impact on the measured contribution of IT investment on total factor productivity growth (TFPG) for the Korean economy.

Another problem with the sample data period 1996–2000 is that it includes a period of unprecedented stock market bubble. For instance, the KOSDAQ index, which is equivalent to the NASDAQ index in the United States, rose from about 80 in late 1998 to over 250 by the end of 1999, but then plummeted to 52 by the end of 2000.

The presence of the stock market bubble during the sample period could have grossly inflated the market value of IT capital to some unknown degree, and the inflated market value of IT capital in turn would have led to an unrealistically high estimate for revised value added, revised TFP, and the extent of IT capital's contribution to economic growth for Korea, as shown in table 10.8.

My final comment is that, given the fact that the sample period 1999–2000 includes a period of severe recession and high unemployment in Korea, it seems quite sensible to test the importance of capacity utilization rate as a determinant of TFPG. The study by Fukao and others shows that capacity utilization rate turns out to be an important determinant of TFPG in the case of Japan.

Comment Dipinder S. Randhawa

Jong-Il Kim provides a nicely structured and informed assessment of the impact of investments in information technology (IT) on firm performance in Korea between 1996 and 2000. The paper concludes that IT investments enhanced productivity by adding value to firms and saving capital and labor. He finds value added reflected further in the finding that the market values investments in IT substantially higher than the acquisition price.

The research question is one of the important issues of our times—the contribution to productivity arising from the substantial investments in information technology. The dilemma in computing the contribution of IT to productivity is evident in two paradoxes: the first at the macro level, encapsulated in the enduring words of Robert Solow dating back to 1987: "we can see the computer age everywhere but in the productivity statistics" (quoted in Brynjolfsson and Hitt 1998). Studies in 1999 and 2000 examining other manifestations of the IT revolution, especially the stock market boom and the resultant increase in spending, deemed the paradox re-

Dipinder S. Randhawa is a teaching fellow at the National University of Singapore Business School.

solved. Events since have of course made this line of reasoning redundant and re-ignited the debate. The second paradox at the firm level is reflected in the inability to find any correlation between IT expenditures and measures of profitability.

At a broader level, a recent NBER paper by Robert Gordon (2002) questions whether the postulated increase in productivity on account of investments in IT in the United States was a one-shot injection in productivity or a productivity increase maintained by the extraordinarily high levels of IT investments until the late 1990s, or whether it has indeed led to a sustained increase in productivity. The same questions are pertinent for the Korean experience.

The Empirics

The studies on the impact of IT on productivity in the Korean economy offer conflicting evidence. Kim offers an articulate and comprehensive account of the major issues in measuring productivity. Five series of tests are conducted to gauge the impact on firm performance:

1. Using a modified Cobb-Douglas production function, investment in IT is treated as an additional factor of production. The marginal productivity of IT investments is computed.
2. To assess firms' profitability, turn to firms' financial statements.
3. For firms' productivity, compute total factor productivity.
4. Market valuation is drawn from firms' stock price.
5. Finally, a growth accounting exercise is used to see how much IT investments affected economic growth toward the end of the 1990s.

The expectation is that the use of a number of metrics would provide a comprehensive and nuanced view of firm performance. Kim notes that the benefits from IT spending lie in reduced coordination and transaction costs, making it easier for companies to adopt flexible coordination system over rigid hierarchical organization.

Kim further notes that during 1997–2000 many Korean firms introduced unprecedented reform of internal organization and corporate governance structure. Although overall fixed investments fell, investment in IT accelerated. Coincidence of structural reform and massive IT investments may imply that IT investments could have worked as a complementary factor to reorganization of Korean firms. The postcrisis period has arguably been one of unprecedented turmoil. A sizable body of literature has documented structural reforms in the corporate sector encompassing the streamlining of operations and management of the capital structure of firms. The largest *chaebols* have not been immune to change. At a time when firms are attempting to rehabilitate their balance sheets to stave off bankruptcy, it is a moot point whether they will have the incentives or the wherewithal to invest in IT on a large scale.

The current work assesses the contribution of IT to firms on the basis of IT spending. The impact of IT spending on a firm can be measured in different ways: (1) as the author has done, in terms of expenditure on IT; (2) on the nature of investments in IT; and (3) by examining the efficiency with which IT investments are managed within the firm.

In order to gain insights into how firms were responding to the crisis, one needs considerably disaggregated sector-level data on IT investments. I share Jong-Il Kim's clearly enunciated concerns about the lack of data. Data problems for such research projects have been endemic, and this paper is no exception. Data on IT spending at the firm level is available only for 1996. Kim extrapolates these numbers over the next three years to gauge the impact of IT. The time frame for the study coincides with the period when IT expenditures in Korea grew at an exponential rate. Assuming a correspondence between expenditures for the reported year and a linear extrapolation of this data for the next three years could lead to considerable distortions. Firms' strategies and corresponding expenditures on IT vary significantly across years and across firms. This extrapolation could lead to a misleading picture of firms' investments in IT.

The sample consists of firms listed on the Korean Stock Exchange. Most of these firms would be among the largest firms in the economy. Evidence from the United States has shown that small and medium-sized enterprises, especially the latter, have adopted some of the most robust strategies for IT investments. Few, if any, of these firms are listed, as most do not meet the minimum listing requirements. These firms have also demonstrated some of the most impressive productivity improvements following IT investments. The absence of this class of firms could conceivably understate the contribution of IT to productivity. Furthermore, studies have found significant differences across industries.

The results, as seen in table 10C.1, are mixed, offering no clear evidence on the impact of IT spending on firm performance. When measuring productivity it isn't clear whether the results reflect a substitution of inputs or an increased efficiency (i.e., a shift along the isoquant or a shift in the isoquant). Furthermore, the data do not enable us to identify the channels through which IT spending benefits the firm. The marginal increase in productivity without a commensurate increase in profitability suggests that

Table 10C.1 **Effects of Information Technology Investments**

	Impact
MP of IT capital	net returns = 0
Profitability	insignificant
Productivity	TFP growth 1% per annum
Market valuation of IT capital	by a factor of 7

the substantial costs incurred on IT investments negate the increases in productivity. The contradictory results for profitability and market valuation reflect a myopia, at worst outright mispricing in the market, an anomaly seemingly rectified following the market crash in 2001.

The Institutional Context

A useful corollary drawing upon the American experience is the role of universities, government research funding, and purely commercial enterprises in nurturing and disseminating IT innovations.

An explanation for the uneven adoption and dissemination of IT between the United States and Europe draws upon labor market regulations. Labor market regulations can have a profound impact on the adoption and dissemination of IT investments both at the firm and economywide levels—the contrast between Europe and the United States suggests they are significant for explaining cross-country differences in performance. It may be useful to examine this issue in the Korean context given the powerful union movement.

The spurt in IT spending in Korea lagged behind that in the United States by nearly a decade.

As the author points out in an analogy with the benefits from the introduction of electricity, there may well be a considerable lag before the beneficial effects of IT investment percolate down in the economy. An important question for researchers is identification of the channels through which these benefits manifest themselves. With the limited data resources, Kim has done an admirable job of providing a fairly comprehensive overview of the impact of IT spending.

References

Brynjolfsson, E., and L. M. Hitt. 1998. Beyond the productivity paradox. *Communications of the ACM* 41 (8): 49–56.

Gordon, R. 2002. Technology and economic performance in the American economy. NBER Working Paper no. 8771. Cambridge, Mass.: National Bureau of Economic Research, February.

11

How Important Is Discrete Adjustment in Aggregate Fluctuations?

Andrew Caplin and John Leahy

11.1 Introduction

The papers in this volume tend to fall into two camps: those that take a microeconomic perspective on growth and productivity and those that take a more aggregate perspective. This paper contributes to the ongoing effort in macroeconomics to link the two perspectives.

One of the factors that makes this link difficult is that adjustment at the level of the individual or firm is often discrete, whereas adjustment at the macroeconomic level is more smooth and continuous. This is especially true of the decisions that contribute to growth and productivity. Individual decisions, such as the decision to build a new factory, the decision to adopt a new technology, or the decision to enter a new market, are all decisions that carry large fixed costs at the microeconomic level. Individuals and firms therefore tend to take these actions infrequently. Other decisions, such as the decision to buy a new car or to change a price, also share this characteristic. Few people, for example, change the car that they drive every day in response to the current value of their stock portfolio or their current utility from driving. Rather, they let their car depreciate over time

Andrew Caplin is professor of economics at New York University and a faculty research fellow of the National Bureau of Economic Research. John Leahy is professor of economics at New York University and a research associate of the National Bureau of Economic Research.

We are grateful to Orazio Attanasio, Russell Cooper, Chris Foote, Chris House, Alejandro Micco, David Laibson, Greg Mankiw, Torsten Persson, Thomas Sargent, Christopher Sims, and two anonymous referees for helpful comments and discussions. We gratefully acknowledge support from the National Science Foundation (NSF). Leahy thanks the Sloan Foundation for financial support.

and occasionally upgrade to a new one that is consistent with their current tastes and wealth.

In spite of the discreteness of many microeconomic decisions, the standard approach to modeling in macroeconomics is to ignore all of this discrete behavior and assume that all firms are represented by a single representative firm that makes all of the investment decisions or that all consumers are represented by a single representative consumer that makes all of the consumption decisions. The decisions, which look so infrequent and discontinuous when viewed from the perspective of the individual firm or consumer, become quite smooth and continuous when viewed from the perspective of these representative agents. These representative agents typically care only about the total stock of capital or durable goods or the average level of technology or prices. They make minor adjustments to these variables in every period in order to equate the relevant marginal costs and marginal benefits of adjustment. While this abstraction provides a tractable microeconomic foundation for the modeling of aggregate investment or durable demand, it is clearly the wrong microeconomic foundation. The question is whether this makes any difference.

Whereas this paper is more theoretical and abstract than most of the other papers in this volume, the issue of how to go from realistic microeconomic analysis to realistic macroeconomic analysis is an important one for all researchers interested in growth and productivity. There is a trade-off between realism and complexity in macroeconomic modeling. We want models with dependable microfoundations, models that reflect the influence of factors such as discrete and infrequent adjustment. We also want simple and useful models of the economy as a whole, models like the representative agent model. The message of this paper is that this trade-off is not as costly as one might think. In spite of the importance of discrete adjustment at the microeconomic level, representative agent models can capture aggregate dynamics fairly accurately. The catch is that the representative agent must be parameterized to represent the market and not any given individual. This means that standard macroeconomic analysis need only be altered slightly in order to incorporate microeconomic discreteness at the microeconomic level.

In recent years there has developed a large body of research that appears to indicate the opposite. This literature suggests that microeconomic frictions might have large macroeconomic consequences.[1] The potential for discrete adjustment to matter lies in the potential for the distribution of

1. Discrete adjustment, particularly in the form of sS policies, has been studied in the context of pricing (Caplin and Spulber 1987; Caplin and Leahy 1991, 1997; Dotsey, King, and Wolman 1999), labor hiring and firing (Caballero, Engel, and Haltiwanger 1997), investment (Cooper, Haltiwanger, and Power 1995; Thomas 2001), and the demand for durable goods (Bertola and Caballero 1990; Bar-Ilan and Blinder 1996; Adda and Cooper 2000a,b; Caplin and Leahy 2002a).

durable goods, capital, prices, or technology to vary over time. For concreteness consider the capital stock. The capital stock of a representative agent is simply the capital stock. In a discrete adjustment model, a given aggregate stock of capital may be consistent with many distributions of capital across firms. A typical firm will allow its capital holdings to drift away from its optimal level, adjusting only when it hits some adjustment trigger. The distribution of capital relative to these adjustment triggers will affect current productivity and influence future investment. The greater the misallocation of capital, the more inefficient the economy and the greater the need for subsequent adjustment. If there are relatively many agents near an upward adjustment trigger then investment will tend to be high in the future. If there are relatively many near a downward adjustment trigger then disinvestment is possible. In this way the distributional dynamics can add an additional source of aggregate fluctuation as misalignment rises and falls over time. This added noise complicates both forecasts and the interpretation of aggregate statistics.

In spite of this flurry of recent research, the importance of discrete adjustment in macroeconomics is still an unsettled question. Bar-Ilan and Blinder (1996) simply claim that "one implication of [discrete adjustment] at the microeconomic level is that aggregate data cannot be generated by a representative agent." They base this claim on the fact that their model has margins of adjustment not present in the representative agent model, namely the number of agents adjusting and the size of individual adjustment. They do not, however, compare the dynamics of their model to the dynamics of a representative agent model. Caballero and coauthors (Caballero 1993; Caballero, Engel, and Haltiwanger 1997) report statistically significant effects of discrete adjustment, but they do not show that these effects are economically significant, nor do their models endogenize prices. On the other hand, Caplin and Spulber (1987) present a model in which discrete behavior aggregates to a representative agent, and Thomas (2001) argues that equilibrium feedback may smooth out the effects of discrete adjustment. Moreover, Adda and Cooper (2000b) argue empirically that most aggregate fluctuations in durable goods markets are associated with fluctuations in price rather than the distribution of holdings.

Investigations of the role of discrete adjustment have been hampered by the difficulty of constructing equilibrium models that can be easily compared to their smooth representative agent counterpart. Given the importance of the distributional dynamics, the dimension of the state space quickly becomes unmanageable. The literature tends to deal with this problem in one of two ways. Much of the literature simply assumes that prices are exogenous to agents' actions. This severs the links among agents, so that the decision problem of each agent can be studied in isolation. Aggregation simply involves integrating across agents' actions. Other papers reduce the dimensionality of the problem by making assumptions on the allowable distributions. For example, Caplin and Leahy (1997) restrict attention to distributions that are uniform in relative prices, and Dotsey, King, and Wolman (1999) assume that the support contains a bounded number of points.

In this paper, we use a more realistic approximation to compare the aggregate dynamics of a discrete adjustment model to that of a representative agent model with continuous adjustment.[2] The approximation was developed by Caplin and Leahy (2002a) in the context of durable goods. The idea behind the approximation is that if there is enough time between an agent's purchases then individual heterogeneity will smooth the echoes of previous cycles. Consider a market in which agents with holdings of a durable below some trigger "little s" rebuild their stocks to some level "big S." High demand today then creates a lump in the cross-sectional distribution of holdings at big S. If there is no individual heterogeneity, then this lump passes through the (S,s) bands as holdings depreciate and produces an echo in demand when it reaches little s. This echo creates a link between the market today and the market in the far future. Breaking this link greatly simplifies the analysis. In this paper we break this link by assuming that the durable goods holdings of different agents depreciate at different rates. This heterogeneity tends to disperse the lump and reduce the echo.

It is important to note that, in assuming pervasive microeconomic heterogeneity, we are taking to heart one of the principal conclusions of the accumulating microeconomic literature on discrete adjustment. It is a common finding in this literature that the variance of the idiosyncratic shocks faced by an individual or firm is many times greater than that of aggregate shocks.[3] This heterogeneity tends to weaken the correlation of adjustment across firms. From a theoretical perspective, it is not important that we put this heterogeneity in the depreciation rate. Any form of heterogeneity will do the trick. We could just as well have assumed that tastes, income, wealth, or demographic variables were heterogeneous. The advantage of our approximation is that it produces a comparatively simple equilibrium model that can be solved analytically and compared to the representative agent model.

It may seem that by smoothing the echoes we are eliminating the distributional dynamics that make the discrete adjustment model distinctive. This is only partially true. Whereas we rule out fluctuations in the density of holdings at the purchase trigger, we still allow the distribution to shift with movements in "big S" and "little s." We would argue that most of the

2. This paper draws heavily on work presented in Caplin and Leahy (2002a,b). The approximation is worked out in Caplin and Leahy (2002a). The mapping between the representative agent model and the discrete choice model is worked out under more general assumptions in Caplin and Leahy (2002b).

3. See, in particular, Bertola and Caballero (1990) and Cooper and Haltiwanger (2000). Many of the papers cited previously are also relevant to this issue.

distributional dynamics that people associate with the business cycle are in fact shifts in these thresholds. When the stock market crashes and people feel less wealthy, they tend to hold on to their cars a bit longer and then purchase less expensive cars. These decisions are well captured by shifts in the adjustment trigger and target. They are not directly related to the density of holdings.[4] Our model is consistent with the observation that fluctuations in aggregate investment activity are driven to a large extent by variation in the number of firms making large investments.[5]

We present the representative agent model and the Caplin-Leahy approximation to the discrete choice model in the next section and compare them in section 11.3. It turns out that the representative agent model and the Caplin-Leahy approximation are observationally equivalent. Each implies that the first difference in sales follows an ARIMA(1,1). In principle, this means that one could construct a mapping between the two models: Choose realistic microeconomic parameters that characterize the discrete adjustment model and then find a representative agent model that yields similar dynamics. We construct such a mapping and analyze some of its properties. First, we consider the special case in which the supply curve is perfectly elastic and find that in this case the mapping between the parameters of the two models is the identity mapping; the models are equivalent.[6] We then show that the mapping is nontrivial when there is a price response to high demand. In particular, the depreciation rate and the real interest rate for the representative agent model need to be adjusted in order to match the dynamics of the discrete adjustment model.

To get a sense of the importance of the differences that arise, we use data from the U.S. automobile industry to calibrate the Caplin-Leahy model. The model fits the data well, with a depreciation rate of 31 percent per annum, which compares favorably to the estimate of 33 percent reported by Jorgenson and Sullivan (1981). We then use the mapping to find the corresponding representative agent model. The representative agent model that mimics the dynamics of the Caplin-Leahy model has a depreciation rate of 27 percent and a real interest rate of 12 percent. Although these differences may appear large, it turns out that the market dynamics are relatively insensitive to these two parameters. Therefore when the two models are calibrated with the same parameters their dynamics do not differ greatly.

We conclude that in the case of the U.S. automobile industry not much is lost by ignoring discrete adjustment at the microeconomic level and instead modeling demand according to the continuous adjustment of a representative agent. In more general settings, care needs to be taken in para-

4. Adda and Cooper (2000b) argue that this extensive margin is more important to distributional dynamics than the intensive margin.

5. See Cooper, Haltiwanger, and Power (1995).

6. It is ironic that in this case our model is a more fleshed-out version of the model employed by Bar-Ilan and Blinder, from which the foregoing quotation was taken.

meterizing the representative agent model. Parameters that appear reasonable on a microeconomic level may not be appropriate for a representative agent who proxies for a group of consumers facing adjustment costs. This distinction may be especially important when conducting policy experiments, since in this case the representative agent model that mimics the discrete choice model might change with the change in policy regime.

We conclude the paper with some observations on when our approximation should hold and when it may not.

11.2 Two Models

In this section we present log-linearized versions of the representative agent model and Caplin and Leahy's approximation of the (S,s) model.

11.2.1 Representative Agent

We consider the problem of a representative agent who derives utility from a stock of a durable good K_t. Utility is separable between durable and nondurable consumption.[7] Utility from durables takes a constant elasticity form, $U(K) = K^{\alpha}/\alpha$. The durable depreciates at a rate Δ. The price of the durable is p_t and the marginal utility of wealth is λ_t.

The consumer maximizes the present value of utility less the cost of new purchases:

$$\max_{\{K_t\}} \sum \beta^t \{U(K_t) - p_t \lambda_t [K_t - (1 - \Delta)K_{t-1}]\},$$

where β is the discount factor. The first-order condition for this problem is to set the marginal utility from the durable equal to a form of Jorgenson's user cost:

$$U'(K_t) = p_t \lambda_t - (1 - \Delta)\beta E_t p_{t+1} \lambda_{t+1}.$$

We close our description of the market with assumptions on price and the marginal utility of wealth. Let $Q_t = K_t - (1 - \Delta)/K_{t-1}$ denote purchases of the durable in period t. We assume that price is equal to marginal cost and that marginal cost is a function of purchases and a cost shock

$$p_t = Q_t^{\gamma} c_t.$$

We assume that both shocks, c_t and λ_t, follow random walks.[8]

11.2.2 The Caplin-Leahy Model

Because many of the parameters, such as α and β, have the same meaning in the two models we will reuse them. If it becomes important to dis-

7. This is a fairly standard assumption in the literature on durable goods. It receives some empirical support from Bernanke (1985).

8. For the marginal utility of wealth to follow a random walk it must be the case that the discount factor is equal to the interest rate.

tinguish between the parameters of one model or the other we will use subscripts or superscripts. For example, α_{rep} will refer to α in the representative agent model, and q^{cl} will refer to q in the Caplin-Leahy model.

Consider a continuum of consumers indexed by $i \in [0, 1]$ who derive utility from their holdings of a durable. As with the representative agent model, we assume that each agent receives utility $U(K_{it}) = K_i^{\alpha}/\alpha$, that the price of a unit of the durable is p_t, and that the marginal utility of wealth is λ_t.[9] We make two changes to the individual's problem. First, when individuals alter their holdings of the durable good they must pay a fixed cost equal to a fraction c of their current holding of the durable. This cost generates intermittent adjustment. Agents will wait until the gain from adjustment justifies incurring the fixed cost. Second, in order to spread purchases of the durable over time we introduce heterogeneity in the form of random depreciation. We assume that in each period each agent's durable depreciates by an amount Δ_{it} which is independently and identically distributed (i.i.d.) with a mean equal to Δ.

Let $V(K_t, \boldsymbol{\omega}_t)$ denote the value of an optimal policy for a consumer holding a durable of size K_t given that the state of the market, to be discussed in detail later, is $\boldsymbol{\omega}_t$. This problem may be written as

$$(1) \quad V(K_{it}, \boldsymbol{\omega}_t) = \max_{\{T_j, S_{T_j}\}} E_t \sum_{s=t}^{\infty} \beta^{s-t} U(K_{is}) - \sum_{j=1}^{\infty} \beta^{T_j - t} p(\boldsymbol{\omega}_{T_j}) \lambda(\boldsymbol{\omega}_{T_j}) [S_{T_j} + (1-c)(1-\Delta_{it}) K_{T_j - 1}],$$

where

$$K_{is} = \begin{cases} K_{it} & \text{if } s = t \text{ and } T_1 > t; \\ S_{T_j} & \text{if } s = T_j; \\ (1-\Delta_{it}) K_{is-1} & \text{otherwise.} \end{cases}$$

Here E_t is the mathematical expectation conditional on date t information. The first summation represents the utility that the agent receives from the durable. β is the consumer's discount rate, and $U(K_s)$ is the utility from holding a durable of size K_s. The second summation represents the cost of successive purchases of the durable. T_j is a random time representing the date of the jth purchase. On these dates the consumer sells a fraction $1 - c$ of his or her current holdings of the durable and purchases S_{T_j} new units of the durable good. Both purchase and sale take place at a price p_{T_j}. λ_{T_j} is the marginal utility of wealth and translates the purchase price into utility terms. Between purchase dates the durable depreciates by an amount Δ_{it}.

If the depreciation rate is great enough and the cost of adjustment is high

9. With perfect capital markets the marginal utility of wealth will be equal across agents.

enough, then it will be rare for agents to reduce their holdings of the durable.[10] Adjustment will be one-sided. Given the state of the market $\boldsymbol{\omega}_t$, there will be a purchase target $S(\boldsymbol{\omega}_t)$ and a purchase trigger $s(\boldsymbol{\omega}_t) < S(\boldsymbol{\omega}_t)$ such that all agents with holdings less than $s(\boldsymbol{\omega}_t)$ adjust their holdings to $S(\boldsymbol{\omega}_t)$.

We close the model in the same manner as the representative agent model. We assume that price is equal to marginal cost and that marginal cost depends on total sales and a cost shock:

$$p_t = Q_t^{\gamma} c_t.$$

In this case total sales are equal to the product of the number of purchases and the size of each purchase.

Solving for equilibrium in such a setting is made difficult by the fact that included in the state vector $\boldsymbol{\omega}_t$ is the entire distribution of durable goods holdings across agents. The number of agents with small holdings matters because this will influence demand and hence price. The rest of the distribution helps to predict the evolution of this lower tail. The Caplin-Leahy model makes two assumptions that simplify these dynamics. Both assumptions are motivated by the idea that when the time between purchases is sufficiently long the present will exert very little impact on the future. The first assumption is that the value of a new durable is exogenous to the current state of the market and can therefore be expressed as $V(K)$. The idea is that current market influences will die out before the next purchase is made. The second assumption is that the density of holdings in the neighborhood of the purchase trigger is log uniform. This assumption requires that there be sufficient time between purchases that the heterogeneity in depreciation smooths out the lumps in the distribution that may occur if a large number of agents purchase the durable at one time. The precise conditions necessary to support these assumptions are discussed in Caplin and Leahy (2002a). The assumption that heterogeneity smooths away the echoes of past shocks removes some of the distributional dynamics associated with discrete adjustment models. It is important to note, however, that an important source of distributional dynamics remains, namely movement in the adjustment trigger s_t. When s_t lies below its steady-state level there will be "pent-up demand," and when s_t lies above its steady-state level demand will be below average for some time. Simulations of the model calibrated to the U.S. automobile market indicate that the assumptions hold remarkably well (Caplin and Leahy 2002a).

Given these assumptions, the first-order conditions for an optimal policy are

10. Depreciation creates a natural tendency toward one-sided adjustment. If the adjustment cost is too small, however, increases in price or in the marginal utility of wealth may create sufficient incentive for agents to reduce durable holdings.

$$V'(S_t) = p_t \lambda_t$$

$$V(S_t) - [S_t - (1-c)s_t] p_t \lambda_t = \frac{S_t^\alpha}{\alpha} + \beta E_t \{ V(S_{t+1}) - [S_{t+1} - (1-c)(1-\Delta)s_t] p_{t+1} \lambda_{t+1} \}$$

The first equation states that the optimal target is determined by equating the value of the marginal purchase to the cost. Note that the adjustment cost does not appear here since it is sunk once the agent decides to purchase. Note also that the determination of the optimal purchase size S_t is essentially a static decision, in much the same way that nondurable consumption is a static decision. This is a consequence of the unpredictability of the future. The second equation states that the optimal trigger is determined by indifference between buying today and buying tomorrow. Note here that we have replaced Δ_{it+1} with its mean.

V will inherit certain homogeneity properties from the constant elasticity utility function and the proportional depreciation rate. It will be useful to normalize V by the level of holdings of the durable good that would occur in steady state in the absence of frictions. Let κ_t denote this level of holdings. Caplin and Leahy (2002a) show that V will be homogeneous of degree α in κ_t:

$$V(S_t) = v\left(\frac{S_t}{\kappa_t}\right)\kappa_t^\alpha.$$

Note that from our analysis of the representative agent model we know that

$$\kappa_t^{\alpha-1-\gamma} = [1 - \beta(1-\Delta)]\Delta c_t \lambda_t.$$

Finally, the number of purchases is determined by depreciation and the evolution of the purchase trigger. With the assumption that the distribution of holdings is log uniform, the number of purchases becomes

$$n_t = \mu(\ln s_t - \ln s_{t-1} + \delta),$$

where μ is the density of holdings and $\delta = -\ln(1-\Delta) \sim \Delta$. Sales are therefore

$$Q_t = \mu S_t(\ln s_t - \ln s_{t-1} + \delta).$$

The evolution of cost and the evolution of marginal utility are as before. This completes the presentation of the model.

11.2.3 Linearization

Our interest is in the first-order differences between the two models. We therefore log-linearize the dynamics. Appendix A presents the details of the derivation. Here we present the results.

The representative agent model is defined by the following system of equations:

(2) $$(\alpha - 1)[1 - (1 - \Delta)\beta]\hat{k}_t = (\hat{p}_t + \hat{\lambda}_t) - \beta(1 - \Delta)E_t(\hat{p}_{t+1} + \hat{\lambda}_{t+1})$$

(3) $$\Delta\hat{q}_t = \hat{k}_t - (1 - \Delta)\hat{k}_{t-1}$$

(4) $$\hat{p}_t = \gamma\hat{q}_t + \hat{c}_t$$

(5) $$\hat{c}_t = \hat{c}_{t-1} + \eta_{ct}$$

(6) $$\hat{\lambda}_t = \hat{\lambda}_{t-1} + \eta_{\lambda t}$$

There are three endogenous variables, $\hat{k}_t$, $\hat{p}_t$, and $\hat{q}_t$, and two state variables, $\hat{c}_t$ and $\hat{\lambda}_t$. All variables are in log deviations from their steady-state values. Equation (2) is the first-order condition for the optimal holding of the durable good. Equation (3) defines sales as a function of the change in durable holdings. Equation (4) defines marginal cost, and equations (5) and (6) define the evolution of the exogenous variables.

Appendix A shows that these equations may be combined to yield a second-order difference equation in $\hat{k}_t$, which has a solution of the form

$$\hat{k}_t = x_{\text{rep}}\hat{k}_{t-1} + y_{\text{rep}}\hat{e}_t,$$

where $x_{\text{rep}} \in [0, 1]$, $y_{\text{rep}} < 0$, and $\hat{e}_t = \hat{c}_t + \hat{\lambda}_t$.

The Caplin-Leahy model is defined by the following system of equations:

(7) $$(\alpha - 1)\hat{S}_t = \hat{p}_t + \hat{\lambda}_t$$

(8) $$\{s^{\alpha} - [1 - \beta(1 - \Delta)](1 - c)sp\lambda\}\hat{s}_t = -p\lambda[S - (1 - c)s](\hat{p}_t + \hat{\lambda}_t) + p\lambda[S - (1 - c)(1 - \Delta)s] \cdot \beta E_t(\hat{p}_{t+1} - \hat{\lambda}_{t+1}) + (\alpha v \kappa^{\alpha} - p\lambda S) \cdot (\hat{\kappa}_t - E_t\beta\hat{\kappa}_{t+1})$$

(9) $$\hat{q}_t = \hat{S}_t + \frac{1}{\delta}(\hat{s}_t - \hat{s}_{t-1})$$

(10) $$(\alpha - 1 - \gamma)\hat{\kappa}_t = \hat{\lambda}_t + \hat{c}_t$$

(11) $$\hat{p}_t = \gamma\hat{q}_t + \hat{c}_t$$

(12) $$\hat{c}_t = \hat{c}_{t-1} + \eta_{ct}$$

(13) $$\hat{\lambda}_t = \hat{\lambda}_{t-1} + \eta_{\lambda t}$$

There are four endogenous variables, $\hat{S}_t$, $\hat{s}_t$, $\hat{p}_t$, and $\hat{q}_t$, and two state variables, $\hat{c}_t$ and $\hat{\lambda}_t$ ($\hat{\kappa}_t$ is a function of these). As before, all variables are in log deviations from their steady state values. Equation (7) is the first-order condition for purchase target. Equation (8) is the first-order condition for purchase trigger. Equation (9) defines sales as a function of the target and the change in the purchase trigger. Equation (10) defines the frictionless steady-state holdings. Equations (11), (12), and (13) are the same as their representative agent counterparts.

Appendix A shows that these equations may be combined to yield the following second-order difference equation in $\hat{s}_t$, which has the form

$$\hat{s}_t = x_{\mathrm{cl}}\hat{s}_{t-1} + y_{\mathrm{cl}}\hat{e}_t, \tag{14}$$

where $x_{\mathrm{cl}} \in [0, 1]$ and $y_{\mathrm{cl}} < 0$.

At this point we note several differences between the two models. First, purchases in the Caplin-Leahy model depend separately on the number of individual purchases and the size of each individual purchase. Second, there is no role for the aggregate stock of durables as in the representative agent model. Only the agents who make purchases affect sales. Third, whereas purchases in the representative agent model depend on the current price and the price next period, the purchase target in the Caplin-Leahy model depends on the current price and the price in the distant future as reflected in the steady-state target. Finally, there is no role for the adjustment cost in the representative agent model.

There are also similarities. Most notable is that both $\hat{s}_t$ and $\hat{k}_t$ follow second-order difference equations.

11.3 A Comparison

In this section, we compare the dynamic properties of the two models. We begin by solving for the dynamics of sales in each case. The price dynamics follow from the supply curve.

The stock of durables in the representative agent model evolves according to

$$\hat{k}_t = x_{\mathrm{rep}}\hat{k}_{t-1} + y_{\mathrm{rep}}\hat{e}_t.$$

Hence, sales are equal to

$$\hat{q}_t^{\mathrm{rep}} = \frac{1}{\Delta}\hat{k}_t - \frac{1-\Delta}{\Delta}\hat{k}_{t-1} = x_{\mathrm{rep}}\hat{q}_{t-1}^{\mathrm{rep}} + y_{\mathrm{rep}}\left[\frac{1}{\Delta}(\hat{\lambda}_t + \hat{c}_t) - \frac{1-\Delta}{\Delta}(\hat{\lambda}_{t-1} + \hat{c}_{t-1})\right].$$

Sales in the Caplin-Leahy model evolve according to

$$\hat{q}_t = \hat{S}_t + \frac{1}{\delta}(\hat{s}_t - \hat{s}_{t-1}).$$

Substituting for $\hat{S}_t$ and $\hat{s}_t$ yields

$$\begin{aligned}
\hat{q}_t^{\mathrm{cl}} &= \frac{1-\alpha}{1-\alpha+\gamma}\cdot\frac{1}{\delta}(\hat{s}_t - \hat{s}_{t-1}) - \frac{1}{1-\alpha+\gamma}\hat{e}_t \\
&= x_{\mathrm{cl}}\hat{q}_t^{\mathrm{cl}} + \left[\frac{1-\alpha}{1-\alpha+\gamma}\cdot\frac{1}{\delta}y_{\mathrm{cl}} - \frac{1}{1-\alpha+\gamma}\right]\hat{e}_t \\
&\quad - \left[\frac{1-\alpha}{1-\alpha+\gamma}\cdot\frac{1}{\delta}y_{\mathrm{cl}} - \frac{x_{\mathrm{cl}}}{1-\alpha+\gamma}\right]\hat{e}_{t-1}.
\end{aligned}$$

In each case, the first difference of sales follows an ARIMA(1,1). There is therefore a sense in which the two models are observationally equivalent. This equivalence is remarkable since it relates a model with discrete adjustment at the microeconomic level to a representative agent model with *no* adjustment costs.

We can think about how to parameterize the representative agent model to mimic the dynamics of the Caplin-Leahy model. For this we need to match the coefficients on $\hat{q}_t$, $\hat{e}_t$, and $\hat{e}_{t-1}$. This requires

$$x_{\text{rep}} = x_{\text{cl}}$$

$$\frac{y_{\text{rep}}}{\Delta} = \frac{1-\alpha}{1-\alpha+\gamma} \cdot \frac{1}{\delta} y_{\text{cl}} - \frac{1}{1-\alpha+\gamma}$$

$$y_{\text{rep}} \frac{1-\Delta}{\Delta} = \frac{1-\alpha}{1-\alpha+\gamma} \cdot \frac{1}{\delta} y_{\text{cl}} - \frac{x_{\text{cl}}}{1-\alpha+\gamma}$$

or

(15)
$$x_{\text{rep}} = x_{\text{cl}}$$

$$y_{\text{rep}} = \frac{x_{\text{cl}} - 1}{1-\alpha+\gamma}$$

$$\Delta = \frac{x_{\text{cl}} - 1}{\frac{1-\alpha}{\delta} y_{\text{cl}} - 1}$$

In principle, a mapping between the parameters of the two models can be constructed as follows. Given any parameterization of the Caplin-Leahy model (α_{cl}, β_{cl}, δ_{cl}, and c), solve for x_{rep}, y_{rep}, and Δ_{rep} using equation (15). Given x_{rep}, y_{rep}, and Δ, derive α_{rep}, β_{rep}, and K using the definitions of x_{rep} and y_{rep} and the steady-state relationship

$$K_{\text{rep}}^{\alpha-1} = [1 - (1 - \Delta_{\text{rep}})\beta_{\text{rep}}]p\lambda.$$

How do the two models differ? We attempt to answer this question in two ways. First, we consider a simple situation in which the supply curve is perfectly elastic and the equations simplify greatly. Second, we match the parameters of the two models to data from the market for new cars in the United States, and ask whether and how much they differ in this case.

11.3.1 A Simple Case

We begin with a situation in which the mapping is simple. If $\gamma = 0$, then it can be shown that $x_{\text{cl}} = 0$ and $y_{\text{cl}} = 1/(\alpha_{\text{cl}} - 1)$. This implies that $x_{\text{rep}} = 0$, $y_{\text{rep}} = 1/(\alpha_{\text{rep}} - 1)$, and $\Delta_{\text{rep}} = \delta_{\text{cl}}/(1 + \delta_{\text{cl}})$. Hence, $\alpha_{\text{rep}} = \alpha_{\text{cl}}$ and Δ_{rep} is equal to Δ_{cl} to a first order. Note that in this case β_{rep} and K_{rep} do not affect the dynamics of the representative agent model and c does not affect the dynamics of the

Caplin-Leahy model. In sum, identical parameterizations of the two models yield identical dynamics. In this case, the two models are identical.

PROPOSITION 1. *If* $\gamma = 0$, *then the response of the Caplin-Leahy model to a shock is identical to the response of a similarly parameterized representative agent model.*

This result is similar to the neutrality result of Caplin and Spulber (1987) in that a heterogeneous agent model with fixed costs delivers dynamics similar to a representative agent model without frictions. The intuition is straightforward. In the absence of a price response, a shock in the Caplin-Leahy model causes a once-and-for-all shift in both $\hat{S}_t$ and $\hat{s}_t$ by an amount $1/(\alpha - 1)$. The intuition is the same as for the permanent income hypothesis: A shift in price or marginal utility causes a proportional shift in policy. Total purchases, $\hat{q}_t$, depend on $\hat{S}$ and the first difference of $\hat{s}_t$. $\hat{S}$ rises permanently, but $\Delta\hat{s}_t$ rises only for one period. The result is that total purchases follow an MA(1). Since $\Delta\hat{s}_t$ receives a weight $1/\delta$ in $\hat{q}_t$, the lagged moving average (MA) coefficient is approximately $1 - \Delta$ as in Mankiw's (1982) representative agent model.

11.4 Evidence from the U.S. Auto Market

In the general case in which $\gamma > 0$, this exact mapping between the two models fails to hold. This can easily be seen from the fact that the adjustment cost c enters the equations that determine x_{cl} and y_{cl}. This cost plays no role in the representative agent model.

In order to see how important these differences may be in practice, we fit the model to data from the market for new cars in the United States. We take data on the number of new cars sold from the Bureau of Economic Analysis (BEA). $\hat{n}$ is the log of this number. The BEA also has data on the average purchase price of new cars. We normalize this number by the price index for new cars obtained from the Bureau of Labor Statistics and take logs to get $\hat{S}$. $\hat{q}$ is the sum of $\hat{n}$ and $\hat{S}$. We construct the relative price of new cars, $\hat{p}$, by dividing the Consumer Price Index (CPI) for new cars by the gross domestic product (GDP) deflator for nondurable goods and taking logs.

Although most of the data are available at a monthly frequency, we estimate the model at a quarterly frequency. The monthly data contain a lot of noise and are dominated at times by movements in inventories, which we have not modeled. Aggregating lessens these problems and yields sensible results. We leave the inclusion of inventory movements for future work.

We restrict the analysis to the period beginning with the first quarter of 1967 and ending in the first quarter of 1990. We begin in 1967 because there are some violent movements in the average price of used cars in the early 1960s, which appear to be more problems with the data than real economic phenomenon. We end in 1990 because there is a trend break in the series

Table 11.1 **Instrumental Variables Estimation of the Effect of Durable Demand on the Relative Price of Durables**

Variable	Coefficient	Standard Error	Probability
$\hat{q}_t$	.171	.036	.000
Constant	4.548	.207	.000
Trend	–.018	.003	.000
100 · trend^2	.012	.005	.001
10,000 · trend^3	–.002	.002	.293

sometime in the late 1980s when minivans and sport utility vehicles (SUVs) begin to replace the station wagon. Whereas station wagons were categorized as cars, minivans and SUVs are categorized as light trucks.

We choose to work with seasonally adjusted data. In principle the model should work as well with seasonally adjusted data. Including seasonality, however, complicates the error structure without adding anything to the analysis.

11.4.1 The Response of Prices

We begin with the response of prices, since if the supply curve is elastic the models are identical. To estimate γ, we regress $\hat{p}$ on $\hat{q}$. We instrument for the demand for autos using the current and lagged change in nondurable consumption, the CPI for energy, and the federal funds rate, as well as the lagged number of purchases. All instruments were expressed in logs. The consumption Euler equation implies that nondurable consumption should be proportional to the marginal utility of wealth, which acts as a demand shock in our model. The lagged number of purchases should be correlated with s_{t-1} and hence the current number of purchases. The federal funds rate and the price of energy were included under the hypothesis that they primarily shift durable demand.

Table 11.1 presents the second-stage results from the two-stage least squares (TSLS) estimation.

The coefficient on $\hat{q}_t$ is significantly different from zero. The t-statistic is about 4.75. We conclude that supply is not perfectly elastic and there is a potential for the two models to differ. Given the positive value for γ, it is difficult to justify modeling the demand for durable goods under the assumption of exogenous prices, as is the practice in much of the literature.[11]

This result is fairly stable. The coefficient on $\hat{q}$ is little changed if only

11. Mankiw (1982), Bernanke (1985), Caballero (1993), and Chah, Ramey, and Starr (1995) all make this assumption. All of these papers (implicitly or explicitly) assume that the price of durable goods is independent of demand and find that the estimated parameters do not make sense within the context of the model. It is possible, however, that price is not perfectly elastic and that the estimated parameters need to be reinterpreted in light of the mapping between the representative agent model and the sS model.

Table 11.2 **Estimation of $\hat{n}_t = x_{cl}\hat{n}_{t-1} + \varepsilon_t$**

Variable	Coefficient	Standard Error	Probability
$\hat{n}_{t-1}$	.711	.075	.000
Constant	1.631	.749	.032
Trend	.027	.036	.416
$100 \cdot \text{trend}^2$	–.037	.046	.433
$10{,}000 \cdot \text{trend}^3$	.016	.021	.439

lagged instruments are used or if only the consumption of nondurables is used as an instrument. It is also similar to other results in the literature. Bils and Klenow (1998) find that the prices of a large number of durable goods are procyclical. Adda and Cooper (2000b) estimate a structural model of the market for new cars. Using data for France and the United States, they find that they need a positive correlation between their demand shock and their price shock in order to fit the data.

We next estimate α and x, since these can be observed from the data.

11.4.2 The Number of Purchases

The number of purchases $\hat{n}$ is related to the change in the purchase trigger $\hat{s}$. If $\gamma > 0$, then $\hat{s}$ follows an AR(1). It is easy to see that $\hat{n}$ also follows a first-order autoregressive process (AR[1]) and that the autoregressive coefficient is x_{cl}.

$$\hat{n}_t = x_{cl}\hat{n}_{t-1} + y_{cl}(\eta_{ct} + \eta_{\lambda t})$$

According to the model, the error in this equation is independent of $\hat{n}_{t-1}$. We can therefore estimate x_{cl} from the data on $\hat{n}$ using ordinary least squares (OLS).

Table 11.2 fits an AR(1) to our data on $\hat{n}$.

x_{cl} is estimated fairly precisely. It is significantly different from both zero and one. This relationship is also very stable. Further lags are insignificant. Dropping the trend variables has no effect on the autoregressive coefficient; neither does including the change in nondurable or the price of energy in the regression.[12]

11.4.3 The Elasticity of Demand

We can calibrate the elasticity of demand α from the reaction of the average size of purchases to price

$$\Delta\hat{S}_t = \frac{1}{\alpha - 1}(\Delta\hat{p}_t + \Delta\hat{\lambda}_t). \tag{16}$$

12. It is also interesting that lagged disposable income is insignificant. This equation therefore passes a Hall orthogonality test of the rational expectations permanent income hypothesis.

Table 11.3 Estimation of Equation (16)

Variable	Coefficient	Standard Error	Probability
$\Delta\hat{p}_t$	−.403	.179	.027
Constant	.003	.042	.936
Trend	−.001	.002	.787
$100 \cdot \text{trend}^2$	.001	.003	.609
$10{,}000 \cdot \text{trend}^3$	−.001	.001	.490
Δcons	.551	.274	.047
Δp_{energy}	−.086	.072	.232
Δffunds	.000	.001	.824

We estimate equation (16) using data on nondurable consumption to control for changes in the marginal utility of wealth. We also include the change in the federal funds rate and the change in the price of energy as controls. The results are reported in table 11.3.

The coefficient on $\Delta\hat{p}_t$ is fairly stable. It does not change if we estimate the equation in levels, omit the trend terms, or omit the other controls. The coefficient implies a value of α approximately equal to −1.5.

11.4.4 Fit

Whether the models differ depends on how one interprets the data. We do two experiments. First, we use the data to back out parameters of the Caplin-Leahy model and then use the mapping described previously to derive the corresponding parameters of the representative agent model. Given our estimates of $\alpha = -1.5$, $x = .71$ and $\gamma = .17$, and we can calculate Δ_{cl} given values for c and β. We calibrate $\beta = .99$, which is consistent with a real interest rate of 4 percent per annum, and select a number of values for $c \in [0, 1]$. It turns out that Δ_{cl} is relatively insensitive to the choice of c. For $c = 1$, we obtain $\Delta_{\text{cl}} = .094$. For $c = .2$, we obtain $\Delta_{\text{cl}} = .091$. The former implies an annual depreciation rate of 32.6 percent, whereas the latter implies 31.7 percent. Both of these are nearly identical to the calculations of 33.33 percent per annum estimated for autos by Jorgenson and Sullivan (1981). The parameterization of the representative agent model that mimics the Caplin-Leahy model has a value for Δ_r of .074 if $c = .2$ and .076 if $c = 1$, and a value for β of .971 if $c = .2$ and .977 if $c = 1$. These depreciation rates are approximately 15 percent lower and are consistent with annual rates of depreciation of 26.5 and 27.2. These discount factors are consistent with real interest rates in the neighborhood of 12 percent per annum. Seen in this light the models appear very different.

The second look that we take is to use our derived parameters for the Caplin-Leahy model and insert these into the representative agent model to derive x_{rep}. This exercise yields a value for x_{rep} of .68 if $c = .2$ and .67 if $c = 1$. These values are within one standard deviation of the estimate of x.

Seen this way, similar parameterizations of the two models yield similar results.

11.5 Conclusions

The search for microfoundations for macroeconomics has brought to the fore the trade-off between realism and tractability in macroeconomic modeling. We need models that reflect the choices that agents actually make in order to make accurate measurements, to forecast and to predict and evaluate the effects of policy experiments. Models that are too realistic, however, quickly become as incomprehensible as the world that they are trying to explain.

In this paper we have developed an approximation of discrete choice that is simple enough that we can solve for the equilibrium dynamic of a market. We found that the discrete choice model and the representative agent shared similar dynamics but that their parameterization potentially differed. Although in the case of the U.S. automobile market these differences did not appear to be too great, care should be taken in parameterizing the representative agent model. Parameters that appear reasonable on a microeconomic level may not be appropriate for a representative agent who proxies for a group of consumers facing adjustment costs. This distinction may be especially important when conducting policy experiments, since in this case the representative agent model that mimics the discrete choice model might change with the change in policy regime.

At this point it might be useful to comment on a number of potential effects of discrete adjustment that are ruled out in our approximation. Most obviously, our assumption that there was enough time between purchases that heterogeneity in depreciation smoothed out lumps in the cross-sectional distribution of holdings ruled out echoes of previous booms in sales. In our view, this is probably not an important difference between the discrete adjustment model and the representative agent model, since individual heterogeneity is pervasive. More important, in our view, is the distinction between one-sided and two-sided adjustment. We implicitly assumed that adjustment was one-sided—that is, that agents only adjust from small cars to large cars. With one-sided dynamics, heterogeneity tends to flatten the distribution of holdings between the (S,s) bands. With two-sided adjustment this is no longer the case. The distribution of holdings tends to be tent-shaped: It peaks near the purchase target and slopes downward toward the triggers. Changes in the purchase triggers therefore lead to changes in the density near the trigger. This adds an additional source of dynamics. How these dynamics relate to the representative agent model remains an open question.

Whether dynamics are one-sided or two-sided depends on the context. Situations with strong drift, such as inflation in prices or depreciation in investment or durable goods, tend to be well modeled as one-sided. Our results apply mainly to these cases.

Appendix A
Linearization

Representative Agent Model

We linearize the model about the nonstochastic steady state. We begin with the first-order condition for the durable stock:

$$(\alpha - 1)K^{\alpha-1}\hat{k}_t = p\lambda(\hat{p}_t + \hat{\lambda}_t) - \beta(1 - \Delta)p\lambda E_t(\hat{p}_{t+1} + \hat{\lambda}_{t+1})$$

Hats represent log deviations from steady-state values. Variables without time subscripts denote steady-state values. Since $K^{\alpha-1} = (1 - [1 - \Delta]\beta)p\lambda$, in steady state, the first-order condition becomes

$$\text{(A1)}\quad (\alpha - 1)[1 - (1 - \Delta)\beta]\hat{k}_t = (\hat{p}_t + \hat{\lambda}_t) - \beta(1 - \Delta)E_t(\hat{p}_{t+1} + \hat{\lambda}_{t+1}).$$

Linearizing the definition of sales yields

$$Q\hat{q}_t = K\hat{k}_t - (1 - \Delta)K\hat{k}_{t-1},$$

or, since $Q = \Delta K$ in steady state,

$$\text{(A2)}\qquad \Delta\hat{q}_t = \hat{k}_t - (1 - \Delta)\hat{k}_{t-1}$$

Log-linearizing marginal cost, we get

$$p\hat{p}_t = Q^{\gamma}c(\gamma\hat{q}_t + \hat{c}_t),$$

or, since $p = Q^{\gamma}c$,

$$\text{(A3)}\qquad \hat{p}_t = \gamma\hat{q}_t + \hat{c}_t.$$

Together with the evolution of the shocks, equations (A1)–(A3) define the model.

Finally, substituting for price in the first-order condition yields the following second-order difference equation:

$$p\lambda(\hat{c}_t + \hat{\lambda}_t) - \beta(1 - \Delta)p\lambda E_t(\hat{c}_{t+1} + \hat{\lambda}_{t+1}) = \frac{\gamma(1 - \Delta)}{\Delta}p\lambda\hat{k}_{t-1}$$
$$+ \left[(\alpha - 1)K^{(\alpha-1)} - \frac{\gamma p\lambda}{\Delta} - \beta(1 - \Delta)\frac{\gamma(1 - \Delta)}{\Delta}p\lambda\right]\hat{k}_t + \beta(1 - \Delta)\frac{\gamma p\lambda}{\Delta}\hat{k}_t,$$

which has the following solution:

$$\hat{k}_t = x_{\text{rep}}\hat{k}_{t-1} + y_{\text{rep}}\hat{e}_t,$$

where

$$x = \frac{-\left\{(\alpha - 1)K^{(\alpha-1)} - \frac{\gamma}{\Delta}p\lambda[1 + \beta(1 - \Delta)^2]\right\}}{2\beta(1 - \Delta)\frac{\gamma}{\Delta}p\lambda} - \sqrt{\left\{\frac{(\alpha - 1)K^{(\alpha-1)} - \frac{\gamma}{\Delta}p\lambda[1 + \beta(1 - \Delta)^2]}{2\beta(1 - \Delta)\frac{\gamma}{\Delta}p\lambda}\right\}^2 - \frac{1}{\beta}}$$

$$y = \frac{p\lambda[1 - \beta(1 - \Delta)\theta]}{-\left\{(\alpha - 1)K^{(\alpha-1)} + \frac{\gamma}{\Delta}p\lambda[1 - \beta(1 - \Delta)^2]\right\} - \beta(1 - \Delta)\frac{\gamma}{\Delta}p\lambda(x + \theta)}$$

Caplin-Leahy Model

We first linearize the first-order condition for the optimal purchase size:

$$-\varepsilon_s(\hat{S}_t - \hat{\kappa}_t) + (\alpha - 1)\hat{\kappa}_t = \hat{p}_t + \hat{\lambda}_t$$

Here $\varepsilon_s = -[v''(S/K)(S/K)]/(v'(S/K)]$. If the time between purchases is sufficiently long ε_s will be approximately equal to $1 - \alpha$.[13] For simplicity, we adopt this approximation, so that the first-order condition becomes

(A4) $$(\alpha - 1)\hat{S} = \hat{p}_t + \hat{\lambda}_t.$$

Linearizing sales, we get

$$Q\hat{q}_t = \mu S\delta\hat{S}_t + \mu S(\hat{s}_t - \hat{s}_{t-1}),$$

which, since $Q = \mu S\delta$, becomes

(A5) $$\hat{q}_t = \hat{S}_t + \frac{1}{\delta}(\hat{s}_t - \hat{s}_{t-1})$$

The marginal cost equation is the same as in the representative agent model:

(A6) $$\hat{p}_t = \gamma\hat{q}_t + \hat{c}_t$$

Finally, we linearize the first-order condition for the purchase trigger:

$$v'S\kappa^\alpha(\hat{S}_t - \hat{\kappa}_t) + \alpha v\kappa^\alpha\hat{\kappa}_t - p\lambda S\hat{S}_t + (1 - c)sp\lambda\hat{s}_t - [S - (1 - c)s]p\lambda(\hat{p}_t + \hat{\lambda}_t)$$
$$= s^\alpha\hat{s}_t + E_t\beta\{v'S\kappa^\alpha(\hat{S}_{t+1} - \hat{\kappa}_t) + \alpha v\kappa^\alpha\hat{\kappa}_{t+1} - p\lambda S\hat{S}_{t+1} + (1 - c)(1 - \Delta)sp\lambda\hat{s}_t$$
$$- [S - (1 - c)(1 - \Delta)s]p\lambda(\hat{p}_{t+1} + \hat{\lambda}_{t+1})\}$$

13. If the time between purchases were fixed then ε_s would be exactly $1 - \alpha$. The difference arises since an increase in S postpones the next purchase.

Using the first-order condition for S, the $\hat{S}_t$ terms cancel, leaving

$$(\alpha v\kappa^{\alpha} - p\lambda S)(\hat{\kappa}_t - E_t\beta\hat{\kappa}_{t+1}) - p\lambda[S-(1-c)s](\hat{p}_t + \hat{\lambda}_t) + p\lambda[S-(1-c)(1-\Delta)s]\beta E_t(\hat{p}_{t+1} - \hat{\lambda}_{t+1}) = \{s^{\alpha} - [1-\beta(1-\Delta)](1-c)sp\lambda\}\hat{s}_t \tag{A7}$$

Finally, linearizing the frictionless capital stock yields

$$(\alpha - 1 - \gamma)\hat{\kappa}_t = \hat{\lambda}_t + \hat{c}_t. \tag{A8}$$

Equations (A4)–(A8) define the model.

To derive the second-order difference equation in $\hat{s}_t$, we begin with equation (A7). We replace $v(S/\kappa)\kappa^{\alpha}$ using the steady-state relationship

$$(1-\beta)\left[v\left(\frac{S}{\kappa}\right)\kappa^{\alpha} - Sp\lambda\right] + [1-\beta(1-\Delta)](1-c)sp\lambda = \frac{s_t^{\alpha}}{\alpha}$$

to get

$$\begin{aligned}
&\{s^{\alpha} - [1-\beta(1-\Delta)](1-c)sp\lambda\}\hat{s}_t \\
&= \left\{\frac{s_t^{\alpha}}{(1-\beta)} + (\alpha-1)Sp\lambda - \frac{[1-\beta(1-\Delta)](1-c)}{(1-\beta)}sp\lambda\right\}(\hat{\kappa}_t - E_t\beta\hat{\kappa}_{t+1}) \\
&\quad - p\lambda[S-(1-c)s](\hat{p}_t + \hat{\lambda}_t) + p\lambda[S-(1-c)(1-\Delta)s]\beta E_t(\hat{p}_{t+1} + \hat{\lambda}_{t+1}).
\end{aligned}$$

Next, combining the expressions (A4)–(A6) yields

$$\hat{p}_t = \frac{\varepsilon_S}{\varepsilon_S + \gamma}\left[\frac{\gamma}{\delta}(\hat{s}_t - \hat{s}_{t-1}) - \frac{\gamma}{\varepsilon_S}\hat{\lambda}_t + \hat{c}_t\right],$$

which allows us to replace $\hat{p}_t$:

$$\begin{aligned}
&-p\lambda[S-(1-c)s]\frac{\varepsilon_S}{\varepsilon_S+\gamma}\frac{\gamma}{\delta}\hat{s}_{t-1} + \Bigg(s^{\alpha} - [1-\beta(1-\Delta)]\,(1-c)sp\lambda \\
&\quad + p\lambda\frac{\varepsilon_S}{\varepsilon_S+\gamma}\frac{\gamma}{\delta}\{(1-\beta)S - [1-\beta(1-\Delta)](1-c)s\}\Bigg)\hat{s}_t \\
&\quad - p\lambda[S-(1-c)(1-\Delta)s]\beta E_t\frac{\varepsilon_S}{\varepsilon_S+\gamma}\frac{\gamma}{\delta}\hat{s}_{t+1} \\
&= \left[\left(\frac{s_t^{\alpha}}{(1-\beta)} + \alpha\left\{S - \frac{[1-\beta(1-\Delta)](1-c)s}{(1-\beta)}\right\}p\lambda\right) - p\lambda S\right](\hat{\kappa}_t - E_t\beta\hat{\kappa}_{t+1}) \\
&\quad - p\lambda[S-(1-c)s]\left(\frac{\varepsilon_S}{\varepsilon_S+\gamma}\right)(\hat{\lambda}_t + \hat{c}_t) \\
&\quad + p\lambda[S-(1-c)(1-\Delta)s]\beta\left(\frac{\varepsilon_S}{\varepsilon_S+\gamma}\right)E_t(\hat{\lambda}_{t+1} + \hat{c}_{t+1}).
\end{aligned}$$

Finally, we use equation (A8) and the assumption that the shocks are permanent,

$$E_t(\hat{\lambda}_{t+1} + \hat{c}_{t+1}) = \hat{\lambda}_t + \hat{c}_t,$$

to get

$$-p\lambda[S-(1-c)s]\frac{\varepsilon_S}{\varepsilon_S+\gamma}\frac{\gamma}{\delta}\hat{s}_{t-1}$$
$$+\left(s^\alpha + p\lambda\frac{\varepsilon_S}{\varepsilon_S+\gamma}\frac{\gamma}{\delta}(1-\beta)S - \left(1+\frac{\varepsilon_S}{\varepsilon_S+\gamma}\frac{\gamma}{\delta}\right)\{[1-\beta(1-\Delta)](1-c)sp\lambda\}\right)\hat{s}_t$$
$$-p\lambda[S-(1-c)(1-\Delta)s]\beta E_t\frac{\varepsilon_S}{\varepsilon_S+\gamma}\frac{\gamma}{\delta}\hat{s}_{t+1}$$
$$=\frac{1}{\alpha-1-\gamma}\{s_t^\alpha - [1-\beta(1-\Delta)](1-c)sp\lambda\}(\hat{\lambda}_t+\hat{c}_t).$$

This second-order difference equation has a solution of the form

$$\hat{s}_t = x\hat{s}_{t-1} + y\hat{e}_t,$$

where

$$x = \frac{s^\alpha + \chi(1-\beta)S - \left(1+\dfrac{\chi}{p\lambda}\right)\{[1-\beta(1-\Delta)](1-c)sp\lambda\}}{2[S-(1-c)(1-\Delta)s]\beta\chi}$$
$$-\left\{\left(\frac{s^\alpha + \chi(1-\beta)S - \left(1+\dfrac{\chi}{p\lambda}\right)\{[1-\beta(1-\Delta)](1-c)sp\lambda\}}{2[S-(1-c)(1-\Delta)s]\beta\chi}\right)^2\right.$$
$$\left.-\frac{[S-(1-c)s]}{\beta[S-(1-c)(1-\Delta)s]}\right\}^2$$

and

$$y = \frac{1}{\alpha-1-\gamma}$$
$$\cdot\frac{s_t^\alpha - [1-\beta(1-\Delta)](1-c)sp\lambda}{s^\alpha + \chi(1-\beta)S - (p\lambda+\chi)[1-\beta(1-\Delta)](1-c)s + [S-(1-c)(1-\Delta)s]\beta\chi(1+x)}$$

and $x = p\lambda\dfrac{\varepsilon_S}{\varepsilon_S+\gamma}\dfrac{\gamma}{\delta}$.

References

Adda, Jérôme, and Russel Cooper. 2000a. Balladurette and Jeppette: A discrete approach. *Journal of Political Economy* 108 (4): 778–806.

———. 2000b. The dynamics of car sales: A discrete choice approach. Boston University, Department of Economics. Mimeograph.

Bar-Ilan, Avner, and Alan Blinder. 1996. Consumer durables: Evidence on the optimality of usually doing nothing. *Journal of Money, Credit and Banking* 24: 258–72.

Bernanke, Ben. 1985. Adjustment costs, durables, and aggregate consumption. *Journal of Monetary Economics* 15 (1): 41–68.

Bertola, Giuseppe, and Ricardo Caballero. 1990. Kinked adjustment costs and aggregate dynamics. In *NBER Macroeconomics Annual 1990,* ed. Olivier Blanchard and Stanley Fischer, 237–88. Cambridge: MIT Press.

Bils, Mark, and Peter Klenow. 1998. Using consumer theory to test competing business cycle models. *Journal of Political Economy* 106:233–61.

Caballero, Ricardo. 1993. Durable goods: An explanation for their slow adjustment. *Journal of Political Economy* 101:351–84.

Caballero, Ricardo, Eduardo Engel, and John Haltiwanger. 1997. Aggregate employment dynamics: Building from microeconomic evidence. *American Economic Review* 87:115–37.

Caplin, Andrew, and John Leahy. 1991. State-dependent pricing and the dynamics of money and output. *Quarterly Journal of Economics* 106:683–708.

———. 1997. Aggregation and optimization with state-dependent pricing. *Econometrica* 65:601–27.

———. 2002a. Durable goods cycles. New York University, Department of Economics. Working Paper.

———. 2002b. On the relationship between sS models and representative agent models. New York University, Department of Economics. Working Paper.

Caplin, Andrew, and Daniel Spulber. 1987. Menu costs and the neutrality of money. *Quarterly Journal of Economics* 102:703–25.

Chah, Eun Young, Valerie Ramey, and Ross Starr. 1995. Liquidity constraints and intertemporal consumer optimization: Theory and evidence from durable goods. *Journal of Money, Credit, and Banking* 27:272–87.

Cooper, Russell, and John Haltiwanger. 2000. On the nature of capital adjustment costs. NBER Working Paper no. 7925. Cambridge, Mass.: National Bureau of Economic Research.

Cooper, Russell, John Haltiwanger, and Laura Power. 1995. Machine replacement and the business cycle: Lumps and bumps. NBER Working Paper no. 5260. Cambridge, Mass.: National Bureau of Economic Research.

Dotsey, Michael, Robert King, and Alexander Wolman. 1999. State-dependent pricing and the general equilibrium dynamics of money and output. *Quarterly Journal of Economics* 104:655–90.

Jorgenson, Dale, and Martin Sullivan. 1981. Inflation and corporate capital recovery. In *Depreciation, inflation, and the taxation of income from capital,* ed. C. Hulten, 178–238, 311–13. Washington, D.C.: Urban Institute Press.

Mankiw, N. Gregory. 1982. Hall's consumption hypothesis and the real interest rate. *Journal of Monetary Economics* 10:417–25.

Thomas, Julia. 2001. Is lumpy investment relevant for the business cycle? University of Minnesota, Department of Economics. Working Paper.

Comment Jong-Il Kim

Caplin and Leahy's (1991) model made a great contribution to the microfoundation of macroeconomics. The model suggested a theoretical possibility that the dynamics of price change may have different characteristics from those simply expected from microeconomic behavior. Under certain conditions, the discrete adjustment of price or fixed price that plays a critical role in generating aggregate fluctuation and nonneutrality of money cannot be taken for granted based on microeconomic behavior of economic agents.

In this paper, they show that the framework could be applied to the fluctuation of consumption of durable goods such as automobiles. This so-called Ss model introduces the state-dependent discrete adjustment behavior specifically in the model. The economic agents do not adjust their behavior continuously. Instead they stick with the current level of consumption until the changing situation hits a trigger point (small s). At the trigger point, they jump to the new level (big S). The most important contribution of this model is that it shows the possibility that the discrete adjustment by itself may not lead to aggregate fluctuation. As long as there is heterogeneity of agents in their timing of this discrete adjustment, the model will behave like the model with continuous adjustment as the representative agent model. When the agents are uniformly distributed in terms of their timing of adjustments and the economic situation changes smoothly, then there would be a constant proportion of agents changing their behavior. Therefore, discrete adjustment does not generate aggregate fluctuation because it is smoothed out.

Furthermore, they show that the representative agent model could be observationally equivalent with the Ss model under certain conditions. That is, it is possible to parameterize the representative agent model to mimic the dynamics of the Ss model. When the supply curve is perfectly elastic, they showed that the SS model and the representative agent model yield identical dynamics if parameterized identically. However, if the price responds to the demand, then they show the relation is not that simple. Thus they caution that with the discrete price adjustment, we cannot parameterize the representative agent model with seemingly reasonable parameters based on a simple guess on micro behavior. They provide the evidence from data from the automobile industry in the United States that the supply curve of automobiles is not elastic. They also add a caution that it is especially important when conducting policy experiments.

The Ss model provided an interesting point that even with discrete adjustment its impact on aggregate economy can be faded away if the structure of the economy allows enough heterogeneity of timing of adjustment

Jong-Il Kim is associate professor of economics at Dongguk University.

among economic agents. As the basic idea and theoretical proposition are interesting and useful, it seems that more work is needed to link the theory to the empirical studies.

The motivation of the paper is to find out how aggregate variables behave dynamically. The paper also started from a general discussion about the effect of discrete adjustment on the dynamics of aggregate variables. The empirical part uses data on the automobile industry to discuss the model. However, there are many different types of durable goods in the economy. For instance, huge information technology (IT) investments in the 1990s are now blamed for the current recession. It may be an example that past lumpy investment has a lasting echo. It is possible that we will see a cycle of IT investment some time in the future. One may find differences in the dynamics of various types of durable goods. Then it would be interesting if the sources of the differences are investigated and modeled theoretically.

The paper reports as empirical evidence that the model fits the data that the implied estimate of depreciation rate is about 32 percent per year, quite similar to the depreciation rate reported by Jorgenson and Sullivan (1981). It should be checked whether Jorgenson and Sullivan's estimate is the rate of physical depreciation or the rate of depreciation in the market value. Conceptually the right depreciation for the model in the paper is physical depreciation. A depreciation rate of about 30 percent per year seems too high for the physical depreciation.

The research done in this paper would contribute much to many issues in macroeconomics such as labor hiring, investment, and consumption of durable goods, as well as price adjustment if further studies on the issues provide more interesting empirical findings to be attacked theoretically.

References

Caplin, Andrew, and John Leahy. 1991. State-dependent pricing and the dynamics of money and output. *Quarterly Journal of Economics* 106:683–708.

Jorgenson, Dale, and Martin Sullivan. 1981. Inflation and corporate capital recovery. In *Depreciation, inflation, and the taxation of income from capital,* ed. C. Hulten, 178–238, 311–13. Washington, D.C.: Urban Institute Press.

Comment Assaf Razin

I must emphasize at the outset that I am a bit of an "outsider" to this strand of the literature. Nevertheless, I read the paper, and I was impressed by the

Assaf Razin is Mario Henrique Simonsen Professor of Public Economics at Tel Aviv University, Friedman Professor of International Economics at Cornell University, and a research associate of the National Bureau of Economic Research.

technical skills of the authors in solving what looks like a difficult dynamic problem.

In macroeconomics we tend to simplify complex problems and ignore some microeconomic behavior patterns that get washed out when the individual behavior is aggregated into a stylized macro behavior of the group of consumers. Discrete adjustments are hard to formulate dynamically. The hope is that discrete adjustments of investment in durable goods on the level of individual consumers could be smoothed out in the aggregate, so as to lead to continuous aggregate adjustment. Most of the macro analysis is therefore based on continuous adjustments.

The main scope of the paper is such a comparison between the representative agent's continuous adjustment of investment in consumption durables and discrete adjustment of such investment by an individual consumer.

The scope for applications of the analysis to other issues is broad: investment booms and busts, ex ante price setting by monopolistically competitive firms, and labor hiring and firing.

The aggregation problem of discrete adjustments is hard because the equilibrium price of durables depends on aggregate demand, which in turn depends on how many people adjust their purchases; and the latter depends on what is the price that people expect will prevail when they execute the transactions.

The main simplifying assumptions are (1) the marginal utility of wealth is constant, and (2) only upward adjustment is permitted. That is, the individual will let the car that he or she owns depreciate for a few years, and at some optimal time or state he or she will purchase a new, upgraded car.

The main finding is that the representative agent, continuous adjustment model and the aggregate of the discrete adjustment individual models are observationally equivalent.

The assumption of no downward adjustment may, however, limit the applicability of the analysis. For example, labor hiring and firing, consisting of both upward and downward adjustments, are excluded as an application. Concerning the application for the theory of inventories, I would like the authors to expand. It would be interesting to see what are the patterns over time of inventory accumulation. Specifically, can the simulations from the discrete adjustment model have a different dynamic path than the continuous model around the time that inventories accumulate—after the business cycle peak when the economy is hit by unexpected negative shocks, and after the trough when the economy expects larger future sales?

The implications of the analysis for dynamic models that are estimated econometrically are not pursued here at all. Examples of useful applications of discrete adjustments in econometrics-based models are Caballero and Engel (1999, 2000). I encourage the authors to highlight applications of this kind, as they are related to the theory they developed.

References

Caballero, Ricardo, and Eduardo Engel. 1999. Explaining investment dynamics in US manufacturing: A generalized (S,s) approach. *Econometrica* 67 (4): 741–82.

———. 2000. Lumpy adjustment and aggregate investment equations: A "simple" approach relying on Q and cash flow information. Massachusetts Institute of Technology. Mimeograph.

Contributors

Daron Acemoglu
Department of Economics, E52-380B
Massachusetts Institute of Technology
50 Memorial Drive
Cambridge, MA 02142-1347

Muhammad Chatib Basri
Institute for Economic and Social Research (LPEM-FEUI)
University of Indonesia
Jl. Salemba Raya no 4
Jakarta 10430, Indonesia

Andrew Caplin
Department of Economics
New York University
269 Mercer Street
New York, NY 10003

Steve Dowrick
School of Economics
Crisp Building 026
Australian National University
Canberra ACT 0200, Australia

Peter Drysdale
Australia-Japan Research Centre
The Australian National University
Canberra ACT 0200, Australia

Kyoji Fukao
Institute of Economic Research
Hitotsubashi University
Naka 2-1, Kunitachi
Tokyo 186, Japan

Chin Hee Hahn
Korea Development Institute
P.O. Box 113 Cheongryangri Dong
Seoul 130-012, Korea

Tomohiko Inui
College of Economics
Nihon University
3-2 Misaki-cho 1-chome, Chiyoda-ku
Tokyo 101-8360, Japan

Keiko Ito
The International Centre for the Study of East Asian Development (ICSEAD)
11-4 Otemachi, Kokurakita
Kitakyushu 803-0814, Japan

Takatoshi Ito
Research Center for Advanced Science and Technology
University of Tokyo
4-6-1, Komaba, Meguro-ku
Tokyo 153-8904, Japan

Simon Johnson
Sloan School of Management, E52-562
Massachusetts Institute of Technology
50 Memorial Drive
Cambridge, MA 02142-1347

Hiroki Kawai
Faculty of Economics
Keio University
2-15-45, Mita, Minato-ku
Tokyo 108-8345, Japan

Jong-Il Kim
Department of Economics
Dongguk University
Pil-dong Jung-gu
Seoul, Korea

John Leahy
Department of Economics
New York University
269 Mercer Street
New York, NY 10003

David D. Li
Department of Economics
Hong Kong University of Science and Technology
Clear Water Bay
Kowloon, Hong Kong

Youngjae Lim
Korea Development Institute
207-41, Chongnyangri-Dong
Dongdaemun-Gu, P.O. Box 113
Chongnyang, Seoul, Korea

Francis T. Lui
Department of Economics
Hong Kong University of Science and Technology
Clear Water Bay
Kowloon, Hong Kong

Tsutomu Miyagawa
Faculty of Economics
Gakushuin University
1-5-1 Mejiro, Toshima-ku
Tokyo 171-8588, Japan

Chong-Hyun Nam
Department of Economics
Korea University
5-1 Anam-Dong, Sungbuk-Gu
Seoul 136-701, Korea

Dean Parham
General Research Branch
Productivity Commission
P.O. Box 80
Belconnen ACT 2616, Australia

Epictetus E. Patalinghug
College of Business Administration
University of the Philippines
Diliman, Quezon City, The Philippines

Dipinder S. Randhawa
NUS Business School
National University of Singapore
1 Business Link
Singapore 117592

Assaf Razin
Eitan Berglas School of Economics
Tel Aviv University
Tel Aviv 69978, Israel

James Robinson
780 Barrows Hall
Departments of Political Science and Economics
University of California, Berkeley
Berkeley, CA 94720-1950

Andrew K. Rose
Haas School of Business Administration
University of California, Berkeley
Berkeley, CA 94720-1900

Kuen-Hung Tsai
Department of Shipping and Transportation Management
National Taiwan Ocean University
2 Pei-Ning Road
Keelung, Taiwan, 202

Jiann-Chyuan Wang
Chung-Hua Institution for Economic Research
75 Chang-Hsing Street
Taipei, Taiwan, 106

Changqi Wu
Department of Economics
Hong Kong University of Science and Technology
Clear Water Bay
Kowloon, Hong Kong

Jungho Yoo
Center for Economic Information
Korea Development Institute
207-41, Chongnyangri-Dong, Dongdaemun-Gu
P.O. Box 113, Chongnyang
Seoul, Korea

Author Index

Abramovit, Moses, 19n5
Acemoglu, Daron, 3–4, 71, 72, 73, 76, 77, 78, 82, 84n9, 85, 85n11, 102, 104
Adda, Jérôme, 352n1, 353, 365
Aghion, Philippe, 13n1, 16, 17, 19n8
Aitken, Brian J., 230n1
Aizcorbe, A., 55n13
Anas, Titik, 233–34n5, 233n4, 234
Apps, Patricia, 10
Ashenfelter, Orley, 10
Aswicahyono, Haryo, 230, 233–34n5, 233n4, 234, 236, 236n6, 270, 271, 272
Aten, Bettina, 83
Austria, Myrna, 146
Avila, John Lawrence, 146
Aw, Bee Yan, 198n21, 310n6, 312, 312n9, 313n10, 314

Baily, Martin Neil, 198, 199, 247n13, 310n6
Baldwin, John R., 173
Bar-Ilan, Avner, 352n1, 353
Barnes, P., 59
Barney, J. B., 280
Barro, Robert, 2, 19, 19n6, 20, 22, 23n11, 25, 84n9, 95
Barth, James R., 93, 93n14
Baruch, Y., 281n5
Basri, Titik, 230, 236, 236n6, 270, 271, 272
Basu, Susanto, 184
Bean, C., 55, 60
Begg, C. B., 279
Benhabib, Jess, 21n10, 22, 23, 24
Bergoeing, Raphael, 298n1
Berlin, J. A., 279
Bernanke, Ben, 356n7, 364n11
Bertola, Giuseppe, 352n1, 354n3
Bhagwati, Jagdish N., 144, 147
Bils, Mark, 365
Blinder, Alan, 352n1, 353
Blomström, Magnus, 150, 230n1
Borensztein, Magnus, 152n1
Borland, Jeff, 13n1
Bosworth, Barry P., 152, 152n1, 173
Bound, J., 283
Brecher, Richard, 110
Bresnahan, T., 57
Brynjolfsson, E., 57, 330, 335n13, 335n14, 342, 346
Burnside, Craig, 184

Caballero, Ricardo, 352n1, 353, 354n3, 364n11, 375
Campbell, David, 198, 199, 247n13, 310n6
Caplin, Andrew, 6, 352n1, 353, 354, 354n2, 358, 363, 373
Caprio, Gerard, 93, 93n14
Caselli, Francesco, 23, 23n11
Caves, Richard E., 150, 229, 310n5
Chah, Eun Young, 364n11
Chen, Xiaomin, 198n21, 310n6, 312, 312n9, 313n10, 314
Chung, B., 339n20
Clark, Colin, 197
Clark, K. B., 278

Coe, David T., 29
Colecchia, Alessandra, 187n11
Collins, Susan M., 152, 152n1, 173
Cooper, Russel, 352n1, 353, 354n3, 365
Cuneo, P., 278
Curtin, Philip D., 77

DeGregorio, Jose, 152n1
Dewan, S., 333n12
Dhaliwal, Naginder, 173
Diaz-Alejandro, Carlos, 110
Dollar, David, 85, 92
Domar, Evsey, 188
Doms, Mark E., 230n1
Dotsey, Michael, 352n1, 354
Dowrick, Steve, 2–3, 19n5, 20n9, 22, 24, 58, 60
Dunne, Timothy, 312n8
Dunning, John H., 229

Easterly, William, 66, 85, 87, 92, 92n13, 144
Eaton, Jonathan, 29
Eichenbaum, Martin, 184
Engel, Eduardo, 352n1, 353, 375
Esquivel, Gerardo, 23, 23n11

Fernandez de Cordoba, Gonzalo, 111
Folbre, Nancy, 10
Forsyth, P., 60
Foster, Lucia, 198, 199, 299, 310n5, 310n6, 314, 315
Frantzen, Dirk, 24, 29
Froot, Kenneth A., 149, 150
Fukao, Kyoji, 5, 178, 178n1, 184n7, 198, 199n22, 200, 225
Fuss, Mevyn A., 256

Gali, J., 55, 58
Gerschenkron, Alexander, 110
Globerman, Steven, 150, 230n2
Good, David H., 313n10
Gordon, Robert, 51n9, 347
Goto, A., 277, 278, 279, 282, 283, 286
Greene, W. H., 281
Gretton, P., 55, 58
Griffith, Rachel, 230n1, 231
Griliches, Zvi, 198n21, 277, 278, 279, 282, 283, 287, 294, 310n6, 342
Grossman, Gene M., 28, 314
Grubel, Herbert G., 28
Gullickson, W., 47n5
Gurr, Robert, 78
Gutierrez, Hector, 77

Hahn, Chin Hee, 6, 299, 310, 310n7, 312, 312n9, 313n10, 317n12
Haim, Regev, 198n21
Hall, B. H., 283n7, 342
Haltiwanger, John, 198, 199, 299, 310n5, 310n6, 314, 315, 352n1, 353, 354n3
Hanel, P., 279
Hanushek, Eric A., 23
Harper, M., 47n5
Harrison, Ann E., 110, 230n1
Hart, Oliver, 150
Hayashi, Fumio, 178, 180, 186, 208, 222, 298n1
Hecht, Joel, 156n2
Heckman, James, 118, 120
Helpman, Elhanan, 28, 29, 150, 314
Heston, Alan, 83
Hill, Hal, 230, 233, 236, 236n6, 270, 271, 272
Hitt, L., 57, 330, 335n13, 335n14, 346
Ho, Mun S., 182, 182n4
Hopehayn, Huga A., 313, 314
Hotz, V. Joseph, 118, 120
Howitt, Peter, 13n1, 16, 17, 19n8
Hsin, P. H., 289
Hulten, Charles, 198, 199, 247n13, 310n6

Inui, Tomohiko, 5, 196, 226
Ishizaki, Yukiko, 233
Islam, Nazrul, 20n9, 23, 87
Ito, Keiko, 5, 231

Jaffe, A., 283
Jensen, J. Bradford, 230n1
Johnson, Simon, 3–4, 72, 73, 76, 77, 78, 82, 85, 102, 104
Johnston, A., 57, 61
Jones, Charles, 16, 19, 19n7, 21
Jorgenson, Dale W., 51n9, 178, 182, 182n4, 187, 187n9, 355, 366
Jovanovic, Boyan, 313, 314

Kang, L., 327
Kawai, Hiroki, 5, 256
Keefer, Philip, 71
Kehoe, Timothy J., 111
Kennard, S., 59
Kenny, Charles, 110
Kim, H., 327, 339n20
Kim, Jong-Il, 6
Kim, Joong-Kyung, 300n3
Kimko, Dennis D., 23
Kindleberger, Charles P., 163

King, Robert, 352n1, 354
Kinukawa, Y., 282, 283n8
Kiyota, Kozo, 198n21, 226
Klenow, Peter J., 66, 365
Knack, Stephen, 71
Knowles, Stephen, 23n11
Kokko, Ari, 150
Koo, Bon Cheon, 303n4
Kortum, Samuel, 29
Krizan, C. J., 198, 199, 299, 310n5, 310n6, 314, 315
Krueger, Alan B., 10, 23
Krugman, Paul, 2
Kwon, Hyeog Ug, 184n7, 198, 199n22, 200

La Porta, Rafael, 76, 111, 118
Lau, L. J., 331
Leahy, John, 6, 352n1, 354, 354n2, 358, 373
Lee, Frank C., 56, 327
Lee, Jong-Wha, 19n6, 21n10, 25, 95, 152n1
Lee, Kevin, 20n9
Lee, X. F., 283
Lefort, Fernando, 23, 23n11
Levine, Ross, 85, 92, 92n13, 93, 93n14
Li, David D., 4
Lichtenberg, Frank R., 28, 29, 30, 277, 278, 279, 286, 288, 331
Lim, Youngjae, 6
Lin, H. L., 283
Lindahl, Mikael, 23
Link, A. N., 278
Lorgelly, Paula K., 23
Lucas, Robert E., Jr., 2, 13n1, 14, 16, 16n4

MacKinlay, Graig, 111n1
Maddison, A., 42
Mairesse, J., 278, 283, 283n7, 287
Mankiw, Greg, 18, 19, 20, 22, 23, 65, 364n11
Mansfield, E., 277, 284
Markusen, James R., 229
Martin, B. R., 288
Martin, F., 288
Martin, Nick, 10
Matsumoto, Kazuyuki, 197
McGuckin, R., 46, 46n4
McLachlan, Rosalie, 197
Miller, Paul W., 10
Milthrop, Peter, 111
Min, C.-K., 333n12
Miyagawa, Tsutomu, 5, 178n1
Mody, Ashoka, 154
Monday, Ian, 197
Mori, Minako, 233
Morrison, Caterine J., 184n7
Motohashi, Kazuyuki, 178, 187, 187n9
Mulvey, Charles, 10
Mutti, Jack, 111

Nadiri, M. Ishaq, 28, 256, 313n10
Nakajima, Takanobu, 198n21, 225, 225n2, 226
Nakanishi, Kiyohko G., 196, 226
Nam, Il Chong, 300n3
Nandi, Banani, 256
Nelson, Julie A., 10
Nelson, Richard R., 22, 24
Nguyen, Duck Tho, 19n5
Nishimura, Kiyohiko, 198n21, 226
Nordhaus, W., 56
North, Douglass C., 71

Odagiri, H., 282, 283n8
Oh, Soogeun, 300n3
Okamoto, Yumiko, 230, 231, 232, 247n13, 270
Oliner, S., 51n9, 55
Olley, G. S., 330n6
Olson, Mancur, 71
Owen, P. Dorian, 23

Pakes, A., 283, 330n6
Parham, Dean, 3, 45n3, 49n6, 52, 55, 58
Pesaran, M. Hashem, 20n9, 21n10
Peteraf, M. A., 280
Phelps, Edmund S., 22, 24
Pilat, Dirk, 56, 327
Pitchford, John, 13n2
Pivovarsky, Alexander, 90n1
Power, Laura, 352n1
Prescott, Edward C., 178, 180, 186, 208, 222, 298n1
Pritchett, John, 23

Radelet, Steven, 144
Rajan, Raghuram, 144
Ramey, Valerie, 364n11
Ramstetter, Eric D., 230n1, 230n2, 234
Razin, Assaf, 4, 150, 151, 154, 156n2
Rebelo, Sergio, 13n1, 184
Rees, Ray, 10
Regev, Haim, 310n6
Ries, John C., 230n2
Rizal, Jose, 233n4, 233–34n5, 234
Roberts, Mark J., 198n21, 310n6, 312, 312n8, 312n9, 313n10, 314

Roberts, P., 49n6, 52
Robinson, James, 3–4, 72, 73, 76, 77, 78, 82, 85, 102, 104
Rodriguez, Francisco, 110
Rodriguez-Clare, Andres, 66
Rodrik, Dani, 66, 110, 144
Roemer, Paul, 13, 13n1, 16, 17, 18
Rogers, Mark, 20n9, 22, 24
Romeo, A., 284
Romer, Paul, 2, 18, 19, 20, 22, 23, 27, 65
Rose, Andrew K., 111
Rosenthal, R., 279
Rouse, Cecilia, 10

Sachs, Jeffrey, 19, 19n6, 87, 144
Sadka, Efraim, 150, 151, 154
Sala-i-Martin, Xavier, 20, 22, 23n11
Salter, A. J., 288
Sampson, Rachelle, 111
Samuelson, Larry, 312n8
Sato, Yuri, 236
Schankerman, M., 283, 289
Scherer, F. M., 277, 279
Schreyer, Paul, 187n11
Schumpeter, J. A., 286
Selgado, R., 60
Shi, Heling L., 13n1
Shin, I., 327, 339n20
Shinar, Nitsan, 156n2
Sichel, D., 51n9, 55
Sickles, Robin, 313n10
Siegel, Donald, 28, 278, 279, 286, 288
Simon, J., 51n9
Simpson, Helen, 230n1
Sjöholm, Fredrik, 230, 230n1, 231, 232, 270
Smith, Ron, 20n9, 21n10
Solow, Robert, 1, 2, 11–12, 18, 346
Song, J., 327
Spiegel, Mark, 21n10, 22, 23, 24
Spulber, Daniel, 352n1, 353, 363
Starr, Ross, 364n11
Stiglitz, Joseph E., 87, 110, 144
Stiroh, K., 51n9, 56, 182, 182n4
Sullivan, Martin, 355, 366
Summers, Robert, 83
Sun, H., 49n6, 52
Suzuki, K., 277, 278, 279, 282, 283, 286
Swan, Trevor, 11–12
Switzer, L., 284

Takayasu, Kenichi, 233
Takii, Sadayuki, 230n1
Teh, Robert, 146
Temple, Jonathan R. W., 23
Terleckyj, N. E., 279
Thaicharoen, Yunyong, 90n1
Thomas, Julia, 352n1, 353
Thomas, Robert P., 71
Timmer, M., 62n16
Tokutsu, I., 331
Tsai, Keun-Hung, 5, 283, 289
Tybout, James R., 310n5, 312n8

van Ark, B., 46, 46n4, 62n16
van Maijl, H., 279
van Pottelsberghe de la Potterie, Bruno, 30
Vertinsky, Ilan, 230n2
Vuori, S., 279

Wakelin, K., 278, 279, 286
Wang, Jiann-Chyuan, 5–6, 283, 289
Wardrop, S., 51n9
Warner, Andrew M., 19n6, 87, 144
Waverman, Leonard, 256
Weder, Rolf, 28
Weil, David N., 18, 20, 22, 23, 65
Wernerfelt, B., 280
Williams, David, 110
Wolman, Alexander, 352n1, 354
Wu, Chinqi, 4

Xu, T. D., 283

Yang, S., 342
Yang, Xiaokai, 13n1
Yeung, Bernard, 111
Yoshikaw, Hiroshi, 178, 197

Zilibotti, Fabrizio, 84n9
Zingales, Luigi, 144

Subject Index

Advantage of backwardness, theory of, 110, 111
Australia: aging of population of, 33–34; contribution of ICT to productivity growth in, 49–58; educational attainment record of, 25–27; evidence on education and growth in, 25–27; growth performance of, 41; growth rate of, 2–3; history of productivity in, 42–44; industry use of ICTs in, 56–58; multifactor productivity in, 44–48; policy reforms and increased productivity in, 59–62; predicted increase in economic growth in, due to increased years of schooling, 24–25; productivity benefits of investment in education and research for, 34; productivity growth in, 3; productivity surge in 1990s in, 44–48; R&D in, 30–32; relationship between education and GDP in, 10; relationship between education and wages in, 10; role of education and skills and increased productivity in, 58–59; TFP growth rates for, 197
Automobile industry: Caplin-Leahy model and, 355–56; development of Indonesian, 232–35; in Indonesia, 230–31; major Indonesian manufacturers in, 236–40; productivity differences between foreign and local firms in Indonesia in, 247–51; productivity differentials of local and foreign plants in, 231; productivity trajectories between foreign and local firms in Indonesia in, 251–54; TFP growth for Indonesian foreign and local firms in, 254–60

Banking crises, institutions and, 93–95
Bankruptcy policy reforms, overview of, in Korea, 297–99. *See also* Exit barriers; Korea
Birth entry, 310
Births, plant, 310–12

Canada, productivity of local vs. foreign-owned plants in, 230n2
Capacity utilization, adjustment of, for growth accounting, in Japan, 184–87
Capital, accumulation of, and economic growth, 12
Capital utilization rates, 289
Caplin-Leahy model, 355, 356–59; comparing dynamic properties of, with representative agent model, 361–62; linearization of, 359–61, 369–71; simple case of, 362–63; U.S. auto market and, 363–68. *See also* Discrete adjustment; Representative agent model
Chaebols, 312; use of bankruptcy procedures by, after crisis, 304–6
Chile, plant entry rate in, 312
Colombia, plant entry rate in, 312
Colonization, 72
Complementarity, of investment, 14

Conditional convergence, 18–19
Cumulative feedback, 11

Data sources: for impact of GATT/WTO accession study, 111–17; for Indonesian automobile industry, 231–32, 240–47, 262–66; Japan Industrial Productivity Database, 178, 178n1, 187n12, 209–17; for R&D in Taiwan, 281–84
Death exits, 310
Death rates. *See* Mortality rates, settler
Death rate, of plants, in Korea, 312–13
Deregulation, and acceleration of TFP growth in Japanese nonmanufacturing sector, 195–98
Development. *See* Research and development (R&D)
Discrete adjustment, 351–53; approximation of, 354; Caplin-Leahy model of, 355, 356–59; investigations into role of, 353–54; macroeconomics and, 353; models for, 352; representative agent model of, 355, 356; smoothing echoes and, 354–55
Disembodied human capital, 9, 10–11. *See also* Embodied human capital; Human capital
Dynamic feedback, 14–15

Economic development: institutions and, 71–72; mortality rates and, 72–73
Economic growth: contribution of R&D to, 27–29; endogenous, 13–14; evidence on education and, 22–27; human capital and, 9, 33; and information technology, in Korea, 327–29; knowledge and, 11; models of, 2–3; neoclassical model of, 9, 12, 12f; object-oriented approach to, 11–12
Education: attainment record, for Australia, 25–27; dynamic feedback of, 14–15; as engine of long-run growth, 15–16; evidence on growth and, 22–27; long-run technological progress and, 24–25; productivity benefits of, 34; relationship between wages and, 10; role of, growth and, 2; role of, increased Australian productivity and, 58–59; of women, effect on Australian economy and, 33–34
Embodied human capital, 9. *See also* Disembodied human capital; Human capital
Endogeneity, 118–19
Endogenous growth models, 2, 13–14; challenges to, 17–19; complementarity and, 14; dynamic feedback and, 14–15
Entries, types of, 310
Entry barriers, 6
Error Correction Model (ECM), 20–21
European Union (EU), 144
Event study, 111
Exchange rate crises, institutions and, 90–93
Exchange rates, FDI inflows and, 150
Exit barriers, 6; for controlling shareholders, in Korea prior to economic crisis, 300–302; for large firms, in Korea prior to economic crises, 299–300; overview of, in Korea, 297–99. *See also* Bankruptcy policy reforms
Exits, types of, 310

Feedback: cumulative, 11; dynamic, 14–15
Firms, entry and exit barriers for, 6. *See also* Foreign-owned plants
Foreign direct investment (FDI), 4–5; advantages of, over types of investments, 151–52; as engines of growth, 149; findings for domestic investment and flows of, 157–59; findings for output growth and, 159–63; gravity model of flows of, 154–55; inward, 110; literature on impact of, on domestic investment, 152–54; macro finance theories of, 150; micro theories of, 150; by multinational corporations, 229–30; panel-data analysis of, 156–57; portfolio investment and, 150–51
Foreign-owned plants: productivity differentials of, vs. local, in automobile industry, 231; productivity of, vs. local firms, 230n1, 230n2; productivity of, vs. local plants, in Indonesian automobile industry, 247–51; productivity trajectories of, vs. local plants, in Indonesian automobile industry, 251–54; TFP growth for Indonesia, 254–60. *See also* Multinational corporations (MNCs)

General Agreement on Tariffs and Trade (GATT)/World Trade Organization (WTO), 109–11; accession to, 109–10, 110–12; data set and methodology for study of before and after economies be-

fore of members of, 111–21; impact of, 4; impact on gross domestic product growth and accession to, 132–35; impact on imports, exports, and foreign direct investment and accession to, 123–32; impact on total factor productivity and accession to, 135–39, 138t, 139t, 140t, 141t; predictions for countries qualifying for accession to, 122–23
Globalization, controversies about, 110
Gross domestic product, relationship between education and, in Australia, 10
Growth. *See* Economic growth
Growth accounting, 2; with adjustment of capacity utilization, 184–87; comparison of studies of, for Japan, 186–87; Japan's low growth and, 177–78; at macro level, for Japan, 179–1184; of U.S. economy vs. Japan's economy, 182–84
Growth theories, 1–2; neoclassical revival in, 33; new vs. old, 2; reconciling conflicting, 19–22

Human capital: economic growth and, 9, 33; embodied vs. disembodied, 9; multifactor productivity and, 59; role of, growth and, 2

Ideas: cumulativeness of, 11; nonrivalry of, 10–11, 17
Illegal Check Control Act, 304
Indonesia, 5; automobile industry in, 230–31; data sources for automobile industry in, 240–47; development of automobile industry in, 232–35; major auto manufacturers in, 236–40; productivity differences between foreign and local firms in automobile industry, 247–51; productivity of local vs. foreign-owned plants in, 230n1; TFP growth for foreign vs. local automobile firms in, 254–60
Information and communications technologies (ICTs), 42; aggregate growth accounting for, 49–55; multifactor productivity and, 48–55; role of, and Australia's productivity surge, 48–49; use of, by industries, 56–58
Information technology (IT): capital, market valuation of, 335–37; and economic growth, in Korea, 327–29; effect of, on aggregate economic growth, 337–40; effects of investment in, on productivity, 332–35; effects of investment in, on profitability, 331–32; effects of investments in, 6; investment in, and aggregate economic growth, 337–40; marginal product of investment in, 329–31
Innovation. *See* Research and development (R&D)
Institutions: banking crises and, 93–95; consequences of, 3–4; economic development and, 71–72; economic outcomes and, 79–83; exchange rate crises and, 90–93; measuring contemporary, 78–79; output volatility and, 85–88; strategy for measuring crises and, 83–85; worst drop in output and, 88–90
International Adult Literacy Survey, 26–27
International Monetary Fund, 4
Investments: complementarity of, 14; effects of IT, 6; model of discrete, 6

Japan: comparison of growth accounting studies for, 186–87; conclusions for TFP growth in, 208; decomposition analysis of TFP growth in manufacturing sector of, 198–208; deregulation, and acceleration of TFP growth in nonmanufacturing sector, 195–98; factors contributing to low growth in 1990s in, 177–78; growth accounting of economy for, vs. U.S., 182–84; growth accounting with adjustment of capacity utilization for, 184–87; sectoral productivity growth in, 187–94; supply-side causes for stagnation of, 179–87; TFP growth rates for, 197
Japan Industrial Productivity (JIP) Database, 178, 178n1, 187n12; data sources and estimation methods of, 209–17

Keio Database (KDB), 187n12
Knowledge: accumulation of, 17; economic growth and, 11
Korea: bankruptcy policy reform in, 297–99; corporate bankruptcy system prior to economic crisis in, 299–302; effects of IT investments in, 6; exit barriers for failing firms in, 6; information technology and economic growth in, 327–29; plant death rate in, 312–13; plant

Korea (*cont.*)
deaths and productivity in, 315–17; plant entry rate in, 312; postcrisis bankruptcy policy reforms in, 302–4; pre-exit productivity of bankrupt cohorts in, 306–9; pre-exit productivity performance and plant deaths in, 317–19; productivity differentials among plant groups in, 313–15; types of bankruptcy filings in, before and after crisis, 301–2. *See also* Information technology (IT)
Korea Asset Management Corporation (KAMCO), 300n2

Mortality rates, settler: economic development and, 72–73; effect of, on institutions and economic stability, 75–76; instability and crises and, 73–74; measuring, 76–78. *See also* Death rate, of plants
Multifactor productivity (MFP) growth: foreign direct investment by, 229–30; human capital and, 59; ICT and, 48–55; surge in Australian, 44–48
Multinational corporations (MNCs): vs. local firms, 5, 229–30; productivity of, 229. *See also* Foreign-owned plants

Neoclassical growth theories, reconciling, with new growth theories, 19–22
New growth theories, 9; reconciling, with neoclassical growth theories, 19–22
Nonrivaly of ideas, 10–11, 17

Object-oriented approach, to economic growth, 12
Output volatility, institutions and, 85–88

Patent rights, 17
Plant births, 310–12
Plant death rate, in Korea, 312–13
Plant deaths: pre-exit productivity performance and, in Korea, 317–19; productivity and, in Korea, 315–17
Plants. *See* Foreign-owned plants
Policy reforms, Australian, and increased productivity, 59–62
Political crises, institutions and, 95–97
Productivity: in Australia, 41; Australian policy reforms and increased, 59–62; benefits of, education and, 34; conclusions about R&D and, for Taiwan, 288–90; determinants of quality of life and, 1; differences in, between foreign and local firms in Indonesian automobile industry, 247–51; differentials in, among plant groups in Korea, 313–15; effects of information technology investment, on, 332–35; foreign ownership and, 5; history of Australian, 42–44; impact of research and development on, 5–6; of local vs. foreign plants in automobile industry, 231; of multinational corporations, 229; plant deaths and, in Korea, 315–17; research and development and, 277–78; surge in 1990s, in Australia, 44–47; trajectories, between foreign and local firms in Indonesian automobile industry, 247–51. *See also* Sectoral productivity
Productivity growth, consequences of, 5
Profitability, effects of information technology investment on, 331–32

Quality of life, productivity and, 1

Representative agent model, 352, 355, 356; comparing dynamic properties of, with Caplin-Leahy model, 361–62; linearization of, 359–60, 368–69; simple case of, 362–63; U.S. auto market and, 363–68. *See also* Caplin-Leahy model; Discrete adjustment
Research and development (R&D): in Australia, 30–32, 34; conclusions about productivity and, for Taiwan, 288–90; contribution of, to economic growth, 27–29; cross-country studies of expenditures on, 29; data and variables for, 281–84; expenditures on, 28; funding for, 27–28; international spillovers of, 29; literature review on, 278–79; model for, 279–81; productivity and, 5–6, 277–78; rates of return on, 28–30, 34; spillover effects of, 29; study results for, 284–88

Schumpeterian hypothesis, 280, 286
Sectoral productivity, 5; growth in, for Japan, 187–94. *See also* Productivity
Settler mortality rates. *See* Mortality rates, settler
Social capital, 14

Switch-in entry, 310
Switch-out exits, 310

Taiwan, 5–6; conclusions about effect of R&D and productivity, 288–90; plant entry rate in, 312; research and development in, 278. *See also* Research and development (R&D)
Tariffs, 109–10
Technological progress, 22
Thailand: productivity of automobile industry in, 231; productivity of manufacturing sector in, 230n2
Third International Maths and Science Study, 27
Total factor productivity (TFP), 2, 112; accession to GATT/WTO and, 135–37; adjustment of capacity utilization for, 184–87; decomposition formula, 267–73; growth accounting for, 179–84; Japan's low growth and, 177–78
Total factor productivity (TFP) growth: conclusions for Japan's, 208; deregulation and acceleration of, in Japan's nonmanufacturing sector, 195–98; for foreign vs. local Indonesian automobile firms, 254–60; for Japan, at sectoral level, 187–94; in Japanese manufacturing sector, 198–208

United Kingdom, productivity of automobile industry in, 231
United States: contribution of ICT to productivity growth in, 49–58; factors attributed to growth in, 21; growth accounting of economy for, vs. Japan's, 182–84; plant entry rate in, 312; productivity of automobile industry in, 231; productivity of local vs. foreign-owned plants in, 230n1; TFP growth rates for, 197

Venezuela, plant productivity in, 230n1

Wages, relationship between education and, 10
World Bank, 4
World Trade Organization (WTO). *See* General Agreement on Tariffs and Trade (GATT)/World Trade Organization (WTO)
Worst drop output, institutions and, 88–90